T0263871

Spoken Dialogues with Computers

Signal Processing and its Applications

Spoken Dialogues with Computers

RENATO DE MORI

McGill University, Montréal, Québec, Canada
and
Université d'Avignon, France

With contributions from:

Bianca Angelini, Giuliano Antoniol, Yoshua Bengio,
Fabio Brugnara, Mauro Cettolo, Anna Corazza,
Daniele Falavigna, Marcello Federico, Roberto Fiutem,
Cesare Furlanello, Diego Giuliani, Roberto Gretter, Denis Jouvet,
Roland Kuhn, Gianni Lazzari, Chafic Mokbel,
Jean Monné, Maurizio Omologo, David Sadek,
Christel Sorin, Piergiorgio Svaizer, Edmondo Trentin

Academic Press

London · San Diego · New York · Boston
Sydney · Tokyo · Toronto

Academic Press
525 B Street, Suite 1900, San Diego, California 92101-4495, USA
http://www.apnet.com

Academic Press Limited
24–28 Oval Road, London NW1 7DX, UK
http://www.hbuk.co.uk/ap/

ISBN 0-12-209055-1

A catalogue record for this book is available from the British Library

Spoken dialogues with computers edited by Renato de Mori.
    p.   cm. – (Signal processing and its applications series)
    ISBN 0-12-209055-1 (alk. paper)
    1. Human-computer interaction.   2. Automatic speech recognition.
I. De Mori, Renato.   II. Series: Signal processing and its applications.
QA76.9.H85S66   1997
006.4'54–dc21   97-43104
                                                              CIP

Typeset by the Alden Group, Oxford
Transferred to digital printing 2005
Printed and bound by Antony Rowe Ltd, Eastbourne

Series Preface

Signal processing applications are now widespread. Relatively cheap consumer products through to the more expensive military and industrial systems extensively exploit this technology. This spread was initiated in the 1960s by introduction of cheap digital technology to implement signal processing algorithms in real-time for some applications. Since that time semiconductor technology has developed rapidly to support the spread. In parallel, an ever increasing body of mathematical theory is being used to develop signal processing algorithms. The basic mathematical foundations, however, have been known and well understood for some time.

Signal Processing and its Applications addresses the entire breadth and depth of the subject with texts that cover the theory, technology and applications of signal processing in its widest sense. This is reflected in the composition of the Editorial Board, who have interests in:

(i)   Theory – The physics of the application and the mathematics to model the system;
(ii) Implementation – VLSI/ASIC design, computer architecture, numerical methods, systems design methodology, and CAE;
(iii) Applications – Speech, sonar, radar, seismic, medical, communications (both audio and video), guidance, navigation, remote sensing, imaging, survey, archiving, non-destructive and non-intrusive testing, and personal entertainment.

Signal Processing and its Applications will typically be of most interest to postgraduate students, academics, and practising engineers who work in the field and develop signal processing applications. Some texts may also be of interest to final year undergraduates.

Richard C. Green
The Engineering Practice,
Farnborough, UK

Sic parvis componere magna solebam
Virgilius, Bucolica, 1.23

**To Giosetta
and
Andrea**

Contents

1

Problems and Methods
for Solution

Renato De Mori[*]

1.1. INTRODUCTION

Spoken dialogue (the term "dialogue" rather than "dialog" will be used throughout this book) with computers is becoming a reality, receiving increasing attention even outside research laboratories. A collection of results obtained from research in different countries has generated valid technologies that are now used in new products. Applications in the area of office systems (automatic call-back systems), telephone services, training and aid to handicapped persons are now developed with more confidence than in the past.

Just in the area of automatic speech recognition (ASR), dictation systems capable of accepting continuous speech and very large vocabularies (>10 000 words) from many speakers are now deployed in many languages (e.g., English,

---

[*]School of Computer Science, McGill University, Montreal, P.Q. H3A 2A7, Canada.

French, German, Italian, Spanish, Japanese, Chinese) and for a variety of application sectors in the medical, legal, political and news fields.

Which elements of progress have made this possible? What makes these achievements still incomplete?

In this book, these questions will be addressed on the basis of an experience gained by reading a large number of papers, summarizing presentations attended at conferences or during visits to laboratories, and supervising or performing research at different sites. Major reading sources have been the *Institute for Electrical and Electronic Engineers (IEEE) Transactions on Speech and Audio Processing* (including its predecessors on acoustics, speech and signal processing and on signal processing); the *IEEE Transactions on Pattern Analysis and Machine Intelligence* (PAMI); *Computer Speech and Language*; *Speech Communications*; and the Proceedings of the *International Conference on Acoustics, Speech and Signal Processing* (ICASSP), the *International Conference on Spoken Language Processing* (ICSLP), the *Eurospeech* Conference, the IEEE, the European Speech Communications Association (ESCA), the Advanced Research Project Agency (ARPA) Speech and Human Language Technology (HLT) workshops, and the NATO advanced study institutes.

The book will describe the content of the basic components of a spoken dialogue system. The methods and techniques that appear to be the most useful in practice will be covered in detail. Other contributions, important from a conceptual or historic point of view will also be covered in some detail or in qualitative terms. In principle, each chapter will be based on the following sequence of items: introduction, problem statement, details on the most effective solution(s), overview of other possible solutions, evaluations, problems and trends.

In recent years, large-vocabulary word dictation systems have been developed (Jelinek, 1976). They accepted fairly large vocabularies (a few thousand words) but were speaker-dependent (they had to be trained on each speaker who had to record a number of predetermined sentences) and required the speaker to make a short pause at the end of each word. This requirement characterizes discrete word recognition systems.

Speech technologies that are acceptable today are based on a set of methods leading to technical solutions which work together in a satisfactory way in pure software systems, running on commonly available workstations and advanced personal computers (PCs), with a response time close to real-time. These systems accept continuous speech from different speakers with very large vocabularies ranging from thousands to tens of thousands of words. They use knowledge at different levels, generating and scoring hypotheses in order to recognize words and produce written texts. In addition to that, dialogue systems extract conceptual representations from hypothesized words and reason about them, taking into account dialogue histories, contexts, plans and goals. Spoken messages can be produced by a dialogue unit on PCs, in real-time and in many languages with good quality.

1.2. PROBLEM POSITION AND METHODS FOR SOLUTION

Person–machine communication (PMC) can be seen as an exchange of information coded in a way suitable for transmission through a physical medium. *Coding* is the process of producing a representation of what has to be communicated. The content to be communicated is structured using words represented by sequences of symbols of an alphabet and belonging to a given lexicon. Phrases are made by concatenating words according to the rules of a grammar and associated in order to be consistent with a given semantics. These various types of constraints are *knowledge sources (KS)* with which a symbolic version of the message to be exchanged is built. The symbolic version undergoes further transformations that make it transmittable through a physical channel.

Dictation and interpretation systems perform a *decoding process* using KSs to transform the message carried by a speech signal into different levels of symbolic representation. Decoding can produce word sequences or conceptual hypotheses.

Unlike person-to-person communication, PMC is expected to produce instances of computer data structures in a deterministic way. Deterministic here means that a computer system has to produce the same representation for the same signal, every time this signal is processed. So, with current technology, speech interpretation by machine is not "creative" in the sense that it is performed by predesigned, predictable reactions to the data. The KSs used by machines in the decoding process are only *models* of the ones used by humans for producing their messages.

One of these KSs is the *language model* (LM). An LM is a collection of constraints on the sequence of words acceptable in a given language. These constraints can be represented by rules of a *generative grammar G. G* can be used to produce sentences of a language LG(*G*). *G* is defined as a 4-tuple: $G = (\sigma, V_T, V_N, P)$, where V_T is a set (an alphabet, in the case of natural language, a lexicon) of all the words of LG(*G*), V_N is a set of non-terminal symbols representing abstractions of language components, for example, syntactic categories. $\sigma \in V_N$ indicates the abstract category of all the sentences in LG(*G*). *P* is a set of rewriting generative rules of the type $\alpha \rightarrow \beta$, where α is a sequence of symbols that should contain at least one in V_N; $\beta \in (V_T \cup V_N)^*$ is a string of symbols in V_T or V_N with which, starting with a rule of the type $\sigma \rightarrow \beta$ and further rewriting the components of β, it is possible to generate a sentence in LG(*G*). If α can be only one symbol in V_N, then *G* and LG(*G*) have the property of being *context-free*.

An important difficulty in natural language (NL) analysis is that it is almost impossible to conceive a grammar *G* capable of generating all and only the sentences of an NL. This is due to many factors, probably the most important one being that NL evolves in a way difficult to characterize with formal models. Nevertheless, with grammars it is possible to build very useful, but approximate LMs. Grammars with a large number of detailed rules can accurately model certain NL aspects but be too limited for other aspects. These grammars are said to have limited *coverage*. Other grammars can have a complete coverage but, being too general, they can generate sentences that do not belong to an NL. A good example of these *overgenerating* grammars is one that can generate every pair of words in an NL vocabulary (*word pair grammar*). Overgeneration can be mitigated by associating probabilities to grammar rules in such a way that undesired sentences will be generated with lower probability than legal sentences in a given NL. Some of these grammars are particularly useful for ASR because they can be represented by *stochastic finite state automata (SFSA)* in which states correspond to symbols in V_N and arcs are labeled with words in V_T. Probabilities are associated to arcs. For example, *bigram* probabilities can be associated to word pairs in a stochastic word pair grammar.

Arcs in these SFSA can be replaced by other (possibly stochastic) automata, one for each word representing alternate pronunciations of each word. Arcs of these word automata are labelled with phonemes and pronunciations are obtained with a *lexical model (LeM)*. In turn, each model can be replaced by a corresponding *acoustic model (AM)* relating each phoneme to distributions of acoustic parameters or features that can be observed when that phoneme is uttered.

In this way, an *integrated network (IN)* can be obtained and effectively used to generate word or interpretation hypotheses about a given speech signal.

The decoding process has to deal with *ambiguity* due to distortions introduced by the transmission channel, the limits of the knowledge used, and often to intrinsic imprecision of the spoken message. The imprecision is due to the fact that the speaker's intention may not be that of producing exactly an instance of the data structures belonging to the knowledge of the decoder.

To a certain extent, ambiguities can be reduced by exploiting message *redundancy*. In practice, knowledge is used to transform the input signal into more suitable sequences of vectors of parameters and to obtain from them various levels of symbolic representations. The first level of symbolic representation can be a word, a syllable, a phoneme or simply an acoustic descriptor.

Interpretation is usually obtained by a *search* process that considers an IN to be the generator of an observable description

$$X = x_1 x_2 \ldots x_n \ldots x_N$$

of the signal to be interpreted. The search process attempts to find the best sequence of IN states identifying a path through which X is generated. Competing sequence candidates are ranked based on *scoring methods*. Scores are used by search strategies for progressively growing partial IN paths. These candidates are often called *theories*. Expansion is constrained by knowledge imposing consistency among components. Redundancy can help in making coherent components more evident.

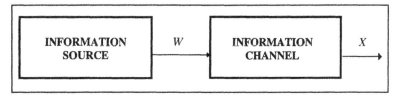

Figure 1.1 A simple decoder model.

Modern systems are based on probabilistic scores for candidate hypotheses. The speech waveform is sampled and quantized (now by standard devices available in many workstations and advanced PCs). A window, displaced by fixed time steps on the time sequence of generated samples, groups them into frames. Each frame is transformed into a vector of coefficients that are more suitable than the samples for further processing. The parameter vector obtained from the nth frame is considered as an acoustic observation x_n. A spoken sentence is thus described by a sequence X of such vectors. Details on speech transducers will be given in Chapter 2; details on speech processing and transformations will be given in Chapters 3 and 4.

A simple, popular probabilistic model for scoring hypotheses has a decoder knowledge that considers the sequence of acoustic observations

$$X = x_1 x_2 \ldots x_n \ldots x_N$$

as the output of an information channel shown in Figure 1.1 that receives at the input a sequence of symbols representing the intention of the speaker. If these symbols are words, then they are usually represented by the sequence

$$W = W_1 \ldots W_k \ldots W_K$$

X is a coded version of W. The objective of recognition is to reconstruct W based on the observation of X. This is done by using knowledge about the coding process. If the same X can be generated by different W, or knowledge is incomplete or imperfect, then reconstruction may not be successful.

In the case of dictation, ambiguity and imprecision make it necessary to consider recognition a search process that generates word hypotheses by selecting candidates for which $\Pr(W|X)$ is maximum. If the source model provides $\Pr(W)$ and the channel model provides $\Pr(X|W)$, then the quantity $\Pr(X, W) = \Pr(X|W)\Pr(W)$ can be computed. Notice that, as $\Pr(X)$ is the same for all the considered candidates W, the sequence W' for which $\Pr(X, W)$ is maximum is also the sequence for which $\Pr(W|X)$ is maximum. $\Pr(X|W)$ is the probability of observing X when W is pronounced. In practice, this probability cannot be computed directly from data. It has to be computed using an acoustic model (AM).

$\Pr(W)$ is the probability of a sequence of words and is computed using a language model (LM).

Current machine dictation systems tend not to employ semantic knowledge in transcribing an acoustic signal into a sequence of words. Instead, given a description X of the signal, such systems output the word sequence W' such that W' maximizes $\Pr(X, W)$ with respect to all possible word sequences W.

Model parameters are estimated with imprecision from corpora of data. As imprecision is model dependent, probabilities computed with different models are weighted differently. For example, for dictation, generation of a sequence W' of word hypothesis can be based on the following score:

$$W' = \arg\max_{W}\{\log \Pr(X|W) + \beta \log \Pr(W)\} \tag{1.1}$$

where β is a "fudge" factor that accounts for difference in model imprecision.

Equation (1.1) can also be seen as a decision criterion that combines scores for candidate hypotheses W provided by two different experts.

The maximum likelihood approach to ASR is extensively discussed in Bahl *et al.* (1983). The problem of classifying parametric information sources whose statistics are available through training data is discussed in Ziv (1985) for application in digital communication. The problem of testing with empirically observed statistics is discussed in Gutman (1989) and Ziv (1988).

If the objective is understanding, then the system has to find the conceptual representation C' that maximizes $\Pr(C|X)$ over all the possible conceptual representations C. This can be expressed as:

$$C' = \arg\max_{C} \Pr(C|X) = \arg\max_{C} \sum_{W} \Pr(CW|X) \cong \arg\max_{CW} \Pr(CW|X)$$

$$= \arg\max_{CW} \Pr(X|CW) \Pr(CW) \cong \arg\max_{CW} \Pr(X|W) \Pr(CW) \tag{1.2}$$

$\Pr(CW)$ can be expressed as $\Pr(C|W)\Pr(W)$ where $\Pr(W)$ is computed by the LM and $\Pr(C|W)$ is computed by a semantic model.

The choice of KSs and the way they are used in a system determines the *system architecture*. System architecture design should be based on a number of performance indices; the most important of them are now briefly reviewed.

A first requirement that has already been discussed is *coverage*. The system has to be able to recognize virtually all the sentences that can be pronounced.

Another requirement is *precision*. KSs and methods for their use should produce the lowest recognition or understanding error rates.

A third requirement is acceptable *computational complexity*, both in terms of *time* and *space*. This has an impact on the central memory requirements for the hardware system. Having responses close to real-time is a necessary condition. This implies methods based on algorithms with linear time complexity or with polynomial time complexity only if the input size is very small.

Knowledge can be manually compiled or obtained by automatic *learning* from a corpus of data. Coverage and precision of manually derived knowledge are often limited. The best results so far have been obtained using component models having a simple, manually decided structure. Statistical parameters of these models are estimated by automatic training. Complex knowledge structures are obtained by composition of basic models.

The requirements for speech synthesis are quite different since it is acceptable to produce only those sentences that can be generated by a suitable grammar with just one or few voice types for the same sentence. In this case, the new dimension of *quality* becomes of fundamental importance.

The structure of the book will be introduced in the next section. Models and KSs specify the components of system architectures. Each chapter describes one of these components.

1.3. BOOK STRUCTURE

The structure of the book is based on a simplified version of many software system architectures existing in these days. Most of the chapters describe components of such an architecture or ways for deriving useful data structures. Parameters of these structures are often obtained by statistical analysis of experimental corpora.

The acoustic and the language models are only an approximation of the reality and interact so that, very often, one compensates for the weakness of the other.

Performance depends on many factors. The first one has to do with the environment, the microphone that captures the speech signal and transforms it into an electrical signal that is then sampled and quantized. Currently, a noticeable degradation in performance is observed if the environment is noisy and the microphone is not close to the speaker's mouth. Considerable research effort is in progress for designing microphone arrays, and for conceiving new signal processing and post-processing techniques that will improve recognition robustness in situations in which actual systems do not perform well. Chapter 2 deals with microphone arrays which are considered a promising technology for allowing computer systems to capture voices of speakers at a variable distance from the transducers and to attenuate noise sources located at directions other than that of the speaker.

Chapter 3 discusses signal analysis. It introduces the type of analysis that produces observations X that are well suited for hidden Markov models (HMMs), the most popular AMs today. Other speech analysis techniques are also introduced, namely those based on sophisticated auditory models. They appear to greatly increase computational load without necessarily yielding a corresponding improvement in recognition performance. Nevertheless, these methods have great potential because the human ear is by definition the standard device for extracting linguistically meaningful acoustic properties from speech even in highly adverse conditions.

Chapter 4 discusses acoustic transformations that may lead to a more suitable representation for the AM. Speech coding transformations are described for representing a speech frame by a symbol. With this type of description, the AM can be seen as a stochastic source of symbol strings with symbols belonging to a specific code alphabet.

Chapter 5 is about acoustic modelling. It formally introduces HMMs, their theory, the types that are useful for modelling speech units and the type of units they can model. Different HMMs are characterized by their topology, the type of observation they accept, and their statistical distributions. These distributions have statistical parameters that have to be estimated from data.

Model training techniques are discussed in Chapter 6. There may be one model per phoneme or several allophone models for the same phoneme. Each allophone corresponds to a specific context or a cluster of contexts. The motivation is that the articulation of a phoneme is influenced by previous and following phonemes (speech units like vowels and consonants described in Chapter 3) because of the inertia and mechanical constraints in the movements of the vocal tract articulators. This phenomenon is known as coarticulation. It is rare that allophone models take into account contexts beyond the previous and the following phoneme. The quality of the models affects the recognition performance of the system using them. This quality, among many factors, depends on the training corpus, its structure, its size, the number, age, sex, and geographic distribution of speakers who uttered the sentences in the corpus.

Statistical language models (LMs) are introduced in Chapter 7. These models are used for computing $\Pr(W)$ for a sequence: $W = W_1 \ldots W_k \ldots W_K$. Various models and methods for computing the model parameters are described. In order to properly train these models, large corpora of written material are necessary. As a consequence, the model parameters depend on the topics covered by the training corpus. This is the case for which dictation systems perform relatively well. Otherwise, there are still problems to be solved. Intense research activity is in progress to attenuate the effects of the bias introduced by the content of the training corpora. For this purpose, mixtures of models and adaptive or dynamic models are also proposed. They have probabilities that can be adapted to a specific topic or the preferences of a speaker. These methods can be used to adapt language models to dialogue states so that the recognizer can build expectations on the set of words to recognize as a dialogue progresses.

Words are represented by a sequence of phonemes and phonemes are modelled by HMMs. Thus, it is possible to represent a lexicon by a collection of finite-state networks, each network being a word model. In principle, every word can follow every word with a certain probability; this is represented by connecting each pair of models by a link associated with a bigram probability given by the LM. Each word model is made of one or more pronunciations. Ways for building lexical representations are discussed in Chapter 8. Most of the systems have one representation per word. This is a limitation especially if potential users of the ASR system come from different regions of a country or are non-native speakers. Determining a useful and tractable set of alternate representations for a word is still a research issue. In fact, multiple representations may capture speaker variability but may also introduce additional recognition errors. Furthermore, word pronunciations are affected by boundary effects or between-word coarticulation. These effects have to be properly modelled by using phonological knowledge.

Generation of word hypotheses given the signal of a spoken sentence is a search problem. Search has to determine which sequence of states in the lexical network is the most likely generator of the acoustic description obtained from the speech signal. Obviously the most likely sequence may not correspond to sequence of phonemes and words perceived by a human listener. Errors may be due to many reasons: the poor information content of the extracted acoustic observations, the model imprecision, the fact that the search algorithm may be inadmissible (not guaranteed to find the optimal solution) in order to run within acceptable time and space complexity. A reasonable compromise between theory and practice has led to the choice of model complexity and non-admissible, but effective search algorithms implemented in pure software systems and running in close to real-time on modern computers and PCs. These solutions are presented in Chapter 9. In the future, more powerful computers will support more accurate acoustic parameters, better models and search algorithms that explore a wider portion of the search space.

Chapter 10 discusses the possible use of neural networks (NNs) for ASR. NNs are basically function approximators. They can approximate classification functions producing class symbols that can be phonemes or acoustic descriptors. NNs can compute probabilities from data. Recurrent NNs (RNNs) containing memory elements can perform the function of HMMs. NNs or RNNs can also be used to extract acoustic observations from data with a joint estimation of feature extraction and HMM specification parameters in order to achieve optimal recognition performance.

A simple software architecture scheme of a system containing the components outlined in the first 10 chapters is shown in Figure 1.2. Each component in the scheme is associated the chapter number in which the component is described.

Actual recognition systems, even if they operate in a quiet environment, exhibit performance that varies from speaker to speaker with generally substantial degradation for speakers whose mother tongue is not the one on which the AMs have been trained. It is possible to partially overcome these problems by adapting the system to a new speaker. This topic is the object of a large research effort reviewed in Chapter 11.

More difficult and still under investigation is the problem, covered in Chapter 12, of conceiving transformations and models that make systems more robust in the presence of noise.

Figure 1.3 shows an adaptation scheme to new speakers, pronunciations, language and background noise. Some of the most advanced systems follow the schemes of Figures 1.2 and 1.3 for word hypothesis generation. The way components are implemented in these systems are described in the corresponding chapters mentioned in the figures.

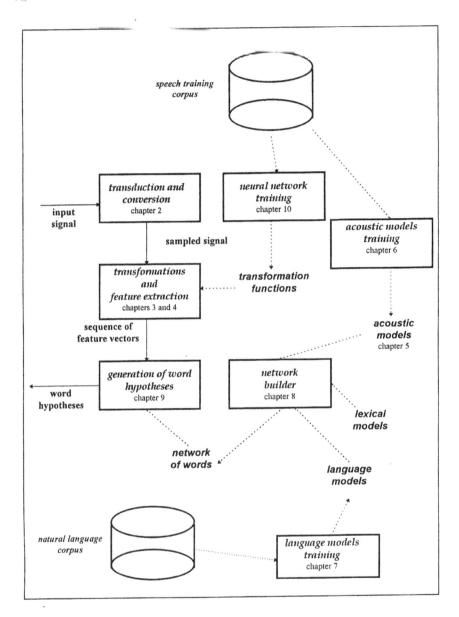

Figure 1.2 Word hypotheses generation scheme.

Chapter 13 introduces the concept of stochastic context-free grammars (SCFG) and reports theoretical results that suggest how these tools can be used in ASR. The problem of training these grammars from a corpus is also discussed.

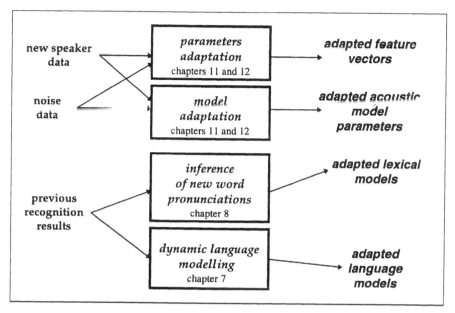

Figure 1.3 Various types of model adaptation.

Chapter 14 describes how to generate conceptual representations from word hypotheses. These representations are intermediate data structures from which database queries or dialogue units can be generated. The application to database query is discussed with the problem of automatic learning interpretation rules from examples made of sentences and the corresponding query.

The use of conceptual representations in dialogue models is discussed in Chapter 15 together with models, knowledge representations and strategies.

Chapter 16 deals with response generation. It covers text generation from concepts and speech generation from text with a presentation of various speech synthesis systems with particular emphasis on the most successful ones.

Chapter 17 discusses system architectures with particular attention to the pure software solutions that can be implemented with modern workstations and PCs. Solutions for client–server architecture are described in great detail. Areas of applications are also described and discussed.

Figure 1.4 shows the scheme of the entire dialogue system in which word hypothesis generation is represented by a single component.

1.4. SYSTEM ARCHITECTURES

The architecture represented in Figures 1.2–1.4 is an example of a *hierarchical structure* in which computation follows a rigid sequential sequence of phases.

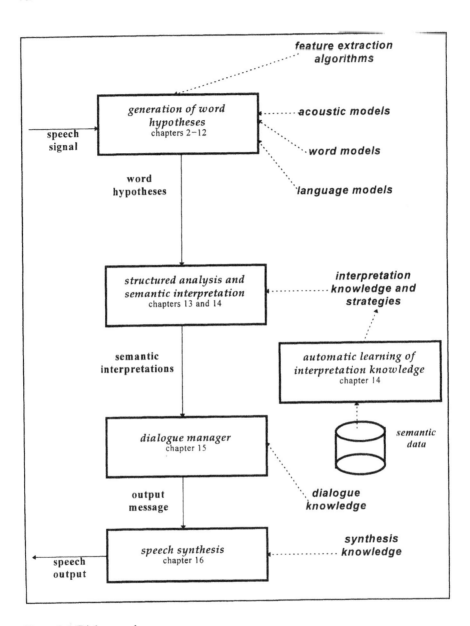

Figure 1.4 Dialogue scheme.

A different family of architectures has a *heterarchical structure* that is characterized by the fact that different modules write the results of their computation into a common shared memory called blackboard (BB). At the beginning, the data acquisition module stores the signal samples into the BB. The appearance of certain conditions in the BB may trigger the activation of other modules that read data from the BB, apply private algorithms and knowledge and deposit the results onto the BB. This architecture was developed for a speech understanding system (SUS) developed in the 1970s and called Hearsay (Erman *et al.*, 1980).

Architectures for speech synthesis proposed so far are hierarchical ones. A rule-based module performs a syntactic and semantic analysis of the message to be synthesized in text form. With the aid of a pronunciation dictionary, a phonetic representation with prosodic markers of the message to be synthesized is produced. These symbols are translated into continuously time-varying control parameters that drive the speech synthesizer that eventually produces the speech waveform. Extensive reviews are provided by Flanagan (1972b), Olive *et al.* (1996) and Van Santen *et al.* (1996).

In the last decade, hierarchical structures have been very popular because they can be implemented in many types of workstations with performance close to real-time. In a strictly hierarchical structure, the choice of the functions to be performed is critical, and a replacement of a function with another is likely to have a great impact on performance.

In recent years, pure hierarchical structures have shown superior performance. These structures perform generation of word hypotheses with a search process that selects the word sequence in the word network that has the best score with a given sequence of input feature vectors. For years this approach has been contrasted with another using separate modules in a hierarchical or heterarchical structure for generating lattices of hypotheses about phonetic, phonemic and syllabic structures. The latter approach, inspired by a speech perception model (Klatt, 1979), had the advantage of being based on specific knowledge about speech production and perception, but had the disadvantage of using manually compiled knowledge with limited coverage and variable precision.

The advent of low-cost multiprocessor systems may inspire new system structures in which specific and effective knowledge can be used even for limited coverage. An interesting solution is the one that performs a *progressive search* to generate a sequence of recognized words or an interpretation based on a conceptual representation.

A two-phase search scheme suitable for large (>1000) or very large (10 000) vocabulary connected speech recognition (LCSR or VLCSR) as well as for SUS performs a cascaded decision process, following the scheme of Figure 1.5. In the first phase, the entire vocabulary is used with simple (e.g. context-independent) AMs and a simple LM for generating a word lattice.

This lattice should be represented by a data structure made of words containing, for each word, a set of parameters such as beginning and ending time, score

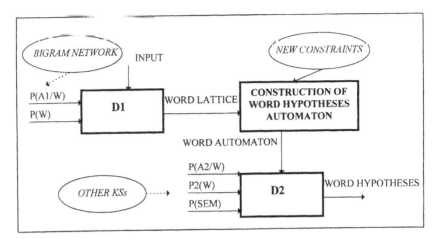

Figure 1.5 Multistage decision process.

etc. It should have a density (number of words in the lattice per pronounced word) that is a fraction of the system vocabulary size, and a very low probability of not containing all the pronounced words in the right precedence order. It is preferable for this phase to use a single integrated KS with the largest possible coverage with a search algorithm having computational complexity compatible with time and space requirements.

As the lattice contains hypotheses with segment bounds, it is possible to apply selective knowledge to prune or to rescore them. Coverage is no longer important, but performance is still very important. Features and algorithms based on all types of knowledge can be applied only where there are preconditions for which it is known that, if the hypothesis is correct, reliable new information is produced. A further search phase can be performed under the control of a finite-state automaton (FSA) generated from the pruned lattice, in which more powerful and perhaps adapted AMs and LMs are used.

Semantic constraints can also be imposed in this phase, in such a way that sequences of words in the FSA are semantically consistent.

1.5. HISTORICAL NOTES[1]

The first machines for producing an artificial voice were developed in the 18th century by Kratzenstein and Von Kempelen. More sophisticated versions of these machines were built in the last century by Wheatstone and Bell. The first electrical synthesizer was demonstrated in 1939 (Dudley, 1939).

---

[1]References in this section that are difficult to find have been replaced where possible by more recent but easier to find ones.

H. Dudley, in 1941, also proposed, in the US patent 2,238,555, an electronic limited-vocabulary word recognizer. In 1950, J. Dreyfus-Graf described in the *Journal of Acoustical Society of America (JASA*, vol. 22, pp. 731–739) the "typo-sonography" for French, an experimental system for voice printing with phonetic symbols. In 1951, C. P. Smith proposed a phoneme detector (*JASA*, vol. 23, pp. 446–451) In 1952, Davis, Biddulph and Balashek made a first demonstration (described in *JASA*, vol. 24, pp. 637–642, 1952) of a limited-word recognizer in English. Work in the UK is described by Fry and Denes (*JASA*, vol. 29, pp. 364–369, 1957).

Early systems were capable of recognizing isolated words from a single speaker using phonetic features detected by special circuits or templates. Templates were made of the time evolution of these features or by binary patterns in which each bit in a given time interval represented the presence of energy above a threshold in a frequency band. An interesting description of one of these systems with a review of the field in the 1950s can be found in Dudley and Balashek (1958). Pioneer work for Japanese is described in Sakai and Doshita (1962). In the 1950s, speech synthesis from low bit-rate driving signals was proposed. An overview of speech synthesis techniques in this period can be found in Fant (1959).

In the 1960s, speech synthesis by rules became available with the possibility of producing phoneme strings and continuous control signals for electronic speech synthesizers starting from text (Kelly and Gerstman, 1961; Holmes *et al.*, 1964; Liljencrants, 1968).

Great inspiration came from Chomsky and Halle (1968). Interesting studies also appeared on the geometry of the vocal tract preparing the advent of synthesizers based on advanced articulatory models (Schroeder, 1967). The subject is briefly, but effectively reviewed in Rahim (1994).

In the same period, circuits for feature extraction were proposed, some based on the perceptron model, the precursor of modern artificial neural networks (ANN). Furthermore, programs for obtaining and classifying acoustic patterns were also developed. Results of research along these lines are reported for Dutch (Pols, 1971), Italian (De Mori *et al.*, 1970), Japanese (Kurematsu *et al.*, 1971; Kohda *et al.*, 1970; Itahashi and Kido, 1971), Russian (Bondarko *et al.*, 1968) and Swedish (Fant, 1970b). Commercial systems capable of recognizing isolated words with a vocabulary of 100 words are described by Martin (*Proceedings of the IEEE*, vol. 64, no. 4, pp. 487–501, April 1976). An excellent review of early work in ASR was provided in Hyde (1972).

Starting in late 1960s and continuing in the 1970s, the use of dynamic programming for isolated word recognition was proposed in Russia (Slustker, 1968; Vintsjuk, 1968; Velichko and Zagoruiko, 1970), in Japan (Sakoe and Chiba, 1971), in the UK (Bridle and Brown, 1974), in the US (see Rabiner and Levinson, 1981 for review) and in Germany (Ney, 1982). This approach is based on an elastic matching of a word pattern with a set of templates. A distance between the unknown pattern and each template is obtained. The recognized word is the label of the template having minimum distance with respect to the input pattern. Better distance measures (Itakura, 1975b) and improved algorithms made it possible to implement speaker-dependent systems capable of recognizing 1000 isolated words. By clustering templates from different speakers, speaker-independent systems were also developed.

At the end of the 1960s, the first attempts were made to recognize continuous speech (Vicens, 1969). The effort was reviewed in Reddy (1974) and continued in the 1970s, leading to effective systems for the recognition of connected digits using statistical modeling (Bahl and Jelinek, 1975). In the early 1980s, it became evident that statistical modeling was the most effective approach to speaker-independent connected word recognition.

An ambitious project was undertaken in the 1970s in the area of speech understanding. Experimental systems were developed for the generation of conceptual interpretations from the analysis of the speech signal using search strategies and KSs inspired by artificial intelligence. Speaker-independent systems capable of recognizing and interpreting continuously spoken sentences using a 1000-word vocabulary were demonstrated in the US, at Carnegie Mellon University (CMU), Stanford Research Institute (SRI) and Bolt and Newman (BBN) in Cambridge, Mass. in cooperation with the Massachusetts Institute of Technology (MIT), in Japan at the Universities of Kyoto, Kyushu, Yamanashi and at the Nippon Telephone and Telegraph (NTT) Musashino Labs, in France at the Centre National d'Etudes de Telecommunications (CNET) and at the University of Nancy and in Italy at the University of Turin.

Some of these systems were based on a statistical approach. Worth mentioning are the HARPY (Lowerre, 1976) and DRAGON (Baker, 1975) systems developed at CMU and a system developed by the researchers of International Business Machines (IBM) (Bahl *et al.*, 1978). Tests on limited-domain tasks resulted in close or above 90% of sentence recognition.

Overviews of these speech understanding systems can be found in Reddy (1976) and Klatt (1977).

In the same period, speaker-dependent and speaker-independent systems with interesting performance were developed for limited vocabulary isolated or connected word recognition at the ATT Bell Labs and at Nippon Electric Company (NEC) in Japan. Other interesting research was performed in Russia, at the Institute of Problems for Information Transmission in Moscow and the University of Novosibirsk, and in Germany, at the Universities of Erlangen and Munich.

A comparative overview of ASR and ASU in the 1970s and in different countries can be found in De Mori (1979).

In the area of speech synthesis, a fundamental book appeared on the theory of speech production (Fant, 1970a); speech synthesis by rule systems were also developed for Japanese, French, Italian, German, Swedish and Russian, and further progress took place, as described in Flanagan (1972b). A new technique for speech analysis and synthesis based on linear prediction coefficients (LPC) was proposed and became very popular (Atal and Hanauer, 1971). Studies in articulatory model dynamics and control contributed to the progress of speech synthesis (Coker, 1967).

In the 1980s, great attention was paid to integrating various types of knowledge into HMMs. New algorithms were proposed for training HMMs and for using them in networks where lexical and language models were integrated. Artificial neural networks (ANN) were also proposed for learning by examples various types of relations including the ones implemented by HMMs. Many aspects of modern ASR systems are covered in detail in Lee and Waibel (1990) as well as in Chapters 4–12 of this book together with historical comments and new developments in the 1990s which led to commercial systems for speaker-independent continuous speech dictation of very large vocabularies and spoken language understanding in restricted domains.

For speech synthesis, effective software systems based on sophisticated models and rules were proposed (Klatt, 1980), progress was made in modelling the vocal tract (Maeda, 1982). The quality of synthesized voice was enhanced by concatenating special segments of synthesis parameters (Charpantier and Moulines, 1990) and successful ANNs were trained for translating orthographic forms into phonetic ones (Sejnowski and Rosenberg, 1986). Recent reviews of progress in speech synthesis can be found in Allen *et al.* (1987), Sagisaka (1990) and Carlson (1994).

ASR and ASU technologies are mature enough to start appearing in real-life systems. Nevertheless, many problems still deserve further investigation. These problems will be discussed in Chapters 2–14. Speech synthesis and language generation are also mature fields in which practical good-quality multilingual systems are available. These systems will be discussed in Chapter 16.

1.6. ACTIVITIES AND PROBLEMS IN DIFFERENT LANGUAGES FOR ASR

In recent years, an impressive amount of work has been reported in ASR (more than in speech synthesis). Recent papers (Lamel and De Mori, 1995; Sagisaka and Lee, 1995) address issues in acoustic modelling, lexical representation, and language modelling in various languages. Due to the very many results recently reported in these fields, a brief summary of activities and problems will be presented in the following. A good review of problems in speech synthesis can be found in Carlson (1994).

1.6.1. Major Active Groups

ASR and ASU systems developed in English in many countries make use of corpora in American English. Research involving dictation of the *Wall Street*

Journal (WSJ) and *North American Business News* has been sponsored by the Advanced Research Project Agency (ARPA) and involves, among others, AT&T, Bolt Beranek and Newman (BBN), Boston University (BU), Carnegie Mellon University (CMU), Cambridge University (CU), Centre de Recherche en Informatique de Montréal (CRIM), Dragon Systems, IBM, Karlsruhe University, the French LIMSI-CNRS of the Centre National de la Recherche Scientifique, MIT Lincoln Labs, New York University, Philips and Stanford Research Institute (SRI). Some of these groups as well as a group at the Massachusetts Institute of Technology (MIT), have also worked in ASU designing an air traffic information system (ATIS). Details and evaluations can be found in SLS95 (1995).

Among the Institutions where there are ASR and ASU activities for French worth mentioning are, in France, Centre National d'Etudes de Telecommunications (CNET), Centre de Recherche en Informatique de Nancy (CRIN), LIMSI-CNRS, IBM-France, and in Canada, CRIM and the Institut National pour la Recherche Scientifique (INRS). In the context of the linguistic research engineering (LRE) SQALE project of the European Community (Steeneken and Van Leeuwen, 1995), CU (Pye *et al.*, 1995) and LIMSI-CNRS and Philips (Dugast *et al.*, 1995) have developed dictation systems for French.

More than 60 groups are active in Japan performing research and developing various types of systems (Nagai *et al.*, 1992; Singer and Takami, 1994; Matsunaga *et al.*, 1995) notably at ATR, NEC, NTT, various companies and universities.

Work in German is performed at the University of Erlangen (Schukat-Talamazzini *et al.*, 1994) and at the University of Karlsruhe specialized in spoken language translation (Geutner, 1995). Philips and the University of Aachen interact in the development of a large-vocabulary dictation system. In the context of the LRE Sqale project, CU Philips and LIMSI-CNRS have developed systems for German (Lamel *et al.*, 1995). Much activity in spoken language translation is under way in the Verbmobil project, sponsored by the German Ministry of Science and Technology. This project includes large-scale recognition and evaluation effort using spontaneous speech corpora for translation of scheduling conversations. The effort involves other European partners in France, Italy and the UK, and others in Japan, Korea and the US. Various groups in these countries have formed a Consortium for Speech Translation and Research (C-STAR).

About 100 research groups are working on Mandarin Chinese. Most of them are in China, a few in Taiwan, others in Hong Kong, Singapore and the US. Very-large-vocabulary dictation systems have been developed for Mandarin Chinese (Lyu *et al.*, 1995, Ho *et al.*, 1995). Other activities are in progress for Cantonese and Taiwanese dialects including research on modelling tone behaviour, an important feature for recognition (Lee *et al.*, 1995).

The major groups active in Italy are at the Centro Studi Elettronica e Telecomunicazioni (CSELT) in cooperation with the Politecnico di Torino (Giachin, 1995), the Istituto per la Ricerca Scientifica e Tecnologica (IRST) and IBM Italy. A 20 000-word dictation system for the Italian business journal *Il sole 24 ore* is available at IRST (Federico, 1996b). An Italian version of ATIS is also available. In Belgium, various ASR and synthesis activities are developed at Lennout and Hanspie.

Groups working in European Spanish Continuous Speech Recognition are at the Universidad Politecnica de Valencia (Vidal *et al.*, 1995), Universidad Politecnica de Madrid, Universidad Politecnica de Catalunya, and Universidad del Pais Vasco. IBM-Sevilla has produced the Spanish version of an isolated word dictation machine.

The most active Korean centres are the Electronics and Communication Research Institute (ETRI), Korean Telecom (KT) and Korean Advanced Institute of Science and Technology (KAIST). An interesting Korean ASR system is described in Han *et al.* (1995).

A major research effort in Sweden at the Royal Institute of Technology (KTH) is the design of the Waxholm spoken language system. KTH is involved in a cooperative project with SRI to develop a speech-to-speech translator between Swedish and English in the ATIS domain.

Hindi is the most commonly studied language in India. A system for railway reservation has been developed at the TATA Institute of Fundamental Research in Bombay (Rao, 1993).

1.6.2. Acoustic and Lexical Modelling

Acoustic modelling is performed with HMMs in almost all systems. Different languages have different sets of units for modelling coarticulation influences among adjacent phonemes.

Lexica are typically represented with symbols of basic sounds, *phonemes* or *phones*. The lexicon is used for building a graph in which each word is expanded according to its lexical pronunciation(s). Words are connected together with probabilistic links whose probabilities are derived from LMs. Efficient tree lexical structures have been developed for several languages (Haeb-Umbach and Ney, 1994; Lamel *et al.*, 1995; Federico *et al.*, 1995).

The fact that words are often composed of more than one morpheme has more complex realizations in certain languages.

Differences in pronunciations of the same word are more frequent in certain languages and affect recognition accuracy.

American English is the language for which the largest amount of data is available, thus allowing extensive experiments on various models to be performed.

Comparable systems have been developed for British as well as for American English with similar performance on the WSJ task. English is usually represented with a set of 40 phonemes.

French has about 34 phonemes, with 14 vowels (three nasal) and 20 consonants. Most systems in French make use of HMMs for acoustic modelling, with context-dependent (CD) phone models. For close to real-time systems, reduced CD model sets or context-independent (CI) models may be used. In French words are frequently represented by a single phoneme. The large number of such *monophones*, the complex *liaison* system and the problem of having words with different orthography but the same phonetic representation (homophones), make ASR a particularly difficult task.

Japanese has five vowels and 21 consonants used in 101 native, mostly consonant-vowel syllables and in 30 additional syllables used in foreign words. There is good correspondence between the *kana* graphemic representation and pronunciation.

German has 25 vowels often including distinctions in the manner of articulation of the same vowel type. Vowel-initial words and morphemes are often, but not systematically, preceded by a glottal stop or by glottalization. German also has a large number of consonant clusters that are subject to reduction at word boundaries. CD and CI phone modelling have been used in speech recognition.

German ASR systems have to deal with many inflections and many different endings of words that require the use of a large lexicon and are hard to recognize. Furthermore, there is a strong tendency to create compound words which enlarge the lexicon. Long-distance agreement between words affects language modelling. In German, there is good correspondence between spelling and pronunciation, but there are large dialectal variations.

Chinese has some 10 000 characters, almost each being a morpheme with its own meaning. There are about 400 basic syllables made of 32 phones and five tones in Mandarin with a total of about 1350 distinct syllables. About 500 CD phone models are used in practical systems.

Italian has only seven vowels that can be reduced to five for practical purposes. The number of consonant clusters is not as large as in English. Detailed phoneme recognition experiments have been conducted at IRST with the Italian corpus APASCI (Angelini *et al.*, 1994b).

Acoustic modelling in Spanish is similar to Italian.

French, Italian and Spanish have rich sets of terminations for verbs. A large proportion of verbs is regular, so there are repetitive structures representing common termination (suffix) of many verbs (three or four basic sets of terminations are sufficient for regular verbs).

Korean is well modelled with seven vowels, 39 consonants and about 1500 syllables. The use of CD models has shown substantial advantage compared to CI models.

Swedish has 18 vowels, long/short consonants, some with considerable length duration (e.g. more than 100 ms occlusion). The Swedish /r/ has many different allophones that cause problems in ASR. Retroflexation and nasality spread over syllable and word boundaries. Prosody plays an important role in communication because Swedish is a tone language with two tones. Swedish verb forms used to be quite a bit more complicated but have been recently simplified. Like German, Swedish has many compound words which are sometimes difficult to decompose. This creates problems both for speech understanding and synthesis.

Hindi has nine vowels and 41 consonants. European Portuguese is difficult for ASR because of the high degree of vocalic reduction.

1.6.3. Language Modelling

Statistical *n*-gram language models (LM) are more or less efficient in the different languages. For languages in which agreement can span several words (like French, Italian, Spanish...), high order *n*-grams ($n > 3$) may be needed. This requires substantially more LM training text materials.

N-gram LMs have been successfully used for French. It has been demonstrated that a bigram LM is not strong enough to account for agreement.

Japanese and Korean are characterized by case structures in which cases correspond to phrases in a sentence. Context-free grammars (formally introduced in Chapter 13) with special parsers are used for Japanese. Word-class-based LMs have been used for Chinese. Finite-state networks are used for Korean and Hindi.

Important results have been obtained in statistical language modelling for German with bigrams and polygrams (Schukat-Talamazzini *et al.*, 1994) and phrase clustering (Kneser and Ney, 1993).

Various types of bigram and trigram models have been developed for Italian (Federico *et al.*, 1995). Stochastic and non-stochastic context-free grammars and grammar constructs (Giachin, 1995) have also been used for specific applications with medium and large vocabularies.

Spanish LMs have been developed using stochastic regular grammars automatically learned with grammatical inference techniques for a task concerning an oral query to a Spanish geographical database. The application of techniques based on *N*-grams to Spanish have also been explored for the same task.

Swedish is a Germanic language and has a grammar exhibiting similarities with both German and English. The Waxholm project uses a parser to model both dialogue and grammar (Blomberg, 1993).

The most widely-known evaluation activities of large vocabulary, continuous speech recognition systems are those carried out under the ARPA CSR program, starting with the Resource Management task (1000 words, word pair grammar), and continuing with the *Wall Street Journal* task (originally 5000 and 20 000 word vocabulary tests) and the *North American Business News* tests with unlimited vocabulary size. The most commonly used measures of performance are the word error and the sentence error. Statistical tests of significance can be applied to each of these, as a way of assessing apparent difference in performance between different systems. The word error is based on counts of word insertions (I), deletions (D) and substitutions (S), after performing a dynamic programming alignment between the reference and hypothesized strings.

Acknowledgements

This book is the result of research and literature survey carried out in the last ten years. This has been made possible by a number of graduate students and research assistants at McGill University. In addition to those who contributed to this book, we should mention with gratitude R. Abu Hosn, P. Boucher, R. Cardin, M. Contolini, S. Doyle, G. Flammia, M. Galler, R. Kompe, R. Lacouture, Y. Normandin, C. Pateras, C. Snow, A. Takahashi and Q. Yi. They were supported in various ways by the Natural Science and Engineering Research Council of Canada (NSERCC). Most of them worked in a program of the Institute for Robotics and Intelligent Systems (IRIS), a Canadian network of centres of excellence. Thanks also go to Hisham Petry, Nicholas Roy and Lise Minogue from McGill University for helping in various ways.

In addition to an extensive exchange of reviews from the authors of various chapters, external reviews were provided by J. G. Bauer, L. Fissore, E. Giachin, P. Heeman, M. Jardino, R. Kneser, P. Laface, E. Marschall, M. Matassoni, G. A. Mian, G. Micca, D. Petrelli, D. V. Rabinkin, R. Rosenfeld, G. Satta, P. Tonella and C. Vair.

It is important to acknowledge the inspiration provided by many conversations with eminent researchers in the field who deserve warm thanks in addition to a continuous admiration: G. Doddington, J. Flanagan, H. Fujusaki, S. Furui, J. P. Haton, F. Jelinek, L. Lamel, J.P. Maertens, H. Ney, H. Niemann, L. Rabiner, R. Reddy, A. Rubio, Y. Sagisaka, S. Seneff, E. Vidal, A. Waibel and V. Zue.

Gratitude go to those who kindly provided advice and suggestions and who are no longer with us: E. Caianielo, R. Capocelli, P. Deuijver, F. Fallside, K. S. Fu, Y. Kato, R. Santori, M. Wajskop and S. Young.

2

Acoustic Transduction

Maurizio Omologo, Piergiorgio Svaizer* and Renato De Mori†

*Istituto per la Ricerca Scientifica e Tecnologica – 38050 Pantè di Povo, Trento, Italy.
†School of Computer Science, McGill University, Montréal, P.Q. H3A 2A7, Canada.

2.1. INTRODUCTION

Speech sounds are generated as rapid variations of air pressure and velocity around their normal values. These variations are converted into electrical signals or are generated from electrical signals by transducers. Speech processing is performed by computers on numerical representations of these electrical signals.

As transducers are not perfect, they introduce distortion to the information carried by the signals they transform. Furthermore, a sound to electrical signal transducer, or microphone, often captures a variety of signals present in the surrounding environment (e.g. speech and noise, or multiple conversation). In many cases, only one of the components is relevant for a given application and this important component has to be singled out from the mixture of sounds captured by the sensor.

Performance of man–machine dialogue systems based on available technologies is influenced by a large number of factors, including type and use of microphones, while the quality and intelligibility of speech produced by synthesis systems is much less affected by the choice of the loudspeaker. For this reason, the emphasis of this chapter is on input (i.e. acoustic to electric) transduction.

Section 2.2 will review basic principles of sound propagation, and introduce the major source of alteration for the signal produced by a sound source and captured by a microphone.

Alteration may cause serious problems if the source is not very close to the sensor. Even when the transduction is performed by a microphone close to the source, the sensor may degrade the original information. Types of microphones, their properties and distortions they may introduce are discussed in section 2.3.

Section 2.4 introduces microphone arrays, that are presently the object of important investigation for their use in selective sound acquisition. Talker location, discussed in section 2.5, is an important operation in applications as hands-free speech interaction and teleconferencing.

The content of sections 2.4 and 2.5 is not essential for understanding the rest of the book, so the reader may choose to read these sections after having read other chapters. Section 2.6 provides a brief overview of the investigation conducted so far on the use of microphones and microphone arrays in automatic speech recognition (ASR).

2.2. SOUND PROPAGATION

2.2.1. The Wave Equation

Sounds originate when air particles are induced to vibrate around their mean position with consequent changes in the air pressure with respect to a static value. This results in a *sound field* in which variations of air density and pressure are function of time and space and propagate as *acoustic waves*.

A simplified but realistic hypothesis in room acoustics, is to assume that air is a homogeneous medium at rest. The speed c of acoustic wave propagation in air then depends only on temperature and is given by the following formula:

$$c = 331.45\sqrt{\frac{T}{273}} \text{ m/s} \tag{2.1}$$

where T is the temperature in kelvins.

Basic laws of physics, such as conservation of momentum and conservation of mass, and the ideal-gas equations, lead to a relationship between pressure and density of a fluid in a general differential equation governing sound propagation (Kinsler *et al.*, 1982; Morse and Ingard, 1986). This relationship is the so-called *wave equation*:

$$\nabla^2 p = \frac{1}{c^2}\frac{\partial^2 p}{\partial t^2} \tag{2.2}$$

where p denotes sound pressure, t denotes time and ∇^2 is the laplacian operator.

If pressure is represented as a scalar field $p(\boldsymbol{a}, t)$, where $\boldsymbol{a} = [x, y, z]^T$ is the vector of the cartesian coordinates in three-dimensional space, the wave equation becomes:

$$\nabla^2 p(\boldsymbol{a}, t) = \frac{\partial^2 p}{\partial x^2} + \frac{\partial^2 p}{\partial y^2} + \frac{\partial^2 p}{\partial z^2} = \frac{1}{c^2}\frac{\partial^2 p(\boldsymbol{a}, t)}{\partial t^2} \tag{2.3}$$

One solution of this equation is the *monochromatic plane wave* of frequency $f = \omega/2\pi$:

$$p(\boldsymbol{a}, t) = A\, e^{j(\omega t - \boldsymbol{k}\cdot\boldsymbol{a})} \tag{2.4}$$

where A is the wave amplitude and $\boldsymbol{k} = [k_x, k_y, k_z]^T$ is called the *wavenumber vector*. The vector $\boldsymbol{k}$ has a direction normal to the propagating wavefronts and a magnitude equal to the number of cycles per unit length of the plane wave along this direction. Here, only the real part of the complex exponential $p(\boldsymbol{a}, t)$ should be considered to have the physical meaning of sound pressure. The distance $\lambda = 2\pi/|\boldsymbol{k}| = c/f$ is called the *wavelength* and corresponds to the spatial period of the propagating wave.

The wave equation can also be expressed in spherical coordinates (r, ϕ, θ). If there is spherical symmetry, i.e. the sound pressure depends only on the distance r from the origin but not on the direction, then equation (2.3) becomes:

$$\frac{\partial^2 p}{\partial r^2} + \frac{2}{r}\frac{\partial p}{\partial r} = \frac{1}{c^2}\frac{\partial^2 p}{\partial t^2} \tag{2.5}$$

The solution:

$$p(r, t) = \frac{A}{r}\, e^{j\omega(t - r/c)} \tag{2.6}$$

corresponds to a monochromatic spherical wave propagating outward from the origin, with a wavelength $\lambda = 2\pi c/\omega$.

The wave equation is a linear equation and complex exponentials are solutions of it. Since any function with a convergent Fourier integral can be expressed as a weighted superposition of complex exponentials, it is possible to assert that, thanks to linearity, any signal described by this type of function satisfies the wave equation.

As a consequence of the superposition principle, any sound field can be thought of as resulting from the superposition of elementary plane or spherical waves. Waves propagate undistorted (under the hypothesis of nondispersive, lossless and homogeneous medium) and carry along the information generated by distant sources.

2.2.2. Room Acoustics

Generally when we listen to someone talking in a room, unless we are face to face with her/him, most of the acoustic energy captured by our ears is carried by indirect sounds arising from reflection at various surfaces inside the room.

The original signal produced by the speaker undergoes an alteration of its perceptual features such as level, timbre and spatial impression, due to reflections from surfaces and diffusion and diffraction by objects inside the room.

This phenomenon, known as *reverberation*, is the most noticeable acoustical phenomenon directly perceivable in an enclosure. For this reason the most important objective measure in room acoustics is *reverberation time*. Reverberation time, T_{60}, of a room is defined as the time needed for the acoustic power of a received signal to decay by 60 dB from a steady state value after the sound source is abruptly stopped.

The reverberation time is nearly independent from the listening position since it is almost constant in a given enclosure. It can be calculated, with reasonable accuracy, by the approximated Sabine formula (Kuttruff, 1991):

$$T_{60} = 0.163 \frac{V}{\alpha S} \tag{2.7}$$

where V denotes the room volume in m^3, S is the total surface area of the room in m^2 and α is the average absorption coefficient of the surfaces.

Reverberation times up to 1 s (measured for frequencies between 500 and 1000 Hz) do not cause any loss in speech intelligibility.

The space separating a sound source from a receiving transducer can be seen as a transmission channel in which the acoustic signal is conveyed and modified, according to the acoustic characteristics of the environment. The *impulse response* $h(t)$ of the acoustic channel between source and sensor in a reverberant room represents all the multiple reflections from the surrounding surfaces that

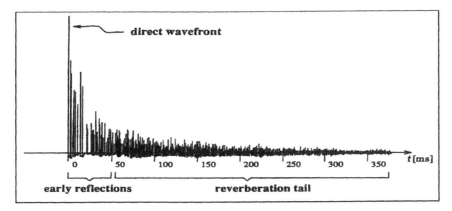

Figure 2.1 Typical impulse response of an acoustic channel between source and sensor in a reverberant environment.

reach the sensor in addition to the direct sound. Reflections from walls and objects produce a variety of paths between the source and the sensor. Since paths have different length, the propagation delay differs from one path to another and several replicas of the radiated signal reach the sensor after the direct wavefront.

Every time a wavefront hits a surface, it is partially absorbed and partially reflected. All the reflections contribute to create the complicated impulse response typical of an enclosure, as shown in Figure 2.1. The effect is more pronounced when the source is placed further from the sensor: the original waveform is distorted by constructive and destructive interference at various frequencies. It should be noted that, in ordinary reverberation conditions ($T_{60} < 0.7\,\text{s}$), the listener is generally unaware of the distortion of the direct signal caused by reflections. The reflected wavefronts are perceived by human ears only when their delay from the direct sound is longer than 50 ms. Reflections exceeding this threshold generally have a negative effect on speech intelligibility, because they result in a merging of basic speech sounds.

On the contrary, for delays shorter than 50 ms, reflections ("early reflections") are perceived as part of the direct sound. Their effect on sound perception is an increase in loudness and a spectral alteration, known as "coloration", that characterizes the "acoustics" of each room.

The total energy contained in the impulse response is obtained by integration of the instantaneous power:

$$E_{tot} = \int_0^\infty h^2(t)\,dt \tag{2.8}$$

The portion of this energy that is useful for intelligibility is given by:

$$D = 1/E_{tot} \int_0^{50\,\text{ms}} h^2(t)\,dt \tag{2.9}$$

and is referred to as the "Deutlichkeit", or "definition" index (Kuttruff, 1991).

Another index related to speech intelligibility is the centre-of-gravity time:

$$t_s = 1/E_{tot} \int_0^\infty t.h^2(t)\,dt \tag{2.10}$$

The higher the value of D and the smaller the value of t_s, the better the speech intelligibility.

A different approach to characterizing speech intelligibility is based on the concept of the modulation transfer function (MTF) and on the reduction of a "modulation index", as a consequence of the smearing effect due to reverberation (Houtgast and Steeneken, 1985).

The flattening of power fluctuations produced by reverberation and noise in different octave bands and at several modulation frequencies is converted into one single indicator, the speech transmission index (STI), which very closely relates to the speech intelligibility measured in listening tests (Steeneken and Houtgast, 1980).

2.2.3. Impulse Response Measurement

A direct approach to measuring the impulse response of a channel consists of applying an impulsive excitation and observing the response of the system. When the channel is an acoustic one, two basic difficulties arise: generating an impulse with enough energy to ensure that signal-to-noise ratios are high at all frequencies of interest, and making sure that the excitation has a sufficiently flat spectrum. Popping balloons, gun shots or short pulses through loudspeakers may not completely satisfy the above requirements.

To overcome these difficulties, maximal length pseudo-random sequences have been used as excitatory signals (Schroeder, 1979). Pseudo-random sequences are binary sequences generated using feedback shift registers, and are therefore periodic and deterministic signals. If the shift register is based upon a primitive polynomial, then the period of the sequence is the maximum achievable with a given number of register cells (MacWilliams and Sloane, 1976). These sequences have a flat spectrum (except at 0 Hz frequency) exactly as white noise. As a matter of fact, the autocorrelation $\phi_{pp}(k)$ of a maximal length sequence $p(n)$ of length L becomes a close approximation of a delta function when L is large:

$$\phi_{pp}(k) = \begin{cases} 1/L & \text{if } k \neq 0 \\ L & \text{if } k = 0. \end{cases} \tag{2.11}$$

As a consequence, the room impulse response $h(t)$ between source and sensor in a room can be obtained by reproducing the acoustic signal corresponding to the sequence and then by simply cross-correlating the excitation sequence $p(n)$ with the signal $y(n)$ acquired by the sensor.

As an alternative to maximal length sequences, time stretched pulses (TSP) have been used as excitatory signals. They are chirp-like signals sweeping all frequencies of interest (Berkhout *et al.*, 1980). Again, the impulse response is then recovered through deconvolution of the received signal.

A reasonable approximation of the impulse responses of the acoustic channels in a room can also be derived by starting from a geometrical model of the room and using some simplifying hypotheses (Allen and Berkley, 1979). If the dimensions of the room and its walls are large compared to the wavelength of sound (e.g. 34 cm at 1 kHz), the concept of *wave* can be replaced by the concept of *sound ray* (similar to a light ray in geometrical optics). If we ignore all the sound portions diffracted by edges and scattered by small obstacles, then, according to Snell's law, the reflection angle of each ray is equal to the incident angle.

Let us examine the sound transmission from the source to the receiver according to the scheme of Figure 2.2(a). Besides the direct path, there is a reflection from the wall. To find the contribution of the reflected ray we first consider the mirror image of the source with respect to the wall. By connecting the image to the receiver we can determine the reflection point. The effect of the wall can be replaced by that of the image source if we take into account the fraction of energy absorbed and not reflected by the wall. Here, the frequency dependence of the wall reflectivity is neglected and it is assumed that its value is constant.

If the enclosure consists of N plane walls, N images of the original source are obtained. Each of these first-order images is then mirrored again by each wall. By iteration of this procedure, a rapidly growing number of images is produced at increasing distances from the original source, as illustrated in Figure 2.2(b). All the images are assumed to emit the source signal synchronously. The rays originating from the images reach the receiver from various directions, with different energy and different delay with respect to the direct sound, according to the total path lengths they have covered (Peterson, 1986). The sum of all the contributions arriving at the receiver after the source has emitted a sound pulse, gives the acoustic impulse response of the room.

A more sophisticated simulation method that takes into account diffuse reflections of sound waves is the method of *sound particles* (Kuttruff, 1994). A sound source is assumed to emit imaginary sound particles, or energy units, that travel along straight trajectories until they hit an obstacle. As a consequence of each collision, the particles lose a part of their energy by absorption and are then reflected either specularly or in a random direction, according to a diffusion model. Whenever a particle reaches the volume associated to the receiver, its arrival time, energy and direction are registered. A histogram of a very large number of received particles as a function of time accounts for the impulse response of the room.

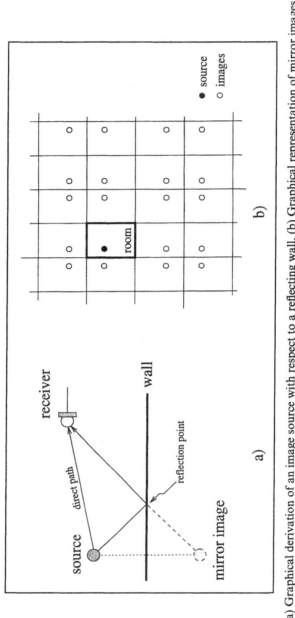

Figure 2.2 (a) Graphical derivation of an image source with respect to a reflecting wall. (b) Graphical representation of mirror images of various orders for a source inside a rectangular room. The pattern of source images is extended indefinitely in all directions, as well as in the third spatial dimension.

2.3. ACOUSTIC SENSORS

2.3.1. Introduction

Present acoustic-transduction technology makes available precise, robust, small microphones, often at fairly or very low cost. The type of microphone, the way in which it is used, and the environmental conditions in which it operates may have a fundamental impact on the performance that can be obtained in applications such as speech recognition.

Speech acquisition involves a number of transformation steps, as information flows from the talker's mouth to a digital representation. Any poorly performed transformation step can cause an unrecoverable distortion of information and, consequently, a deterioration in recognition performance.

An important contribution to distortion is due to microphone transduction. In telephone applications, the microphone cannot be chosen to maximize recognition performance and the AMs of the ASR system must account for different types of telephone handsets. But, for other applications (e.g. dictation, data entry, voice-driven interfaces, voice-command games, etc.) an optimal transducer choice can be made depending on microphone mounting conditions, directional response and other specifications that are discussed in the following.

General characteristics

A microphone is a device that converts the acoustic energy of sounds into a corresponding electrical energy. This transduction is generally realized with a diaphragm whose movements are produced by sound pressure and vary the parameters of an electrical system (a variable resistance conductor, a condenser, etc.) inducing a variable voltage that constitutes the microphone output. As other electrical systems, a microphone may be characterized by a *frequency response* and a *signal-to-noise ratio (SNR)*. In high-fidelity speech applications, the whole transduction process should take place with negligible loss of information in a frequency range of at least six octaves (e.g. from 100 Hz to 6400 Hz). The power of the noise produced by the microphone itself should be well below the power of the electrical signal that conveys the speech information. In practice, noise power is also influenced by the electrical equipment that is connected to the microphone.

Two other important parameters in microphone performance are *impedance* and *sensitivity*. Generally, microphone impedance does not affect the acquisition quality. Low-impedance microphones connected to low-impedance pre-amplifiers often represent the best choice, because this reduces hum and electrical noise picked up by the connections (especially when long cables are used). On the other hand, high-impedance microphones and system input connections are easier to realize and cheaper. Note that the impedance declared on commercial products indicates a range around which the actual impedance will assume its value. As an example, most low-impedance microphones are declared as "150 ohm" impedance, but their actual impedance range is from 100 to 300 ohm, while "150 ohm" is specific of 94 dB sound pressure level (SPL).[1]

The sensitivity of a microphone is determined by measuring either the output voltage (generally expressed in millivolts across a given impedance) or the power (that can be expressed in dBm) relative to a standard condition.[2] Given two closely spaced microphones, A and B, and an active sound source placed at the same distance from them, the output voltage of each microphone is measured: if the output voltage of microphone A is N dB higher than that of microphone B, A is N dB more sensitive than B. The sensitivity is evaluated after measurements over the entire frequency range specified by the manufacturer. The measurement is taken with the microphone open-circuited within a reflection-free field, such as that found in an anechoic chamber.

Another significant parameter that affects the microphone response characteristics is the *directional response* provided by the *polar pattern*. Since the air-pressure waves arrive at the microphone diaphragm from all directions, the directional response of a microphone should be represented in a three-dimensional space. However, the most common way to depict it is by a polar diagram with concentric circles that correspond to different sensitivity levels on a particular plane.

Generally, the polar pattern is computed for different input frequencies and graphically represented in a diagram of the type shown in Figure 2.3. According to the polar response shape, the microphones can be classified as either omnidirectional or directional. The former type has a near constant response to sound coming from all directions. The latter type can be further subdivided into categories that depend on the directionality characteristics and can be roughly classified into cardioid (supercardioid, hypercardioid, shotgun, etc.), and bidirectional (or figure-of-eight). There is also the category of polidirectional microphones, that have a switch for selecting the desired polar pattern.

A property, deriving from the previously introduced characteristics, is the so-called *reach*, that may be defined as the potential distance range at which the microphone can pick up the sound without a considerable reduction of SNR. The reach factor depends on the polar pattern and the sensitivity characteristics but also on the capability of the device to reduce noise and reverberation. An example of very high reach is that of shotgun microphones, that may be used to acquire sounds at up to a range of 100 m.

---

[1]SPL is a unit of sound pressure measurement that is expressed in decibels and is sometimes used in place of the microbar (basic unit of atmospheric pressure). As a reference, "0 dB SPL" corresponds to 0.0002 μbar and represents the threshold of hearing.
[2]0 dBm corresponds to 0 dB referenced to 1 mW.

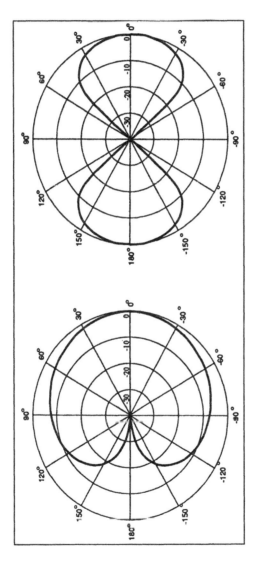

Figure 2.3 Two basic microphone polar responses, representing a cardioid pattern (left) and a figure-of-eight pattern (right).

Microphone mountings

Microphones can be classified along many criteria. An important criterion describes how they are to be mounted. For speech recognition, the most common mounting options are: *hand-held, head-mounted,* and *table-stand* (or desktop). Recently, improvement in local transmitter-receiver technology has led to the flexible solution of head-mounted wireless microphones (with a radio-frequency connection to the sound acquisition system).

Each of these solutions has advantages and disadvantages. The hand-held microphone has critical effects related to the user's experience in managing such a device. A careless use of the microphone can lead to high variability of speech dynamics (due to change in talker–microphone distance), overload, distortion, clipping (caused by the talker's mouth being placed too close to the microphone), handling noise, etc. Hand-held microphones must be chosen in order to reduce the influence of these factors. For instance, some microphones (e.g. condenser) are very robust to handling vibrations. Moreover, the angle between the axis normal to the microphone diaphragm and the mouth–microphone direction may influence the quality of the acquisition: for hand-held cardioid microphones, an angle of about 45° is generally suggested. Another improvement can be obtained by applying a windscreen to the microphone in order to prevent breath pop (typical of words that begin with a stop consonant).

The head-mounted microphones have the advantage of reducing the variations in the "talker's mouth to microphone" distance and the effects of the environment (e.g. background noise, reverberation, echoes, etc.). Since vibration noise can influence the acquisition, mounting must be kept stable. In this case, breath noise and pop effects are more prominent, due to the proximity between the talker's mouth and the microphone.

Table-stand and *Lavalier*[3] microphones belong to the category of microphones that allow the user to have hands-free interaction. However, they are better suited for teleconferencing, film and television applications than for speech recognition. In fact, they pick up different kinds of environmental and vibrational noise. Also highly directive or autodirective table-stand microphones, such as the two-dipole based one described in Chu (1995), are now available on the market. However, their usability in ASR applications may be affected by a non-uniform behaviour caused by variations in the position of the talker. Besides, a non-optimal noise reduction/compensation performed in the device may alter the speech input spectrum.

2.3.2. Basic Transduction Categories

Microphones can be classified according to the type of transduction they

---

[3]Lavalier microphones are small microphones that are suspended from the neck or attached to clothing.

perform (Davis and Davis, 1989; Kinsler *et al.*, 1982; Clifford, 1986). The first classification is between *passive transducers* and *active transducers*. Passive transducers are those in which sound is directly converted to electrical energy. Active transducers require an external energy source (e.g. battery) that is modulated by the effect of sound vibrations.

A second classification is based on the physical quantity that is transduced (i.e. pressure or pressure gradient).

Another possibility of classifying microphones is given by the material and physical principles on which the transduction is based. In the following a classification is given according to the type of transduction employed.

Electromagnetic and electrodynamic microphones

The most common microphones belonging to these two categories are: *ribbon microphones* and *moving-coil microphones*. Both these microphones are widely utilized, reliable for indoor and outdoor use, have extended and smooth frequency response, good transient response, and are available at moderate cost.

Ribbon microphones (also called velocity microphones) consist of a thin, stretched duralumin ribbon suspended between the poles of a permanent magnet and clamped at both ends, but free to move back and forth. AC voltage is induced across the magnetic field depending on the frequency of the impinging sound waves. Generally, ribbon microphones provide a bidirectional response (also called "figure-of-eight pattern"). Their low inertia results in an excellent transient response.

Moving-coil microphones (also called dynamic microphones) can be thought of as the inverse of a loudspeaker. The wire coil is attached to and suspended by a light diaphragm made of a non-metallic material such as plastic. The moving-coil microphone induces a much larger voltage than the ribbon microphone, due to the greater length of the coil.

Electrostatic microphones

Electrostatic microphones are based on variation of sensor capacity caused by air-pressure waves. The most common types are *condenser microphones* and *electret microphones*.

Condenser microphones contain a capacitor that consists of a pair of metal plates, separated by an insulating material, called the dielectric. One of the plates is free to move: its motion produces variations in voltage across the capacitor. The voltage changes in steps with the incoming sound pressure level. An amplifier is needed to reinforce such a "small" voltage. The output impedance of a condenser microphone is extremely high. So, the amplifier acts as an impedance adaptor. Condenser microphones have excellent frequency response, low distortion and an excellent transient response. They require a power supply (with batteries or phantom power systems) both for the amplifier and for the condenser element.

Electret microphones are special types of condenser microphones with a specially designed capacitor that can hold a charge for a very long time. A voltage, known as a "bias voltage" (that can be more than 100 V), is impressed on the electret at the time of manufacturing. Also in this case, a power supply is used by an internal impedance converter circuit. Electret microphones can be very small: they are suitable for high-quality recording and provide uniform frequency response and good transient capability (i.e. given a sound level that passes almost instantaneously from zero to a high peak as well as from a high peak to zero, the diaphragm of the microphone must respond equally rapidly). However, the dynamic range and sensitivity values in electrets are lower than standard values for condenser units.

Piezoresistive and piezoelectric microphones

Piezoresistive and piezoelectric microphones are based on the variation of electric resistance of their sensor induced by the variations of sound pressure level.

Carbon microphones consist of a small cylinder ("button") packed with tiny granules of carbon. A diaphragm produces pressure against the button containing the carbon granules. The acoustic energy impinging on the diaphragm causes it to vibrate, giving the granules a chance to separate. Since carbon is a conductor, the device acts as a variable resistor (the diaphragm does not move at its periphery, because it is fastened): when the granules are compacted, its resistance is lowered. Pickup range, frequency range, and transient response of carbon microphones are limited.

Crystal microphones and *ceramic microphones* are based on the same principle as carbon microphones. Crystal microphones contain a crystal of Rochelle salt between two metal plates with the upper one free to move. Varying pressure of the metal plate transmitted to the surface of the crystal tends to deform it (piezoelectric effect). This deformation generates an alternating voltage at the rate of sound pressure change. Crystal microphones can be very small and are characterized by low cost and high voltage output. However, the average quality of crystal microphones is not satisfactory for ASR, and the crystal can easily be damaged by high temperatures and humidity.

2.3.3. Specific Microphones

Pressure-zone microphones

The *pressure-zone microphone* (*PZM*) has an electret placed approximately in the centre of a plate, with a gap of less than 1 mm between the transducer cover and the plate. The PZM takes advantage of the fact that, at the primary boundary, the direct wave coming from the source and waves reflected from the plate are so close in time that they act as one reinforced signal. PZMs are used particularly in the area of speech reinforcement. They are characterized by a hemispherical pickup pattern and are able to transduce sound levels of up to 150 dB without distortion. It is worth noting that, when using a conventional microphone, at some particular frequencies sound cancellation effects caused by the combination of direct and reflected waves may occur. PZMs are conceived to prevent this effect.

Pressure-gradient microphones

Pressure-gradient microphones have a response proportional to the gradient of the pressure wave. They are suitable for directional acquisition, and generally are based either on a single diaphragm, both sides of which are exposed to the direct sound field, or on a more complex device that can acquire sounds from different directions and compensate for relative delay of the wavefront arrival. The most common types of pressure-gradient microphones are the first-order and the second-order gradient, and the toroidal (Flanagan *et al.*, 1991; Sessler *et al.*, 1969, 1989). It is worth noting that a very simple example of a pressure-gradient microphone is the ribbon microphone.

Noise-cancelling microphones

Differential or noise-cancelling microphones are useful in noisy environments, where it is important to reduce the effect of background noise. Differential microphones contain two parallel diaphragms, one of which faces the talker's mouth. Sound arriving from lateral directions will produce equal pressures on both sides resulting in signal cancellation. On the basis of the differential principle, noise cancelling microphones can also be realized using two transducers, of those previously described (e.g. two electrodynamic microphones).

Micromechanical silicon microphones

Digital processing of audio signals is gradually replacing traditional analogue processing systems. The microphone (as well as the loudspeaker for reproduction) remains as the last component that operates entirely in the analogue domain.

Present silicon technology allows building micromechanical sensors that can be combined with microelectronic components for digital signal processing, leading to integrated sensors for acoustic transduction.

Silicon microphones (Sessler, 1996) offer an advantage over standard microphones because they can be made considerably smaller in size (1 mm^2 compared to 5 mm^2). They have low sensitivity to vibration and electromagnetic interference and can be manufactured at low cost depending on the underlying transduction principle. So far, the transduction principles explored have led to the realization of the following silicon microphones: condenser, modulated field-effect-transistor (FET), piezoelectric and piezoresistive, and optical waveguide. In particular, the optical waveguide microphone is based on the principle of conversion of an acoustic signal into an intensity or phase modulation of a light wave. It has been introduced in 1994 and consists in a two-chip set (a membrane chip and a waveguide chip). Light is coupled into the waveguide chip via a transmitting fibre. Present prototypes have a flat frequency response only up to 4 kHz.

2.4. MICROPHONE ARRAYS

2.4.1. Introduction

The ideal method for capturing an acoustic message is to use a transducer placed close to the emitting source. In this configuration, the captured power of the noise produced by other sound sources is often negligible when compared with the power of the signal produced by the source of interest.

For ASR, available modelling techniques are based on the assumption that a single, clear speech message is conveyed by the acquired signal. However, this assumption is clearly not valid in many practical situations where the message to be processed is generated at some distance from the transducer and, therefore, is mixed with other sounds.

In these conditions, it could be advantageous to exploit the spatial selectivity of a microphone array to acquire the signal of the desired source. A microphone array consists of a set of acoustic sensors placed at different locations to spatially sample a sound pressure field. Using a microphone array it is possible to selectively pick up a speech message, while avoiding the undesirable effects due to distance, background noise, room reverberation and competitive sound sources. This objective can be accomplished by means of a spatio-temporal filtering approach (Flanagan *et al.*, 1985; Silverman, 1987).

The directivity of a microphone array can be electronically controlled, without changing the sensor positions or placing the transducers very close to the speaker (Flanagan *et al.*, 1991). Moreover, detection, location, tracking, and selective acquisition of an active talker can be performed automatically to improve the intelligibility and quality of a selected speech message in applications such as teleconferencing and hands-free communication (e.g. car telephony).

2.4.2. Beamforming

A beamformer exploits the spatial distribution of the elements of a microphone array to perform spatial filtering (Van Veen and Buckley, 1988). The microphone signals are appropriately delayed, filtered and added to constructively combine the components arriving from a selected direction while attenuating those arriving from other directions. As a consequence, signals originating from distinct spatial locations can be separated even if they have overlapping bandwidths.

Delay-and-sum beamforming is the simplest and most straightforward array signal processing technique. A proper delay τ_n is applied to each microphone signal $s_n(t)$, $n = 1 \ldots N$, in order to cophase the desired component by compensating for the difference in path lengths from the source to each microphone. Each signal amplitude can be weighted by a coefficient w_n in order to shape the overall polar pattern, and finally the N signals associated to N microphones are summed together as follows:

$$z(t) = \sum_{n=0}^{N-1} w_n s_n(t - \tau_n) \tag{2.12}$$

By adjustment of the delays, the array can be electronically steered towards different locations. Desired main beam width and sidelobe level can be obtained with a proper choice of the coefficients w_n.

A delay, in the time domain, is equivalent to a linear phase shift in the frequency domain. Therefore the beamformer can also be implemented by a proper phase alignment in the frequency domain according to the relationship:

$$Z(f) = \sum_{n=0}^{N-1} w_n S_m(f) \, e^{-j2\pi f \tau_n} \tag{2.13}$$

A more general beamforming structure is the *filter-and-sum* beamformer described by the equation:

$$z(t) = \sum_{n=0}^{N-1} w_n h_n(t) * s_n(t - \tau_n) \tag{2.14}$$

In this case, an additional linear filtering with impulse response $h_n(t)$ is inserted in each channel prior to summation, according to the scheme of Figure 2.4, in

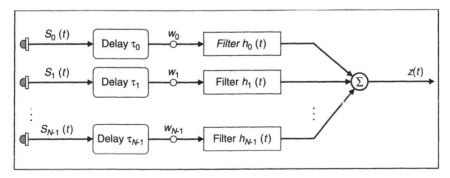

Figure 2.4 Configuration of a filter-and-sum beamformer.

order to perform more complex spatiotemporal filtering and directivity shaping, especially when dealing with broadband signals (e.g. speech). Moreover, the transfer functions of the filters can be chosen according to the statistical characteristics of the desired signal and interfering noise.

The directional characteristics of the microphones, the locations of the array elements, and the overall array geometry provide additional degrees of freedom in designing the directivity pattern of a beamformer.

2.4.3. Uniform Linear Array

The uniform linear array is the most commonly used sensor configuration in multichannel signal processing. It consists of N transducers located on a straight line and uniformly spaced by a distance d.

If a source is far from the array (in the so-called "far-field" region), then the arrival direction of the sound wavefronts is approximately equal for all sensors, and the propagating field can be considered to consist of plane waves. If a wavefront reaches the sensors from a direction forming an angle θ with the normal to the array, as depicted in Figure 2.5, then the relative delay τ_a between wavefront arrivals at two adjacent microphones is given by:

$$\tau_a = \frac{d}{c}\sin\theta \qquad (2.15)$$

If the source is located close to the array (in the "near-field" region), then the wavefronts of the propagating waves are perceivably curved with respect to the dimensions of the array and the arrival direction differs from an element to another. In this case, the relative delays of wavefront arrival at successive sensors lie on a hyperbolic curve (Silverman and Kirtman, 1992).

The frequency response of an unsteered ($\tau_n = 0 \quad \forall n$) linear array of $N = (2M + 1)$ equispaced omnidirectional microphones, hit by a plane wave

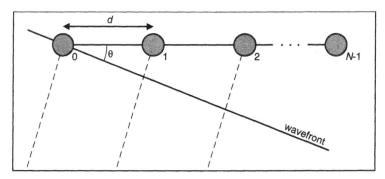

Figure 2.5 Uniform linear array of N elements and intersensor distance d. A plane wavefront reaches the array from a direction identified by the angle θ.

arriving with a direction angle θ, is expressed as:

$$H(\omega) = \sum_{m=-M}^{M} w_m \, e^{-j\omega m \tau_a} \tag{2.16}$$

where τ_a is given by relation (2.15).

With the substitution $z = e^{j\omega\tau_a}$, it becomes apparent that a linear array with equispaced elements is analogous to a digital FIR filter. Therefore, the same design procedures used for FIR filters can be applied to obtain a desired directivity pattern. For a given width of the main beam, for example, using Chebyshev coefficients, will result in minimized sidelobes for a given amplitude of the main lobe.

In the case of uniform weights (i.e. $w_n = 1$ for every value of n) from expression (2.16), identity $\sum_{k=0}^{K-1} z^k = (1 - z^K)/(1 - z)$ and Euler's formulae may be applied resulting in a frequency response of the unsteered beamformer (Johnson and Dudgeon, 1993):

$$H(\omega) = \frac{\sin\left(\dfrac{N}{2}\omega\tau_a\right)}{\sin\left(\dfrac{1}{2}\omega\tau_a\right)} \tag{2.17}$$

If the beamformer is steered towards an angle of arrival ϕ, and the wavefront still arrives from direction angle θ, then the frequency response becomes:

$$\hat{H}(\omega, \phi, \theta) = \frac{\sin\left[\dfrac{N}{2}\omega\dfrac{d}{c}(\sin\theta - \sin\phi)\right]}{\sin\left[\dfrac{1}{2}\omega\dfrac{d}{c}(\sin\theta - \sin\phi)\right]} \tag{2.18}$$

Therefore, if the array is steered to a direction different from the wavefront arrival direction, then the spectrum of the array's output is distorted by the beamformer transfer function $\hat{H}(\omega, \phi, \theta)$. Typically, this distortion results in an attenuation of the high-frequency components of the source signal.

If $\phi = 0°$ (broadside steering), then the first zero of $\hat{H}(\omega, \phi, \theta)$ as a function of the arrival angle θ, is found at $\theta_0 = \sin^{-1}(2\pi c/N\omega d)$ and the width BW of the main beam is given by:

$$BW = 2\sin^{-1}\frac{2\pi c}{N\omega d} \tag{2.19}$$

From (2.19) it appears that the beam width is inversely proportional to frequency. Furthermore, the beam width can be reduced either by increasing the number of elements or by increasing the interelement distance.

Figure 2.6(a) shows the directivity pattern, at a frequency $f = 2\,\text{kHz}$, of a uniform unweighted linear array with 16 elements and an intersensor distance of 10 cm, steered to broadside. Figure 2.6(b) shows the effect of beamforming

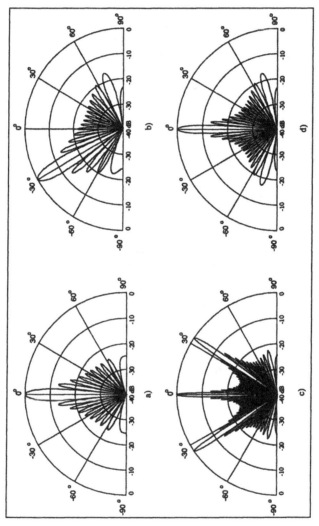

Figure 2.6 Directivity patterns of a uniform unweighted linear array with 16 elements: (a) directivity at the frequency $f = 2\,\text{kHz}$ when the intersensor distance is $d = 10\,\text{cm}$ and the array is steered to broadside ($\phi = 0°$); (b) directivity of the same array steered towards $\phi = -30°$; (c) $\phi = 0°$, $f = 6\,\text{kHz}$, $d = 10\,\text{cm}$; two grating lobes have appeared; (d) $\phi = 0°$, $f = 6\,\text{kHz}$, $d = 5\,\text{cm}$: the spatial aliasing has been avoided by a shorter element separation.

towards arrival angle $\phi = -30°$. It is interesting to notice that since $\hat{H}(\omega, \phi, \theta)$ depends on $\sin \theta$, the directivity pattern exhibits an asymmetric beam shape when the array is not steered to broadside. Maximum peaks of $\hat{H}(\omega, \phi, \theta)$ occur when

$$\sin \theta - \sin \phi = m \frac{2\pi c}{\omega d} \tag{2.20}$$

where m is an integer. The main beam corresponds to $m = 0$. If other values of m solve equation (2.20), then the corresponding peaks are called *grating lobes* and are produced by the "spatial aliasing" effect. Figure 2.6(c) illustrates how the directivity pattern of Figure 2.6(a) is transformed at the frequency $f = 6\,\text{kHz}$; two grating lobes appear at $\theta_{gl} = \pm 34.5°$.

Signals propagating from the directions of grating lobes cannot be discriminated from those propagating from the main beam direction. The spatial aliasing phenomenon is analogous to frequency-domain aliasing due to time sampling at an insufficient rate. Spatial aliasing can be avoided by setting the interelement distance to satisfy the constraint:

$$d < \frac{\lambda}{1 + |\sin \theta|} \tag{2.21}$$

In the general case, the requirement is $d < \lambda/2$ (or conversely the maximum frequency of the source signal should satisfy $f_{\max} < c/2d$) that corresponds to the Nyquist criterion for spatial sampling. In Figure 2.6(d) the intersensor distance was reduced to $5\,\text{cm}$ in order to avoid the spatial aliasing at $6\,\text{kHz}$ observed in Figure 2.6(c).

Equation (2.18) and relationships (2.19) and (2.21) hold in the plane-wave (far-field) hypothesis, and are only indicative of amplitude response in short distance situations in which near-field distortion (of both amplitude and phase) must be compensated (Khalil *et al.*, 1994; Kennedy *et al.*, 1996).

2.4.4. Constant Beamwidth Beamforming

It is clear from equation (2.19) that the beamwidth of a linear array decreases as frequency increases. As a consequence, even slight inaccuracy in steering of the beamformer may result in an undesirable effect of low-pass filtering a broadband source signal. In fact, it will be shown in Chapter 3 that a speech signal contains significant information over a frequency range of at least four octaves, thus an array having a practical beamwidth at lower speech frequencies would present an exceedingly narrow beamwidth at higher frequencies.

Constant beamwidth may be obtained by frequency weighting of array elements such that the number of active sensors is gradually reduced as frequency increases (Flanagan, 1985). An alternate solution consists of subband processing that uses subarrays of different dimensions for different frequency ranges.

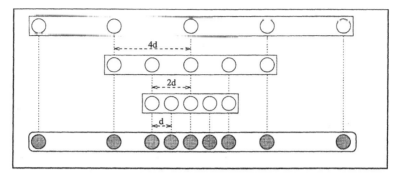

Figure 2.7 Harmonic array composed of three subarrays, operating in adjacent octaves. Some elements are shared by different subarrays.

Of particular interest is the *harmonic array*, which employs a distinct subarray for each frequency octave. In this case, the beamwidth remains unchanged across different frequency subbands, provided that the intersensor spacing is progressively halved from each octave to the higher one (so that the product ωd in (2.19) does not change). Several octaves can be processed by harmonically nested subarrays, and the final output is obtained by subband recomposition. Thus, the wideband beamforming design is reduced to the easier task of constant beamwidth design over a single octave (Goodwin and Elko, 1993; Chou, 1995). Due to a distance-halving relationship between subarrays covering adjacent octaves, it is possible to efficiently exploit element sharing between the subarrays, as exemplified in Figure 2.7.

2.4.5. 2-D and 3-D Arrays

Linear arrays (1-D arrays) provide spatial capture selectivity as a function of only one angular coordinate (the *azimuth*). Their directivity in the three-dimensional space is independent of the elevation angle.

A two-dimensional array is required in order to form a beam pattern confined in two dimensions (azimuth and elevation). With a planar array (2-D array), it is possible to form a "pencil beam" that exhibits improved spatial selectivity. In a reverberant room, only sound reflections propagating along the steering direction are "captured" by the beam, whereas all other reflections as well as the interfering sources are attenuated. Directivity analysis, the FIR filter design analogy, and the harmonic nesting approach are easily extended from 1-D to 2-D arrays (Flanagan *et al.*, 1985, 1991).

By using two orthogonal two-dimensional arrays with intersecting beams it is possible to achieve spatial selectivity in three dimensions (volume selectivity) with an additional improvement in the quality of sound pick-up from the desired source. This is a particular case of a three-dimensional sensor distribution. Cubic 3-D arrays have been shown (Flanagan, 1987) to provide directivity patterns with beam width independent of the steering direction over 4π steradians.

2.4.6. Linearly Constrained Adaptive Beamformers

In a delay-and-filter beamformer, the filter coefficients can be made automatically adjustable in order to obtain a dynamically modifiable directional pattern. Such an adaptive array has the capability of reducing or eliminating directional interference by modifying its filters in order to cancel signals arriving from directions other than a specified steering angle.

A classical adaptive beamforming algorithm has been proposed by Frost (1972). This algorithm iteratively adapts the weights of a broadband sensor array in order to minimize the interference power at the beamformer output, while maintaining the desired frequency response in the steering direction ("Frost constraint"). The interferences, which are assumed to be uncorrelated with the desired signal, contribute additional power to the system output. Hence, minimization of the overall output power, constrained by the imposed frequency response in the steering direction, causes the adaptive beamformer to create nulls in its sidelobe structure in order to eliminate these additional undesired components. In this way, the algorithm progressively "learns" the statistics of the jammer signals and attempts to eliminate their effect.

Figure 2.8 shows an adaptive beamformer with N microphones. Each sensor is connected to a steering delay element followed by a FIR digital filter with L adaptive weights. Consider the matrix $W(n)$ of the weights at discrete time instant n:

$$W(n) = \begin{bmatrix} w_1(n) & w_2(n) & \ldots & w_L(n) \\ w_{L+1}(n) & w_{L+2}(n) & \ldots & w_{2L}(n) \\ \vdots & \vdots & & \vdots \\ w_{(N-1)L+1}(n) & \ldots & & w_{NL}(n) \end{bmatrix} \tag{2.22}$$

and the matrix $X(n)$ representing the state of the FIR filters at instant n:

$$X(n) = \begin{bmatrix} x_1(n) & x_2(n) & \ldots & x_L(n) \\ x_{L+1}(n) & x_{L+2}(n) & \ldots & x_{2L}(n) \\ \vdots & \vdots & & \vdots \\ x_{(N-1)L+1}(n) & \ldots & & x_{NL}(n) \end{bmatrix} \tag{2.23}$$

The beamformer output is given by $y(n) = \sum_{i=1}^{NL} w_i(n)x_i(n)$.

The steering delay elements cophase the desired signal components at the input of the filters. If only these input components are taken into account,

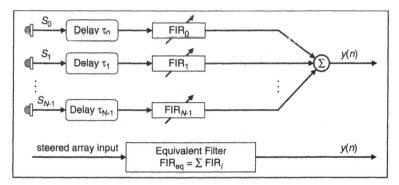

Figure 2.8 Diagram of the Frost beamformer. The multichannel processor can be viewed as a single equivalent filter that must satisfy the Frost constraint represented by a fixed frequency response in the direction of the target signal.

the multichannel processor can be replaced, as shown in Figure 2.8, by an equivalent FIR filter having coefficients c_i, $i = 1 \ldots L$, given by the column sum vector of the original weight matrix:

$$[1\ 1 \ldots 1]\boldsymbol{W}(n) = [c_1\ c_2 \ldots c_L] \tag{2.24}$$

The Frost constraint corresponds to imposing the values c_i, $i = 1 \ldots L$, according to a desired frequency response for the equivalent filter. At each time instant n, the LMS (least mean square) algorithm (Widrow and Stearns, 1985) is applied to minimize the output power. Then a correction of the weights is applied to reestabilish the constraint (2.24):

$$\boldsymbol{W}(n+1) = \boldsymbol{W}(n) + 2\mu y(n)\boldsymbol{X}(n) + \boldsymbol{E}(n) \tag{2.25}$$

where μ is the convergence parameter of the LMS algorithm, $y(n)$ is the output of the beamformer, and $\boldsymbol{E}(n)$ is a matrix that performs a weight readjustment (Widrow and Stearns, 1985) necessary to satisfy relationship (2.24).

If the constraint (2.24) corresponds to a filter with unit gain and linear phase (e.g. $c_1 = 1$, $c_i = 0$ for $i = 2 \ldots L$), then the output consists of an undistorted version of the desired signal with added noise of minimal power. It represents a minimum variance estimate of the desired signal.

An alternate version of a linearly constrained adaptive beamformer, which produces a desired frequency response in the steering direction, has been proposed by Griffiths and Jim (1982). This implementation, illustrated in Figure 2.9, is called the *generalized sidelobe canceller*, and achieves precisely the same overall result as the Frost beamformer, but does not require any constraint in the adaptive process. Signals containing only undesired components are obtained by pairwise subtractions of the input channels and are processed by adaptive filters to minimize the variance of the system output.

Frost's constraint is very strong since it requires the frequency response in the steering direction to be uniquely predetermined. A softer constraint may be

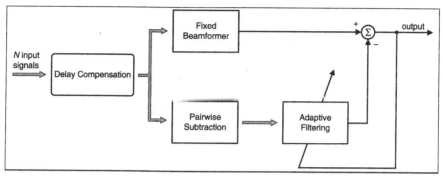

Figure 2.9 Block diagram of the generalized sidelobe canceller (GSC), a linearly constrained adaptive beamformer proposed in Griffiths and Jim (1982).

adopted (Kaneda and Ohga, 1986) by allowing a small degree of degradation in the response to the desired signal. The benefit of this approach is an improved noise reduction capability at the expense of a limited response degradation that can be tolerated in most applications.

The linearly constrained adaptive beamformers may suffer the major drawback of the partial *cancellation* of the desired signal. Cancellation can be caused by non-ideal conditions that can arise in real applications in which talkers may not behave as far-field point sources and the array steering angle estimate may be affected by error. Such conditions will cause part of the desired signal to be interpreted as interference and therefore cause the filters adapt to cancel it. It is found that, in this eventuality, the cancellation becomes stronger as the interference power diminishes.

Another cause of cancellation is reverberation. When multipath propagation conditions exist, many replicas of the desired signal impinge on the array with various angles of incidence. The adaptive filters perceive incoming reflections as unwanted noise and thus adapt to remove also these signal components. This results in partial cancellation or in spectral modification of the desired speech signal.

A possible method of reducing signal cancellation due to inaccurate steering is the use of additional constraints (Grenier, 1993; Hoffman and Buckley, 1995) that incorporate tolerances for inaccurate steering or array imperfections. In a multipath environment, signal cancellation can be reduced by allowing filter adaptation only during the intervals in which the desired signal is not present (Van Compernolle, 1990; Van Compernolle *et al.*, 1990; Oh and Viswanathan, 1992; Greenberg and Zurek, 1992).

Noise propagating in a reverberant enclosure is often characterized by low spatial coherence. It can then be modelled as a noise field with a strong diffuse component. Adaptive beamformers fail to suppress such a noise component, in that they can only place nulls in the directivity pattern towards a limited number of discrete noise sources. In this case an effective technique for noise reduction is post-filtering the output of a conventional beamformer with a Wiener filter (Zelinski, 1988).

Microphone array processing which combines adaptive beamforming and adaptive Wiener post-filtering has been proposed in a unified scheme (Fischer and Simmer, 1995). Such a system was demonstrated to be effective in noise suppression independently of the spatial correlation characteristics of the noise field. Thus both coherent and incoherent noise components can be simultaneously attenuated (Fischer and Simmer, 1996).

2.4.7. Dereverberation

As discussed in section 2.2, speech propagating inside an enclosure is subject to linear distortion due to reverberation and spectral coloration. Reverberant speech is the result of a convolution of the original signal with a room impulse response $h(t)$. In principle, reverberation could be removed by an equalizing filter that exactly inverts the room effect. Denoting the room frequency response with $H(\omega) = \mathcal{F}\{h(t)\}$, the inverse filter $H_{inv}(\omega) = 1/H(\omega)$ is stable only if $H(\omega)$ is a minimum phase function, i.e. if its Laplace transform contains no poles or zeros in the right half-plane. In this case, $H_{inv}(\omega)$ is also minimum phase.

In practice, a room impulse response $h(t)$ is generally a non-minimum phase function (Neely and Allen, 1979). Therefore, it is impossible to obtain a direct and exact inverse filter because the inverse function is either unstable or anticausal (anticipatory). The corresponding frequency response $H(\omega)$ can be decomposed as follows: $H(\omega) = H_{mp}(\omega)H_{np}(\omega)$, where $H_{mp}(\omega)$ is a minimum phase component and $H_{np}(\omega)$ is a non-minimum phase component (Oppenheim and Schafer, 1989).

$H_{mp}(\omega)$ has a causal and stable inverse filter, while a stable inverse of $H_{np}(\omega)$ can be obtained only with an infinite anticausal filter. However, a truncation and shifting operation produces a causal approximation (Mourjopoulos, 1994) of this filter that is practically feasible with the introduction of a suitable delay.

The exact inverse filtering of the reverberation effect produced by an enclosure has been shown to be possible if more than one sensor is used (Miyoshi and Kaneda, 1988). This method is based on a principle called multiple-input/output inverse theorem (MINT). Consider a source and two microphones in a reverberant room, and let $H_1(z)$ and $H_2(z)$ be the z-transforms of the digitized impulse responses between the source and the two microphones. The method requires to find two equalizing FIR filters $G_1(z)$ and $G_2(z)$ such that:

$$H_1(z)G_1(z) + H_2(z)G_2(z) = 1 \qquad (2.26)$$

The equalizing FIR filters are applied to the input channels, as shown in Figure 2.10, and then the filter outputs are added together to obtain a spectrally unaltered replica of the source signal.

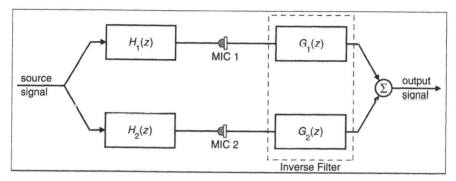

Figure 2.10 Principle of the MINT inverse filter: by using two input channels the exact inverse filtering of reverberation becomes possible.

A unique solution $(G_1(z), G_2(z))$ exists if $H_1(z)$ and $H_2(z)$ do not have common zeros. The orders of $G_1(z)$ and $G_2(z)$ are less than those of $H_2(z)$ and $H_1(z)$ respectively. It has been shown that the effectiveness of this method can be affected by numerical errors resulting from the inversion of poorly conditioned matrices (Putnam *et al.*, 1995).

The above described dereverberation techniques may be difficult to implement in practice since the impulse response of the inverse filter may be extremely long. Moreover, dereverberation performance is very sensitive to the accuracy of the measured impulse responses and to the variations related to source and receiver positions inside the room (Mourjopoulos, 1994), as well as to environmental conditions (Hikichi and Itakura, 1994).

The computational complexity resulting from long inverse filters can be reduced by the use of a subband MINT technique in which the full speech signal bandwidth is divided into many subbands (Yamada *et al.*, 1991). Each subband is decimated and processed by the MINT method to remove the effect of reverberation. Then, the inverse filtered subband signals are resynthesized into a full-band speech signal

Another subband approach to dereverberation (Wang and Itakura, 1991) considers that the feasibility of inverse filtering a subband signal depends on the z-plane distribution of the zeros of the transfer function in that subband. In a multi-microphone system, the transfer functions between the sound source and the various microphones have different zero distributions. By choosing, in each subband, the microphone with the most easily invertible transfer function, it is possible to reconstruct a resulting full-band signal in which the effect of reverberation has been equalized. The method is based on the assumption that, if the numbers of subbands and microphones are large enough, it is likely that each subband has at least one minimum phase source-to-microphone transfer function. All dereverberation subband filter coefficients are obtained by a least mean square estimation. Then, in each subband, the filter with minimum estimation error is used to compensate for the effect of reverberation.

2.4.8. Multiple Beamforming and Matched Filter Array

Performance of beamformers may be severely degraded by reverberation and multipath distortion. In fact, although a conventional beamformer mitigates the effect of reflections arriving from directions unaligned with its main lobe, it nevertheless collects reflections arriving from its steering direction.

Beamforming techniques that can exploit the energy of multipath components in useful ways have been proposed to reduce the effects of reverberation (Flanagan *et al.*, 1993). Such an approach is implemented in the *multiple-beamforming* technique. Assume that it is possible to identify the arrival directions of the most significant signal reflections at each microphone in an N-element array. Separate beams are then steered to the direction of the sound source and to the directions of the K major images. All the beamformed outputs are realigned and summed. The multiple beamformer provides a gain in the ratio of undistorted signal power to interfering reverberant power that can be shown to approach a value N compared with the value N/K provided by a single beamformer.

A more sophisticated approach (Flanagan *et al.*, 1993) considers the whole impulse response of each source-to-microphone channel, and applies *matched-filter* processing. The traditional matched-filter impulse response $h^{mf}(t)$ is the time inverse of the impulse response $h(t)$ of the system to be matched, i.e. $h^{mf}(t) = h(-t)$. In a matched-filter array, all the microphone signals are processed by their matched filter and the outputs of the filters are summed up. Denoting the source signal with $r(t)$, the ith microphone signal with $s_i(t)$, the ith impulse response with $h_i(t)$, the total output of an N-microphone matched-filter array can be expressed as:

$$\sum_{i=0}^{N-1} s_i(t) * h_i^{mf}(t) = \sum_{i=0}^{N-1} r(t) * h_i(t) * h_i(-t) = r(t) * \sum_{i=0}^{N-1} \phi_i(t) \qquad (2.27)$$

Here $\phi_i(t)$ denotes the autocorrelation of the ith impulse response.

Every matched filter $h_i^{mf}(t) = h_i(t)$ is the time-inverse of a causal filter and is therefore anticausal. Delay and truncation must be applied to $h^{mf}(t)$ to obtain a causal filter that approximates the desired response. It is evident from equation (2.27) that the output of each single matched filter is a spectrally modified version of the source signal $r(t)$, but the overall frequency response obtained with the use of a large number of microphones is generally fairly flat (Jan, 1995). Furthermore, the impulse responses of the various channels should be as uncorrelated as possible (Jan and Flanagan, 1996) to provide high-quality sound pick-up and high spatial selectivity (Jan *et al.*, 1995).

2.5. TALKER LOCATION

2.5.1. Introduction

Acoustic source location is of practical importance for various applications. A possible use for source location may be found in video conferencing applications, where automatic moving of the camera may be performed based on acoustic source tracking. In hands-free ASR applications, one can envision a target scenario where the microphone array system realizes selective acquisition of a speech message, based on estimated position of the dominant talker, and on a reduction of the captured noise, including background noise produced by other talkers.

Acoustic source location can be accomplished following different approaches, which may be grouped into four main categories.

Time difference of arrival (TDOA)

The methods of the first category are based on *time difference of arrival* (*TDOA*) estimation techniques. In principle, the TDOA-based location procedure consists in a *relative delay estimation* (RDE) step followed by a *source position computation* (SPC). The remainder of this section will focus on this category of location algorithms, with a particular emphasis to the use of a TDOA technique based on generalized cross-correlation analysis. The accuracy of the relative delay estimate of wavefront arrival between two microphones is crucial to source location performance. Another critical issue is the method of combining the resulting delay estimates in the SPC step. Exact solution methods, for a direct derivation of the source position, can be proposed only for simple geometrical models. For unconstrained microphone geometries, procedures based either on approximated closed-form solution algorithms or on iterative algorithms are adopted to approach the optimal maximum likelihood solution (Brandstein, 1995; Rabinkin *et al.*, 1996).

Power field scanning

A second category of source location methods consists of *power field* location techniques, that are based on steering the array to various positions in space and on looking for the maximum either of the power field (PF) or of an equivalent objective function (e.g. global coherence field), that will be introduced later. From the reliability point of view, the PF-based approaches have some limitations. Furthermore, the computational complexity of the PF may be too high for real-time implementation on common inexpensive hardware platforms.

Human perception models

A third category consists of techniques based on *human perception models*. The ultimate goal of this approach is to develop a system that simulates the localization ability of humans and animals. This capability enables them to find the source position quickly and accurately, using only two sensors. Humans and animals are capable of performing this task accurately, even under adverse acoustical conditions. Literature is rich on this field: starting from the work described in Wallach (1949), many advance studies have been conducted on sound source localization.[4] A thorough description of the main principles of auditory space perception can be found in Blauert (1983).

In the human auditory system, fundamental information that enables auditory space perception is provided by the pinnae (Musicant and Butler, 1984) located in the outer ear and, to a lesser extent, by conduction through bones and other secondary paths to the inner ear. Thirty years ago, Batteau (1967) reported on the role of the pinna in sound source localization, showing that possible front/back and up/down confusions are resolved due to the shape characteristics of the outer ear. The outer ear exhibits a direction-dependent frequency response, which varies with sound source elevation as well as with possible diffraction and reflections due to shoulders, head, torso, etc. for sounds coming from above, below, and behind the listener. In particular, the head plays an important role in the process of sound localization, since it introduces frequency-dependent wave diffraction at the ears. Clearly, this so-called head-shadow effect is more evident for lateral sources than for frontal ones. Moreover, head movements can improve the ability of source localization, especially in noisy and reverberant environments. According to physiological and psychoacoustic studies, interaural time difference (ITD) is considered the most important mechanism for sound source localization. Also, interaural intensity difference (IID) can play a significant role as described in Rayleigh (1907), especially in the case of a source located far away from the median plane or in the case of acoustic events whose energy is concentrated in the upper frequency region (above 1.6 kHz).

Virtual-reality experiments based on binaural recording[5] show that when binaural-recorded signals are reproduced through a stereo headphone set, subjects perceive a realistic 3-D spatial-effect reconstruction. The basic principles of binaural modelling and its extensions are described in Blauert (1983), Colburn and Durlach (1978), Lindemann (1986), Stern (1988), Gaik (1993) and Stern and Trahiotis (1995). An attempt to exploit binaural modelling

---

[4]In the literature both the term "location" and the term "localization" can be found, without a clear distinction between the two. Here, the former has been preferred to denote the task of finding the acoustic source position, while the latter one has been maintained only for what concerns references to studies on perception, where it is more prevalent.

[5]Binaural recording is based on an acquisition made by two small microphones placed in the ear canals of a dummy head.

for automatic sound source localization is described in Bodden (1993), where ITD is related to the peak positions of the neural excitation patterns that represent the output of the binaural processor.

Eigendecomposition

A fourth category that deserves to be mentioned is that known as the *eigendecomposition*-based techniques. The most representative class of this category is that of the MUSIC (multiple signal classification) algorithms (Haykin, 1995; Johnson and Dudgeon, 1993; Schmidt, 1979; Bienvenu and Kopp, 1980) generally used for processing narrowband signals and multiple sources. The approach of eigendecomposition techniques should also be investigated to solve the problem of talker location when dealing with multiple speakers in a noisy environment.

Other approaches

Finally, the literature in areas outside talker location (e.g. underwater acoustics) proposes other approaches to source location (see as an example Krause (1987) for GPS navigation), that are based on the use of high-resolution spectral analysis, maximum-likelihood estimation, ARMA (autoregressive moving average) modelling (Compton, 1988; Bar-Shalom and Fortmann, 1988; Monzingo and Miller, 1980; Wang and Kaveh, 1985; Hassab, 1990; Kay, 1993). These techniques are generally used for narrowband signals processing and require some assumptions about the input signals that are not applicable to speech signals (e.g. the signal is often assumed to be stationary over a long interval).

2.5.2. Problem Definition

Let us consider an acoustic source, positioned in $p = (x, y, z)$, that generates an acoustic signal $r(t)$, and a set of M sensors, with an arbitrary three-dimensional array geometry, placed in positions $p_0 = (x_0, y_0, z_0), \ldots, p_{M-1} = (x_{M-1}, y_{M-1}, z_{M-1})$, and capturing the respective electrical signals $s_0(t), \ldots, s_{M-1}(t)$. Figure 2.11 describes the geometrical configuration of the system in the far-field case, where a linear array consisting of two sensor pairs is used.

Assuming that the acoustic waves associated with $r(t)$ propagate in a noisy environment, the signal acquired by acoustic sensor i can be expressed as follows:

$$s_i(t) = \alpha_i r(t - \mathsf{t}_i) + n_i(t) \qquad (2.28)$$

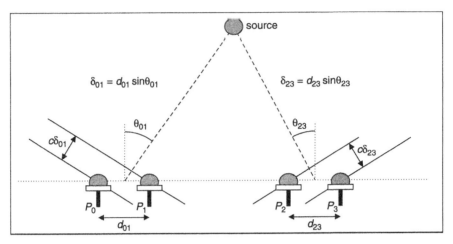

Figure 2.11 Wavefront propagation of an acoustic stimulus. Signals s_0, s_1, s_2, s_3 are acquired through an array of microphones organized in two pairs. The figure shows the relation between relative delays of the wavefront arrival and positions of the source and the microphones.

where α_i is an attenuation factor due to propagation effects, $n_i(t)$ includes all the undesired components, which can be correlated with $r(t)$ if the environment is reverberant, and t_i denotes[6] the propagation time of the wavefront from p to the ith sensor. This propagation time can be expressed as follows:

$$t_i = \frac{d_i}{c} = \frac{\sqrt{(x_i - x)^2 + (y_i - y)^2 + (z_i - z)^2}}{c} \tag{2.29}$$

where c is the speed of sound and d_i is the distance between the source and the ith microphone.

The relative delay of the wavefront arrival between microphones i and k, can be expressed as:

$$\delta_{ik} = t_k - t_i \tag{2.30}$$

In near-field conditions, this delay identifies a set of points lying on half a hyperboloid: all these points represent possible source positions. When the source lies in the far-field region, this set of points can be approximated to a cone that is asymptotic to the near-field hyperboloid. Note that, if the source and the microphone pair are assumed to lie on a common plane, the hyperboloid can be replaced by a hyperbola (obtained by intersection with that plane) and the cone can be replaced by a straight line identifying the

---

[6]t_i depends on the position p. For sake of simplicity, in most of the following the notation of dependence of variables from the source position p will be implicit.

angle of wavefront arrival θ_{ik}:

$$\theta_{ik} = \arcsin\left(\frac{c\delta_{ik}}{d_{ik}}\right) \tag{2.31}$$

where d_{ik} indicates the distance between microphones i and k.

2.5.3. Generalized Cross-Correlation for Time Delay Estimation

Given two array signals $s_i(t)$ and $s_k(t)$, the most direct method for determining the relative time delay δ_{ik} is to estimate for every lag τ, the cross-correlation function:

$$R_{ik}(\tau) = E[s_i(t)s_k(t+\tau)] \tag{2.32}$$

where $E[\cdot]$ denotes expectation. Given the model (2.28), (2.32) can be expressed as:

$$R_{ik}(\tau) = \alpha_i\alpha_k R_{rr}(\tau - \delta_{ik}) + R_{n_i n_k}(\tau) + \alpha_i R_{rn_k}(\tau - t_i) + \alpha_k R_{n_i r}(\tau - t_k) \tag{2.33}$$

where $R_{rr}(\tau)$ represents the autocorrelation of the source signal $r(t)$, evaluated at lag τ, and the remaining terms refer to the correlation functions involving the noise components $n_i(t)$ and $n_k(t)$. If the direct wavefront component $r(t)$ is assumed to dominate over noise and reverberation, then these terms may be neglected in a first approximation.

The delay δ_{ik} can be theoretically derived by maximizing the cross-correlation function $R_{ik}(\tau)$ with respect to τ. However, due to the finite observation time, expression (2.32) can only be estimated for a given temporal window of length T_w, centred at time t. We denote this estimate as:

$$\widehat{R}_{ik}(t, \tau) = \frac{1}{T_w}\int_{t-T_w/2}^{t+T_w/2} s_i(u)s_k(u+\tau)\, du \tag{2.34}$$

When dealing with real noisy signals, the simple maximization based approach applied to (2.34) may fail, due to the nature of the signal and to the limits of the mathematical model. An improvement (Silverman and Kirtman, 1992) is obtained by normalizing $\widehat{R}_{ik}(t, \tau)$ with respect to signal energies, leading to:

$$\widehat{R}_{ik}^{(N)}(t, \tau) = \frac{\displaystyle\int_{t-T_w/2}^{t+T_w/2} s_i(u)s_k(u+\tau)\, du}{\sqrt{\displaystyle\int_{t-T_w/2}^{t+T_w/2} s_i^2(u)\, du}\sqrt{\displaystyle\int_{t-T_w/2}^{t+T_w/2} s_k^2(u+\tau)\, du}} \tag{2.35}$$

In an ideal situation, where expression (2.28) may be simplified with the assumption that $\alpha_i = 1$ for every i (i.e. there is no attenuation) and that noise components $n_i(t)$ are uncorrelated, $\widehat{R}_{ik}^{(N)}(t, \tau)$ has a peak equal to 1 at lag τ

corresponding to the delay δ_{ik}. But, if $r(t)$ is a periodic signal with period T_P, then $\hat{R}_{ik}^{(N)}(t,\tau)$ contains other unit peaks, for each lag $\tau = \delta_{ik} + mT_P$ (with m integer). This fact is related to the periodic characteristic of $R_{rr}(\tau)$ and is evident when the technique is applied to speech, since the signal is often quasi-periodic. Signals captured in a reverberant environment may also cause the application of cross-correlation analysis techniques to produce incorrect results. In fact, in analogy with pitch and formant structure in voiced speech (see Chapter 3), reverberation must be interpreted as the sum of delayed replicas of a given source signal, where delays depend on paths that were followed by the reflected signals.

All the above facts should also be considered with respect to the distance between microphones and to the relation between the wavefront arrival delays and the dominant frequencies in the signals. Keeping an adequately small distance between microphones can avoid some of the above-mentioned problems but will reduce the resolution in estimating the angle of arrival. In a digital implementation, this effect can be compensated either by using interpolation techniques or by increasing the sampling frequency.

A maximum-likelihood estimator for determining time delays between two signals s_i and s_k was proposed in Knapp and Carter (1976), where the generalized cross-correlation (GCC) function is introduced as a combination of cross-correlation and of "optimal" filtering.

Here, a specific case of GCC is considered that leads to the so called cross-power spectrum phase (CSP) analysis discussed in Omologo and Svaizer (1997). The GCC between $s_i(t)$ and $s_k(t)$ is defined as:

$$R_{ik}^{(g)}(t,\tau) = \int_{-\infty}^{+\infty} \psi(t,f) G_{ik}(t,f)\, e^{j2\pi f\tau}\, df \qquad (2.36)$$

where $G_{ik}(t,f)$ is the cross-power spectrum at instant t and $\psi(t,f)$ is a frequency weighting filter. In order to facilitate the successive maximization step in the generic broadband signal case, a way to "sharpen" the GCC peak is to "whiten" the input signals. The choice:

$$\psi(t,f) = \frac{1}{|G_{ik}(t,f)|} \qquad (2.37)$$

leads to the so-called phase transform technique (Knapp and Carter, 1976) that is based on using only phase information. The following GCC is obtained:

$$R_{ik}^{(p)}(t,\tau) = \int_{-\infty}^{+\infty} \frac{G_{ik}(t,f)}{|G_{ik}(t,f)|}\, e^{j2\pi f\tau}\, df \qquad (2.38)$$

In the ideal situation, when noise signals are uncorrelated, only the first term of the sum in (2.33) remains, leading to:

$$\frac{G_{ik}(t,f)}{|G_{ik}(t,f)|} = e^{-j2\pi f\delta_{ik}} \qquad (2.39)$$

In practice, the procedure for estimating the GCC starts from the computation of the spectra $\widehat{S}_i(t, f)$ and $\widehat{S}_k(t, f)$ through Fourier transforms applied to windowed segments of s_i and s_k, centred around the time t. These power spectra are used to estimate the normalized cross-power spectrum:

$$\phi(t, f) = \frac{\widehat{S}_i(t, f)\widehat{S}_k^*(t, f)}{|\widehat{S}_i(t, f)||S_k(t, f)|} \tag{2.40}$$

that preserves only information about phase differences between s_i and s_k. Finally, the inverse Fourier transform of $\phi(t, f)$ can be obtained as follows:

$$\tilde{R}_{ik}(t, \tau) = \int_{-\infty}^{+\infty} \phi(t, f)\, e^{j2\pi f\tau}\, df \tag{2.41}$$

It is worth noting that, unlike other delay estimation techniques, the GCC given by (2.38) is virtually independent from the input waveform characteristics. This means that, in the ideal case, it is reduced to a delta function centred at the correct delay δ_{ik}, at every instant t. In real conditions, the function $\tilde{R}_{ik}(t, \tau)$ has a constant energy, mainly concentrated on the delay $\tau = \delta_{ik}$. This fact reinforces the assumption that the secondary terms of expression (2.33) are negligible, in a first approximation, but it emphasizes the limits of this assumption when noise is correlated with the source signal. In the latter case, the energy will be accumulated at delays corresponding to dominant correlated noise components (e.g. echoes).

2.5.4. Coherence Measure

Information on mutual delay between microphone pair signals can be associated to a coherence measure (CM) function $C_{ik}(t, \tau)$ that expresses, for a hypothesized delay τ, the similarity between segments (centred at time t) extracted from two generic signals s_i and s_k. This measure can be derived from the CSP analysis or from other signal processing techniques as shown in Omologo and Svaizer (1994). In the former case, the relation $C_{ik}(t, \tau) = \tilde{R}_{ik}(t, \tau)$ is used.

Figure 2.12(a) shows that the CM function $C_{ik}(t_0, \tau)$, computed for a time interval centred at the time instant t_0, has a prominent peak at delay $\tau = \delta_{ik}$ corresponding to the direction of wavefront arrival. As shown in Figure 2.12(b), the analysis of noisy signals also provides a fairly clear peak. It is worth noting that the peak magnitude can represent an effective cue also for acoustic event detection.

Once the CM function has been computed, a bidimensional CM representation can be obtained as shown in Figures 2.13 and 2.14, where the CSP-CM analysis was applied both for stationary and for moving sources. In this representation, time is on the horizontal axis, while the delay is on the vertical axis, and the coherence magnitude is represented by grey levels. A similar

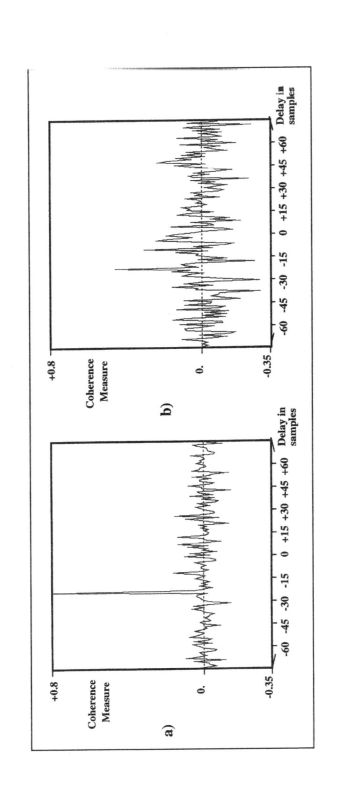

Figure 2.12 CSP coherence measure functions for a frame of two input signals acquired under (a) low noise conditions (SNR = 30 dB); (b) under higher noise conditions (SNR = 0 dB). The acoustic event was generated in a position corresponding to a relative delay equivalent to −25 samples.

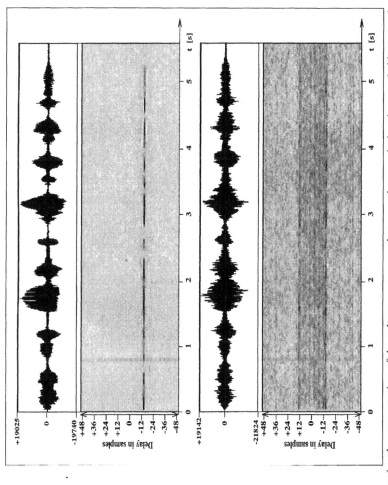

Figure 2.13 Graphical representation of the coherence measure between the speech signals recorded by two microphones (the signal of one of the two channels is also illustrated). In the upper part of the figure the SNR is 30 dB, and there is no reverberation. In the lower part the reverberation time is 0.3 s. Distance between microphones is 30 cm, signals were sampled at 48 kHz and the theoretical delay is −14 samples.

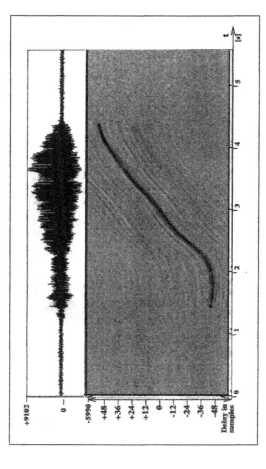

Figure 2.14 Coherence measure representation based on the CSP analysis between signals $s_0(t)$ (plotted in the upper part of the figure) and $s_1(t)$ acquired by a microphone pair. The acoustic stimulus was a vowel /a/, uttered in a noisy environment by a speaker that was walking from the left to the right of the microphone pair.

representation for the cross-correlation-based CM function can be found in Simmer *et al.* (1992).

2.5.5. Power Field

The delay and sum beamformer, expressed by (2.12), can be steered to an arbitrary spatial location by employing a proper set of steering delays $\tau = (\tau_0, \ldots, \tau_{M-1})$. If the location space is subdivided by a grid Σ of potential source locations $p_s = (x_s, y_s, z_s)$ and the corresponding sets τ_s of steering delays are used to "scan" the space by means of the array, the power of the output signal, when the array is steered at a given location, can be used to derive a degree of plausibility that the source is located at that point.

The power field (PF) is defined on the grid Σ and it represents the power of the signal obtained at the output of the beamformer, as a function of the point of space at which the array is steered. A similar representation can be obtained by considering the average coherence between signals realigned by the beamformer, instead of the power of its output. An example is the global coherence field (GCF) that derives from the coherence measure.

Let us consider a set Ω of Q microphone pairs and denote with $\delta_{ik}(x, y, z)$ the theoretical delay for the microphone pair (i, k) if the source is at position (x, y, z). Once the coherence measure $C_{ik}(t, \delta_{ik}(x, y, z))$ has been computed at instant t, for each microphone pair (i, k) belonging to Ω, the GCF is expressed as:

$$\text{GCF}(t, x, y, z) = \frac{1}{Q} \sum_{(i,k) \in \Omega} C_{ik}(t, \delta_{ik}(x, y, z)) \qquad (2.42)$$

Maximizing (2.42) over all the possible coordinates $(x, y, z) \in \Sigma$ provides a reliable source position hypothesis (as shown in Figure 2.15). For a high number of microphone pairs, this solution tends to be accurate and robust enough, since the source position error is not influenced by inaccuracy of a few time delay estimators. However, the higher the number of microphone pairs the higher the computational load.

In Alvarado (1990) an optimization method called stochastic region contraction (SRC) is presented to reduce the complexity of the optimal location search. In Silverman and Kirtman (1992) a two-stage algorithm is described, which is based on the PF computed through the evaluation of the cross-correlation functions between microphone array signals.

2.5.6. CSP-Based Relative Delay Estimation

Section 2.5.3 introduced a cross-correlation-based time delay estimation and described some of its limitations. In the case of normalized cross-correlation

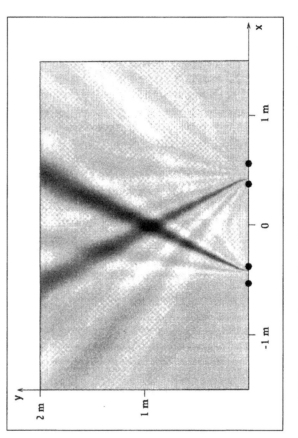

Figure 2.15 Global coherence field for an acoustic event located in position (0 m, 1 m) and acquired by a microphone array consisting of two pairs at a distance of 90 cm. The distance between the two microphones of each pair is 15 cm.

these limitations are confirmed in Silverman and Kirtman (1992). The authors describe problems arising when a simple peak-picking algorithm is applied to the corresponding CM function.

During recent years, GCC-based time delay estimators, and in particular those emphasizing the phase information carried by the cross-power spectrum, have been preferred to cross-correlation based ones, due to their accuracy and robustness to noise and reverberation.

A delay estimator based on the CSP analysis is described in Omologo and Svaizer (1994, 1997). The source is assumed to be stationary and its position is searched by a two-dimensional location algorithm.[7] Two microphone pairs are used to derive the two corresponding coherence measure matrices. Starting from the coherence measure $C_{ik}(n, l)$, that is the digital counterpart of (2.41), for all physically admissible delays l $(-l_{MAX} \leq l \leq l_{MAX})$ and frames n $(1 \leq n \leq N)$ including the acoustic event, a lag $\hat{l}_{ik}(n)$ is estimated with one-sample precision as follows:

$$\hat{l}_{ik}(n) = \operatorname*{argmax}_{l}[C_{ik}(n, l)] \tag{2.43}$$

In the specific case of a stationary source, expression (2.43) collapses into a maximum search over the components of the vector $C'_{ik}(l) = \sum_n C_{ik}(n, l)$. Once the maximum is found, a subsample refinement of the estimate $\hat{l}_{ik}$ is provided by a suitable interpolation. Given the two resulting delay estimates, the source position is derived as intersection point between the two corresponding bearing lines.

In Omologo and Svaizer (1996) performance of the same location technique is studied under different noise and reverberation conditions, showing that an average location error of less than 10 cm can be attained, using a linear microphone array of two microphone pairs. Further details on this subject and on possible derivations can be found in Rabinkin *et al.* (1996), Stephenne and Champagne (1995) and Champagne *et al.* (1996).

Another source location method based on the use of the CSP is described in Brandstein *et al.* (1995). In this approach, the inverse Fourier transform described by (2.41) is replaced by phase slope computation, where the delay estimate is related to the slope of the line that "fits" the series of phase terms. The substantial difference between this method and those previously mentioned is that an implicit step of phase unwrapping is required in the slope computation (since phase is modulo 2π). Brandstein (1995) describes different effective methods that can be adopted for this purpose (worth mentioning is the method described in Tribolet, 1977).

---

[7]Two-dimensional location implies that both the microphones and the source are assumed to lie on the same plane.

2.5.7. Source Position Computation

Given a set of relative delay estimates, obtained by processing a set of microphone pair signals, the source position can be derived by triangulation techniques, as shown for instance in Jan (1995) and Omologo and Svaizer (1997), or by solving a problem that is generally non-linear, but that can be simplified to a closed-form solution or solved via an iterative procedure. This simplification leads to a suboptimal solution, that is satisfactory in most cases. Only when the number of spatial dimensions is equal to the number of delay estimates, an exact solution can be derived (Fang, 1990). In the general case, iterative procedures (Foy, 1976; Delosme *et al.*, 1980) start from an initial position hypothesis and converge to an optimal solution, for instance applying at each step local linearized corrections. In these cases, the solution can be influenced by the initial guess and by the ability of the algorithm to converge to a unique location, that is not always guaranteed. On the other hand, closed-form location estimation procedures generally correspond to simple methods for deriving a suboptimal solution of the given non-linear problem (Smith and Abel, 1987; Chan and Ho, 1994; Schau and Robinson, 1987; Friedlander, 1987). Other closed-form location procedures can be found in the literature. In particular, the work of Brandstein *et al.* (1997), concerning 3-D talker location, discusses on the use of a closed-form location algorithm when using microphone pairs arranged in clusters of four microphones (based on a square geometry). In the case of a large number of sensors, a suitable choice of the array geometry as well as an effective source location procedure are required. For instance, to compensate for a different "reliability" in the relative delay estimation, the algorithm of source position computation can be rendered more robust by exploiting the dependence of error statistics of the delay estimates, on source position, on array geometry, and on environmental characteristics. These issues are addressed in Brandstein (1995) and Brandstein *et al.* (1996).

2.6. MICROPHONES IN SPEECH RECOGNITION

2.6.1. Introduction

Even though some methodological aspects and results, concerning the use of microphones in ASR, will be described in successive chapters, a few qualitative considerations can be anticipated here.

The first consideration is that acoustic models (AM) have to be trained using a speech corpus. As a result of this training, the microphone characteristics become part of the acquired knowledge. Intuitively, it can be concluded that the microphone used for recognition tests, or in real-life operation, should be of the same type as the microphone used in the acquisition of the training data in order to obtain good ASR results. Microphone dependency can be avoided only if very robust microphone normalization (or adaptation) techniques are utilized.

Apart from microphone characteristics, the channel, the environmental conditions, and the usage style should be similar during testing and training. For instance, a non-ideal position of the talker's mouth with respect to the microphone can cause a substantial degradation in performance (as a result, in some cases a very high-quality microphone can represent a useless expense).

As discussed in the following section, the use of either specific microphones or microphone arrays can make less stringent some constraints between training and testing conditions (further improvement in channel characteristic alignment can be performed by techniques for normalization/compensation described in Chapter 12).

2.6.2. On the Use of a Single Microphone

When operating in a quiet environment, the use of a single microphone can allow high performance. As previously emphasized, using different microphones during training and testing may cause a performance loss.

In recent years, many works have been devoted to investigating on the impact of the microphone on recognition performance. For instance, specific research issues (e.g. "microphone independence" and "known alternate microphones") were addressed under the ARPA Continuous speech recognition Corpus Coordinating Committee (CCCC) programme on dictation of *Wall Street Journal* (*WSJ*) and *North American Business* (*NAB*). For these activities, speech corpora are created by collecting stereo (or multichannel) speech data through a high-quality head-mounted close-talking microphone, used as reference and for training, and through other microphones (e.g. omnidirectional, directional, desk-mounted, telephone, etc.) for testing.

In a work on the DARPA-resource management task Acero (1993) reports on a drop in performance under quiet conditions from 85% WRR (word recognition rate), when using a close-talking microphone (the same used for training) during test, to 19% when using a PZM desktop microphone. Note that when using the latter microphone for training, performance was about 77%.

Recently, Chang and Zue (1994) investigated the nature of the recognition errors that occurred in experiments running on a stereo acoustic-phonetic corpus (TIMIT), and showed that significant influence of microphone mismatching on the recognition performance persists even if the acquisition is conducted in a quiet environment. In this work, a noise-cancelling close-talking microphone was compared with another microphone placed at some distance away from the talker's mouth; in this case, the contribution to the phone error increased from 27% to 34%, mostly due to distortion in low-frequency spectral range.

Other recent results confirm the importance of microphone matching as well as the partial effectiveness of adaptation/compensation techniques, as described in Pallett *et al.* (1995), Anastasakos *et al.* (1994), Neumeyer and Weintraub (1994a), Liu *et al.* (1994).

Another application where the influence of the microphone has been deeply investigated is ASR in the car environment (a near-field case). As shown in Smolders *et al.* (1994), the microphone position plays a fundamental role. Its optimal position does not necessarily correspond to the point where the noise level is minimum (or, more generally, where the SNR is high). Note that the SNR in a moving car is often lower than 0 dB (e.g. when air-conditioning is switched on) and that another typical effect is the increase in the spectrum power at low frequencies (generally below 500 Hz).

Under these adverse conditions, one common way to improve recognition performance is to use a secondary noise-cancelling microphone. However, this microphone may cause some drawbacks, due to the implicit subtraction realized by the "secondary" microphone that could pick-up and subtract both part of the direct talker's message (if the microphone position is not optimal) and its first reflections (in case of reverberant environment). A pressure-gradient noise-cancelling microphone was shown very useful in a car environment but only when its position was optimized and fixed (that is very close to the talker's mouth) (DalDegan and Prati, 1988). Similar results can be found in Viswanathan and Henry (1986) where first-order and second-order gradient microphones were used, in extremely adverse conditions such as in a fighter aircraft cockpit. The use of first-order gradient microphones for connected digit recognition in a moving car is also discussed in (Gupta *et al.*, 1996).

In general, it appears that the use of a single special transducer can be effective for low-noise conditions, while further analysis has to be made for more adverse conditions.

2.6.3. Microphone Arrays

The microphone array represents a natural alternative to the use of a single special microphone. Autodirectivity characteristics and noise reduction capabilities allow the microphone array to compensate for degradation due to the acoustical environment or to speaker movements.

The car environment was one of the first experimental contexts considered for microphone array application, mostly due to legal constraints that impose hands-free interaction and to the limitations in performance shown when a single microphone is used.

As shown in Oh and Viswanathan (1995), an effective solution is to combine the microphone array acquisition with a generalized sidelobe canceller (GSC).

Results were superior to those obtained either with a single microphone or when using a non-adaptive delay-and-add beamformer. A variant of the GSC algorithm may be proposed as shown by Grenier (1992, 1993), which highlights the limitations of this system under severely noisy conditions.

Recent works have been conducted to show the microphone array processing potential for speech recognition in office or large-room environments for hands-free command interaction, dictation, and telephone applications. As an example, Giuliani *et al.* (1995) report on the effectiveness of a linear microphone array consisting of four omnidirectional PZM microphones when a delay-and-sum beamformer is used to reconstruct the input to the recognizer. The improvement due to the time delay compensation is shown to be "independent" from that added when adaptation/compensation techniques are introduced to improve the acoustic-phonetic models of the recognizer. To a certain extent, this result remains valid under different noise and reverberation conditions as shown by simulation experiments described in Giuliani *et al.* (1996). Similar experiments and results are described in Adcock *et al.* (1996), where an array of 16 pressure gradient microphones was used.

Most of the mentioned experiments were conducted with the talker in a fixed position, a distance of some metres from the array. An important aspect of these research studies is that the final system should be flexible in order to provide high recognition performance independently of talker position. Hence, further studies are needed on this issue. As an example, Che *et al.* (1994a) describes an ASR application that uses a neural network (NN) to perform a transformation/normalization of acoustic features extracted from the delay-and-add beamformed signal. Since during the training the NN learns some information related to the talker position, the influence of the talker location is addressed in Lin *et al.* (1996), showing the effectiveness of location-independent NN.

3

Basic Speech Sounds,
their Analysis and Features

Bianca Angelini, Daniele Falavigna, Maurizio Omologo*
and Renato De Mori[†]

*Istituto per la Ricerca Scientifica e Tecnologica – 38050 Pantè di Povo, Trento, Italy.
[†]School of Computer Science, McGill University, Montreal, P.Q. H3A 2A7, Canada.

3.1. INTRODUCTION

Speech recognition requires the solution of problems of very different nature. A basic question is how to deal with the redundancy in the speech information, in order to derive a compact representation in terms of acoustic features. Speech sounds are characterized by some properties related to their production. The relationship between the nature of these sounds and the physiological mechanisms at the basis of their production (and perception) has a fundamental importance for the derivation of a set of acoustic features as well as for the consequent acoustic modelling, which will be introduced in Chapter 5.

Section 3.2 describes the fundamentals of speech production at the articulatory, phonetic, and acoustic level. Section 3.3 reviews speech analysis principles including windowing, short-time spectral analysis and linear predictive modelling. Section 3.4 briefly introduces auditory modelling, a topic that will be discussed in detail in Chapter 12 because of its importance when ASR is performed in noisy environments. Section 3.5 describes acoustic features used for ASR and section 3.6 deals with the time evolutions of these features and other dynamic parameters useful for characterizing speech sounds. Some conclusions are given in section 3.7.

3.2. THE NATURE OF SPEECH SOUNDS

3.2.1. Fundamentals of Speech Production

Speech is produced by pressure waves coming out, primarily, from the mouth and the nostrils of the speaker. These waves are non-stationary and have amplitudes that depend on the strength of the airflow coming out of the lungs, and on the configuration of the speech production organs. Figure 3.1 shows an outline of the human speech production apparatus.

Although there is a large number of possible speech organ configurations resulting in different airflow paths from the lungs to the lips, some broad categories can be defined that have generally a direct correspondence with sound classes. For some short time intervals, one can assume the stationarity[1] of a configuration based on which the speech waveform can be acoustically

---

[1]Actually, ther term "quasi-stationary" is more appropriate than "stationary" to describe a slow variation inside these intervals.

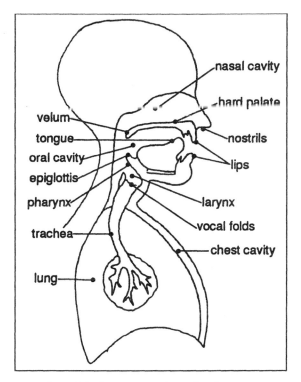

Figure 3.1 Representation of the human speech production apparatus.

characterized. The duration of these intervals can vary from a few milliseconds to more than 100 ms. Consequently, the production of a speech message[2] can be seen as the result of a sequence of target configurations of the phonatory organs. However, during fluent speech production the speech organs do not complete their evolution from one target configuration to the successive one. This phenomenon is generally unintentional and mainly due to the inertia of the articulators: some of them start to move toward a new target (next phone) while others still attempt to reach the stable configuration of another target (previous phone). These dynamic effects are known as *coarticulation.*

3.2.2. Basic Speech Sounds

Every speech message can be seen as composed of a sequence of basic speech sounds. Every language has a set of basic units that represent the building blocks for the composition of every word or sentence. These basic units can

---

[2]It is worth recalling that replicas of a given sentence, even if uttered by the same speaker, under the same conditions, and during consecutive instants, are never represented by exactly the same signal.

be classified at different levels: articulatory, acoustic, and phonetic (or sub-phonetic).[3]

It is worth noting that the number and the type of units used for acoustic modelling in ASR can be very different, according to the characteristics of the recognition task (as discussed in the following chapters). The simplest choice is to associate a basic speech unit with each phoneme of the language. However, the introduction of other subphonetic or subword units may be necessary to better account for different realizations of the same phoneme. For this reason, beside *phone-like unit* and *phone unit*, other terms such as *acoustic-phonetic unit, context dependent unit, diphone, triphone, syllable* are used.

This section has the purpose of introducing some of these concepts and high-lighting specific aspects that concern the realization of the basic speech sounds in the spoken language and the consequent problems that can be encountered in modelling them. An extended overview on acoustic phonetics can be found in Fry (1976), Lieberman and Blumstein (1988), Kent and Read (1992), Laver (1994) and Hardcastle and Laver (1997).

Articulatory level

The articulatory level deals with the configuration of the speech organs as they vary in time while the air flows from the lungs to the lips. These aspects are the object of *articulatory phonetics* studies.

The airflow can first find a partial or total constriction of the vocal folds at the larynx level. The amount of constriction depends on the degree of opening of the glottis. The resulting airflow represents the glottal *excitation* at the entrance of the vocal tract, which acts as sound modulator before radiation from the lips (and the nostrils). While the glottal excitation is produced, the vocal fold constriction can vary periodically in time with rapid opening and closing of the glottis. Such a vibration is characteristic of *voiced sounds* (also called *sonorants*) and its rate is called *fundamental frequency* (or *pitch*[4]). *Nasal* sounds are also voiced; however, in this case the production is based on lowering the velum, with radiation from the nostrils.

Speech sounds produced without any vibration of the glottis are called *unvoiced*. In particular, those generated with narrow vocal tract constrictions are called *obstruent* or *occlusive* sounds. On the other hand, if the air pressure behind the constriction is large enough, a turbulent airflow (called frication)

---

[3]The auditory level is introduced to consider perceptual cues as discriminant for basic speech unit distinction. Here this aspect will not be addressed; a specific discussion can be found in O'Shaughnessy (1987).

[4]The terms pitch and fundamental frequency are generally used without a clear distinction between the two; the correct use of the term pitch should preferably refer to the perception of the fundamental frequency than to the periodicity of the vocal fold vibration (that can be detected in the speech waveform).

can arise providing the so called *fricative* sounds. In this case, it can be assumed that the point of excitation of the vocal tract is the position at which frication occurs. It is worth noting that some speech sounds are characterized by a mixed excitation, due to simultaneous glottis movement and frication.

From the point of view of articulatory phonetics, the basic speech sounds can be classified according to the *manner of articulation* and the *place of articulation*. The manner of articulation specifies the way in which the air flows and the degree of constriction it encounters in the vocal tract. As mentioned above, for some sounds (e.g. vowels) the airflow crosses the vocal tract without finding any obstacle, while for other sounds (e.g. obstruents), it may be inhibited by some constriction. The point of major constriction identifies the place of articulation.

Phonetic level

A *phoneme* is an abstract linguistic unit, the smallest discriminant one in the phonology of a given language. Each language has its own set of phonemes that, generally, contains a few tens of elements. The term *allophone* is used to indicate members of a given phoneme, accounting for its different pronunciations. In principle, for each phoneme, there can be an infinite number of physical realizations, each of them resulting in different acoustic events. The term *phone* is used to indicate the acoustic realization of a phoneme.

Note that, while phonemes and allophones are abstract units, phones correspond to acoustic events, produced by the articulators of the human vocal tract. Furthermore, although some phonemes are shared among different languages, their realizations can be substantially language dependent.[5]

Phonemes are divided into two broad categories, namely *vowels* and *consonants*. Both classes can be further subdivided, according to some cues.

Each phoneme can be described by a set of *articulatory gestures*, that is a sequence of target positions of the articulators. Some phonemes are characterized by being steady-state during most of their realizations, while others correspond to quite complex realizations, based on changes of voicing, manner of articulation, and place of articulation (an example is represented by the diphthongs, consisting of a non-complete continual evolution between two vowel configurations). In these cases, two or more subunits can be identified inside a phone unit, with each subunit characterized by distinct acoustic cues (e.g. the closure that precedes obstruent sounds). Also for this reason, the concept of subphonetic unit is needed in addition to that of phone unit.

---

[5]For the sake of brevity, only the phonemes of the English language will be considered in this book. A detailed discussion and a comparison of phoneme sets of different languages can be found in Maddieson (1987) and Ladefoged and Maddieson (1990, 1996).

Acoustic level

Basic speech units can also be classified according to the properties of the corresponding speech waveforms. These properties are generally described by the amplitude evolution of the waveform or by the corresponding spectral content, obtained with an appropriate spectral analysis method. The most popular method is based on the *power spectrum* estimation provided by the *Fourier transform* (see Appendix A). The power spectrum $|S(f)|^2$ gives information about the energy content of a given signal $s(t)$ at each frequency f. As discussed in section 3.3, the analysis is performed on finite energy signals after applying a *windowing* process.

In order to describe the time evolution of power spectrum the *spectrogram* representation is introduced, as shown in Figure 3.2. In this representation, the horizontal axis corresponds to time while the vertical axis corresponds to frequency. The intensities of different time–frequency regions are represented by the darkness of the plotted points. According to the length of the analysis interval as well as to the window characteristics, the spectrogram is distinguished in *wideband* (short analysis window) and *narrowband* (long analysis window).

Concentrations of the power spectrum at some frequency regions denote vocal tract resonances, also called *formants*. Each formant has a central frequency, a bandwidth, and a magnitude. The spectrogram representation shows the position and the movement of each formant frequency and highlights the time extension of both speech units and transitions between adjacent units.

The power spectrum and the spectrogram exhibit other useful information, such as spectral tilts and antiresonances (mostly evident in spectra of nasal consonants). Figures 3.3 and 3.4 show some examples of spectral envelopes for vowels and nasals.

Another important visible cue is voicing information. It is highlighted by the periodicities in the speech waveform; it can also be detected by inspection of either the power spectrum or the spectrogram. A voiced speech segment is generally characterized by a "peaky" fine structure of the spectrum, obtained by narrowband analysis: a corresponding horizontal striation can be seen in the spectrogram, at multiples of the fundamental frequency. In the case of voiced segments, the wideband spectrogram also shows vertical striations due to spectral discontinuities related to the narrowness of the analysis window (which can be comparable or smaller than the pitch period).

Looking at the speech waveform representation, it is possible to observe a correspondence between the temporal and the frequency domain representation for most of the speech units. As an example, voiced sounds are characterized by a pitch period duration inversely proportional to the peak-to-peak distance in the "fine structure" of the power spectrum, as shown in Figure 3.5. Even if more difficult to observe, formants also have a direct relation with oscillations that can be seen inside a *pitch epoch* (the interval between two consecutive instants

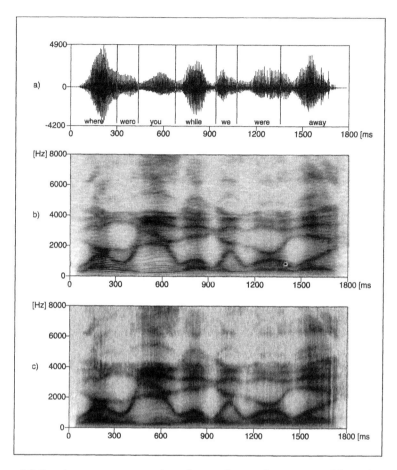

Figure 3.2 Spectrogram representation of a speech waveform extracted from the TIMIT database (Lamel, 1986). The sentence was "Where were you while we were away?" (a) The waveform; (b) a narrowband spectrogram and (c) a wideband spectrogram.

of closure of the vocal chords) of the speech waveform. The higher the formant magnitude, the more evident the oscillation at the corresponding frequency. In Figure 3.5, one can note that the first formant of the vowel /ae/ has a central frequency near 800 Hz, and that its counterpart in the time domain is represented by waveform oscillations with periodicity of about 1.2 ms.

Two examples of speech waveforms, including fricative and occlusive sounds, and the corresponding spectrograms are given in Figure 3.6. In these cases, the spectrogram highlights complex temporal evolutions. As an example, the occlusive /t/ of the first example is divided in a first phase of obstruction /tcl/, and a second phase of burst /t/; a final phase of release, included in the following vowel /ah/, can be noted as well. In the second example, one can note an analogous distinction in two phases in the realization of the occlusive /b/.

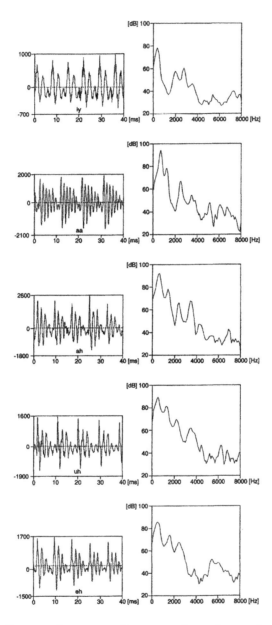

Figure 3.3 Waveforms and corresponding spectral envelopes of some vowels of American English (the phonetic symbols are defined in Table 3.1).

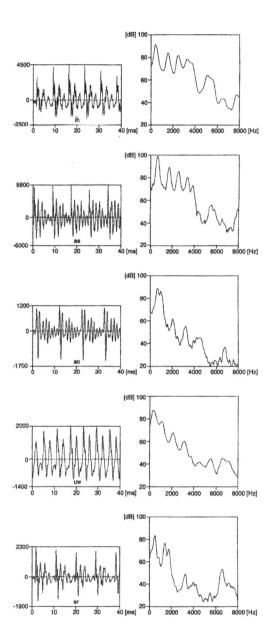

Figure 3.3 Continued.

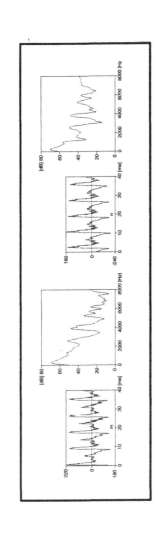

Figure 3.4 Waveform and corresponding spectral envelope of two nasal sounds (/m/ and /n/).

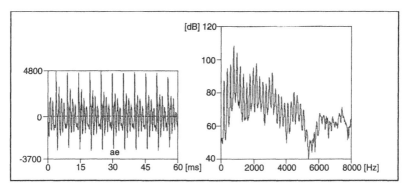

Figure 3.5 Waveform and power spectrum of a portion of the vowel /ae/. The fundamental frequency corresponds to the peak-to-peak distance of about 5 ms in the time domain and of about 200 Hz in the spectrum. The first formant, F_1 (~800 Hz), corresponds to a peak-to-peak distance of about 1.2 ms in the time domain.

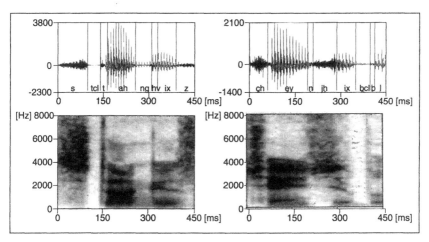

Figure 3.6 Waveforms and corresponding spectrograms of speech segments including fricatives and occlusives

The speech waveforms of these examples show how critical the application of a short-time spectral analysis to speech sounds can be where abrupt changes in the signal characteristics occur in very short time intervals.

3.2.3. Phoneme Classification

In this section, a classification of English phonemes is given according to articulatory phonetics.

For every language, a set of symbols belonging to a *phonetic alphabet* is used to represent all the phonemes. Due to the overlapping between phonetics of

Table 3.1 The list of symbols of the ARPAbet phonetic alphabet. For each symbol, the corresponding broad phonetic class is given. The example highlights (with bold characters) the part of the word where the symbol is used

Long	Short	Broad ph. class	Example	Long	Short	Broad ph. class	Example
AA	a	vowel	**ho**t	EN	N	nasal	so**n**
AE	@	vowel	h**a**d	M	m	nasal	**m**e
AH	A	vowel	c**u**d	N	n	nasal	**n**o
AO	c	vowel	l**aw**	NG	G	nasal	ha**ng**
AX	x	vowel	**a**go	B	b	stop	**b**ed
EH	E	vowel	b**e**t	D	d	stop	**d**one
ER	R	vowel	h**er**	G	g	stop	**g**ain
IH	I	vowel	h**i**t	P	p	stop	**p**ot
IX	X	vowel	ros**e**s	T	t	stop	**t**one
IY	i	vowel	h**ee**d	K	k	stop	**k**id
UH	U	vowel	c**oo**k	DX	F	stop	bu**tt**er
UW	u	vowel	l**oo**p	CH	C	affricate	**ch**eck
AW	W	diphthong	**ou**t	JH	J	affricate	**j**udge
AY	Y	diphthong	h**i**de	F	f	fricative	**f**ive
EY	e	diphthong	**ai**d	V	v	fricative	**v**ex
OW	o	diphthong	**ow**e	DH	D	fricative	**th**is
OY	O	diphthong	b**oy**	TH	T	fricative	**th**in
W	w	glide	**w**itch	S	s	fricative	**s**ix
Y	y	glide	**y**es	Z	z	fricative	**z**oo
EL	L	liquid	catt**le**	SH	S	fricative	**sh**ine
L	l	liquid	**l**awn	ZH	Z	fricative	plea**s**ure
R	r	liquid	**r**ace	HH	h	fricative	**h**elp
EM	M	nasal	so**me**	Q	Q	glottal stop	—

different languages, an International Phonetic Alphabet (IPA) has been introduced. Since not all the IPA symbols can be typed by conventional computer keyboards, another alphabet, called *ARPAbet*,[6] was proposed based on an ASCII representation of all the phonemes of the English language. In Table 3.1, derived from Lea (1980), a short and a long version of each phonetic symbol is given.[7] For languages different from English, phonetic alphabets similar to ARPAbet have been proposed. A discussion on different types of transcription and principles for their classification can be found in Laver (1994).

From the point of view of articulatory phonetics, phonemes can be classified, according to their manner of articulation, into *sonorants* and *obstruents*. Within sonorants there are *vowels*, *diphthongs*, *glides*, *liquids* and *nasals*. All of these, except vowels and diphthongs, involve some vocal tract restrictions. Obstruents consist of *stops*, *fricatives* and *affricates*.

---

[6]The development of ARPAbet was sponsored by the US Advanced Research Projects Agency (ARPA).

[7]There is an almost complete equivalence between ARPAbet long symbols and acoustic-phonetic symbols (denoted here with small letters between bars) used to transcribe the TIMIT corpus (Lee, 1988b).

Note that diphthongs, glides, stops and affricates give rise to *transient sounds*, because they involve a sequence of different articulatory gestures, while the other phonetic classes include *continuant sounds*, because they are essentially generated by a steady-state configuration of the vocal tract. In Table 3.1 these broad phonetic classes are associated with the ARPAbet symbols.

The place of articulation allows another fine subdivision of phonemes. In particular, consonants can be distiguished, according to the configuration of the vocal tract (positions of tongue and lips), into: *labials, dentals, alveolars* and *palatals*. Two more constrictions at the glottis and at the pharynx originate *glottals* and *pharingeals*.

In the following, some acoustic properties of the phonetic classes of Table 3.1 will be described.

Vowels are characterized by formants in their power spectrum. The central frequencies of the first three formants, called F_1, F_2, F_3, are generally sufficient to characterize all the vowels. In Figure 3.7 the distributions of vowels of the American English language are reported in the F_1-F_2 plane. One can note that the various vowels are distributed along a triangle known as *vowel triangle* (whose vertices are placed in the regions referred to as the cardinal vowels /iy/, /uw/, /aa/). Place of articulation of vowels is related both to the horizontal/vertical positions of the tongue body and to the restriction caused by the lips. According to the horizontal position of tongue, vowels can be divided into *back, middle* and *front* while, referring to the vertical position of the tongue, vowels can be *low* or *high*. In particular, a middle horizontal

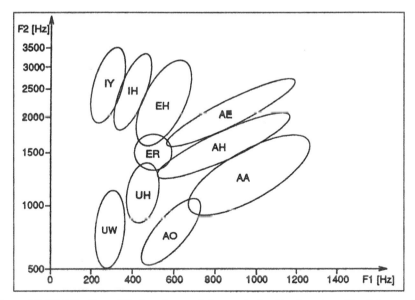

Figure 3.7 Distribution of first and second formants for the American English vowels.

tongue position is specific of the "schwa" vowel /ax/, that is characterized by a low-energy signal of short duration. Finally, vowels can be divided into *lax* and *tense*, depending on the duration and the displacement of the tongue from the neutral position typical of schwa, and into *rounded* and *unrounded*, depending on the lip positioning. For example, /aa/ is back, low, unrounded, /iy/ is front, high, unrounded, /uw/ is back, high, rounded. Further details can be found in O'Shaughnessy (1987).

Glides are similar to vowels but are articulated more quickly, due to narrower constrictions. Generally, they are characterized by a short duration, by a signal amplitude reduction, and they look like transient sounds with associated formant transitions from or toward target values.

Diphthongs can be seen, in principle, as sequences of vowels and glides, but their classification is often a matter of discussion. In English, only some of the possible sequences *vowel + glide* are classified as diphthongs. Table 3.1 includes in this category only the following symbols: /ey/, /ay/, /oy/, /aw/ and /ow/. Also *glide + vowel* sequences are sometimes classified as diphthongs. It is worth noting that in some European languages, diphthongs are not considered as a single phonetic symbol.

Liquids have spectra similar to vowels. However, since they involve narrow constrictions of the vocal tract (mainly determined by the tongue position), they have lower energy than vowels. Note that, in some languages (e.g. French and Italian), the liquid /r/ is produced by vibration of the tongue tip, generating a speech waveform characterized by a sort of amplitude modulation.

Nasals are produced by obstructing the oral cavity and diverting the airflow across the nasal cavity. They are characterized by a spectral zero in the vocal tract transfer function, which generates an antiresonance in the frequency range 750–1250 Hz for /m/, 1450–2200 Hz for /n/ and above 3000 Hz for /ng/ (Fujimura, 1962). A first energy concentration at low frequency (generally less than 300 Hz) dominates the spectrum. Generally, the nasal resonances are characterized by a higher bandwidth than that of vowel formants. Note that nasal sounds influence the spectra of adjacent phonemes (especially vowels).

Stops (often called occlusives) are transient sounds characterized by a vocal tract occlusion (*closure*) followed by a sudden release, which has an effect similar to a small explosion, and which is called *burst*. The speech sound, related to the closure portion, can be either a silence (*unvoiced stops*) or a weak energy signal (*voiced stops*). In the latter case, the occlusion segment is also called *voice bar* and consists of an oscillation at a low frequency, caused by the radiation of the glottal pulses. Depending on the place of articulation, stops can be bilabial (/p/, /b/), alveolar (/d/, /t/) or velar (/g/, /k/). The release of the occlusion creates a burst noise that presents energy concentrations at frequencies of a fricative having the same place of articulation. When a stop occurs between two vowels (as in the word "matter"), it is often produced as a *flap* (/dx/) (Zue and Laferriere, 1979).

Fricatives, as occlusives, are produced by constricting the vocal tract and may be either voiced or unvoiced. In unvoiced fricatives the excitation mostly occurs at the point of major constriction, and it consists of turbulent noise. On the contrary, frication noise can be mixed with glottal pulses for producing voiced fricatives (in this case there are two excitation points of the vocal tract). Generally, unvoiced fricatives exhibit energy concentration at high frequency, while voiced fricatives exhibit a voice bar.

Affricates are transient phones formed by a stop followed by a fricative. In American English, affricates are /ch/ (as in "check") and /jh/ (as in "judge"). The former is unvoiced, while the latter is voiced.

3.2.4. Coarticulation

Phones exhibit consistent spectral characteristics, if pronounced in isolation or in isolated syllables. On the other hand, large acoustic variations may appear if they are uttered in different contexts. One reason for these variations is *coarticulation*. It is determined by the physiology of the speech production mechanism. During sentence generation the phonetic articulators move from target positions of a phoneme to target positions of the succeeding one. These movements are planned by the brain, in such a way that the effort of the muscles is kept to a minimum. Furthermore, articulatory gestures are not instantaneous, following dynamics constrained by mechanical time constants associated with each articulator.

If an articulator must reach a certain position to produce a phone and the preceding phone does not need that articulator, then the articulator itself may anticipate its movement toward the next target position, before the production of the previous phone is finished. This phenomenon is called *forward coarticulation*. On the contrary, an articulator may slow down to release a target position, corresponding to the pronounced phone, if it is not required by the next phoneme. This second type of coarticulation is known as *backward coarticulation* (O'Shaughnessy, 1987).

As an example, let us consider the pronunciation of a vowel followed by a nasal consonant. In this case, the *velum* starts lowering before the vowel has finished so that the final part of the vowel is strongly influenced by the following nasal. This effect is visible in the spectrogram of the vowel, where the anti-resonance is present and the first formant becomes wider (i.e. the corresponding bandwidth is enlarged) and sometimes shifted upward. A similar effect is observed in vowels preceded by nasals and in vowels between nasals. Since coarticulation involves all articulatory organs, its effects are the source of many problems for ASR and speech synthesis. Coarticulation effects may extend beyond the phones immediately adjacent to that currently uttered. Furthermore, it has effects not only on speech spectra but also on sound durations. Perceptual experiments show that some phones may not be correctly perceived, if not properly coarticulated (Gottfried and Strange, 1980).

Generally, during speech production, articulators do not reach steady state positions. Therefore, the corresponding acoustic features hardly ever assume target values. For this reason, the dynamics of articulatory gestures, as well as the temporal trend of acoustic parameters, have to be used for modelling both speech production and perception. An example is given by the so called *locus theory* (Delattre *et al.*, 1955) for the second formant F_2 of occlusives. In perceptual experiments using synthetic speech produced by a formant synthesizer, if the F_2 temporal pattern starts from a locus at 1.8 kHz and moves toward target values of different vowels, then the occlusives are correctly perceived; on the contrary, if the initial part of the F_2 pattern is substituted by silence, a dental occlusive is always heard.

Coarticulation is a complex aspect of speech production and is investigated using sophisticated technologies, such as x-rays, magnetic resonance, ultrasound and electromyography. However, due to the high costs of the instruments, articulatory models of speech production are often obtained, indirectly, from the acoustic analysis of the speech signal. In this case, it is necessary to use methods for mapping spectral estimates into vocal tract shapes. A review of some of these methods can be found in Schroeter and Sondhi (1994).

3.3. SPEECH ANALYSIS PRINCIPLES

3.3.1. Introduction

The speech signal can be considered as a non-stationary stochastic process (Papoulis, 1991). Thus, its spectral analysis must take into account variability both in time and in frequency. As discussed in the previous section, the signal is produced by articulatory organs moving from one position to another with intrinsic mechanical time constants. Therefore, it is possible to define a time interval (*stationarity interval*) within which the signal can be considered time-invariant (i.e. stationary). On a segment of length comparable with that of the stationarity interval, standard spectral analysis methods (e.g. based on the Fourier transform or on autoregressive models) can be applied. In ASR, the main goal of the so-called *feature extraction* step is the computation of a sequence of feature vectors that provide a compact representation of the given input signal. In this section, some analysis methods for feature extraction will be reviewed.

3.3.2. Start–End-Point Detection

Given the input signal, a first problem to address is that of removing the silence and the background noise, preceding and following the utterance to be recognized. Several techniques have been developed (Rabiner and Schafer, 1978; Rabiner and Sambur, 1975; Lamel *et al.*, 1981; Ney, 1981; Junqua *et al.*, 1994), based either on the same acoustic features used during the recognition process or on other specific ones such as energy and zero-crossing rate (see Appendix A).

Furthermore, the start–end-point detection can be performed simultaneously with the recognition phase or before it. This problem, which becomes critical especially when dealing with recognition in noisy environment, will be addressed in more detail in Chapter 12.

3.3.3. Signal Preprocessing

In order to render more effective the use of a generic spectral analysis method, a preprocessing technique can be conveniently applied to the input signal. For instance, preprocessing may be aimed at noise reduction or formant enhancement in the power spectrum. This aspect will be discussed in Chapter 12.

A common characteristic that can be found in the power spectrum of voiced speech is the low magnitude of high-frequency formants. A way to overcome this effect is that of preemphasizing the input signal. *Preemphasis* is generally realized by applying a fixed first-order FIR-filter (see Appendix A) with z-transfer function $H(z) = 1 - az^{-1}$, where a is the preemphasis parameter (a typical choice is $a = 0.95$, while the most common one for fixed-point implementations is $a = \frac{15}{16}$). In this way, the spectrum magnitude of the resulting preemphasized speech is increased in the upper frequencies of more than 20 dB (approximately 30 dB at the Nyquist frequency).

3.3.4. Spectral Analysis

As mentioned above, due to the non-stationarity of speech signals, standard spectral analysis methods can be applied only to short time intervals.

Short-time Fourier transform

The so-called *short-time Fourier transform* (STFT) (Rabiner and Gold, 1975), $S(n, e^{j\omega})$ of a digital signal $s(m)$ is defined as:

$$S(n, e^{j\omega}) = \sum_{m=-\infty}^{+\infty} s(m)w(n-m)\,e^{-j\omega m} \tag{3.1}$$

where $w(n-m)$ is a window sequence which emphasizes a specific portion of the given signal, at the nth time instant. For a given value of n, $S(n, e^{j\omega})$ represents the standard Fourier transform of the signal $s(m)w(n-m)$. For a given value of

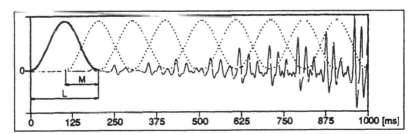

Figure 3.8 Short-time spectral analysis of a speech waveform.

ω, the time signal $S(n, e^{j\omega})$ represents the frequency content of $s(n)$ around ω, within a band "equivalent" to that of the window $w(n)$.

Short-time spectral analysis

In practice, the short time spectral analysis can be described as follows:

- The sampled speech signal, $s(n)$, is multiplied by a finite length window $[w(n)]_{n=0}^{L-1}$, running in time (see Figure 3.8). The window is displaced by steps of fixed duration M, where $M \le L$ is the *analysis step*: its position identifies an analysis *frame*. The tth frame results in a sequence $[s_t(n)]_{n=0}^{L-1}$ that can be written as:

$$s_t(n) = w(n)s(n + tM) \qquad 0 \le t \le T - 1 \tag{3.2}$$

where T is the total number of frames. Usual durations for the analysis window (Hockel and Gray, 1976) are of the order of 15:40 ms. To avoid undesired edge effects, the most common windows are tapered, i.e. they assume values close to 1 in the central part and values that gradually go to zero at the two extremities. An example is represented by the Hamming window (Rabiner and Schafer, 1978).

- Assuming the stationary of the signal within the given tth frame, a standard spectral analysis technique (e.g. STFT) is applied, that produces a vector of coefficients representing instantaneous spectral estimates of the signal (given the temporal resolution corresponding to the window length L).

Spectrogram

Let us assume that, at every instant t, the log-power spectrum $\mathbf{S}_t$ has been computed, that is:

$$\mathbf{S}_t = [\log(|S_t(e^{j\omega_0})|^2), \ldots, \log(|S_t(e^{j\omega_K}|^2)]^{\mathrm{T}}, \quad 0 \le t \le T - 1 \tag{3.3}$$

where T denotes transposition and $K = (L - 1)/2$.

Let us indicate with:

$$S_t(e^{j\omega_k}) = \sum_{n=0}^{L-1} s_t(n)\, e^{-j\frac{2\pi}{L}kn}, \quad 0 \le k \le \frac{L-1}{2} \tag{3.4}$$

the kth discrete Fourier transform (DFT) coefficient (see Appendix A) of the sequence $[s_t(n)]_{n=0}^{L-1}$. The above DFT sequence represents exact samples of the Fourier transform, $S_t(e^{j\omega})$, at $\omega_k = 2\pi k(F_s/L)$, where F_s is the sampling frequency (Oppenheim and Schafer, 1989).

Then, a spectrogram representation (see Figure 3.2) is provided by the matrix $S = [S_0, \ldots, S_{T-1}]$.

Critical issues

The power spectrum (see Appendix A), obtained from the DFT in (3.4), is also known as *sample spectrum* of the sequence $[s_t(n)]_{n=0}^{L-1}$ and allows estimating the power spectral density (PSD) of the corresponding stationary stochastic process (Marple, 1987). This estimation method, as well as the others based on the Fourier transform, is subject to the following limitations:

- The multiplication of the signal with the analysis window corresponds, in the frequency domain, to the convolution of the signal spectrum with the window spectrum. Generally, the window spectrum has a main lobe, centred on $\omega = 0$ (with width inversely proportional to the length of the window itself), and sidelobes of lower intensities (see Rabiner and Schafer (1978) for a detailed description of these aspects). To improve frequency resolution of spectral estimates, a window having a narrow main lobe should be used. However, the only way to do this is by lengthening the analysis window, thus reducing the temporal resolution. In practice, a trade-off between time and frequency resolution has to be made depending on the desired objectives. Furthermore, sidelobes introduce a bias in the spectral estimate, often called *leakage*, due to aliasing effects between adjacent frequency bands. A class of optimal windows for spectral analysis is discussed in Adams (1991).
- Generally, the position of the analysis window falls randomly within the pitch period of voiced sounds. This fact can cause fluctuations in the spectral estimate, especially for analysis based on short windows.
- The sample spectrum is a biased estimator of the PSD (it would be unbiased only as the window length approached infinity). Furthermore, the sample spectrum is not a consistent estimator and, therefore, the variance of the estimate, at each frequency, does not tend to zero as the window length tends to infinity.

Autoregressive modelling techniques, introduced later on, can be used to reduce leakage and fluctuations in the spectrum. Alternatively, other kinds of

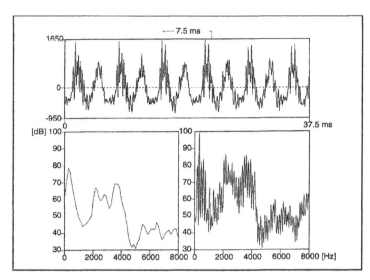

Figure 3.9 Speech waveform of a portion of a vowel and corresponding power spectra, obtained with two different window lengths (7.5 ms and 37.5 ms).

smoothing can be applied to the sample spectrum by using either *periodogram-*based estimators (Oppenheim and Schafer, 1989), or filter bank analysis (see section 3.3.6).

The second limitation mentioned above can be addressed by using *pitch synchronous* analysis. In this case, the analysis window always fits the same number of pitch periods (one or more) in order to reduce the distortion due to the windowing process (Hess, 1983; Markel and Gray, 1976; Medan and Yair, 1989; Medan *et al.*, 1991; O'Shaughnessy, 1987). Note that this approach requires a preliminary accurate pitch estimation and implies that the window length changes in time according to the instantaneous pitch period.

Figure 3.9 shows the power spectra of a speech signal analysed with two windows having different lengths. The signal corresponds to a portion of a vowel, and the windows have durations of 7.5 ms and of 37.5 ms, respectively. As mentioned above, the longer window provides a more irregular fluctuating spectrum, where it is difficult to distinguish some features (e.g. formant frequencies). This is due to the quasi-periodic glottal source whose spectrum, when multiplied by the vocal tract frequency response, exhibits peaks at the fundamental frequency and at its harmonics.

Although spectrographic analysis may manifest all the above mentioned drawbacks, it has been largely used for speech analysis (Koenig *et al.*, 1946; Flanagan, 1972a) because it produces useful time–frequency patterns. Another analysis method, more suitable for non-stationary signals, is that of time–frequency distributions, described in the next subsection.

3.3.5. Time–Frequency Distributions

The objective of time–frequency analysis is to characterize frequency components of the signal at given time instants. In the following, the theory of time–frequency distributions (TFDs) will be summarized by considering a continuous time signal $s(t)$. A generalization to the discrete time case is straightforward.

According to Cohen (1989b) the TFD, $P_s(t, \omega)$, of a signal $s(t)$ must satisfy the following conditions:

$$\int P_s(t, \omega)\, d\omega = |s(t)|^2 \tag{3.5}$$

$$\int P_s(t, \omega)\, dt = |S(\omega)|^2 \tag{3.6}$$

$$\int |s(t)|^2\, dt = \int |S(\omega)|^2\, d\omega = 1 \tag{3.7}$$

where $S(\omega)$ is the Fourier transform of $s(t)$. Conditions (3.5) and (3.6) are called *marginals* of the TFD, while condition (3.7) corresponds to having a signal, $s(t)$, with unit energy (in the following the signal is normalized so that (3.7) is always satisfied). It is worth noting that, although the equations above resemble those for statistical distributions, the signals considered here are deterministic.

It was found that an infinite number of TFDs exist that satisfy (3.5), (3.6) and (3.7), specifically those generated by the following equation:

$$P_s(t, \omega) = \frac{1}{4\pi^2} \int \int \int e^{-j(\theta t + \tau\omega - \theta u)} \phi(\theta, \tau) s^*\left(u - \frac{\tau}{2}\right) s\left(u + \frac{\tau}{2}\right) du\, d\tau\, d\theta \tag{3.8}$$

where * denotes complex conjugate. In the equation above, the function $\phi(\theta, \tau)$ is called the *kernel*, that defines the type of TFD for the signal. For example, some TFDs like Wigner–Ville, Rihaczec and Page, widely investigated in the past, have kernels 1, $e^{j\theta\tau/2}$ and $e^{j\theta|\tau|/2}$, respectively.

It can be shown that from the conditions on the distribution, expressed by (3.5), (3.6) and (3.7), one can derive the following kernel properties:

$$\phi(0, 0) = 1 \tag{3.9}$$
$$\phi(\theta, 0) = 1 \tag{3.10}$$
$$\phi(0, \tau) = 1 \tag{3.11}$$

It is interesting to derive the relation between TFDs and the spectrogram. The spectrogram[8] $|S(t, \omega)|^2$ can be expressed by means of the following equation:

$$|S(t, \omega)|^2 = \frac{1}{2\pi}\left|\int e^{-j\omega\tau} w(t - \tau) s(\tau)\, d\tau\right|^2 \tag{3.12}$$

---

[8] For the sake of clarity, in this section the spectrogram is interpreted as short-time power spectrum of the signal $s(t)$ instead of that as log-power spectrum (see equation (3.3)).

where $w(t)$ is the analysis window shifted by a fixed step. By expanding (3.12) and after a change of variables, we obtain:

$$|S(t,\omega)|^2 = \frac{1}{2\pi} \int \int e^{-j\omega\tau} \mathcal{K}(t-u,\tau) s\left(u+\frac{\tau}{2}\right) s^*\left(u-\frac{\tau}{2}\right) d\tau\, du \qquad (3.13)$$

where

$$\mathcal{K}(t-u,\tau) = w\left(t-u-\frac{\tau}{2}\right) w^*\left(t-u+\frac{\tau}{2}\right) \qquad (3.14)$$

Considering that the Wigner–Ville TFD (we remind it has unitary kernel) of the signal $s(t)$ is given by the following equation:

$$W_s(t,\omega) = \frac{1}{2\pi} \int e^{-j\omega\tau} s\left(t+\frac{\tau}{2}\right) s^*\left(t-\frac{\tau}{2}\right) d\tau \qquad (3.15)$$

one can note that the spectrogram, expressed by means of (3.13), is a smoothed version of the Wigner–Ville TFD of the signal itself.

It can also be shown (Cohen, 1989b) that, in order to match (3.8), the spectrogram should have the following kernel function:

$$\phi_S(\theta,\tau) = W_w(\theta,\tau) = \int w\left(t+\frac{\tau}{2}\right) w^*\left(t-\frac{\tau}{2}\right) e^{-j\theta t}\, dt \qquad (3.16)$$

where $W_w(\theta,\tau)$ is the Wigner–Ville TFD of the analysis window. As a consequence, given the kernel properties of (3.9), (3.10) and (3.11), we obtain:

$$\phi_S(0,0) = \int |w(t)|^2\, dt = 1 \qquad (3.17)$$

$$\phi_S(\theta,0) = \int |w(t)|^2 e^{-j\theta t}\, dt = 1 \qquad (3.18)$$

$$\phi_S(0,\tau) = \int |W(\omega)|^2 e^{-j\tau\omega}\, d\omega = 1 \qquad (3.19)$$

where $W(\omega)$ is the Fourier transform of the analysis window. Equation (3.17) is satisfied if the analysis window has unit energy, while (3.18) and (3.19) are satisfied if either $w(t)$ or $W(\omega)$ are delta functions. The latter two conditions cannot be simultaneously fulfilled, since $W(\omega)$ becomes broader as $w(t)$ is shortened. Hence, the spectrogram is not a TFD of the general class (3.8), since it does not satisfy the marginal conditions. Some kernels that match the marginals of a TFD, without requiring particular constraints for the analysis window (thus allowing a more effective time–frequency respresentation), are described in Cohen (1989b), Zhao *et al.* (1990) and Pitton *et al.* (1994).

A particular class of TFDs is represented by positive TFDs (in this case $P_s(t,\omega)$ must be non-negative for all t and ω). In Cohen (1989b) and Cohen and Posch (1985) it is shown that such TFDs can be generated with the following equation (a particular case of (3.8)):

$$P_s(t, \omega) = |S(\omega)|^2 |s(t)|^2 \Omega_s(u(t), v(\omega)) \qquad (3.20)$$

where

$$u(t) = \int_{-\infty}^{t} |s(\tau)|^2 \, d\tau \qquad (3.21)$$

$$v(\omega) = \int_{-\infty}^{\omega} |S(\theta)|^2 \, d\theta \qquad (3.22)$$

and $\Omega_s(u(t), v(\omega))$ is a non-negative function kernel. An iterative method to derive positive TFDs was proposed in Pitton *et al.* (1994).

The spectrogram representation of equation (3.13) allows covering of the time–frequency plane with a uniform resolution determined by the analysis window length. An improved time–frequency representation can be obtained with *multiresolution analysis*. The main principle of this analysis is based on the fact that one can decide to cover the time–frequency plane with "elementary cells" of different sizes (the spectrogram makes use of cells of the same size). A general theory that deals with this kind of analysis is based on the *wavelet transform*, as described in Cohen and Kovacevic (1996) and Rioul and Vetterli (1991). An efficient method, based on the filter bank theory,[9] for implementing the wavelet transform is reported in Nielsen and Wickerhausek (1996). Finally, an application of the wavelet transform to speech enhancement can be found in Pinter (1996).

3.3.6. Filter Bank Analysis

Speech analysis techniques described so far give, for each frame, spectrum magnitude and phase at equally spaced frequency intervals, from 0 to the Nyquist frequency $F_s/2$. However, the most significant cues of the signal are located in specific frequency bands. Filter bank analysis has the objective of focusing on different bands of the spectrum and of extracting a correspondingly more compact representation. Filter banks are made of band-pass filters, each characterized by a central frequency, a bandwidth and an impulse response. Band-pass filters generally overlap in frequency and have an overall coverage of the frequency range where "useful" speech information can be found. As an example, for telephone applications, a filter bank may cover an approximate range between 200 Hz and 3200 Hz and may consist of filters having a bandwidth increasing with frequency, as shown in Figure 3.10. Note that each band-pass filtered signal, due to its limited bandwidth, can be conveniently decimated to obtain an equivalent lower sampling frequency rate.

---

[9]The quadrature mirror filters, cited in the next section, are a particular case of the general wavelet transform.

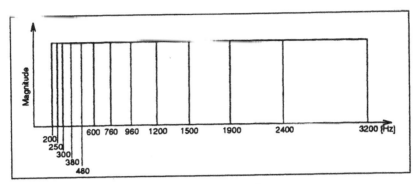

Figure 3.10 A filter bank used for telephone applications.

As mentioned above, the accuracy of the representation depends on the purpose of the analysis. For speech coding applications, a filter bank analysis must allow a successive speech reconstruction from the coding of each band. Quadrature mirror filters (QMF) represent the most accurate solution for perfect reconstruction (Crochiere and Rabiner, 1983; Vaidyanathan, 1987). On the other hand, in most speech recognition applications, a simple evaluation of the average magnitude in each band may be sufficient (Rabiner and Juang, 1993).

Let us consider a bank of I band-pass FIR filters,[10] each of them having an impulse response $h_i(m)$. The output signal $y_i(n)$ (see the left part of Figure 3.11) of the ith filter can be expressed as follows:

$$y_i(n) = s(n) * h_i(n) = \sum_m h_i(m)s(n - m) \quad 1 \leq i \leq I \tag{3.23}$$

where $*$ denotes convolution. Assuming that the impulse response of the generic ith filter is represented by a window, $w(n)$, modulated by a complex exponential as follows:

$$h_i(n) = w(n) \, e^{j\omega_i n} \tag{3.24}$$

a new relationship can be derived from (3.23):

$$\begin{aligned} y_i(n) &= \sum_m w(m) \, e^{j\omega_i m} s(n - m) \\ &= \sum_m s(m)w(n - m) \, e^{j\omega_i(n-m)} \\ &= e^{j\omega_i n} \sum_m s(m)w(n - m) \, e^{-j\omega_i m} \\ &= e^{j\omega_i n} S(n, e^{j\omega_i}) \end{aligned} \tag{3.25}$$

---

[10]Given a FIR filter basic module, the filter bank analysis can be performed in a straightforward manner using the direct form structure. Other possible realizations of the filter are discussed in Rabiner and Gold (1975) and Oppenheim and Schafer (1989). The advantage of FIR filtering is that it ensures a linear phase response. The alternative use of an IIR filter basic module does not guarantee this property but allows an efficient implementation and a lower computational load.

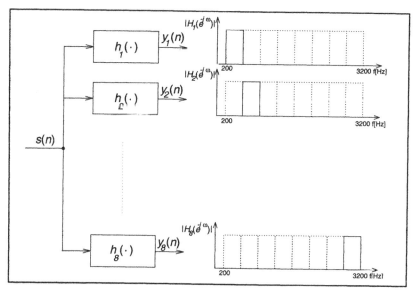

Figure 3.11 Bank of eight filters and corresponding set of ideal frequency responses.

where $S(n, e^{j\omega_i})$ is the short-time Fourier transform (see equation (3.1)) of the windowed input signal (evaluated at time n at the central frequency $f_i = (\omega_i/2\pi)F_s$ of the ith filter), which is expressed as:

$$S(n, e^{j\omega_i}) = \sum_m s(m)w(n-m)\, e^{-j\omega_i m} \tag{3.26}$$

From equations above we note that the computation of (3.23) can be performed with an efficient procedure based on the DFT.[11] Note again that the quantity $S(n, e^{j\omega_i})$ can also be interpreted as a time signal (function of n) that represents the content of $s(n)$, both in terms of amplitude and phase, within a band centred at ω_i and whose width depends on the characteristics of the window $w(n)$.

The energy of the signal at the output of a band-pass filter can also be approximated as a weighted sum of squared DFT coefficients, where the weights define a filter "mask" (typically having triangular or trapezoidal shape). For a given analysis frame t, let us indicate with $[S_t(e^{j\omega_k})]_{k=0}^{L-1}$ the short-time DFT sequence (see section 3.3.4) obtained from the input signal $[s_t(n)]_{n=0}^{L-1}$, and let us consider the mask for the ith filter being centred at the DFT point k_i and placed in the interval $[k_i - d_i, k_i + d_i]$. Denoting with $\varpi_i = [\varpi_{k_i-d_i}, \ldots, \varpi_{k_i+d_i}]$ the weighting vector representing this "mask", the approximation of the

---

[11] The fast Fourier transform (FFT) algorithm can be used to reduce computation time as discussed in Rabiner and Gold (1975).

spectrum in the corresponding band can be expressed as:

$$S'_t(i) = \sum_{l=-d_i}^{d_i} \varpi_{k_i+l} S_t(e^{j\omega_{k_i}+l})$$ (3.27)

where each sum must be limited to values of $S_t(e^{j\omega_k})$ included in the range $[0,(L-1)/2]$ of the DFT sequence. An example of a filter bank consisting of rectangular masks is given in the right part of Figure 3.11. Section 3.5.2 will further discuss this approximation process.

3.3.7. Linear Predictive Coding

Linear prediction (LP) was first introduced in Wiener (1966) on time series analysis and then applied to speech processing in many different contexts (Saito and Itakura, 1966; Atal, 1970b). In a previous work (Fant, 1970a), a linear vocal tract model was proposed, based on a cascade of a small number of two-pole resonators. In fact, the theory of linear predictive coding (LPC) leads to the derivation of an all-pole model that is suitable for simple but quite accurate approximation of the vocal-tract transfer function, with reference to the production of voiced speech segments. For unvoiced as well as for nasal sounds and transients, LPC analysis has limitations because the basic model does not include zeros. Nevertheless, LPC analysis provides effective spectral estimation for low- and very low-bit-rate coding, for speech synthesis and for speech recognition (Atal, 1970b; Atal and Hanauer, 1971). In the following, only the basic concepts will be described; more details can be found in Markel and Gray (1976), Rabiner and Schafer (1978), Makhoul (1973, 1975) and Marple (1987).

Basic principles

The LPC model can be seen as a particular case of the more general autoregressive (AR) moving average (MA) model that accounts for the use of a pole–zero transfer function $H(z)$ expressed, in terms of z-transform, as:

$$H(z) = \frac{\sum_{k=0}^{q} b_k z^{-k}}{1 - \sum_{k=1}^{p} a_k z^{-k}}$$ (3.28)

The equivalent time-domain relationship between the input signal $u(n)$ and the output signal $s(n)$ is:

$$s(n) = \sum_{k=1}^{p} a_k s(n-k) + \sum_{k=0}^{q} b_k u(n-k)$$ (3.29)

where p and q indicate the orders of the pole filter (denominator of (3.28)) and the zero filter (numerator of (3.28)), respectively, while $[a_k]_{k=1}^p$ and $[b_k]_{k=0}^q$ represent the two corresponding sets of coefficients.

The LPC model accounts only for the AR part of an ARMA model, by imposing that the numerator of equation (3.28) is a constant. The main principle of the analysis is that, for a given time interval where the speech signal is assumed to be stationary, a sample $\hat{s}(n)$ can be computed by means of a linear combination of the p previous samples $[\hat{s}(n-p), \ldots, \hat{s}(n-1)]$ and of an excitation signal. Given this assumption, the following expression holds:

$$\hat{s}(n) = Gu(n) + \sum_{k=1}^{p} a_k \hat{s}(n-k) \tag{3.30}$$

where p indicates the *predictor order*, G is a scaling factor for the excitation signal $u(n)$, and $[a_k]_{k=1}^p$ are the predictor coefficients. The same relationship can be expressed in terms of z-transform as:

$$\hat{S}(z) = GU(z)H(z) \tag{3.31}$$

where

$$H(z) = \frac{1}{A(z)} = \frac{1}{1 - \sum_{k=1}^{p} a_k z^{-k}} \tag{3.32}$$

is the transfer function of the all-pole filter that is used to produce the speech signal.

Computing the set of coefficients $[a_k]_{k=1}^p$ from the input signal $s(n)$ requires the definition of the prediction error signal (also called *residual signal*):

$$e(n) = s(n) - \sum_{k=1}^{p} a_k s(n-k) \tag{3.33}$$

that corresponds to the z-transform relationship:

$$E(z) = S(z)A(z) \tag{3.34}$$

The parameters $[a_k]_{k=1}^p$ can be derived, directly, from the input speech samples by applying a least-square criterion to (3.33). The most common choice is to minimize a total-squared error $E = \sum_n e^2(n)$. Once the predictor coefficients have been estimated, the "ideal" excitation signal $e(n)$ can be used for a perfect signal reconstruction, that is $\hat{s}(n) = s(n)$. The most critical issue in speech coding is the quantization of the LPC model parameters as well as of the excitation signal.

An example of LPC application is shown in Figure 3.12 that describes the block diagram (see equation (3.30)) of a *buzz and hiss* LPC-based speech synthesizer. In this case, the excitation signal can be either a random noise source (for unvoiced speech) or a periodic pulse train source (for voiced speech), according to a voiced/unvoiced preclassification of the speech units (this is a crude approximation, as the residual signal $e(n)$ is neither a white

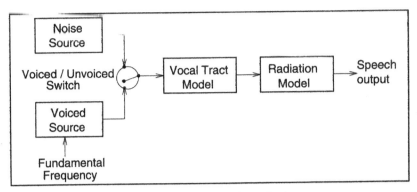

Figure 3.12 Block diagram of an LPC-based speech synthesizer.

noise nor a periodic sequence, unless $s(n)$ has been produced by an AR model of order equal to the predictor order p). Note that the radiation model is introduced to account for radiation effects at the lips. For speech coding and synthesis, many variants (Atal *et al.*, 1993; Klein and Paliwal, 1995) of this module have been proposed to take into account the inadequacy of the binary preclassification (buzz–hiss) of the glottal excitation.

Predictor coefficient computation

The LPC filter described by (3.32) can be implemented with variations of the basic direct-form structure. The coefficients can be obtained using different techniques and can be represented in different but equivalent ways, as discussed later on. Two common approaches for the calculation of the LPC coefficients are the *least-square* and the *lattice* approaches. The former one minimizes the energy of the residual defined in (3.33) and gives rise either to the *autocorrelation* or to the *covariance methods* described below. The latter one is typically used for speech coding and synthesis applications, where the lattice structure is preferred for its advantages in terms of stability and quantization effects (Honig and Messerschmidt, 1984).

    Autocorrelation method. Let us consider the windowed signal $[s_t(n)]_{n=0}^{L-1}$, obtained by multiplying the input signal $s(n)$ by a window of length L. The total-squared prediction error for the given interval is defined as:

$$E = \sum_{n=0}^{L-1} e^2(n) = \sum_{n=0}^{L-1} \left[s_t(n) - \sum_{k=1}^{p} a_k s_t(n-k) \right]^2 \qquad (3.35)$$

The minimum of E can be found by differentiating E with respect to each a_k and setting the result to zero, that is:

$$\frac{\partial E}{\partial a_k} = 0, \quad 1 \le k \le p \qquad (3.36)$$

A system of p linear equations in p unknowns is obtained as follows:

$$\sum_n s_t(n-i)s_t(n) = \sum_{k=1}^{p} a_k \sum_n s_t(n-i)s_t(n-k), \quad 1 \leq i \leq p \qquad (3.37)$$

Since the signal $s_t(n)$ is zero outside the interval $[0, L-1]$, the autocorrelation function $R(i)$ can be expressed as:

$$R(i) = \sum_{n=i}^{L-1} s_t(n-i)s_t(n), \quad 1 \leq i \leq p \qquad (3.38)$$

Taking into account the finite duration of the windowed signal and the symmetry of the autocorrelation function (i.e. $R(i) = R(-i)$), equation (3.37) can be written as:

$$R(i) = \sum_{k=1}^{p} a_k R(|i-k|), \quad 1 \leq i \leq p \qquad (3.39)$$

The linear system above is represented by a $p \times p$ Toeplitz matrix (symmetric with the same values along each diagonal) and can be solved efficiently using the Levinson–Durbin recursive algorithm or other methods (as described in Markel and Gray, 1976). It is usually referred to as the *Yule–Walker equation.*

Covariance method. Assuming that the total-squared prediction error E is computed in the interval $[0, L-1]$, but without explicit hypothesis on the windowed signal extension (as in the autocorrelation method), let us indicate the covariance function $\phi(i,k)$ as:

$$\phi(i,k) = \sum_{n=0}^{L-1} s_t(n-i)s_t(n-k), \quad 1 \leq i \leq p, \quad 1 \leq k \leq p \qquad (3.40)$$

The computation of $\phi(i,k)$ involves samples from $s_t(-p)$ to $s_t(-1)$ that are outside the analysis interval. The set of equations (3.37) can be rewritten as:

$$\phi(i,0) = \sum_{k=1}^{p} a_k \phi(i,k), \quad 1 \leq i \leq p \qquad (3.41)$$

The resulting matrix is symmetric but it is not Toeplitz. It can be efficiently solved with the Cholesky decomposition method as described in Markel and Gray (1976).

On the choice of analysis conditions

The all-pole model described by (3.32) represents an accurate approximation of the vocal tract response, whose spectrum results from the "best match"[12] with

---

[12]In linear prediction analysis the term "best match" often refers to the optimization of a specific criterion for the computation of the LPC coefficients. For example, under specific hypotheses, the use of either the autocorrelation method or the covariance method lead to a *maximum likelihood* model estimation.

the spectrum of the corresponding speech frame. The level of accuracy for the match depends both on the minimization error criterion (El-Jaroudi and Makhoul, 1991) and on the predictor order.

Various papers (Atal, 1970a; Atal and Hanauer, 1971; Wakita, 1972) report on the use of linear prediction for lossless acoustic-tube modelling and on its application to vocal-tract modelling. As a result, an all-pole transfer function with p poles, that can be obtained by linear prediction analysis of order $2p$, was introduced to model an acoustic tube of p cylindrical sections of equal length. More details on this issue can be found in Markel and Gray (1976).

An example of the effect of LPC analysis with different predictor orders is shown in Figure 3.13, where LPC spectra, obtained with variable order models, are plotted corresponding to the same portion of a vowel. Generally, one or two poles can be considered sufficient for a good modelling of a basic resonance of the vocal tract, represented by a peak in the corresponding spectral envelope. Markel and Gray (1976) suggested using an LP order equal to $(F_s + 5)$ for voiced sounds and equal to F_s for unvoiced sounds, where F_s represents the sampling frequency expressed in kHz. In this way, the LP analysis allows for a more accurate modelling of formants in the spectrum of vowels and of antiresonances that can be present in the spectrum of other sounds (e.g. nasals).

Note that an antiresonance in the spectrum could also be modelled with a substantial increase of the number of poles (proportional to the predictor order), as discussed in Makhoul (1975). However, this increase would imply higher analysis complexity and would not always guarantee more accurate modelling of poles and zeros of the spectrum. In fact, in some cases increasing the order introduces the effect shown in Figure 3.13, where the additional poles "at disposal" are used to model peaks corresponding to the "fine" structure of the power spectrum (pitch harmonics).

The analysis window should be selected according to the coefficient computation method. For instance, the rectangular window can lead to undesired effects such as a concentration of poles to characterize the most prominent formant (Markel and Gray, 1976) when autocorrelation method is used; on the other hand, the rectangular window is the only reasonable solution when the covariance method is used. Furthermore, the choice of the analysis window and its location with respect to pitch epochs can be critical. The most common LPC analysis for speech recognition is pitch-asynchronous and is based on the use of a Hamming window. It results in a slightly degraded spectral estimate and in discontinuities between adjacent frames, but its performance is satisfactory and it is simple to implement. On the other hand, as mentioned above, a pitch-synchronous analysis requires a reliable pitch estimator and additional complexity, due to the use of the covariance method, which is preferred to the autocorrelation method for the analysis of short frames (Paliwal, 1984).

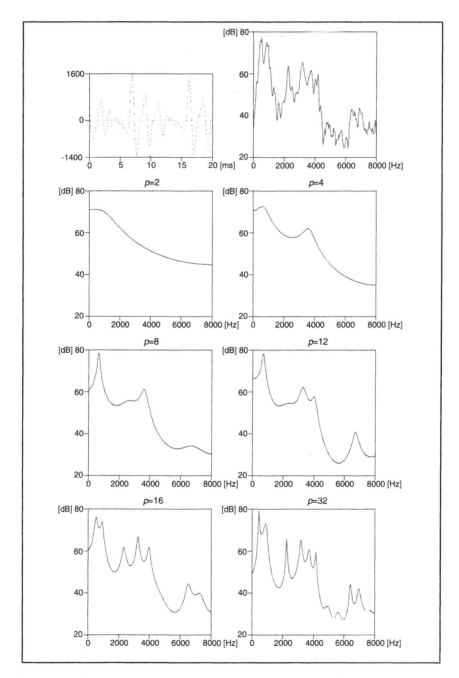

Figure 3.13 Waveform, power spectrum and corresponding LPC spectral envelopes, obtained with different predictor orders, for a portion of a vowel.

3.3.8. Homomorphic Cepstral Analysis

Homomorphic analysis (Rabiner and Gold, 1975; Rabiner and Schafer, 1978; Oppenheim and Schafer, 1989) is a technique for decomposing a signal into components having different spectral characteristics.

It has been mentioned that the human vocal-production apparatus can be modelled by a cascade of two blocks, a source generator and a time-varying linear system. The latter can be viewed as a non-uniform acoustic tube that varies its sectional areas according to the sounds to be pronounced. The reflection coefficients (see section 3.5.3) of the acoustic tube are univocally correlated with the coefficients of the linear system. By varying them in time, it is possible to simulate the dynamics of the vocal tract during sound production. The source model can be schematically represented by a periodic pulse generator or by a random number generator (see Figure 3.12): these two generators are used for the production of voiced sounds and unvoiced sounds, respectively. It is worth noting that, in this case, the voice source and the vocal tract are assumed to be independent.

The objective of homomorphic analysis is to decompose the given signal $s(n)$ into the components related to the source, $e(n)$, and to the impulse response, $h(n)$, of the vocal tract. Since $s(n)$ is the convolution of $e(n)$ with $h(n)$, then in the frequency domain we have:

$$S(e^{j\omega_k}) = E(e^{j\omega_k})H(e^{j\omega_k}) \tag{3.42}$$

where capital letters indicate DFTs. Taking the logarithm of $|S(e^{j\omega_k})|$ one gets:

$$\log(|S(e^{j\omega_k})|) = \log(|E(e^{j\omega_k})|) + \log(|H(e^{j\omega_k})|) \tag{3.43}$$

The frequency response of the vocal tract, $\log(|H(e^{j\omega_k})|)$, is a slowly varying function of frequency and can be represented by the envelope of $\log(|S(e^{j\omega_k})|)$. On the contrary, the part of the log-spectrum related to the excitation source, $\log(|E(e^{j\omega_k})|)$, varies more rapidly with respect to frequency; therefore it is possible, in the log-spectral domain, to separate the two types of information by linear filtering (Rabiner and Gold, 1975). In practice, instead of using linear filters, the inverse Fourier transform of $\log(|S(e^{j\omega_k})|)$ is computed and the corresponding lowest-order coefficients are retained to account for the vocal-tract transfer function. The inverse Fourier transform of $\log(|S(e^{j\omega_k})|)$ is called the *cepstrum* of the signal $s(n)$. It is also called the *real cepstrum*, to distinguish it from the *complex cepstrum*, which is the inverse Fourier transform of the complex logarithm, $\log(S(e^{j\omega_k}))$ (Oppenheim and Schafer, 1989). In Figure 3.14 a block diagram of homomorphic analysis is given.

Figures 3.15 and 3.16 show the results of the various steps of homomorphic analysis applied to a single speech frame of phones /s/ and /eh/, respectively. The cepstrally smoothed spectra were obtained by applying a rectangular window, of length 2.5 ms, to the two cepstral sequences derived from the log-spectra, as shown in Figure 3.14.

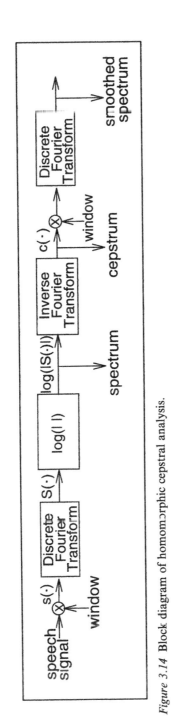

Figure 3.14 Block diagram of homomorphic cepstral analysis.

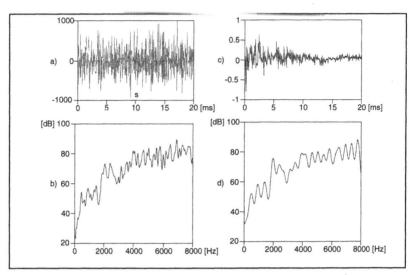

Figure 3.15 Waveform (a), power spectrum (b), cepstral sequence (c), and cepstrally smoothed spectrum (d) of a speech frame corresponding to a portion of the phone /s/.

The result of the application of homomorphic analysis to a whole speech utterance is shown in Figure 3.17. In the figure the cepstral vectors of the various frames are plotted as in the spectrogram representation. Here, this representation will be called "cepstrogram". In the "cepstrogram" one can

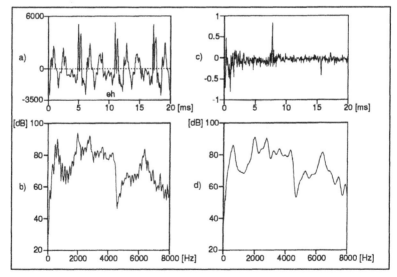

Figure 3.16 Waveform (a), power spectrum (b), cepstral sequence (c) and cepstrally smoothed spectrum (d) of a speech frame corresponding to a portion of the phone /eh/. Note the presence in the cepstral sequence of the peak corresponding to the

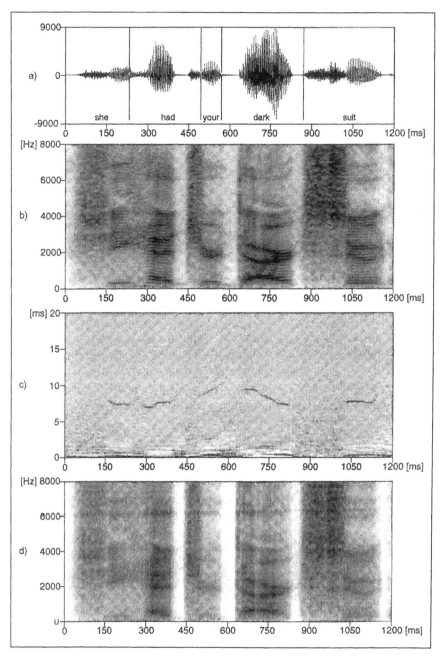

Figure 3.17 Speech waveform (a) and corresponding spectrogram (b), "cepstrogram" (c) and cepstrally smoothed spectrogram (d). In the cepstrogram, the peak curve corresponds to the pitch period evolution.

note the curve corresponding to the peaks at the pitch periods: other curves, not easily detectable, would correspond to lower peak values due to formant frequencies. Furthermore, the cepstrally smoothed spectrogram, obtained by Fourier transform of windowed cepstral sequences, may be interpreted as a low-pass-filtered version of the spectrogram itself.

The cepstrum is largely used in pattern-matching problems, because the Euclidean distance between two cepstral vectors represents a good measure for comparing the corresponding log-spectra (see Chapter 4).

Note that the zero-order cepstral coefficient, that is the inverse Fourier transform of the log-spectrum at point zero, represents the log-energy of the signal itself, as stated by the Parseval theorem (see Appendix A). Generally, when the analysis is performed for speech recognition, this coefficient is discarded.

3.4. AUDITORY MODELS

3.4.1. Introduction

Physiologically-based models of the human auditory system have also been considered for ASR, especially for their capability of separating the message of interest from redundant information. This capability is very important for speech decoding in adverse conditions, for example in a noisy environment where many people are talking simultaneously ("cocktail-party effect").

Many experiments were conducted in the past to understand how humans process and recognize speech (Allen, 1994, 1996). During the last decade, there have been some attempts to use auditory modelling for speech recognition (Seneff, 1988; Ghitza, 1988; Lyon and Mead, 1988; Cohen, 1989a). It is still uncertain whether or not an auditory-modelling-based set of features is more convenient than a set of perceptually based features deriving from short-term spectral analysis. At present, performance obtained using an auditory model shows little improvement with respect to other techniques, generally more evident under noisy conditions (Jankowski *et al.*, 1995). The counterpart of this improvement is that auditory modelling analysis techniques require a very high computational load, which makes them impractical (Lyon and Mead, 1988; Cosi *et al.*, 1991).

In the following, a brief description will be given of the physiology of human hearing and of the main criteria applied in the development of the most common auditory modelling schemes.

3.4.2. Physiology of Hearing

The main problem in modelling the human auditory system is that most of what is known about the physiology of the ear concerns the auditory periphery and,

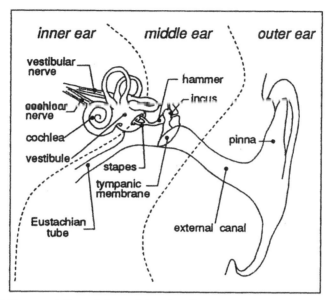

Figure 3.18 Representation of the peripheral auditory system.

in particular, the information that constitutes the output of the cochlear neural transduction, while little is known about the subsequent auditory nerve activity. Nevertheless, there is evidence that some of the auditory periphery functions are, at least partially, responsible for the way a speech message is understood (Greenberg, 1988).

A simplified scheme of the human ear is shown in Figure 3.18. The peripheral part of the auditory system can be modelled as a cascade of three modules: the *outer ear*, the *middle ear* and the *inner ear*. The outer ear has the role of increasing the sound pressure (through the concha that creates resonances that enter the external canal) at the *tympanic membrane*. As mentioned in Chapter 2, the outer ear helps also in sound-source localization.

The acoustic waves are collected at the outer ear by the *pinna* and are conveyed through the *external canal* toward the middle ear, where three small bones, the *hammer* (or *malleus*), the *incus* and the *stapes* convert the sound pressure into mechanical vibrations. In practice, the middle ear has the role of an acoustic impedance converter, coupling the sound energy (that otherwise would be mostly reflected) from the air (low impedance) to the cochlear fluid (high impedance).

In the inner ear, the mechanical vibrations activate a fluid that is present in the *cochlea*; while travelling along it, this fluid makes the *basilar membrane* vibrate at different places, each of them associated with a specific frequency. The auditory transduction at the basilar membrane is realized by the *organ of Corti*, in which one row of about 25 000 *inner hair cells* and five rows (of equivalent size) of *outer hair cells* are placed. The inner hair cells at the extremity of the auditory nerve fibres are responsible for the conversion from the mechanical displacement of the basilar membrane into a firing activity, then transmitted to the auditory nerve. More details can be found in Pickles (1982).

3.4.3. Auditory-Based Analysis Models

In the last four decades, several attempts (Seneff, 1988; Ghitza, 1988; Lyon and Mead, 1988; Cohen, 1989a) were made to model the information at the output of the cochlea (the application of these models to robust ASR is further discussed in Chapter 12).

Most of the models are based on a processing scheme that consists of two or more stages. The first one attempts to model the auditory processing up to the activation of the inner hair cells by the basilar membrane vibrations. This simulation is often realized through a frequency selective linear model, implemented with a filter bank whose centre frequencies are log-spaced in the frequency axis, in order to resemble the uniform distribution of inner hair cells along the basilar membrane.

The most common criterion of placing filters along the frequency axis is that based on the use of the critical-band scale. The most common critical band scales are the *mel scale* and the *bark scale*. According to these scales, filter placing along the frequency scale is linear up to about 1000 Hz and logarithmic above 1000 Hz.

The basilar membrane is modelled by a number of segments each of them corresponding to a frequency range. The basilar membrane simulation includes also a compressive non-linear filter that accounts for the non-linearities at the tip of the basilar membrane. The successive processing stages are non-linear and simulate the transformation from the hair-cell output to the auditory-nerve firing rate.

3.5. ACOUSTIC FEATURES

3.5.1. Introduction

Section 3.3 introduced some basic principles and analysis techniques commonly used for speech processing. Starting from those techniques, different acoustic features can be derived for use in ASR. The *static* acoustic features are aimed at representing the power spectrum in a compact way and are derived from a short-interval analysis (generally the interval duration is between 20 ms and 50 ms). On the other hand, the *dynamic* features, discussed in the following section, account for the time evolution of the power spectrum in a longer interval (usually more than 100 ms).

3.5.2. Filter-Bank-Based Coefficients

A basic concept of the filter bank analysis, introduced in section 3.3.6, is that the output of each filter can be represented by a signal or by its energy. An effective way to estimate this energy is to apply a cascade of a non-linear module (e.g. a half-wave rectifier), a low-pass filter, and a sampling rate reduction step, to the filtered signal (Rabiner and Juang, 1993). The filter bank outputs can be further processed for dimensionality reduction to make the spectral representation more compact and efficient and to diminish the complexity of acoustic modelling in the ASR system (see also Chapter 4).

A fundamental choice concerns the structure of the bank, which is specified by the number of filters, their response and their spacing in frequency. A uniform structure is characterized by filters that have the same shape and that are equally spaced in frequency. However, the most general case is when filters are spaced non-linearly, according to auditory perceptual considerations (e.g. using mel scale or bark scale), and have a bandwidth increasing with frequency. These filters can have overlapping frequency responses, as discussed in Dautrich *et al.* (1983).

Another common choice involves the use of symmetric triangular filter masks to weight the DFT values. In this case, an approximate computation of the energy of each band-pass signal is performed by (3.27). In Rabiner and Juang (1993) it is shown that this operation can be considered as a "quick and dirty" method for approximating the energies of the filter-bank signals. Along the same line, let us consider a symmetric triangular weight vector $[\varpi_{k_i+l}]_{l=-d_i}^{d_i}$ (see Figure 3.19) that is applied to the DFT sequence $[S_t(e^{j\omega_k})]_{k=0}^{L-1}$ (obtained from the windowed signal $[s_t(n)]_{n=0}^{L-1}$) to derive an approximate average power spectrum value $|S_t'(i)|^2$, associated with the ith filter of the bank, as:

$$|S_t'(i)|^2 = \sum_{l=-d_i}^{d_i} \varpi_{k_i+l}|S_t(e^{j\omega_{k_i+l}})|^2 \tag{3.44}$$

It can be shown that:

$$|S_t'(i)|^2 = \varpi_{k_i}|S_t(e^{j\omega_{k_i}})|^2 + 2\sum_{l=1}^{d_i} \varpi_{k_i+l}[|X_t^c(e^{j\omega_{k_i}},l)|^2 + |X_t^s(e^{j\omega_{k_i}},l)|^2] \tag{3.45}$$

where $[X_t^c(e^{j\omega_{k_i}},l)]_{k_i=0}^{L-1}$ and $[X_t^s(e^{j\omega_{k_i}},l)]_{k_i=0}^{L-1}$ are the DFT sequences of the signals $[x_t^c(l,n)]_{n=0}^{L-1}$ and $[x_t^s(l,n)]_{n=0}^{L-1}$, respectively, defined as follows:

$$x_t^c(l,n) = s_t(n)\cos\left(\frac{2\pi ln}{L}\right), \quad 0 \le n \le L-1 \tag{3.46}$$

$$x_t^s(l,n) = s_t(n)\sin\left(\frac{2\pi ln}{L}\right), \quad 0 \le n \le L-1 \tag{3.47}$$

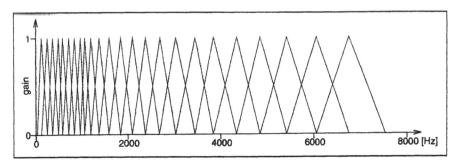

Figure 3.19 Example of a filter bank (consisting of 24 triangular filters), where filters are spaced in frequency according to the mel scale.

Expression (3.45) shows that $|S_t'(i)|^2$ is a weighted sum of k_ith components of power spectra obtained multiplying the given signal by cosine and sine sequences in the time domain.

Mel-based cepstral coefficients

The most common parameter set, presently used for ASR, is the set of *mel-scaled cepstral coefficients* that are computed from energies at the output of a filter bank similar to that presented above. The mel-scaled cepstral coefficients were evaluated by Davis and Mermelstein (1980) and often compared favourably with other alternative feature sets, both in terms of recognition performance and in terms of practical computational complexity. In practice, they are obtained by applying an inverse DFT to the log-energy output $[\log |S'(i)|]_{i=1}^{I}$ of the filter bank consisting of I triangular filter masks, as follows:

$$c_n = \sum_{i=1}^{I} \log |S'(i)| \cos \left[n \left(i - \frac{1}{2} \right) \frac{\pi}{I} \right], \quad 1 \leq n \leq M \qquad (3.48)$$

where c_n is the nth mel cepstral coefficient and M denotes the dimensionality of the parameter vector.

The coefficient c_0 approximates the average log-energy of the signal, but it is generally replaced by the energy directly computed from the signal. Note that, low-order coefficients can be interpreted as representations of the log-energy balance in frequency. For instance, c_1 provides the log-energy ratio between the frequency bands in the intervals $[0, F_s/4]$ and $[F_s/4, F_s/2]$. High values of c_1 occur with sonorant sounds, while low values are typical of fricative sounds. An interpretation of higher-order coefficients is more difficult, but it can be provided, taking into account the relation between the order n and the cosine function that "weights" the log-energy outputs. As a matter of fact, higher-order coefficients are generally influenced by the "fine" structure of the spectrum and by "idiosyncrasies" due to the analysis method (e.g. windowing).

Generally, the filter bank dimension I ranges from 20 to 40, while the feature set dimension M ranges from 8 to 16. Given these ranges, some attempts can be made to find an optimal combination of the parameters (M, I) and of the structure of the filter bank but, in most of the cases, variations around a standard configuration do not exhibit important fluctuations in terms of recognition performance.

Finally, note that the inverse DFT is an orthogonal transformation (Jayant and Noll, 1984), i.e. it not only provides a more compact representation of the filter bank output energies but it also produces approximately uncorrelated features, leading to simplified acoustic models as discussed in Chapter 5.

3.5.3. LPC-Based Coefficients

In most cases the LPC predictor coefficients do not appear to be the best features and are transformed into equivalent representations that are more effective for the given application. The LPC-derived features commonly used in ASR are now briefly introduced. A complete discussion about this issue can be found in Rabiner and Schafer (1978) and Markel and Gray (1976).

Reflection coefficients

An important set of features is that of *reflection coefficients*, which can be directly obtained by the solution of (3.39), when the autocorrelation method and the Levinson–Durbin recursion procedure are used.

Let us indicate with $E^{(i)}$ the total-squared prediction error at the ith recursion step and with $a_l^{(i)}$ the lth coefficient calculated at the same step. The initial condition is to set $E^{(0)} = R(0)$, where $R(i)$ denotes the autocorrelation coefficient computed by (3.38). Then, the following set of equations is solved recursively for $i = 1, \ldots, p$:

$$
\begin{aligned}
k_i &= \frac{[R(i) - \sum_{l=1}^{i-1} a_l^{(i-1)} R(i-l)]}{E^{(i-1)}} \\
a_i^{(i)} &= k_i \\
a_l^{(i)} &= a_l^{(i-1)} - k_i a_{i-l}^{(i-1)} \quad 1 \leq l \leq i-1 \\
E^{(i)} &= (1 - k_i^2) E^{(i-1)}
\end{aligned} \tag{3.49}
$$

where $[k_i]_{i=1}^p$ is the set of reflection coefficients, also called PARCOR coefficients. Since the total-squared error cannot be negative, the magnitude of the reflection coefficients is always lower or equal to 1. The minimum total-squared error $E^{(p)}$, measured in the final step of this recursive procedure, represents also the gain G of the resulting pth-order LPC model. Note that each reflection coefficient is computed at its corresponding recursion step once and for all. At the generic ith step, the new set of predictor coefficients describes the optimal ith order linear predictor and the new reflection coefficient k_i allows for adding a new cylindrical section to the generic $(i-1)$th section of the acoustic-tube model. Denoting with $\mathcal{A}_i$ and $\mathcal{A}_{i+1}$ the corresponding cross-sectional areas, the following relationship holds:

$$g_i = \frac{\mathcal{A}_{i+1}}{\mathcal{A}_i} = \frac{1-k_i}{1+k_i}, \quad 1 \le i \le p \tag{3.50}$$

where $\mathcal{A}_{p+1} = \mathcal{A}_p$ for impedance matching at the glottis, and g_i indicates the ith area ratio, more commonly replaced by the log-area ratio (LAR) when the corresponding logarithm $\log(g_i)$ is used.

It is worth noting that the relationship between predictor polynomials $A_{i-1}(z)$ and $A_i(z)$ can be expressed as follows:

$$A_i(z) = A_{i-1}(z) - k_i z^{-1} \hat{A}_{i-1}(z) \tag{3.51}$$

where $\hat{A}_i(z) = z^{-i} A_i(z^{-1})$. A discussion about a recursive generation of the polynomials $A_i(z)$ and $\hat{A}_i(z)$ can be found in Markel and Gray (1976).

Finally, an important alternative formulation of PARCOR coefficients can be derived from the lattice-based approach to the definition of LPC analysis and synthesis filtering, as discussed in Rabiner and Schafer (1978) and Markel and Gray (1976).

Line spectral frequencies

Another parametric representation of LPC coefficients is given by the line spectral frequencies (LSFs), also denoted in the literature as line spectrum pairs (LSPs). It was originally introduced in Itakura (1975a) and successively used for speech coding (Paliwal and Atal, 1993; Soong and Juang, 1993).

Given the pth-order stable all-pole filter $H(z) = 1/A(z)$, two $(p+1)$th-order polynomials $P(z)$ and $Q(z)$ are defined as follows:

$$P(z) = A(z) + z^{-(p+1)} A(z^{-1}) \tag{3.52}$$

$$Q(z) = A(z) - z^{-(p+1)} A(z^{-1}) \tag{3.53}$$

This condition corresponds to defining two new acoustic-tube models of $(p+1)$ sections (see (3.51)), where the extremity at the last section is entirely open ($k_{p+1} = -1$) or entirely closed ($k_{p+1} = 1$), respectively. Two important properties of LSFs are the following:

- $P(z)$ and $Q(z)$ are linear-phase FIR transfer functions whose roots are on the unit circle.
- The roots of these polynomials are interlaced, that is:

$$0 = \omega_0 < \omega_1 < \ldots < \omega_{p-1} < \omega_p < \omega_{p+1} = \pi \tag{3.54}$$

where even indexes correspond to $P(z)$ roots, while odd indexes correspond to $Q(z)$ roots.

The roots of $P(z)$ and $Q(z)$ are called LSFs and can be used to recompute the original predictor coefficients. Although the LSF values are altered (for instance by quantization), the two mentioned properties ensure that the corresponding $A(z)$ is minimum-phase and that the resulting $H(z)$ represents a stable filter (see Appendix A). Many other interesting and useful properties characterize these parameters, as described in Soong and Juang (1984) and Lepschy *et al.* (1988). Thanks to these properties, very efficient computation procedures were conceived (see for example Kabal and Ramachandran, 1986). Concerning their use for speech recognition, the most interesting aspect is the direct correspondence between LSF parameters and the related LPC spectrum envelope. Denoting with $|H(e^{j\omega})|^2$ the LPC all-pole power spectrum, the following relationship holds:

$$|H(e^{j\omega})|^2$$

$$= \frac{2^{-p}}{\left[\cos\dfrac{\omega}{2}\displaystyle\prod_{o=1}^{p-1}(\cos\omega - \cos\omega_o)\right]^2 + \left[\sin\dfrac{\omega}{2}\displaystyle\prod_{e=2}^{p}(\cos\omega - \cos\omega_e)\right]^2} \quad (3.55)$$

in the case of p even and:

$$|H(e^{j\omega})|^2 = \frac{2^{-(p-1)}}{\left[\displaystyle\prod_{o=1}^{p}(\cos\omega - \cos\omega_o)\right]^2 + \left[\sin\omega\displaystyle\prod_{e=2}^{p-1}(\cos\omega - \cos\omega_e)\right]^2} \quad (3.56)$$

in the case of p odd. In these relationships, o, e indicate odd and even indexes, respectively.

As a result, a concentration of two or more LSF in a narrow frequency interval indicates the presence of a resonance in the LPC spectrum envelope. Figure 3.20 shows a set of LSFs and the corresponding LPC envelope.

This correspondence leads to a frequency selective spectral sensitivity that ensures an excellent behaviour when quantization errors occur (as in the case of speech coding applications), and that may justify the use of LSFs for formant tracking and speech recognition, as discussed in Paliwal (1988, 1992a).

LPC cepstral coefficients

Cepstral coefficients can be computed not only from the logarithm of the speech magnitude spectrum, but also from the LPC coefficients. Given the set of coefficients $[a_k]_{k=1}^p$ and denoting with G the gain of the LPC model, the LPC

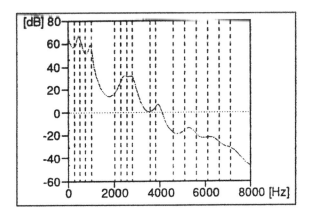

Figure 3.20 Line spectral frequencies (indicated by the dashed lines) and the corresponding LPC spectrum envelope, obtained with an LPC of order 16. Note the correspondence between concentration of LSFs and resonances.

cepstral coefficients are computed through the following recursion:

$$c_0 = \log(G)$$

$$c_n = a_n + \sum_{k=1}^{n-1} \binom{k}{n} c_k a_{n-k}, \quad n \geq 1 \tag{3.57}$$

with $a_n = 0$ for $n > p$.

As for the case of mel cepstral coefficients, there is experimental evidence that LPC cepstral coefficients computed using a critical-band frequency scale are more effective for ASR. LPC cepstral coefficients (as mel-based cepstral coefficients) can be obtained via critical-band frequency warping, first computing the log-magnitude LPC spectrum, and then warping the frequency axis. In Lee (1988b) a bilinear transformation of the frequency axis is proposed to approximate the mel-scale warping. Other details on linear prediction with respect to a warped frequency scale can be found in Atal (1974a), Makhoul (1975) and Furui (1981).

Perceptual linear prediction analysis

One of the most evident limitations of LPC analysis is that it provides an all-pole model that approximates all the frequencies of the spectrum with the same accuracy. As mentioned above, just using a mel-scale-based frequency warping gives benefits to the recognizer.

Aspects of human speech perception are taken into account in an LPC-based analysis system described in Hermansky (1990). The resulting perceptual linear prediction (PLP) analysis provides an effective and compact representation. A discussion on the use of PLP analysis for ASR is reported in Chapter 12. Here, the procedure for PLP coefficient computation is briefly outlined.

The first step is to obtain a bark-scale spectral analysis. The frequency-warped power spectrum is then convolved with a set of relatively broad critical-band masking curves in order to reduce the spectral resolution. A product of the resulting low-resolution spectrum with a fixed equal loudness curve and a successive magnitude reduction stage (realizing a cubic-root compression) account for the non-equal sensitivity of human hearing at different frequencies and for the non-linear relation between the intensity of sound and its perceived loudness. The resulting low-resolution spectrum is suitable for an all-pole modelling approximation: an inverse DFT provides an autocorrelation function that leads to the final computation of the predictor coefficients of the all-pole model and eventually of the equivalent cepstral coefficient representation.

The PLP analysis represents a good example of the use of well-known hearing properties in an established modelling framework such as the LPC analysis. The PLP analysis was recently combined with time filtering of cepstrum trajectories to obtain the so-called RASTA parameters (Hermansky and Morgan, 1994), a more robust representation for speech recognition under various environmental conditions.

3.5.4. Fundamental Frequency and Formants

As mentioned so far, the speech signal can be separated in a component related to the glottal source activity and in a component related to the vocal-tract response. At least for voiced sounds, fundamental frequency (as well as the excitation signal produced at the glottis) and formant frequencies (as well as their bandwidths) may be more useful than other features, to derive a reliable and compact representation of the speech spectrum.

However, accurate formant tracking is still an investigation issue and the usefulness of fundamental frequency for ASR is an open question. In fact, fundamental frequency varies not only from speaker to speaker but also within an utterance, and can take different values inside the same phone (it can be assumed to be uniformly distributed within a predefined range). Therefore, it could be useful as an additional acoustic parameter only in specific cases, as when a prosodic analysis is required for syntactic or semantic disambiguation.

Fundamental-frequency estimation

In the past, many pitch detection algorithms were proposed and evaluated. An extended review of methods for pitch estimation is presented in Hess (1983). Other details can be found in Markel (1972), Gold and Rabiner (1969), Rabiner (1977), Ramachandran and Kabal (1989) and Markel and Gray (1976).

In principle, fundamental-frequency estimation requires determining the main period of a quasi-periodic waveform, in a given time interval of adequate length. For this purpose, it is possible to use analysis techniques in the time domain or in the frequency domain. Usually, the pitch contour of a speech waveform is determined by computing, for every analysis frame, a function of the lag.

Two common functions are the autocorrelation function and the average magnitude difference function (AMDF). The autocorrelation function is given by equation (3.38), while the AMDF, of a generic frame t, is defined as follows:

$$\text{AMDF}_t(m) = \frac{1}{N_p} \sum_{n,m} |s_t(n) - s_t(n-m)|, \quad 0 \le n - m \le L - 1 \qquad (3.58)$$

where L is the frame length and N_p is the total number of sample pairs involved in the computation. In Figure 3.21 an example of autocorrelation function and of AMDF for a speech frame is given. Note the peak in the autocorrelation and the valley in the AMDF corresponding to a pitch period of 8 ms.

Also the normalized cross-correlation, described in Medan and Yair (1989), Medan *et al.* (1991) and De Mori and Omologo (1993), represents a very effective function that can be used for a detailed, even if more computationally expensive, pitch analysis.

To reduce the influence of formants on pitch estimation, a low-pass filter can be first applied to the speech waveform. Post-processing techniques (e.g. median filters) are generally used at the end of the estimation phase so that the overall pitch pattern satisfies some continuity constraints (Markel and Gray, 1976).

An alternative approach makes use of homomorphic cepstral analysis (Noll, 1964, 1967). The algorithm exploits the fact that the sequence of cepstral coefficients of a voiced frame exhibits a peak at the pitch period (see Figure 3.16). The main problem of this method is that, sometimes, the cepstral sequence provides a prominent peak corresponding to half the fundamental frequency so that the estimate of the pitch period is twice the real one (Hess, 1983).

In the past, it has been observed that many other parameters derived from the spectrum (e.g. formants, energy, etc.) exhibit different degrees of correlation with the fundamental frequency (Atal, 1974b; Singer and Sagayama, 1992). This fact makes sound discrimination more difficult and represents a further problem for speech recognition. Also for this reason, some attempts have been made to use pitch in speech recognition. A method for estimating the spectra of voiced frames that takes into account a pitch measure has been proposed in Erell and Weintraub (1991, 1994). Another one is that described in Singer and Sagayama (1992). In this case, pitch information is used to normalize cepstral parameters to obtain what the authors call *pitch neutral* parameters. The normalization method makes use of linear regression (Press

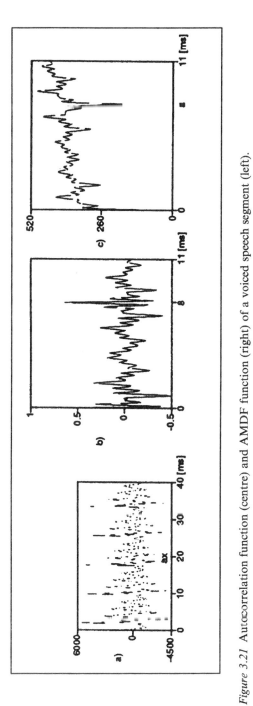

Figure 3.21 Autocorrelation function (centre) and AMDF function (right) of a voiced speech segment (left).

et al., 1988) with which a normalized cepstral vector $\tilde{c}$ is obtained by subtracting from the corresponding unnormalized vector c a quantity proportional to a normalized measure $\tilde{F}_0$ of the fundamental frequency:

$$\tilde{c} = c - \alpha \tilde{F}_0 \tag{3.59}$$

where α is the regression vector. It was observed (Singer and Sagayama, 1992) that the correlation between the resulting normalized components and the pitch diminishes.

Formant estimation

Techniques based on linear prediction (Markel and Gray, 1976) or on cepstral analysis (Schafer and Rabiner, 1970) can be used to estimate formant parameters. In fact, as the LPC spectral envelope represents an estimation of the frequency response of the vocal tract, the formant frequencies can be obtained by searching for the peaks in the LPC envelope itself.

Furthermore, the resonances of the vocal tract are also related to the complex poles, $z_k = \text{Re}(z_k) + j\,\text{Im}(z_k)$, of the LPC model (see equation (3.32)), according to the following equations:

$$B_k = -\frac{F_s}{\pi \log(|z_k|)} \tag{3.60}$$

$$F_k = \frac{F_s}{2\pi} \arctan\left(\frac{\text{Im}(z_k)}{\text{Re}(z_k)}\right) \tag{3.61}$$

where F_k is the kth formant frequency, B_k the corresponding bandwidth, $|z_k|$ is the module of the kth pole, and F_s is the sampling frequency. An alternate way to evaluate the formant frequencies is to use the cepstrally smoothed spectrum, introduced in section 3.3.8. Assuming that the cepstrally smoothed spectrum is an estimate of the vocal-tract frequency response, then peak-picking techniques can be used to obtain formant frequencies. In analogy with the case of fundamental-frequency estimation, a post-processing is needed, at the end of the formant estimation phase, in order to make formant trajectories satisfy some continuity constraints.

Tracking of consistent formant frequency trajectories is still an open problem. Particularly critical is line tracking in rapid transient sounds, while frequency hops (the case in which higher-order formants take the role of lower-order ones) can arise especially at the beginning or at the end of an entire trajectory. However, promising results were obtained by using statistical methods (Kopec, 1986; Streit and Barrett, 1990), sophisticated interpolation schemes (Sun, 1995) or time-varying analysis techniques (Nathan *et al.*, 1991). In Zolfaghari and Robinson (1996) an effective method for formant tracking based on modelling formants by mixtures of Gaussians is discussed.

3.6. DYNAMIC FEATURES

Cepstral coefficients and the log-energy of the corresponding spectrum are popular *static features* computed at every short-time frame. On the other hand, the voice signal is not stationary and various acoustic realizations of a phoneme may depend on the context. Hence, for speech recognition, temporal variations of features and contextual dependency of speech spectra can be conveniently taken into account. While coarticulation phenomena can be explicitly represented by context specific models, temporal trajectories of acoustic features can be modelled in two different ways:

- by considering acoustic parameters (*dynamic features*) computed in intervals longer than the analysis window
- by explicitly modelling the correlation, among the static parameters, with parameter trajectories (Afify *et al.*, 1996; Ostendorf and Roukos, 1989).

The vector that represents the input to the recognizer is generally formed by static and dynamic features and it is often called *observation vector*.

3.6.1. Time Derivative Features

The most common dynamic features used in speech recognition are based on the computation of time derivatives of the corresponding static features. As an example, Furui (1981) describes how temporal trajectories of cepstral coefficients can be modelled by their time derivatives. An advantage of using time derivatives is that they are not sensitive to slow channel-dependent variations of the static parameters.

In principle, given the acoustic feature set $x_t^{(0)}(j)$, time derivatives can be computed by means of finite differences, as follows:

$$x_j^{(i)}(t) = x_j^{(i-1)}(t+1) - x_j^{(i-1)}(t-1) \tag{3.62}$$

where $x_j^{(i)}(t)$ is the ith-order time derivative of the generic jth acoustic feature and t is the frame index. However, the first-order finite difference is affected by various types of noise, so that some sort of smoothing is required, for instance by fitting each cepstral trajectory with a linear combination of orthogonal polynomials of order from zero to two. The first- and second-order coefficient of the expansion are considered as slope and curvature of the trajectory. This method was used for speaker verification (Furui, 1981) to fit a trajectory of 90 ms computed with an analysis step of 10 ms (hence the trajectory extends over nine frames). Time derivatives, evaluated by means of a polynomial expansion, can be computed according to the following equation:

$$x_j^{(i)}(t) = \sum_{\tau=t-M_i}^{t+M_i} \kappa(i, j, \tau) x_j(\tau) \tag{3.63}$$

where M_i specifies a window around the current analysed frame t and $\kappa(i, j, \tau)$ are coefficients that depend on the orthogonal polynomials used.

Experimental evidence supports the importance of time derivatives of cepstral coefficients for ASR (Wilpon *et al.*, 1991, 1993). Using an observation vector consisting of first- and second-order time derivatives of cepstral coefficients and log-energy, in a telephone digit recognition task, the recognition error was reported to decrease from 2.9% to 1.4%. The first version of the SPHINX ASR system (Lee and Hon, 1989a) used LPC cepstral coefficients, log-energy and the corresponding first-order time derivatives, computed on a 40 ms window. The error rate in a 1000-word continuous speech recognition task dropped from 6.9% to 5.7% (Huang *et al.*, 1991) by incorporating into the feature vector both differenced cepstral coefficients evaluated on a 40 ms window and differenced cepstral coefficients evaluated on a 80 ms window.

Usually, between eight and 16 cepstral coefficients, with their first- and second-order time derivatives, are used as feature observation vector in modern ASR systems (Bocchieri and Wilpon, 1993).

3.6.2. Other Types of Dynamic Features

A parameter that may be useful for speech analysis and, in some cases, for speech recognition, is the measure of spectral variation among adjacent speech frames. This measure should be low if a given spectrum is highly correlated with neighbouring spectra. In Brugnara *et al.* (1992b) a spectral variation function (SVF) is presented, whose temporal pattern is characterized by valleys corresponding to stationary parts of the signal and by peaks corresponding to acoustic transitions. This function was experimented as additional parameter for speech recognition on the TI-digit task (Leonard, 1984). A reduction in the error rate of 20% was attained with respect to the use of a standard observation vector (energy, mel-based cepstral coefficients and corresponding derivatives). This type of SVF is evaluated, given a context of $2D$ frames around the instant t, by means of the following equation (Brugnara *et al.*, 1993):

$$\text{SVF}(t, D) = \frac{1}{2} \left(1 - \frac{\langle x_l(t, D) x_r(t, D) \rangle}{|x_l(t, D)||x_r(t, D)|} \right) \tag{3.64}$$

where $\langle \ \rangle$ denotes the scalar product, while $x_l(t, D)$ and $x_r(t, D)$ are two vectors derived from the left and the right context of the current frame t, respectively. Specifically, $x_l(t, D)$ represents the average filter bank output vector evaluated on D frames on the left side of t, and $x_r(t, D)$ is that evaluated on D frames on the right side. The parameter D is fixed according to the type of variation (long-term or short-term) that is desired. In Figure 3.22 a speech waveform and two corresponding spectral variation functions, evaluated with different values of D, are reported. The normalized inner product used in the equation above is considered an appropriate similarity measure in pattern classification

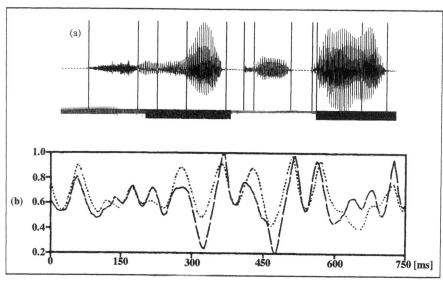

Figure 3.22 Speech waveform (a) and two spectral variation functions (b): the solid and the dotted line SVF curves were obtained using a window of six frames (30 ms) and 10 frames (50 ms), respectively.

tasks (Duda and Hart, 1973). Other types of SVF were proposed and used for automatic speech segmentation (Svendsen and Soong, 1987; Andre-Obrecht, 1988; Marzal and Vidal, 1990; Brugnara *et al.*, 1993; Hemert, 1991; Li and Gibson, 1996).

Another dynamic feature, called *dynamic cepstrum*, was proposed in Aikawa *et al.* (1993) and Beppu and Aikawa (1995). Its use was suggested by research on human perception. In Aikawa *et al.* (1993), the dynamic cepstrum accounts for the forward masking effect of the human auditory system (Seneff, 1988; Hirahara, 1991). It is evaluated, at time *t*, by subtracting a masking coefficient $m_j(t)$ from each cepstral coefficient $c_j(t)$. The masking pattern, $m_j(t)$, is obtained by filtering the standard cepstral coefficients as follows:

$$m_j(t) = \sum_{\tau=0}^{M-1} c_j(t-\tau)h_j(\tau) \qquad (3.65)$$

where $[h_j(\tau)]_{\tau=0}^{M-1}$ is the impulse response of the masking filter and M represents the overall duration of the masking effect. In Aikawa *et al.* (1993) two different masking filter impulse responses, a rectangular window and a Gaussian window, were tested and in Beppu and Aikawa (1995) both forward and backward masking effects were considered, obtaining improvements with respect to the use of either forward masking or backward masking.

Other dynamic features are those based on the Karhunen–Loeve transformation (KLT) (Fukunaga, 1990). As reported in Brown and Algazi (1991) and

Algazi *et al.* (1993) the KLT allows segmenting the speech signals into subword units depending only on acoustic properties, so that no relation exists between these acoustic subwords and *a priori* defined units, such as phones.

Further useful dynamic features can be obtained by applying the technique known as *RASTA processing* (Hermansky and Morgan, 1994). This technique can be used to compensate for the effects of different channels through which the speech signal is transmitted. It essentially consists of band-pass filtering the temporal trajectories corresponding to some of the cepstral coefficients described in section 3.5. The technique was first proposed and applied with PLP analysis of speech (Hermansky, 1990). If the channel is supposed to have convolutive effects and if it varies in time more slowly than the signal, the suppression of low-frequency components (see section 3.3.8) corresponds, in the time domain, to approximately deconvolve the signal itself with the transfer function of the channel. It was demonstrated (Hermansky and Morgan, 1994) that RASTA filtering improves recognition performance when convolutive noise is added to clean signals. Furthermore, RASTA filters were also applied (Mokbel *et al.*, 1994) directly to the mel-scaled cepstral trajectories to improve recognition over the telephone network.

3.7. CONCLUSIONS

The purpose of this chapter was to provide an overview of some fundamental issues on basic speech sounds and signal-processing techniques commonly applied in the front-end processor of ASR systems. Currently, most speech recognizers use "standardized" feature extraction modules. A common set of features consists of cepstral coefficients and their derivatives. These coefficients are extracted either from a short-term power spectrum or from LPC analysis. In both cases, a spectral representation on a warped frequency axis (e.g. mel scale) is generally preferred to the linear frequency one. Static features are computed on a short-term window at a regular rate (e.g. every 10 ms). First-order and second-order derivatives are computed on larger time intervals (whose length may range from 50 ms to 150 ms). Features based on auditory modelling are commonly determined at a regular analysis rate (e.g. 10 ms): however, in this case each feature set is representative of both short-term and long-term history of the input signal, because of the simulation of physiological mechanisms realized in these models.

A limitation of these acoustic feature sets is represented by the regularity of the analysis rate as well as by the fixed range over which dynamic features are computed. Although speech may be assumed to be quasi-stationary, the degree of stationarity varies substantially in time. As a result, fixed-rate analysis techniques lead to feature vector sequences that can be either highly correlated over time (e.g. long vowels) or insufficient to represent the various acoustic phenomena occurring inside the associated intervals (e.g. occlusives). Some attempts have been made to use variable-frame-rate analysis techniques (Ponting and Peeling, 1991) or to preprocess the speech signal in order to represent it in a multilevel acoustic segmentation (Glass and Zue, 1989) or, more generally, in a sequence of "uniform" speech units.

Another limitation of many front-end processors is the poor spectral representation from which acoustic features are derived. Time–frequency distributions as well as higher-order spectral analysis techniques (Nikias and Mendel, 1993) may represent alternative and more reliable methods of spectral estimation.

A further issue, that may be explored to overcome these limitations, is the use of subband analysis techniques in order to derive specific features for each frequency band. Each subband feature set may be used as input to a specific recognition process, independent from those associated with other bands (Bourlard *et al.*, 1996). In this way, various hypotheses based on the spectral content in a given frequency range could also be used. A particular advantage of this approach is foreseen when noise is concentrated in some (unpredictable) frequency bands.

4

Parameter Transformation

Diego Giuliani,[*] Daniele Falavigna[*] and Renato De Mori[†]

4.1. INTRODUCTION

In Chapter 3, methods of acoustic analysis for the speech signal were introduced. These methods can provide acoustic features to automatic speech recognition (ASR) systems which make use of basic speech units represented by hidden Markov models (see Chapters 5 and 6). The choice of the features for the models has a major impact on system performance. In fact, the use of a large number of features for each frame yields a large number of statistical parameters to estimate and requires a great amount of data for system training. Furthermore, adding new features to a given original set does not necessarily improve recognition accuracy.

Generally, in ASR it is useful to employ methods for reducing the dimensionality of the feature vectors, obtained from a given acoustic front end. To cope with this task, two main approaches, namely *feature selection* and *feature extraction* (Fukunaga, 1990; Leggetter, 1995), have been proposed.

---

[*]Istituto per la Ricerca Scientifica e Tecnologica – 38050 Pantè di Povo, Trento, Italy.
[†]School of Computer Science, McGill University, Montréal, P.Q. H3A 2A7, Canada.

In feature selection, given a set of features, the objective is to select the most *effective* subset of them according to a given optimal criterion. Exhaustive search, among all possible subsets of features has, in general, a prohibitive computational cost. Therefore, techniques have been investigated for ranking features according to their contribution to recognition performance and for selecting the most significant ones (Bocchieri and Wilpon, 1993; Paliwal, 1992a).

In feature extraction, a transformation is applied to the feature vectors in order to reduce their dimensionality while preserving their information content as much as possible. The transformation can be linear or non-linear. In the first case, the two most popular techniques are *principal component analysis* and *linear discriminant analysis* (Fukunaga, 1990; Brown, 1987; Hunt and Lefebvre, 1989; Paliwal, 1992a; Haeb-Umbach and Ney, 1992; Beulen *et al.*, 1995).

Among the non-linear transformations, *vector quantization* (VQ) has been widely investigated and used in both ASR (Lee and Hon, 1989a; Huang *et al.*, 1993) and speech coding (Jayant and Noll, 1984). It allows a real-valued feature vector to be mapped onto a symbol belonging to a given finite alphabet. Hence, the spoken utterance is represented by a sequence of symbols rather than by a sequence of real-valued vectors.[1] The major drawback of the method is that VQ introduces a loss of information, because different vectors can be mapped onto a same representation (prototype) in the feature space. To overcome this problem the size of the symbol alphabet can be enlarged, increasing modelling and recognition complexity.

Finally, other types of non-linear transformations can be obtained with artificial neural networks (ANNs) as, for example, in hybrid ASR systems described in Chapter 10.

This chapter is organized as follows. Section 4.2 describes dimensionality reduction using feature selection and extraction methods. Section 4.3 describes VQ, metrics for the feature space, techniques for clustering this space and for obtaining a representative vector for each cluster. Section 4.4 provides a summary of some significant work regarding parameter transformation for speech recognition.

4.2. DIMENSIONALITY REDUCTION

A vector of acoustic features contains, in general, static and dynamic features; the former are obtained via spectral analysis, the latter are time *derivatives* of static features (as described in Chapter 3). Intuitively, enlarging the number of features should lead to better recognition performance. However, the introduction of extra features does not necessarily imply higher discrimination

---

[1]When VQ is employed in speech coding the receiver needs to realize the inverse transformation, from symbols to feature vectors and, hence, to speech.

among acoustic classes if new features do not contain further useful information (i.e. they are redundant). In this last case, the marginal benefit of adding extra features, in terms of improvement of recognition performance, may vanish.

The type and number of acoustic features for an ASR system should be selected as a compromise among different factors such as: the effective contribution to the recognition performance, the amount of training data needed for robust parameter estimation, the computational requirements.

4.2.1. Feature Extraction

Feature extraction allows to obtain a reduced set of new features from the ones provided by the acoustic front end.

In the simplest case, the new features are linear combinations of the original ones. Therefore, original feature vectors are projected into a new, reduced feature space by means of a linear transformation. This is, in general, carried out by means of either *linear discriminant analysis* or *principal component analysis* (Fukunaga, 1990). In both cases the optimal transformation results in the projection of data along the eigenvectors of a matrix, although different matrices are considered in the two cases.

A more sophisticated feature extraction is performed by hybrid HMM/ANN speech recognition systems (described in Chapter 10) where feature extraction and acoustic modelling are performed by the same optimization process. In this case the new features are obtained by a non-linear transformation of the original ones.

Linear discriminant analysis

Linear discriminant analysis (LDA) is widely adopted in pattern recognition to approach the problem of dimensionality reduction. In LDA a linear transformation is sought that maps the feature space into a lower-dimensional space such that a given *class separability* criterion is optimized.

Let $\{x_n\}_{n=1}^{N}$ be a sample of D-dimensional feature vectors, each categorized into one of L classes, $\{\omega_l\}_{l=1}^{L}$. The sample covariance matrix Σ and mean vector μ are defined as follows:

$$\Sigma = \frac{1}{N}\sum_{n=1}^{N}(x_n - \mu)(x_n - \mu)^{\mathrm{T}} \tag{4.1}$$

$$\mu = \frac{1}{N}\sum_{n=1}^{N}x_n \tag{4.2}$$

where T denotes transpose.

Given the sample, a measure of separation among classes can be specified. Although other choices are possible (Fukunaga, 1990), class separability is usually expressed in terms of a function of scatter matrices, namely, the *within-class scatter* matrix and the *between-class scatter* matrix. The within-class scatter matrix, S_w, represents the scatter of samples around their class mean vector while the between-class scatter matrix, S_b, represents the scatter of the class means around the *total* mean μ of the sample vectors. The within-scatter matrix is defined as follows:

$$S_w = \frac{1}{N} \sum_{l=1}^{L} \sum_{x \in \omega_l} (x - \mu_l)(x - \mu_l)^T = \frac{1}{N} \sum_{l=1}^{L} N_l \Sigma_l \qquad (4.3)$$

where μ_l and Σ_l denote the mean vector and the covariance matrix of class ω_l, which contains N_l samples. S_w is symmetric, since it is the average within-class covariance matrix, and usually non-singular if $N > D$. The between-scatter matrix is specified as follows:

$$S_b = \frac{1}{N} \sum_{l=1}^{L} N_l (\mu_l - \mu)(\mu_l - \mu)^T \qquad (4.4)$$

and, for the moment, we assume it is full rank. The scatter matrices, S_w and S_b, are invariant under coordinate shift, and are used to express a measure of separation among classes. Two of these measures are defined as follows:

$$J_1 = \text{tr}(S_w^{-1} S_b) \qquad (4.5)$$

and

$$J_2 = \frac{\det(S_b + S_w)}{\det(S_w)} \qquad (4.6)$$

where $\text{tr}(\ )$ and $\det(\ )$ denote the trace and the determinant of a matrix, respectively. In some sense, they express the ratio of the between-class separation to the average within-class dispersion. The class separability measures J_1 and J_2 are invariant under any nonsingular linear transformation (Fukunaga, 1990).

The class separability measure J_1, can be seen as a generalization, to the multidimensional case, of the *Fisher ratio* measure (Duda and Hart, 1973; Paliwal, 1992a). The Fisher ratio F_i, for the ith feature, is defined as the ratio of the between-class variance to the average within-class variance:

$$F_i = \frac{B_i}{W_i} \qquad (4.7)$$

where B_i and W_i are the ith diagonal elements of the scatter matrices S_b and S_w, respectively. F_i is large when class means are well scattered with respect to the average within-class variance. A feature showing a large Fisher ratio should allow to discriminate well between different classes. In general, the Fisher ratio is a good measure of class separability when class distributions are unimodal and separated by the scatter of the class means (Fukunaga, 1990).

Consider a linear transformation from the original D-dimensional feature space to a D'-dimensional feature space, with $D' < D$, expressed as follows:

$$y = U^T x \qquad (4.8)$$

where U is a $D \times D'$ matrix having linearly independent column vectors.

It can easily be proven that the between-class scatter matrix $\hat{S}_b$ and the within-class scatter matrix $\hat{S}_w$, in the transformed feature space, can be expressed as (Fukunaga, 1990):

$$\hat{S}_b = U^T S_b U \quad \text{and} \quad \hat{S}_w = U^T S_w U \qquad (4.9)$$

In the new feature space the class separability measure J_1 can be expressed as:

$$\hat{J}_1(D') = \mathrm{tr}(\hat{S}_w^{-1} \hat{S}_b) = \mathrm{tr}((U^T S_w U)^{-1}(U^T S_b U)) \qquad (4.10)$$

and matrix U has to be determined in order to maximize $\hat{J}_1(D')$.

It can be shown that the linearly independent columns of the optimal transformation matrix U that maximizes $\hat{J}_1(D')$ are the D' eigenvectors corresponding to the D' largest ordered eigenvalues of the matrix $S_w^{-1} S_b$. As $S_w^{-1} S_b$ is not necessarily symmetric, its eigenvectors and eigenvalues can be effectively obtained by means of simultaneous diagonalization of the matrices S_w and S_b (Fukunaga, 1990). Therefore, matrix U^T represents a linear transformation that projects a D-dimensional feature vector into a D'-dimensional feature space spanned by D' eigenvectors, also called *principal discriminants*, of the matrix $S_w^{-1} S_b$.

When the D-dimensional sample vectors are projected on a line, the Fisher ratio can be used as a class separability measure for the projected data. Consider the projection of feature vectors on a line passing through the origin. For some orientation of the line, the projected samples result in well separated data classes and therefore in a high Fisher ratio.

Matrix U is determined so that the projection of the training data onto its first column vector, i.e. the first principal discriminant, provides a maximum Fisher ratio, equal to the largest eigenvalue of matrix $S_w^{-1} S_b$. Projection of training data on the second column vector, which is linearly independent with respect to the first one, provides the second largest value of the Fisher ratio. This value corresponds to the second largest eigenvalue of matrix $S_w^{-1} S_b$. Projections of training data along the remaining linearly independent column vectors of the matrix U give a decreasing sequence of the Fisher ratio values. Therefore, the eigenvalues of matrix $S_w^{-1} S_b$ suggest which eigenvectors have to be selected for determining matrix U: the ones associated to the smallest eigenvalues are in general discarded, as projections of sample vectors along them do not result in well separated classes.

When $L \le D$, matrix $S_w^{-1} S_b$ has at most rank $L - 1$ (provided that S_b has rank $\le L - 1$). In this case, matrix $S_w^{-1} S_b$ has at most $L - 1$ non-zero eigenvalues, and matrix U can be formed by considering at most $L - 1$ eigenvectors.

The effectiveness of feature reduction through projection along a reduced set of *principal discriminants* depends on how well the adopted class separability measure reflects the structure of the data. In fact, the class separability measures, J_1 and J_2, are appropriate when class distributions are unimodal and well separated by the scatter of the class means (Fukunaga, 1990). In general, this is not the case; however, LDA can be still performed but it is less effective.

Principal component analysis

Principal component analysis (PCA) generates a lower-dimensional representation which preserves as much as possible the variance of the original features (Fukunaga, 1990). PCA is also known as Karhunen–Loéve expansion.

When PCA is carried out to reduce the number of the features for pattern classification, it is assumed that the directions in the feature space, where large variations of the acoustic parameters occur, are the most informative about the classes to recognize.

Let us consider a sample $\{x_n\}_{n=1}^N$ of feature vectors having dimension D. The sample covariance matrix and mean vector are specified as in equations (4.1) and (4.2), respectively.

In PCA, feature vectors are projected in a feature space where coordinate axes are oriented in the directions of maximum variance. Coordinate axes of the new feature space represent the *principal components* of the sample distribution. It can be shown (Fukunaga, 1990) that the principal components correspond to the orthogonal eigenvectors of the sample covariance matrix Σ and that the corresponding eigenvalues account for the variance of the sample distribution along principal components.

A linear transformation which projects, by rotation, D-dimensional feature vectors along principal components can be expressed, as specified by equation (4.8), by means of a $D \times D$ matrix U having as column vectors the orthogonal eigenvectors of Σ. This transformation leaves the between-class distances unchanged. In the new space, the coordinate axes correspond to the eigenvectors of Σ, the sample covariance matrix has diagonal form and the variance along each axis is equal to the eigenvalues (Fukunaga, 1990). Furthermore, a pure scale transformation can be applied after projection along principal components, resulting in a whitening process, in order to obtain unit variance for each dimension (Fukunaga, 1990).

To select a lower dimensional feature space, preserving most of the variance of the original features, the D' eigenvectors, with $D' < D$, of matrix Σ corresponding to the D' largest eigenvalues, are selected as columns of matrix U.

When feature reduction is carried out for pattern classification, PCA may not be as effective as expected (Duda and Hart, 1973; Brown, 1987). In fact, although principal components are oriented in the directions of greatest variation, they do not necessarily account for information about class membership. Furthermore, principal components depend on parameter scale.

Application of LDA to speech recognition

Both PCA and LDA are widely used, in ASR, to transform the output of an acoustic front end in order to produce lower-dimensional feature vectors or to decorrelate the features (Brown, 1987; Hunt and Lefebvre, 1989; Hunt *et al.*, 1991; Haeb-Umbach and Ney, 1992; Class *et al.*, 1993; Ljolie, 1994; Siohan, 1995; Eisele *et al.*, 1996).

To apply LDA, it is necessary to assign training feature vectors to the acoustic classes to discriminate. Labelled data, when not available, can be obtained with an available speech recognizer (Brown, 1987; Aubert *et al.*, 1993; Beulen *et al.*, 1995). Each training utterance is time aligned with the concatenation of models corresponding to its phonetic transcription and feature vectors in the utterance are labelled according to the segmentation produced by the Viterbi algorithm (see Chapters 5 and 9). Segments may correspond to either speech units or model states, according to choice of the classes to discriminate.

After labelling is performed, within-class and between-class statistics are computed and the LDA matrix transformation is estimated. This transformation matrix is then applied to the output of the acoustic front end to produce feature vectors for a new recognition system (Haeb-Umbach and Ney, 1992).

The number of features to retain depends on many factors such as the type and number of emission distributions, the definition of the classes to discriminate and the amount of available training data (Brown, 1987; Beulen *et al.*, 1995). Also the benefit in terms of recognition performance depends on these factors.

Usually, an enlarged set of acoustic features is considered to capture as much information as possible (Haeb-Umbach and Ney, 1992). After having assigned a class label to each frame in the training set, an augmented feature vector can be obtained by adding to a given vector the k preceding and following vectors in the utterance (k is in general a small integer, such as 1 or 3) (Beulen *et al.*, 1995). In this way contextual information is captured. In building augmented feature vectors, static features alone or both static and dynamic features can be considered (Beulen *et al.*, 1995; Eisele *et al.*, 1996). Scatter matrices are then computed using the augmented feature vectors and exploiting the already assigned class labels.

4.2.2. Feature Selection

In this approach, given a set of features, on which a recognizer is based, the objective is to select the most *effective* subset of them (Fukunaga, 1990). The effectiveness should be measured in terms of recognition performance.

Generally, exhaustive search, among all possible subsets of features, is unfeasible due to its computational cost. Therefore, suboptimal feature ordering methods have been proposed with the aim of ranking individual features according to a given figure of merit (Paliwal, 1992a; Bocchieri and Wilpon, 1993). In these approaches, once individual basic features have been ranked, the most promising are selected and used to form lower-dimensional observation vectors for a new recognition system.

In Paliwal (1992a) both recognition rate and Fisher ratio have been proposed as figures of merit for feature ordering. Experiments were carried out using continuous-density HMMs with mixtures of Gaussians having diagonal covariance matrices. The baseline system was trained using as acoustic parameters 12 cepstral coefficients, their corresponding first- and second-order time derivatives, the first- and second-order time derivatives of the energy (for a total of 38 basic features). Training and test material was acquired from the same speakers over the telephone line and recognition results were reported for a small-vocabulary isolated word task. When the recognition rate was used as figure of merit, a recognition system was trained for each of the acoustic features and the recognition rates obtained on the training set, were used to rank the features. When the Fisher ratio (see equation (4.7)) was used as a figure of merit, training utterances were aligned, by the Viterbi algorithm, against corresponding baseline models (all the features were used in this phase). Assuming a suitable definition of classes (see the cited article for the details), between-class and within-class variances were computed for each basic feature.

Using the same set of features, another feature ordering method, called discriminative feature selection, has been proposed (Bocchieri and Wilpon, 1993). Also in this case the baseline system used continuous HMMs with mixtures of Gaussian densities, having diagonal covariance matrices, associated to model states. Before training, each model state was expanded into parallel states, thus resulting in a single Gaussian density per state. During training, the Viterbi algorithm assigned each feature vector x_t to a Gaussian density. Successively, continuous phone recognition was performed on the training set. For each training utterance, insertion and substitution phone errors were identified. Frames assigned to models corresponding to phone insertion or substitution errors were classified as *incorrect*. Furthermore, the states aligned with the incorrect frames were identified.

Denoting with $\tilde{x}_t$ an incorrect feature vector, at time t, and with s_t the state to which its results aligned, the following index, used later as figure of merit, was computed for each basic feature:

$$\mathcal{D}(i) = E\left[\frac{(\tilde{x}_t(i) - \mu_{s_t}(i))^2}{\sigma_{s_t}(i)}\right], \quad i = 1, \ldots, D \qquad (4.11)$$

where D is the number of basic features, E denotes arithmetic average, μ_{s_t} and σ_{s_t} denote the mean and the variance vectors characterizing the Gaussian density associated to state s_t. Intuitively, features with largest $\mathcal{D}(i)$ provide less overlap between classes and should be selected. The statistical meaning of the proposed index is discussed in Bocchieri and Wilpon (1993) where feature selection, based on the proposed method, was investigated using different corpora.

Applying the reported feature ordering methods for dimensionality reduction it was found that it is possible to use about half of the basic features without tangibly affecting recognition performance (Paliwal, 1992a; Bocchieri and Wilpon, 1993). However, the optimal number of features to be included in the reduced set has to be empirically determined.

Furthermore, it was noted that feature selection methods based on feature ordering suffer from the fact that they ignore correlation among features (Paliwal, 1992a; Leggetter, 1995). In fact, the use of a selection criterion based on physical considerations (Paliwal, 1992a), provided better recognition performance than the use of the automatic feature selection methods based on feature ordering.

Finally, feature-ordering methods may lead to different orderings of the features that are likely to be dependent on both the recognition system and the training speech corpus (Paliwal, 1992a).

4.3. VECTOR QUANTIZATION

To obtain a discrete parametric representation of speech signals, the feature vectors, obtained with spectral analysis, are transformed into symbols belonging to a finite alphabet. In principle, such transformation can be carried out in two different ways:

- by discretizing, separately, the various components of the feature vectors
- by partitioning the whole feature space and assigning the same symbol to all vectors contained in a given element of the partition.

In the first case the process is called *scalar quantization*, while in the second case it is called *vector quantization* (VQ).

VQ has been used to produce symbolic descriptions of speech patterns to be used as observations for HMMs. This parameter transformation results in a substantial reduction of storage requirements and computational complexity (Huang *et al.*, 1993). In fact, in this case, the probability densities of the HMMs are discrete functions and the corresponding likelihood values can be simply evaluated with lookup tables. With discrete probability densities special and very effective model training algorithms, based on *maximum mutual information* estimation, have been developed (Normandin, 1991).

VQ can also be used for speech coding (Makhoul *et al.*, 1985; Jayant and Noll, 1984; Buzo *et al.*, 1980; Gray, 1984), especially when a very low bit rate is required. In fact, the transmission of a limited number of symbols, at a given rate, requires less bandwidth than the transmission of continuous values.

In this chapter only some basic concepts of VQ are introduced; more details can be found in Makhoul *et al.* (1985) and Linde *et al.* (1980).

VQ consists of mapping a multidimensional feature vector x ($x \in \mathcal{R}^D$) onto a vector q belonging to a finite set $\mathcal{Q} = \{q_k\}_{k=1}^K$. The set $\mathcal{Q}$ is called *codebook*, while its elements q_k, that have the same dimensionality of the original space $\mathcal{R}^D$, are called *codewords*. The total number, K, of codewords is called *size* or *level* of the codebook.

The quantization map, $q = \Lambda(x)$:

$$\Lambda : \mathcal{R}^D \to \mathcal{Q} \qquad (4.12)$$

is generally estimated from a training set of data and is designed to satisfy a predefined criterion (e.g. to minimize a distortion or an error measure).

Equation (4.12) yields a subdivision of the feature space $\mathcal{R}^D$ (in the following this space will be called *pattern space*) into non overlapped regions, called *cells*, as depicted in Figure 4.1. Each cell contains the feature vectors that are mapped onto the same codeword. Therefore, a codebook of size K is specified by both

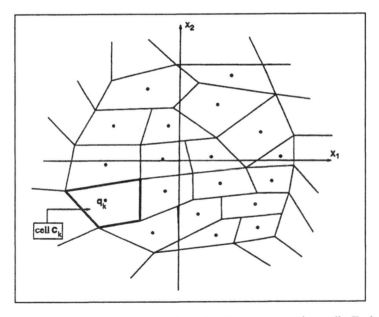

Figure 4.1 Partition, using VQ, of a two-dimensional pattern space into cells. Each point within a cell, say C_k (denoted with a bold line), is transformed into the corresponding codeword q_k (the centroid of the cell). Note the different sizes and shapes of the cells. With scalar quantization only cells of different sizes but with the same shape can be obtained.

the set $\{q_k\}_{k=1}^K$ of the codewords and the set $\{C_k\}_{k=1}^K$ of the corresponding cells[2].

VQ reduces to scalar quantization when the pattern space $\mathcal{R}^D$ is one-dimensional (i.e. $D = 1$). Furthermore, if each component of the input vector x is scalar quantized independently of the others (i.e. each dimension is subdivided into intervals), the resulting partition consists of cells that can have different sizes but the same shape. On the other hand, VQ allows cells to be defined with different shapes, as shown in Figure 4.1. This has some advantages over scalar quantization, as will be seen later.

The VQ process requires addressing the two following problems:

- Define a method for designing the codebook (i.e. for partitioning the pattern space).
- Specify the transformation expressed by equation (4.12).

Both problems require the definition of a *distortion measure*, over the pattern space, in order to quantify the similarity (or the dissimilarity) between two vectors. Once this measure is defined, an optimal criterion, for transformation (4.12), is that of minimizing the distortion, $d(x, q)$, between the feature vector x and the codewords. Hence, the codeword q is selected as follows:

$$q = \operatorname*{argmin}_{q_k \in \mathcal{Q}}(d(x, q_k)). \tag{4.13}$$

The equation is an expression of the so called *nearest neighbour* rule.

An optimal criterion for selecting the codewords is that of minimizing the average distortions of the cells. Hence, the codeword q_k, associated to cell C_k, is the one that minimizes the quantity Δ_k defined as:

$$\Delta_k = E[d(x, q_k)], \quad x \in C_k \tag{4.14}$$

where operator E denotes expectation. The codeword q_k is also called *centroid* of cell C_k. Since, in practice, only a finite set of vectors $\mathcal{X} = \{x_n\}_{n=1}^N$ is available for codebook design the average cell distortion is simply evaluated as:

$$\hat{\Delta}_k = \frac{1}{N_k} \sum_{x_n \in C_k} d(x_n, \hat{q}_k) \tag{4.15}$$

where N_k is the number of vectors contained in C_k and $\hat{q}_k$ is an estimate of the corresponding codeword. If the distance measure corresponds either to the mean squared error or to the weighted mean squared error (see next section) the codeword $\hat{q}_k$ that minimizes the equation (4.15) is the sample mean of the vectors in C_k:

$$\hat{q}_k = \frac{1}{N_k} \sum_{x_n \in C_k} x_n \tag{4.16}$$

---

[2]In ASR applications only the knowledge of the indices of the cells is required, while for speech coding the values of the components of all the codewords must be known in order to reconstruct the speech signal.

Given the codewords, the cells are determined with the distortion measure. Alternatively, given the cells, the codewords are determined by evaluating the centroids of the cells. Hence, codebook design can be done by finding, equivalently, the codewords or the cells.

In the following, some of the most well known distortion measures for speech processing as well as the method known as *k-means* algorithm for codebook design are described.

4.3.1. Spectral Distances

The most popular distortion, or *distance measure*, between two multidimensional vectors, $x \in \mathcal{R}^D$ and $y \in \mathcal{R}^D$, can be expressed as follows:

$$d_p(x, y) = \frac{1}{D} \sum_{k=1}^{D} |x_k - y_k|^p. \tag{4.17}$$

For $p = 1$, d_p represents the *average absolute error* while, for $p = 2$, the *mean squared error* (MSE) is obtained. For $p \to \infty$, $(d_p(x, y))^{1/p}$ tends to the maximum error between x and y. When $p = 2$, a weighted mean squared error measure can be introduced. This has the purpose of differently weighting the various components of x and y. The measure has the following expression:

$$d_W(x, y) = (x - y)^\mathsf{T} W^{-1} (x - y) \tag{4.18}$$

where W is square matrix of dimension D. In pattern recognition, W is often the estimated covariance matrix of the pattern space; in this case the distance, given by equation (4.18), is called *Mahalanobis distance*. The MSE (or the weighted counterpart) between cepstral vectors has been largely used in speech processing. The reason for this is given below.

It is worth noting that, to optimize the performance of the VQ process, the distortion measure is strictly related to the type of acoustic parameters in the feature vector (i.e. to the type of spectral analysis used to derive them). In principle, the distance between two speech vectors should resemble the difference in the areas of the corresponding two spectra (or spectral envelopes). If we consider two autoregressive models (see Chapter 3):

$$S_A(z) = \frac{\sigma_a}{A(z)} \tag{4.19}$$

$$S_B(z) = \frac{\sigma_b}{B(z)}$$

derived by applying LPC analysis (see Chapter 3 for details) to two different speech frames, then a *log-spectral distance* $L_p(S_A, S_B)$ can be defined as:

$$L_p(S_A, S_B) = \left[\frac{1}{2\pi} \int_{-\pi}^{\pi} \left| \log\left(\frac{\sigma_a^2}{|A(e^{j\omega})|^2} \right) - \log\left(\frac{\sigma_b^2}{|B(e^{j\omega})|^2} \right) \right|^p d\omega \right]^{1/p} \tag{4.20}$$

where p is a positive integer, varying from 1 to $+\infty$, and $\sigma_a^2/|A(e^{j\omega})|^2$ and $\sigma_b^2/|B(e^{j\omega})|^2$ are the spectral envelopes corresponding to the two LPC models. For a given value of p, the log-spectral distance is a metric, i.e. it is symmetric, positive definite and satisfies the triangle inequality. Furthermore, for $p = 1$, equation (4.20) represents the *mean absolute log-spectral distance*, for $p = 2$, it represents the root of the *mean squared log-spectral distance* while, for $p \rightarrow \infty$, L_p tends to the maximum error between the two envelopes. Finally, it can be shown (Gray *et al.*, 1980) that L_p increases with p, i.e. $L_1 \leq L_2 \leq \ldots \leq L_\infty$.

Since computation of $L_2(S_A, S_B)$, in the form of equation (4.20), is extremely complex an approximate method has been proposed in Gray and Markel (1976). The method is based on the cepstral representation (defined in Chapter 3) of the spectral envelopes $|S_A(e^{j\omega})|^2$ and $|S_B(e^{j\omega})|^2$. By expressing the logarithms of the envelopes as Fourier transforms one can write:

$$\log\left(\frac{\sigma_a^2}{|A(e^{j\omega})|^2}\right) = \sum_{k=-\infty}^{+\infty} c_k^a e^{-jk\omega} \tag{4.21}$$

$$\log\left(\frac{\sigma_b^2}{|B(e^{j\omega})|^2}\right) = \sum_{k=-\infty}^{+\infty} c_k^b e^{-jk\omega} \tag{4.22}$$

where $c^a = [c_k^a]_{k=-\infty}^{\infty}$ and $c^b = [c_k^b]_{k=-\infty}^{\infty}$ are cepstral sequences, $c_0^a = \log(\sigma_a^2)$ and $c_0^b = \log(\sigma_b^2)$. Since the logarithm of a squared magnitude is a real function it turns out that $c_{-k}^{(a,b)} = c_k^{(a,b)}$ and, by applying Parseval's theorem to equation (4.20), one obtains:

$$L_2^2(S_A, S_B) = \sum_{k=-\infty}^{+\infty} (c_k^a - c_k^b)^2 = (c_0^a - c_0^b)^2 + 2\sum_{k=1}^{+\infty}(c_k^a - c_k^b)^2 \tag{4.23}$$

Note from equation above that the square of the L_2 distance between two spectral envelopes is equal to the squared error between the two corresponding cepstral sequences. Furthermore, it was shown (Gray and Markel, 1976) that the distance expressed by equation (4.23) is well approximated even if the summation is truncated to the degree M of the polynomials $A(z)$ and $B(z)$ (i.e. to the predictor order used in LPC analysis):

$$L_2^2(S_A, S_B) \approx \sum_{k=-M}^{M} (c_k^a - c_k^b)^2. \tag{4.24}$$

Other measures for comparing speech spectral envelopes can be derived from the maximum likelihood formulation of LPC analysis. Itakura and Saito (1968) have shown that a maximum likelihood estimate of the parameters of an autoregressive model can be obtained by minimizing the following distance (*Itakura–Saito distance*) between a given signal spectrum, $S(e^{j\omega})$, and the corresponding autoregressive spectrum, $S_A(e^{j\omega})$:

$$d_{IS}(S, S_A) = \frac{1}{2\pi} \int_{-\pi}^{\pi} \left[\left| \frac{S(e^{j\omega})}{S_A(e^{j\omega})} \right|^2 + \log \left(\left| \frac{S_A(e^{j\omega})}{S(e^{j\omega})} \right|^2 \right) - 1 \right] d\omega \qquad (4.25)$$

Although the Itakura–Saito distance is important from a theoretical point of view, it is not suitable for comparing speech spectral envelopes, because of its sensitivity to LPC gain. Therefore, a modified version of the distance has been defined in order to reduce this sensitivity. This new distance, called *Itakura distance*, has the following expression:

$$d_I(S_A, S_B) = \log \left(\frac{1}{2\pi} \int_{-\pi}^{\pi} \left| \frac{A(e^{j\omega})}{B(e^{j\omega})} \right|^2 d\omega \right) \qquad (4.26)$$

The above distance is often referred as *log-likelihood ratio*, while the quantity inside the logarithm is simply called *likelihood ratio*.

The Itakura distance has also an interpretation in terms of the prediction errors associated to the models $S_A(z)$ and $S_B(z)$. In fact, called $x^a(n)$, $x^b(n)$ the data sequences used to estimate the coefficient vectors $\boldsymbol{a} = [a_i]_{i=0}^M$ and $\boldsymbol{b} = [b_i]_{i=0}^M$ of the LPC polynomials $A(z)$ and $B(z)$, respectively, the following four types of errors can be evaluated:

$$E_a^a = \sum_n \left(\sum_{i=0}^M a_i x^a(n-i) \right)^2 \qquad (4.27)$$

$$E_a^b = \sum_n \left(\sum_{i=0}^M a_i x^b(n-i) \right)^2 \qquad (4.28)$$

$$E_b^a = \sum_n \left(\sum_{i=0}^M b_i x^a(n-i) \right)^2 \qquad (4.29)$$

$$E_b^b = \sum_n \left(\sum_{i=0}^M b_i x^b(n-i) \right)^2 \qquad (4.30)$$

In the equations above a_0 and b_0 are set to 1. As shown in Figure 4.2, the various errors can be obtained by filtering each data sequence with the LPC inverse filters $A(z)$ and $B(z)$ and summing the corresponding outputs over time. The log-likelihood ratios, $d_I(S_A, S_B)$ and $d_I(S_B, S_A)$, can be expressed in terms of the above errors, as follows (Gray and Markel, 1976):

$$d_I(S_A, S_B) = \log \left(\frac{E_a^b}{E_a^a} \right) = \log \left(\frac{1}{2\pi} \int_{-\pi}^{\pi} \left| \frac{A(e^{j\omega})}{B(e^{j\omega})} \right|^2 d\omega \right) \qquad (4.31)$$

$$d_I(S_B, S_A) = \log \left(\frac{E_b^a}{E_b^b} \right) = \log \left(\frac{1}{2\pi} \int_{-\pi}^{\pi} \left| \frac{B(e^{j\omega})}{A(e^{j\omega})} \right|^2 d\omega \right) \qquad (4.32)$$

Since, by definition, $E_a^a \leq E_a^b$ and $E_b^b \leq E_b^a$, both ratios are greater or equal to 1 and their corresponding logarithms are greater or equal to 0. Furthermore,

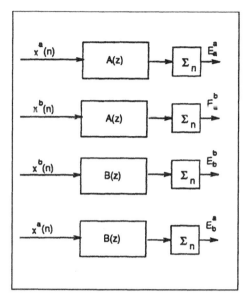

Figure 4.2 The different residual errors obtained by "inverse filtering" the data sequences, $x^a(n)$ and $x^b(n)$, used to estimate the parameters of the autoregressive models $\sigma_a/A(z)$ and $\sigma_b/B(z)$, respectively.

from equations (4.31) and (4.32) it turns out that $d_I(S_A, S_B) \neq d_I(S_B, S_A)$, i.e. the log-likelihood ratio is not symmetric.

Finally, the Itakura distance can be conveniently computed with the following matrix form (Itakura, 1975b):

$$d_I(S_A, S_B) = \frac{b^T \Phi_A b}{\sigma_a^2} \tag{4.33}$$

where $b = [1, b_1, \ldots, b_M]$ is the vector of coefficients of $B(z)$ and Φ_A is the Toeplitz autocorrelation matrix (see Chapter 3) obtained from the sequence $x^a(n)$.

Further discussion on distances and distortions will be presented in Chapter 12.

4.3.2. Codebook Design

One of the most popular algorithms for codebook design is the *k-means algorithm*. It is an iterative clustering algorithm that, given a set of training data $\mathcal{X} = \{x_n\}_{n=1}^{N}$, searches for a partition of the pattern space that minimizes the overall distortion of the codebook. The algorithm divides the training set into K *clusters*[3] whose centroids, $\{q_k\}_{k=1}^{K}$, are the codewords. It can be summarized

---

[3] The concept of cluster has to be distinguished from that of cell. In fact a cluster is a subset of vectors that are mapped onto a same codeword, while a cell is a region of the pattern space that is associated to a codeword.

as follows:

(a) First the codewords are initialized (e.g. using one of the methods described in Makhoul *et al.*, 1985).
(b) The clusters associated to the codewords are evaluated by means of equation (4.13).
(c) A new set of codewords, as well as the corresponding cell distortions, are computed by applying equations (4.15) and (4.16) to the clusters obtained in the previous step.
(d) Steps (b) and (c) are repeated until a stop criterion is fulfilled (e.g. the decrease in the overall distortion of the clusters is below a predefined threshold).

Since the algorithm has been shown to converge to a local optimum (Linde *et al.*, 1980), different codebooks can be derived by using different initial codewords. To overcome this problem, the algorithm is generally executed several times, with different initializations. The configuration that provides the minimum global distortion is retained.

4.4. APPLICATIONS AND TRENDS

The k-means algorithm has been used in ASR to provide discrete observations for HMMs. Generally, the feature vector is subdivided into subsets of features and a specific codebook is designed for each one of them. For example, in Lee and Hon (1989a) and Gupta *et al.* (1987) three different codebooks are used: one for the mel-scaled cepstral coefficients (see Chapter 3), one for their first-order time derivatives, and one for the energy and its corresponding first-order time derivative. The output probabilities, in the HMMs, are thus evaluated by factorizing the probabilities provided by each separate codebook (see Chapter 5).

In Rigoll (1992) VQ is performed by means of a multilayer neural network. The codewords of the codebook are represented by the indices of the output neurons. During recognition, the output that provides the maximum value for a given speech frame is selected as the codeword for that frame. The network weights are estimated in order to maximize the mutual information between the codewords and the words to recognize. This codebook design method, as the one based on the k-means algorithm, is *unsupervised*.

A *supervised* method for codebook design is presented in Cerf *et al.* (1994). In this work, a multilayer perceptron network is used as a phonetic frame labeller for an ASR system based on discrete HMMs. Hence, the network outputs correspond to a predefined set of phonemes, or allophones. In this case the output corresponding to the highest score provides the frame label for the recognizer.

Methods for simultaneously estimating both codebook and HMMs parameters can be found in Huang and Jack (1989a) and Pcinado *et al.* (1996). Furthermore, to take into account contextual variations of acoustic features, due to coarticulation effects, a context dependent VQ method has been proposed and investigated in Bahl *et al.* (1993a).

In the past, the *k*-means algorithm has also been largely used to cope with the task of speaker identification and verification (Rosenberg and Soong, 1987; Brunelli and Falavigna, 1995). In this case a codebook is designed for each speaker in a reference database, while, in the recognition phase, the distortions between the input speech signal and the reference codebooks are evaluated and sent to a suitable classifier (Brunelli and Falavigna, 1995).

Finally, it is worth noting that the advent of more powerful workstations has reduced the importance of VQ in ASR applications redirecting the attention to linear transformations.

Discriminant analysis has been used in various ASR systems. Experimental results with small- and large-vocabulary continuous-speech recognition systems show that the use of LDA can tangibly improve recognition performance (Aubert *et al.*, 1993; Haeb-Umbach *et al.*, 1993; Beulen *et al.*, 1995). Also for small-vocabulary recognition tasks over a telephone line, LDA has shown to be effective (Eisele *et al.*, 1996).

The use of PCA and LDA, for dimensionality reduction in speech recognition, is discussed in Brown (1987), Paliwal (1992a) and Jankowski *et al.*, (1995). Further details on LDA, to reduce noise effects, are given in Chapter 12.

5

Acoustic Modelling

Fabio Brugnara[*] and Renato De Mori[†]

5.1. INTRODUCTION

As introduced in Chapter 1, acoustic models (AMs) are stochastic models used with language models (LMs) and other types of models to make decisions based on incomplete or uncertain knowledge. Given a sequence of feature vectors $\mathbf{x}_1^T \triangleq [x_t]_{t=1}^T$ extracted from a speech waveform by the signal processing front end, the purpose of the AMs is that of computing the probability that a particular linguistic event (i.e. a word, a sentence, etc.) has generated the sequence. These probabilities can then be combined with *a priori* probabilities

---

[*]Istituto per la Ricerca Scientifica e Tecnologica – 38050 Pantè di Povo, Trento, Italy.
[†]School of Computer Science, McGill University, Montreal, P.Q. H3A 2A7, Canada.

given by the LM to find the sentence in the recognition language that is the most probable generator of the utterance described by x_1^J.

AMs have to be flexible, accurate and efficient. Flexibility is required because the characteristics of the recognition task are often quite different from the training conditions, and because of the complexity of the language used in many ASR applications. Accuracy is needed because of the ambiguity which is inherent in the relation between speech sounds and linguistic contents. Finally, efficiency is important when a recognition system is used interactively, to avoid forcing the user to wait for the computer response to spoken input.

Even if these problems have not been completely solved, hidden Markov models (HMMs) are a satisfactory solution, and most of the recent systems are based on their use. Therefore, the next two chapters will describe theory and applications of HMMs.

Markov chains were first used by Markov (1913) to analyse the letter sequence in the text of a literary work. The extension to HMMs only appeared later on, and their diffusion began when efficient methods for training and using them were proposed by Baum *et al.* in the 1960s (Baum and Eagon, 1967; Baum *et al.*, 1970). The first works on application of HMMs to ASR were published in the 1970s (Baker, 1975; Jelinek *et al.*, 1975; Jelinek, 1976).

Section 5.2 introduces HMM theory. Section 5.3 describes the entities modelled by HMMs. Section 5.4 discusses the possibility of sharing components among different models or parts of the same model. Section 5.5 deals with problems encountered in HMM implementation. Extensions and variations of basic models are briefly discussed in section 5.6. Section 5.7 summarizes recent phoneme recognition results using HMMs.

5.2. HIDDEN MARKOV MODEL THEORY

5.2.1. Definition

An HMM can be defined as a pair of discrete time stochastic processes (I, X). The process I takes values in a finite set $\mathcal{I}$, whose elements are called *states* of the model, while X takes values in a space $\mathcal{X}$ that can be either discrete or continuous, depending on the nature of the data sequences to be modelled, and is called the *observation* space. The two processes satisfy the following relations:

$$\Pr(I_t = i | I_0^{t-1} = i_0^{t-1}) = \Pr(I_t = i | I_{t-1} = i_{t-1}) \qquad (5.1)$$

$$\Pr(X_t = x | I_0^{t+h} = i_0^{t+h}, X_1^{t-1} = x_1^{t-1}) = \Pr(X_t = x | I_{t-1}^t = i_{t-1}^t) \qquad (5.2)$$

where the probabilities on the right-hand side are independent of time t.

Equation (5.1) is the expression of the so-called "first-order Markov hypothesis", and states that history before time t has no influence on the future evolution of the process if the present state is specified. Process I is therefore a first-order homogeneous Markov chain. Equation (5.2) states the "output independence hypothesis", that neither evolution of I nor past observations influence the present observation if the last two states are specified. For notational convenience, in the following, when an equation concerning the sequence of values taken by the process, such as $I_0^t = i_0^t$, is the argument of the probability function, it will be denoted as i_0^t when no ambiguity arises. In this way, for example, hypotheses (5.1) and (5.2) become $\Pr(I_t = i|i_0^{t-1}) = \Pr(I_t = i|i_{t-1})$ and $\Pr(X_t = x|i_0^{t+h}, x_1^{t-1}) = \Pr(X_t = x|i_{t-1}^t)$, respectively. Moreover, the same operator Pr will be used to denote the probability of discrete events, and the value of a probability density function for events in a continuous space.

The random variables of process X represent the variability in the realization of the acoustic events for a given speech unit, while process I models various possibilities in the temporal concatenation of these events.

In equation (5.2), output probabilities at time t are conditioned by the states of process I at time $t-1$ and t, that is, by the *transition* at time t. It is also common practice to express conditional probabilities by making reference only to the state of process I at time t. There are no strong arguments for preferring one of the formulations over the other, and the resulting models are virtually equivalent.

From the above introduced hypotheses, a few elementary properties of an HMM can be immediately derived, which will be useful in proving the correctness of several formulae for probability computation. They are expressed as follows:

$$\Pr(x_s^t|i_0^{t+h}, x_1^{s-1}) = \Pr(x_s^t|i_{s-1}^t) \tag{5.3}$$

$$\Pr(I_t = i|i_0^{t-1}, x_1^{t-1}) = \Pr(I_t = i|i_{t-1}) \tag{5.4}$$

$$\Pr(x_{t+1}^{t+h}|i_0^t, x_1^t) = \Pr(x_{t+1}^{t+h}|i_t) \tag{5.5}$$

where $0 \le s \le t \le T$ and $h > 0$.

- Proof of (5.3):

$$\Pr(x_s^t|i_0^{t+h}, x_1^{s-1}) = \prod_{r=s}^t \Pr(x_r|i_0^{t+h}, x_1^{r-1}) \tag{5.6}$$

$$= \prod_{r=s}^t \Pr(x_r|i_{r-1}^r) \tag{5.7}$$

$$= \Pr(x_s^t|i_{s-1}^t) \tag{5.8}$$

Equation (5.7) is a consequence of (5.2).

- Proof of (5.4):

$$\Pr(I_t = i | i_0^{t-1}, x_1^{t-1}) = \frac{\Pr(i_0^{t-1}, I_t = i)}{\Pr(i_0^{t-1})} \frac{\Pr(x_1^{t-1} | i_0^{t-1}, I_t = i)}{\Pr(x_1^{t-1} | i_0^{t-1})} \tag{5.9}$$

$$= \frac{\Pr(i_0^{t-1}, I_t = i)}{\Pr(i_0^{t-1})} \tag{5.10}$$

$$= \Pr(I_t = i | i_{t-1}) \tag{5.11}$$

The second factor in (5.9) is equal to 1 by virtue of (5.3), and (5.11) follows from (5.1).

- Proof of (5.5):

$$\Pr(x_{t+1}^{t+h} | i_0^t, x_1^t) = \sum_{i_{t+1}^{t+h} \in \mathcal{I}^h} \Pr(x_{t+1}^{t+h} | i_0^{t+h}, x_1^t) \Pr(i_{t+1}^{t+h} | i_0^t, x_1^t) \tag{5.12}$$

$$= \sum_{i_{t+1}^{t+h} \in \mathcal{I}^h} \Pr(x_{t+1}^{t+h} | i_t^{t+h}) \Pr(i_{t+1}^{t+h} | i_t) \tag{5.13}$$

$$= \Pr(x_{t+1}^{t+h} | i_t) \tag{5.14}$$

Equation (5.13) follows from (5.3) and (5.4).

5.2.2. Observation Probability and Model Parameters

The model is well defined if it is possible to compute the joint probability density of every finite sequence X_1^T of observable random variables. This probability can be decomposed as:

$$\Pr(x_1^T) = \sum_{i_0^T \in \mathcal{I}^{T+1}} \Pr(x_1^T | i_0^T) \Pr(i_0^T) \tag{5.15}$$

By using the hypotheses (5.1) and (5.2), the terms appearing in the above sum can be expressed as follows:

$$\Pr(i_0^T) = \Pr(i_0) \prod_{t=1}^{T} \Pr(i_t | i_0^{t-1})$$

$$= \Pr(i_0) \prod_{t=1}^{T} \Pr(i_t | i_{t-1})$$

$$\Pr(x_1^T | i_0^T) = \Pr(x_1 | i_0^T) \prod_{t=2}^{T} \Pr(x_t | x_1^{t-1}, i_0^T)$$

$$= \prod_{t=1}^{T} \Pr(x_t | i_{t-1}^t)$$

From these equations, it follows that an HMM can be defined by specifying the following parameter set ϑ:

$$\vartheta \triangleq (\pi, A, B)$$

$$\pi_i \triangleq \Pr(I_0 = i), \qquad\qquad \forall i \in \mathcal{I}$$

$$a_{ij} \triangleq \Pr(I_t = j | I_{t-1} = i), \qquad\qquad \forall i, j \in \mathcal{I}$$

$$b_{ij}(x) \triangleq \Pr(X_t = x | I_{t-1} = i, I_t = j), \quad \forall i, j \in \mathcal{I}, \forall x \in \mathcal{X}$$

The *initial state density* π and the *transition probability matrix* A constitute the parametrization of the Markov chain I. If the set $\mathcal{I}$ has N states, then π is an N-dimensional stochastic vector and A is an $N \times N$ stochastic matrix, which means that they satisfy the following relations:

$$\pi_i \geq 0, \quad \forall i \in \mathcal{I}$$

$$\sum_{i \in \mathcal{I}} \pi_i = 1$$

$$a_{ij} \geq 0, \quad \forall i, j \in \mathcal{I}$$

$$\sum_{j \in \mathcal{I}} a_{ij} = 1, \quad \forall i \in \mathcal{I}$$

The parametrization of the output densities b_{ij} varies according to the form of the observation space $\mathcal{X}$ and is discussed in section 5.2.5, as it plays an important role in HMM applications.

With the above definitions, the probabilities in expression (5.15) can be computed with the model parameters as follows:

$$\Pr(i_0^T) = \pi_{i_0} \prod_{t=1}^T a_{i_{t-1} i_t} \tag{5.16}$$

$$\Pr(x_1^T | i_0^T) = \prod_{t=1}^T b_{i_{t-1} i_t}(x_t) \tag{5.17}$$

$$\Pr(x_1^T) = \sum_{i_0^T \in \mathcal{I}^{T+1}} \pi_{i_0} \prod_{t=1}^T a_{i_{t-1} i_t} b_{i_{t-1} i_t}(x_t) \tag{5.18}$$

Expression (5.18) is important, because it shows that the model parameters are sufficient for computing the probability of a sequence of observations. Nevertheless, it is impractical because it requires an exceedingly high number of operations.

In HMM applications, however, probability computations are never carried out by applying this formula, as faster algorithms, described in section 5.2.4, have been proposed.

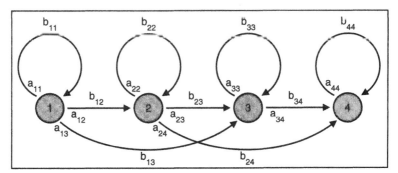

Figure 5.1 A graph representation of an HMM. A transition probability a_{ij} and an output density b_{ij} is associated to each arc $i \rightarrow j$.

5.2.3. HMMs as Probabilistic Automata

HMMs are often seen as a special case of probabilistic automata, or graphs. Nodes of the graph correspond to states of the I Markov chain, while directed arcs correspond to allowed transitions, i.e. pairs of states i, j such that $a_{ij} > 0$. A sequence of observations can be thought of as the emission of a system which, at each time instant, makes a transition from a node to another node, randomly chosen according to a node-specific probability density, and generates a random vector according to an arc-specific probability density. The number of states in a model and its set of arcs define what is often referred to as the model *topology*. In speech recognition applications, it is common to encounter *left-to-right* topologies, in which $a_{ij} = 0$ for $j < i$, as in the example shown in Figure 5.1, corresponding to a topology proposed in Bakis (1976). Moreover, when left-to-right topologies are adopted, the first and last states of the model are often indicated as *source* state and *final* state, respectively. The choice of the first state as a source state is equivalent to setting the initial state density to $\pi = [\delta(i, 0)]_{i \in \mathcal{I}}$. Indicating by F the last state and considering it as a final one means that in the evaluation the emission probability of a sequence of observations, the summation in (5.18) is carried out only on "complete" paths, i.e. paths that end in state F at time T. In such a case, state F does not have outgoing transitions, and the stochasticity constraint on the transition matrix is violated, since $a_{Fi} = 0, \forall i \in \mathcal{I}$. This affects the interpretation of the equations, as will be briefly discussed in the following. Nevertheless, it has little impact on the algorithms that use these relations. In this case equation (5.16) can be used to *define* a probability density on the set of all the finite-length paths ending in the final state. These paths are seen as elementary events. If the transition matrix satisfies the obvious condition that the final state is reachable from every other state, it follows that:

$$\sum_{T=1}^{\infty} \sum_{i_0^T, i_T = F} \Pr(i_0^T) = 1$$

The "state" of the system at time t cannot be seen as the value of a random variable, but it is still possible to define the event $(I_t = i)$ as the set of the complete paths i_0^T for which $i_t = i$, and (5.16) is still a valid expression of $\Pr(I_0^T = i_0^T)$ for partial paths. The main difference with respect to Markov chains is that, in general, $\sum_{i \in \mathcal{I}} \Pr(I_t = i) < 1$. It holds, in fact, that $\sum_{i \in \mathcal{I}} \Pr(I_t = i) \to 0$ as $t \to \infty$. Then, expression (5.17) can be used to define a family of conditional joint densities on finite sequences of observations with a specific length:

$$\Pr_T(x_1^T | i_0^T) \triangleq \prod_{t=1}^{T} b_{i_{t-1} i_t}(x_t) \tag{5.19}$$

The following definition:

$$\Pr(x_1^T) \triangleq \sum_{i_0^T, i_T = F} \Pr(i_0^T) \Pr_T(x_1^T | i_0^T) \tag{5.20}$$

introduces a probability density on the space $\mathcal{X}^* \triangleq \bigcup_{T=1}^{\infty} \mathcal{X}^T$ of finite sequences of observations since:

$$\begin{aligned}
\int_{\mathcal{X}^*} \Pr(x) \, dx &= \sum_{T=1}^{\infty} \int_{\mathcal{X}^T} \Pr(x_1^T) \, dx_1^T \\
&= \sum_{T=1}^{\infty} \int_{\mathcal{X}^T} \sum_{i_0^T, i_T = F} \Pr(i_0^T) \Pr(x_1^T | i_0^T) \, dx_1^T \\
&= \sum_{T=1}^{\infty} \sum_{i_0^T, i_T = F} \Pr(i_0^T) \int_{\mathcal{X}^T} \Pr(x_1^T | i_0^T) \, dx_1^T \\
&= \sum_{T=1}^{\infty} \sum_{i_0^T, i_T = F} \Pr(i_0^T) \\
&= 1
\end{aligned}$$

It is no longer possible to have a sequence of random variables for which expression (5.20) represents a finite-dimensional marginal density, but it is still possible to assign probabilities to the events of interest. For a given input sequence of length T, probabilities will be referred to the T-dimensional defective density defined by (5.20). The independency assumptions stated in section 5.2.1 apply now to the corresponding marginal densities.

To summarize, if state evolution is modelled by a Markov chain, the source model emits infinite sequences, finite subsequences of which are interpreted as partial realizations of a process in which the possible emission, at a given instant, is a random variable. When there is a final state, the source is supposed to emit arbitrarily long finite sequences, and the model directly gives a probability density on the whole set of possible observation sequences. The formulae for expressing probabilities in the two cases are almost the same. The use of a final state is convenient in speech recognition applications, especially when basic models are combined to form composite models, as will be seen in the following sections.

5.2.4. "Forward" and "Backward" Coefficients

As anticipated in section 5.2.2, computation with HMMs does not involve direct application of expression (5.18). Instead, partial probabilities are defined that can be efficiently computed by means of iterative algorithms, and allow to retrieve, beside the total emission probability, other quantities useful in solving the *parameter estimation* and *decoding* problems, that will be defined in the following sections. This section introduces the definitions of these quantities and the recurrent algorithms used for their computation.

- *Forward probability* $\alpha_t(x_1^T, i)$ is the probability that X emits the partial sequence x_1^t and process I is in state i at time t:

$$\alpha_t(x_1^T, i) \triangleq \begin{cases} \Pr(I_0 = i), & t = 0 \\ \Pr(I_t = i, x_1^t), & t > 0 \end{cases}$$

It can be computed iteratively by the following formula:

$$\alpha_t(x_1^T, i) = \begin{cases} \pi_i, & t = 0 \\ \sum_{j \in \mathcal{I}} a_{ji} b_{ji}(x_t) \alpha_{t-1}(x_1^T, j), & t > 0 \end{cases} \tag{5.21}$$

- *Backward probability* $\beta_t(x_1^T, i)$ is the probability that X emits the partial sequence x_{t+1}^T given that the process I is in state i at time t:

$$\beta_t(x_1^T, i) \triangleq \begin{cases} \Pr(x_{t+1}^T | I_t = i), & t < T \\ 1, & t = T \end{cases}$$

The recurrent formula for its computation, strongly analogous to (5.21) except that it is applied in reverse time order, is the following:

$$\beta_t(x_1^T, i) = \begin{cases} 1, & t = T \\ \sum_{j \in \mathcal{I}} a_{ij} b_{ij}(x_{t+1}) \beta_{t+1}(x_1^T, j), & t < T \end{cases} \tag{5.22}$$

- *Best-path probability* $\nu_t(x_1^T, i)$ is the maximum joint probability between the partial sequence x_1^t and a state sequence ending at state i at time t:

$$\nu_t(x_1^T, i) \triangleq \begin{cases} \Pr(I_0 = i), & t = 0 \\ \max_{i_0^{t-1}} \Pr(i_0^{t-1}, I_t = i, x_1^t), & t > 0 \end{cases}$$

It is computed with the following formula:

$$\nu_t(\boldsymbol{x}_1^T, i) = \begin{cases} \pi_i, & t = 0 \\ \max_{j \in \mathcal{I}} a_{ji} b_{ji}(x_t) \nu_{t-1}(\boldsymbol{x}_1^T, j), & t > 0 \end{cases} \tag{5.23}$$

The total probability of an observation sequence can be computed by means of the α and β coefficients by using one of the following relations:

$$\Pr(\boldsymbol{x}_1^T) = \sum_{i \in \mathcal{I}} \alpha_T(\boldsymbol{x}_1^T, i) \tag{5.24}$$

$$= \sum_{i \in \mathcal{I}} \pi_i \beta_0(\boldsymbol{x}_1^T, i) \tag{5.25}$$

$$= \sum_{i \in \mathcal{I}} \alpha_t(\boldsymbol{x}_1^T, i) \beta_t(\boldsymbol{x}_1^T, i) \tag{5.26}$$

The coefficient ν is used to compute another form of "score" that the model assigns to an observation sequence. It corresponds to the probability along the path that gives the highest contribution to the summation in (5.18):

$$\hat{\Pr}(\boldsymbol{x}_1^T) \triangleq \max_{i \in \mathcal{I}} \nu_T(\boldsymbol{x}_1^T, i) \tag{5.27}$$

This is in fact the quantity on which the recognition decision is often made, as will be shown in the following. If the model has initial and final states, then the final probabilities are obtained by taking only the value of the appropriate coefficient at the final state.

All these algorithms have a time complexity $O(MT)$, where M is the number of transitions with non-zero probability and T is the length of the input sequence. M can be at most equal to N^2, if N is the number of states in the model, but is usually much lower, since the transition probability matrix is generally sparse.

The computation of the above probabilities is performed in a common framework, and exploit a data structure named *trellis*, which corresponds to the unfolding of the graph structure of the model along the time axis (see Figure 5.2). Nodes in the trellis are pairs (t, i), where t is a time instant and i is a model state. Arcs represent model transitions composing possible paths in the model from the initial time instant to the final one. Each interval between two columns corresponds to an element of the observed sequence. Each trellis column holds the values of one of the above probabilities for a partial sequence ending at different model states. Once an observation sequence $\boldsymbol{x}_1^T$ is given, each arc $(t-1, i) \rightarrow (t, j)$ carries a "weight" given by $a_{ij} b_{ij}(x_t)$. Each path can then be assigned a score corresponding to the product of the weights of the arcs traversed by the path. This score corresponds to the probability of emission of the observed sequence along the path, given ϑ, the current set of model

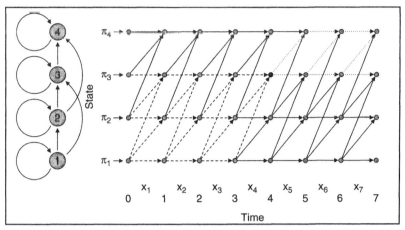

Figure 5.2 A state–time trellis. A trellis column holds values corresponding to different states at a fixed time. Arcs correspond to model transitions at different times, and are weighted by the product of the arc probability and the emission probability.

parameters:

$$q(\boldsymbol{x}_{t+1}^{t+h}, \boldsymbol{i}_t^{t+h}, \vartheta) \triangleq \prod_{s=t+1}^{t+h} a_{i_{s-1}i_s} b_{i_{s-1}i_s}(x_t) = \Pr(\boldsymbol{x}_{t+1}^{t+h}, \boldsymbol{i}_{t+1}^{t+h} | I_t = i_t) \qquad (5.28)$$

All the above coefficients can then be expressed by means of operations on path scores:

$$\alpha_t(\boldsymbol{x}_1^T, i) = \sum_{i_0^t, i_t = i} \pi_{i_0} q(\boldsymbol{x}_1^t, \boldsymbol{i}_0^t, \vartheta) \qquad (5.29)$$

$$\beta_t(\boldsymbol{x}_1^T, i) = \sum_{i_t^T, i_t = i} q(\boldsymbol{x}_{t+1}^T, \boldsymbol{i}_t^T, \vartheta) \qquad (5.30)$$

$$\nu_t(\boldsymbol{x}_1^T, i) = \max_{i_0^t, i_t = i} \pi_{i_0} q(\boldsymbol{x}_1^t, \boldsymbol{i}_0^t, \vartheta) \qquad (5.31)$$

From this point of view, the recurrent computations of α, β and ν correspond to appropriately combine, at each trellis node, the scores of paths ending in or starting at that node.

The computation proceeds in a column-wise manner, synchronously with the appearance of the observations. At every time frame, the scores of the nodes in a column are updated by means of the recursion formulae which involve the values of an adjacent column, the transition probabilities of the models, and the values of the output densities for the current observation. For α and ν, the computation starts from the leftmost column, whose values are initialized with the values of π, and ends at the opposite side, computing the final value with (5.24) or (5.27). For β, computation goes from right to left.

In Figure 5.2 a node is marked in the trellis along with the sets of paths contributing to its score for α and β. The dashed arrows indicate the paths whose score is added to obtain the α probability, while the dotted arrows show the paths contributing to the β probability. The ν probability corresponds to the highest scoring path among the dashed ones.

Proofs of the forward–backward relations

The trellis representation gives an intuitive explanation of formulae (5.21), (5.22), (5.23), but they can also be formally derived by exploiting the definition and the elementary properties of an HMM given in section 5.2.1.

- Proof of (5.21):

$$
\begin{aligned}
\alpha_t(x_1^T, i) &= \Pr(I_t = i, x_1^t) \\
&= \sum_{j \in \mathcal{I}} \Pr(I_{t-1} = j, I_t = i, x_1^t) \\
&= \sum_{j \in \mathcal{I}} \Pr(I_{t-1} = j, x_1^{t-1}) \Pr(I_t = i | I_{t-1} = j, x_1^{t-1}) \\
&\quad \times \Pr(x_t | I_{t-1} = j, I_t = i, x_1^{t-1}) \\
&= \sum_{j \in \mathcal{I}} \Pr(I_{t-1} = j, x_1^{t-1}) \Pr(I_t = i | I_{t-1} = j) \Pr(x_t | I_{t-1} = j, I_t = i) \\
&= \sum_{j \in \mathcal{I}} a_{ji} b_{ji}(x_t) \alpha_{t-1}(x_1^T, j)
\end{aligned}
$$

- Proof of (5.22):

$$
\begin{aligned}
\beta_t(x_1^T, i) &= \Pr(x_{t+1}^T | I_t = i) \\
&= \sum_{j \in \mathcal{I}} \Pr(I_{t+1} = j, x_{t+1}^T | I_t = i) \\
&= \sum_{j \in \mathcal{I}} \Pr(I_{t+1} = j | I_t = i) \Pr(x_{t+1} | I_t = i, I_{t+1} = j) \\
&\quad \times \Pr(x_{t+2}^T | I_t = i, I_{t+1} = j, x_{t+1}) \\
&= \sum_{j \in \mathcal{I}} \Pr(I_{t+1} = j | I_t = i) \Pr(x_{t+1} | I_t = i, I_{t+1} = j) \Pr(x_{t+2}^T | I_{t+1} = j) \\
&= \sum_{j \in \mathcal{I}} a_{ij} b_{ij}(x_{t+1}) \beta_{t+1}(x_1^T, j)
\end{aligned}
$$

- Proof of (5.23):

$$\nu_t(x_1^T, i) - \max_{i_0^{t-1}} \Pr(i_0^{t-1}, I_t = i, x_1^t)$$

$$= \max_{i_0^{t-2}} \max_{j \in \mathcal{I}} \Pr(i_0^{t-2}, I_{t-1} = j, I_t = i, x_1^t)$$

$$= \max_{j \in \mathcal{I}} \left(\Pr(I_t = i | I_{t-1} = j) \Pr(x_t | I_{t-1} = j, I_t = i) \right.$$

$$\left. \times \max_{i_0^{t-2}} \Pr(i_0^{t-2}, I_{t-1} = j, x_1^{t-1}) \right)$$

$$= \max_{j \in \mathcal{I}} a_{ji} b_{ji}(x_t) \nu_{t-1}(x_1^T, j)$$

5.2.5. Output Probabilities

In order for an HMM to be representable, its parameter set has to be finite. While this is obvious for the initial and transition probabilities, it may not be the case for the output probability densities, that are, in general, functions defined on the observable space. If the observation sequences are composed of symbols drawn from a finite alphabet of O symbols, then a density is a real-valued vector $[b(x)]_{x=1}^O$, having a probability entry for every possible symbol, and subject to the constraints:

$$b(x) \geq 0, \quad \forall x = 1 \ldots O$$

$$\sum_{x=1}^O b(x) = 1$$

Alternatively, observations can be composed of Q-uples of symbols $[x^h]_{h=1}^Q$, which are, in this case, usually considered mutually statistically independent. An output density is then represented by the product of Q independent densities, as follows:

$$b(x) = \prod_{h=1}^Q b^h(x^h)$$

and the marginal densities b^h are again subject to the above stated normalization constraints.

Hidden Markov models with this kind of output densities are referred to as *discrete* HMMs. The first HMM-based recognition systems used these models because of their simplicity and efficiency. In fact, computation of a discrete probability density only involves direct access in an array, and a few multiplications if the sequences are multidimensional. However, coding speech events with a small set of symbols is a heavy simplification, prone to a considerable loss of information. For this reason, most recent implementations directly model the real-valued vector sequences resulting from acoustic parameter extraction. Even if this approach increases the model resolution, it imposes that assumptions must be made about the form of the output densities, since they must belong to some parametric family in order to be representable with a limited number of coefficients. One of the most obvious choices for a parametric continuous density is the multivariate *Gaussian* density:

$$\mathcal{N}_{\mu,\Sigma}(x) = \frac{1}{\sqrt{(2\pi)^D \det(\Sigma)}} \exp\left(-\frac{1}{2}(x-\mu)^*\Sigma^{-1}(x-\mu)\right) \qquad (5.32)$$

where D is the dimension of the vector space, that is the length of a feature vector. The parameters of the Gaussian density $\mathcal{N}_{\mu,\Sigma}$ are the *mean vector* μ and the symmetric *covariance matrix* Σ. Gaussian (or *normal*) densities are a common choice for modelling random variables whose values spread around an average value as a result of many unknown factors. The mean vector μ is a location parameter, while the matrix Σ expresses the dispersion of the data around the value μ. Application of Gaussian densities is widespread in statistics, and their parameters are relatively easy to estimate. Their most notable limit in modelling general random variables is that they are *unimodal*, i.e. they are concentrated in the proximity of a value, which is inappropriate in modelling speech parameters. To overcome this limitation, *Gaussian mixtures* are often used, which are weighted sums of Gaussian densities:

$$\mathcal{M}(x) = \sum_{k=1}^{K} w_k \mathcal{N}_{\mu_k,\Sigma_k}(x) \qquad (5.33)$$

Mixture densities are in principle flexible enough to sufficiently approximate "arbitrary" densities, when an appropriate number of components is used. On the other hand, they considerably increase the number of parameters needed for representing a single output density. A D-dimensional Gaussian mixture with K components is identified by means of $K[1 + D + (D(D+1)/2)]$ real numbers. If, for example, $D = 30$ and $K = 20$, the number of required parameters is 9920. A way of reducing the number of free parameters without reducing the modelling capability too much is that of constraining the covariance matrix Σ to be diagonal, which means that the different components of the feature vector are considered to be mutually conditionally independent, given a particular mixture component. The joint density is therefore the product of one-dimensional Gaussian densities corresponding to the individual vector elements. A diagonal-covariance Gaussian is identified by means of $2D$

parameters, and is expressed as:

$$\mathcal{N}_{\mu,\sigma}(x) = \frac{1}{\sqrt{(2\pi)^D \prod_{h=1}^D \sigma_h}} \exp\left(-\frac{1}{2}\sum_{h=1}^D \frac{|x_h - \mu_h|^2}{\sigma_h^2}\right)$$

Diagonal-covariance Gaussians are widely used in speech applications. They can be estimated more reliably because they have fewer degrees of freedom when compared to full-covariance Gaussians, and are faster to evaluate on input frames. However, when the number of densities is on the order of several thousands, even Gaussians with diagonal covariances may cause the computational complexity of a recognizer to be practically unacceptable. In this case *distribution tying*, or *sharing* is often adopted. This corresponds to imposing that different transitions, possibly in different models, share the same output density. The tying scheme can be chosen by applying *a priori* knowledge, resulting, for example, in sharing distributions among different allophones of the same phoneme, or among automatically clustered transitions. This is an important issue in modern systems and it will be discussed in more detail in section 5.4.

While the choice of the Gaussian family is by far the most common, there are notable exceptions. In Ney and Noll (1994), Laplacian mixture components are used, which are defined as follows:

$$\mathcal{L}_{\mu,\sigma}(x) = \frac{1}{\sqrt{2^D} \prod_{h=1}^D \sigma_h} \exp\left(-\sqrt{2}\sum_{h=1}^D \frac{|x_h - \mu_h|}{\sigma_h}\right)$$

A Laplacian density has a slower decay than a Gaussian as its argument moves away from μ, and can be marginally more efficient to compute.

5.2.6. Empty Transitions

It is often useful to augment the hidden Markov chain of an HMM with *empty transitions* (Bahl *et al.*, 1983), i.e. transitions that the chain can undertake without emitting any observation. This causes a desynchronization between the hidden and the observable processes, because a sequence of length t can be emitted along a path which is longer than t, being partially composed of empty transitions. However, the correct handling of empty transitions requires just a slight modification of the basic probability computation algorithms introduced before, provided that it is assumed that *no loops of empty transitions exist*. A model with empty transitions has an additional transition matrix $A^\varepsilon = \{a_{ij}^\varepsilon, i, j \in \mathcal{I}\}$, which satisfies the following relation with matrix A:

$$\sum_{j \in \mathcal{I}} a_{ij} + a_{ij}^\varepsilon = 1, \quad \forall i \in \mathcal{I}$$

The recurrent algorithms for α, β and ν computations are modified as follows:

$$
\alpha_t(\boldsymbol{x}_1^T, i) = \begin{cases} \pi_i + \sum_{j \in \mathcal{I}} a_{ji}^\varepsilon \alpha_0(\boldsymbol{x}_1^T, j), & t = 0 \\ \sum_{j \in \mathcal{I}} a_{ji} b_{ji}(\boldsymbol{x}_t) \alpha_{t-1}(\boldsymbol{x}_1^T, j) + \sum_{j \in \mathcal{I}} a_{ji}^\varepsilon \alpha_t(\boldsymbol{x}_1^T, j), & t > 0 \end{cases}
\tag{5.34}
$$

$$
\beta_t(\boldsymbol{x}_1^T, i) = \begin{cases} 1 + \sum_{j \in \mathcal{I}} a_{ij}^\varepsilon \beta_T(\boldsymbol{x}_1^T, j), & t = T \\ \sum_{j \in \mathcal{I}} a_{ij} b_{ij}(\boldsymbol{x}_{t+1}) \beta_{t+1}(\boldsymbol{x}_1^T, j) + \sum_{j \in \mathcal{I}} a_{ij}^\varepsilon \beta_t(\boldsymbol{x}_1^T, j), & t < T \end{cases}
\tag{5.35}
$$

$$
\nu_t(\boldsymbol{x}_1^T, i) = \begin{cases} \max\left\{ \pi_i, \ \max_{j \in \mathcal{I}} a_{ji}^\varepsilon \nu_0(\boldsymbol{x}_1^T, j) \right\}, & t = 0 \\ \max\left\{ \max_{j \in \mathcal{I}} a_{ji} b_{ji}(\boldsymbol{x}_t) \nu_{t-1}(\boldsymbol{x}_1^T, j), \ \max_{j \in \mathcal{I}} a_{ji}^\varepsilon \nu_t(\boldsymbol{x}_1^T, j) \right\}, & t > 0 \end{cases}
\tag{5.36}
$$

These formulae appear to be recursive, in that they refer to values belonging to the same time column of the coefficients to be computed. However, loops of empty transitions are forbidden, so it is always possible to order the computation steps in such a way that the computation of a coefficient only requires values that are already available. To make this easier, for example, states can be renumbered so as to have only left-to-right empty transitions.

5.2.7. HMM Composition

ASR with stochastic models is performed by *probabilistic decoding*, which consists of choosing, in the set of the possible linguistic events, the one that corresponds to the observed data with the highest probability. This implies that a model has to be available for every possible event, allowing to "score" the hypothesis that a linguistic event has generated the observed data. In ASR, an observation often does not correspond to the utterance of a single word, but of a sequence of words. If the language considered has a limited set of sentences, then it is reasonable to have a different model for every possible utterance, but when the set of valid sentences is large, or even infinite, a different approach has to be considered. A large number of models causes problems both in training and recognition. If the target vocabulary is composed of several thousands of words, and a specific model was needed for each word, then, in order to properly train the set of models, it would be necessary to have many occurrences of each word in a training corpus. It may be practically impossible to collect these samples. Moreover, with this approach, the recognition language could not be extended to include words not observed in the training

data. These problems can be solved by representing the events of interest by
means of concatenation of basic units coming from a list of manageable size.
Only these units will have specific models, and more complex units will then
be modelled by composing the models of their constituent basic units.

This framework is especially suited for HMM-based ASR for the following
reasons. First, the production of speech is in fact based on the emission of a
sequence of basic sounds coming from a limited inventory, the phonemes of
the language. Second, the graph structure of HMMs makes it easy to build
compound models. In the English language, for example, there are about 40
basic phonemes. Suppose an HMM is available for each one of them, and
that the HMMs have a topology with distinguished initial and final states. In
order to evaluate the probability that a given speech signal corresponds to the
utterance of the word *"one"*, we could use the phoneme models corresponding
to the phonemic transcription, i.e. *w ah n*, and build a word model by simply
concatenating the phoneme models, as shown in Figure 5.3. With the use of
empty transitions, the same result can be achieved by connecting with a single
empty transition the final state of a phoneme in the chain representing a
word, with the initial state of the following one.

It is then clear that, if a complete model set of phonemes is available, a model
can be constructed for each word in a language, once its phonemic transcription
is known. The importance of model composition is not only related to
probability evaluation, but also to model training. In order to train a model,

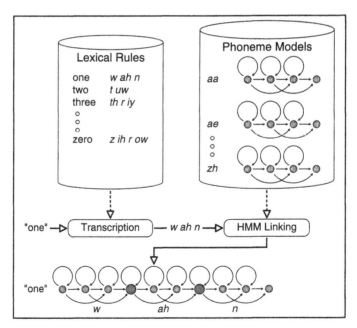

Figure 5.3 The construction of a word model by linking phoneme models.

a set of examples has to be available. When the basic units are phonemes, it is not possible to collect isolated examples, as only complete words or sentences can be naturally spoken. Therefore, training phoneme models with pertinent data requires performing a "segmentation" of the training data, specifying the identity and location of every phoneme in every utterance. A similar task is at best tedious, or even impossible to carry out on a large training corpus. However, by using the concatenation of basic models, the processing of training data is much simpler. As will be shown in the next chapter, HMM training consists of an iterative procedure where, at each step, the new values for the model parameters are computed depending on the previous values and on the training data. An iteration of the procedure consists of two steps: first, every training utterance is used to update a set of intermediate values, each corresponding to a model component, then, these "accumulated" values are used to compute the new parameter set. This allows to use model composition in training basic models with continuously spoken sentences. For every training utterance, only its phonemic transcription has to be known. According to it, a compound HMM, representing the whole sentence, can be built and the accumulators of its constituents can be updated. After all the training data have been processed, parameters of every phoneme model are reestimated by exploiting all the phoneme occurrences in the training set. It is to be noted that, with this procedure, accumulators for a phoneme model are influenced even by training data which do not belong to it, with a contribution that depends on how well these data fit the current model. It may be surprising, but there is experimental evidence, that, in spite of this fact, it is possible to initialize the training with a set of "neutral" models (e.g. all models being equal) and obtain a good convergence toward a set of selective phoneme models.

Model composition is easily extended to more general connecting rules beside concatenation. By connecting extremal states with empty transitions, it is possible to build arbitrary networks of models, as will be shown in Chapter 8. In spite of its simplicity, the use of these models with the Viterbi algorithm gives good performance on actual recognition systems.

5.2.8. The Viterbi Algorithm

The algorithm for computing the ν probabilities (Viterbi, 1967; Forney, 1973) is known as the *Viterbi algorithm*, and can be seen as an application of dynamic programming for finding a best scoring path in a directed graph with weighted arcs, which, in this case, is the trellis. Allowing for the presence of empty transitions, the algorithm is based on the recursion formula (5.36). When the whole observation sequence x_1^T has been processed, the score of the best path can be found by computing $\hat{\Pr}(x_1^T) = \max_{i \in \mathcal{I}} \nu_T(x_1^T, i)$. While applying the recursion formula, it is possible to keep track of the identity of the state that attains the maximum, creating a matrix of *backpointers* $\phi_t(x_1^T, i)$. With these backpointers it is possible to retrieve the highest probability path along the state–time trellis. The path is composed of a sequence of state–time pairs $[\hat{\imath}_l, \hat{\imath}_l]_{l=0}^L$ and can have a length $L + 1$ greater than $T + 1$, since more states can be visited at the same time instant if models have empty transitions.

The optimal path constitutes a time alignment of input speech frames with model states. It is therefore especially useful when states have an associated meaning, which is the case when the model is a compound model. In these models, different states may correspond to different phonemes, and the time alignment then locates the occurrences of the phonemes in the utterance, by indicating when the optimal path enters and leaves each basic model. The Viterbi algorithm applied to compound models gives even more when models are connected with empty transitions to build arbitrarily complex models, as will be shown in the following example.

Suppose the recognition vocabulary is composed of the 11 English digits (*"oh"*, *"zero"*, *"one"*, ..., *"nine"*) and that words are spoken in isolation. In order to make a recognition decision about the word corresponding to an incoming utterance, one could compute the emission probability of the input data with each digit model and then choose the model that gives the highest value. A more efficient solution consists of building a compound model as shown in Figure 5.4, performing the Viterbi algorithm and retrieving the most probable path. Due to the topology of the compound model, each complete path uniquely corresponds to the utterance of a digit. It is therefore possible to make a decision on the recognized digit by examining the states visited by the best path. A detailed description of Viterbi scoring on HMM networks can be found in Lee and Rabiner (1989). As shown in Figure 5.4, the construction of a compound model for recognition includes three steps. First, the recognition language is represented by a network (or "finite-state automaton") with word-labelled arcs. The connections between words are made by means of empty transitions, which could have assigned a probability. This is trivial for the present example, but it is still possible with many language specifications used in ASR, including *n*-gram language models, as will be discussed in Chapter 8. Given the network representing the recognition language, each word-labelled arc is replaced by a sequence, or possibly a network, of phoneme-labelled arcs, according to a set of lexical rules. Finally, each phoneme-labelled arc is replaced by an instance of the corresponding HMM, obtaining the final compound model. Special labels can be assigned to word-ending states, so as to simplify the work of retrieving the word sequence from the state sequence. It should be noted that, when the recognition is performed with a Viterbi search in a compound model, the criterion used for scoring competing hypotheses is not the total emission probability, but the best-path probability. In this respect this approach is a suboptimal solution. However, by comparing the two scoring criteria it can be verified that their difference does not considerably affect the recognition rate, and the Viterbi

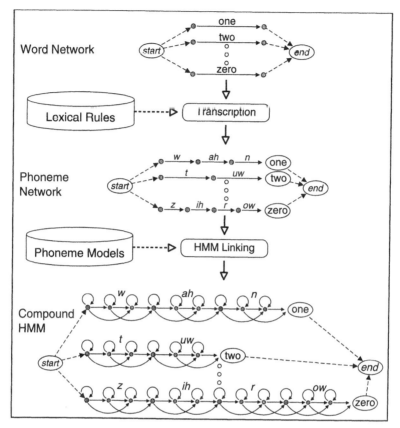

Figure 5.4 The construction of a compound model for recognizing the utterance of a digit. Dashed lines in the networks represent empty transitions used for connecting models.

approach has many desirable properties that make it preferable over the optimal one in most situations. Application of the Viterbi algorithm to continuously spoken sentences will be described in Chapter 9. By simply connecting the final state of the network depicted in Figure 5.4 with its initial state through an empty transition, it would be possible to recognize digit sequences of arbitrary length.

Given the importance of the Viterbi algorithm in speech recognition applications, a description of the basic procedures needed to implement a Viterbi-based HMM recognizer is given in Figure 5.5 in a PASCAL-like language. It is supposed that an observation sequence x_1^T is given and that N is the number of states in the model. The two main functions are **viterbi** and **backtrack**. The former one fills the matrix $[\nu_t(i)]$ with the partial path scores while also storing backtracking information in the two matrices $[\phi_t(i)]$ and $[\tau_t(i)]$. Here the state index i ranges from 1 to N, while the time index t ranges from 0 to T. The

```
function viterbi                        function backtrack
begin                                   begin
  t: =0;                                  t := T; j : =1;
  for i: =1 to N do begin                 for i: =2 to N do begin
    ν_t(i): =π_i; φ_t(i): = nil; τ_t(i): = nil    if ν_t(j) < ν_t(i) then  j : =i;
  end                                     end
  expand_empty_trans;                    l: =-1;
  for t: =1 to T do begin                while j ≠ nil do begin
    for i: =1 to N do ν_t(i): =0;          l: =l + 1;
    expand_full_trans;                     î_l: =j; t̂_l: =t;
    expand_empty_trans                     j := φ_t(î_l) ; t := τ_t(î_l) ;
  end                                     end
  Ď: =ν_T(1) ;                           reverse(î_0^l) ;
  for i: =2 to N do begin                reverse(t̂_0^l) ;
    if Ď < ν_T(i) then  Ď :=ν_T(i) ;     return  (î_0^l, t̂_0^l)
  end                                   end
  return Ď
end


procedure expand_empty_trans           procedure expand_full_trans
begin                                   begin
  for i: =1 to N do push(i) ;             for i: =1 to N do begin
  i := pop;                                 for j : =1 to N do begin
  while i ≠nil do begin                       Ď : =ν_{t-1}(i) a_{ij}b_{ij}(x_t) ;
    for j : =1 to N do begin                  if ν_t(j) < Ď then begin
      Ď : =ν_t(i) a_{ij}^ε;                      ν_t(j) : =Ď;
      if ν_t(j) < Ď then begin                   φ_t(j) : =i;
        ν_t(j): =Ď;                              τ_t(j) : =t - 1
        φ_t(j): =i;                            end
        τ_t(j): =t                           end
        push_unique(j)                     end
      end                                end
    end
  end
  i := pop
  end
end
```

Figure 5.5 A PASCAL-like description of the basic functions needed to implement a Viterbi recognizer.

value $φ_t(i)$ represents the last state visited by the best path ending in state i at time t, while $τ_t(i)$ is used to know whether the last transition of the path was empty or not. The **viterbi** function calls, at every time instant, the two procedures **expand_empty_trans** and **expand_full_trans** which update a trellis column by taking into account empty and full transitions, respectively. The algorithm for expanding empty transitions does not impose any particular restriction, and could be made more efficient if, for example, empty transitions were only allowed to be left-to-right. This, however, is often difficult to guarantee in a compound model. The algorithm relies on a stack accessed by means of the usual **push** and **pop** functions, with the addition of a **push_unique** function which only inserts an item in the stack if it is not already present. The **backtrack** function exploits the information stored by the **viterbi** function to retrieve the time alignment between input frames and model states. The path is returned in the two arrays $\hat{i}_0^l$ and $\hat{t}_0^l$. The **reverse** procedure is called to reverse the order of the arrays, since they are built in inverse time order.

5.3. ENTITIES MODELLED

In the design of an ASR system, even when the recognition language is well specified, the choice of the model set is still an open problem. The identification of the basic events, for which explicit models have to be built, is in fact an important step in the design of an HMM-based ASR system. This choice depends on many factors, among which are the complexity of the task, the confusability among target events, the size and quality of the training corpus, and the similarity between training data and test data. In speech modelling, the first natural choice is to use phonemes as basic units. This indeed allows achievement of good recognition performance, but it can be improved by better considering the nature of speech sounds. Describing the utterance of a word by means of a concatenation of phonemes is an abstraction that does not take into account a number of important details. It is known, for example, that the acoustic realization of a phoneme can be considerably influenced by the surrounding phonemes. For example a vowel in the context of two plosives, as in *"bad"*, is often "reduced" in the sense that its acoustic parameters do not reach a stationary target value but evolve continuously from the target value (*locus*) of the preceding plosive to the locus of the following plosive. A very different transition behaviour is observed in a word like *"cap"*. This means that a more realistic description of the basic sounds can be achieved by dedicating different models to the same phoneme in different contexts, leading to the definition of *allophone* models, or *context-dependent* units. *Triphone* models, in which the context of a phoneme is made of the previous and the following phonemes were proposed in Schwartz *et al.* (1985) and have been widely used since then. Phoneme models can have left-to-right topologies with the first (set of) state(s) representing the *onset* part of the phoneme, a central (set of) state(s) representing the *body* of the phoneme and the last (set of) state(s) representing the *coda*. Although the three main components of a phoneme may all have context-dependent (CD) emission probabilities, it is often assumed that these probabilities are context-independent (CI) in the body, they depend on the left context in the onset and on the right context in the coda. In fact the body should correspond to the central part of the phoneme where the acoustic parameters are expected to be stable around the so-called "phoneme target values", while the onset and the coda should exhibit more variation due to coarticulation with their contexts.

Note that if the phoneme context includes both the preceding and the following phoneme, and the basic unit set is composed of say 40 units, the set of possible context-dependent allophones includes $40^3 = 64\,000$ units. Of course not all of the possible context combinations appear in practice, due to phonotactic constraints, but the number of units to consider is nonetheless very high, thus requiring a large training set for providing an adequate number of examples for every unit. For a given training set, one can choose to explicitly model only those allophones whose number of occurrences exceeds a given threshold. Another approach is that of considering units that span more that one phoneme. Instead of modelling a phoneme in a particular context, a model is defined that describes the actual concatenation of two or more phonemes (Schukat-Talamazzini *et al.*, 1992). Selection of multiphone units can again be based on the criterion of minimum number of occurrences in the training data.

Choosing only the most frequent context combinations greatly reduces the number of required models, but can still lead to a set of thousands of basic units. It is then evident that the specialization of basic models cannot be applied blindly. The following section suggests some techniques to reduce the explosion of the number of free model parameters to be estimated.

The above mentioned methods of introducing detailed basic units have a common starting point: an association between words and phonemes that is based on *a priori* phonetic knowledge.

A different approach to the definition of basic models is proposed in Bahl *et al.* (1988), where the selection of basic models and the association between words and units are automatic and completely data-driven. As a first step, the set of all the vectors in the training data is partitioned by means of an unsupervised clustering procedure. The corresponding centroids are taken as starting distributions for a set of basic units, called *fenones*, all of which have a very simple topology as that of Figure 5.6.

The fenone-based transcription of the vocabulary words (the *fenonic base-forms*) are then automatically generated by applying maximum likelihood decoding of sample word utterances in terms of fenone sequences. Word models are built by combining the fenones according to their fenonic baseform. Finally, fenone parameters are reestimated with maximum likelihood training, by using the fenonic baseform as transcriptions of the training data. The fenonic approach was introduced in the paradigm of isolated word recognition, using word models as a reference, which is not practical for large-vocabulary speech recognition. However, the idea of data-driven parameter tying inspired several developments which are used in many state-of-the-art systems today.

In order to better characterize parameter distributions for a large population of speakers, instead of associating a single probability distribution to a transition of a fenone, a weighted mixture of distributions can be considered.

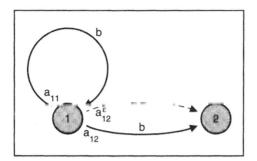

Figure 5.6 Topology of a fenone. The two full transitions share the same output distribution.

Fenonic baseforms enriched with multiple distributions are called *multonics* baseforms (Bahl *et al.*, 1993b). Among the other types of units that have been proposed, is is worth mentioning *semiphones*, consisting of the combination of a left diphone, a central monophone and a right diphone (Paul, 1991b), *micro-segment* models (Deng and Erler, 1991), syllable and demi-syllable models (Hunt *et al.*, 1980; Ruske and Schotola, 1981), complex phoneme networks for modelling microfeatures of speech parameter evolution (Wolferstetter and Ruske, 1995).

5.4. PARAMETER TYING

In principle a great number of different allophone models and of different model parameters means high resolution in acoustic modelling. In order for the models to be effective, they must have a high precision that depends on the number of samples used for estimating each parameter. A good trade-off between resolution and precision is obtained by *parameter tying*. Parameter tying consists in imposing an equivalence relation between different components of the parameter set of a model, or components of different models. Even subword modelling can be seen as a form of parameter tying. Word models expressed by means of phoneme units can be seen as tied-parameter models, where the sharing involves whole portions of the models. However, the term is generally used to denote the sharing of simpler items like states, distributions, Gaussians and just means or variances, as discussed in Takahashi and Sagayama (1995b). The use of tying is a key factor for obtaining a balanced trade-off between the need for detailed acoustic modelling and the constraint of having a manageable number of free parameters to estimate. The definition of a tying relation in principle involves a decision about every parameter of the model set, and, as such, is a difficult task. A first broad classification of tying schemes can be made by separating methods which define an *a priori* knowledge-based equivalence relation from methods which automatically determine how parameters are to be tied by means of objective measurements on training data. An emblematic example of the former approach are the so-called *semicontinuous* HMMs (Bellegarda and Nahamoo, 1990; Huang and Jack, 1989b), where the output distributions in the HMMs are mixtures, all of which share the same set of basic Gaussian components, called the *codebook* in analogy with vector quantization. What makes the difference between distributions are therefore the mixture weights only. As their name suggests, semicontinuous HMMs (SCHMMs) were introduced as a bridge between VQ-based discrete HMMs and mixture-based continuous density HMMs. The rationale was that of adding fuzziness to VQ-based models, without imposing the computationally heavy evaluation of many Gaussian densities. This approach compares favourably with discrete HMMs and continuous density HMMs when the training set is of moderate size, but if the training corpus is large, it is possible to use more detailed tying schemes. An evolution of this approach related to context-dependent modelling is the use of *phonetically tied mixtures* (PTM) (Lee *et al.*, 1990a). A PTM-based system is a set of context-dependent HMMs in which the mixtures of all the allophones of a phoneme share a phoneme-dependent codebook.

In the above methods, the equivalence between parameters (in this case Gaussian components) was established *a priori*. In the case of PTM, the choice of the equivalence classes is based on phonetic considerations. Several methods have been proposed for determining equivalence relations between probability densities that integrate both phonetic knowledge and data-driven clustering.

These methods are directed at finding an optimal tying scheme between states, also called *senones* in this context, of different allophones of a phoneme. Sharing a state means in practice sharing a mixture density, as transition probabilities are not taken into account.

In Young and Woodland (1994), state tying is achieved with a clustering procedure. First, a large set of context-dependent units is identified, and a set of completely untied models is trained. The models have a single Gaussian associated to each state. Then, states belonging to allophones of the same phones are clustered with an agglomerative algorithm, based on a divergence measure between Gaussians. After the tying scheme has been established, the densities are converted to mixtures and the models are trained again. During the last stage, the acoustic resolution can be progressively incremented by adding mixture components.

Other methods rely on the use of *phonetic decision trees* (Bahl *et al.*, 1991b; Hwang *et al.*, 1993; Young *et al.*, 1994) to single out the distributions that have to be shared between different allophonic models. A phonetic decision tree is a binary tree, described in Appendix B, which has a question and a set of HMM densities attached to each node. A node is connected with two children containing the sets of densities corresponding to positive and negative answers to the question. The root node contains the whole set of densities under consideration, and each level of the tree is a refinement of the partition defined by the previous level. The tying relation is then defined by tying distributions that belong to the same leaf node. In general, a coarse subdivision of distributions is *a priori* made, and then a decision tree is constructed for each class. For example, one can decide to allow tying only among allophones of a phoneme, or only among initial (or central, or final) portions of allophones of a phoneme. The questions related to nodes generally concern the context of a phoneme, as for example "is the right context a vowel?".

The construction of a phonetic decision tree uses a predefined set of questions, a set of observations labelled with the corresponding distribution, and a *goodness-of-split* evaluation function (Bahl *et al.*, 1991b). Initially, all the training data are put at the root node of the tree. Then, the impact of each question is evaluated by means of the goodness-of-split function, which assess the improvement obtained by splitting the data according to the question. The question with the highest score is selected, and the two children of the node are created and added to the tree. This process is repeated at each node, and the splitting ends when a termination criterion is met, which is related both to the relative improvements and to a threshold in the occupancy of the nodes. The evaluation function can be based on likelihood or on entropy.

An important feature of the approach based on phonetic decision trees is that it allows to build context-dependent models regardless of the fact that examples are available on the training data or not. Given the specification of a CD unit, in fact, it suffices to find the tree leaves in which its distributions fall, by answering the questions at the nodes. Then, the model can be built by connecting the corresponding tied distributions with transitions probabilities taken from a context-independent model. This is especially useful when the system includes cross-word contexts.

Yet another approach is presented in Digalakis and Murveit (1994), where parameter sharing involves codebooks of Gaussians, called *genones*. Semi-continuous HMMs or PTM-based HMMs are seen as special cases of genonic models, with a single genone in the former case, and a phoneme-dependent genone in the latter. Genones, however, can be automatically determined by means of a three-step procedure, which starts from a PTM-based system and progressively relaxes the tying relation between Gaussians. In the first step, the mixtures of allophones of each model are clustered with an agglomerative algorithm using an entropy-related measure of similarity between the sets of mixture weights. This partition defines the sets of mixtures that will have common components. In the second step, the genones are assigned to each cluster element by selecting the most likely set of components. The third step consists of a retraining of the system with the resulting tying relation. In this case, only the Gaussians are shared between different allophones, while the mixture weights remain distribution-specific. The assignment of Gaussians to multiple genones, in the second step, implies the reduction of the degree of tying, thus resulting in a data-driven increase of the acoustic resolution, alternative to the above-mentioned methods.

5.5. HMM IMPLEMENTATION ISSUES

The expressions for α, β and ν, given in section 5.2.4, show that the values of these quantities decay exponentially with the length of the observation sequence. When working with finite precision, underflow is likely to occur, especially when processing long sequences. To overcome this problem, two techniques can be applied: *scaling* and *log-probabilities*. The former one consists in multiplying each value in a trellis column with a coefficient in such a way that the dynamic range of the arithmetic unit that performs computation is not exceeded. The multiplicative coefficients have to be taken into account when the computed probabilities are used. The second method simply consists of storing the logarithms of the probabilities instead of the probabilities them-selves. Logarithms have a much lower dynamic range than their arguments; this allows underflow in typical HMM computations. The use of log-probabilities has the advantage of not requiring additional information to be associated to the trellis. Moreover, log-probabilities are especially appropriate when dealing with continuous Gaussian or Laplacian densities, since, in this case, only the argument of the exp function has to be computed. In the following, some details on log-probabilities implementation will be discussed, while details on scaling can be found in Levinson *et al.* (1983). Storing probabilities in logarithmic format requires of course modifications in the algorithms. This is trivial as long as multiplications are concerned, because it suffices to replace them by additions. This is all that is needed for the Viterbi algorithm. When summations are also required, some consideration have to be made, in order to avoid losing the advantages of logarithmic representation. Performing a sum in log-probabilities means that, given the two logarithmic values x, y, one computes:

$$z = \log(e^x + e^y) \tag{5.37}$$

If this expression was applied directly, underflow might occur in the evaluation of the exp function, causing a dramatic loss in precision. However, the expression can be rewritten as:

$$\log(e^x + e^y) = \log(e^x(1 + e^{y-x})) = x + \log(1 + e^{y-x}) \tag{5.38}$$

By defining the function:

$$\Lambda(h) \triangleq \log(1 + e^{-h}), \quad h \in [0, +\infty) \tag{5.39}$$

a "logsum" can be computed as:

$$z = \begin{cases} x + \Lambda(x - y), & \text{if } y \le x \\ y + \Lambda(y - x), & \text{if } x < y \end{cases} \qquad (5.40)$$

This method has several advantages over the computation expressed by (5.37). First, if underflow occurs in evaluating (5.39), this is because the two addends have a small difference, so expression (5.40) still gives a good approximation. Besides, it requires two evaluations of functions as opposed to three in (5.37), thus reducing the overhead due to logarithmic representation. Moreover, Λ is a bounded function which smoothly decreases from $\log 2$ to 0, and, as such, it can be conveniently discretized in a table of precomputed values, completely removing the need of executing mathematical functions. The size of the table can be determined on the basis of the precision needed. In typical HMM applications, in fact, a very high numerical accuracy is not required.

This fact is also reflected in another commonly used technique for reducing the computational load in HMM implementation, namely computation *thresholding*. When updating the trellis by means of the algorithms presented in section 5.2.4, it is rather common that some nodes have an accumulated probability which is much lower than the highest one on the same trellis column. Such nodes will then give only a minor contribution when used for updating the adjacent column. If the ratio between their score and the best one is sufficiently low, their contribution may become negligible. It is then possible to choose a threshold value c for this ratio and, after the computation of a column, force to zero those nodes whose score is lower than c times the best score. In the next step, these nodes will thus be neglected. A good implementation of the algorithms and a judicious choice of the threshold can lead to considerable efficiency improvements at the expense of a small decrease in accuracy. When applied to the Viterbi algorithm, this technique is known as *beam search*, and will be discussed in Chapter 9.

Another approximation is often made when evaluating continuous mixture densities, reducing the computational load in speech recognition applications. In order to completely avoid the logsum operation, the sum in (5.33) is replaced by a maximization, that is, the value of the mixture is assumed to be the value of the most significant term. This is motivated by the empirical observation that, in practice, the sum is often dominated by a single component, given the fast decrease of exponential densities.

5.6. EXTENSION AND VARIATIONS

HMMs have proven to be a good choice for ASR, but they are by no means a definitive answer to the need for detailed acoustic modelling. Several alternatives have been proposed and are under investigation. Some of them appear to be very different, as for example the ones based on neural networks (discussed in Chapter 10), others are variations which try to address specific problems. An example are HMMs with explicit state-duration modelling. In HMMs, the probability of remaining in a state exhibits an exponential decrease in time, and this is not appropriate. A control on duration can be inserted at the innermost level with state-specific duration distributions, which can be non-parametric, as in Ferguson (1980), or parametric, as in Russel and Moore (1985) and Levinson (1986). Alternatively, phone-level or word-level duration constraints can be applied by a postprocessor (Rabiner *et al.*, 1989).

Another attempt to improve the modelling of duration and frame correlation in standard HMMs is the introduction of *second-order HMMs* (Mari and Haton, 1994). In these models, the first-order hidden Markov chain is replaced by a second-order chain, where transition probabilities depend not only on the current state, but also on the previous one.

Of special interest are *stochastic segment models* (SSM) (Ostendorf and Roukos, 1989). An SSM is composed of a set of joint densities, and a map which assigns one of these densities to every possible phone length. A general SSM could allow complete modelling of frame correlation inside an acoustic unit, as there are no independence assumptions on the marginal densities of the joint densities. In practice, however, independence assumptions are often introduced, in order to reduce the number of free parameters. With these assumptions, an SSM can be represented by means of an HMM with a complex topology. A unified view of several variations of the segment-based approach can be found in Ostendorf *et al.* (1996). In Afify *et al.* (1996), a related method, based on *stochastic trajectory modelling*, is proposed. *Dynamic HMMs* using a state-dependent dynamical system to model local behaviour of parameter trajectories are proposed in Ephraim (1992b). Other techniques for state-dependent parameter trajectory modelling are proposed in Ghitza and Sondhi (1993) and Deng *et al.* (1994). The possibility of modelling a unit with multiple interacting HMMs is proposed in Brugnara *et al.* (1992a). Interesting aspects of multiple but not necessarily interacting HMMs can be found in White (1992) and Woodard (1992). A comprehensive discussion on multiple HMMs for modelling speech in noise is presented in Gales and Young (1996).

5.7. PHONEME RECOGNITION RESULTS WITH HMMs

The simplest task which allows to evaluate the acoustic modelling capability of a speech recognition system is that of phonetic recognition, whose target is to extract the phonetic contents of a sentence without imposing any constraints on the possible phone sequences. The attribute "simple" refers to the easiness of implementation, and not to an easiness of the task itself. A state-of-the-art system can in fact make an error every third or fourth phone in unconstrained phonetic recognition.

A phonetic recognizer can be implemented by building a compound IIMM including all the phonetic units in a loop, and then performing a Viterbi decoding as explained in section 5.2.8. Alternatively, probabilistic constraints on the phoneme sequence can be imposed by employing bigram probabilities for phoneme concatenation, and integrated again in a compound model by means of empty transitions.

To evaluate the recognizer performance, it is supposed that the exact phonetic transcription of the incoming utterance is known. The phone sequence output by the recognizer is thus compared with the reference transcription by evaluating their distance according to the *Levenshtein* metric, which gives the number of operations needed to transform the former string into the latter, in terms of *insertions, deletions* and *substitutions*. These numbers are accumulated on the whole set of testing utterances. Assuming that N is the total number of phoneme occurrences in the testing set, and that S, I, D are the total numbers of substitutions, insertions and deletions, respectively, the performance of the recognition system is expressed by the following two measures:

$$Phone\ accuracy\ (PA) \triangleq 100\frac{N - (S + I + D)}{N}$$

$$Phone\ correct\ (PC) \triangleq 100\frac{N - (S + D)}{N}$$

The phone-correct measure does not account for insertion errors, which are in fact less severe since they are considerably reduced when linguistic constraints are imposed.

The evaluation of a phoneme recognizer requires a sizeable corpus of accurately labelled speech data. The TIMIT corpus (Zue *et al.*, 1990) was collected to be a reference tool for training and evaluating speaker-independent phoneme recognition systems. It contains speech of 630 speakers, with 10 sentences per speaker, with a suggested subdivision in training and testing data. The sentences were designed to provide a good coverage of phonetic contexts, and for each sentence both word labelling and accurate phonetic labelling are available. An experimental setup for TIMIT was presented in Lee and Hon (1989b), defining a set of reference units for performance evaluation, which has since been used by several laboratories to compare experiments. In that work it is also reported that expert human spectrogram readers were able to achieve around 69% PC in unconstrained phone recognition. The performance of the system, based on 1450 context-dependent discrete IIMMs, was 73.8% PC and 66.1% PA when bigram probabilities were used. Subsequently, continuous HMM-based systems have also been evaluated on TIMIT, giving a performance of about 77% PC and 73% PA (see e.g. Young and Woodland, 1994; Lamel and Gauvain, 1993). In Robinson (1994) a recognition system based on recurrent neural networks is shown to compare favourably to several HMM-based systems. In the last few years, the interest in phone recognition as an evaluation framework for recognition systems has reduced in favour of more application-oriented tasks, such as large-vocabulary dictation. Performance of dictation systems depends on many factors besides acoustic accuracy, and they are discussed further in Chapter 9.

6

Training of Acoustic Models

Fabio Brugnara[*] and Renato De Mori[†]

6.1. INTRODUCTION

Usually the choice of HMM topologies, as well as the type of probability distributions, is performed by a designer. The values of the parameters characterizing these distributions, as well as transition probabilities, are instead estimated by a training algorithm, which processes a set of labelled examples, the *training set*, with the purpose of computing an "optimal" set of values for the HMM parameters. Optimality is defined by means of an objective function depending both on the HMM parameters and on the observations contained in the training set. Once this objective function has been chosen, model training

---

[*]Istituto per la Ricerca Scientifica e Tecnologica – 38050 Pantè di Povo, Trento, Italy.
[†]School of Computer Science, McGill University, Montreal, P.Q. H3A 2A7, Canada.

becomes a constrained maximization problem. Training algorithms can differ in the optimality criterion and/or in the method of performing the optimization. In HMM modelling, however, there is a method which is widely accepted for its simplicity and effectiveness, and is based on use of the Baum–Welch algorithm to compute maximum likelihood estimates of the parameters. The availability of this algorithm is in fact one of the reasons for the success of HMMs in ASR applications. In section 6.2, the Baum–Welch algorithm will be described in detail, and then applied to the two most commonly used objective functions, namely likelihood and *a posteriori* probability. Section 6.3 introduces maximum likelihood (ML) parameter estimation. Section 6.4 describes maximum *a posteriori* (MAP) estimation. Section 6.5 discusses the generation of initial models for the previously introduced estimation methods. In section 6.6, some comments about the Baum–Welch algorithm are presented, together with a discussion on the statistical interpretation of the computation steps. Finally, section 6.7 briefly overviews several alternatives to maximum likelihood estimation of HMM parameters.

6.2. THE BAUM–WELCH ALGORITHM

The Baum–Welch algorithm, as described in Baum *et al.* (1970) and Baum (1972), is related to the maximization, with respect to a variable ϑ, of a function P with the following representation:

$$P(\vartheta) = \int p(\xi, \vartheta)\, d\xi \tag{6.1}$$

Here p is a "smooth" positive function, and the integration is performed in a space with finite measure.

Consider the following auxiliary function:

$$Q(\vartheta, \vartheta') = \frac{1}{P(\vartheta)} \int p(\xi, \vartheta) \log p(\xi, \vartheta')\, d\xi \tag{6.2}$$

The Baum–Welch algorithm relies on the following inequality:

$$Q(\vartheta, \vartheta') - Q(\vartheta, \vartheta) \leq \log P(\vartheta') - \log P(\vartheta) \tag{6.3}$$

which is derived as follows:

$$Q(\vartheta, \vartheta') - Q(\vartheta, \vartheta) = \int \frac{p(\xi, \vartheta)}{P(\vartheta)} \log \frac{p(\xi, \vartheta')}{p(\xi, \vartheta)}\, d\xi$$

$$\leq \log \int \frac{p(\xi, \vartheta')}{P(\vartheta)}\, d\xi$$

$$= \log \frac{P(\vartheta')}{P(\vartheta)} \tag{6.4}$$

Inequality (6.4) is a consequence of the Jensen inequality applied to the strictly concave log function and to the unitary measure $[p(\xi, \vartheta)/P(\vartheta)] \, d\xi$. It is therefore strictly satisfied unless $p(\xi, \vartheta) = p(\xi, \vartheta')$ *almost everywhere* in ξ, that is, for every ξ except at most for a set of measure zero.

From inequality (6.3) it follows that the transformation T, defined as:

$$T(\vartheta) \triangleq \operatorname*{argmax}_{\vartheta'} Q(\vartheta, \vartheta') \tag{6.5}$$

is a *growth transformation* for the function P on the domain of ϑ, i.e. it satisfies the condition:

$$P(T(\vartheta)) \geq P(\vartheta) \tag{6.6}$$

A sequence $\{\vartheta_{(n)}, n = 1, 2, \ldots\}$ that monotonically increases the objective function P can thus be generated as follows, starting with an arbitrary initial guess $\vartheta_{(0)}$:

$$\vartheta_{(n)} = T(\vartheta_{(n-1)}), \quad n = 1, 2, \ldots \tag{6.7}$$

The problem of maximizing P thus becomes a sequence of optimization problems for the function Q, and this is the essence of the so-called Baum–Welch algorithm. The method is effective, of course, only if these problems can be easily solved. This is fortunately the case in HMM training and in other statistic estimation problems involving "hidden" variables, i.e. random variables which cannot be directly sampled, but only indirectly observed through samples of related random variables. In these problems, function Q often turns out to be strictly concave in the second argument, allowing for an easy analytical unique solution of (6.5). In this case, it is possible to prove that the sequence of $\vartheta_{(n)}$ actually converges to a local maximum of P, which is not guaranteed by (6.6) alone. To this end, one can apply Theorem 2 in Baum and Sell (1968), which gives local convergence of the estimates if, besides (6.6), the following conditions are met:

$$\nabla P(\vartheta) = 0 \quad \Rightarrow \quad T(\vartheta) = \vartheta \tag{6.8}$$

$$P(T(\vartheta)) = P(\vartheta) \quad \Rightarrow \quad \nabla P(\vartheta) = 0 \tag{6.9}$$

If Q has a unique maximum, then the solution to (6.5), i.e. the value $T(\vartheta)$, can be found as the solution of the following gradient equation in ϑ':

$$\nabla_{\vartheta'} Q(\vartheta, \vartheta') = 0 \tag{6.10}$$

From the identity:

$$\nabla_{\vartheta'} Q(\vartheta, \vartheta') = \frac{1}{P(\vartheta)} \int p(\xi, \vartheta) \nabla_{\vartheta'} \log p(\xi, \vartheta') \, d\xi = \frac{1}{P(\vartheta)} \int \frac{p(\xi, \vartheta)}{p(\xi, \vartheta')} \nabla_{\vartheta'} p(\xi, \vartheta') \, d\xi$$

it follows that:

$$\nabla_{\vartheta'} Q(\vartheta, \vartheta')|_{\vartheta' = \vartheta} = \frac{1}{P(\vartheta)} \nabla_{\vartheta} \int p(\xi, \vartheta) \, d\xi = \frac{1}{P(\vartheta)} \nabla P(\vartheta) = \nabla \log P(\vartheta) \tag{6.11}$$

Now, if ϑ is a *critical point* of P, i.e. $\nabla P(\vartheta) = 0$, this equality shows that the value $\vartheta' = \vartheta$ solves equation (6.10), and hence $T(\vartheta) = \vartheta$, that is to say, ϑ is a *fixed point* of T. Condition (6.8) is thus satisfied.

Furthermore, if $P(T(\vartheta)) = P(\vartheta)$, from the definition of T and inequality (6.3) it follows that $Q(\vartheta, T(\vartheta)) = Q(\vartheta, \vartheta)$, which implies $T(\vartheta) = \vartheta$. By applying equation (6.11) again, one gets $\nabla P(\vartheta) = 0$, proving that condition (6.9) is satisfied as well.

By referring to the above-mentioned theorem, one can conclude that, for every isolated local maximum $\tilde{\vartheta}$ of P, there is a neighbourhood U such that, if $\vartheta_{(0)} \in U$ and $\vartheta_{(n)}$ is defined by (6.7), then $\vartheta_{(n)} \to \tilde{\vartheta}$ as $n \to \infty$.

With general assumptions like these, it is clearly impossible to draw conclusions about the *speed* of convergence; that would require an examination of the differential properties of the objective function. In the case of HMMs, the objective function sharply increases in the first few iterations, after which the relative improvements achieved by the algorithm progressively decrease. In practice, the iterative process can be stopped when the relative increase of the objective function falls below a predefined threshold.

It has to be noted that the above arguments apply practically unmodified when the maximization problem includes constraints, as in the case of the estimation of some HMM parameters.

6.3. MAXIMUM LIKELIHOOD ESTIMATION

6.3.1. Problem Definition

The objective of maximum likelihood estimation (MLE) for HMMs is to find a set of model parameters $\tilde{\vartheta}$ which maximizes the emission probability of a given "training" observation sequence x_1^T. MLE thus becomes the following optimization problem:

$$\tilde{\vartheta} = \operatorname*{argmax}_{\vartheta} \operatorname{Pr}_\vartheta(x_1^T) \qquad (6.12)$$

where the optimization variable is the set of HMM parameters. i.e. $\vartheta \triangleq (\pi, A, B)$.

6.3.2. Baum–Welch ML Reestimation Formulae

The Baum–Welch reestimation formulae for the parameters of an HMM are obtained by applying the algorithm to the objective function corresponding to the total emission probability:

$$P(\vartheta) \triangleq \operatorname{Pr}_\vartheta(x_1^T) = \sum_{i_0^T \in \mathcal{I}^{T+1}} \operatorname{Pr}_\vartheta(x_1^T, i_0^T) = \sum_{i_0^T \in \mathcal{I}^{T+1}} \pi_{i_0} \prod_{t=1}^{T} a_{i_{t-1}i_t} b_{i_{t-1}i_t}(x_t)$$

where x_1^T is the given training observation sequence, and ϑ is the parameter set of the HMM. The role of the variable ξ in (6.1) is thus played by the state sequence i_0^T, while the p function is defined by:

$$p(i_0^T, \vartheta) \triangleq \pi_{i_0} \prod_{t=1}^{T} a_{i_{t-1}i_t} b_{i_{t-1}i_t}(x_t) \tag{6.13}$$

and the integral is replaced by a summation. In the following, the observed sequence x_1^T is considered given and fixed, so that explicit reference to the dependence of the values on it will be removed.

The auxiliary function Q takes the following form:

$$Q(\vartheta, \vartheta') = \frac{1}{P(\vartheta)} \sum_{i_0^T \in \mathcal{I}^{T+1}} p(i_0^T, \vartheta) \left(\log \pi'_{i_0} + \sum_{t=1}^{T} \log a'_{i_{t-1}i_t} + \sum_{t=1}^{T} \log b'_{i_{t-1}i_t}(x_t) \right) \tag{6.14}$$

and can thus be decomposed as follows into the sum of three terms which depend only on some component of the parameter set:

$$Q(\vartheta, \vartheta') = Q_\pi(\vartheta, \pi') + Q_a(\vartheta, A') + Q_b(\vartheta, B') \tag{6.15}$$

$$Q_\pi(\vartheta, \pi') \triangleq \frac{1}{P(\vartheta)} \sum_{i_0^T \in \mathcal{I}^{T+1}} p(i_0^T, \vartheta) \log \pi'_{i_0} \tag{6.16}$$

$$Q_a(\vartheta, A') \triangleq \frac{1}{P(\vartheta)} \sum_{i_0^T \in \mathcal{I}^{T+1}} p(i_0^T, \vartheta) \left(\sum_{t=1}^{T} \log a'_{i_{t-1}i_t} \right) \tag{6.17}$$

$$Q_b(\vartheta, B') \triangleq \frac{1}{P(\vartheta)} \sum_{i_0^T \in \mathcal{I}^{T+1}} p(i_0^T, \vartheta) \left(\sum_{t=1}^{T} \log b'_{i_{t-1}i_t}(x_t) \right) \tag{6.18}$$

Problem (6.5) can be solved by separately maximizing these terms.

Transition probabilities

Estimation of transition probabilities requires maximization of the following function:

$$F_a(A') \triangleq \frac{1}{P(\vartheta)} \sum_{i_0^T \in \mathcal{I}^{T+1}} p(i_0^T, \vartheta) \sum_{t=1}^{T} \log a'_{i_{t-1}i_t}$$

with the constraints:

$$a'_{ij} \geq 0, \quad \forall i, j \in \mathcal{I}$$

$$\sum_{j \in \mathcal{I}} a'_{ij} = 1, \quad \forall i \in \mathcal{I}$$

The function F_a can still be decomposed into a sum of functions, each of which depends only on the ith row a'_i of the matrix A':

$$F_a(A') = \frac{1}{P(\vartheta)} \sum_{i_0^T \in \mathcal{I}^{T+1}} p(i_0^T, \vartheta) \sum_{t=1}^T \log a'_{i_{t-1} i_t}$$

$$= \frac{1}{P(\vartheta)} \sum_{i_0^T \in \mathcal{I}^{T+1}} p(i_0^T, \vartheta) \sum_{t=1}^T \log a'_{i_{t-1} i_t} \sum_{i,j \in \mathcal{I}} \delta(i_{t-1}, i) \delta(i_t, j)$$

$$= \frac{1}{P(\vartheta)} \sum_{i,j \in \mathcal{I}} \log a'_{ij} \sum_{i_0^T \in \mathcal{I}^{T+1}} p(i_0^T, \vartheta) \sum_{t=1}^T \delta(i_{t-1}, i) \delta(i_t, j)$$

$$= \sum_{i \in \mathcal{I}} F_{a_i}(A'_i)$$

where:

$$F_{a_i}(A'_i) \triangleq \sum_{j \in \mathcal{I}} \gamma(i, j) \log a'_{ij}$$

$$\gamma(i, j) \triangleq \sum_{t=1}^T \gamma_t(i, j)$$

$$\gamma_t(i, j) \triangleq \frac{1}{P(\vartheta)} \sum_{i_0^T \in \mathcal{I}^{T+1}} p(i_0^T, \vartheta) \delta(i_{t-1}, i) \delta(i_t, j)$$

$$= \frac{1}{P(\vartheta)} \sum_{\{i_0^T \in \mathcal{I}^{T+1} : i_{t-1} = i, i_t = j\}} p(i_0^T, \vartheta)$$

This problem can be easily solved analytically, by applying the method of Lagrange multipliers for constrained optimization. This requires finding (λ, a'_i) such that:

$$\begin{cases} \dfrac{\partial}{\partial a'_{ij}} F_{a_i}(a'_i) + \lambda = 0, & \forall j \in \mathcal{I} \\ \sum_{j \in \mathcal{I}} a'_{ij} = 1 \end{cases}$$

Now, given that:

$$\frac{\partial}{\partial a'_{ij}} \sum_{l \in \mathcal{I}} \gamma(i, l) \log a'_{il} = \frac{\gamma(i, j)}{a'_{ij}}$$

the system of equations becomes:

$$\begin{cases} \gamma(i, j) + \lambda a'_{ij} = 0, & \forall j \in \mathcal{I} \\ \sum_{j \in \mathcal{I}} a'_{ij} = 1 \end{cases}$$

By summing the first set of equations and applying the constraints one gets:

$$\lambda = -\sum_{j \in \mathcal{I}} \gamma(i, j)$$

which leads to a solution expressed as:

$$a'_{ij} = \frac{\gamma(i, j)}{\sum_{l \in \mathcal{I}} \gamma(i, l)}$$

It remains to show how the quantities $\gamma_t(i, j)$ can be computed by means of the forward–backward coefficients presented in section 5.2.4. From equations (6.13), (5.28), (5.29) and (5.30), it follows that one can write, for every t:

$$\gamma_t(i, j) = \frac{1}{P(\vartheta)} \sum_{\{i_0^T : i_{t-1} = i, i_t = j\}} p(i_0^T, \vartheta)$$

$$= \frac{1}{P(\vartheta)} \sum_{\{i_0^T : i_{t-1} = i, i_t = j\}} \pi_{i_0} q(x_1^{t-1}, i_0^{t-1}, \vartheta) a_{ij} b_{ij}(x_t) q(x_{t+1}^T, i_t^T, \vartheta)$$

$$= \frac{1}{P(\vartheta)} \left(\sum_{i_0^{t-1}, i_{t-1} = i} \pi_{i_0} q(x_1^{t-1}, i_0^{t-1}, \vartheta) \right) a_{ij} b_{ij}(x_t) \left(\sum_{i_t^T, i_t = j} q(x_{t+1}^T, i_t^T, \vartheta) \right)$$

$$= \frac{\alpha_{t-1}(x_1^T, i) a_{ij} b_{ij}(x_t) \beta_t(x_1^T, j)}{\mathrm{Pr}_\vartheta(x_1^T)}$$

Output probabilities

The estimation of output distribution parameters requires the maximization of the following function:

$$F_b(B') \triangleq \frac{1}{P(\vartheta)} \sum_{i_0^T \in \mathcal{I}^{T+1}} p(i_0^T, \vartheta) \left(\sum_{t=1}^{T} \log b'_{i_{t-1}i_t}(x_t) \right) \tag{6.19}$$

In analogy with the previous section, the function can be expressed as a sum of independent terms, each of which related to a specific distribution:

$$F_b(B') = \sum_{i,j \in \mathcal{I}} F_{b_{ij}}(B'_{ij})$$

$$F_{b_{ij}}(B'_{ij}) \triangleq \sum_{t=1}^{T} \gamma_t(i, j) \log b'_{ij}(x_t) \tag{6.20}$$

where B_{ij} is the parameter set of distribution b_{ij}. We thus have:

$$\nabla_{B'_{ij}} F_{b_{ij}}(B'_{ij}) = \sum_{t=1}^{T} \gamma_t(i, j) \frac{\nabla_{B'_{ij}} b'_{ij}(x_t)}{b'_{ij}(x_t)} \tag{6.21}$$

The above general equations are used in developing reestimation formulae that depend on the parametrization of the output distributions.

Discrete output probabilities

The parameters of discrete distributions on a set of O symbols are the probabilities of the different symbols, i.e. $B_{ij} = [b_{ij}(x)]_{x=1}^{O}$. By applying the above relations a constrained maximization problem can be formulated, in analogy with the estimation of transition probabilities, leading to the following solution with the method of Lagrange multipliers:

$$b'_{ij}(x) = \frac{\sum_{t=1}^{T} \gamma_t(i,j)\delta(x, x_t)}{\gamma(i,j)}$$

Gaussian output densities

If output densities are Gaussian, as in (5.32), the unknown parameters of the density b_{ij} are the mean μ_{ij} and the covariance matrix Σ_{ij}, i.e. $B_{ij} = (\mu_{ij}, \Sigma_{ij})$. The corresponding formulae are more conveniently derived if derivatives are expressed with respect to Σ_{ij}^{-1}, the *precision matrix*. From the equalities:

$$\nabla_x (x^* \Sigma^{-1} x) = 2\Sigma^{-1} x$$

$$\nabla_\Sigma \det(\Sigma) = \det(\Sigma)\Sigma^{-1}$$

$$\nabla_{\Sigma^{-1}} (x^* \Sigma^{-1} x) = xx^*$$

where * denotes matrix transposition, one gets:

$$\nabla_{\mu_{ij}} b_{ij}(x) = b_{ij}(x)\Sigma_{ij}^{-1}(x - \mu_{ij})$$

$$\nabla_{\Sigma_{ij}^{-1}} b_{ij}(x) = \frac{1}{2} b_{ij}(x)\left(\Sigma_{ij} - (x - \mu_{ij})(x - \mu_{ij})^*\right)$$

and hence:

$$\nabla_{\mu'_{ij}} F_{b_{ij}}(\mu'_{ij}, \Sigma'_{ij}) = \sum_{t=1}^{T} \gamma_t(i,j)\Sigma_{ij}'^{-1}(x_t - \mu'_{ij}) \tag{6.22}$$

$$= \Sigma_{ij}'^{-1}\left(\sum_{t=1}^{T} \gamma_t(i,j)x_t - \gamma(i,j)\mu'_{ij}\right)$$

$$\nabla_{\Sigma_{ij}'^{-1}} F_{b_{ij}}(\mu'_{ij}, \Sigma'_{ij}) = \frac{1}{2}\sum_{t=1}^{T} \gamma_t(i,j)\left(\Sigma'_{ij} - (x_t - \mu'_{ij})(x_t - \mu'_{ij})^*\right) \tag{6.23}$$

In this case the solutions can be found simply by setting to zero these derivatives:

$$\mu'_{ij} = \frac{\sum_{t=1}^{T} \gamma_t(i,j) x_t}{\gamma(i,j)}$$

$$\Sigma'_{ij} = \frac{\sum_{t=1}^{T} \gamma_t(i,j)(x_t - \mu'_{ij})(x_t - \mu'_{ij})^*}{\gamma(i,j)}$$

$$= \frac{\sum_{t=1}^{T} \gamma_t(i,j) x_t x_t^*}{\gamma(i,j)} - \mu'_{ij}\mu'^*_{ij}$$

It is evident from the above relations that the constraints on the covariance matrix Σ_{ij}, namely symmetricity and positive definiteness, are satisfied in the reestimation step.

Mixture output densities ·

In the case of mixture densities, the probability density associated to every transition has the form:

$$b_{ij}(x) = \sum_{k \in \mathcal{K}} w_{ijk} b_{ijk}(x)$$

where $\mathcal{K}$, the set of mixture indexes, for the sake of conciseness, is supposed to be the same for all transitions. The likelihood function $P(\vartheta)$ can be rewritten as follows in a form which is compatible with (6.1):

$$P(\vartheta) \triangleq \mathrm{Pr}_\vartheta(x_1^T)$$

$$= \sum_{i_0^T \in \mathcal{I}^{T+1}} \mathrm{Pr}_\vartheta(x_1^T, i_0^T)$$

$$= \sum_{i_0^T \in \mathcal{I}^{T+1}} \pi_{i_0} \prod_{t=1}^{T} \left(a_{i_{t-1} i_t} \sum_{k \in \mathcal{K}} w_{i_{t-1} i_t k} b_{i_{t-1} i_t k}(x_t) \right)$$

$$= \sum_{i_0^T \in \mathcal{I}^{T+1}, k_1^T \in \mathcal{K}^T} \pi_{i_0} \prod_{t=1}^{T} a_{i_{t-1} i_t} w_{i_{t-1} i_t k_t} b_{i_{t-1} i_t k_t}(x_t)$$

$$= \sum_{i_0^T \in \mathcal{I}^{T+1}, k_1^T \in \mathcal{K}^t} p(i_0^T, k_1^T, \vartheta)$$

where:

$$p(i_0^T, k_1^T, \vartheta) \triangleq \pi_{i_0} \prod_{t=1}^{T} a_{i_{t-1} i_t} w_{i_{t-1} i_t k_t} b_{i_{t-1} i_t k_t}(x_t) \qquad (6.24)$$

The role of the variable ξ in (6.1) is thus played by the pair of sequences (i_0^T, k_1^T). Then, the corresponding auxiliary function is:

$$Q(\vartheta, \vartheta') = \frac{1}{P(\vartheta)} \sum_{i_0^T, k_1^T} p(i_0^T, k_1^T, \vartheta)$$

$$\times \left(\log \pi'_{i_0} + \sum_{t=1}^{T} \left(\log a'_{i_{t-1}i_t} + \log w'_{i_{t-1}i_t k_t} + \log b'_{i_{t-1}i_t k_t}(x_t) \right) \right)$$

which again can be split into different terms depending only on different components of the parameter set ϑ. Considering the term corresponding to the mixture weights:

$$Q_w(\vartheta, w') \triangleq \frac{1}{P(\vartheta)} \sum_{i_0^T, k_1^T} p(i_0^T, k_1^T, \vartheta) \sum_{t=1}^{T} \log w'_{i_{t-1}i_t k_t}$$

it is possible to decompose as before the objective function in terms which only depend on the weights of a single mixture:

$$F_w(w') = \sum_{i,j} F_{w_{ij}}(w'_{ij}) \tag{6.25}$$

where:

$$F_{w_{ij}}(w'_{ij}) \triangleq \sum_{k} \gamma(i,j,k) \log w'_{ijk} \tag{6.26}$$

$$\gamma(i,j,k) \triangleq \sum_{t=1}^{T} \gamma_t(i,j,k)$$

$$\gamma_t(i,j,k) \triangleq \frac{1}{P(\vartheta)} \sum_{i_0^T, k_1^T} p(i_0^T, k_1^T, \vartheta)\delta(i_{t-1}, i)\delta(i_t, j)\delta(k_t, k)$$

The maximization of $F_{w_{ij}}(w_{ij})$ is easily carried out by means of the Lagrange method, leading to the following solution:

$$w'_{ijk} = \frac{\gamma(i,j,k)}{\sum_{l \in K} \gamma(i,j,l)} \tag{6.27}$$

By applying the same method used to find the expression of $\gamma_t(i,j)$, one gets:

$$\gamma_t(i,j,k) = \frac{w_{ijk}b_{ijk}(x_t)}{b_{ij}(x_t)}\gamma_t(i,j) \tag{6.28}$$

The reestimation formulae for the parameters of the mixture components are analogous to those of single Gaussians, with the $\gamma_t(i,j)$ coefficients replaced by $\gamma_t(i,j,k)$.

6.3.3. Summary of Baum–Welch ML Reestimation Formulae

This section is a summary of the formulae for Baum–Welch reestimation of HMM parameters. The discussion in previous sections assumed a single observation sequence, which is clearly too limited for ASR applications, especially when left-to-right topologies are used. However, the above method can be generalized to consider multiple examples. The following formulae will thus assume that a set $\mathcal{L}$ of training samples is available. A sample in $\mathcal{L}$ will be denoted by x, without explicit reference to its length; that will be denoted by $T(x)$ when necessary. In the case of multiple training sequences, the objective function is $\mathrm{Pr}_\vartheta(\mathcal{L}) = \prod_{x \in \mathcal{L}} \mathrm{Pr}_\vartheta(x)$ and the auxiliary function Q becomes the sum of the individual auxiliary functions of the sequences. The discussion in section 6.2 then applies unmodified, leading to the expressions appearing in this summary. Furthermore, if an observation is composed of a vector with independent components, so that the output probability is computed as a product of the probabilities of each component, as frequently happens in discrete modelling, the factors of the product density are individually estimated with these formulae.

In the following expressions, $i, j \in \mathcal{I}$ will denote model states, $k \in \mathcal{K}$ will denote a mixture component index, and $h = 1 \ldots D$ will be used as an index for the components of observation vectors or means and standard deviations of Gaussians. With the above assumption, the basic quantities needed for the reestimation are defined as follows:

$$\gamma(i) \triangleq \sum_{j \in \mathcal{I}} (\gamma(i,j) + \gamma^\varepsilon(i,j)) \tag{6.29}$$

$$\gamma(i,j) \triangleq \sum_{x \in \mathcal{L}} \sum_{t=1}^{T(x)} \gamma_t(x,i,j) \tag{6.30}$$

$$\gamma^\varepsilon(i,j) \triangleq \sum_{x \in \mathcal{L}} \sum_{t=0}^{T(x)} \gamma_t^\varepsilon(x,i,j) \tag{6.31}$$

$$\gamma(i,j,k) \triangleq \sum_{x \in \mathcal{L}} \sum_{t=1}^{T(x)} \gamma_t(x,i,j,k) \tag{6.32}$$

$$\gamma_t(x,i,j) \triangleq \frac{\alpha_{t-1}(x,i) a_{ij} b_{ij}(x_t) \beta_t(x,j)}{\mathrm{Pr}_\vartheta(x)} \tag{6.33}$$

$$\gamma_t^\varepsilon(x,i,j) \triangleq \frac{\alpha_t(x,i) a_{ij}^\varepsilon \beta_t(x,j)}{\mathrm{Pr}_\vartheta(x)} \tag{6.34}$$

$$\gamma_t(x,i,j,k) \triangleq \frac{w_{ijk} b_{ijk}(x_t)}{b_{ij}(x_t)} \gamma_t(x,i,j) \tag{6.35}$$

For the relations corresponding to Gaussian densities, the following quantities are also defined:

$$s(i,j,k) \triangleq \sum_{x \in \mathcal{L}} \sum_{t=1}^{T(x)} \gamma_t(\boldsymbol{x},i,j,k) x_t \tag{6.36}$$

$$s_*(i,j,k) \triangleq \sum_{x \in \mathcal{L}} \sum_{t=1}^{T(x)} \gamma_t(\boldsymbol{x},i,j,k) x_t x_t^* \tag{6.37}$$

$$s_2(i,j,k)_h \triangleq \sum_{x \in \mathcal{L}} \sum_{t=1}^{T(x)} \gamma_t(\boldsymbol{x},i,j,k) x_{th}^2 \tag{6.38}$$

together with their analogous $s(i,j)$, $s_*(i,j)$ and $s_2(i,j)_h$ that are obtained by ignoring the mixture component index k.

Once the above quantities have been computed, the parameter values are updated as shown in the following relations, that include expressions for empty transitions and different types of output distributions. In the case of Gaussian distributions, Σ refers to the full covariance matrix, while σ refers to the standard deviations of the components when the covariance matrix is assumed to be diagonal.

Initial probabilities

$$\pi_i' = \frac{\pi_i \sum_{x \in \mathcal{L}} \beta_0(\boldsymbol{x},i)}{\sum_{x \in \mathcal{L}} \mathrm{Pr}_\vartheta(\boldsymbol{x})} \tag{6.39}$$

Transition probabilities

$$d_{ij}' = \frac{\gamma(i,j)}{\gamma(i)} \tag{6.40}$$

$$d_{ij}'^\varepsilon = \frac{\gamma^\varepsilon(i,j)}{\gamma(i)} \tag{6.41}$$

Discrete output probabilities

$$b_{ij}'(x) = \frac{\sum_{x \in \mathcal{L}} \sum_{t=1}^{T(x)} \gamma_t(\boldsymbol{x},i,j)\delta(x,x_t)}{\gamma(i,j)} \tag{6.42}$$

Gaussian output probabilities

$$\mu'_{ij} = \frac{s(i,j)}{\gamma(i,j)} \tag{6.43}$$

$$\Sigma'_{ij} = \frac{s_*(i,j)}{\gamma(i,i)} - \mu'_{ij}\mu'^*_{ij} \tag{6.44}$$

$$\sigma'^2_{ijh} = \frac{s_2(i,j)_h}{\gamma(i,j)} - \mu'^2_{ijh} \tag{6.45}$$

Gaussian mixture output probabilities

$$w'_{ijk} = \frac{\gamma(i,j,k)}{\gamma(i,j)} \tag{6.46}$$

$$\mu'_{ijk} = \frac{s(i,j,k)}{\gamma(i,j,k)} \tag{6.47}$$

$$\Sigma'_{ijk} = \frac{s_*(i,j,k)}{\gamma(i,j,k)} - \mu'_{ij}\mu'^*_{ij} \tag{6.48}$$

$$\sigma'^2_{ijkh} = \frac{s_2(i,j,k)_h}{\gamma(i,j,k)} - \mu'^2_{ijkh} \tag{6.49}$$

6.3.4. Training Models with Shared Distributions

The reestimation formulae can be easily adapted to take into account shared distributions. In this case, γ accumulators can be associated to the distributions themselves. A shared distribution can be referred to by different arcs, or even by different mixtures if it is a single Gaussian in a mixture-based system. In the former case, for a distribution b, there will be a set $\mathcal{A}(b)$ of pairs (i,j) for which $b_{ij} = b$. The associated accumulators are then defined as:

$$\gamma(b) \triangleq \sum_{x \in \mathcal{L}} \sum_{t=1}^{T(x)} \gamma_t(x, b)$$

$$\gamma_t(x, b) \triangleq \sum_{(i,j) \in \mathcal{A}(b)} \gamma_t(x, i, j)$$

These quantities are then substituted in the reestimation formulae in place of the arc-related ones. For example, the new mean of a Gaussian is computed as follows:

$$\mu'_b = \frac{\sum_{x \in \mathcal{L}} \sum_{t=1}^{T(x)} \gamma_t(x, b) x_t}{\gamma(b)}$$

If a Gaussian is referred to as mixture component, then the set $\mathcal{A}(b)$ will be composed of triples (i, j, k) including a pair of states and a mixture index, and the consequent formulae are obtained accordingly.

6.3.5. Dealing with Singularities

The sequence of estimates for a parameter may converge at the boundary of the allowed region. This means, for example, that transition probabilities may tend to zero. Given that transition probabilities have only few degrees of freedom, if compared to other components of the parameter set, it is reasonable to accept this as statistical evidence, if it happens, and remove the transition from the model. The case of discrete output probabilities is different. It may happen that the numerator in (6.42) for a particular symbol $\hat{x}$ is zero because $\hat{x}$ never occurs in the training data. The direct application of (6.42) would yield a null estimated probability for that symbol in all the distributions, resulting in a model which assigns a null probability to a sequence if it happens to contain an occurrence of $\hat{x}$. This often happens in HMM modelling of speech, and can be solved in different ways. A possibility is to choose a floor ε and ensure that no probability value is lower than that. The behaviour of the resulting models is not highly sensitive to the actual value of ε (Levinson *et al.*, 1983). A simple way of imposing a floor on the probabilities is to replace (6.42) by:

$$b'_{ij}(x) = (1 - O\varepsilon) \frac{\sum_{x \in \mathcal{L}} \sum_{t=1}^{T(x)} \gamma_t(\boldsymbol{x}, i, j) \delta(x, x_t)}{\gamma(i, j)} + \varepsilon \qquad (6.50)$$

where O is the size of the symbol alphabet. Alternatively, a post-processing iterative procedure on the estimated densities can be applied, where the probability values lower than ε are replaced by ε, and the other ones are properly rescaled to satisfy the stochasticity constraint (Levinson *et al.*, 1983). This is repeated until no values fall below the threshold. It is easily seen that (6.50) performs an interpolation between the density estimated with (6.42) and a uniform density on the O symbols, with weights given by $(1 - O\varepsilon)$ and $O\varepsilon$, respectively. Instead of using a uniform density, one could also choose to "smooth" the density by interpolating it with a more general one, such as an average distribution on symbols. Moreover, instead of fixing the weights, it is possible to automatically determine them by means of *deleted interpolation* (Bahl *et al.*, 1983). Another possible consequence of sparseness in the training data appears when using continuous densities. In this case, it may happen that the covariance matrix of some Gaussian densities approaches a singular matrix. In the diagonal-covariance densities, this means that some of the variances of the components approach zero. Again, a simple solution is to set a threshold on the variances, or to interpolate them with those coming from a Gaussian with a greater variance. Instead of substituting small variances with a lower bound, a constant value can be added to every variance, as discussed in

Paul (1995). However, the vanishing of variances is most often a consequence of the fact that some densities get very low counters during the processing of the training data, indicating that the tying scheme should be modified.

6.4. MAXIMUM *A POSTERIORI* (MAP) ESTIMATION

In MAP estimation, it is supposed that an unknown parameter is a random variable itself, with a given probability density $g(\vartheta)$. This density is supposed to embody some *a priori* knowledge on the possible parameter values. Instead of seeking the value that maximizes $\Pr_\vartheta(x_1^T) = \Pr(x_1^T|\vartheta)$, it is natural, in this case, to look for the values that has maximum probability of occurring given the training data, that is the one which maximizes $\Pr(\vartheta|x_1^T)$ or equivalently $\Pr(\vartheta, x_1^T)$. The optimization problem to be solved then becomes:

$$\tilde{\vartheta} = \operatorname*{argmax}_{\vartheta} g(\vartheta) \Pr_\vartheta(x_1^T) \tag{6.51}$$

This estimation procedure is often used for parameter *adaptation* problems, when the parameter set of a model has to be modified by using a limited amount of training data in order to compensate for the adverse effect of a mismatch between training and testing data. In this case, the prior density on the parameters often has a mode which is located around the values corresponding to an already trained model, and prevents large deviations of the parameters unless a strong evidence is present in the adaptation examples.

ML estimation can be seen as a case of improper MAP estimation, when the *a priori* density is not informative. If $P(\vartheta) = \Pr_\vartheta(x_1^T)$ is expressed as in (6.1), then the objective function for MAP estimation is

$$R(\vartheta) = g(\vartheta)P(\vartheta) = \int g(\vartheta)p(\xi, \vartheta) \, d\xi \tag{6.52}$$

which is still in a form compatible with formulation (6.1) with the substitution $p(\xi, \vartheta) \to g(\vartheta)p(\xi, \vartheta)$. This means that the Baum–Welch algorithm can be applied also in this case. The corresponding auxiliary function is:

$$Q_{\text{MAP}}(\vartheta, \vartheta') = \log g(\vartheta') + \frac{1}{P(\vartheta)} \int p(\xi, \vartheta) \log p(\xi, \vartheta') \, d\xi$$

$$= \log g(\vartheta') + Q(\vartheta, \vartheta') \tag{6.53}$$

The results of section 6.2 can thus be applied without modifications to this problem, requiring the solution of a series of optimization problems involving the function Q_{MAP}. The actual expression of this function and the resulting formulae depend, in this case, also on the assumptions made about the *a priori* density $g(\vartheta)$, which has to be statistically meaningful and allow for an easy solution of the intermediate problems. A discussion on this subject can be found in Gauvain and Lee (1994) and Huo *et al.* (1995), whose approach will be followed here to derive MAP reestimation formulae for HMMs. Prior density parameter estimation and incremental estimation are discussed in Chapter 11 in the framework of speaker adaptation.

6.4.1. Assumptions on the Prior Density

The prior densities of the different components of the ϑ parameter set will be assumed to be mutually independent. In the case of models with mixture distributions, for example, the global prior density has the form:

$$g(\vartheta) = g(\pi, A, w, B)$$

$$= g_\pi(\pi)\left(\prod_{i\in\mathcal{I}} g_{a_i}(a_i)\right)\prod_{i,j\in\mathcal{I}}\left(g_{w_{ij}}(w_{ij})\prod_{k\in\mathcal{K}} g_{b_{ijk}}(\mu_{ijk}, \Sigma_{ijk})\right) \quad (6.54)$$

This choice allows the optimization problem to be split into different subproblems involving only a single component of the parameter set, as for the MLE case.

For a parameter set component involving a set of discrete probabilities, as is the case of initial probabilities, transition probabilities, discrete output probabilities, and mixture weights, a Dirichlet prior will be assumed, which is defined on the simplex:

$$\left\{r \in \mathbb{R}^L : r > 0, \sum_{l=1}^L r_l = 1\right\}$$

by:

$$f(r) \triangleq c\prod_{l=1}^L r_l^{\zeta_l - 1} \quad (6.55)$$

This density is parametrized by the vector of positive exponents $[\zeta_l]_{l=1}^L$. In this section, the variable c appearing in the definitions of densities refers to different normalization constants whose values do not influence the following computations.

For the parameters of full covariance D-dimensional Gaussian densities, the prior density will be a normal-Wishart density:

$$f(\mu, \Sigma) \triangleq c\sqrt{\det(\Sigma)^{(D-\eta)}}\exp\left(-\frac{\tau}{2}(\mu - m)^*\Sigma^{-1}(\mu - m) - \frac{1}{2}\mathrm{tr}(S\Sigma^{-1})\right) \quad (6.56)$$

which is parametrized by the the two values $\eta > D - 1$, $\tau > 0$, the vector m and the symmetric positive definite matrix S.

For diagonal covariance matrices, a product of normal-gamma is used:

$$f(\mu, \sigma) = c \left(\prod_{l=1}^{D} \sigma_l^{(1-2\eta_l)} \right) \exp\left(-\sum_{l=1}^{D} \frac{\tau_l(\mu_l - m_l)^2}{2\sigma_l^2} + \frac{\rho_l}{\sigma_l^2} \right) \tag{6.57}$$

whose parameters are the D-dimensional vectors $\eta > 0$, $\tau > 0$, $\rho > 0$ and m.

6.4.2. Baum–Welch MAP Reestimation Formulae

To obtain relations for the MAP reestimation of HMM parameters, one can apply the same procedure as for MLE in section 6.3.2. The auxiliary function Q_{MAP} is decomposed into a sum of terms each of which depends only on some components. These terms are then maximized separately. Computations are made more complex by the presence of the prior densities, without qualitative changes. In the following, the reestimation of the parameters of Gaussian mixture densities, which is the most complex case, will be considered.

Mixture weights

The independence assumption about prior densities of different components of the parameter set, expressed by equation (6.54), together with expression (6.53) for the auxiliary function Q_{MAP} and the properties of the Q function found in section 6.3.2, allow one to conclude that the reestimation of the mixture weights of the density associated with transition $i \rightarrow j$ can be carried out by considering only the following objective function:

$$G_{w_{ij}}(w'_{ij}) \triangleq \log g_{w_{ij}}(w'_{ij}) + F_{w_{ij}}(w'_{ij}) \tag{6.58}$$

where $F_{w_{ij}}(w'_{ij})$ is given by (6.26), and $g_{w_{ij}}$ is the Dirichlet density defined by:

$$g_{w_{ij}}(w'_{ij}) \triangleq c \prod_{k \in \mathcal{K}} w'^{\zeta_{ijk}-1}_{ijk} \tag{6.59}$$

By applying the method of the Lagrange multipliers, the system of equations to be solved becomes:

$$\begin{cases} \dfrac{\partial}{\partial w'_{ij}} \left(\log g_{w_{ij}}(w'_{ij}) + F_{w_{ij}}(w'_{ij}) \right) + \lambda = 0, & \forall k \in \mathcal{K} \\ \displaystyle\sum_{k \in \mathcal{K}} w'_{ijk} = 1 \end{cases} \tag{6.60}$$

that is:

$$\begin{cases} \gamma(i, j, k) + \zeta_{ijk} - 1 + \lambda w'_{ijk} = 0, & \forall k \in \mathcal{K} \\ \displaystyle\sum_{k \in \mathcal{K}} w'_{ijk} = 1 \end{cases} \tag{6.61}$$

whose solution is:

$$w'_{ijk} = \frac{\zeta_{ijk} - 1 + \gamma(i,j,k)}{\sum_{l \in \mathcal{K}} (\zeta_{ijl} - 1 + \gamma(i,j,l))} \tag{6.62}$$

A comparison between this equation and the ML estimate of the mixture weights, expressed by (6.27), shows that the MAP estimate is an average between the mode of the prior density and the ML estimate, with proportions given by $\sum_{l \in \mathcal{K}}(\zeta_{ijl} - 1)$ and $\sum_{l \in \mathcal{K}} \gamma(i,j,l)$, respectively. The mode of the Dirichlet density is in fact given by

$$\left[\frac{\zeta_k - 1}{\sum_l (\zeta_l - 1)} \right]_{k \in \mathcal{K}}$$

in the hypothesis that $\zeta_k > 1, \forall k \in \mathcal{K}$.

Gaussian means and variances

The function to be maximized for the reestimation of mean and covariance matrix of a Gaussian mixture component $b_{ijk} = \mathcal{N}_{\mu_{ijk}, \Sigma_{ijk}}$ is:

$$G_{b_{ijk}}(\mu'_{ijk}, \Sigma'_{ijk}) = \log g_{b_{ijk}}(\mu'_{ijk}, \Sigma'_{ijk}) + F_{b_{ijk}}(\mu'_{ijk}, \Sigma'_{ijk}) \tag{6.63}$$

where:

$$F_{b_{ijk}}(\mu'_{ijk}, \Sigma'_{ijk}) = \sum_{t=1}^{T} \gamma_t(i,j,k) \log \mathcal{N}_{\mu'_{ijk}, \Sigma'_{ijk}}(x_t) \tag{6.64}$$

is the objective function corresponding to ML estimation. In this case the solution of the optimization problem is found by solving the following system of equations:

$$\begin{cases} \nabla_{\mu'_{ijk}} G_{b_{ijk}}(\mu'_{ijk}, \Sigma'_{ijk}) = 0 \\ \nabla_{\Sigma'^{-1}_{ijk}} G_{b_{ijk}}(\mu'_{ijk}, \Sigma'_{ijk}) = 0 \end{cases} \tag{6.65}$$

From equation (6.56) one can compute the derivatives of the prior distributions:

$$\nabla_{\mu'_{ijk}} \log g_{b_{ijk}}(\mu'_{ijk}, \Sigma'_{ijk}) = \tau_{ijk} \Sigma'^{-1}_{ijk}(m_{ijk} - \mu'_{ijk})$$

$$\nabla_{\Sigma'^{-1}_{ijk}} \log g_{b_{ijk}}(\mu'_{ijk}, \Sigma'_{ijk}) = \frac{(\eta_{ijk} - D)\Sigma'_{ijk} - S - \tau_{ijk}(\mu'_{ijk} - m_{ijk})(\mu'_{ijk} - m_{ijk})^*}{2}$$

By substituting into the system (6.65) these expressions and the derivatives of $F_{b_{ijk}}$, which are analogous to (6.22) and (6.23), a system of equations is obtained which can be explicitly solved, leading to:

$$\mu'_{ijk} = \frac{\tau_{ijk} m_{ijk} + \sum_{t=1}^{T} \gamma_t(i,j,k) x_t}{\tau_{ijk} + \gamma(i,j,k)}$$

$$\Sigma'_{ijk} = \frac{S_{ijk} + \tau_{ijk}(\mu'_{ijk} - m_{ijk})(\mu'_{ijk} - m_{ijk})^* + \sum_{t=1}^{T} \gamma_t(i,j,k)(x_t - \mu'_{ijk})(x_t - \mu'_{ijk})^*}{\gamma(i,j,k) + \eta_{ijk} - D}$$

$$= \frac{S_{ijk} + \tau_{ijk} m_{ijk} m_{ijk}^* + \sum_{t=1}^{T} \gamma_t(i,j,k) x_t x_t^* - (\tau_{ijk} + \gamma(i,j,k))\mu'_{ijk}\mu'^{*}_{ijk}}{\gamma(i,j,k) + \eta_{ijk} - D}$$

6.4.3. Summary of Baum–Welch MAP Reestimation Formulae

In this section, a summary of MAP reestimation formulae obtained by applying the Baum–Welch algorithm is presented. The same considerations and definitions of section 6.3.3 are still valid here. The hyperparameters, i.e. the parameters of the prior distributions, are referenced in accordance to the definitions in section 6.4.1. In order to simplify notations, hyperparameters of Dirichlet densities will always be denoted by the symbol ζ. This should not induce confusion, since prior densities are local to the parameter set components (i.e. transitions leaving a state, discrete output probabilities of a single distribution, etc.), and it is always clear from the context which density has to be applied. If empty transitions are present, then the prior densities hyperparameters are composed of two N-dimensional vectors, ζ and ζ^ε. Expressions for single Gaussians are not given here, as they are immediately obtained from those related to mixture components by neglecting the mixture component index.

Initial probabilities

$$\pi'_i = \frac{\zeta_i - 1 + \pi_i \sum_{x \in \mathcal{L}} \beta_0(x,i)}{\sum_{x \in \mathcal{L}} \mathrm{Pr}_\vartheta(x) + \sum_{j \in \mathcal{I}}(\zeta_j - 1)}$$

Transition probabilities

$$d'_{ij} = \frac{\zeta_{ij} - 1 + \gamma(i,j)}{\gamma(i) + \sum_{l \in \mathcal{I}}(\zeta_{il} - 1) + \sum_{l \in \mathcal{I}}(\zeta^\varepsilon_{il} - 1)}$$

$$a'^{\varepsilon}_{ij} = \frac{\zeta^\varepsilon_{ij} - 1 + \gamma^\varepsilon(i,j)}{\gamma(i) + \sum_{l \in \mathcal{I}}(\zeta_{il} - 1) + \sum_{l \in \mathcal{I}}(\zeta^\varepsilon_{il} - 1)}$$

Discrete output probabilities

$$b'_{ij}(x) = \frac{\zeta_{ijx} - 1 + \sum_{x \in \mathcal{L}} \sum_{t=1}^{T(x)} \gamma_t(x, i, j)\delta(x, x_t)}{\gamma(i, j) + \sum_{y=1}^{O} (\zeta_{ijy} - 1)}$$

Gaussian mixture output probabilities

$$w'_{ijk} = \frac{\zeta_{ijk} - 1 + \gamma(i, j, k)}{\gamma(i, j) + \sum_{l \in \mathcal{K}} (\zeta_{ijl} - 1)}$$

Full covariance matrix:

$$\mu'_{ijk} = \frac{\tau_{ijk} m_{ijk} + s(i, j, k)}{\tau_{ijk} + \gamma(i, j, k)}$$

$$\Sigma'_{ijk} = \frac{S_{ijk} + \tau_{ijk} m_{ijk} m^*_{ijk} + s_*(i, j, k) - (\tau_{ijk} + \gamma(i, j, k))\mu'_{ijk}\mu'^{*}_{ijk}}{\gamma(i, j, k) + \eta_{ijk} - D}$$

Diagonal covariance matrix:

$$\mu'_{ijkh} = \frac{\tau_{ijkh} m_{ijkh} + s(i, j, k)_h}{\tau_{ijkh} + \gamma(i, j, k)}$$

$$\sigma'^2_{ijkh} = \frac{2\rho_{ijkh} + \tau_{ijkh} m^2_{ijkh} + s_2(i, j, k)_h - (\tau_{ijkh} + \gamma(i, j, k))\mu'^2_{ijkh}}{\gamma(i, j, k) + 2\eta_{ijkh} - 1}$$

6.5. GENERATION OF SEED MODELS

The iterative nature of the parameter estimation procedure requires an initial guess for the model parameter set. When applying MAP reestimation, the initial parameter set often comes from an already trained model, which embodies some characteristics of the corresponding acoustic unit. For ML estimation, the starting model has to be built differently. A uniform initialization is often a reasonable choice for distributions on discrete spaces, such as discrete output distributions and transition probabilities, reflecting a total lack of information about the value of the parameters. For continuous unbounded spaces, there is no such thing as a uniform density.

In the case of single Gaussian densities, a neutral choice is a Gaussian whose mean and covariance matrix are taken from the statistics of the training data. All the densities in the model are initialized in the same way. They are expected to specialize during training. If the transition matrix is full, however, a flat initialization of the transition probabilities, coupled with an identical starting point for the output densities, would make all the states equivalent, a property that would be preserved by the training algorithm. To avoid this inconvenience, the means of the initial densities can be randomly perturbed.

Densities based on Gaussian mixtures have a high number of degrees of freedom, and a more careful initialization is thus important. A common method for generating an initial Gaussian mixture is based on the use of an unsupervised clustering procedure. Once the number of mixture components has been chosen, the training data are clustered in the desired number of clusters, and the centroids are then taken as means for the Gaussian components. The variances can be computed with statistics on the clusters. In this way, all the mixtures will have the same number of components. An alternative method of initializing mixtures which allows for a more specific control of the number of components in different mixtures relies on a progressive increase of the number of Gaussians. The distributions are initially defined with a single Gaussian. After a few training iterations, some of the Gaussians are "split", that is, they are replaced by a mixture of two or more Gaussians whose means are obtained by perturbations of the original mean. The weights associated to the newly generated Gaussians are computed by uniformly distributing the weight of the generating Gaussian. Then, the model is trained again. The splitting procedure can be repeated so as to reach a desired number of basic densities. This number can be decided on the basis of the amount of training data. The choice of which densities are to be split can be based on different criteria. One can decide to split the Gaussians with the broadest variances, or those with the highest mixture weights, or finally those with the highest accumulators as computed during the training step.

6.6. NOTES ON THE BAUM-WELCH ALGORITHM

The first references to Baum Welch reestimation formulae were based on the following theorem (Baum and Eagon, 1967).

Baum–Eagon Theorem. *Let F be a homogeneous polynomial with non-negative coefficients in the variable*

$$x = [x_{ij}]_{i=1,\dots,N, i=1\dots M_i}$$

Let U be the domain defined by:

$$U \triangleq \left\{ x : x_{ij} \geq 0, \sum_{j=1}^{M_i} x_{ij} = 1, i = 1\dots N, j = 1\dots M_i \right\}$$

Then the transformation $T : U \to U$ defined by:

$$T(x) \triangleq \left[\frac{x_{ij}(\partial F(x)/\partial x_{ij})}{\sum_{h=1}^{M_i} x_{ih}(\partial F(x)/\partial x_{ih})} \right]_{i=1\ldots N, j=1\ldots M_i} \tag{6.66}$$

is a growth transformation for F on U, i.e.

$$F(T(x)) > F(x) \text{ unless } T(x) = x$$

The proof of the above proposition relies on purely geometrical arguments and depends on the polynomial nature of function F. It can be directly applied to the problem of estimating discrete HMMs, since, in this case, the likelihood function is exactly a homogeneous polynomial with respect to the model parameters. By computing the derivatives and applying relation (6.66), one gets exactly the same formulae found in section 6.3.3 for the discrete parameters. However, the above approach would not be suitable for different functions, or different optimization domains. A completely different derivation, which greatly generalized the applicability of the formulae, can be found in Baum *et al.* (1970). This is the approach followed in the present chapter, since it allows to find a unified framework for discrete and continuous parameter estimation.

In Dempster *et al.* (1977), the *EM algorithm* is presented in the paradigm of a statistical estimation problem involving *incomplete* data and *complete* data, giving a unified formalization of several specialized estimation methods used in statistics.

It is assumed that two random variables Y in $\mathcal{Y}$ and Z in $\mathcal{Z}$ are given, related by a functional relation $Z = o(Y)$, where o is a mapping $o : \mathcal{Y} \to \mathcal{Z}$. If a parametric density f_ϑ is given on the complete data space $\mathcal{Y}$, then the density induced on the incomplete data space $\mathcal{Z}$ is:

$$g_\vartheta(z) = \int_{\mathcal{Y}} f_\vartheta(y)\delta(o(y) - z) \, dy \tag{6.67}$$

The symbol δ, with a single argument, denotes here the Dirac functional. Given a sample in the incomplete data space, the objective is to find ϑ so as to maximize the sample likelihood, which is only indirectly known through (6.67). In the above-mentioned paper, the EM algorithm is proposed in two formulations, the first one of which is restricted to the case where the f_ϑ density is a member of the exponential family. In its most general formulation, the EM algorithm relies on the use of the function:

$$Q(\vartheta'|\vartheta) \triangleq E(\log(f_{\vartheta'}))|z, \vartheta) \tag{6.68}$$

where E is the expectation operator, and generates a sequence of estimates $\vartheta_{(n)}$ as follows:

$$\vartheta_{(n)} \triangleq \operatorname*{argmax}_{\vartheta'} Q(\vartheta'|\vartheta_{(n-1)}) \tag{6.69}$$

The sequence generated according to (6.69) is shown to increase the likelihood at every iteration and to converge under some assumption about the differential properties of the densities.

With the substitutions $f_\vartheta(y) \to p(y, \vartheta)$ and $dy \to \delta(o(y) - z)\, dy$, the likelihood expressed by (6.67) turns out to be exactly in the same functional form as (6.1). Moreover, by expanding (6.68), one gets:

$$Q(\vartheta' | \vartheta) = E(\log(f_{\vartheta'}) | z, \vartheta)$$

$$= \frac{1}{g_\vartheta(z)} \int_y \log(f_{\vartheta'}(y)) f_\vartheta(y) \delta(o(y) - z)\, dy \qquad (6.70)$$

which is analogous of (6.2). Therefore, the EM algorithm expressed by (6.67), (6.68) and (6.69) is in fact an instance of the Baum–Welch algorithm, which was formulated in section 6.2 without assigning a statistical meaning to the functions involved.

In the case of HMMs, the incomplete data correspond to observation sequences x_1^T, the complete data correspond to observation sequences aligned with model states, i.e. to pairs (i_0^T, x_1^T), and the o function is a projection, $o(i_0^T, x_1^T) = x_1^T$. By examining the quantities computed for applying the Baum–Welch algorithm, one sees that they correspond to making an estimation of the *sufficient statistics* (see e.g. DeGroot, 1970) of the complete-data densities given the current value of the parameter ϑ and the training observation. For example, the numerator used for reestimating transition probabilities is the expected number of times that the transition has been taken in emitting the observation. To see this, let $c(i, j, i_0^T)$ be the number of times transition $i \to j$ is contained in path i_0^T, i.e:

$$c(i, j, i_0^T) \triangleq \sum_{t=1}^{T} \delta(i_{t-1}, i) \delta(i_t, j)$$

If the state sequence could be observed directly, a sample would consist of a sequence i_0^T, and the corresponding maximum likelihood estimation of the transition probability a'_{ij} would be obtained through the above counters as:

$$a'_{ij} = \frac{c(i, j, i_0^T)}{\sum_{l \in \mathcal{I}} c(i, l, i_0^T)} \qquad (6.71)$$

The counters $\left[c(i, j, i_0^T)\right]_{j \in \mathcal{I}}$ are sufficient statistics for the discrete probability density $[a_{ij}]_{j \in \mathcal{I}}$. When the state sequence is only indirectly observed through the emission sequence x_1^T, the direct solution given by (6.71) is replaced by an iterative procedure in which successive approximations of the unknown probabilities are computed by replacing the counters $c(i, j, i_0^T)$ with $\gamma(i, j, x_1^T)$, their expected values given the observation and the current value of the parameters. In fact, by looking at the definitions of the γ quantities, one can write:

$$\gamma(i, j, x_1^T) = \sum_{t=1}^{T} \gamma_t(i, j, x_1^T)$$

$$= \sum_{t-1}^{T} \sum_{i_0^T} \Pr_\vartheta(i_0^T | x_1^T) \delta(i_{t-1}, i) \delta(i_t, j)$$

$$= \sum_{i_0^T} \Pr_\vartheta(i_0^T | x_1^T) \left(\sum_{t=1}^{T} \delta(i_{t-1}, i) \delta(i_t, j) \right)$$

$$= \sum_{i_0^T} \Pr_\vartheta(i_0^T | x_1^T) c(i, j, i_0^T)$$

Similar considerations apply to the other components of the HMM parameter set, giving an intuitively appealing explanation of the Baum–Welch (or EM) algorithm.

The "geometric" formulation of the Baum–Eagon theorem, mentioned at the beginning of this section, was later generalized from polynomial functions to a class of rational functions in Gopalakrishnan *et al.* (1991), allowing the construction of Baum–Welch algorithms for problems where the objective function is different from the sample likelihood.

6.7. OTHER TRAINING METHODS

The ML and MAP methods for training HMMs are actually methods for estimating distributions. Given an assumption on the parametric form of the unknown distribution on the observation space, they are directed at finding the "best" representation of the distribution inside the considered family. This is separately made for each acoustic model, and there is no direct relation between the objective function used during training and the ultimate performance measure of interest, namely the recognition rate. Other methods have been proposed that approach the training of a set of models as a problem of estimating the optimal parameters of a classifier, with criteria that are more closely related to classification accuracy.

For example, estimation of parameters based on *maximum mutual information* (MMI) has been proven to increase performance in several situations (Bahl *et al.*, 1987; Brown, 1987). As discussed in the previous sections, the function to be maximized in ML estimation, given a training set $\mathcal{L}$, is the total likelihood function. Assuming that $m(x)$ is defined as the model corresponding to the utterance contained in the observation x, and that $\vartheta(m)$ is the parameter set of model m, the objective function of ML estimation is expressed as follows:

$$F_{\text{ML}} = \prod_{x \in \mathcal{L}} \text{Pr}_{\vartheta(m(x))}(x) \tag{6.72}$$

$$= \prod_{m \in \mathcal{M}} \prod_{x \in \mathcal{L}, m(x)=m} \text{Pr}_{\vartheta(m)}(x) \tag{6.73}$$

where $\mathcal{M}$ is the set of models. The ML objective function is therefore a product of functions that only depend on the parameters of the individual models. In MMI estimation, the following function is used instead:

$$F_{\text{MMI}} = \prod_{x \in \mathcal{L}} \frac{\text{Pr}_{\vartheta(m(x))}(x)\,\text{Pr}(m(x))}{\sum_{m \in \mathcal{M}} \text{Pr}_{\vartheta(m)}(x)\,\text{Pr}(m)} \tag{6.74}$$

This function results from considering the mutual information between two random variables representing the production of linguistic events and acoustic events, and making some assumptions reflecting the fact that the true distributions of these random variables are not known. When the training sequences include continuously spoken sentences, the denominator in (6.74) is computed by means of a compound model that can integrate unit HMMs and LM probabilities. In practice, it follows from (6.74) that MMI estimation consists of maximizing the *a posteriori* probability of the unit sequence corresponding to the training data. There are no known algorithms which make the optimization of (6.74) as simple as that of (6.72). In Bahl *et al.* (1987), a gradient descent method is used to maximize F_{MMI} for continuous density HMMs. The extension of the Baum–Welch algorithm proposed in Gopalakrishnan *et al.* (1991) is suitable for MMI estimation of parameters of discrete models. As shown in that work, an analogy of the Baum–Eagon theorem still holds when F is a rational function, if the transformation T defined by (6.66) is replaced by:

$$T(x) \triangleq \left[\frac{x_{ij}\left(\dfrac{\partial \log F(x)}{\partial x_{ij}} + C\right)}{\sum_{h=1}^{M_i} x_{ih}\left(\dfrac{\partial \log F(x)}{\partial x_{ih}} + C\right)} \right]_{i=1\ldots N, j=1\ldots M_i} \tag{6.75}$$

where C is an appropriate constant, to be determined. Gopalakrishnan *et al.* show that, for every rational function F, there exists a number C_F such that expression (6.75) defines a growth transformation for every $C > C_F$. They also observe that, in order to achieve a fast convergence, the value of C should be set as low as possible. For this reason they propose to choose a small positive constant ε and compute C at every step as follows:

$$C(x) \triangleq \varepsilon + \max\left\{ \max_{i,j}\left\{ -\frac{\partial \log F(x)}{\partial x_{ij}} \right\}, 0 \right\} \tag{6.76}$$

This choice of C does not ensure that the objective function is increased at every step, nor that the generated sequence converges, but it has been proven to work well in practice. In Normandin *et al.* (1994) an improvement to this algorithm is proposed and applied to MMI estimation of both discrete and continuous HMMs in a connected digit recognition task. The extension to continuous HMMs is achieved by approximating Gaussian densities with discrete densities. A unified view of ML and MMI estimation, under the more general paradigm of *minimum discrimination information* estimation, is presented in Ephraim and Rabiner (1990).

Though well formalized and intuitively appealing, MMI estimation is unfortunately much more computationally intensive than Baum–Welch estimation, especially for systems with a high number of parameters. A more pragmatic approach is the *corrective training* proposed in Bahl *et al.* (1993c). It is inspired by an error-correcting procedure which is known to be effective for training linear classifiers, and is applied to discrete-word HMMs. First, a set of word models is trained by standard ML estimation, and the counters associated with each parameter, i.e. the numerators of the reestimation formulae in section 6.3.3, are kept. Then, for every training utterance, the forward–backward counters for the correct word and those of a few acoustically confusable words are computed. These are used to update the global counters for each parameter by increasing those of the correct word and decreasing those of the others, by an amount depending linearly on the difference between the log-probabilities of the wrong models and the correct model assigned to the utterance. After all utterances have been processed, the HMM parameters are reestimated with the updated global counters. This procedure is repeated until no adjustment occurs during the corrective step. There is no theoretical proof that such a procedure converges, but in spite of that it has been shown to outperform both ML and MMI estimation in several experiments. In fact, MMI estimation was introduced in an attempt to find a consistent formalization for an algorithm which works in this way, by increasing the probability of the correct word and decreasing that of incorrect words, but it did not appear to be superior to this empirical solution.

Another method for training models with an objective function which is strongly related to classification accuracy is presented and compared to standard ML estimation in Juang *et al.* (1995). In this case, the objective function is an estimation of the error probability, appropriately smoothed to make it suitable for gradient-based optimization.

While the above-mentioned methods were all inspired by the need to directly relate the training criterion to the performance of the recognizer, the method proposed in Rabiner *et al.* (1986) is an alternative to Baum–Welch training and is motivated by a reduction in computation complexity. It is based on the consideration that the *most likely state sequence* (MLSS), that is the one retrieved by the Viterbi algorithm, in many typical situations has a dominant contribution to the summation in (5.18), which gives the total emission probability of an observation sequence (Merhav and Ephraim, 1991). Therefore, it often happens that, during Baum–Welch training, many local γ_t weights give a marginal contribution to the counters. In K-means training, for every incoming utterance x, the MLSS $\hat{i}$ is first found through a Viterbi alignment, and then only the counters of transitions along this path are incremented. This is equivalent to the set $\gamma_t(x, i, j) = \delta(\hat{i}_{t-1}, i)\delta(\hat{i}_t, j)$. Analogously, if the distribution associated with the transition is a mixture, only the counter of the component giving the highest likelihood on the current frame is incremented. This procedure corresponds to maximizing the joint probability of a path and the observation, instead of the total emission probability. The performance of models trained with Baum–Welch or K-means training are very similar in most typical situations, making K-means a convenient choice especially for training large-scale systems.

As stated in the introduction to this chapter, the *topology* of HMMs is usually decided *a priori* and it is not modified by automatic procedures. For ASR application, a simple left-to-right topology is often effective enough for acoustic units. However, methods for automated topology design have been proposed, and shown to be useful is some situations. In Casacuberta *et al.* (1990) and Lockwood and Blanchet (1993), techniques for the inference of regular grammars are adapted to the estimation of the topology of the hidden chain of an HMM. Random search and simulated annealing are used in De Mori *et al.* (1995a) to optimize model topologies along with other discrete features of the HMM system, such as parameter tying and context clusters for context-dependent units.

7

Language Modelling

Marcello Federico[*] and Renato De Mori[†]

[*]Istituto per la Ricerca Scientifica e Tecnologica – 38050 Pantè di Povo, Trento, Italy.
[†]School of Computer Science, McGill University, Montréal, P.Q. H3A 2A7, Canada.

7.1. INTRODUCTION TO STOCHASTIC LANGUAGE MODELS

This chapter describes in detail language models (LMs) following the introduction of section 1.2. The purpose of LMs is to compute the probability $\Pr(W_1^T)$ of a sequence of words $W_1^T = w_1 \ldots, w_t, \ldots, w_T$. The probability $\Pr(W_1^T)$ can be expressed as

$$\Pr(W_1^T) = \prod_{t=1}^{T} \Pr(w_t \mid h_t) \qquad (7.1)$$

where $h_t = w_1, \ldots, w_{t-1}$ can be considered the *history* or *context* of word w_t. The probabilities $\Pr(w_t \mid h_t)$ may be difficult to estimate as the sequence of words h_t grows. A simplification can be introduced by defining equivalence classes on the histories h_t in order to considerably reduce their cardinality. An *n*-gram LM approximates the dependence of each word (regardless of t) to the $n - 1$ words preceding it:[1]

$$h_t \approx w_{t-n+1} \cdots w_{t-1} \qquad (7.2)$$

The *n-gram* approximation is based on the formal assumption that language is generated by a *time-invariant* Markov process (Cover and Thomas, 1991). This

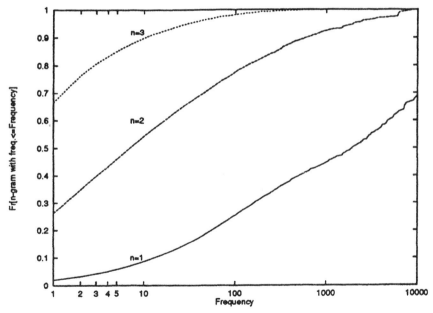

Figure 7.1 Empirical cumulative distributions of *n*-gram $(n = 1, 2, 3)$ frequencies in the LOB corpus. For each frequency value on the abscissa, the relative number of *n*-grams occurring a number of times less than or equal to that value is plotted.

---

[1]With the convention, however, that h_t cannot span beyond w_t.

greatly reduces the statistics to be collected in order to compute $\Pr(W_1^T)$. Clearly, such an approximation causes a reduction in precision. Nevertheless, even a 3-gram (trigram) model may require a large amount of data (text corpus) for reliably estimating a large number of model parameters. For example, a trigram LM with a vocabulary of 1000 words requires estimating about 10^9 probabilities.

Another important aspect that makes n-gram estimation a difficult task is the inherent data sparseness of real text corpora. Experimentally, most correct word sequences appear to be rare events, as they generally occur only very few times, if ever, even in very large corpora. This phenomenon is shown by the curves plotted in Figure 7.1, which represent some empirical cumulative distributions of n-gram frequencies computed on the LOB corpus (Garside *et al.*, 1987), a 1.2 Mw (million word) collection of English texts from different sources published by the universities of Lancaster, Oslo and Bergen. Here, the empirical frequency of n-grams ($n = 1, 2, 3$) occurring less than or equal to a certain number of times is plotted against this number. It appears that more than 20% of bigrams and 60% of trigrams occur only once in the considered corpus, and that about 85% of trigrams occur less than five times.

Figure 7.2 shows instead the likelihood of finding *new* n-grams after having examined increasing portions of the same corpus. Here, the corpus is examined

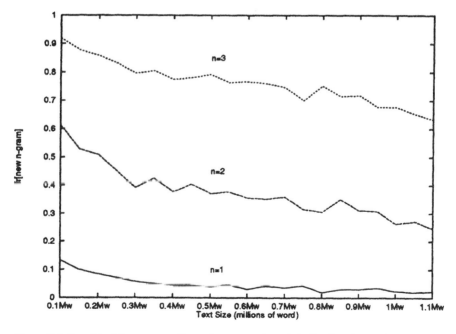

Figure 7.2 Empirical frequency of novel n-grams ($n = 1, 2, 3$) when increasing portions of the LOB corpus are observed. Frequencies are computed by considering the fraction of never-observed n-grams found in the last stretch of 50 kw.

with steps of 50 kw (thousand words), and, for each step, the fraction of the *n*-grams not observed so far is computed. The result is that the percentage of new *n*-grams decreases on the average as larger numbers of texts are being observed. After examining almost the entire corpus, the expected chances of finding new bigrams and trigrams are still around 22% and 65%, respectively. For this reason, estimation methods have to be used for providing reliable probability estimates also for infrequent or never observed (i.e. zero-frequency) events.

Section 7.2 deals with LM assessment. Section 7.3 introduces the basic estimation theory for *n*-gram LMs. Section 7.4 describes the two most widely used smoothing techniques for computing *n*-gram probabilities, i.e. interpolation and backing-off. Both techniques try to cope with the estimation of a large number of parameters despite the data sparseness of texts. Section 7.5 describes a different class of *n*-gram LMs, which are specified on the basis of constraints on marginal probabilities that are estimated (observed) from empirical data. Section 7.6 reviews improvements and variations on the standard *n*-gram paradigm. Section 7.7 concludes the chapter by presenting different applications, practical issues and prospective improvements of stochastic LMs.

7.2. PERPLEXITY AS A MEASURE FOR LM EVALUATION

In general, LMs for ASR are evaluated with respect to their impact on the recognition accuracy. However, LMs can be also evaluated separately by considering, for instance, their capability of predicting words in a text. The most widely used performance measure is the so-called *perplexity*. Unfortunately, even if perplexity is usually a good indicator of the quality of an LM for ASR, its correlation with the recognition accuracy is not perfect. In fact, recognition accuracy is surely influenced by the acoustic similarity of words, which is not taken into account by perplexity.

Perplexity is based on the following *log-prob* quantity:

$$LP = -\frac{1}{M} \log_2 \hat{\mathrm{Pr}}(W_1^M) \tag{7.3}$$

where $W_1^M = w_1 \ldots w_M$ is a sufficiently long *test sequence* and $\hat{\mathrm{Pr}}(W_1^M)$ is the probability of W_1^M computed with a given stochastic LM. Hence, the LM perplexity is defined as:

$$PP = 2^{LP} \tag{7.4}$$

By test sequence is meant a text independent of that used to estimate the LM. Assuming that the considered language source is *ergodic*, i.e. its behaviour can be statistically described by analysing a sufficiently long word sequence, it can be shown (Cover and Thomas, 1991) that *LP* converges in probability to the source *cross-entropy* measured by the LM:

$$H(\text{Pr}, \hat{\text{Pr}}) = \lim_{M \to \infty} -\frac{1}{M} \sum_{W_1^T} \text{Pr}(W_1^T) \log \hat{\text{Pr}}(W_1^T) \tag{7.5}$$

which is an upper bound of the source *entropy*:[1]

$$H(\text{Pr}) = \lim_{M \to \infty} -\frac{1}{M} \sum_{W_1^T} \text{Pr}(W_1^T) \log \text{Pr}(W_1^T) \tag{7.6}$$

According to basic information theory principles, perplexity indicates that the prediction task of the LM is about as difficult as guessing a word among PP equally likely words. Hence, the smaller the log-prob and the perplexity statistics are, the better the LM is. The requirement that W_1^M is a test sequence produces better statistics because computation involves n-grams unseen in the training data. Because new n-grams may be quite frequent (see Figure 7.2), a major issue for the LM is the ability to anticipate every possible event with a non-zero probability. For an n-gram LM, the logarithm of the probability (*log-prob*) in (7.3) is easily computed by exploiting the probability factorization (7.1):

$$LP = -\frac{1}{M} \sum_{t=1}^{M} \log_2 \hat{\text{Pr}}(w_t \mid h_t) \tag{7.7}$$

The above formula shows that the LP statistic rewards LMs assigning high probabilities to the n-grams of the test sequence. On the other hand, LP goes to $+\infty$ as soon as a zero probability is assigned to an n-gram.

The perplexity measure in (7.4) can be seen as a function with arguments, an LM and a text sequence. According to this point of view, the measure used here is often called *test-set perplexity*, to distinguish it from the *train-set perplexity*, which is computed on the same text used to estimate the LM. While the test-set perplexity evaluates the generalization capability of the LM to predict words inside new texts, the train-set perplexity measures how much the LM fits or explains the training data. It can be shown that the train-set perplexity is strictly related to the train-set *likelihood* (Mood *et al.*, 1974).

Another important issue of LMs is the choice of the vocabulary size. In fact, due to the exponential growth of the n-gram population with respect to the vocabulary size, an increase of the vocabulary requires much additional training

---

[1] An empirical upper bound of the entropy of English was computed in Shannon (1951), with the assumption that the English vocabulary consists of 27 characters (26 letters and a space symbol). During an experiment, a subject was asked to make guesses about the continuation of a given English text. More precisely, the subject had to guess the unknown text, letter by letter, under supervision of the experimenter. By taking the empirical frequency distribution of the number of guesses required to guess each letter, an entropy estimate of 1.3 bits per symbol was found ($PP = 2.46$). More recently, by using a character-based trigram LM, estimated on a 583 Mw corpus of English texts, an upper bound of 1.75 bits ($PP = 3.36$) was computed (Brown *et al.*, 1992b).

Table 7.1 Some test-set perplexity values measured on newspaper corpora of different languages. For each text source, the language, the corpus size, the vocabulary size (Voc.) and the out-of-vocabulary (OOV) rate are indicated. Test-set perplexities are given for 2-gram and 3-gram LMs

Source	Language	Corpus (Mw)	Voc. (kw)	OOV rate (%)	2-gram PP	3-gram PP
Wall Street Journal	English	37	20	4	114	111
Le Monde	French	37.7	20	4	95	91
Frankfurter Rundschau	German	31	20	9	109	100
Il Sole 24 Ore	Italian	19	20	3	133	67

Sources: Jardino (1996); Federico (1996a).

data and computational resources for estimating the *n*-gram probabilities. This trade-off is some way optimized by limiting the vocabulary to the most frequent *k* words occurring in the corpus. This choice also provides the lowest rate of out-of-vocabulary (OOV) words, i.e. the probability of finding never-observed 1-grams. Hence, LM estimation and test-set perplexity are usually performed in *closed vocabulary* modality, i.e. by only involving in-vocabulary *n*-grams.

In Table 7.1 some experimental results are reported for *n*-gram LMs estimated on newspaper corpora of different languages. Interestingly, for the same vocabulary size, quite similar OOV rates are reported for French, English and Italian, while for German a significantly higher rate results. Besides possible differences in the homogeneity of texts, among the considered corpora, a reason for this gap is surely due to the many compound words of German. Another remarkable fact emerges by looking at the perplexity reduction obtained by moving from a bigram LM to a trigram one. In particular, the significant improvement observed on the Italian task is probably due to the high number of function words, i.e. prepositions, articles, conjunctions, etc., which occur in the text corpus (i.e. about one word every two and a half). Because the bigram LM has difficulties in guessing words which follow function words, great benefits are achieved when a trigram LM is employed instead.

7.3. BASIC ESTIMATION THEORY

In the following, a simple formulation of the *n*-gram estimation problem is presented that allows basic estimation criteria to be introduced for more sophisticated models used in the next section.

Let one consider a *training text* $W = w_1 \ldots w_T$ made of words belonging to a finite vocabulary V. (Note that the sequence of words W_1^T is simply indicated as W if there is no need to make explicit reference to its length T.) From the

Markovian assumption that h_i is limited to the last $n-1$ words, the training text W can be mapped, without loss of information, into the ordered sample of n-grams:

$$S = h_n w_n, h_{n+1}, w_{n+1}, \ldots, h_T w_T$$

Given a fixed history h, a sample S_h can be extracted from S by taking the subsequence of all n-grams in S that begin with h. This ordered sample:

$$S_h = h w_{h_1}, \ldots, h w_{h_m}$$

where $\{h_1, h_2, \ldots, h_m\} \subseteq \{n, n+1, \ldots, T\}$, can be seen as a realization of m word occurrences independently drawn according to the probability law $\Pr(w \mid h)$. In other words, the sample is made of *independent and identically distributed* (IID) random variables.

In the following, for the sake of simplicity, the context h will be assumed to be fixed and will be omitted from the notation. Hence, the objective is that of estimating the discrete probability distribution $\Pr(w)$, defined on w, from a *training sample*

$$S = w_1, \ldots, w_m$$

of IID random variables. Notice that w refers to a word of the vocabulary, while w_i refers to the ith word in a sequence. The distribution $\Pr(w)$ is assumed to belong to a known parametric family $\{\Pr(w; \theta), \theta \in \Theta\}$, where θ is an unknown parameter vector specifying the distribution, and Θ is the parameter space. Two simple and general distributions will be investigated, here called *discrete* and *(discrete) symmetric* distributions.

Discrete distribution

The parameter space of the discrete distribution is the simplex:

$$\Theta = \left\{ \theta = [\theta_w]_{w \in V} \colon \theta_w \geq 0 \;\; \forall w \in V, \sum_{w \in V} \theta_w = 1 \right\}$$

that directly assigns one parameter to each word w of the word vocabulary V. In fact,

$$\Pr(w; \theta) = \theta_w \tag{7.8}$$

This distribution belongs to the *exponential family* (Mood et al., 1974), as well as the corresponding *likelihood* of S, which is the multinomial distribution:

$$\Pr(S; \theta) = \frac{m!}{\prod_{w \in V} c(w)!} \prod_{w \in V} \theta_w^{c(w)}, \quad \text{where } c(w) = \sum_{i=1}^{m} \delta(w_i = w) \tag{7.9}$$

with $\delta(e) = 1$ if e is true and 0 otherwise. The multinomial distribution (7.9) also belongs to the exponential family, and the count vector $[c(w)]_{w \in V}$ represents a *sufficient statistic* of S (Mood et al., 1974).

Symmetric distribution

A slightly different parametric distribution can be defined by assuming the *symmetry requirement* that words having the same frequency in S must have the same probability. Hence:

$$\Pr(w; \theta) = \frac{\theta_r}{n_r}, \quad \text{where } r = c(w)$$

θ_r represents the total probability of all words of w occurring r times in S, while n_r denotes the number of different words occurring r times in S. The above model introduces less parameters, as it partitions w with respect to the frequency of each word in S. Hence, the parameter space Θ of the symmetric distribution is the simplex with dimension equal to the size of this partition. The likelihood of S with the symmetric distribution is:

$$\Pr(S; \theta) = \frac{m!}{\prod_{w \in V} c(w)!} \prod_{w \in V} \left(\frac{\theta_{c(w)}}{n_{c(w)}} \right)^{c(w)} = \frac{m!}{\prod_{w \in V} c(w)!} \prod_{r \geq 0} \left(\frac{\theta_r}{n_r} \right)^{r n_r} \quad (7.10)$$

Given a parametric model $\Pr(w; \theta)$ the problem is to find the *best* value for its parameter vector. The problem of point estimation is a classical problem in parametric statistics and can be approached in several ways. In the following, three different estimation criteria or principles will be introduced: *maximum likelihood*, *Bayesian* and *cross-validation*.

7.3.1. Maximum Likelihood Estimation

This criterion considers the parameter θ as an unknown quantity to be determined. The best estimate is defined to be the one that maximizes the probability (or likelihood) of observing the sample S. Given a sample $S = w_1, \ldots, w_m$ of m IID random variables, the maximum likelihood (ML) estimate of θ is:

$$\theta^{ML} = \underset{\theta \in \Theta}{\operatorname{argmax}} \Pr(S; \theta)$$

$$= \underset{\theta \in \Theta}{\operatorname{argmax}} \prod_{i=1}^{m} \Pr(w_i; \theta) \quad (7.11)$$

Example 1. The ML estimate of the discrete distribution can be easily computed by maximizing the logarithm of the likelihood in place of the likelihood itself. By taking into account the constraints on Θ, and eliminating a constant factor, the following Lagrangian function is obtained:

$$L(\theta; \lambda) = \sum_{w \in V} c(w) \log \theta_w + \lambda \left(1 - \sum_{w \in V} \theta_w \right)$$

By deriving with respect to θ_w ($w \in V$) and equating to zero, one gets:

$$\frac{\partial L}{\partial \theta_w} = \frac{c(w)}{\theta_w} - \lambda = 0, \quad \forall w \in V$$

After reordering the terms and summing up with respect to w, one gets:

$$\sum_{w \in V} c(w) = \left(\sum_{w \in V} \theta_w\right)\lambda = \lambda$$

By substituting λ, the required estimate follows:

$$\theta_w^{\mathrm{ML}} = \frac{c(w)}{\sum_{w \in V} c(w)} = \frac{c(w)}{m} \tag{7.12}$$

Example 2. Maximizing the log-likelihood of the symmetric distribution with respect to θ gives:

$$\theta_r^{\mathrm{ML}} = \frac{n_r r}{m} \tag{7.13}$$

which provides the same word probability as the discrete distribution.

7.3.2. Bayesian Estimation

As discussed in Chapter 6, Bayesian estimation (Mood *et al.*, 1974; Duda and Hart, 1973) is conceptually different from the maximum likelihood one. In fact, the parameter vector θ is considered as a random variable for which an *a priori* distribution is assumed to be known. In this case, the problem is to find a point estimate of θ, given a training sample $S = w_1, \ldots, w_m$ of IID random variables and an *a priori* distribution $\Pr(\theta)$ of the parameter θ. By applying the well known Bayes' rule, the *a posteriori* distribution of θ is:

$$\Pr(\theta \mid S) = \frac{\Pr(S \mid \theta)\,\Pr(\theta)}{\Pr(S)} \tag{7.14}$$

The posterior distribution of θ combines the *a priori* evidence with the empirical evidence provided by the sample. It must be noted that the two different expressions of the likelihood, namely $\Pr(S \mid \theta)$ and $\Pr(S; \theta)$, indeed denote the same distribution. The notation just makes evident that in the latter case θ is a parameter while in the former one it is random variable.

Point estimates of θ can be derived from the posterior distribution in several ways. Two of them are discussed now.

The *maximum a posteriori* (MAP) criterion looks for the value of θ that maximizes the *a posteriori* probability. By eliminating the constant factor $\Pr(S)$ in

(7.14), the MAP criterion appears as a generalization of the ML one:

$$\theta^{MAP} = \underset{\theta \in \Theta}{\operatorname{argmax}}\ \Pr(\theta \mid S)$$

$$= \underset{\theta \in \Theta}{\operatorname{argmax}}\ \Pr(S \mid \theta)\Pr(\theta)$$

The simplest but also less informative *a priori* knowledge for the vector θ is the uniform distribution:

$$\Pr(\theta) = s(\theta) = \frac{1}{\operatorname{vol}(\Theta)} \tag{7.16}$$

where $\operatorname{vol}(\Theta)$ indicates the volume of the parameter space Θ. Clearly, with this prior distribution, the MAP estimate is equivalent to the ML one.

The *Bayesian* (B) criterion instead considers the expectation of θ with respect to the posterior distribution:

$$\theta^B = E[\theta \mid S]$$

$$= \int_\Theta \theta\,\Pr(\theta \mid S)\,d\theta$$

$$= \frac{\int_\Theta \theta\,\Pr(S \mid \theta)\Pr(\theta)\,d\theta}{\int_\Theta \Pr(S \mid \theta)\Pr(\theta)\,d\theta} \tag{7.17}$$

It can be shown that this criterion minimizes the risk on the guess of θ with respect to a squared-error risk function. A sufficient condition for the practical computation of the posterior distribution (7.14) is that S admits sufficient statistics, which is guaranteed if the parametric form $\Pr(w; \theta)$ belongs to the *exponential family*. In fact, the existence of sufficient statistics also implies the existence of *reproducing priors*, i.e. distributions $\Pr(\theta)$ for which the posterior distribution belongs to the same family as the prior.

Example 1. Assuming a uniform prior distribution, the Bayesian estimate of θ for the discrete distribution is (Vapnik, 1982):

$$\theta^B_w = \frac{\int_\Theta \theta_w \prod_{z \in V} \theta_z^{c(z)}\,d\theta}{\int_\Theta \prod_{z \in V} \theta_z^{c(z)}\,d\theta} = \frac{c(w) + 1}{m + k}, \qquad \forall w \in V$$

where k is the size of the vocabulary V.

Interesting reproducing priors, called *natural conjugates* (Spragins, 1965) or *kernel densities* (Duda and Hart, 1973), can be computed if a special sample S', called *a priori sample*, and a uniform distribution $s(\theta)$ are made available. The resulting natural conjugate is:

$$\Pr(\theta \mid S') = \frac{\Pr(S' \mid \theta)s(\theta)}{\Pr(S')} \tag{7.18}$$

Given an *n*-gram context *h*, the *a priori* sample could correspond, for instance, to the sample $S_{h'}$ of the less specific $(n-1)$-gram context h' (see for instance Kawabata and Tamoto, 1996).

Example 2. The natural conjugate prior of the multinomial distribution is the Dirichlet distribution (Spragins, 1965):

$$\Pr(\theta \mid S') = \frac{(m'+k-1)!}{c'(1)! \dots c'(k)!} \prod_{w \in V} \theta_w^{c'(w)}$$

where $c'(w) = \sum_{i=-m'+1}^{0} \delta(w_i = w)$ are sufficient statistics computed on the prior sample $S' = w_{-m'+1}, \dots, w_0$. By applying the Bayesian criterion (7.17) with this prior distribution, a ratio similar to the one of the previous example is obtained:

$$\theta_w^B = \frac{\int_\Theta \theta_w \prod_{z \in V} \theta_t^{c(z)+c'(z)} d\theta}{\int_\Theta \prod_{z \in V} \theta_z^{c(z)+c'(z)} d\theta} = \frac{c(w)+c'(w)+1}{m+m'+k}, \quad \forall w \in V$$

The MAP estimate is instead similar to the ML one with the multinomial distribution:

$$\theta^{\mathrm{MAP}} = \underset{\theta \in \Theta}{\mathrm{argmax}} \prod_{w \in V} \theta_w^{c(w)+c'(w)} = \left(\frac{c(w)+c'(w)}{m+m'} \right)_{w \in V}$$

7.3.3. Cross-Validation Estimation

Cross-validation is a well-known technique that can be applied both for estimating and evaluating a generic parametric model (Stone, 1974; Duda and Hart, 1973). For the problem of estimating a parametric distribution, cross-validation can be combined with maximum likelihood estimation. In particular, cross-validation estimation can be applied when the parametric model $\Pr(w; \theta)$ uses some functions (statistics) that are computed on the training sample *S*. In fact, cross-validation allows to reduce the bias resulting from using the training data *S* both to estimate the unknown parameters and to compute the statistics of the model. In order to overcome the problem, two different samples should be used, one for computing the statistics and the other for estimating the parameters. Unfortunately, this technique, called the *held-out method* (Duda and Hart, 1973) requires additional data. A better solution consists of replacing the factors in the ML formula (7.11) with others in which the probability of each sample point uses statistics computed on the entire sample with the exception of that point. Hence, the cross-validation (CV) estimation of θ is defined as:

$$\theta^{\mathrm{CV}} = \underset{\theta \in \Theta}{\mathrm{argmax}} \prod_{i=1}^{m} \Pr(w_i; \theta \mid S^{(i)}) \tag{7.19}$$

where $S^{(i)}$ indicates the sample *S* in which the *i*th point has been removed. In fact, this technique, also called *deleted estimation* (Jelinek and Mercer, 1980), simulates in some way the occurrence of new events inside the sample.

An interesting result can be derived when CV estimation is applied to the symmetric distribution.

Example. The cross-validation likelihood function of the symmetric distribution is:

$$\Pr(S; \theta) \propto \prod_{i=1}^{m} \left(\frac{\theta_{c(w_i)} - 1}{n_{c(w_i)} - 1} \right) = \prod_{r \geq 1} \left(\frac{\theta_r - 1}{n_r - 1} \right)^{rn_r}$$

In fact, in each sample point w_i, the statistic $n_{c(w_i)}$ is computed on the sample S with the point w_i removed. Taking the logarithm of the above function, results in the following Lagrangian function:

$$L(\theta, \lambda) = \sum_{r \geq 0} (r+1) n_{r+1} \log \left(\frac{\theta_r}{n_r} \right) + \lambda \left(1 - \sum_{r \geq 0} \theta_r \right)$$

By equating to zero the derivative with respect to θ, the following equation system is obtained:

$$\frac{\partial L}{\partial \theta_r} = \frac{(r+1) n_{r+1}}{\theta_r} - \lambda = 0 \qquad r = 0, 1, 2, \ldots$$

After some reordering and summing up with respect to r, one gets:

$$\sum_{r \geq 0} (r+1) n_{r+1} = \lambda \left(\sum_{r \geq 0} \theta_r \right) = \lambda$$

whose solution is:

$$\theta_r^{CV} = \frac{(r+1) n_{r+1}}{m} \tag{7.20}$$

Assuming, without loss of generality, that the word $w \in V$ occurs r times, the resulting probability estimate is:

$$\Pr(w; \theta) = \frac{\theta_r^{CV}}{n_r} = \frac{r^*}{m}, \quad \text{where } r^* = (r+1) \frac{n_{r+1}}{n_r} \tag{7.21}$$

The expression of the corrected frequency r^* is known as the Good–Turing formula (Good, 1953). The derivation of the Good–Turing formula through cross-validation estimation is by Nadas (1985).

7.4. INTERPOLATION AND BACKING-OFF LMs

In this section, the most popular estimation methods for *n*-gram LMs are introduced. Given an *n*-gram *hw*, where *h* indicates an $(n-1)$-word context, parametric models for the conditional distribution $\Pr(w \mid h)$ are in general obtained by combining two components:

- a discounting model
- a redistribution model.

Discounting is related to the zero-frequency estimation problem (Witten and Bell, 1991), in the sense that a probability for all the words never observed after the history h must be estimated by discounting the n-gram ML estimate, i.e. the relative frequency:

$$fr(w \mid h) = \frac{c(hw)}{c(h)} \qquad (7.22)$$

where by definition $c(h) = 0$ implies $fr(w \mid h) = 0$. More formally, discounting produces a *discounted conditional frequency* $fr^*(w \mid h)$, such that:

$$0 \leq fr^*(w \mid h) \leq fr(w \mid h)$$

$\forall hw \in V^n$. The *zero-frequency probability* $\lambda(h)$, defined as:

$$\lambda(h) = 1.0 \; - \; \sum_{w \in V} fr^*(w \mid h)$$

is redistributed among the set of words never observed in the context h. In particular, it can be shown that from the definition of $fr(z \mid h)$, it follows that $c(h) = 0$ implies that $\lambda(h) = 1$. Redistribution of the probability $\lambda(h)$ is performed proportionally to a less specific distribution $\Pr(w \mid h')$, where h' denotes a less specific context. Typically, the bigram distribution is used when trigrams are computed, and the uniform distribution when unigrams are estimated. Recent improvements to this basic method are reported in Kneser and Ney (1995). Discounting and redistribution are usually combined according to two main *smoothing schemes*: *backing-off* and *interpolation*.

7.4.1. Backing-Off and Interpolation Schemes

The introduction of the backing-off and interpolation smoothing methods are, respectively, by Katz (1987) and Jelinek and Mercer (1980). In order to provide a unified presentation, both methods have been here generalized in terms of recursive schemes that can be applied with different discounting methods. In fact, the original models will be presented when specific discounting methods will be considered.

According to the *backing-off scheme*, the n-gram probability is smoothed by selecting the most significant available approximation:

$$\Pr(w \mid h) = \begin{cases} fr^*(w \mid h), & \text{if } fr^*(w \mid h) > 0 \\ \alpha_h \lambda(h) \Pr(w \mid h') & \text{otherwise} \end{cases} \qquad (7.23)$$

where α_h is an appropriate normalization term:

$$\alpha_h = \left(\sum_{w:fr^*(w|h)=0} \Pr(w \mid h') \right)^{-1}$$

assuring that $\Pr(w \mid h)$ sums up to 1.

In the *interpolation scheme*, the two approximations are directly combined:

$$\Pr(w \mid h) = fr^*(w \mid h) + \lambda(h)\Pr(w \mid h') \tag{7.24}$$

Clearly, both the interpolation and the backing-off schemes recursively apply to the lower-order distributions. In particular, for LMs whose probabilities are smoothed with interpolation, it is possible to build efficient integrated networks for driving a speech decoding algorithm as will be described in Chapter 8.

Several frequency discounting methods as well as zero-frequency estimators have been proposed in the literature of information theory, statistics, pattern recognition, speech recognition, etc. Four of the best-known techniques will be reviewed here, namely, floor discounting, Good–Turing discounting, absolute discounting and linear discounting. Table 7.2 shows the single discounted conditional frequencies and zero-frequency probabilities that will be derived.

Before introducing the methods, some notation is briefly introduced. The following quantities, computed on the training corpus, will be used throughout:

Table 7.2 Estimators for the discounted function $fr^*(w \mid h)$ and the zero frequency probability $\lambda(h)$

Discounting model	$fr^*(w \mid h)$	$\lambda(h)$	Remarks
FL	$\delta(c(hw) > 0)\dfrac{c(hw) + 1}{c(h) + k}$	$\dfrac{n_0}{c(h) + k}$	
GT	$\delta(c(hw) > 0)\dfrac{c(hw)^*}{c(h)}$	$1 - \sum_{w:c(hw)>0} fr^*(w \mid h)$	$r^* = (r+1)\dfrac{n_{r+1}}{n_r}$
S1	$\max\left\{\dfrac{c(hw) - 1}{c(h)}, 0\right\}$	$\dfrac{n(h)}{c(h)}$	
Sβ	$\max\left\{\dfrac{c(hw) - \beta}{c(h)}, 0\right\}$	$\beta\dfrac{n(h)}{c(h)}$	$\beta \approx \dfrac{n_1}{n_1 + 2n_2} < 1$
LE	$\dfrac{c(hw)}{c(h) + n(y)}$	$\dfrac{n(h)}{c(h) + n(h)}$	
LP	$(1 - \lambda(h))fr(w \mid h)$	$\dfrac{n_1(h)}{c(h)} - \dfrac{n_2(h)}{c(h)^2} + \dots$	
LB	$(1 - \lambda(h))fr(w \mid h)$	$\dfrac{n_1(h)}{c(h)}$	
LI	$(1 - \lambda(h))fr(w \mid h)$	$\lambda(h)$	EM estimation

- $c(\cdot)$ denotes the number of occurrences of a specified word sequence.
- $n(\cdot)$ denotes the number of different words occurring after a specified context.
- n_r denotes the number of different n-grams occurring exactly r times.
- $n_r(\cdot)$ denotes the number of different words occurring exactly r times after a specified context.

Given a training text W_1^T, a vocabulary V of size k, a context h of length $n-1$, and a word w, and assuming the n-gram approximation $h_t = w_{t-n+1} \ldots w_{t-1}$, the above statistics are computed as follows:

$$c(hw) = \Sigma_{t=n}^T \delta(h_t w_t = hw), \quad n_r(h) = \Sigma_{w \in V} \delta(c(hw) = r)$$

$$c(h) = \Sigma_{t=n}^T \delta(h_t = h), \quad n(h) = \Sigma_{w \in V} \delta(c(hw) > 0)$$

$$c = \Sigma_{t=n}^T 1 = T - n, \quad n_r = \Sigma_{hw \in V^n} \delta(c(hw) = r)$$

7.4.2. Floor (FL) Discounting

Floor discounting is a simple method that can be derived by applying the Bayesian estimation criterion, discussed in section 7.3.2, to the discrete distribution $\Pr(w \mid h)$ and assuming a uniform *a priori* distribution. This technique simply adds a constant 1 to all the n-gram counts and assigns a probability, proportionally to their number, to all never-seen events. Hence, the resulting discounted conditional frequency is:

$$fr^*(w \mid h) = \begin{cases} \dfrac{c(hw) + 1}{c(h) + k} & \text{if } c(hw) > 0 \\ 0 & \text{otherwise} \end{cases} \tag{7.25}$$

while the zero probability is:

$$\lambda(h) = 1 - \sum_{w \in V} fr^*(w \mid h) = \frac{n_0(h)}{c(h) + k} \tag{7.26}$$

Despite its solid statistical motivation, this method has some drawbacks. In fact, it tends to overestimate the probability of rare events, as well as the zero-frequency probability, in presence of very sparse data. For this reason, this discounting method is usually employed only for smoothing unigram probabilities.

Example. The application of the FL discounting method to unigrams, with the back-off smoothing scheme, gives:

$$\Pr(z) = \begin{cases} \dfrac{c(z) + 1}{c + k} & \text{if } c(z) > 0 \\ \dfrac{1}{c + k} & \text{otherwise} \end{cases} \tag{7.27}$$

where the zero-frequency probability is redistributed according to the uniform distribution on V, also called *zero-gram* distribution.

7.4.3. Good–Turing (GT) Discounting

The Good–Turing (Good, 1953) formula can be derived (see section 7.3.3) by assuming the symmetry requirement that same frequencies correspond to equal probability estimates. For each n-gram hw, the Good–Turing formula computes the corrected frequency $c(hw)^*$ as follows:

$$c(hw)^* = (c(hw) + 1)\frac{n_{c(hw)+1}}{n_{c(hw)}} \tag{7.28}$$

From the above formula, an estimate of the probability of the never-observed n-grams can be computed by subtracting the ML estimate with the Good–Turing estimate over all observed n-grams:

$$\sum_{hw\,:\,c(hw)>0} \frac{c(hw)}{c} - \frac{c(hw)^*}{c} = \frac{n_1}{c} \tag{7.29}$$

The above estimate practically approximates the probability of all the zero-frequency n-grams with the relative frequency of the n-grams occurring once. The soundness of this estimate can be empirically verified by looking at the curves plotted in Figures 7.1 and 7.2. In fact, it results that the most reliable empirical frequencies of novel n-grams (right side of Figure 7.2) almost coincide with the empirical frequencies of the n-grams occurring once (left side of Figure 7.1).

From (7.28) the following conditional discounted frequency can be derived:

$$fr^*(w \mid h) = \begin{cases} \dfrac{c(hw)^*}{c(h)} & \text{if } c(hw) > 0 \\ 0 & \text{otherwise} \end{cases} \tag{7.30}$$

whose corresponding zero-frequency estimate is:

$$\lambda(h) = 1 - \sum_{w\,:\,c(hw)>0} \frac{c(hw)^*}{c(h)} \tag{7.31}$$

The Good–Turing formula was first introduced for backing-off n-gram estimation by Katz (1987) and has inspired bigram and trigram LMs used in practical applications.

In order to properly apply this method, it is important to consider that the statistics n_r generally have positive values for small frequencies r and have many zero values as r becomes large. Hence, the expression for obtaining r^* may be undefined for many n-grams. Different authors have suggested solutions to this problem. For instance, Church and Gale (1991) suggested smoothing the

n_r values so that they are always positive. Katz (1987) proposed replacing the Good–Turing corrected frequency r^* with a modified one r', such that $r' = r$ when the frequency r is larger than a given threshold l, and the balance equation (7.29) is satisfied, i.e.:

$$\sum_{0 < r \leq l} \left(\frac{r}{c} - \frac{r'}{c} \right) n_r = \frac{n_1}{c} \tag{7.32}$$

In other words, the original Good–Turing zero-frequency estimate is left intact and no discounting is applied to frequencies higher than l (a practical value is $l = 5$), as they are considered reliable. By looking at a solution of the form $(r - r') = \mu(r - r^*)$, the following corrected frequency r' ($1 \leq r \leq l$) can be derived:

$$r' = \frac{r^* - \alpha r}{1 - \alpha}, \quad \text{where } \alpha = (l + 1) \frac{n_{l+1}}{n_1} \tag{7.33}$$

Example. The original backing-off model by (Katz, 1987) for a trigram LM is computed as follows:

$$\Pr(z \mid xy) = \begin{cases} \dfrac{c(xyz)'}{c(xy)} & \text{if } c(xyz) > 0 \text{ and } c(xy) > 0 \\[2mm] \lambda(xy)\alpha_{xy} \Pr(z \mid y) & \text{if } c(xyz) = 0 \text{ and } c(xy) > 0 \\[2mm] \Pr(z \mid y) & \text{if } c(xy) = 0 \end{cases} \tag{7.34}$$

where:

$$\lambda(xy) = 1.0 - \sum_{z : c(xyz) > 0} \frac{c(xyz)'}{c(xy)}$$

and

$$\alpha_{xy} = \left(\sum_{z : c(xyz) = 0} \Pr(z \mid y) \right)^{-1}$$

The less specific (bigram) distribution can be expressed in a similar way.

7.4.4. Absolute Discounting

Absolute or "shift" discounting methods (Ney *et al.*, 1994; Witten and Bell, 1991) subtract a small positive constant β from all non-zero n-gram counts. The resulting parametric model for the discounted frequency is:

$$fr^*(w \mid h) = \max\left\{ \frac{c(hw) - \beta}{c(h)}, 0 \right\} \tag{7.35}$$

and the zero-frequency probability is:

$$\lambda(h) = \beta \frac{n(h)}{c(h)} \tag{7.36}$$

S1 method

By taking $\beta = 1$, all singletons are deleted from the counts and treated as if they were novel events. The zero-frequency probability becomes directly proportional to the number of different words occurring after the context h. Experimentally, this method provides lower zero-frequency probabilities than the floor method. Another advantage is that a significantly smaller amount of n-grams have to be kept in storage, as most n-grams in real texts occur few times (see Figure 7.1).

Sβ method

By assuming instead $0 < \beta < 1$ and applying the CV estimation criterion, the following estimate of β is proposed (Ney and Essen, 1991):

$$\beta \approx \frac{n_1}{n_1 + 2n_2} < 1 \tag{7.37}$$

where no significant performance improvements were reported by making β a function of the context h.

7.4.5. Linear Discounting

According to this method, empirical conditional frequencies are discounted in proportion to their value, i.e.:

$$fr^*(w \mid h) = (1 - \lambda(h))fr(w \mid h) \tag{7.38}$$

LP method

An estimate of $\lambda(h)$ can be derived under the assumption that new words appear after a given context h according to independent Poisson processes. Without going into the mathematical details, which can be found in Witten and Bell (1991), the resulting estimate is

$$\lambda(h) = \frac{n_1(h)}{c(h)} - \frac{n_2(h)}{c(h)^2} + \frac{n_3(h)}{c(h)^3} - \cdots \tag{7.39}$$

Interestingly, a first-order approximation of (7.39) is the zero-frequency estimate provided by the Good–Turing formula:

$$\lambda(h) \approx (r+1) \frac{n_{r+1}(h)}{n_r(h)} \left. \frac{n_r(h)}{c(h)} \right|_{r=0} = \frac{n_1(h)}{c(h)}$$

LE method

An empirical solution was described by Witten and Bell (1991) and recently used for LM estimation (Placeway *et al.*, 1993). The basic idea is to make the zero-frequency probability $\lambda(h)$ proportional to the number of "new events" that occurred in the context h during the production of the text sample. Hence, the resulting zero-frequency estimate is:

$$\lambda(h) = \frac{n(h)}{c(h) + n(h)} \qquad (7.40)$$

where the corresponding discounted frequency can be written as:

$$fr^*(w \mid h) = \frac{c(hw)}{c(h) + n(h)} \qquad (7.41)$$

LB method

Estimates for $\lambda(h)$ can also be derived by applying the estimation principles discussed in section 7.3 and under specific assumptions on the form of the conditional distribution $\Pr(w \mid h)$. In fact, by assuming the linear discounting model (7.38) and the backing-off smoothing scheme (7.23), the following parametric model results:

$$\Pr(w \mid h) = \begin{cases} (1 - \lambda(y))fr(w \mid h) & \text{if } c(hw) > 0 \\ \alpha_h \lambda(h) \Pr(w \mid h') & \text{otherwise} \end{cases} \qquad (7.42)$$

where α_h is a suitable normalization constant. By applying the CV estimation principle, Ney and Essen (1991) derived the linear Good–Turing estimate:

$$\lambda(h) = \frac{n_1(h)}{c(h)} \qquad (7.43)$$

LI method

By assuming the linear discounting model and the interpolation smoothing scheme, different estimates of $\lambda(h)$ can be derived either with the ML or CV criteria. In the linear interpolation scheme, n-gram conditional frequencies are recursively smoothed with the lower order frequencies. The basic n-gram probability is expressed as follows.

$$\Pr(w \mid h) = (1 - \lambda(h)) fr(w \mid h) + \lambda(h) \, \Pr(w \mid h') \qquad (7.44)$$

where the same scheme applies to the lower-order distribution $\Pr(w \mid h')$. The $\lambda(h)$ are such that $0 < \lambda(h) \leq 1$ if $c(h) > 0$, and $\lambda(h) = 1$ otherwise.

Each interpolation parameter can be estimated with a training sample W_1^T by means of the EM (*expectation maximization*) algorithm (Dempster *et al.*, 1977) that numerically approximates their ML estimates. The EM algorithm leads to iterating the following formula, also independently derived by Baum (1972):

$$\lambda^{(n+1)}(h) = \frac{1}{c(h)} \sum_{t=n}^{T} \frac{\delta(h_t = h) \lambda^{(n)}(h) \Pr(w_i \mid h_t')}{(1 - \lambda^{(n)}(h)) fr(w_i \mid h_t) + \lambda^{(n)}(h) \Pr(w_i \mid h_t')} \qquad (7.45)$$

where the summation is taken over all the n-grams with context h occurring in the training sequence. To avoid estimating the statistics $fr(w \mid h)$ and the other parameters on the same sample, the CV estimation criterion can be applied. The resulting iterative formula is equal to (7.45), but the relative frequency is replaced with:

$$fr(w \mid h, S^{(i)}) = \frac{c(hw) - 1}{c(h) - 1} \qquad (7.46)$$

Moreover, in order to reduce the number of parameters $\lambda(h)$ to be estimated, contexts h can be grouped into equivalence classes, or *buckets*. Several criteria to form such buckets have been presented in the literature (see Chen (1996) for a review). A reasonable method consists in grouping parameters on the basis of context frequencies (Federico, 1996a). Buckets are formed so that rare contexts share the same parameters, while frequent contexts have their own parameters.

Example. A trigram LM can be computed as follows:

$$\Pr(z \mid xy) = (1.0 - \lambda([xy])) fr(z \mid xy) + \lambda([xy]) \Pr(z \mid xy)$$

where:

$$[xy] = \begin{cases} 0 & \text{if } c(xy) \leq k_1 \\ c(xy) & \text{if } k_1 < c(xy) \leq k_2 \\ ord(xy) + k_2 & \text{if } c(xy) > k_2 \end{cases} \qquad (7.47)$$

$ord(xy)$ assigns an ordinal number to all the observed word pairs xy, and the thresholds k_1 and k_2 are determined empirically. The less specific (bigram) distribution can be expressed in an analogous way.

Another important aspect concerns the criterion used to stop the iterations of formula (7.45). Training can be terminated, for example, as soon as the value of the parameter stops changing significantly. In general, better results are obtained by evaluating the likelihood of a small *development-test* sample, after each iteration. Iterations are stopped just before the likelihood of the development-test sample starts decreasing. The drawback of this procedure is that precious data have to be taken away from the training sample. A solution to this problem has been proposed in Federico *et al.* (1995). A *stacked* estimation technique is used that randomly partitions l times the data sample into two samples: a training sample and a development-test sample. Parameters are estimated l times and, at the end, they are linearly combined together. This method shows on the average a reduction in perplexity.

To conclude, it can be noticed that linear interpolation itself can be seen as a general smoothing scheme, that allows to combine an arbitrary number of distributions, or even LMs. In fact, the original version of the linear interpolated trigram LM (Jelinek, 1990) was not defined recursively, but as a linear combination of all order empirical distributions:

$$\Pr(z \mid xy) = \lambda_1(xy) fr(z \mid xy) + \lambda_2(xy) fr(z \mid y) + \lambda_3(xy) fr(z)$$

where $\forall xy \in V^2$, $\lambda_i(xy) \geq 0$ $(i = 1, 2, 3)$ and $\sum_i \lambda_i(xy) = 1$.

Parameter estimation of a linear combination of known distributions:

$$\Pr(w; \lambda) = \sum_{i=1}^{l} \lambda_i \{\backslash \Pr\} - i \tag{7.48}$$

with λ defined on the l-dimension simplex, can be carried out through the EM iterative formula:

$$\lambda_i^{(n+1)} = \sum_{t=1}^{m} \frac{\lambda_i^{(n)} \Pr_i(w_t)}{\sum_{j=1}^{l} \lambda_j^{(n)} \Pr_j(w_t)} \tag{7.49}$$

The general mixture model in (7.48) will be referred to in a following section, in which variations on the n-gram LMs will be reviewed. For a discussion on the estimation of mixture distributions the reader may refer to McLachlan (1992).

7.5. CONSTRAINT-BASED LMs

In the previous section, different backing-off and interpolation parametric models for n-gram LMs have been presented. All these models try to combine knowledge of different information sources according to some fixed smoothing scheme. For example, the LI model smooths the n gram conditional frequency with the less specific $(n - 1)$-gram distribution by means of a linear combination. The estimation problem reduces to that of estimating the weights of the interpolation formula.

A different way to combine sources is provided by the *maximum entropy* and *minimum discrimination information estimation* criteria, which are now briefly introduced.

7.5.1. Maximum Entropy Estimation

The maximum entropy (ME) principle has roots in classical statistical mechanics and was extended to statistical applications in Jaynes (1957). The concept of ME estimation is introduced now for the discrete distribution. For the sake of simplicity, let one identify any discrete distribution with its parameter vector $\theta = [\theta_w]_{w \in V}$.

The *entropy* (Cover and Thomas, 1991) of a discrete distribution θ is defined as:

$$H(\theta) = - \sum_{w \in V} \theta_w \log_2 \theta_w \qquad (7.50)$$

where $0 \cdot \log_2 0 = 0$ by definition.

Now, let one consider d linearly independent constraints $(d < k)$:

$$\sum_{w \in V} \alpha_i(w)\theta_w = p_i, \quad i = 1, \dots, d \qquad (7.51)$$

where $p_1, \dots, p_d$ are the only available observations on θ, measuring some *macro-properties*, defined by d known constraint functions $\alpha_1, \dots, \alpha_d$. For instance, the constraint functions could specify a partition of v for which the marginal probabilities are known.

The ME principle suggests estimating θ so that the constraints are satisfied and the entropy H is maximized. A justification of this principle is the following one. Let one group all possible random samples of θ of size m $(m \to \infty)$ into equivalence classes of the count vector $[c(w)]_{w \in V}$. Each of these equivalence classes, $[\hat{c}(w)]_{w \in V}$, corresponds to a possible *macro-state* of the sample population V^m, whose elements (*micro-states*) all provide the same empirical estimate $\hat{\theta} = [\hat{c}(w)/m]_{w \in V}$. The ME principle selects the macro-state that satisfies the constraints (7.51) and has the largest number of micro-states. In fact, the size of a macro-state $[\hat{c}(w)]_{w \in V}$ is:

$$\frac{m!}{\prod_{w \in V} \hat{c}(w)!}, \quad \text{where} \sum_{w \in V} \hat{c}(w) = m$$

by applying Stirling's approximation $n! \approx (n/e)^n$ it follows that:

$$\frac{m!}{\prod_{w \in V} \hat{c}(w)!} \approx \prod_{w \in V} \left(\frac{m}{\hat{c}(w)}\right)^{\hat{c}(w)} = 2^{-m \sum_{w \in V} \frac{\hat{c}(w)}{m} \log_2 \frac{\hat{c}(w)}{m}} = 2^{mH(\hat{\theta})}$$

Hence, it results that maximizing the entropy of θ under the constraints (7.51) is equivalent to looking for the largest macro-state satisfying the constraints.

7.5.2. Minimum Discrimination Information Estimation

Maximum entropy estimation can be seen as a special case of *minimum discrimination information* (MDI) estimation. Given a set of constraints (7.51) on the distribution θ, and a *prior* distribution θ', the MDI estimate of θ is a distribution that satisfies the constraints and minimizes the *discriminatory information function* or *Kullback–Leibler distance*:

$$D(\theta, \theta') = \sum_{w \in V} \theta_w \log \frac{\theta_w}{\theta'_w} \qquad (7.52)$$

In fact, it can be shown (Cover and Thomas, 1991) that $D(\theta, \theta') \geq 0$, with equality holding if and only if $\theta = \theta'$. In other words, the MDI distribution is the distribution satisfying the constraints that is *closest* to the prior distribution, with respect to the distance D. In particular, if a uniform prior is considered, MDI estimation reduces to ME estimation.

7.5.3. MDI *n*-gram LMs

MDI estimation were first applied to language modelling by Della Pietra *et al.* (1992). The basic idea is that knowledge sources are introduced in terms of *constraints* that the desired distribution should satisfy. An interesting case for LM estimation is the one for which constraint functions define marginal probabilities on the sample space V^n:

$$\sum_{hw} \alpha_i(hw) \Pr(hw) = p_i, \quad i = 1, \ldots, d \qquad (7.53)$$

where $\alpha_i : V^n \to \{0, 1\}$, and $p_i \geq 0$ $(i = 1, \ldots, d)$. Each constraint function α_i is the characteristic function of a subset of the sample space and p_i represents its required marginal probability. Typically, a large number d of such constraints is set and the marginal probabilities are empirically estimated from a training corpus.

Example. If a trigram *LM* has to be estimated, constraints are in general introduced for unigrams, bigrams and trigrams. Constraints are usually set only where marginal probabilities can be reliably estimated from a corpus, e.g. for sufficiently frequent events. For example, bigram constraints are set for all bigrams occurring at least 10 times as follows:

$$\sum_{xy \in V^2} \alpha_{\hat{x}\hat{y}}(xy) \Pr(xy) = fr(\hat{x}\hat{y})$$

where $\hat{x}\hat{y}$ is a specific bigram whose ML probability estimate is $fr(\hat{x}\hat{y})$, and:

$$\alpha_{\hat{x}\hat{y}}(xy) = \begin{cases} 1 & \text{if } xy = \hat{x}\hat{y} \\ 0 & \text{otherwise} \end{cases}$$

Constraints for other *n*-grams can be set in a similar way.

7.5.4. The GIS Algorithm

Let one focus on the MDI estimation of the joint n-gram distribution $\Pr(hw)$. It can be shown (Darroch and Ratcliff, 1972) that every MDI distribution has the parametric form:

$$\Pr(hw) = \Pr'(hw)\mu_0 \prod_{i=1}^{d} \mu_i^{\alpha_i(hw)} \tag{7.54}$$

where $\Pr'(hw)$ is any prior distribution, $\mu_0, \ldots, \mu_d$ are determined so that d linear constraints:

$$\sum_{hw \in V^n} \alpha_i(hw) \Pr(hw) = p_i, \quad i = 1, \ldots, d \tag{7.55}$$

are satisfied, and $\Pr(hw)$ sums up to 1. Moreover, it can be shown that an algorithm exists, called *generalized iterative scaling* (GIS) (Darroch and Ratcliff, 1972), which converges to a unique solution of the form (7.54), given that the constraints (7.55) are consistent. In particular, when the observations p_i ($i = 1, \ldots, d$), are based on empirical frequencies observed on a corpus, consistency is guaranteed as the empirical frequency distribution $fr(hw)$ is itself a distribution satisfying the constraints. The GIS algorithm requires some normalization condition on the constraint functions, i.e. α_i ($i = 1, \ldots, d$) must be real-valued functions such that:

$$\sum_{i=1}^{d} \alpha_i(hw) = k, \quad \forall hw \in V^n \quad k > 0 \tag{7.56}$$

The GIS algorithm can be summarized as follows. First, the initialization with the prior distribution is carried out, i.e. $\Pr^{(0)}(hw) = \Pr'(hw)$.[2] Then, the following iterative computations are performed:

$$\Pr^{(m+1)}(hw) = \Pr^{(m)}(hw)\mu_0^{(m)} \prod_{i=1}^{d} \left(\frac{p_i}{p_i^{(u)}}\right)^{\frac{\alpha_i(hw)}{k}} \tag{7.57}$$

where:

$$p_i^{(n)} = \sum_{hw \in V^n} \alpha_i(hw)\Pr^{(m)}(hw), \quad i = 1, \ldots, d$$

and $\mu_0^{(m)}$ is the normalization factor.

It can be observed that the algorithm must be iterated on all possible values of hw, which could become prohibitive even for estimating bigram probabilities. A solution to this problem was suggested by Della Pietra and Della Pietra

---

[2]ME estimation is performed by initializing with 1.

(1994). The following constraints are added for every observed history $\hat{h}$:

$$\sum_{hw \in V^n} \alpha_{\hat{h}}(hw) \Pr(hw) = fr(\hat{h}) \qquad (7.58)$$

where:

$$\alpha_{\hat{h}}(hw) = \begin{cases} 1 & \text{if } h - \hat{h} \\ 0 & \text{otherwise} \end{cases} \qquad (7.59)$$

With these additional constraints, the iterative algorithm only needs to iterate on the observed histories, which are indeed very much less than all the possible ones. In fact, the constraints require that for the not-observed histories h, the MDI estimate $\Pr(hw)$ must be zero. However, it can be shown that this does not imply that the conditional probability $\Pr(w \mid h)$ must be zero. An exhaustive dissertation about ME estimation of LMs can be found in Rosenfeld (1994, 1996), while computational improvements on the GIS algorithm have been recently proposed in Lafferty and Suhm (1995).

7.6. VARIATIONS ON *n*-GRAM LMs

The *n*-gram models introduced in the previous sections are essential components of practical systems. Other models, that are frequently used in ASR systems are briefly reviewed in this section.

7.6.1. Models Based on Parts of Speech

These models were introduced for highly inflected languages, like French, German or Italian. In fact, for these languages, given the large number of terminations or variations that a word stem may assume, the data are very sparse. *Part-of-speech* (POS) models are inspired by syntactic knowledge. Let $g(w_t) = g_t$ denote the POS of the word occurring at time t and let G be the set of all POSs. Note that a given word in the vocabulary can belong to different POSs at different times: for instance, "light" can be a noun, a verb or an adjective. By definition, each occurrence of a word has only one POS. In practice, it may be difficult to single out the right POS of a word, in a given context, among the set of POSs associated with that word. A trigram POS model (3g-gram) is in general approximated with the formula:

$$\Pr(w_t \mid g_{t-2} g_{t-1}) \approx \sum_{g_t \in G} \Pr(w_t \mid g_t) \Pr(g_t \mid g_{t-2} g_{t-1}) \qquad (7.60)$$

The implied assumptions are that the word at time t only depends on the POS at time t, and that the latter only depends on the last two POSs. The trigram probabilities $\mathrm{Pr}(g_t \mid g_{t-2}, g_{t-1})$ can be estimated with any of the n-gram models proposed in this chapter. Moreover, estimating probabilities of POS models requires that each word of the training corpus is labelled by a POS symbol. For those words having only one POS, labels can be assigned by dictionary look-up. For words having more that one POS label, special programs called *taggers* are used. They assign each word a *tag* representing the specific class it belongs to, given its actual context. Recently, automatic taggers based on probabilistic models have been developed (Derouault and Merialdo, 1986; Garside *et al.*, 1987; DeRose, 1988; Church, 1988; Cutting *et al.*, 1992). Training of such taggers can be carried out through a bootstrap procedure that starts from some manually labelled data. Accuracy of such taggers has agreed with more that 95% of the tags placed by human experts. The use of POS language models in German, French and Italian are described, respectively in Steinbiss *et al.* (1990), Cerf-Danon and El-Bèze (1991) and Maltese and Mancini (1992).

7.6.2. Models Based on Morphology

Morphological models (El-Bèze and Derouault, 1990) are an extension of the POS models. A drawback of POS models is that they make no use of any semantic association between words. Thus, a semantic component is introduced at the level of lemma. Different words may indeed correspond to different inflections of a unique lemma, for example like the words "gone" and "went". The number of inflections per lemma generally depends on the part of speech. For instance, verbs show as much as 40 variations for each lemma (specifying time, mode and person), while nouns have just four (number and gender).

In the morphological model the prediction of a word is computed by considering the POS of the two previous words, and the lemmas of the two previous content words (i.e. nouns, adjectives, verbs, adverbs, proper nouns, etc.). Let G and L be the sets of all POSs and lemmas, respectively. The morphological trigram model (3m-gram) is approximated with the formula:

$$\mathrm{Pr}(w_t \mid h_t) = \sum_{g_t \in G} \mathrm{Pr}(g_t \mid g_{t-2}, g_{t-1})(\lambda(g_t)\,\mathrm{Pr}(w_t \mid g_t) + (1 - \lambda(g_t))\mathrm{Pr}_m(w_t \mid g_t))$$

with the morphological component Pr_m computed as follows:

$$\mathrm{Pr}_m(w_t \mid g_t) = \sum_{l_t \in L} \mathrm{Pr}(l_t \mid l_{t-k}, l_{t-j})\,\mathrm{Pr}(w_t \mid p_t, l_t)$$

where l_t is a possible lemma for w_t, and l_{t-k}, l_{t-j} are the lemmas of the two last content words encountered in the history h_t. The interpolation parameters depend on the POS of the word being predicted: i.e., λ is set to 1 for function words (i.e. pronouns, prepositions, articles, conjunctions, etc.) and can take any value between 0 and 1 for content words.

It can be seen that training of the above model requires a corpus labelled both with POSs and lemmas. Nevertheless, this requirement can be simplified by assuming that each valid word-POS assignment identifies a unique lemma. In this way, after a POS tagging phase, which can be carried out automatically, tagging with lemmas can be performed deterministically. Further improvements to the morphological model can be found in Cerf-Danon and El-Bèze (1991).

7.6.3. Models Based on Word Classes

Instead of using POSs based on the syntax of the language, it is possible to determine word classes by automatically clustering words of a given training corpus. Several clustering algorithms for bigrams, based on different optimization criteria have been proposed in the literature (Jelinek, 1990; Brown *et al.*, 1992a). A general word-clustering algorithm proposed by Kneser and Ney (1991) is given in Table 7.3. It can be seen that the algorithm is suboptimal and that the resulting clusters strictly depend on the initial mapping G and from the order in which words are moved from one cluster to another. In general, words should be ordered by decreasing frequency and the most frequent words mapped into individual clusters and the remaining ones into one single cluster. Applicable optimization criteria are maximum likelihood, cross-validation and mutual information between adjacent word classes. An alternative clustering algorithms using simulated annealing is presented in Jardino and Adda (1993). Experimental comparisons of all the above-cited techniques can be found in Moisa and Giachin (1995). Extensive results and computational requirements of bigram and trigram clustering on a 38 Mw corpus are reported in Martin *et al.* (1995). Comparisons between class- and POS-based bigram LMs can be found in Kneser and Ney (1993). Results on large corpora of different languages are reported in Jardino (1996). The perplexity of a given corpus is in general lower if an n-gram word model is used compared to a class model with the same n.

Table 7.3 General word-class clustering algorithm

Start with some initial clustering G: $w \rightarrow G(w)$

Iterate until some convergence criterion is met
Loop over all words $w \in V$
    Loop over all clusters g'
        Check how the optimization changes if w is moved from its current cluster
        $g = G(w)$ to g'
    Move word w to the cluster g' which maximizes the optimization criterion

7.6.4. Long-Distance/Dynamic Models

The need to go beyond trigram models is advocated in Jelinek (1991). Long-distance models try to capture statistical dependencies that go beyond trigrams. Since trigrams use a very limited context, they are in fact unable to capture style or topic variations of the text. Different approaches have emerged that allow application of either *n*-grams for some $n > 3$ or consideration of distribution variations of $\Pr(w_t \mid h_t)$ due to words in h_t up to 100 words distant from w_t. Such models are often called dynamic, as they dynamically modify their statistics according to the hypothesized history.

In Isotani and Matsunaga (1994), bigrams are assumed to depend, among other things, on the last function or content word present in the history. The number of parameters is reduced by introducing particular independence assumptions according to the category of w_t and w_{t-1}. A justification to this approach is that in Japanese, as well as in other languages, function words mainly convey case information about the content word preceding them.

Permugrams (Schukat-Talamazzini *et al.*, 1995) are a generalization of *n*-grams. They are obtained by linear interpolation of a large number of conventional bigram, trigram and higher-order *n*-gram models which operate on different and specific permutations of the history h_t of word w_t. In this way, also dependencies between non-adjacent word sequences can be captured without the requirement of very large *n*-grams.

Phrase bigrams extend ordinary word bigrams to bigrams of short phrases. These allow higher order dependencies to be captured which cannot be considered by a standard bigram LM. In Giachin (1995), algorithms are used that progressively look for suitable word pairs that can be joined to form new compound words. The process is repeated until the LM perplexity does not improve. In Kenne *et al.* (1995), adjacent word pairs which provide high mutual information are joined together. In McCandless and Glass (1994), first a grammar is automatically inferred from the training corpus, then an algorithm tries to reduce the grammar by merging word sequences and non-terminals (i.e. phrases). Finally, the grammar is used to generate a phrase/class LM.

Permugrams and phrase-bigram-based LMs have been shown to be effective for small-vocabulary human–machine dialogue applications, in which a typical feature of sentences is that they contain a consistent number of short phrases that have a very high frequency of occurrence. Thus, much better predictions can be achieved by using larger *n*-grams. Nevertheless, none of these methods tries to cope with the size explosion caused by using large-order models.

Decision-tree-based LMs (Bahl *et al.*, 1989a) determine equivalence classes on the history h_t through successive questions requiring yes/no answers. Hence, for each equivalence class $[h_t]$, a conditional distribution $\Pr(w_t \mid [h_t])$ is estimated. The questions are determined automatically from the training corpus, so that the cross-entropy of each equivalence class distribution is reduced. Decision-tree LMs can be considered within the general framework of classification trees, whose theory is extensively described in Breiman *et al.* (1984).

Prediction-suffix-tree (PST)-based LMs (Pereira and Singer, 1995) model *n*-grams with a special class of learnable probabilistic finite-state automata. *N*-gram history equivalence classes are represented with PSTs and are adaptively extended as long as the extension improves prediction. Thus, for example, certain contexts will activate a 3-gram LM, while others a 4-gram LM, and so on. In this way, the LM size explosion can be kept under control, as high-order *n*-grams are introduced only for some contexts.

Scalable n-gram LMs (Murveit *et al.*, 1994; Seymore and Rosenfeld, 1996; Brugnara and Federico, 1996; Kneser, 1996) consider methods for deleting specific *n*-gram statistics to reduce the memory requirements of the LM, without paying too much in terms of performance. These techniques have been mainly applied to trigrams but can be successfully extended to higher order *n*-grams. In Kneser (1996), improvements on the trigram model are reported by scaling down 4-gram and 5-gram LMs.

Collocation or *word triggers* models use long distance dependencies between word pairs which are significantly correlated inside the training corpus. Practically, word pairs with high mutual information are searched for inside a window of fixed duration. Triggers are introduced either under the form of constraints for ME-trained LMs (Rosenfeld and Huang, 1992), or by interpolating them with an *n*-gram model (Ney *et al.*, 1994).

Cache memory LMs (Kuhn, 1988; Kupiec, 1989; Kuhn and De Mori, 1990) exploit self-triggering words inside the text corpus. The idea is to capture short-term shifts in word-use frequencies that cannot be captured by the pure time-invariant Markov models. The cache component has been used in a 3*g*-gram model to replace the word-in-class probability in (7.60) with:

$$\mathrm{Pr}_{\mathrm{cache}}(w_t \mid g_t) = \lambda fr_{\mathrm{train}}(w_t \mid g_t) + (1 - \lambda) fr_{\mathrm{cache}}(w_t \mid g_t) \qquad (7.61)$$

where the first relative frequency is computed on the training corpus, while the second is based on the content of a cache memory containing the last *N* words which were guessed to have POS equal to g_t. The interpolation parameter $0 < \lambda < 1$ can be estimated either with the EM algorithm or empirically.

Mixture n-gram LMs (Kneser and Steinbiss, 1993) attempt to capture long distance constraints in a sentence or paragraph by interpolating several topic-specific *n*-gram LMs. The interpolation parameters are estimated, through the EM algorithm (7.49), on the text passage preceding the word under consideration. In Iyer *et al.* (1994) a variation of this approach is proposed. In particular, LM interpolation is performed at the level of sentence, and topic-specific LMs are estimated on paragraph samples derived by a text clustering algorithm.

7.6.5. Adapting Language Models

Adapting LMs, like long distance ones, are an attempt to model language variations due to domain or user changes. In general, the paradigm is similar to that for speaker adaptation (see Chapter 11). A general speaker-independent (SI) LM is available, which is progressively adapted to a new user as soon as speaker-dependent (SD) text samples are available. As a difference with dynamic LMs, like the cache or trigger-word ones, LM adaptation is performed from data and not from the current history h_t, which could in fact be just hypothesized.

Interpolation models linearly combine the statistics of the SI LM with those of the SD training data (Jelinek *et al.*, 1991; Chevalier *et al.*, 1995; Federico, 1996a). By applying the general linear interpolation smoothing scheme (7.48), the following LM results:

$$\Pr(w \mid h) = \lambda_1(h) \Pr_{SI}(w \mid h) + \lambda_2(h) \Pr_{SD}(w \mid h)$$

where the notation also specifies the samples on which distributions are estimated. The interpolation parameters can be estimated with the EM algorithm (7.49).

Minimum discrimination information adaptation models (Della Pietra *et al.*, 1992) use SD data statistics to set constraints on some marginal distributions of $\Pr(hw)$. Hence, the distribution is estimated through the MDI estimation criterion (see section 7.5.2), by taking an available SI distribution as the prior distribution.

Fill-up-based adaptation (Besling and Meier, 1995) combines all the statistics on the SI and SD data according to rules that define their reliability:

$$\Pr(w|h) = \begin{cases} fr_{SD}^*(w|h) & \text{if } c_{SD}(h, w) > 0 \\ \alpha(h) fr_{SI}^*(w|h) & \text{if } c_{SD}(h, w) = 0 \text{ and } c_{SD}(h) > 0 \text{ and } c_{SI}(h, w) > 0 \\ \beta(h) \Pr(w|h') & \text{otherwise} \end{cases}$$

where $\alpha(h)$ and $\beta(h)$ are suitable normalizing constants. In Besling and Meier (1995) the discounted frequencies of each sample are computed with the $S\beta$ discounting method presented in section 7.4.4.

7.7. APPLICATIONS OF LMs

Statistical LMs were introduced for ASR but were also used for machine translation, spelling correction, optical character recognition, etc.

In fact, machine translation can be seen as an information channel fed by messages in one language, producing messages in another language. Translation can then be modelled by a channel model having probabilities of words or linguistic structures in one language, given the corresponding ones in the

Table 7.4 Rules from written forms to alternative spoken forms

---

100 → one hundred, a hundred

0.1 → zero point one, point one

1/2 → and one half, and a half

---

other language and a language model. An overview of these concepts can be found in Church and Mercer (1993).

The same paradigm can be applied to spelling correction and optical character recognition (OCR). In both cases, the information channel outputs a text string with possible errors due to typing and recognition errors, respectively. Text correction algorithms may employ a letter based *n*-gram model and a dynamic programming algorithm to restore the corrupted text. An overview of techniques for automatically correcting words in text is in Kukich (1992).

In the field of language modelling for ASR, interesting results were obtained in the framework of the North American Business (NAB) task, for which a 248 Mw corpus of American newspapers is available. Some general results that were found useful in practice are listed below.

- LMs can be improved by modifying the training corpus in order to simulate how people actually read written texts (Schwartz *et al.*, 1994). In fact, written texts often represent in a unique form expressions that can be spoken in different ways. Hence, additional training data can be generated by applying empirical rules like those shown in Table 7.4.
- Using more complex LMs helps speech recognition accuracy significantly. In comparable testing on a 20 Kw dictionary task, using trigrams versus bigram LMs reduced error rates by amounts ranging from 12% to 23% (Pallett *et al.*, 1994).
- Performance improvement of a dictation system is possible by letting the LM adapt to the speaker's vocabulary and word sentences. Supervised LM adaptation, i.e. allowing the use of the correct text to adapt, reduced the error rate to 18.2% as opposed to 21.1% for the same utterances with an unchanged LM (Pallett *et al.*, 1994). A similar improvement was also achieved by using unsupervised adaptation.
- The importance of stochastic LMs in terms of coverage has been discussed in Chapter 1 In particular, the probability of finding a new *n*-gram while examining a text corpus was considered. For $n = 1$ and for a fixed dictionary, this probability represents the fraction of *out-of-vocabulary* (OOV) words that a recognizer can expect at the input. It has been estimated that, on average, each OOV word causes around 1.2 word recognition errors. Experiments, performed on the NAB corpus (Rosenfeld, 1995), showed that lexical coverage

strongly depends on the amount of training data, but it exhibits much slower improvement after a level of 30 Mw–50 Mw is reached. Moreover, the source and the recency of the data are also important in modelling a newspaper language.

- To reduce the expected OOV rate one normally has to increase the lexicon of the recognizer. In fact, a larger vocabulary also increases the acoustic confusability between words, which indeed can be a source of recognition errors. Assuming that the confusability between words grows logarithmically with the lexicon size, in Rosenfeld (1995) it is extrapolated that, for the NAB corpus and with current technology, the optimal trade-off between lexical coverage and acoustic confusability is reached with lexicons of 60 kw–110 kw.
- Moving from read or planned speech to spontaneous speech significantly worsens recognition accuracy. Experiments performed on spontaneous speech collected from newspaper reporters provided error rates at least 34% higher than those obtained on read speech (Pallett *et al.*, 1994). In fact, a major problem of spontaneous speech are disfluence phenomena, like hesitations, repetitions, or deletions, which may significantly alter the acoustic and linguistic form of utterances. At the moment, no satisfactory way to model speech disfluencies has been found.

So far, bigram and trigram LMs have been applied with great success to ASR and appear to be essential components of a successful system. This justifies the extensive description of techniques for the estimation of the parameters of these models and the necessary background. On the other hand, the integration of such LMs in the speech decoding process will be discussed in Chapter 9.

Prospective research topics to improve today's LMs are briefly discussed now. In the immediate future, research is expected to move towards very large vocabulary dictation tasks, for which efficient and precise LMs are needed. A major challenge will be that of automatically extracting linguistic information, relevant to a specific task, from the many corpora that are available on the market. Hence, because of the exponential growth of LM parameters with respect to resolution, LMs should be able to adapt their precision according to the acoustic and linguistic ambiguity of contexts. Dynamic adaptation to topic and style variations will be also an important requisite for general large-vocabulary LMs. Hence, major efforts in improving current adaptation algorithms are expected in the future. For example, in the field of dialogue applications, e.g. phone services, dynamic and adapting LMs may also take advantage of the fact that expectation of certain words may be "modulated" by dialogue situations.

Finally, more attention will also be paid to spontaneous speech in which non-speech events play a very important role. It will be important to understand whether or not spontaneous speech phenomena should be included with the LMs and, in the affirmative case, how.

8

Knowledge Integration

Mauro Cettolo,[*] Roberto Gretter[*] and Renato De Mori[†]

8.1. INTRODUCTION

This chapter deals with the use of AMs, LMs and lexical models for obtaining an integrated network (IN), as outlined in Chapter 1.

Generation of word hypotheses is performed by assembling the results of a search for sequences of states and transitions in the IN that best match the input data. Matching is based on scores that are linear combinations of the logarithms of the probabilities associated with LMs and AMs when acoustic features are used as observations. IN should be organized to obtain the lowest possible time and space complexities of the search algorithms.

The integration of the three types of knowledge can be obtained, for example, with the transition network (TN) formalism. It is a hierarchy of networks, which can represent every type of context-free grammars. Networks are made of states

[*]Istituto per la Ricerca Scientifica e Tecnologica – 38050 Pantè di Povo, Trento, Italy.
[†]School of Computer Science, McGill University, Montreal, P.Q. H3A 2A7, Canada.

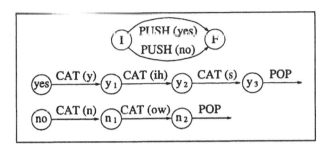

Figure 8.1 Transition network for a simple "yes/no" grammar.

described by symbols and transitions represented by arcs. There are three types of arcs, namely:

$$CAT(x), PUSH(y), POP.$$

The network is used by an algorithm Λ that handles two pointers π_S and π_T. Pointer π_S, at the beginning, points to a special state I of the network. $I \in V_N$, the alphabet of non-terminal symbols of the grammar, is the initial state at the top of the hierarchy. Pointer π_T points to one symbol of a string X of symbols belonging to a terminal alphabet V_T.

When π_S points to a given state, the algorithm Λ can perform an action suggested by the type of arcs coming out of that state. If the arc is $CAT(x)$, $x \in V_T$, and π_T points to a symbol that is x, then π_T will advance one position and π_S will point to the destination of the CAT arc. Otherwise this action cannot be performed.

If the arc is $PUSH(y)$, $y \in V_N$, then y is usually the label of the starting state of a subnetwork of the hierarchy, π_S points to y and the state destination of the $PUSH$ arc is stored into a temporary last-in first-out (LIFO) queue. Each subnetwork ends with a POP type arc. When it is reached, π_S is made to point to the state extracted from the top of the LIFO queue.

Example. Figure 8.1 shows how the TN formalism can be used to represent the knowledge of a simple isolated word recognition system having a vocabulary of two words: {yes, no}. Here the terminal alphabet V_T is phoneme symbols.

The integration of LMs, word models and AMs can be represented by a TN. It is possible to replace phoneme symbols in word models by the corresponding HMMs obtaining a TN of HMMs for each word. This is shown in Figure 8.2 for

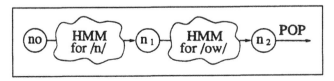

Figure 8.2 Transition network representing the word "no" with embedded HMMs.

the word "no" in the example of Figure 8.1. Bigram or trigram LMs can be represented by finite-state networks, as will be shown in section 8.5 with an example in Figure 8.9. Thus, by replacing each word symbol in the LM network with the corresponding word TN, it is possible to build the IN containing the three types of knowledge. Of course, as the TN formalism can represent context-free grammars, this type of architecture can also be used with n gram LMs.

HMMs are made of states and transitions. They can be seen as subnetworks that reach their final state by recognizing an input segment of speech with the Viterbi algorithm.

When π_S is in a state, usually a large number of transitions are possible and the choice among them is a search problem. Different choices have different scores obtained by combining the probabilities of various models, thus various search strategies can be used in order to generate the best word hypotheses with the best performance of the search algorithm in terms of space and time complexities.

While AMs have been extensively discussed in Chapters 5 and 6 and LMs in Chapter 7, lexical models will be introduced in this chapter.

The basic component for building a lexical model is a *pronunciation dictionary* (PD) in which each word is represented by a *canonical pronunciation form*, i.e. by a sequence of symbols such that each symbol corresponds to an AM.

While particular care has to be taken in building PDs, it is useful to consider multiple pronunciations for each word, to account, for example, for word boundary effects.

After discussing lexical modelling in sections 8.2, 8.3 and 8.4, methods for building INs will be introduced in sections 8.5 and 8.6.

8.2. WHOLE-WORD MODELS VS SUBWORD MODELS

For small-vocabulary systems, it is possible to use and train an HMM for each word. A sufficient number of samples is usually available for each word. For example, corpora are available for the 10 digits in English and in other languages with a number of pronunciations per word and speaker, and data from hundreds of speakers.

Sophisticated discriminative training algorithms can be used in such a case, and word boundary effects can be accurately modelled in a way that is specific for the vocabulary. Very high performance (0.2% word error rate and 0.8% string error rate) has been obtained in this way for the English connected digits of a corpus known as TIDIGITS (Normandin *et al.*, 1994) that contains strings having an unknown variable number of digits pronounced by male and female speakers.

Search is rather complex even for such a small vocabulary because there are no reliable algorithms for detecting word boundaries unless the speaker

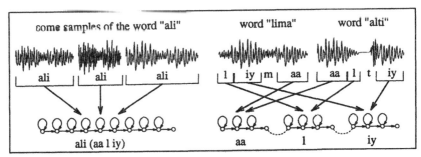

Figure 8.3 Word modelling using HMMs: whole-word model and unit-based models for the word "ali" (aa l iy). The closure before "t" is not represented by a symbol for the sake of simplicity.

intentionally makes a pause at the end of each word. The search algorithm has to assume that each word can start at every time frame.

It is more difficult, if not impossible, to use whole-word models for large vocabularies. In fact, in order to train whole-word models, it is necessary to have a large training corpus with many samples of each word. Furthermore, words that are very similar like "complement" and "compliment" may be easily confused. A better distinction between them can be achieved if their models are built with phoneme models, so that the score difference between the two words will strictly depend only on the scores of the phonemes that are different.

If new words have to be added to the system, new whole-word models have to be trained requiring a number of samples for each new word. This is highly impractical for very-large-vocabulary or speaker-independent systems.

A practically feasible approach consists of making word models by concatenating shareable *subword models*. In principle, there should be fewer subword models than words. Subword models are shorter, with fewer model parameters to estimate, than whole word models. The two possibilities are illustrated in Figure 8.3, which shows the use of three samples to obtain a whole-word model and the use of phoneme models trained from samples in different words.

As was discussed in Chapter 5, subword units can be chosen using linguistic knowledge or determined automatically by learning algorithms executed on a training corpus. In the first case, possible units are phonemes (Lee, 1988b; Lennig *et al.*, 1992; Angelini *et al.*, 1994b), phones that take into account acoustically different realizations of a phoneme (Lee, 1988b; Lee *et al.*, 1992; Riley *et al.*, 1995), syllables (De Mori and Galler, 1996) or segment-sharing sets of articulatory features (Deng *et al.*, 1995). Units that are not chosen based on *a priori* knowledge are obtained by clustering acoustic data (Paliwal, 1990) to obtain a set of a few hundred basic *fenones* (Bahl *et al.*, 1993d) which evolve into *multones* (Bahl *et al.*, 1993b) by representing observation probabilities with mixtures of distributions to model different speakers and contexts.

The main motivation for deriving acoustic representations of words directly from samples, instead of using linguistic knowledge, is that the latter is subjective and, unfortunately, not error-free. The former approach first requires dividing the acoustic space into similar regions by means of vector quantizer (VQ). One baseform of a word, in terms of VQ prototypes, can then be obtained as the label string produced by the VQ. In order to handle variations in the label strings corresponding to different samples of the same word, each label is replaced by a simple fenonic Markov model introduced in Chapter 5.

The use of subword units has several advantages. First, models can be effectively trained with less data than for whole-word models. Second, each word can be represented by a network of subword units, which makes it possible to model multiple pronunciations. Third, in principle it is possible to produce a model for a new word by just concatenating the models of its subword components without a specific training with samples of that word. Flexible vocabulary systems (Lennig *et al.*, 1992) exploit this fact to build a new word model by concatenation of the models corresponding to the sequence of phonemes representing the pronunciation for that word.

The number of AMs can vary between a few tens in the case of phonemes and more than tens of thousands in the case of syllables or context-dependent models with large contexts. There are various desirable properties that unit models should have:

- Their statistical parameters should be "well estimated" with a sufficient (>100) number of sample data.
- Models should properly take into account acoustic context dependencies such as coarticulation.
- If the number of models is high, in order for training to be effective, it may be necessary to share distributions among models.
- Short function words like articles, prepositions, short verbs, and conjunctions may have a large number of different pronunciations depending on the context in which they are used. Special models should be considered for them with multiple pronunciations and even special phone models (Lee, 1988b).

8.3. GENERATION OF CANONICAL PRONUNCIATION FORMS

There are no optimal methods for building lexical representations for an IN starting with a word list in orthographic form. If units based on phonetic knowledge are used, often a good starting point could be a dictionary in electronic form, which provides a *phonemic* baseform for each word. This representation is made of some tens of *phonemes*, which do not specify fine phonetic details, such as flapping or glottal stop insertions. Different contexts induce different modifications or *allophonic variations* on phoneme parameters. Units that take these variations into account are called *phones*, which represent different realizations of the same phoneme in different contexts. Phonemes are often called context-independent units, while phones correspond to context-dependent units.

It has to be possible to progressively modify the PD content for the following reasons.

- Users may require the recognizer to accept words that were not considered at the beginning.
- Usually phonemic transcriptions of words are manually prepared, or at least checked, by an expert. The use of the system may suggest replacing some transcriptions that are phonetically plausible or with which better performance is observed.

In both cases, tools for generating phone sequences for words are useful. Tools can be based on grapheme/phoneme translation rules or other type of algorithms and devices including those that can be trained from examples with machine learning algorithms. These tools can exploit, when available, one or more pronunciations of the new word by the user (Bahl *et al.*, 1991a).

The problem of generating phonemic and phonetic representations of words from their orthographic transcription is common to ASR and speech synthesis and has degrees of difficulty that are language-dependent. This is demonstrated by grapheme–phoneme translation tests (in various languages) performed using HMMs as generators of phonemic representations (Rentzepopoulos and Kokkinakis, 1992). Reported experiments show that for languages like English and Greek it is more difficult to automatically produce phonemic transcriptions with respect to other languages like Italian and German. Thus, transcription tools should have different type of sophistication depending on the language.

Rules defined by humans have been the first solution to this type of problem, but the availability of both corpora of transcribed words and phonetically labelled databases allowed consideration of other approaches, based on machine learning algorithms. The problem of deriving word pronunciations from their orthographic form is also known as letter-to-sound translation. For the English language, various algorithms have been proposed for this purpose based on artificial neural networks (ANN) (Sejnowski and Rosenberg, 1987), decision trees (Bahl *et al.*, 1991a), image processing techniques (Luk and Damper, 1991) and predictive methods (Riley, 1991), which generate a lattice of pronunciations for a given sentence.

Let $F = f_1 \ldots f_i \ldots f_I$ be a phone sequence and $C = c_1 \ldots c_j \ldots c_J$ be a character string forming a sentence in a given language. Let $X = x_1 \ldots x_k \ldots x_K$ be a sequence of acoustic features observed when a speaker reads C. Bahl *et al.* (1991a), following Lucassen and Mercer (1984), proposed finding the sequence $\hat{F}$ that is the most likely to be the phonemic transcription of C with the following decision rule:

$$\hat{F} = \underset{F}{\operatorname{argmax}} \Pr(F \mid C, X) \approx \underset{F}{\operatorname{argmax}} \Pr(X \mid F) \Pr(F \mid C) \qquad (8.1)$$

$\Pr(X \mid F)$ is computed with an acoustic model; $\Pr(F \mid C)$ is the probability of the model for a letter-to-sound translator. This probability can be expressed as:

$$\Pr(F \mid C) = \Pr(f_1 \mid c_1 \ldots c_j \ldots c_J) \times \prod_{i=2}^{I} \Pr(f_i \mid c_1 \ldots c_j \ldots c_J, f_1 \ldots f_{i-1}) \quad (8.2)$$

As the context that conditions the probability of f_i in the (8.2) contains too many items, it can be reduced to containing only a subset of the most relevant elements. They can be found by using classification and regression trees (CART). The approach is applicable to derivation of fenonic or multonic forms as well.

Of great importance is the strategy with which the decoder based on (8.1) is implemented when the most plausible pronunciation of a word has to be found based on its signal. Pronunciations of many words are speaker-dependent. Thus, this method is appropriate for finding the ways a given speaker pronounces a word. Even in this case, the algorithm may produce different phoneme sequences for different pronunciations of the same word. Multiple pronunciations of certain words are inevitable in good systems.

Rule-based systems, in which the rules are obtained automatically or semi-automatically, have been proposed for many languages (Torkkola, 1993; Van Coile, 1991; Huang *et al.*, 1994). In particular, a Japanese vocabulary of 100 000 has been represented in phonetic form with rules (Kimura *et al.*, 1989; Kimura, 1990).

An example of a rule-based system presented in Torkkola (1993) is now briefly described, based on the definition of the growing context of the letters needed to resolve phoneme ambiguities. The algorithm starts by defining a set of single-letter–single-phoneme correspondence rules, from the analysis of a training set, without considering letter contexts. Conflicting rules, i.e., letters leading to different phonemes in different words, are specialized in successive iterations by considering progressively larger contexts. Iteration stops either when all the conflicts within the training set are resolved (in which case the training set will be learned without errors), or when a predefined limit on the maximum allowed context is reached. Rules are organized in a tree; context-free rules are tried first and more specialized rules are considered only when a conflict is found.

In Meng *et al.* (1994), hierarchical tree structures are proposed to describe the spelling and pronunciation of English words. The levels of the structures involve morphs (like root and prefix), syllable stress, syllable components (like onset, nucleus and coda), manner and place of articulation. This leads to a hierarchical representation, an example of which is the tree for the word "given" shown in Figure 8.4.

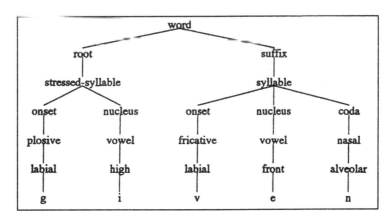

Figure 8.4 Hierarchical tree structure for the word "given".

Special attention should be paid to the phonemic transcription of proper names, acronyms and foreign words (Van Coile *et al.*, 1992; Konst and Boves, 1994; Trancoso *et al.*, 1994). For foreign words, it may be useful to find out which language they originally belong to before attempting to find their phonemic representation in another language. In Vitale (1991), a statistical approach is proposed to the language identification problem, in which probabilities for trigrams of letters are computed and stored for a set of languages. For an unknown name, the language showing the higher probability, averaged over all trigrams of the name, is chosen. It would be very useful to have transcribers capable of proposing candidates with an associated "degree of trustworthiness" that can be used for making a final decision on the acceptance or the modification of a transcription.

An excellent overview of spoken language identification can be found in Zissman (1995).

For languages rich of inflected forms, tools based on morphological knowledge can be very useful (Pachunke *et al.*, 1994; Gulikers and Willemse, 1992; Belrhali *et al.*, 1992; Gretter *et al.*, 1990). Morphological analysers are generally composed of a lexicon of morphemes, a set of rules and a search engine, which must find one or more valid decompositions for an input word. German and Dutch, for example, make great use of compound words, leading to a potentially infinite number of words; to cope with this problem, a morphological approach seems the only viable solution. For German, it is stated in Pachunke *et al.* (1994) that a rule-based transcriber cannot solve some local ambiguities without knowing the morphological decomposition of a word. Moreover, some words may have different possible decompositions, each one having a different pronunciation. These decompositions are provided by a morphological tool described in Pachunke *et al.* (1994). For the Italian language (Gretter *et al.*, 1990), a morphological approach is necessary for stress assignment, at least for verbs. In fact, the general decomposition of a verbal form must account for a prefix, a stem, an inflection and one or more clitics, as in the word "ri-mand-a-me-lo" (send it to me again). As the clitics do not influence the position of the stress, it would be very hard to correctly assign a stress pattern to such words without a morphological decomposition. A study of the factors which affect pitch accent placement is discussed in Ross *et al.* (1992), where a system is also described, based on decision trees, for predicting pitch accents.

Languages like Chinese Mandarin are based on monosyllabic words that may differ only by tone values. In general tone languages have peculiar problems as discussed in Lee *et al.* (1995). AMs of these languages must include suprasegmental acoustic features to be combined with fixed frame features.

8.4. MULTIPLE PRONUNCIATIONS

A word can be pronounced in different ways due to the influence of the previous and successive words or to different habits and culture of speakers.

Some motivations for having word models with multiple pronunciations are given in the following.

- A speaker may have used a valid pronunciation which does not occur in the PD. For example, the word "via" may be pronounced *v iy ae* or *v ay ae* (among other possibilities). The word "zero" may be *z ih r ow* or *z iy r ow*.
- A speaker may have mispronounced a word in such a way that recognition of the uttered word is still possible. For example, "continental" may have the following canonical form, *kcl k ah n tcl t iy n ae n tcl t ah l*, and be pronounced as *kcl k ah n tcl t iy n ih n ah l* or a variant of it which does not correspond to any other English word.
- Word boundary effects may produce a coarticulation where the last phoneme of a word and the first phoneme of the successive word interfere with each other. For example, in the string "six-seventeen", the word final /s/ of "six" and the word initial /s/ of "seventeen" can be merged – only a single /s/ is spoken.

The benefit of multiple pronunciations includes:

- Accommodating multiple valid pronunciations for words, eliminating the first of the above-mentioned problems.
- Accommodating multiple "invalid" pronunciations for words, where a large number of users pronounce a word differently than the PD, e.g. as a result of dialect; this can also be used to correct some major coarticulation errors.
- Some known, consistent but minor errors in the recognizer could be compensated for at the level of the PD, and generally for lower overall cost than repairs elsewhere in the recognizer (e.g. retraining of acoustic models).

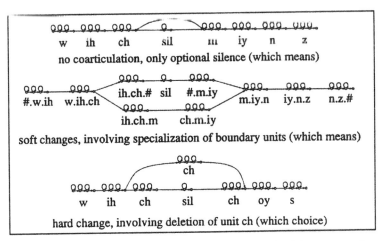

Figure 8.5 Examples of coarticulation between words, realized by means of acoustic units for the phrases "which means" and "which choice".

A difficult problem, in every case, is the appropriate modelling of *coarticulation* at the boundaries of two successive words. A solution to this problem is to consider a number of branches representing possible coarticulation effects at the boundaries of each word model (Giachin *et al.*, 1991, 1992; Chou *et al.*, 1994). At word boundaries, it is possible to consider "soft changes" consisting of introducing various allophones of the first (last) phoneme to take into account the contextual effect of the last (first) phoneme of the preceding (following) word. On the contrary, "hard changes" are the result of the application of phonological rules to produce phoneme insertions, deletions or substitutions at the word boundaries depending on the context. Examples of such situations are shown in Figure 8.5.

Phonological rules can be part of a phonological grammar (Bird and Ellison, 1994). They can be acquired automatically from the analysis of the lexicon (Belrhali *et al.*, 1992; Kimura *et al.*, 1989), using statistical methods (Bahl *et al.*, 1991b; Phillips *et al.*, 1991), starting from the results of a phoneme recognizer (Sloboda, 1995), from manual transcriptions (Flach, 1995) and from rules (Cremelie and Martens, 1995; Hochberg *et al.*, 1991).

With phonological rules, it is possible to generate pronunciation networks, an example of which is shown in Figure 8.6. Various aspects of multiple pronunciations are discussed in Wooters and Stolcke (1994), Chen (1990), De Mori *et al.* (1995b), Zue *et al.* (1990) and Riley (1991).

Learning strategies for obtaining new pronunciations is of fundamental importance. An example of strategy was proposed in De Mori *et al.* (1995b) and is summarized in the following.

The initial assumption is that a new pronunciation has to be added when a recognition error can be corrected based on justifiable distortions of the

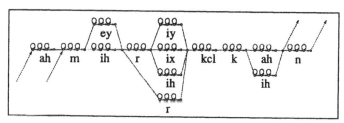

Figure 8.6 Multiple pronunciations network for the word "American".

canonical form of a word or its already accepted pronunciations. A justifiable distortion is one produced by rules which have been accepted based on experimental evidence constrained by speech knowledge. Speech knowledge establishes, for example, unacceptable substitutions like a vowel with a fricative.

Let us assume that sentence W, having a most likely word sequence $W = w_1, w_2, \ldots, w_j, \ldots, w_n$, is misrecognized, and that the first (left-to-right) misrecognized word is w_j. Let $(t_b, t_e)_i$ denote the beginning and ending times (input frame numbers) for word i. The procedure for establishing accepted pronunciations is as follows.

1. Determine time interval τ consisting of at least $(t_b, t_e)_j$.
2. For each alternate pronunciation, assess how well that pronunciation corrects the error, iterating until the error is corrected or no further alternate candidates exist. In this latter situation, if possible, change τ to cover the previous word and perform this step once again. If it is *still* the case that no candidate corrects the error, exit with failure.
3. Infer rules from the proposed form. If these rules already exist, add the current instance as new justification for the existing rules. Otherwise, endeavor to associate new rules with existing rules which may be more detailed and/or might also have corrected the misrecognition, so as to produce more general rules.
4. Update lexicon: check for entries which are similar (e.g., same place of articulation context as the phoneme the newly applied rule modified) and apply the rule(s) to them.

By counting when alternate pronunciations are used, it is possible to associate counts and probability estimation to rules.

Example of inferred rules are reported in Table 8.1. The rule ay → ey is justified by samples of "nine" and "United". A possible generalization of this observation is that it is valid when preceded by n, it contains the main stress, and is followed by n or t. This makes it applicable to "nineteen" but application can be delayed because "nineteen" has a longer string of phonemes following ay than "nine" or "United".

Alternate pronunciations can be ordered according to a measure of the distortion they exhibit with respect to the canonical form.

Table 8.1 Examples of inferred rules

Phoneme and context	Possible rewriting with justification example
aa (ae)	ow (e) Continental
(p) ae (n)	(p) eh (n) Japan Airlines
(n) ao (r)	(n) ow (r) Northwest
ax (m)	ah (m) American
ay	ey nine United
eh	ih Northwest
ih (r)	eh (r) Air Canada
(k) ow	(k) ao Air Mexico

A measure of distortion can be found in the following way. Let X be the sequence of acoustic features of a word, w_k be a particular word which may be pronounced in a variety of ways depending upon the speaker's intentions, and w_{k_j} be the jth variant, or *distortion*, of that word.

Distortions w_{k_j} can be evaluated based on a "belief":

$$B(w_{k_j}) = \Pr(w_{k_j} \mid w_k X) = \frac{\Pr(X \mid w_{k_j} w_k) \Pr(w_{k_j} \mid w_k) \Pr(w_k)}{\Pr(w_k X)}.$$

$\Pr(w_k)$ and $\Pr(w_k X)$, common to all the candidates w_{k_j}, can be ignored in a comparison among candidates w_{k_j}. Furthermore, it is possible to assume: $\Pr(X \mid w_{k_j} w_k) = \Pr(X \mid w_{k_j})$ if we consider distortions w_{k_j} unique to w_k. This leads to:

$$B(w_{k_j}) = c \Pr(X \mid w_{k_j}) \Pr(w_{k_j} \mid w_k).$$

A way to determine $\Pr(w_{k_j} \mid w_k)$ is needed. One way is to use the product of the probabilities of the rules for obtaining w_{k_j} from w_k. If rules not yet inferred have to be applied, a floor probability is assigned to them.

Rule probabilities may have both a static and dynamic component; the latter component can capture individual speaker variations and uses the cache architecture introduced in the previous chapter for dynamic language models.

A final problem remains to be addressed: the generation of candidates w_{k_j} to be evaluated.

Given the time interval τ and a lattice of syllable or phoneme hypotheses, it is possible to extract the syllables or phonemes detected in that interval.

Pronunciation candidates $w^*_{k_j}$ can be constructed by concatenating adjacent syllables or phonemes in the segment τ of the lattice. If none of the elements $w^*_{k_j}$ corrects the observed error, then either w_k is not directly responsible for that error or the error cannot be corrected. Otherwise, candidates w_{k_j} can be found by successively reducing the differences between $w^*_{k_j}$ and the available pronunciations of w_k. Those new forms, which allow correction of the error, are candidates to become new pronunciations in ϕ_k, the set of pronunciations of w_k. The one with maximum belief can be kept.

Candidates can be found by replacing phonemes in $w^*_{k_j}$ in a way which is consistent with constraints imposed by phonetic knowledge. Some procedural rules found useful in practice include the following:

1. Remove insertions in $w^*_{k_j}$.
2. Align vowels in $w^*_{k_j}$ with one of the forms in ϕ_k.
3. Substitute vowels with vowels following an order imposed by the place of articulation.
4. Same as (3) for consonants in the same class and with the following order: fricatives, nasals, semivowels, plosives.

An example of a word network obtained with the just outlined procedure is shown in Figure 8.6. Inferred rules can be applied across the entire lexicon so as to achieve the effect of correcting pronunciations based on observed distortions. Since application of the updates involves dependencies on other, previously applied updates, and retraction of an application (and its consequent applications) may be required, a justification maintenance system is employed to control update application.

It is possible that with enough "training" on individual dialects, clusters of sets of updates may be constructed allowing a generic lexicon to be expeditiously modified to accommodate a speaker's particular dialect.

Word networks have a topology that explicitly reflects phoneme deletions, insertions and substitutions. It is advisable to assign probabilities to different paths since certain distortions are more frequent than others (Wooters and Stolcke, 1994).

The problem of detecting a new word that is not in the vocabulary and of adding its phonemic representation is discussed in Asadi *et al.* (1990, 1991) and Haeb-Umbach *et al.* (1995).

8.5. BUILDING AN INTEGRATED NETWORK FOR SEARCH

8.5.1. Network Topology and Complexity

The accuracy and speed of the search algorithms are affected by the precision of the models integrated into the IN, by the network organization and its use in the

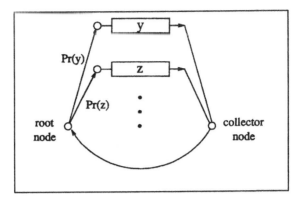

Figure 8.7 Unigram linear representation.

generation of word hypotheses. LMs based on *n*-grams can be represented by a finite TN in which lexical and acoustic models are integrated into a single, iterative but non-recursive, IN.

Let us consider, as a first case, an IN obtained with a unigram LM, i.e. an LM in which $P(w_i \mid \text{history}) = P(w_i)$. The IN based on it has the scheme shown in Figure 8.7. Here, labels *y*, *z* indicate word models. Each word model can be a simple concatenation of the HMMs of the phonemes corresponding to the word canonical form, or a word network representing all the pronunciations of that word.

The final state of the network of each word is connected to a collector that, in turn, is connected to a root node. These links represent transitions with probability 1 and no symbols are associated to them (empty transitions). The root node is connected to the first node of each word model with another empty transition with transition probability equal to the one in the unigram LM of the word reached by the link. This is the portion of IN that represents the LM.

The introduction into the network of a generic model of possible non-speech events between words can be done as shown in Figure 8.8. The non-speech event model has an empty transition in parallel, representing the fact that a word may immediately follow another word.

Considering now bigram LMs, the general network structure shown in Figure 8.9 can be derived. This network contains an explicit representation of all the possible links between word pairs.

The complexity of such a network is in practice too high for large (LV) and very large vocabularies (VLV). In fact, for a vocabulary of 10^3 words, the bigram LM should have a separate bigram for each word following a given word, resulting in 10^3 bigrams for each word, for a total of 10^6 links. From this example, it is possible to conclude that building INs using a bigram LM requires a number of inter-word links equal to the square of the vocabulary

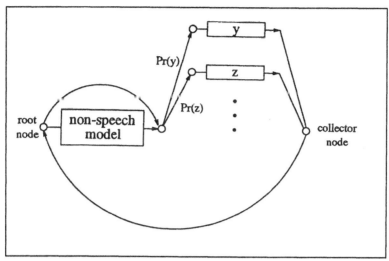

Figure 8.8 Non-speech events within the network.

size. This makes search impractical with the known algorithms that will be reviewed in the next chapter. As the situation is even worse if trigram LMs are used, an optimal trade-off between accuracy and speed suggests to use trigram LMs only after a network of word hypotheses has been generated.

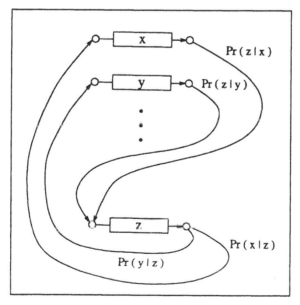

Figure 8.9 Bigram linear representation.

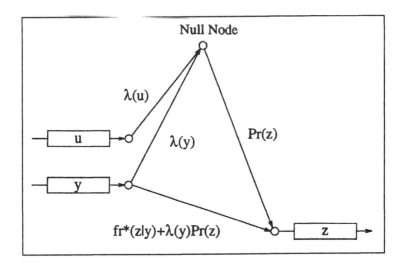

Figure 8.10 Bigram representation by using the "null node".

A practical solution can be proposed even for VLV bigram LMs because only a limited number of bigrams is observable in practically available corpora, forcing the assumption that the probabilities of the other bigrams are all equal and small, as discussed in section 7.4. This situation can be exploited to reduce network complexity by reducing the number of links connecting pairs of words.

As has been shown in section 7.4, bigram probabilities can be expressed as:

$$\Pr(z \mid y) = fr^*(z \mid y) + \lambda(y)\Pr(z) \qquad (8.3)$$

with $0 \le \lambda(y) \le 1$, $\lambda(y) = 1$ when $c(y) = 0$ and where $fr^*(z \mid y)$ is the discounted frequency of observation in the training corpus of the bigram yz.

Following a suggestion in Placeway *et al.* (1993), the scheme shown in Figure 8.10 can be used in the IN to integrate bigram LM probabilities computed with the (8.3). Each word y is linked to a *null node* by an arc with probability $\lambda(y)$ and the null node is linked to the model of z by an arc with probability $\Pr(z)$. This path corresponds to the second addend of (8.3). For bigrams yz for which $fr^*(z \mid y) > 0$, there are also direct links from y to z with probability given by (8.3). Notice that when a direct link exists between two word models, its associated probability is the sum of the two terms. One of them is equal to the probability obtained following the two link path through the null node. In Chapter 9, it will be shown how this network is used by a search process that computes the maximum score for competings paths. In this computation, the probability of the two-link path is ignored because it is always lower than the one of the directed path.

For an unseen bigram uz ($fr^*(z \mid u) = 0$) there will be only an arc from u to the null node and an arc from the null node to the initial state of a word z

with the unigram probability $\Pr(z)$. Thus, for each unseen bigram uz the word models are connected by a path through the null node.

Indicating with V the size of the vocabulary and with n_b the number of different bigrams with non-zero frequency, there are only $n_b + 2|V|$ connecting word links. For LV and VLV systems, this number is much less than $|V|^2$, since the unobserved bigrams can be more than 70%.

For small vocabularies and artificial languages like the one used by air traffic controllers, it is possible to derive an IN from a graphical representation of the language grammar (Brown and Buntschuh, 1994). Compilers for these types of network are available in some commercial products.

8.5.2. Tree-Based Representation

The schemes shown in Figures 8.7 and 8.9 are *linear* because each word has a separate model. The acoustic "similarity" of words is not taken into account in the linear representation. Since in a large vocabulary many words share the initial portion of their phonetic transcription, the lexicon can be represented by a tree in which common beginning phonemes of words are shared and each leaf corresponds to a word as in the scheme of Figure 8.11.

The advantage of using a tree structure for the lexicon becomes evident when search algorithms are considered. Although these algorithms will be introduced in the next chapter, it is possible to anticipate that the most popular ones consider input frames one at a time as in the case of the Viterbi algorithm introduced in section 5.1. For each HMM state, a node in the trellis is generated at each time frame. Factorizing phonemes in the tree organization corresponds to a reduction of the size of the trellis. This aspect is discussed in detail in Ney *et al.* (1992a) and Ney (1995). Moreover, a tree organization results in considerable memory saving with respect to a linear organization. As an example, for the 10 000-word dictation A.Re.S. system developed at IRST (Angelini *et al.*, 1994a; Federico *et al.*,

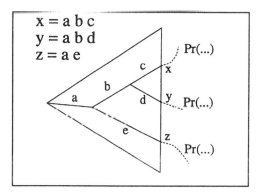

Figure 8.11 Example of a lexical tree.

1995), the ratio of the number of links required by a linear representation of the lexicon and the corresponding tree organization is 2.69.

Unfortunately, unlike the linear representation, in the tree organization a branch may not correspond to a simple word with the exception of branches ending in a leaf. Thus, in order to integrate bigram probabilities, a copy of the whole lexicon tree must follow each word and the bigram probability can be attached only at the end of the second word of each pair that corresponds to a leaf of the second tree. The entire network would require an unmanageable amount of memory, corresponding to 450×10^6 phoneme-labelled links for the above-mentioned A.Re.S. system.

However, the computational efficiency provided by tree-based representation can be effectively exploited if memory requirements are reduced by the network compression algorithms that will be introduced in the following.

8.6. STATIC TREE-BASED NETWORK ALLOCATION

The IN used for search can be compiled and entirely allocated in the main memory before search starts. In this case, two network topologies have been proposed to reduce the number of links. They are based on linear-tree mixtures (Murveit *et al.*, 1994), or on the null node (Federico *et al.*, 1995).

It is also possible to dynamically build only portions of the IN when they are required by the search process. The description of search algorithms in the next chapter will clarify how these portions can be identified.

A static representation of the whole IN is attractive mainly for two reasons: first, there is no overhead in building it during the recognition process; and secondly, the network can be compressed off-line.

The tree-based network organization proposed in Federico *et al.* (1995) is now described. The idea is to extend the use of the null node to the tree-based representation, as shown in Figure 8.12. For each word, a tree is built with the set of successor words that formed a bigram effectively observed in the training data. If word z is a successor of y, then the probability $P(z \mid y)$ given by (8.3) is assigned to the arc connecting the leaf corresponding to z in the successor tree of y with the root of the successor tree of z. The null node is the root of the whole lexicon tree. In Figure 8.12 the left-most triangle represents the whole lexicon tree, while small triangles represent successor trees ($st(\cdot)$). Each leaf of the lexicon tree corresponds to one of the $|V|$ words of the vocabulary and is linked to the root of its successor tree by an arc with the corresponding unigram probability $\Pr(z)$. Another arc, with probability $\lambda(z)$, links the root of the successor tree of z with the null node. Within every tree, when word transcriptions are prefixes of other ones, their last phoneme arc is duplicated in order to have different word-end leaves.

Using successor trees instead of $|V|$ repetitions of the whole lexicon tree, the static representation of the tree-organized network becomes effective. In fact,

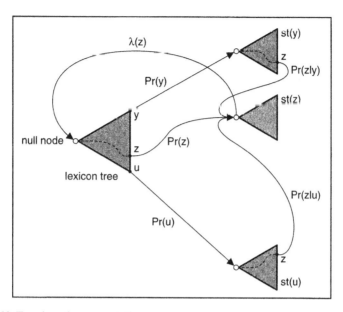

Figure 8.12 Tree-based representation.

the average size of successor trees depends on the number of different bigrams that have been observed in the training corpus, and is usually much smaller than the size of the whole lexicon tree. Successor trees can be further reduced by considering only word pairs that appeared frequently in the training corpus. Some techniques for choosing subsets of bigrams are discussed in Murveit *et al.* (1994).

8.6.1. Factorization of Probabilities

Probabilities of acoustic observations in phoneme HMMs within trees, and bigram probabilities of arcs among trees, are attached at different links of the tree-based network.

Search will, in general, be more efficient if bigram probabilities are factorized within the trees. When more words share a phoneme arc, both in the lexicon tree and in successor trees, the upper bound of their probabilities can be associated to that arc (see Figure 8.13). In Alleva *et al.* (1996) the use of the sum instead of the upper bound is suggested.

The algorithm, summarized in Figure 8.14, performs factorization of probabilities in a tree. Note that using upper bounds is not an approximation, since the correct LM probabilities are given by the product of values encountered along each path from the root to leaves.

Smearing LM scores in a tree-based representation was introduced in Odell *et al.* (1994) and Steinbiss *et al.* (1994), where it is specified that the values

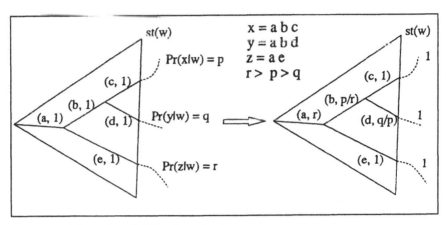

Figure 8.13 Effect of probability factorization.

were calculated on-the-fly during recognition. In Steinbiss *et al.* (1994), to avoid run-time overhead, the use of unigram upper bounds is proposed. Of course, if static tree-based factorization is adopted, the factorization of bigram probabilities can be performed off-line, resulting in no run-time overhead and in the application of correct upper bounds.

8.6.2. Tree-Based Network Reduction

After factorization of the probabilities, empty arcs outgoing from leaves with probability equal to one can be eliminated by collapsing the states linked by them. Moreover, many arcs toward the end of a path corresponding to a

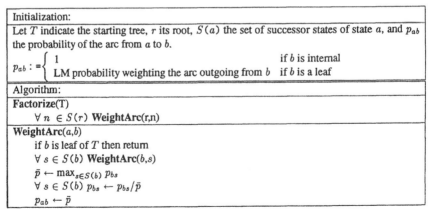

Figure 8.14 Algorithm for probability factorization in a tree.

word (Figure 8.13) have an associated probability equal to 1. This means that, in the tree-based network, there are still redundant paths that can be merged to reduce the network size.

In the following subsections, three possible network reduction algorithms will be discussed. IN compression is also discussed in Lacouture and De Mori (1991).

Optimization

A first possibility is to compress the network by using one of the available algorithms for minimizing the number of states in a deterministic finite state automaton. These algorithms are based on the *indistinguishability* property of states (Linz, 1990). Let T_1 and T_2 be the automata derived from the same automaton T by considering as initial states respectively S_1 and S_2. S_1 and S_2 are said to be indistinguishable if the languages accepted by T_1 and T_2 are exactly the same.

The *partitioning algorithm* (Aho *et al.*, 1974, pp. 157–162), can be used for this purpose. It starts with an initial partition of the automaton states and, iteratively, refines the partition by considering the set of states whose next state, given a symbol, is in one particular block of the current partition. Each time a block is partitioned, the smaller generated subblock is used for further refining. The algorithm ends when, for each given (*block, symbol*) pair, all states that point to some state of the given block with an arc labelled with the given symbol, are in the same block. Each block of the resulting partition consists of states that are indistinguishable and therefore can be merged. The automaton obtained in this way has the minimum number of states among those equivalent to the starting one.

The algorithm is given in Figure 8.15. The starting partition can be obtained by partitioning the states into final and non-final ones. The time complexity is $O(m\,n\log n)$, where m is the number of different symbols labelling arcs, and n the number of states of the starting network.

Note that symbols of the network of Figure 8.13 are pairs (*phoneme, probability*) and their number can be very large depending on the network structure.

Subtree isomorphism

The state optimization algorithm gives the greatest reduction of network size, but it does not take advantage of the particular topology of the network.

An elegant way to exploit the tree topology is to use an algorithm, with quadratic time complexity, that is still based on the indistinguishability property of states. The algorithm simply considers all possible pairs of states and marks those that result indistinguishable. At the end, these marked states are merged

Initialization:
Let a_h, $h=0, \cdots, m-1$, indicate the m symbols labelling links.   Let $\Pi=\{B[i]\ ,\ i=0, \cdots, n-1\}$ be an initial partition of states.   Let $W=\{(i,h): i=0, \cdots, n-1;\ h=0, \cdots, m-1\}$ be the set of all active   block-symbol pairs $B[i]$ and a_h.
Algorithm:
$\forall$ pair $(i,h) \in W$ until $W \neq \emptyset$ $\quad$ Remove (i,h) from W $\quad$ Let I be the set of states having an outgoing arc labelled with a_h to some $\quad\quad$ state of block $B[i]$ $\quad$ $\forall$ block $B[j]$ such that $B[j] \cap I \neq \emptyset$ and $B[j] \not\subset I$ $\quad\quad$ Create a new block $B[n] \leftarrow B[j] \cap I$ $\quad\quad$ Update $B[j] \leftarrow B[j] - B[n]$ $\quad\quad$ $\forall$ symbol a_k $\quad\quad\quad$ if $(j,k) \in W$ $\quad\quad\quad$ then add (n,k) to W $\quad\quad\quad$ else if $\| B[j] \| \leq \| B[n] \|$ $\quad\quad\quad\quad$ then add (j,k) to W $\quad\quad\quad\quad$ else add (n,k) to W $\quad\quad$ $n \leftarrow n+1$

Figure 8.15 Partitioning algorithm.

together and the optimum automaton, with respect to the number of states, is obtained.

If the starting automaton is a tree, the indistinguishability property coincides with that of *subtree isomorphism*. In fact, in this case, two states are indistinguishable if and only if their subtrees are isomorphic.

To apply this idea to the problem of reducing the size of the tree-based network, a tree is built by starting from a new root node and connecting it to the roots of all the successor trees and to the lexicon tree after probability factorization. The new connecting arcs are then labelled with new symbols not in use in the trees. Then, the algorithm depicted in Figure 8.16 is used by considering only non-leaves (internal) nodes, in such a way that the final linking can be done according to the bigram LM.

Initialization:
Let r indicate the root of the starting tree T, $T(v)$ its subtree starting from node v, and $I(v)$ the set of internal nodes of $T(v)$.
Algorithm:
$\forall s \in I(r)$ $\quad$ $\forall v \in I(r): v \neq s$ $\quad\quad$ if $T(v)$ and $T(s)$ are isomorph then $\quad\quad\quad$ Identify v with s in T and remove $T(v)$ from T

Figure 8.16 Subtree isomorphism-based algorithm.

To reduce the number of isomorphism checks, it is convenient to introduce some additional knowledge about a state, such as the length of the longest path to a leaf node. In any case, the time complexity of the algorithm remains $O(n^2)$.

Sharing tails

The third possibility to compress a tree-based network is to share tails of word transcriptions within trees whenever possible (Brugnara and Cettolo, 1995).

Let a *linear tail* in a tree be a path ending in a leaf and going through nodes with a unique successor. Probability factorization "pulls back" the probability attached to the last arc of the linear tail, leaving arcs with unit probability. All the tails corresponding to the same word y in different successor trees are linked to the root of $st(y)$, hence the first state of each one of them will be indistinguishable from one of the states forming the longest linear tail of y. The shared-tail topology exploits this property for reducing redundancy. For each word, only the longest linear tail is kept, and other tails are removed by identifying their origin with an appropriate state within the longest one. Figures 8.17 and 8.18 show a simple LM represented with a tree-based and a shared-tail topology, respectively.

Note that the shared-tail topology does not correspond to an optimized network, because it takes into account, among all the possible sources of redundancy, only a particular one. Nevertheless, comparison with optimized

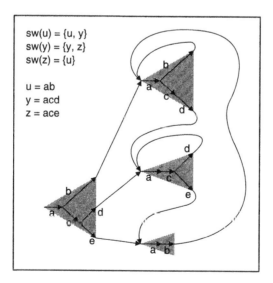

Figure 8.17 Tree-based LM representation example. $sw(w)$ indicates the set of successors of word w. Neither arc probabilities nor back-off arcs are depicted.

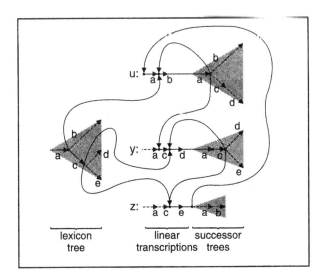

Figure 8.18 Shared-tail LM representation. Neither arc probabilities nor back-off arcs are depicted.

networks shows that duplicated linear tails account for most of the network oversizing introduced by the tree-based topology. Moreover, this criterion can be easily integrated into a single-step network building algorithm, whose computational cost is orders of magnitude smaller compared to the two-step approach of constructing the tree-based network and then reducing it. In fact, merging linear tails introduces only a slight overhead in the tree-based network construction.

Shared-tail compiler

The algorithm for compiling the shared-tail network is given in Figures 8.20 and 8.21, in which the notation of Figure 8.19 is adopted. It starts by inserting into the network the linear transcriptions of all the vocabulary words. For each of them, the tree of successor words observed in the training text is built (function *BuildTree*) in such a way that each leaf has just one successor; word-ending arcs are weighted by bigram probabilities. After the factorization of probabilities (*Factorize*, Figure 8.14), those nodes from which the linear tails start are marked (*MarkTails*). Then, the tree is visited in a depth-first manner, adding to the network all paths from the root to marked nodes and linking these to linear transcriptions by means of empty arcs (*AddTree*).

The final step consists of inserting back-off arcs (*AddBackOff*) and of removing unused initial portions of linear transcriptions. For notational convenience, a dummy word ϑ is used. Its successor tree is defined as the

Notation	
fsn	the shared-tail network
V	the vocabulary
u, y	$\in V$ generic words
$sw(u)$	$= \{y \in V : fr^*(y \mid u) > 0\}$
ϑ	a dummy word with no transcription
$sw(\vartheta)$	$= V$
$Pr(u \mid \vartheta)$	$= Pr(u)$
T	a tree
$S(a)$	set of successors of state a in a tree
p_{ab}	probability of the arc linking states a and b

Figure 8.19 Notation for the shared-tail network compiler.

whole lexicon, and the unigram probabilities are defined as bigram probabilities in the context of ϑ.

Algorithm
$\forall u \in V$
insert in *fsn* the linear transcription of u
$\forall u \in V \cup \{\vartheta\}$
$T \leftarrow$ **BuildTree**(u)
Factorize(T)
MarkTails(T)
AddTree($root(T)$)
$\forall u \in V$
AddBackOff(u, $root(T)$)
delete unused portion of linear transcription of u

Figure 8.20 Shared-tail network compiler.

8.7. CONCLUSIONS

Integrating acoustic, lexical and syntactic knowledge into a single network is an effective practical solution because the proper acoustic-phonetic, lexical and linguistic details are embodied in the structure.

Human knowledge and the results of machine learning can be integrated to obtain the best coverage of the data while keeping computational complexity linear with time and compatible with the size of central memory. Algorithms from automata theory are very useful for this purpose.

The idea of integrating knowledge into a large network for ASR, even with large vocabularies, probably has its roots in the systems developed in the DARPA projects of the 1970s. Good examples of them are DRAGON (Baker, 1975) and HARPY (Lowerre, 1976).

Functions

BuildTree(u)
    $\forall y \in sw(u)$
      insert y in T
      weight the last arc of y with $\Pr(y \mid u)$
    `return` T

MarkTails(T)
    $\forall$ node n of T, *tail_link*$_n \leftarrow \vartheta$
    $\forall$ leaf f of T
      let $\bar{u}$ be the word corresponding to f
      $n \leftarrow f$
      `while`(*tail_link*$_n = \vartheta$)
        $m \leftarrow parent(n)$
        `if` $(\mid S(m) \mid = 1 \wedge m \neq root(T))$
          $n \leftarrow m$
        `else`
          tail_link$_n \leftarrow \bar{u}$

AddTree(n)
    $\forall s \in S(n)$
      $u \leftarrow$ *tail_link*$_s$
      `if` $(u \neq \vartheta)$
        add to *fsn* an empty arc from n to the
        proper state of the linear transcription of u
      `else`
        add to *fsn* the arc (n,s)
        AddTree(s)

AddBackOff(u, r)
    add to *fsn* an empty arc from r to the root of the
    lexicon tree weighted by the back-off value $\lambda(u)$

Figure 8.21 Functions for the shared-tail network compiler.

A practical question is whether or not INs have to be precompiled and fully allocated in central computer memory before recognition starts or IN chunks should be generated only when they are required by the search algorithm. The first solution is faster but requires a larger memory space. The second solution has lower memory complexity but requires a higher computation time. The continuous progress in low-cost computer architectures makes affordable solutions that are more and more complex.

Lexical modelling is an important topic. The problem of letter-to-sound translation is of fundamental importance for speech synthesis as well as for ASR. Problems depend on the language and are the object of an intense research activity in order to improve the actually available solutions.

9

Search and Generation of Word Hypotheses

Mauro Cettolo,* Roberto Gretter* and Renato De Mori[†]

9.1. INTRODUCTION

In Chapter 8 it has been shown how acoustic, lexical and language knowledge can be compiled into a stochastic finite-state integrated network (IN) to be

*Istituto per la Ricerca Scientifica e Tecnologica – 38050 Pantè di Povo, Trento, Italy.
†School of Computer Science, McGill University, Montreal, P.Q. H3A 2A7, Canada.

used for generating word hypotheses. In general, IN is used to produce a match between a description of the input data x_1^T and a sequence of states and transitions, i.e. a path, in IN. A match is evaluated by a *score* that allows matches of the same input data and IN paths to be ranked.

For fast dictation systems, IN may control the generation of a *single* sequence of word hypotheses corresponding to the best match.

Another possibility is to produce an ordered set of sequences of word hypotheses corresponding to paths in IN. Ordering is based on the scores computed by the matching of x_1^T against those paths. The *N-best* sequences of word hypotheses can thus be obtained.

A third possibility is to generate a *lattice* of word hypotheses, each word being part of a path in IN that survived a competition in the matching with x_1^T. Each word in the lattice is associated a score and a pair of time values or intervals indicating when that word hypothesis can begin or end. If word hypotheses are connected to make explicit temporal word dependencies, the generated data structure is known as *word graph*.

All these types of word hypotheses are constructed by *search algorithms* attempting to find prominent matches between x_1^T and IN. A search algorithm is *admissible* if it always gives, as a result, the state sequence with the maximum score. The sequence of words produced by an admissible search algorithm may not be the sequence whose pronunciation generated the observed signal. This is due to various levels of imprecision in signal processing, feature extraction, acoustic, lexical and language modelling. As often admissible algorithms may require a practically unavailable amount of resources, effective *non-admissible* algorithms have been introduced and used with very good recognition performance, because missing the optimal solution may not correspond to missing the correct solution, especially if the first event is rare.

Section 9.2 reviews basic search algorithms. Section 9.3 describes examples of how these algorithms have been applied to ASR. Section 9.4 introduces a non-admissible but effective and very popular algorithm known as "beam search". Examples of its applications in real systems are given in section 9.5. Section 9.6 deals with fast-match techniques, a step of multiple stage search, which, in turn, is introduced in section 9.7. Some recent results in dictation are reviewed in section 9.8. The extraction of keywords, belonging to a limited vocabulary, from continuously spoken sentences, known as word spotting, is described in section 9.9. Some conclusions end the chapter.

9.2. BASIC SEARCH ALGORITHMS

The search for a match between IN and a given description x_1^T of the input signal can be carried out by progressively generating a *search graph*.

If IN is the HMM of a single isolated word w_i, then the search graph is the trellis introduced in section 5.2.4 and reproduced in Figure 5.2.

The search algorithm finds, in this case, the path in the trellis that corresponds to the alignment of x_1^T with a sequence of states in the HMM for which $\Pr(x_1^T \mid \text{HMM})$ is maximum.

Search algorithms are important because they find the optimal alignment without necessarily generating or considering the entire trellis. Reduction in complexity is achieved if it is acceptable to find suboptimal solutions. Different algorithms generate or explore portions of the trellis in different ways. Before discussing them, let us consider the structure of the search space for the networks introduced in Section 8.5 representing a set of words $\{w_1 \ldots w_i \ldots w_I\}$, each word being modelled by a single HMM with a link between the final state of each word w_i and the initial state of each word w_j with associated bigram probability $\Pr(w_j \mid w_i)$ for $i, j = 1, 2, \ldots, I$.

The search space includes a trellis for each word with the uppermost nodes of the trellis of each word w_i connected with the lowest nodes of each other word w_j. This is shown in Figure 9.1 where, for the sake of simplicity, only the trellis of w_i followed by the one of w_j are represented.

Other types of structures for IN lead to different types of trellis in the search space. Nevertheless, each trellis will have a node $\nu_{s,t}$ for each state s in IN and each value for the time index t of input frames. Each node $\nu_{s,t}$ in the trellis can be connected to a node corresponding to the next value of the time index $(t+1)$ and to states in IN that can be reached from s in IN.

INs introduced in Chapter 8 may have millions of nodes in the case of very large vocabularies in which multiple pronunciations are used for each word. In such a case, for practical reasons mainly related to the size of the central memory of a computer, it may be impractical to precompile IN entirely and store it into the central memory. It may be preferable that the search algorithm *dynamically* builds and allocates portions of IN useful to grow partial interpretation hypotheses (Ney *et al.*, 1992b).

In the following subsection, a best first search algorithm is introduced as a first example of graph search.

9.2.1. Best First Search

The theory of the most popular search algorithm, known as A*, is described in detail in Nilsson (1982). The basic steps of the algorithm are summarized in Figure 9.2.

The list *OPEN* contains *theories*. A theory describes the matching between the input data (or part of them) and a partial or a complete path in the search graph; it is represented by that path and the value of an *evaluation function* that will be discussed later on. Additional information characterizing theories and stored in *OPEN* are: the last node ν of the path, the cumulative

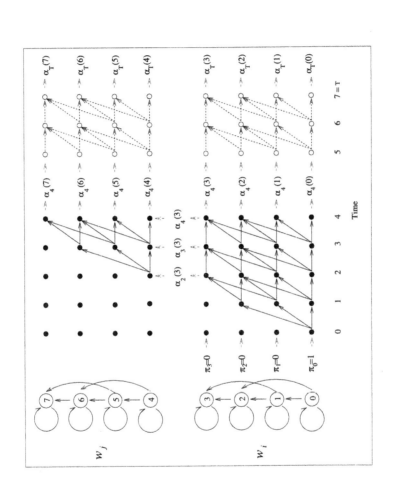

Figure 9.1 Trellis built during graph search.

Initialization:
Create a search graph, consisting solely of the start node
Put the associated starting theory in the list OPEN
Create the empty list CLOSED

Algorithm:

LOOP:
    if OPEN is empty
        exit with failure
    Select the best theory $\bar{\tau}$ in OPEN; let $\bar{\nu}$ be the last node of $\bar{\tau}$
    Remove $\bar{\tau}$ from OPEN
    Put $\bar{\nu}$ in CLOSED
    If $\bar{\nu}$ is a final node
        exit successfully with $\bar{\tau}$ as the solution
    Determine successor nodes $S(\bar{\nu})$ of $\bar{\nu}$
    $\forall \nu \in S(\bar{\nu})$
        if $\tau(\nu) \in$ OPEN
            recombination of paths
        else if $\nu \in$ CLOSED
            re-adjustment of search graph
        else
            add $\tau(\nu)$ to OPEN
    Reorder the list OPEN
    Go LOOP

Figure 9.2 Algorithm for the heuristic search of a graph. $\tau(\nu)$ indicates the theory ending at ν.

probability of the path from the start node to ν, a backward pointer from ν to the previous node in the path.

Ending nodes of theories in the list *OPEN* have still to be considered for further expansions. On the contrary, the list *CLOSED* contains nodes whose successors have already been generated.

Items in the list *OPEN* are ordered according to values of the evaluation function. Ordering is modified every time new theories are generated or old theories are updated (last step of LOOP in Figure 9.2). For this reason, *OPEN* is a *stack* type of data structure. The algorithm using it for ASR is also known as *stack decoder* (Jelinek, 1969).

Figure 9.3 shows a trellis with different representations between the nodes in *OPEN* and those in *CLOSED* and the possible expansions of theories ending with these nodes. Functions $g(\cdot)$ and $h(\cdot)$ will be introduced later.

It is possible that a node at the end of a theory belongs to the path of an already existing theory. If the new node ν is already in *OPEN*, i.e. ν has not yet been expanded, it means that there are two competing paths ending at that node, thus only the path with the best score should be kept. If the winner is the new path, then a *recombination of the path* ending at ν takes place, consisting in keeping just the new path as a theory ending at ν.

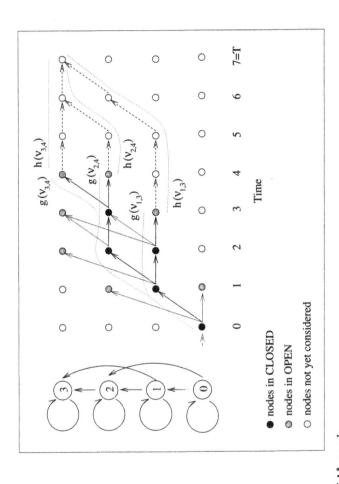

Figure 9.3 Example of A* search.

If the current node ν is already in *CLOSED*, then ν is an internal node of the path P of at least another theory, i.e. ν has already been expanded. If the new path ending at ν has a score better than the subpath of P ending at ν, then the just-found path has to replace the old subpath, with the forward propagation of the new score (*re-adjustment of search graph*).

Re-adjustment may be computationally expensive. It can be avoided if an already-expanded node belongs to the best path among those containing that node. This can be achieved if the evaluation function satisfies certain conditions discussed in the following.

Evaluation function

Given a theory ending with a node ν of the search graph, the *evaluation function* of ν is given by:

$$f(\nu) = g(\nu) + h(\nu) \tag{9.1}$$

where $g(\nu)$ is an estimation of the cost of the best path starting at the initial node and ending at ν.

Assuming, for the sake of simplicity, that a path corresponds to a sequence of words $w_1^k = w_1 \ldots w_k$ hypothesized by matching **IN** with the sequence $x_1^t = x_1 \ldots x_t$ of acoustic feature vectors, and that the end of the path is a node corresponding to the final state of the HMM of w_k, then the cost $g(\nu)$ can be expressed by:

$$g(\nu) = -\log \Pr(x_1^t \mid w_1^k) \Pr(w_1^k) \tag{9.2}$$

The function $h(\nu)$ represents an estimation of the minimum cost of any path from node ν to a final node of the search graph, corresponding to the association of the final state of a word HMM with the last acoustic feature vector in the description of the input signal.

As $f(\cdot)$, $g(\cdot)$ and $h(\cdot)$ are estimates of cost functions, it is important to know how they are related to $f^*(\cdot)$, $g^*(\cdot)$ and $h^*(\cdot)$, the corresponding true cost functions satisfying the following relation:

$$f^*(\nu) = g^*(\nu) + h^*(\nu)$$

If $f^*(\cdot)$ is the opposite of the logarithm of the probability of a complete theory $(-\log \Pr(th))$, then the $g(\cdot)$ in (9.2) is exactly $g^*(\cdot)$; if the Viterbi approximation is adopted, then $g(\cdot)$ is the score of the best path only. This is an approximation of the true probability obtained by summing over all paths.

An estimation $h(\nu)$ can be based on heuristic considerations. For such a reason, $h(\nu)$ is also called *heuristic function* and the algorithm using it is also called *heuristic search*.

It is possible to prove that if $h(\nu)$ is a *lower bound* of $h^*(\nu)$, then an A^* algorithm in which theories are ordered, on the basis $f(\nu)$, is admissible.

Furthermore, if:

$$h(\nu_i) - h(\nu_j) \le c(\nu_i, \nu_j), \quad \forall \nu_i, \nu_j \tag{9.3}$$

where node ν_j is a successor of node ν_i and $c(\cdot)$ is the transition cost, then, if a node is already in *CLOSED*, the associated path is the optimal one containing it and there is no need to perform any re-adjustment of the search graph. Equation (9.3) is known as *monotone restriction*.

Some significant examples of evaluation functions proposed in the literature (Ney, 1992) are briefly discussed in the following.

9.2.2. Introductory Search Strategies

Branch and bound strategy

One of the simplest forms of the evaluation function $f(\cdot)$ is to make it equal to $g(\cdot)$, i.e. assuming $h(\cdot) = 0$, which is certainly a lower bound for $h^*(\cdot)$.

The strategy that uses this assumption is known as *branch and bound*. The corresponding algorithm is admissible and the items in *OPEN* are ordered independently of their duration even if duration affects the cumulated score.

In real applications, the number of theories to be explored with this choice of the evaluation function is so high to make the computation cost prohibitive.

Heuristic absolute and adaptive strategies

An estimation of the cost of the path between the last node of a theory and its completion can be based on the length of the signal that remains to be analysed according to the following evaluation function:

$$f(\nu_{s,t}) = g(\nu_{s,t}) + (T - t)d$$

where d is an estimation of the average cost of a trellis transition. In the so-called *heuristic absolute search*, d is a constant greater than the average cost of a transition. In such a case, the algorithm is no longer admissible, but the evaluation function decreases along the optimal path as time increases, thus ensuring a certain focus on search and the expansion of a limited number of nodes.

Experiments have shown in many cases that better performance is achieved if d is data-dependent (*heuristic adaptive search*) as in the following example:

$$d = a\frac{g(\nu_{s,t})}{t}$$

where a should be chosen either to ensure admissibility or in order to achieve good performance with an acceptable complexity.

Breadth first strategy

The list *OPEN* can be ordered merely based on the length of the stored theories using the following evaluation function:

$$f(\nu_{s,t}) = g(\nu_{s,t}) + Bt$$

where D is a constant greater than the maximum cost of every possible complete theory.

In order for the algorithm to be admissible, when the last time frame of the input data has been reached, all the theories in *OPEN* have to be expanded.

9.3. SEARCH STRATEGIES APPLIED TO ASR

9.3.1. Viterbi Search

The Viterbi search algorithm is time-synchronous. In principle, at every time frame t, all the theories are expanded before moving to the next frame $t + 1$ producing a new set of theories all ending with nodes in the trellis corresponding to the same time frame $t + 1$. The basic algorithm has been introduced in Chapter 5 to compute the score of a word. Now, its application is considered in the case of large vocabularies with word representations and grammars embedded into an IN. In this case, since the search space may be very large, it must be controlled using some heuristics.

In the case of continuous speech, the highest row of each word trellis is fully connected with the lowest row of the trellis of every word (Figure 9.1). In a more realistic case, each word model should be preceded or followed by an optional model of non-speech events. As the complete trellis may be huge, only useful parts of it should be kept as the search progresses.

Viterbi search can be seen as a breadth first strategy. In general, computation cost differences between Viterbi strategy and best first strategies lie on the necessity for the latter to keep an ordered list of theories and to perform readjustment on them. In fact, recombination cost is common to both approaches, as it is the basic step of the dynamic programming on which Viterbi search is based. Although re-adjustment can be avoided also in the best first strategies if monotone restriction is satisfied, finding an efficient evaluation function is difficult. It is perhaps easier and more effective to limit the search space explored by the Viterbi algorithm through a non-admissible, but practically effective, algorithm, known as beam search, which will be introduced in section 9.4.

During the Viterbi search, a set of back-pointers between trellis nodes has to be maintained as well as a set of word labels, as discussed below.

Managing back-pointers during search

The Viterbi search algorithm ends by computing the observation probabilities of the last acoustic feature vector. The best among the scores of the trellis nodes associated with the word final states in IN is used to select the starting point of a backward reconstruction of the best path in the trellis.

In order to build the best path it is necessary to store some back-pointers from trellis nodes as their scores are computed. In theory, a necessary back-pointer is the one from each trellis node to the node that gave the maximum contribution in equation (5.23). In practice, for large vocabulary systems, the memory size required for storing all these pointers may be unacceptable. Furthermore, such a fine resolution in the description of the optimal path (detail on which state contributed to the path every 10 ms) may not be necessary if search has to find the best sequence of word hypotheses. For this purpose, back-pointers have to be kept only for initial and final states of word models.

Figure 9.4 clarifies how this idea can be applied. Let assume, following the trellis on the left of Figure 9.4, that node $\nu_{1,1}$ has a back-pointer to node $\nu_{0,0}$. Furthermore, let assume that node $\nu_{2,2}$ has a back-pointer to node $\nu_{1,1}$. The back-pointer from node $\nu_{2,2}$ can be made to point directly to the destination of the back-pointer of node $\nu_{1,1}$, i.e. to node $\nu_{0,0}$ as shown in the trellis on the right of Figure 9.4.

In general, when a new node ν in the trellis is considered, its back-pointer $p(\nu)$ is determined with its destination $a = dest(p(\nu))$. If a does not correspond to the initial state of a word, then the destination of the back-pointer of a, $dest(p(a))$ replaces $dest(p(\nu))$ and the back-pointer of a is removed. In this way, direct back-pointers from the end of a word to its beginning are generated (see Figure 9.5).

Finding word labels in the optimal path

Once the optimal path has been found in the trellis, the labels of the corresponding words have to be found. This can be easily achieved if word labels have a unique association to states of word models. This is the case, for example, of leaves in a tree structure. If a state n in IN is labelled with a symbol $w \in V$, this label is associated to every node in the trellis $\nu_{n,t}$ associated to n. The sequence of labels associated to words in the optimal path is the best sequence of word hypotheses.

9.3.2. Examples of Strategies Used for ASR

In Kenny *et al.* (1993), IN is a network of phoneme models. Theories correspond to phoneme sequences since matching is between phoneme hypotheses and lexical representations based on phoneme sequences.

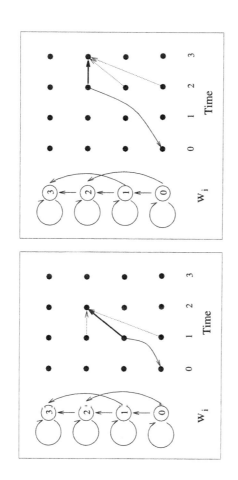

Figure 9.4 Choice of the best path (left) and adjustment of the back-pointer (right).

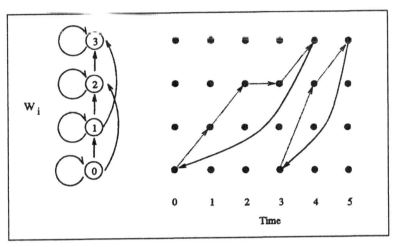

Figure 9.5 Back-pointers between the end and the beginning of a word, skipping internal states. Note that, in general, back-pointers for different ending times link to different starting times.

A node $\nu_{s,t}$ of the search graph corresponds to the final state of a phoneme reached at time t. The evaluation function uses two functions of the forward–backward algorithm described in Chapter 5:

$$f(\nu_{s,t}) = -\log \alpha_t(s) - \log \beta_t(s)$$

where $\beta_t(\cdot)$ is computed using a simple IN conceived for the purpose of achieving acceptable computational complexity while ensuring admissibility.

In Paul (1992), partial theories are word sequences. The expansion of a theory in *OPEN* considers all the words that can possibly follow the sequence in the theory.

A node $\nu_{s,t}$ in the search graph corresponds to the final node of the HMM for word w_i at time t. Let assume that there is no relation between w_i and the following words, i.e. no cross-word acoustic models and no-grammar or uni-gram language model are used. Then the heuristic function $h^*(\nu_{s,t})$ does not depend on s but only on t representing the optimal completion up to the final frame T of all theories ending at t:

$$f(\nu_{s,t}) = g(\nu_{s,t}) + h^*(t) \tag{9.4}$$

Let:

$$f^*(t) = g^*(t) + h^*(t) \tag{9.5}$$

be the true cost of the best theory with a word transition at time t. The function $f^*(\cdot)$ is equal to the true cost of the correct theory at its word boundaries. In Paul (1992), it is claimed that this function is almost constant. Subtracting equation (9.5) from equation (9.4) gives a new evaluation function $\hat{f}(\nu_{s,t})$

which differs from the true evaluation function $f(v_{s,t})$ just for a "constant" term:

$$\hat{f}(v_{s,t}) = f(v_{s,t}) - f^*(t) = g(v_{s,t}) - g^*(t) \qquad (9.6)$$

$\hat{f}(v_{s,t})$ is zero for the time frames corresponding to the transitions between a word and the successive one for the correct theory. Furthermore, it is negative in all other cases and has, in general, little variations which make the search practically admissible.

In practice, $g^*(t)$ in equation (9.6) is replaced by $g^*_{sf}(t)$, the cost of the best available theory ending at t, where sf stands for "so far". This implies that the stack has to be reordered when, at time t, a new value of $g^*_{sf}(t)$ is available.

With this approach, the ending time t of a partial theory is not known, so the score used for positioning a theory in the stack is obtained as follows:

$$\hat{f}_{sc}(v_{s,t}) = \min_t \hat{f}(v_{s,t})$$

(*sc* stands for "stack score"). For such a theory, the ending time is given by:

$$\hat{t}_{sc}(v_{s,t}) = \operatorname*{argmin}_t \left(\hat{f}_{sc}(v_{s,t}) = \hat{f}(v_{s,t}) \right)$$

Theories having the same score are ordered in the stack based on their length giving priority to the shortest ones. In order to achieve computational efficiency, it is possible to ignore theories in the stack with particularly low score.

Introducing a LM more complex than the one based on unigram probabilities requires performing a breadth first search with heuristics for pruning the stack content (Paul, 1992; Bahl and Jelinek, 1988). Of course, removing active candidates in the stack makes search no longer admissible.

Admissible search for phoneme recognition

Admissible algorithms have been used for generating the best string of phoneme hypotheses given an IN of phoneme models and phoneme bigram probabilities. Performance is evaluated by counting insertion (I), deletion (D) and substitution (S) errors. Phoneme *classification error* contains only substitutions and is usually obtained by assuming phoneme segmentation to be known like in the case of the TIMIT (Fisher *et al.*, 1987; Lamel *et al.*, 1986) corpus described in Appendix C.

The following measures are frequently used for phoneme as well as for word recognition:

$$\text{percent correct} = 100 \left(1 - \frac{D+S}{N} \right)$$

$$\text{accuracy} = 100 \left(1 - \frac{I+D+S}{N} \right)$$

where N is the total number of phonemes in the test. Results on phoneme recognition are reported in Chapter 5.

Some ASR systems are based on error (performance) models of phoneme sequences generated by these types of recognizers in a first search phase.

9.4. BEAM SEARCH

The Viterbi algorithm requires that, at every time frame, all possible path extensions are considered in order to update the scores of the network states for the next time frame. This can be a time-consuming operation if the network is large. On the other hand, it often happens that only a small fraction of the network states have a high probability, while a large number of states have a probability that compares unfavourably with the best one, making it unlikely that these states, eventually, can be included in the optimal path. The beam search method (Lowerre, 1976; Ney *et al.*, 1992b) exploits this observation to reduce the amount of computation needed to find the optimal path. While decoding an observation vector, at every time frame $t = 1, \ldots, T$, the cost of the best path "so far" is computed:

$$\bar{g}_t = \min_s g(\nu_{s,t})$$

and only those states $\nu_{s,t}$ are expanded whose cost is less than a threshold obtained as follows:

$$g(\nu_{s,t}) < K\bar{g}_t$$

The value of K determines the aggressivity of the pruning strategy. Discarding paths on the basis of such a simple criterion may obviously prevent from finding the optimal solution, but in practice this rarely happens, while the number of states explored during search is dramatically reduced. Moreover, by varying the threshold level, it is possible to find a good trade-off between loss in accuracy and speed gain.

Several analyses of speech decoding results have shown that the distance between the score of the best global path and the one of the best local paths is not uniform during search. In particular, this difference is lower at word boundaries and for non-linguistic events (see Figure 9.6 and its description in section 9.5). Thus, there are time intervals where the ambiguity in the decision is higher. This observation suggests that the use of a constant threshold is not adequate. More effective solutions include the use of multiple beams (e.g. one for inter-word and another for intra-word states) and adaptive values of K.

In Lacouture and Normandin (1993), a comparison between the use of one fixed threshold with respect to using two thresholds, a narrow one at word endings and a wider one elsewhere, is discussed. The two-beam scheme appears to be convenient, even when the lexicon has a tree organization.

In Steinbiss *et al.* (1994), the effect of setting an upper bound to the maximum number of active nodes is investigated. A variant of this scheme is the use of an upper bound for the maximum number of the active phone models. Along this line, a deactivation of less likely phones obtained through *look-ahead* and *phone pruning* techniques is described in section 9.6.2. Factorization of LM probabilities within trees as discussed in section 8.6.1 can be seen as a linguistic inter-word pruning (Steinbiss *et al.*, 1994).

In Jones *et al.* (1992), an adaptive beam threshold is used in a search strategy controlled by a probabilistic context-free grammar. As the problem, in this case, is the overflow of the path hypotheses stack for highly ambiguous, non-grammatical input segments, the beam width is decreased when the rate of node expansion is high, while if the rate is low, a wide beam is very likely to include the correct path.

9.5. SYSTEMS BASED ON ONE-PASS SEARCH

Two examples of dictation systems that use one-pass search are described in this section.

The ASR system called A.Re.S. (Automatic Reporting by Speech) (Angelini *et al.*, 1994a) developed at Istituto per la Ricerca Scientifica e Tecnologica (IRST) in Trento, Italy, is a significant example of the state of the art in large-vocabulary dictation. This is a speaker-independent continuous speech system which adopts a strategy search based on the beam search Viterbi algorithm.

Lexical models are based on phonetic transcriptions of Italian words with 50 context-independent units. Unit HMMs have simple left-to-right topologies of three or four states, depending on the average length of the unit. Observation distributions are Gaussian mixtures with a variable number of components, resulting from a training process that initializes all mixtures with 24 components, and then prunes rarely used Gaussians. The final configuration used in the experiments reported in this section includes a total of 2863 Gaussians appearing in 281 mixtures.

The signal processing front end provides the recognizer with a 27-dimensional vector every 10 ms, consisting of eight mel-scaled cepstral coefficients, the log-energy, and their first and second time derivatives. The acoustic parameters are scaled to ensure that all the elements of the parameter vector have comparable ranges. In evaluating Gaussian mixtures, the weighted sum is approximated by the component that would give the maximum contribution to the mixture for a given input sample. This reduces computation time without affecting accuracy.

Acoustic models were trained with maximum likelihood estimation on a set of about 2000 sentences belonging to the phonetically rich database APASCI collected at IRST (Angelini *et al.*, 1994b).

Table 9.1 A.Re.S. task: recognition tests

Topology	WER (%)	Processing time vs real time	Memory requirements (Mb)
Tree-based	6.5	0.49	16
Shared-tail	6.5	0.49	9.6

The implementation of the decoding algorithm takes into account the fact that the IN can be very large. Hence, in spite of the network being static, the memory used in intermediate computations is allocated on demand with a simple caching strategy. Moreover, caching of distribution values is performed, ensuring that each distribution is computed at most once in every frame even if the same model appears in many transitions.

Recognition results of the system on an Italian 10 000-word radiological reporting dictation task (Federico *et al.*, 1995; Brugnara and Cettolo, 1995) are discussed below. A performance comparison with the IN structures introduced in section 8.6 is shown in Table 9.1. In all the experiments, a bigram LM was used and the beam threshold was chosen to achieve real-time response on a Hewlett-Packard 735 workstation with 64 Mb of central memory.

The same recognition accuracy is obtained with different IN organizations. Nevertheless, due to the higher average number of hypotheses per frame, recognition with the linear network is five times slower than the one obtained using the tree-based lexical representation. This reduction of the search effort using a tree organization of the lexicon is comparable to that reported in Ney *et al.* (1992a), where a factor of seven is mentioned.

The positive impact of the tree network topology on the beam search Viterbi decoding is preserved both after network optimization and sharing tails; the memory requirements for network storage after the two types of compression are reduced by 60% and 40% respectively. Recognition results for tree-based and shared-tail topologies are shown in Table 9.1 in terms of word error rate (WER), measured as the percentage of word insertions (I) deletions (D) and substitutions (S) over all the words in the test set.

The same architecture was also used in a dictation system for the financial newspaper *Il Sole 24 Ore*, the Italian counterpart of the *Wall Street Journal*. Using the shared-tail topology for a 10 000-word bigram LM, an 11% WER was obtained with a real-time response.

Figure 9.6 shows the evolution of the number of processed IN arcs at each frame of the synchronous search. The speech waveform is in the upper window, with labelling and segmentation resulting from the decoding process. The second window shows how the number of active arcs in the network varies with time: the dashed line refers to the linear network, while the solid line refers to the tree-based network. The third window shows the same

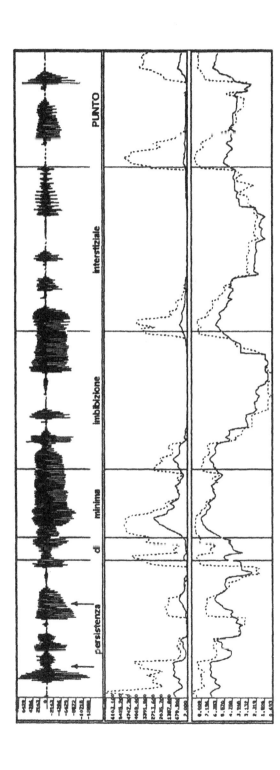

Figure 9.6 Number of active arcs during the decoding of a speech segment with two networks as described in section 9.5.

values, but on a logarithmic scale, to highlight differences in intervals where values are low. This example reflects a qualitative behaviour that was consistently observed in many cases. As one may expect, most of the ambiguities appear in regions corresponding to between-word transitions. Major differences between the two representations are in these regions and the peaks of ambiguity are much higher with the linear network. The within-word peaks correspond to potential word boundaries. For example, for the word *persistenza* ("persistence"), peaks in the number of active arcs, marked by arrows in the upper window of Figure 9.6, appear at the end of the components *per* and *persiste*, which are words by themselves (respectively, "for" and "persists").

An interesting version of the Philips dictation system (Steinbiss *et al.*, 1993) has been applied to dictation tasks in German with 10 k to 20 k words, and to American English tasks such as the 5 k and the 20 k-word *Wall Street Journal* corpora (Aubert *et al.*, 1994).

The acoustic vector, which represents 25 ms of signal every 10 ms, consists of 63 components: 30 spectral intensities, roughly corresponding to a mel-frequency scale in the range from 200 Hz to 6400 Hz, normalized with respect to their mean value, 15 first- and 15 second-order differences (pairs of adjacent spectral intensities are averaged for this computation) and three components representing the signal energy and its differences. Linear discriminant analysis maps acoustic vectors into a space where the discrimination is high in spite of a reduction in dimensionality.

Between 40 and 50 phonemes are modelled with HMMs; the observation distributions are continuous Laplacian mixture densities; for a given vector of acoustic features, the component of the mixture that gives the maximum contribution to the weighted sum replaces the sum itself with a great saving in computation time. Context-dependent units have been used for American English tasks.

LM is based on smoothed *n*-grams, typically word or class bigrams.

The lexicon of word pronunciations has a tree organization. The correct use of bigram LM probabilities requires the activation of a new copy of the lexicon tree when a word ending is reached during a Viterbi beam search. Thus, the search space grows dynamically. Such a growth is constrained by smearing (factorizing) LM probabilities within trees (as described in section 8.6.1) and by phoneme look-ahead (described in section 9.6) resulting in an effective focusing of the search.

With little modification of the search strategy, this system has also been used to produce word graphs in a two-pass search, as described in section 9.7.2.

Word error rates ranging from 4% to 12% were obtained for vocabularies of 5 k and 20 k words.

Another type of one pass search algorithm is used in the system of Cambridge University with comparable high performance (Woodland *et al.*, 1995).

9.6. FAST MATCH FOR CONSTRAINING SEARCH

Heuristic methods can be used for constraining search and reducing the search space size. *Fast match* (FM) (Bahl *et al.*, 1989b) is a method for the rapid computation of a list of candidates that will constrain successive search phases in which a computationally expensive detailed match is performed. FM has to be accurate both to reduce the risk of losing the correct candidate and to keep the candidate list as short as possible.

For example, FM has been used in isolated word recognition to obtain a list of word candidates (Bahl *et al.*, 1989b). Applied to stack decoders, FM reduces the number of successors to be expanded for the current best theory (Paul, 1991a). The same idea is the basis for phoneme look-ahead in which pruning is applied in the synchronous search based on the estimation of the score of possible phoneme chains that may follow a given phoneme (Ney *et al.*, 1992a), whose final state is in the active list of the beam search.

Admissibility

FM algorithms that do not rule out the optimal search solution are *admissible*. For real-time systems, admissibility is often too expensive in terms of computation time. For this reason, some systems are based on non-admissible FM techniques, and admissible algorithms are used for evaluating if the approximation introduced by the non-admissible ones does not significantly deteriorate performance.

In order to guarantee admissibility, FM has to be based on a score that satisfies the constraints discussed in (Bahl *et al.*, 1989b), which are summarized in the following. For the sake of simplicity, decisions are supposed to be taken at the word level. Let V be the vocabulary and $D(x, w)$ the detailed likelihood of the match between input x and word w. Let $F(x, w)$ be an estimator of $D(x, w)$ that is fast to compute and is an upper bound of $D(\cdot)$:

$$F(x, w) \geq D(x, w), \quad \forall x, w \tag{9.7}$$

A word list of an admissible FM is obtained by computing $F(x, w)$ for an acoustic input x and each word w of the vocabulary. Let w_b be the word for which the function has the maximum value:

$$w_b = \underset{w \in V}{\operatorname{argmax}} F(x, w)$$

After computing the detailed score for w_b, the FM word list, NV, is given by:

$$NV = \{w \in V : F(x, w) \geq D(x, w_b)\}$$

It is easy to show that from (9.7) and from the definition of NV, the correct word is contained in NV. Thus, this type of FM is admissible.

9.6.1. A Basic FM Technique

In order to achieve a fast computation of $F(\cdot)$, it is necessary to introduce some approximation in the matching of the unit models with the input. A way to obtain this is to simplify the models. In Bahl *et al.* (1993e), discrete HMM models of phonemes, syllables or words are simplified as follows. Given the HMM which models the generic unit u and an input sequence l_1^T of codebook symbols describing the input signal, the probability that the sequence of states $s_1, \ldots, s_T$ in that model produces l_1^T is given by:

$$\Pr(l_1^T, s_1, \ldots, s_T) = \Pr(s_1, \ldots, s_T) \prod_{i=1}^{T} \Pr(l_i \mid s_i)$$

As shown in Chapter 5, the probability $D(\cdot)$, that an HMM u produces the sequence l_1^T, is given by:

$$D(l_1^T, u) = \sum_{s_1, \ldots, s_T} \Pr(l_1^T, s_1, \ldots, s_T) = \sum_{s_1, \ldots, s_T} \Pr(s_1, \ldots, s_T) \prod_{i=1}^{T} \Pr(l_i \mid s_i) \quad (9.8)$$

where $s_1, \ldots, s_T$ are complete paths in the HMM u, with s_1 being the initial state and s_T the final state.

As the codebook size is finite, it is possible to compute, for each model u and once forever, the highest output probability for every label l_i among all the transitions $s_j \to s_k$ in u:

$$\mu(l_i, u) = \max_{(j,k) \in u} b_{jk}(l_i)$$

With this result and defining the contribution of the transition probabilities for all paths of length T in the model u as:

$$q(T, u) = \sum_{s_1, \ldots, s_T} \Pr(s_1, \ldots, s_T)$$

an upper bound of the (9.8) obtainable with a fast computation is:

$$D(l_1^T, u) \leq q(T, u) \prod_{i=1}^{T} \mu(l_i, u)$$

Indicating with $q_{max}(u)$ the maximum of $q(T, u)$ with respect to T, i.e. the maximum probability of any complete path in u, the following upper bound for the detailed match score can be considered:

$$D(l_1^T, u) \leq F(l_1^T, u) = q_{max}(u) \prod_{i=1}^{T} \mu(l_i, u)$$

where $F(l_1^T, u)$ represents the *acoustic fast-match score* of u for l_1^T. Since it is always greater than or equal to the detailed match score, FM is admissible. The time complexity of the computation of $F(\cdot)$ is linear with T. In Bahl *et al.*

(1993e), it is claimed that the computation time of $F(\cdot)$ is about 10 times lower than that of $D(\cdot)$. In order to further reduce it, the tree organization of the lexicon can be adopted in addition to a pruning strategy. On an isolated 20 k-word dictation task, such computation was about 100 times faster than for the detailed match, achieving real-time performance on a low-cost hardware system, with only a 0.34% increase in the word error rate due to the FM.

An interesting application of the above-described FM method is presented in Bahl *et al.* (1992) where a technique for constructing off-line groups of acoustically similar words, starting from utterances of all vocabulary words made by different speakers, is described. The technique proposes to begin with an aggressive FM which outputs a very short list of candidate words. Then, words acoustically similar to those of the FM list are added to the final set of candidates to be considered for further detailed processing. Results on an isolated 20 k-word dictation task show the effectiveness of the method: at a very low computation cost, the number of candidates is reduced from 20 k to 1500, while the correct word is missed only 2% of the time.

Other effective techniques to group acoustically similar words are presented in Laface *et al.* (1994) and Roe and Riley (1994). In the former paper, artificial utterances of words are obtained by concatenating real subword unit "templates". Sets of acoustically similar words are then identified through the decoding of such utterances on the lexical tree of a very large vocabulary. In the latter paper, a measure of confusability between pairs of words is derived from the phonetic pronunciation of words determined by the grapheme-to-phoneme converter of a synthesizer and the general (independent from the particular words) phonetic confusions exhibited by the recognizer. With these approaches, there is no need to collect acoustic samples of words.

9.6.2. Other FM Techniques

Look-ahead

In Haeb-Umbach and Ney (1991), an FM *look-ahead* technique is presented, which proceeds "synchronously" with Viterbi search. When a word-ending state in the search space is reached during the detailed search, a look-ahead procedure attempts to determine which words are likely to survive the continuation of the search. Only these words are considered for hypothesis growing. The "looking ahead" is performed by matching the acoustic input frames with just a lexical tree, without managing back-pointers. The fast match is a beam search executed at most every other frame. Note that observation probabilities computed during look-ahead can be re-used for detailed match, because the same unit models are involved in the two operations. Results on a 12.3 k-word speaker dependent continuous speech task show a reduction of the search space by a factor of 3–5 compared to standard Viterbi beam search, with an increase in error rate of 1–2%.

A similar technique is described in Ney *et al.* (1992a) and consists of executing the look-ahead routine at phone endings and not at word endings. Results on the above-mentioned 12 k-word task show a reduction of the search space by a factor of 2–4 compared to Viterbi beam search without phoneme look-ahead, with an increase in error rate of 1%.

Both in word and phoneme look-ahead, performance depends on the length of the look-ahead interval. The larger the look-ahead interval, the higher is the number of pruned candidates and the computation time. Optimal, empirically estimated, lengths are a few tens of microseconds for phoneme look-ahead and a few hundreds of microseconds for word look-ahead.

In Phillips and Goddeau (1994), look-ahead is made on the lexicon tree, and increased speed is achieved by collapsing phonemes into phone classes, with a decrease in accuracy.

Phone pruning

In Gopalakrishnan *et al.* (1994) and Renals and Hochberg (1995), the goodness of matching between phonemes and incoming input frames is estimated before a detailed matching phase, with the purpose of disregarding less promising hypotheses. The approach is similar to phoneme look-ahead, except that look-ahead is performed on the whole set of phonemes, no matter which search nodes are active.

In Gopalakrishnan *et al.* (1994), isolated word recognition is performed with discrete HMMs. For each phoneme P and frame time t, the likelihood that P produces the label sequence $l_t^{t+n_P}$ is computed. n_P is a fixed duration of phoneme P, estimated from multispeaker training data. The set of these likelihoods is kept into a matrix called *channel bank*. During detailed search, when a phoneme ending state becomes active in the search process at time t, among all the possible successor phonemes, only those that, in a time interval around t, have a value in the channel bank above a given threshold are activated. Thresholds are phone-dependent. The use of this technique increases the speed of the acoustic FM presented in Bahl *et al.* (1993e), and described above, by a factor of two with a 5–10% increase in error rate.

In Renals and Hochberg (1995), phone pruning is performed in a hybrid connectionist/HMM approach to speech recognition. As will be described in section 10.9, a recurrent network is used to estimate phone posterior probabilities. The presence of a phone in a particular time interval is asserted by comparing the phone posterior probability with a threshold common to all phones. By integrating this method with the single-pass decoder, on a 20 k-word dictation task, an overall speed increase of 15 was obtained at the cost of 7% increase in word error rate.

Decision trees for FM

In Waast and Bahl (1995), a binary classification tree automatically built from data is used for FM. Labelled data are pairs (*phonetic transcription, acoustic sequence*) where the acoustic sequence contains codeword labels. The questions at the nodes are of the type "Does P_i belong to S?", where P_i is a phone of the input phonetic baseform and S is a subset of the phones. Since the possible subsets of a set P of phonemes are $|\mathcal{P}(P)| = 2^{|P|} - 1$, with 40 units there would be 10^{21} different subsets. As this number is too high, only meaningful phone classes are considered. Splits are evaluated by discriminant analysis that leads to a formulation of questions in terms of projection of the input acoustic sequence onto the discriminant axis between the YES and NO classes of nodes. The halting criterion is a simple threshold on the improvement given by the split.

This FM method has been applied to the recognition of isolated syllables with good results. The approach will probably be extended to continuous speech recognition.

9.7. MULTISTAGE SEARCH

The introduction of different knowledge sources (KSs) during the search of the optimal solution may be very complex, depending on the type of KSs used. In fact, if it is possible to integrate AMs, LM and lexical models to form an IN, as outlined in Chapter 8, there are other KSs that either lead to unmanageable INs or simply cannot be integrated in such a structure. This is typically the case of semantic models used for speech understanding.

A possible solution to this problem is to carry out search in successive phases. In the first phase, the most discriminant and computationally cheaper KSs are used, reducing, in some way, the number of hypotheses. In successive phases, progressively reduced sets of hypotheses are considered and more powerful and expensive KSs are used. The resulting search algorithm is, in general, not admissible, because if the optimal solution (considering all the KSs involved) is lost in a phase, it cannot be recovered later. However, the benefits of complexity reduction greatly justify this approach. Moreover, in practice, the use of more and more detailed KSs on a reduced set of candidates may give better results than an admissible algorithm using poor models.

An example of multistage search is described in Fissore *et al.* (1988). An HMM-based speech recognizer generates a lattice of word hypotheses, each of which is characterized by a word identifier, begin and end times, and likelihood scores. Words are ordered according to likelihoods. In one of the reported experiments, the acoustic stage is driven by a word preselection process, based on a presegmentation of the speech signal into six phonetic classes. Then, a linguistic parser tries to build the most probable sentence hypothesis from the word lattice, taking into account word scores, linguistic constraints and temporal constraints between adjacent words. Such an approach has the drawback that good heuristics have to be introduced in order to cope with temporal constraints between adjacent words.

Of great importance in multistage search are the data structures representing word hypotheses. These structures are typically finite-state automata, in which temporal constraints between words are reflected in the automaton topology. Figure 9.7 shows the example of two popular structures, namely, *word lattice* and *word graph*.

9.7.1. Extraction of the *N*-Best Word Sequences

Recently, algorithms have been proposed to find the *N* most likely word sequences, in order to provide a simple and efficient interface for the use of powerful KSs. Note that, although in the following we shall refer to the *N*-best word sequence, it is always possible to consider other units, like phonemes or syllables, instead of words.

Exact N-best and word-dependent N-best

A first version of the *N*-best algorithm, in which the value *N* has to be pre-defined, is now briefly described (Schwartz and Chow, 1990). It is an extension of the time-synchronous Viterbi algorithm, with the difference that it computes probabilities of word sequences rather than state sequences. To do this, each theory ending at node $\nu_{s,t}$ is associated with its *history*, defined as the sequence of complete word hypotheses in the theory path. Theories having the same history are merged and their probabilities are summed together. At each node $\nu_{s,t}$, only the *N* best paths are retained. At the end, the paths of the final nodes of the trellis are simply reordered to obtain the *N*-best sequences. The complexity of this algorithm is proportional to *N*.

This algorithm is computationally expensive for large values of *N*, mainly because of memory requirements and the need to manage the lists of paths at each node. A modification of such algorithm has been proposed in Schwartz and Austin (1991), in which the concept of history has been released following the reasonable assumption that the hypothesized beginning time of a word depends only on the preceding word hypothesis. This assumption, known as word-pair approximation, can be considered true if the preceding word is long, otherwise it is questionable. Note also that frequent short words are function words, which are often poorly articulated. In practice, the loss in performance due to this approximation has been found to be very small (Aubert and Ney, 1995). With this assumption, the history to be considered for a word hypothesis is no longer an entire word sequence starting at the beginning

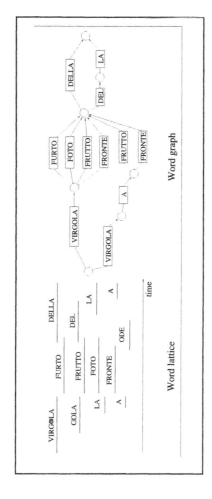

Figure 9.7 Word lattice and word graph for task in Italian. In the lattice, each word has a time interval explicitly associated to it, while in the word graph, temporal constraints implicitly result from the topology.

of the utterance, but only the previous word. Using this approximation, the number of theories to be kept is highly reduced, being $k \ll N$ at each node. At the end, a recursive traceback must be performed to find the N-best list. The algorithm has time complexity proportional to k, but is no longer admissible.

Forward–backward algorithms

The algorithms introduced above do not perform any prediction, in terms of minimum cost to completion, at time t, about the future of the active theories. This makes the algorithms computationally intensive in order to ensure admissibility, or at least to achieve good performance.

This difficulty is alleviated by the so-called forward–backward search algorithms. The idea is to first perform a forward search, during which partial scores α are stored for each node, and then a backward search, driven by the previously computed α scores. The backward search is a search performed on the sentence *reversed*, i.e. considering the last frame T as the beginning one, and the first frame as the last one. Moreover, also AMs and LMs must be reversed. A score β is computed in the backward search.

The forward search must be very fast, and is generally a time-synchronous Viterbi search. For very large vocabularies, simplified AMs or LMs are often used. Different solutions have been proposed for the backward search, which can be time-synchronous as well as time-asynchronous.

If the same AMs and LMs are used during the two phases, then α and β scores can be the ones introduced in Chapter 5.

Time-synchronous forward–backward search

In Austin *et al.* (1991b), an N-best algorithm is proposed in which both forward and backward phases are performed by time-synchronous Viterbi search. Let us define a node $\nu_{e_w,t}$, active at time t, that represents the ending state of the HMM for word w. During the forward stage, the score $\alpha(w, t)$ of each active node $\nu_{e_w,t}$ is recorded. Let us denote as Ω^t the set of active words[1] at time t, and as α^T the global score of the optimal path determined by the forward pass.

The backward phase is, in general, more complex than the forward one. For instance, it can use more sophisticated AMs or LMs, but in this case α and β scores are not comparable and cannot be combined in the same computation as in Chapter 5. Another possibility, discussed in the following, is to use, during the backward phase, the time-synchronous word-dependent N-best algorithm. In this case, the scores are exactly the same of the forward pass,

---

[1]Using a beam search during the forward pass makes the entire algorithm inadmissible, as the words not in Ω^t will no longer be considered during the backward phase.

but the algorithm has a greater complexity. The backward pass starts by activating the words found in Ω^T, and by computing the backward scores $\beta(w, T-1)$ for each active word. In this case, $\beta(w, t)$ represents the best score from node $\nu_{e_w,t}$ to a node corresponding to the end of the sentence.

At a generic node $\nu_{e_{w_1},t}$, the combination of the forward and backward scores $\alpha(w_1, t)\beta(w_1, t)$ represents the maximum score that can be obtained for a generic sentence hypothesis passing through that node. If another node $\nu_{e_{w_2},t}$ has a worse forward–backward score, it can be concluded that there is at least one theory including node $\nu_{e_{w_1},t}$ that will have a final score better than each of the theories including node $\nu_{e_{w_2},t}$. Also, if a word w_3 is not in Ω^t, all theories including node $\nu_{e_{w_3},t}$ would have out-of-beam scores; therefore, word w_3 can be excluded from the computation at time t.

In general, the quantity $\alpha(w, t)\beta(w, t)/\alpha^T$ is equal to 1 for the nodes belonging to the optimal path. If this quantity falls below a pruning threshold at a given node, then all paths passing through that node will have low global scores and will be pruned. This gives a powerful criterion to deactivate words during search. It is important to stress the difference between the beam applied during the forward pass, and the beam of the backward pass. The former causes the algorithm to be inadmissible, because pruning is made with respect to the local optimal score. On the other hand, the backward pass can exploit both the score of the global optimal path (if it is not lost during the forward stage) and the α predictions, to find all and only the theories having a global score inside the backward beam.

As soon as the forward pass is performed, the optimal path (1-best) can be further processed by other modules, while the backward pass starts computing subsequent candidates. An increase in speed of a factor of 40, without any reduction in performance, was observed with respect to the word-dependent N-best algorithm.

Tree–trellis forward–backward search

Another algorithm for N-best computation is described in Soong and Huang (1991). The name given to this algorithm, tree–trellis search, comes from the data structures it uses.

Briefly, a forward Viterbi search is performed synchronously with the input sequence, in order to compute and store the forward scores $\alpha(w, t)$ corresponding to a node $\nu_{e_w,t}$ defined above. A* search is then performed backward, expanding asynchronously one word at a time and using the combination of forward and backward scores as upper bounds for partial theory completion. Forward scores are used as prediction scores. As the same metric (i.e. that given by the HMMs and the language model) is used to compute forward and backward scores, the search is admissible. This means that the first complete hypothesis that is found coincides with the best one found during the forward pass and is the 1-best. Subsequent complete hypotheses correspond sequentially to the N-best, as they are generated in decreasing order of score.

Backward search is based on A^*, i.e. at each step, the most probable theory is removed from the stack, and the list of possible one-word extensions for that theory is generated. A theory th contains a word sequence and all the pertinent scores $\beta(th_{w_j}, t)$, $(t = 0, \ldots, T)$, where w_j is the first word of the sequence (the last expanded). Note that, in this case, $\beta(th_w, t)$ is defined as the best score from node $\nu_{s_w, t}$, corresponding to the starting state of the HMM representing word w at time t, including the word sequence of th and reaching a final node of the search trellis. In practice, a theory accounts for all possible time segmentations of its word sequence. Let us assume that the one-word backward extension leading to theory th' concerns word w_i, as depicted in Figure 9.8, where w_j is represented as the last expanded word of theory th. For each time frame t, the product $\alpha(w_i, t)\beta(th_{w_j}, t)$ represents the score of the best complete path including node $\nu_{e_{w_i}, t}$ (or equivalently $\nu_{s_{w_j}, t}$) and belonging to th. The optimal crossing time t^* between w_i and w_j is the time frame for which $\alpha(w_i, t)\beta(th_{w_j}, t)$ is maximum. The $\beta(th'_{w_i}, t)$, $(t = 0, \ldots, T)$ scores are computed with a backward dynamic programming recursion for word w_i, starting from the backward scores $\beta(th_{w_j}, t)$, $(t = 0, \ldots, T)$. Finally, the theory th' obtained by the one-word extension will be inserted into the stack, ordered by the score $\alpha(w_i, t^*)\beta(th_{w_j}, t^*)$.

This algorithm is computationally attractive, because the backward phase requires only a small fraction of computation with respect to the forward pass. In order to find the N-best word sequences, the size of the stack in the A^* search must be N. In fact, because the stack is reordered and the prediction is exact, at each time, the $(N + 1)$th theory has no chance to become part of the first N. Finally, N-best hypotheses are generated sequentially, which is computationally advantageous if subsequent modules have to process hypotheses to satisfy other constraints.

Advantages and limitations of N-best search

Different uses of the N-best word sequences are described in Schwartz *et al.* (1992) and Nguyen *et al.* (1994). First, the N-best hypotheses are an effective interface between ASR and natural language processing, avoiding search strategies that strongly depend on the characteristics of both components. N-best hypotheses can be further processed by complex KSs such as higher order statistical LMs (e.g. trigrams), or cross-word coarticulation models. The contribution of a new KS can be evaluated starting from the N-best hypotheses without having to integrate it into a complex system. Eventually, a new search strategy can be developed only after an increase in performance with new KSs has been observed.

N-best computation is effective only for N of the order of tens or hundreds. Moreover, in a typical N-best sequence, many of the different sequences are

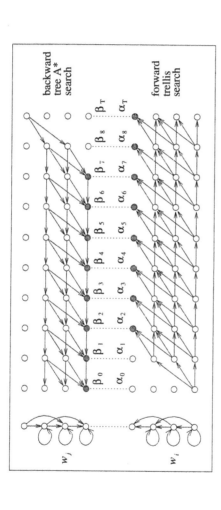

Figure 9.8 Merging of forward–backward scores for the tree–trellis algorithm. Note that α_t and β_t stand respectively for $\alpha(w_i, t)$ and $\beta(th_{w_j}, t)$.

```
           quale citta' e' stato presentato l' articolo
*** in quale citta' e' stato presentato l' articolo
           quale citta' e' stato presentata l' articolo
     in quale citta' e' stato presentata l' articolo
           quali citta' e' stato presentato l' articolo
           quale citta' e' stato presentata l' titolo
     in quale citta' e' stato presentata l' titolo
           quali citta' e' stato presentata l' articolo
      a quale citta' e' stato presentato l' articolo
      a quale citta' e' stato presentata l' articolo
           quali citta' e' stato presentata l' titolo
           quale citta' hanno   presentato l' articolo
     in quale citta' hanno   presentato l' articolo
           quale citta' hanno   presentata l' articolo
     in quale citta' hanno   presentata l' articolo
      a quale citta' e' stato presentata l' titolo
```

Figure 9.9 Example of *N*-best list for the Italian sentence marked with ***, which means "in which town has the paper been presented?".

one-word variations of each other, and subsequent sequences concern all the possible combinations of these independent variations, as shown in Figure 9.9. Thus, the number of sentences needed to include the correct hypothesis grows exponentially with the length of the utterance.

9.7.2. Word Hypotheses Structures

Algorithms trying to overcome the limitations of *N*-best search make use of more compact hypothesis representations such as word lattices or word graphs. Word lattices are composed by word hypotheses, associated with a score and word boundaries, which can be either time frames or time intervals. An interesting example can be found in Alleva *et al.* (1993). Word graphs are composed by a finite-state network, in which arcs are labelled by words. Temporal constraints are implicitly imposed by the network topology.

A word structure can be evaluated based on two parameters: the number of word hypotheses per pronounced word, which is related to the structure size, and the word error rate of the best word string (with respect to the input sentence) inside the structure. The latter gives an upper bound of system performance.

A*-based word graphs

An evolution of the tree–trellis forward–backward search algorithm (Soong and Huang, 1991) includes a path merging step during the backward pass.

This idea was first proposed in Hetherington *et al.* (1993), where each theory during the backward pass is characterized by its optimal crossing time t^*. Briefly, a suitable criterion is applied to collapse, during the backward pass, partial theories reaching the same grammar node at the same optimal crossing time. The algorithm ends when all complete theories whose scores differ from the best one for less than a specified threshold, have been found.

The computational gain with respect to classical N-best search is also discussed in Hetherington *et al.* (1993), and mainly concerns the fact that word sequences which span the same speech interval and are variations of already found hypotheses are simply added to the word graph. In this way, finding all the combinations of independent variations is no longer necessary. Furthermore, it is shown that all the N-best theories, having a score within a specified threshold, are surely contained in the word graph.

A similar algorithm is introduced in De Mori *et al.* (1994) which takes advantage of the fact that, thanks to the tree–trellis organization, no paths having identical words and differing only in time alignment are inserted into the word graph.

This algorithm follows the tree–trellis forward–backward N-best algorithm (Soong and Huang, 1991), still using a forward pass and the forward–backward score merging mechanism. Differences come from the fact that, during the backward phase, a word graph is built incrementally by adding an arc at each theory extension. The backward phase of this algorithm is now described as an example.

Example. A word graph, WG, is built during the backward A^* phase. α scores are associated with states of IN for each $t = 0, \ldots, T$. A theory th_j contains a state s_i in IN, the scores $\beta(th_j, t)$, $(t = 0, \ldots, T)$, the best crossing time t^*, which is the time frame for which $\alpha(s_i, t)\beta(th_j, t)$ is maximum, and the score $\alpha(s_i, t^*)\beta(th_j, t^*)$. Furthermore, for the construction of the WG, the theory must contain the last arc expanded in IN and a destination state in WG.

Let us refer to Figure 9.10, in which an IN composed of three states is shown. α scores have been computed for each state, and the best path leads to a global score α^T. The initial theory th_1 is associated to state s_3, $\beta(th_1, t)$ equals 0 for each t but T, and the optimal crossing time is T. Being an initial theory, the last arc expanded in IN is not defined, while the destination state in WG is a final one, say s_f. Expanding theory th_1 requires identification of all arcs arriving at state s_3 in IN, each one corresponding to a possible extension of that theory. In our case, a single arc goes from state s_2 to s_3, with associated word w_j: let us define theory th_2 as an extension of theory th_1. In order to find $\beta(th_2, t)$, $(t = 0, \ldots, T)$ the dynamic recursion must be performed backwards, on a trellis defined on word w_j, initialized with $\beta(th_1, t)$, $(t = 0, \ldots, T)$. After that, the optimal crossing time for theory th_2 can be found as the time t for which $\alpha(s_2, t)\beta(th_2, t)$ is maximum. Note that, as there is only one path, the maximum must be equal to α^T. At this point, theory th_2 is inserted into the stack, according to its score α^T. Its last expanded arc is identified by w_j, and its destination state in WG

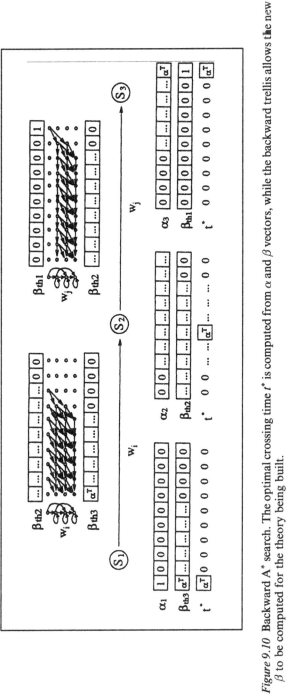

Figure 9.10 Backward A* search. The optimal crossing time t^* is computed from α and β vectors, while the backward trellis allows the new β to be computed for the theory being built.

will be s_f. When th_2 is extracted from the stack, the same procedure generates a theory th_3, which eventually reaches state s_1 with optimal crossing time 0.

The WG is built during backward search. At each ending node ν_{s_i,t^*} of a theory th_j, extracted from the stack, is associated a state in the WG. The initial state of WG is assigned to the node $\nu_{1,0}$, being 1 the initial state of the IN; the final state of WG, s_f, is assigned to all the nodes $\nu_{F,T}$, where F is a final state of IN. When theory th_j is extracted from the stack, the last arc expanded must be inserted in the WG. As the destination state in WG is part of the theory, it remains to define the starting state. If the node ν_{s_i,t^*} has not yet been found, a new state of WG is defined, say s_{s_i,t^*}, and assigned to that node, the last arc expanded is inserted into WG and the theory is expanded. Otherwise, there must have been another theory th_k that already reached that node with a better score, because A* is admissible. Thus, the actual theory will eventually evolve in the same way as th_k, with a worse score. The last expanded arc is linked during path merging to the state previously assigned to the node, s_{s_i,t^*}, and the actual theory is abandoned.[2] The search ends when no more partial hypotheses having score within a given beam are on the stack.

This algorithm leads to small WGs, with several alternatives when there are hypotheses with similar acoustic scores, and few alternatives when acoustic scores are quite different. Figure 9.11 shows an example of a WG, obtained for a dictation task of 10 000 words in Italian. The IN includes smoothed bigrams represented through a null node, as described in section 8.5 (see also Figure 8.10). As the original WG has been rearranged, for the sake of clarity, in order to remove empty transitions, in some cases there is a duplication of word arcs. This is due to the fact that two paths covering the same words are in the beam. The first uses the direct bigram link, the second goes through the null node (described in section 8.5.1). In fact, WG is exactly a subspace of the original search space. Note also that the density of WG is variable and the word subsequences "*DEL PETROLIO VIRGOLA*" and "*DEL GOLFO*" do not have competitors.

Progressive search

The basic idea of progressive search (Murveit *et al.*, 1993) is that of using more and more complex KSs, on a progressively reduced search space. The search space is defined as a word-transition diagram, without temporal and scoring information. In stage p of progressive search the word graph WG, generated at stage $(p-1)$, is used to produce a WG for the successive stage.

A first algorithm, called word-life, generates a WG with a time-synchronous beam search Viterbi forward pass. During search, for each time t, different bit

---

[2]Abandoning a theory does affect admissibility, because it does not account for paths of th reaching state s at a time different from t^*.

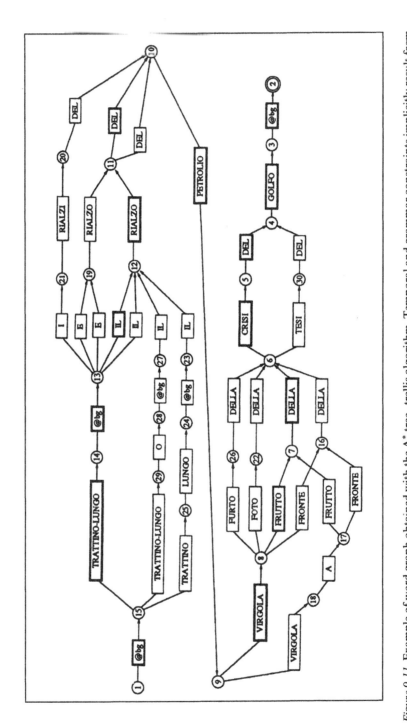

Figure 9.11 Example of word graph obtained with the A* tree–trellis algorithm. Temporal and grammar constraints implicitly result from the network topology.

tables are filled for active words at t, ending words at t, all word-to-word connections active at t. The active word table has a row for each word w and a column for each value of t. A bit is set to 1 in position (w, t) if an internal state of the model of w is active in the beam search at time t. The word-ending table is analogous, with the exception that a bit is set to 1 at position (w, t) if the final state of the model of w is active at t. The connection table has a similar structure with a row for each word to word connection. Words found active for some t, which do not appear to terminate within a reasonable time, are removed, because they were candidates pruned before activating other words. Finally, a WG is built, which contains all surviving words with the corresponding word-to-word transitions. WGs generated by this algorithm do not scale up well, because a small beam has to be used in order to generate WGs of acceptable size, with the possibility of definitively losing the best-scoring hypotheses.

To overcome this problem, the forward–backward word-life algorithm has been introduced. A time-synchronous forward step is performed using beam search and computing $\alpha(w, t)$, the probability of each word w ending at time t. The best complete hypothesis, having score α^T, allows the computation of a global pruning threshold. Then a time-synchronous backward step is performed, which is similar to the word-life algorithm described above. The improvement comes from the fact that before recording a word-to-word connection between w_i and w_j at time t, forward–backward scores are used to check if that transition is below the global pruning threshold θ, i.e.

$$\alpha(w_i, t)\beta(w_j, t)P(w_j \mid w_i) < \alpha^T\theta$$

where $P(w_j \mid w_i)$ represents the bigram LM probability. If the condition is not satisfied, then that connection at that time is blocked.

Progressively introducing more complex KSs allows one to obtain great improvements in complexity, without affecting recognition accuracy.

Word graph algorithm

Two algorithms (Oerder and Ney, 1993; Ney and Aubert, 1994) have been proposed to build word graphs without a backward phase. Both are based on time-synchronous beam search decoding using a tree-organized lexicon. The search space is built dynamically, instantiating a new tree each time a leaf, corresponding to a word end, is reached. Basically, each word ending at a given time corresponds to a word hypothesis, which is kept and then used to build a WG. The WG is defined as a direct acyclic graph, where each arc is labelled with a word and a score, and each node corresponds to a time frame.

In Oerder and Ney (1993), a first algorithm is proposed, in which a word hypotheses generator (WHG) finds, with a beam search, word hypotheses consisting of a word identifier, an acoustic score, start and end times. Hypotheses

```
Algorithm:
∀t
    ∀(wᵢ, wⱼ) ending at t
        store the word boundary th(t; wᵢ, wⱼ)
        store the word score h(wⱼ; th(t; wᵢ, wⱼ), t)
build WG by tracing back the hypotheses stored
```

Figure 9.12 Word graph building algorithm.

can be arranged in a large graph that must be pruned and optimized by the subsequent module, called a word graph optimizer (WGO). A reduction in the number of arcs can be obtained by the WHG if words are allowed to start only every other or every third frame. A possible WGO works as follows: first the graph is unfolded from the start node into a tree structure; then, for each set of partial paths with identical start time, end time and word sequence, only the most probable path is kept; finally edges having a score below a certain threshold, with respect to the best complete score, are removed. Other actions that may be performed by a WGO concern the merging of nodes with identical time, or the merging of subgraphs having identical time boundaries and word labels.

A different word graph builder is presented in Ney and Aubert (1994), which is integrated into a one-pass search algorithm. It exploits the word-pair approximation, assuming that the boundary between two words is independent of previous history. Using this assumption in conjunction with an n-gram language model it is possible to recombine, at time t, all the word sequence hypotheses having identical $n - 1$ final words. The algorithm is based on a dynamic programming recursion that finds, at time t, the optimal word boundary between words w_i and w_j at ending time t, say $th(t; w_i, w_j)$, which, under the word-pair assumption, is independent of previous words; the cumulative score for word w_j from the optimal word boundary to t, say $h(w_j; th(t; w_i, w_j), t)$, is also computed. The algorithm is summarized in Figure 9.12.

Rescoring WGs (Aubert and Ney, 1995) with higher order LMs, such as trigrams, can be carried out without recomputing acoustic scores, because the same acoustic scores and time boundaries can be used. On the contrary, if more detailed AMs are used, for instance by modelling alternative pronunciations or coarticulation between words, then WG must be modified and a new search must be performed.

9.7.3. Systems Based on Multistage Search

In Nguyen *et al.* (1994), a four-pass lattice search algorithm for 20 000 words dictation is introduced, in which each phase constrains the following one. The first phase is a forward time-synchronous beam search which stores high-scoring word ends, using a fast-match technique. A successive time-synchronous backward search uses the previously computed word-ending scores to speed up search. During this phase, a bigram LM and within-word triphone models are used; $\beta_{w_j}^t$ scores and beginning times are stored for each word found. During the third pass – identical to the second one, but running forward – ending times and $\alpha_{w_j}^t$ scores are saved. The fourth phase uses information of phases 2 and 3 to determine possible word-juncture times; in particular, a word pair will be used if the following relation holds:

$$\alpha_{w_j}^t \beta_{w_i}^t \Pr(w_i \mid w_j) > \lambda$$

where $\Pr(w_i \mid w_j)$ is the bigram probability for word w_j followed by word w_i and λ is a threshold. By iteratively connecting word pairs, a word graph is built, which is then expanded to include trigram LMs and cross-word triphones. The most likely hypothesis is then obtained with the fourth backward phase. If other expensive KSs are to be used, the fourth pass may generate, instead of the best word sequence, an N-best sequence or another word graph, which will be further processed.

In Glass *et al.* (1995), a speech understanding system for an air travel information service (ATIS) is described. The first two phases are based on the A* word graph algorithm described previously (Hetherington *et al.*, 1993), using a class bigram LM and representing each word with a pronunciation network of context-independent phones. The third stage is applied on the word graph, and generates the top 50-best sentence hypotheses using a class 4-gram LM. The fourth stage rescores the 50-best hypotheses using a more accurate AM, which includes context-dependent and gender-dependent units. Only the top five reordered hypotheses are passed to the last module, which is a natural language (NL) component. Each hypothesis can be either accepted or rejected by this component; the first one which satisfies NL constraints is eventually used for building a query to a database.

In Seneff *et al.* (1995), an attempt to use a linguistically motivated language model for search is described. After generating a word graph with an A* search, further search is performed using either an *n*-gram LM or the TINA NL processing framework (Seneff, 1992c), in order to compare the two techniques. TINA, which will be described in Chapter 14, was developed to apply NL capabilities for the interpretation of spoken input. It is based on a context-free grammar, augmented with a set of syntactic and semantic constraints which can block linguistically wrong hypotheses during search. Grammar rules can be divided into two sets, the first one representing the language (i.e. English) and the second one specific to the application (i.e. ATIS), thus simplifying porting in different domains. Grammar rules are written by hand, and are automatically converted to a set of transition probabilities involving both terminal words and grammar constituents. Probabilities are estimated on a set of parse trees obtained automatically on a training set of sentences; in this way, a sort of *n*-gram LM is embedded into the context-free grammar. A* search is performed on the word graph, whose basic step is the one-word extension of a theory. A theory is composed of a unique word sequence, a set of partial parses for that word sequence, and a probability for sorting theories. When a theory is selected for expansion, all partial parses are extended to cover the new word, producing a new theory. Results, given both in terms of word error rate and of understanding error rate, show that TINA competes favourably with various *n*-gram LMs.

In Riley *et al.* (1995), a system for 60 000 words dictation is presented. Two stages are involved: in the first one a word graph is generated, while the second one uses context-dependent AMs and an LM which consists of about 34 million *n*-grams, with *n* ranging from 1 to 5. The first stage consists of a cascade of phone recognition, syllable recognition, word recognition, and finally the application of a bigram LM. Each of these operations produces a graph, which is first modified to account for the knowledge source of the next level and then becomes the input for the next operation. In absence of pruning, this cascade of operations is equivalent to performing search with an IN containing all these KSs. Motivations for this choice are thus related to speed and memory requirements, at least for very large vocabulary tasks. It is reported that the intermediate steps reduce the search space and make search faster.

9.7.4. Scoring in Progressive Search

So far, several methods for generating different structures of multiple word hypotheses have been described. Depending on the goal of the system, i.e. dictation, understanding, translation, etc., these multiple hypotheses have to be successively processed by using new KSs in order to make a final decision. Examples of KSs used in progressive search are: higher-order *n*-gram language models, acoustic models with longer context dependence, between-word coarticulation models and segmental models. In the following, some works in which particular types of KSs are used for rescoring multiple hypotheses are briefly presented.

In Fissore *et al.* (1988), a post-processing of the word lattice generated by a continuous speech recognizer is described. The goal is speech understanding that is achieved by parsing the lattice in order to find the most likely sequence of words. Sentence meaning is extracted under the control of caseframes with associated semantic rules which guide the parsing. The parser starts from the most acoustically reliable word hypotheses and extends them in longer phrase hypotheses which, in turn, are chosen for extension following a best-first strategy, until the entire input sentence is covered by a (the best) phrase.

In Boiteau and Haffner (1993), Lokbani *et al.* (1993) and Rayner *et al.* (1994), three different methods for reordering the *N*-best list generated by a speech recognizer are presented. The first two approaches use the same HMM-based isolated-word recognizer that generates an *N*-best list together with the segmentation of each hypothesis.

In Boiteau and Haffner (1993), rescoring uses two artificial neural networks (ANNs) working at the segmental level on information not available to the recognizer: one is the duration of the segment and one is a vector of the average values of the input parameters over the segment. Given an hypothesis, two scores are computed from the ANN outputs of the hypothesis segments. The score of the HMM module and those derived from the two ANNs are finally linearly combined to give a new hypothesis score that is used for reordering the *N*-best list.

In Lokbani *et al.* (1993), each segment is represented by a vector of acoustical and temporal components. Two Gaussian functions, with diagonal covariance matrix, model the emission probability of observation vectors given, respectively, the correct and the incorrect phoneme. The segmental score is obtained as the ratio of the emission probability of the observation vector of the correct model over the emission probability of the incorrect model. For each hypothesis, a global segmental score is obtained combining the segmental scores of its segments. Finally, each hypothesis in the *N*-best list is rescored by linearly combining the segmental score and the acoustic score.

In Rayner *et al.* (1994), reordering of *N*-best list is made through the score obtained by the linear combination of scores from different KSs. The method is automatically trainable and assumes the availability of a training corpus of *N*-best lists with the correct hypothesis marked (if there is one). Some KSs give scores, such as the likelihood of the recognizer and a binary score expressing whether or not the hypothesis could be parsed. Other KSs produce "linguistic items" that have to be associated with numerical scores; this is obtained through "discrimination functions", one for each type of linguistic item. An example of linguistic item is that of word triples, that is the set of surface trigrams. The corresponding discrimination function gives positive scores to triples that occur more frequently in correct hypotheses, and negative scores to those triples often observed in incorrect hypotheses. Another linguistic item takes into account coherence between subjects and predicates. In general, given a linguistic item *L* and its type *T*, the discrimination function for *T* gives a value obtained through a symmetric formula on the two countings of *L* in correct and incorrect hypotheses of the training corpus. Weights of the linear combination of different KS scores are estimated on training data by optimizing a cost function.

9.8. SOME RECENT RESULTS IN DICTATION

Different groups performed experiments in 1994 on a corpus known as North American Business (NAB) containing 248 million words. The corpus includes various test sets. Results of different types of experiments are reported in Pallett *et al.* (1995).

The architectures of some systems are inspired by the Sphinx system developed at Carnegie Mellon University (CMU) (Lee *et al.*, 1990b,c).

Most of the systems involved in the test performed a multiple-step search. Progressive search in the system of Stanford Research Institute (SRI) was based on the following steps: word lattice generated by forward–backward (FB) search using bigrams and within-words context-dependent HMMs, FB *N*-best search on the word lattice, rescoring using across-word HMMs, unseen triphone models, LDA, trigram LM, globally consistent template models and hybrid HMM/ANN models. Scores are combined linearly. An important feature of the SRI system was consistency modelling, based on speaker-adapted HMMs obtained by clustering speakers from the training set (Sankar *et al.*, 1995). Adding ANN and HMM cross-word context-dependent models reduces the word error rate from 15.43% to 14.09%.

The IBM system was based on a two-pass search. First *envelope search* was used to generate the 100-best sentences. Envelope search is a version of the A^* algorithm in which PARTIAL and COMPLETE hypotheses are kept and scored with log-likelihood L. A profile of a path ending with a word is an array of values of $L(t)$. The envelope at time t is the maximum value of the individual path profiles at t. Candidates with L greater than the envelope value minus a threshold are alive, the others are dead. The shortbest (the best among the shortest ones) alive path is expanded. When a path becomes dead, its contribution to the envelope is retracted, the envelope changes and dead paths may become alive again. Search stops when there is an optimal (or *N*-best) complete path and there are no other paths alive (Gopalakrishnan *et al.*, 1995). The best 100 sentences are rescored using the acoustic probability obtained for the maximum (bigrams) based probability path with continuous density models.

In the system developed at Cambridge University (CU), a precursor of which is described in Woodland *et al.* (1994), a word lattice is obtained following the word graph approach and the word-pair approximation (the start time of each word is independent of all words before its immediate predecessor). A lattice is converted into a stochastic FSA introducing *N*-gram language models. An arc of the lattice is pruned if the score of the best path through it is lower that the absolute optimal global path minus a threshold. Lattice performance is defined in terms of density (number of lattice arcs per word in the sentence), sentence error rate (the entire sentence cannot be obtained from the lattice) and word error rate (a word is not in the lattice). With a 65 000-word vocabulary, an average density of 341 hypothesized words per spoken word was observed with 0.65% of out-of-vocabulary (OOV) words and 1.5% of words missed in the lattice.

Other important systems were developed at Philips, based on word graphs described in previous sections and at LIMSI-CNRS (Gauvain *et al.*, 1995). An A^* algorithm was used in the Lincoln Labs system. The BBN system was based on four or five search steps, described in section 9.7.3.

A unique approach was followed at AT&T with a system architecture based on a cascade of phoneme (with bigrams), syllables and word lattice generations performed by weighted transducers, following a theory (without pruning) equivalent to the algebra of rational series (Pereira *et al.*, 1994). A word lattice was generated with this system with a 20 000-word lexicon producing an average density of 827 words, 2.7% OOV and 4 4% of missed words. The lattice was used in a further search step with word HMMs leading to an overall 10% word error rate. By adding the missed words to the lattice (excluding OOVs), it was observed that only 0.2% of words missed in the first pass were correctly recognized in the second pass. With multiple-step search, it was possible to use *n*-grams ($n > 3$), mixtures of LMs and adaptive LMs with remarkable reductions in language model perplexity and up to 10% reduction in word error rate. Semicontinuous and continuous HMM were used with a small number of states. Various types of context dependencies were considered with contexts extending up to five phonemes. Thousands of gender-dependent models were used with different types of parameter sharing. The total number of Gaussian distributions was varying from a few to some tens of thousands with four to a few tens of Gaussians per mixture. Cross-word-phoneme models were separately trained in some systems.

9.9. WORD SPOTTING

There are applications in which it is not necessary nor possible to recognize all the words pronounced by the user. This can happen when either the vocabulary is not completely predictable, or the information one wants to capture is completely contained in a few words of the sentence.

Word spotting aims to detect and recognize a limited number of keywords (KWs) in unconstrained speech. Of great importance are the filler models of all words and speech events that are not keywords. In general, the more information is contained in the fillers, the best performance is reached.

Evaluation criteria

To represent KW spotting performance, two parameters are used, namely precision (PR), which is the percentage of correctly spotted keywords, and the number of false alarms (FAs) (usually normalized with the number of keywords and hours of speech, or FA/(KW × HR)). The receiver operating characteristic (ROC) curve is widely used for a concise representation of these performance parameters. The ROC is a plot of PR versus FA for different operating conditions and allows an operating point to be chosen, based on the trade-off between the two parameters. In addition, a figure of merit can be calculated, as the average percentage of correctly spotted keywords computed with the ROC curve between 0 and 10 FA/(KW × HR). However, this measure does not seem to be very useful when comparing systems working with keyword lexicons of different sizes, because the normalization with respect to the number of keywords makes systems with a large number of keywords look better. Therefore, in the following example, only normalization per hours of speech (FA/HR) are considered.

9.9.1. A Working Example

An example of KW spotting for the Italian language is now described. The system (Gretter, 1996) uses phoneme HMMs, trained on 2140 APASCI (Angelini *et al.*, 1994b) sentences. In order to avoid a specific acoustic training depending on the keyword lexicon, filler models do not depend on keywords. Moreover:

- No "syntactic" constraints on the presence of keywords are imposed (in some tasks it is hypothesized that a known number of keywords is present in each sentence).
- Since some keywords rarely appear in both test and training sets, neither a specific KW training nor a word dependent choice of the operating point are feasible.
- The same framework used for dictation is applied to word spotting. Many word spotting systems vary especially for the IN used during recognition.

The test set is composed of 660 APASCI sentences, with a lexicon of 1552 words. Once a keyword lexicon has been defined, a reference text is generated, starting from the transcriptions of the test sentences, and is used for performance evaluation.

In order to evaluate performance degradation at the increase of keyword length and number, an automatic procedure selects different sets of keywords. Three parameters can be defined to select a keyword: minimum and maximum

Table 9.2 Characteristics of the keyword sets used for word-spotting experiments

Identifier	Imposed parameters		Resulting features	
	Keyword length (phonemes)	Min. occurrences per keyword	Number of keywords	Total keyword occurrences
L4.5-O2	4–5	2	203	1076
L4.5-O10	4–5	10	30	435
L6.7-O2	6–7	2	262	972
L6.7-O5	6–7	5	56	435
L8.30-O2	>8	2	277	847
L8.30-O5	>8	5	32	228

number of phonemes, and minimum (or maximum) number of occurrences of the keyword in the test set. For example, it is possible to define as keywords all the words of the test set which occur at least twice and are composed of four to six phonemes.

Six keyword sets have been considered, whose characteristics are described in Table 9.2. It is worth noting that several keywords are often similar, corresponding to variations in gender and/or number of the same stem, like *figlia–figlio* ("daughter"–"son").

System structure

A typical IN for word spotting is composed of two subnetworks, one for the keywords and the other for the fillers, connected in a loop. Recognition generates sequences of fillers and keywords. The keyword lexicon is organized as a tree, having word labels at the leaves. The simplest filler model used in these experiments does not include any lexical or syntactic information, and is composed of all phonemes in a loop. Figure 9.13 shows an example of such a structure.

Each leaf of the keyword subnetwork is associated a weight w_k, while each arc of the filler subnetwork is associated another weight w_f. The sum of these weights (which can be considered as belonging to a sort of language model) and the acoustic scores (using log(prob)) determines the optimal filler/keyword sequence using the Viterbi algorithm on the whole network. Without these weights, the recognizer would almost always hypothesize a sequence of phonemes from the filler subnetwork. Therefore, w_k and w_f must boost keyword models. Higher values for w_k tend to boost keywords with an increase in false alarms. In order to draw a complete ROC curve, recognition must be performed for different values of the weights.

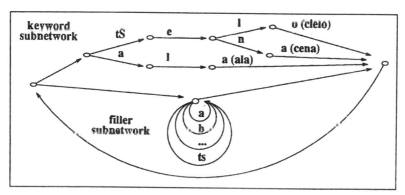

Figure 9.13 Simple spot network for the three keywords *cielo, cena, ala* ("sky", "dinner", "wing"). The filler is composed of all phonemes in loop.

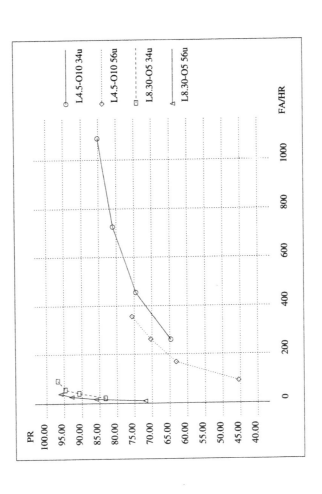

Figure 9.14 Comparison between base units (34u) and extended units (56u): the ROC curves for the extended units, for the same task, show better performance.

Experiments

A first experiment was performed to evaluate the effect of using different unit sets, namely base units (34 units, corresponding to phonemes of the Italian language) and extended units (56 units, i.e. base units plus stressed vowels, geminate consonants and end-word vowels), to model both fillers and keywords. Results on all tasks, represented by ROC curves, show that the more accurate the unit set, the best the performance. Figure 9.14 shows ROC curves for tasks L4.5-O10 and L8.30-O5 defined in Table 9.2. All successive experiments were performed using the extended unit set.

Figure 9.15 shows ROC curves for all tasks, using the extended unit set. It appears in this figure, as expected, that both keyword length and keyword number strongly influence performance. However, it is interesting to note that the most critical factor is the keyword length. Experiments on the most critical task, L4.5-O2, will be reported in the following.

Exploiting lexical knowledge into fillers

Keyword-spotting performance when using short keywords is poor: one of the reasons is that a short keyword is often a substring of longer words, as it happens for the keyword *nato* ("born") and the words *abbonato, raffinato, cucinato* ("subscriber", "sophisticated", "cooked"). Each time one of these long words appears, the system will probably spot the short keyword, generating a false alarm, unless the longer words are explicitly modelled and recognized instead.

Lexical knowledge can easily be added into the filler models by explicitly introducing a lexical tree into the filler network. In this way the whole network will have three typical branches:

- a keyword, represented by its unit sequence, having weight w_k
- a phone filler, represented by a phoneme loop, having each arc weighted by w_f
- a word filler, represented by its unit sequence, having weight w_f (intermediate weights were also tried, but without significant improvements).

The phone filler is kept for two reasons: first of all, in a real word-spotting application, the lexicon must be considered open; secondly, phenomena like phone elisions, false starts, etc. impose to model non-word speech even if the lexicon may be considered fixed.

Experiments were performed by including an increasing number of words into the fillers, ranging from 0 (equivalent to the previous case) to 100% (close vocabulary). Figure 9.16 shows the resulting ROC curves.

Exploiting syntactic knowledge into fillers

Experiments were performed with the introduction of linguistic knowledge by means of a stochastic LM into the filler models. Bigrams were computed

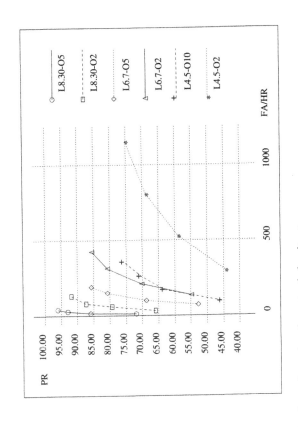

Figure 9.15 ROC curves for the tasks, using the extended unit set.

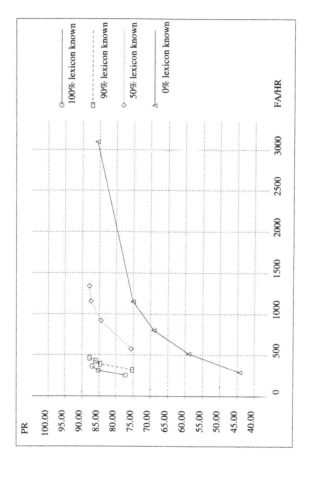

Figure 9.16 Task L4.5-O2: introduction of lexical knowledge.

on the 2140 APASCI training sentences, and considering only words supposed to be known (90% of the test lexicon). Words not belonging to the known lexicon were simply labelled as UNKNOWN, which was added to the original lexicon and resulted the most frequent word. Then, a finite-state automaton was built, which includes bigram probabilities and a null node (introduced in sections 8.5 and 8.6). The word UNKNOWN was then replaced by the phone loop structure, which accounts for unseen words. The resulting network roughly corresponds to a medium-size-vocabulary speech recognizer, capable of labelling some portions of speech as "garbage". Giving more or less weight to the language model probability allows to control the trade-off between false alarms and percentage of keyword detection, at least for a portion of the ROC curve. In fact, the weight w_k is no longer used in this experiment, while both bigram probabilities and w_f, which together form the language model, control the trade-off between precision and FA rate.

Figure 9.17 shows the effect of the introduction of syntactic information into the filler model, when 90% of the lexicon is known. For comparison purposes, also the curve referring to 100% lexicon known, with no syntactical information, is plotted. It results that syntactic information can provide better results than the knowledge of the whole lexicon. Curves A, B, C are obtained by using three values for the weight w_f associated with each phone expanding the word UNKNOWN. In fact, since multiplying the weights by a common factor influences both bigram probabilities and w_f, a good choice of these values must be found. Curves A, B, C are not monotonic because, when the language model gets too much weight with respect to the acoustic model, a performance degradation is observed. Unlike in speech recognition, the number of sentences on which bigrams are estimated seems not to be very important: tests using 1070 and 535 sentences, not reported here, showed only a small decrease in performance.

9.9.2. A Brief History of Word Spotting

Most of the systems described in the literature use a number of KWs ranging from 10 to 50; some systems use artificial vocabularies up to 250 KWs. The most referred corpus in word spotting is the Switchboard (Godfrey *et al.*, 1992), a large multispeaker corpus of conversational speech collected over telephone lines. Early works on word spotting (Bridle, 1973) use template concatenation techniques; in Higgins and Wohlford (1985) there is an explicit modelling of 25 KW templates and 75 filler templates. The use of HMMs for word spotting began in 1989, showing improvements over template techniques.

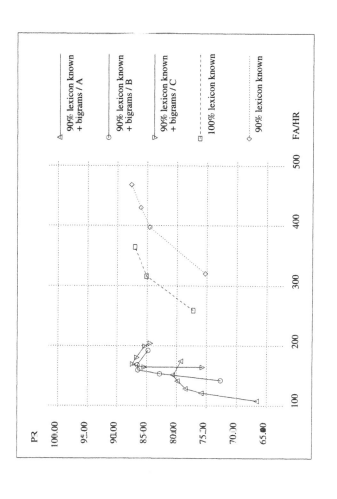

Figure 9.17 Task L4.5-O2, 90% lexicon known: introduction of syntactic knowledge. Three values for w_f generate the curves A, B, C.

Use of HMM

In Rohlicek *et al.* (1989), 20 KWs are modelled by HMM word models. Two filler models are compared: the first is made of some segments of the KW models; the second is a single-state filler, obtained with a uniform weighting of all the distributions in the KW states. The former model results in better performance. As a basis for scores, the Viterbi score at time t for state i is considered:

$$L_i(t) = \Pr(s_t = i, x_1, \ldots, x_t)$$

which is used to compute an *a posteriori* probability:

$$\Pr(s_t = i | x_1, \ldots, x_t) = \frac{\Pr(s_t = i, x_1, \ldots, x_t)}{\Pr(x_1, \ldots, x_t)} = \frac{L_i(t)}{\Sigma_j L_j(t)}$$

where the sum is over all HMM states. Local maxima of the *a posteriori* probability for the ending state of each KW correspond to possible KW ending points. This score is found to be better than a duration normalized likelihood:

$$\Pr(x_{t-d+1}, \ldots, x_t | KWi)^{1/d}.$$

In fact, the duration normalized likelihood may assume lower values for a KW not only when the KW is absent, but also when the KW is present and the whole speech signal does not match KW models well, as it may happen in the presence of noise not seen during training. The use of the posterior probability better accounts for the latter case, because, in the presence of unseen noise, both KWs and filler models will return lower values.

In Rose and Paul (1990), modelling of 20 KWs by subword unit HMMs in a continuous speech recognition system is described. This system outputs a stream of KWs and fillers. Different filler models are investigated: unsupervised clustering of unlabelled speech utterances, explicit word modelling for all the 80 words that are not KWs, triphone and monophone models. All methods, except the unsupervised clustering, provide good performance. By considering that the explicit modelling of all 80 words poorly represents unconstrained speech, the most attractive solution seems to be the one of monophone models, which require less computation than triphones. As a score, a duration normalized word likelihood is used:

$$L_{KW} = \frac{\log \Pr(KW_e, x_{t_b}, \ldots, x_{t_e})}{t_e - t_b}$$

where KW_e is the ending state of the HMM for KW, t_b and t_e are respectively the beginning and ending times for the word. A background filler model (BG), running in parallel, is used to form a log-likelihood ratio score (LR):

$$L_{LR} = L_{KW} - L_{BG}$$

resulting in a significant improvement.

In Wilpon *et al.* (1990) a telephone application, involving 5 KWs with different filler models is reported, including *n* specific non-vocabulary words plus background, non-KW speech and background, all words and background. A large number of extraneous speech models is shown to obtain good performance in terms of recognition of the 5 KWs. Reducing the number of extraneous speech models to just one model, however, results in only a small performance degradation, suggesting computationally simpler solutions.

In Hofstetter and Rose (1992) the problem of using a large task-independent corpus with the addition of a small task-dependent corpus to adapt to a particular speaker or environment is discussed. It is shown that good word-spotting performance can be obtained without collecting any KW sample to train the word spotter.

In Rose (1992) discriminant techniques are proposed for improving the discrimination between KW utterances and background speech. Monophone models, trained from utterances not containing KWs, give the best trade-off between word-spotting performance and computational complexity. Corrective training is used to maximize an error criterion that is directly related to the *a posteriori* keyword probability used in the word spotter.

Use of language models

In Rohlicek *et al.* (1993), following Rohlicek *et al.* (1989), HMM acoustic models, overall HMM structure, and KW-scoring methods with a comparison of different approaches are considered. Important remarks are made about the use of different information sources, including a bigram grammar. This work can be related to Jeanrenaud *et al.* (1993), about different HMM architectures gradually including more KSs (acoustical, lexical, syntactic). As the resulting systems are computationally expensive, methods for reducing the vocabulary size are also investigated, showing only a little decrease in performance. In this context, the concept of "event spotting" is introduced, in which a KW is represented by a proper subgrammar, embedded into a bigram LM. As the event results in units which are larger than the KW alone, it is more easily detected, increasing performance. This work is extended in Jeanrenaud *et al.* (1994), where complex units such as grammatical events (dates, etc.) are spotted, and strategies for generating a consistent score for each event are discussed.

In Weintraub (1993), a task-specific language model is estimated, combining task specific and task-independent text material. Experiments show that varying the vocabulary size from medium (700 words) to large (7000 words) does not affect performance; in addition, the phone loop background model does not seem to help. In Rose (1993) several problems are addressed, among which is the lexicon size needed to model non-KWs. A size of 300 is reported to give satisfactory performance. In addition, a simple word-pair grammar only for KWs and their adjacent words appears to improve performance with respect to the absence of syntactic constraints.

In Bourlard *et al.* (1994), a method for estimating word and garbage penalties is illustrated. Moreover, an "on-line garbage", obtained by averaging *N*-best local scores of phone models, is introduced. Using this approach, no explicit filler models are needed, and a multilayer perceptron (see Chapter 10), can be used to estimate the emission probabilities of the HMMs.

Word spotting in information retrieval tasks

In James and Young (1994), a fast solution to the problem of finding some KWs in a large amount of stored audio material is proposed, without any *a priori* knowledge of the KW lexicon. It is based on an off-line generation of a *phoneme lattice*, which is used at run-time to search the desired KWs. Each KW is matched against the phoneme lattice, by accounting for phone insertions, deletions or substitutions. Comparison with whole-word spotting systems shows similar accuracy with much more computation time.

In Jones *et al.* (1995) and Foote *et al.* (1995), an information retrieval task is introduced, and preliminary experiments are reported with audio retrieval performance very close to that of text. In information retrieval, a query is defined as a set of KWs, and a score has to be computed for each query document. This score is based on the presence/absence of the KWs, possibly weighting their score or their relative frequency. Experiments are also reported with speaker adaptation.

9.10. CONCLUSIONS

Hypotheses generation with a search process is now a commonly used approach. The opportunity of using inadmissible algorithms like "beam search" is widely accepted with multiple-step search, although there are noticeable exceptions. This solution was introduced in Lowerre (1976).

Search can be performed initially with speech frames as input or with phone symbols generated in a previous phase. As early decisions usually involve more errors, the latter solution may require additional error recovery computation that makes the whole approach not advantageous.

Admissible and inadmissible algorithms can be time-synchronous or not. Data structures produced by search can be the word sequence with the highest score, the *N*-best word sequences, a word lattice or a word graph.

Multiple-step search seems to be a flexible and useful approach, since the set of hypotheses is progressively reduced by using more and more sophisticated knowledge sources.

Searching large INs has been made possible by recent progress in workstation and personal computer architectures producing effective and affordable very-large-vocabulary dictation systems.

In laboratory conditions, speaker-independent, continuous speech dictation in given domains with very large vocabularies can be performed in real-time with a word error rate ranging from 5% to 25%, depending on the vocabulary size of the task. Less than 1% string error rate can be obtained for connected digit recognition.

The use of large-vocabulary models appears to be useful even for spotting a small set of words.

10

Neural Networks for Speech Recognition

Edmondo Trentin,[*] Yoshua Bengio,[†] Cesare Furlanello[*] and Renato De Mori[‡]

[*]Istituto per la Ricerca Scientifica e Tecnologica – 38050 Panté di Povo, Trento, Italy.
[†]Dept. Informatique et Recherche Opérationelle, Université de Montréal, Montréal, P.Q. H3C 3J7, Canada.
[‡]School of Computer Science, McGill University, Montréal, P.Q. H3A 2A7, Canada.

10.1. INTRODUCTION

After having described in previous chapters probabilistic models, this chapter introduces a new type of model based on artificial neural networks (ANNs). ANNs are learning machines trainable from examples, loosely inspired by the principles of data processing in the brain. Machine learning algorithms are not limited to ANNs but are also used in statistics and probabilistic modelling (HMMs, linear regression, time-series autoregressive and moving-average models, non-parametric statistical models and many others), and in artificial intelligence (decision trees, rule induction, etc.).

This chapter introduces basic principles with a large set of pointers to the literature, where further details about theory and applications to speech can be found. After an introductory discussion on learning theory, the simple linear perceptron is presented in section 10.2. The multilayer perceptron and its training algorithm is described in section 10.3. Practical training problems are discussed in section 10.4. Networks with radial basis functions are introduced in section 10.5. Connections with statistical methods are in section 10.6. Unsupervised learning is introduced in section 10.7, networks for dealing with time sequences are presented in section 10.8, and ANN/HMM hybrid systems are described in section 10.9. Applications to ASR and, more generally, to speech processing, are described in various sections.

10.1.1. Learning Theory

A modern discussion on the theoretical foundations of machine learning algorithms, called *learning theory*, can be found in Vapnik (1995). We will summarize here some of the basic principles of learning theory, which are important for a successful application of ANNs and HMMs to difficult problems such as ASR.

A machine implementing a learning algorithm is provided with a *training set* of data samples $T = \{z_1, \ldots, z_N\}$ of size N, and attempts to learn a function from the data. In SR applications, we are mostly concerned with supervised learning problems, in which each sample z is an (input, output) pair (x, y) (such as a pair given by a sequence $x_1^L = (x_1, x_2, \ldots, x_L)$ of acoustic features, and the corresponding correct symbolic interpretation $y_1^M = (y_1, y_2, \ldots, y_M)$), which could be a sequence of phonemes, words or other descriptors. In general, we will assume that data examples are independently sampled from some distribution. Statistical models typically make a direct assumption about the form of that distribution, as discussed in section 10.6. The learning theory developed by Vapnik (1982, 1995) assumes that the data are sampled from some distribution $\Pr(z)$ but does not make any assumptions about the form of that distribution. When learning by induction, the learning machine will search for a solution, within a certain set of solutions S (also called *hypothesis space*), which optimizes the average of a certain criterion $Q(z)$ on the training data T. Without loss of generality, we can indicate by $Q(z, \theta)$ the value of the criterion obtained on a sample z, using a solution $\theta \in S$. In HMMs and ANNs, S represents a model, and θ is specified by parameters of the model. The average value of the criterion $Q(z, \theta)$ on the training data is called the *empirical risk* (or *training error*, or *training criterion*):

$$C_{train}(\theta) = \frac{1}{N} \sum_{z_p \in T} Q(z_p, \theta). \tag{10.1}$$

However, the ultimate objective of the learning machine is not to minimize $C_{train}(\theta)$, but rather to minimize the expected error on new samples, also called *generalization error* (or *expected risk*):

$$C_{gen}(\theta) = \int_z Q(z, \theta) \Pr(z) \, dz. \tag{10.2}$$

For example, training algorithms for HMMs tune the parameters θ (e.g., transition probabilities, Gaussian means) of an HMM with a given structure, in order to maximize the likelihood of the observed acoustic features given the corresponding phonemes or words in the training data, i.e., $Q(z, \theta) = -\log \Pr(x_1^L | y_1^M, \theta)$, where x_1^L is an acoustic sequence of length L, and y_1^M is a word sequence of length M. Similarly, many ANN types have parameters (connection weights) which are tuned in order to reduce the average squared error between the outputs of the network $\hat{y}(x, \theta)$, given an input vector x, and the corresponding desired output y in the training set, i.e., $Q(z, \theta) = 0.5(\hat{y}(x, \theta) - y)^2$.

Two major points can be made from learning theory. The first one is that if θ^* is chosen to minimize $C_{train}(\theta)$, then $C_{train}(\theta^*)$ is a biased (optimistic) estimation of the true generalization performance, i.e., averaging over all possible training sets T of size N sampled from $\Pr(z)$, $E_T[C_{train}(\theta^*)] < C_{gen}(\theta^*)$.

The second one is that the expected difference between training performance $C_{train}(\theta^*)$ and generalization performance $C_{gen}(\theta^*)$ can be bounded under some conditions, even without making any assumptions about the data distribution $\Pr(z)$.

To bound this difference, learning theorists have introduced the notion of *capacity*, which can be understood as a measure of the size of the set of solutions S (also called hypothesis space). Such a measure is the so-called VC dimension (for Vapnik–Chervonenkis), indicated by h. In the simple case of classification, the capacity h is the maximum number of training samples that can always be correctly classified (by picking the most difficult task T and the best solution θ within S, for T). The notion of capacity has also been generalized to regression and density estimation problems (Vapnik, 1982, 1995). In general, within a given class of learning machines (such as the polynomial classifiers), the capacity increases with the number of free parameters. In the case of linear models (e.g.,

$\hat{y}(x) = wx + b$ with $\theta = (w, b)$), the capacity is exactly equal to the number of free parameters.

The bounds on the difference between training and generalization error essentially depend on the ratio of capacity to number of training examples, h/N. When the capacity h is fixed, increasing the number of training examples N increases $C_{train}(\theta^*)$ and decreases $C_{gen}(\theta^*)$. As $N \to \infty$, both errors converge to the same asymptotical value (which depends on h, and would be lower for a larger h), if the class of learning machines at hand is consistent (see Vapnik (1982, 1995) for more formal definitions). When the number of examples N is fixed, starting from a low capacity and gradually increasing it, it appears that initially both $C_{train}(\theta^*)$ and $C_{gen}(\theta^*)$ decrease. At some point, called the *optimal capacity h^**, further increase in capacity continues to yield improvements in $C_{train}(\theta^*)$, but on the other hand $C_{gen}(\theta^*)$ starts increasing. This is the well-known phenomenon of *overfitting*.

10.2. SIMPLE LINEAR PERCEPTRONS AND THE WIDROW–HOFF ALGORITHM

For the sake of simplicity, let us introduce a feedforward connectionist model trainable with supervision by providing, for each training input sample, the corresponding desired output. This means that input vectors are presented at the input of the network one at a time. Based on the input, the network computes an output vector.

Let us consider the training set $T = \{(x_k, y_k) | k = 1, \ldots, N\}$, where N input samples $x_1, \ldots, x_N$ have been previously labelled with their corresponding desired (target) outputs $y_1, \ldots, y_N$. The aim is to build a model able to compute for each input of the training data an output close to the desired one, according to some optimality criterion. A particular family of such models is represented by *simple linear perceptrons* (see Figure 10.1).

A simple linear perceptron has a set of input units S_I acting as placeholders for the components of the current input vector. Each input unit is fully connected with all the neurons of the output units set S_O, via direct links (connections, or *synapses*) characterized by a specific connection weight (*synaptic strength*), denoted with $w_{i,j}$ in the figure (in the following figures, connection weights are not explicitly shown). An input signal is propagated forward along the connections, and multiplied by the corresponding connection weight. All the incoming weighted signals to a given output unit are summed together, to form the input to the unit itself. The unit reacts by producing an activation response which is equal to its input. This model is usually referred to as a *layered network*, with the obvious meaning that units are arranged into subsequent layers: the computation proceeds from one layer to the next in bottom-up order, but never in a lateral or backward manner. For this reason the network is called "feedforward".

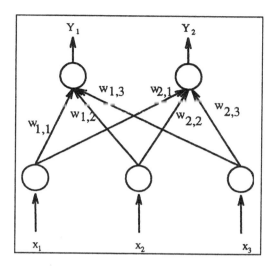

Figure 10.1 Simple linear perceptron.

The family of models considered in this section fits the training data as summarized by the following equation (written for the generic ith output component):

$$\hat{y}_i(\boldsymbol{x}) = \sum_{j \in S_I} w_{ij} x_j. \qquad (10.3)$$

This is a homogeneous linear transformation, but an additive bias can be easily added to the model. Simple linear perceptrons can thus be seen as linear regression models or linear discriminators for classification. Nevertheless, the way these networks *learn* from the training set is quite general, and can be extended to the study of other, more complex, ANN architectures.

Once a training set T and a simple linear perceptron are given, with the obvious assumption that the number of input and output units matches the dimensionality of the input and target vectors, respectively, the *learning problem* can be stated as the search for the network weights $\boldsymbol{w}$ which optimally fit the data, according to a certain criterion. The latter is usually expressed as a functional of the training data (and of the model) that represents a gain to be maximized or a loss (or risk) to be minimized. A sound and common choice for the criterion function is the sum of squared differences between target outputs and actual outputs:

$$C = \frac{1}{2} \sum_{n=1}^{N} \sum_{k \in S_O} (y_{kn} - \hat{y}_{kn})^2 \qquad (10.4)$$

where y_{kn} is the kth component of the nth target, $\hat{y}_{kn}$ is the output of the kth output unit when the network is presented with the nth input vector, and the multiplicative factor $\frac{1}{2}$ is introduced for computational convenience, as we shall see below. The minimization of (10.4) is known as the *least squares criterion*. A general and broadly used optimization technique for the minimization of expression (10.4) is the gradient descent method. Most network training algorithms are based on it. Although it is not guaranteed that the approach will eventually reach the global minimum of the criterion function, these techniques often produce practically useful behaviour in the case of the multi-layer perception. It is worth noting that the estimation of the coefficients of a linear transformation which will minimize a least squares criterion on a training set using gradient descent is an instance of the well-known *Widrow–Hoff algorithm* (Duda and Hart, 1973), used to perform discriminant linear analysis for classification. We will see that gradient descent iterative algorithms are used also for training more complicated ANN architectures.

The iterative approach can be developed in the following way. Given the vector w of the connection weights at a certain iterative step of the algorithm, with an arbitrary choice at the initial step, a new weight vector w' is computed according to the expression:

$$w' = w + \Delta w \tag{10.5}$$

where Δw denotes the weight-change vector, which in turn satisfies the following relation:

$$\Delta w \propto -\nabla_w C. \tag{10.6}$$

In expression (10.6) the symbol $\nabla_w C$ represents the gradient vector of the error functional computed with respect to the weights w. Rewriting equation (10.6) in an explicit form, the gradient descent algorithm moves away from the current weights along the direction opposite to the gradient, by prescribing:

$$\Delta w = -\eta \nabla_w C \tag{10.7}$$

or, equivalently, if individual variations of weights are expressed in terms of the corresponding partial derivatives:

$$\Delta w_{ij} = -\eta \frac{\partial C}{\partial w_{ij}} \tag{10.8}$$

where η is the so-called *learning rate*, a small constant that controls the rate of convergence of the algorithm, i.e. the length of the step away from the current point in weight space. Larger values of η allow for faster convergence, however if the value is too large, the algorithm can diverge (C increases). The optimal value of η depends on the largest eigenvalue of the Hessian matrix of second-order derivatives of the cost function with respect to the weights (see next section). The above iterative step is repeated, starting from the initial weights and evolving along a trajectory in weight space, until convergence to a minimum of the criterion function is reached, or when a stopping criterion is met. The latter can be related to the availability of computational resources, or can be expressed in terms of an estimation of generalization performance at each iteration (*early stopping*). From a theoretical point of view, the gradient descent technique can always reach a minimum of the criterion function (if the learning rate is reduced during training, that is if $\sum_{t=1}^{\infty} \eta_t = \infty$ and $\sum_{t=1}^{\infty} \eta_t^2 < \infty$), but it may get stuck in the case of the multi layer perceptron in local minima without reaching the global minimum. Starting a few times the algorithm from different initial weights is a common practice. The problem of local minima has been widely investigated: Baldi and Hornik (1989) discuss the case of linear networks, while Gori and Tesi (1992) face the same problem for the more general case of nonlinear networks.

In practical cases, instead of computing the gradient of function (10.4), with a summation over all the training samples (*batch mode*), an *on-line* variant of the algorithm is used, by taking the partial derivatives of the following error functional:

$$C = \frac{1}{2} \sum_{k \in S_O} (y_k - \hat{y}_k)^2 \tag{10.9}$$

which is locally computed over each training pair (x, y), and the weight changes are still determined using equation (10.8) every time the network is presented with a new input vector. This approach, also known as *stochastic gradient descent*, proves to be quite effective when the number of training patterns is large (several thousands or more). The whole training set is repeatedly fed through the net for a certain number of *epochs*. An important consequence of stochastic gradient descent is the ability of incremental training, since the network can potentially learn more from new examples without requiring a complete, batch retraining. This is an historical reason why the terms *learning* or *adaptation*, rather than *optimization*, are often used to describe this process. Stochastic gradient descent has also proven to be more effective than standard gradient in many cases, particularly for its generalization ability.

In order to obtain an explicit form for equation (10.8) suitable for an efficient implementation, the partial derivatives of equation (10.9) with respect to a generic weight w_{ij} have to be computed. We can write:

$$\frac{\partial C}{\partial w_{ij}} = \frac{1}{2} \sum_{k \in S_O} \frac{\partial (y_k - \hat{y}_k)^2}{\partial w_{ij}}$$

$$= \frac{1}{2} \frac{\partial (y_i - \hat{y}_i)^2}{\partial w_{ij}}$$

$$= -(y_i - \hat{y}_i) \frac{\partial \hat{y}_i}{\partial w_{ij}}. \tag{10.10}$$

Recalling equation (10.3) we can now write the partial derivative of the output

$\hat{y}_i$ from the ith output unit with respect to the weight w_{ij} as:

$$\frac{\partial \hat{y}_i}{\partial w_{ij}} = \frac{\partial f_i(x_i)}{\partial w_{ij}}$$

$$= \frac{\partial \sum_{l \in S_l} w_{il} x_l}{\partial w_{ij}}$$

$$= x_j \tag{10.11}$$

where x_i denotes the input to output unit i. Substituting equations (10.10) and (10.11) into equation (10.8) we obtain:

$$\Delta w_{ij} = \eta (y_i - \hat{y}_i) x_j \tag{10.12}$$

which gives the weight changes for each connection weight of the network in terms of the product of the component of the current input to the connection, by the difference between the desired and the actual output from the corresponding neuron. If the difference is small, i.e. the network response resembles the target value, then only a small adjustment of the weight is performed. Larger differences imply larger modifications of the synaptic strengths.

If we define the quantity δ_i as:

$$\delta_i = y_i - \hat{y}_i \tag{10.13}$$

we can rewrite equation (10.12) in the form:

$$\Delta w_{ij} = \eta \delta_i x_j \tag{10.14}$$

which is known as the *delta rule* and provides a more compact representation of the learning rule (10.12).

Equation (10.14) can be written as the difference of two terms as follows:

$$\Delta w_{ij} = \eta y_i x_j - \eta \hat{y}_i x_j \tag{10.15}$$

where the first term is a typical example of *Hebbian learning*, which expresses the tendency to strengthen the synaptic weight whenever the input and the desired output of a neuron (pre- and post-synaptic activations) are both high. The second term, on the contrary, is referred to as *anti-Hebbian learning*, with the intuitive, opposite meaning.

A direct and important extension to the simple linear perceptron model uses a more general activation function $f_i()$ of the output units. The output $\hat{y}_i$ of the ith unit will be written $\hat{y}_i = f_i(a_i)$, where a_i is the input to the unit, usually $a_i = \sum_{l \in S_l} w_{il} x_l$. Typically, $f_i()$ is either the identity or a squashing non-linearity, such as the hyperbolic tangent $f_i(a_i) = \tanh(a_i)$ or the sigmoid $f_i(a_i) = 1/(1 + e^{-a_i})$. The only constraint that must be imposed, if the gradient descent technique is still used, is that the activation functions must be continuous and differentiable functions. In this general case, equation (10.11) must be rewritten in the following form:

$$\frac{\partial \hat{y}_i}{\partial w_{ij}} = \frac{\partial f_i(a_i)}{\partial w_{ij}}$$

$$= \frac{\partial f_i(a_i)}{\partial a_i} \frac{\partial a_i}{\partial w_{ij}}$$

$$= f_i'(a_i) \frac{\partial \sum_{l \in S_i} w_{il} x_l}{\partial w_{ij}}$$

$$= f_i'(a_i) x_j \tag{10.16}$$

where $f_i'(a_i)$ is the derivative of the activation function computed over the current input a_i to ith unit, and equation (10.8) becomes:

$$\Delta w_{ij} = \eta(y_i - \hat{y}_i) f_i'(a_i) x_j \tag{10.17}$$

that easily reduces to equation (10.12) in the linear case. It is still possible to define the quantity δ_i to be:

$$\delta_i = (y_i - \hat{y}_i) f_i'(a_i) \tag{10.18}$$

which, in turn, is a straight generalization of equation (10.13) and includes the latter as a special case, leading to:

$$\Delta w_{ij} = \eta \delta_i x_j \tag{10.19}$$

that is identical to equation (10.14). In the next section, the above concepts are further developed in the context of multilayered networks and, surprisingly enough, the calculation of the learning algorithm for these models will lead to expressions substantially identical to the delta rule.

10.3. MULTILAYER PERCEPTRONS AND THE BACKPROPAGATION ALGORITHM

The most popular neural network architecture is the *multilayer perceptron* (MLP), also known as feed-forward neural network. This is an extension of the simple linear Perceptron with additional layers of units, called *hidden layers*. In the hidden layers an internal, intermediate representation of data is formed. An MLP is fed by an input vector and subsequent computations are passed from layer to layer in the usual feedforward manner. This produces an output vector of values of the units of the last (output) layer of the network. Activation functions associated to hidden and output units can be linear or non-linear, and can be different for different units. Input units still act as place-holders for the components of the current input vector. A training algorithm estimates a set of weights to be assigned to the connections between each pair of units belonging to adjacent layers, in order to optimize a training criterion.

Training is generally supervised. Let us consider a labelled training set $T = \{(x_k, y_k)|k = 1, \ldots, N\}$. The learning problem for MLPs is to find the weights that result in a (generally non-linear) model that best fits the training data, given a certain criterion function. The most common choice for the criterion is the sum of squared differences between target and actual outputs, just as in the case of simple linear perceptrons. We will illustrate an on-line gradient descent technique (Werbos, 1974; LeCun, 1986; Rumelhart *et al.*, 1986a) to minimize the cost function:

$$C = \frac{1}{2} \sum_{n \in S_O} (y_n - \hat{y}_n)^2 \qquad (10.20)$$

computed after the presentation of a certain input pattern x associated with a desired output vector y of a layered network with a set of input units S_I, hidden units S_H, and output units S_O. An example of such a network is shown in Figure 10.2. Extension to more hidden layers is straightforward.

The learning algorithm is similar to the one for simple linear perceptrons. The weight change Δw_{ij} of the connection strength between the jth hidden unit and the ith *output* unit is computed as follows:

$$\Delta w_{ij} = -\eta \frac{\partial C}{\partial w_{ij}}. \qquad (10.21)$$

The calculation begins as in equation (10.10), by writing:

$$\frac{\partial C}{\partial w_{ij}} = \frac{1}{2} \sum_{n \in S_O} \frac{\partial (y_n - \hat{y}_n)^2}{\partial w_{ij}}$$

$$= \frac{1}{2} \frac{\partial (y_i - \hat{y}_i)^2}{\partial w_{ij}}$$

$$= -(y_i - \hat{y}_i) \frac{\partial \hat{y}_i}{\partial w_{ij}} \qquad (10.22)$$

where the term $\partial \hat{y}_i / \partial w_{ij}$ can be calculated as:

$$\frac{\partial \hat{y}_i}{\partial w_{ij}} = \frac{\partial f_i(a_i)}{\partial w_{ij}}$$

$$= \frac{\partial f_i(a_i)}{\partial a_i} \frac{\partial a_i}{\partial w_{ij}}$$

$$= f_i'(a_i) \frac{\partial \sum_{l \in S_H} w_{il} \hat{y}_l}{\partial w_{ij}}$$

$$= f_i'(a_i) \hat{y}_j \qquad (10.23)$$

where $f_i'(a_i)$ still denotes the derivative of the activation function computed over

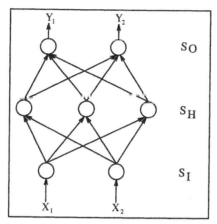

Figure 10.2 Multilayer perceptron.

the current input a_i to the ith unit. We define:

$$\delta_i = (y_i - \hat{y}_i)f_i'(a_i) \tag{10.24}$$

and we write:

$$\Delta w_{ij} = \eta \delta_i \hat{y}_j \tag{10.25}$$

as in the delta rule for simple perceptrons. Let us now consider a unit of the *hidden layer*, say j. The variation of a weight w_{jk} associated to a connection between the kth input unit and the jth hidden unit

$$\Delta w_{jk} = -\eta \frac{\partial C}{\partial w_{jk}} \tag{10.26}$$

can be computed considering that:

$$\frac{\partial C}{\partial w_{jk}} = \frac{1}{2} \sum_{n \in S_O} \frac{\partial(y_n - \hat{y}_n)^2}{\partial w_{jk}}$$

$$- \sum_{n \in S_O} (y_n - \hat{y}_n) \frac{\partial \hat{y}_n}{\partial w_{jk}}. \tag{10.27}$$

This equation resembles (10.22), but takes into consideration the influence that changes in weight w_{jk} have on the whole set of output units, i.e. each hidden unit affects all of the outputs in some way. Now we can write:

$$\frac{\partial \hat{y}_n}{\partial w_{jk}} = \frac{\partial f_n(a_n)}{\partial w_{jk}}$$

$$= \frac{\partial f_n(a_n)}{\partial a_n} \frac{\partial a_n}{\partial w_{jk}}$$

$$= f_n'(a_n) \frac{\partial a_n}{\partial w_{jk}} \tag{10.28}$$

where a further development of term $\partial u_n/\partial w_{jk}$ leads to:

$$\frac{\partial a_n}{\partial w_{jk}} = \frac{\partial \sum_{l \in S_H} w_{nl}\hat{y}_l}{\partial w_{jk}}$$

$$= \sum_{l \in S_H} w_{nl} \frac{\partial \hat{y}_l}{\partial w_{jk}}$$

$$= w_{nj} \frac{\partial \hat{y}_j}{\partial w_{jk}} \tag{10.29}$$

and, in turn:

$$\frac{\partial \hat{y}_j}{\partial w_{jk}} = \frac{\partial f_j(a_j)}{\partial w_{jk}}$$

$$= \frac{\partial f_j(a_j)}{\partial a_j} \frac{\partial a_j}{\partial w_{jk}}$$

$$= f_j'(a_j) \frac{\partial \sum_{m \in S_I} w_{jm} x_m}{\partial w_{jk}}$$

$$= f_j'(a_j) x_k. \tag{10.30}$$

Substituting equations (10.27), (10.28), (10.29) and (10.30) into equation (10.26) we finally obtain:

$$\Delta w_{jk} = \eta \sum_{n \in S_O} \left[(y_n - \hat{y}_n) f_n'(a_n) w_{nj} \right] f_j'(a_j) x_k$$

$$= \eta \left\{ \sum_{n \in S_O} \left[w_{nj}(y_n - \hat{y}_n) f_n'(a_n) \right] \right\} f_j'(a_j) x_k$$

$$= \eta \left(\sum_{n \in S_O} w_{nj} \delta_n \right) f_j'(a_j) x_k \tag{10.31}$$

where δ_n is defined as in equation (10.18), for each output unit. For a generic unit j in the hidden layer we can similarly define:

$$\delta_j = \left(\sum_{n \in S_O} w_{nj} \delta_n \right) f_j'(a_j) \tag{10.32}$$

that brings to evidence the fact that the deltas for hidden units can no longer be computed as a direct function of the difference between the desired target output and the actual network output, because the units themselves have an indirect influence on it. The deltas can rather be expressed as a weighted sum of the deltas already computed at the upper layer, thus backpropagating deltas from one layer to the next (lower) one. In summary, the current input vector is propagated forward through the network, obtaining an output. The error, that is a squared difference between the obtained and the target output, is computed and used to determine deltas at the output layer. Weight changes for the weights of the output layer are immediately computable, according to the delta rule. These deltas are then propagated backward to the hidden layer, allowing for the computation of weight changes by application of equation (10.31). This is usually referred to as error backpropagation, and the resulting algorithm is known as the *backpropagation (BP) algorithm* (Rumelhart *et al.*, 1986a). The compact formulation of the latter can be written as:

$$\Delta w_{jk} = \eta \delta_j x_k \tag{10.33}$$

which, when used together with equation (10.25), is called *generalized delta rule*. If more than one hidden layer is present, the calculation proceeds exactly in the same way, backpropagating the deltas down to the next (lower) hidden layer and yielding a rule identical to equation (10.33). The BP algorithm is the most popular training technique for neural networks, and it has been successfully used in a wide range of applications. The ability of MLPs to model a linear or non-linear discriminant function for classification tasks, or a regressor in multivariate spaces, makes the feedforward connectionist approach a suitable method for many applications in speech processing. Important examples will be given in the next sections, especially concerning the integration of MLPs in an ASR system based on hidden Markov models. MLPs have been used for recognizing phonemes from portions of spectrograms (Bengio, 1996), for grapheme-to-phoneme translation (Sejnowski and Rosenberg, 1986, 1987), and for mapping acoustic features obtained with a microphone array with the same features obtained with a close-mouth microphone (Che *et al.*, 1994b).

10.4. IMPORTANT HEURISTICS FOR TRAINING MLPs

Although the implementation of MLPs and of most ANNs is generally straightforward (and is certainly one reason for their appeal), there are several simple tricks, generally not mentioned in the literature, which should be used to obtain speedy convergence of the training algorithm and good generalization.

Many of these tricks are motivated by the idea that the speed of convergence of gradient directly depends on the *conditioning* of the Hessian matrix (of second derivatives of the training criterion with respect to the parameters). Although it is not generally practical to compute, and invert, this matrix (which would allow one to have perfect conditioning), some of these tricks are computationally simple ways to improve the conditioning. The latter depends on the ratio of the largest to the smallest of the eigenvalues.

10.4.1. Normalization of the Input Data and Use of the Symmetric Sigmoid

One way to improve conditioning, and therefore speed up convergence is to make sure that the average value of the activations of hidden and input units is small in comparison to their variance.

Therefore, it is useful to normalize the inputs to have approximately zero mean, and near unity variance. A rotation of the inputs (using the eigenvectors of their covariance matrix) also improves convergence.

Concerning the hidden units, it is clearly better to use a symmetric sigmoid such as the hyperbolic tangent, with a range from -1 to 1, rather than the asymmetric sigmoid:

$$y = \frac{1}{1 + e^{-x}} \tag{10.34}$$

(which ranges from 0 to 1), since this brings the average activation closer to 0.

10.4.2. Choice of Targets and a Non-linear Output for Classification

For classification problems, two target output values are usually defined, a "low" and a "high" target, for each output unit. For these tasks, it is advisable to use a saturating non-linearity on the output units, such as the sigmoid, hyperbolic tangent, or softmax (defined in equation 10.43). The main advantage of this non-linearity is that it penalizes the network less for producing outputs above the "high" target or below the "low" target. On the other hand, one should not choose these targets too close to the asymptotic values of the non-linearity (e.g., 0 or 1 for the sigmoid), since this will yield very large weights on the output layer, and will stall training because of the near zero derivatives through the output non-linearity. It is advisable to choose target outputs near the inflection points of the non-linearity, i.e., 0.2 and 0.8 for the sigmoid.

10.4.3. Use of Stochastic Gradient Descent or Conjugate Gradient Descent

Stochastic gradient descent updates the ANN parameters after each pattern presentation, whereas batch gradient descent updates the parameters after having processed the whole training set (summing all the gradient contributions).

For large training sets (several hundreds or thousands), stochastic gradient descent usually gives significantly faster convergence than batch gradient descent (sometimes hundreds of times faster). The main reason for faster convergence is the redundancy present in training sets. Furthermore, stochastic gradient descent appears to be more robust to local minima and to generalize better. The resistance to shallow local minima is due to the "noise" in the gradient, since only one or few patterns are used to "estimate" it. This often causes small (temporary) uphill jumps in the error function, thus allowing it to escape shallow (but not wide) minima. Finally, better generalization is generally observed because stochastic gradient descent tends to find solutions in wide basins of the error function. In these wide basins, many similar values of the parameters yield similar performance, therefore the solution obtained is robust to small changes in the parameters (which could occur when a different training set is used, for example). The set of solutions within wide basins require less precision for the parameters and therefore correspond to a smaller effective capacity (hence better control of the overfitting problem).

When stochastic gradient descent is used, convergence can be further accelerated by presenting more "surprising" examples more often (where surprise can be defined by the error performed by the network on these patterns). The first application of this simple idea is to randomly *shuffle* all the examples from the training set. A very bad training set for stochastic gradient descent would have grouped all the examples of the same class together. Shuffling guarantees that such dependencies on the sequence of patterns are removed. A more general application of this idea is to present examples that have generated a large error in the past more often, therefore focusing on the more ambiguous patterns near the decision surface, and yielding faster and more discriminant training. However, one has to be careful with outliers (e.g., wrongly labelled data), and not concentrate the training efforts on these cases.

For small training sets (less than a thousand examples), and especially if high-precision outputs are required (as in regression problems), conjugate gradient descent appears to be the best choice. Conjugate gradient descent (Gill *et al.*, 1981) is a second-order batch method that does not require direct computation of the Hessian and has been found to work well for ANNs (Vogl *et al.*, 1988; Moller, 1992; Battiti, 1989; Hinton *et al.*, 1992).

10.4.4. Early Stopping

When an iterative training algorithm (such as gradient descent) is used, the *effective capacity* (Vapnik, 1995) of the learning machine increases as training proceeds. The effective capacity is smaller than the actual capacity (Bengio, 1996), and takes into account the constraints (and the limitation of resources) of the training algorithm. Before the training iterations start, the "size" of the set of solutions explored by the learning algorithm is very small (i.e., 1). As training proceeds, the algorithm is allowed to explore a larger set of solutions, and the effective capacity increases.

By estimating after each training epoch the generalization performance on a *validation set* (not used for training), training can be stopped early. When the estimated generalization does not improve any more (or even worsens), the effective capacity is too large and the machine starts to overfit.

10.4.5. Use of *a priori* Knowledge

Learning can be seen as combining two different types of information: prior knowledge (or *hints* (Abu-Mostafa, 1990)) and training data. Prior knowledge can be any information about the problem that can be used to impose constraints on the learning process or help it to reach a "better" solution. Constraints can be used to reduce the size of the hypothesis space S. However, the fact that the "prior knowledge" can be partially incorrect may introduce some undesirable bias. Three categories of constraints can be considered, namely: architectural constraints, constraints that guide training, and constraints used for initialization (see Bengio (1996) for further discussions).

Architectural constraints can be introduced in several ways. The network architecture itself can be constrained by reducing connectivity, using shared weights, or more generally using a weight space transformation (LeCun, 1989). Input preprocessing and coding, as well as output representation and coding are also important. Finally, the system can be partitioned into modules by decomposing the problem into subproblems (e.g., see Waibel, 1989; Waibel *et al.*, 1989b; Bengio, 1996; Pratt and Kamm, 1991) introducing intermediate state variables. Prior knowledge can be used to decide on a representation for these intermediate states.

An important training constraint is in the choice of cost function and possible *penalty* terms (such as weight decay (Rumelhart *et al.*, 1986a)). A particularly interesting type of training constraint imposes some *invariance* on the function computed by the network. For example, Simard *et al.* (1992) show how to train a backpropagation network to perform image classification constrained to be locally invariant to input transformations such as translation, rotation, scaling and thinning.

Input representation

Similar to other learning algorithms, it is very important for ANNs to appropriately select preprocessing schemes and the input representation. In the case of ASR (Bengio, 1996; Rossen, 1989) there is evidence of the importance of the type of signal processing used. For example, in experiments described in Cosi *et al.* (1990), an auditory model performed better as a preprocessor for a feedforward neural network than a mel-scaled filter bank. This network received at the input the normalized energies of a spectrogram in a time–frequency grid covering about 10 time frames, and selected frequency bands. The ANN generated hypotheses about the place of articulation of vowels from the analysis of their spectra. Other examples can be found in Bengio *et al.* (1992b), Bengio (1996) and Rossen (1989).

For some tasks, one may be able to decompose the problem into multiple parallel problems, for example, discriminating among different sets of phonemes. There is evidence suggesting that some particular input features or preprocessing are relevant to some subtasks and not to others, and that it is worth using *specialized networks* (Bengio *et al.*, 1992a,b). This is shown in an application to the recognition of plosive sound, described in section 10.8.2.

Output representation

Most ANNs designed for phoneme recognition have a simple output coding scheme consisting of one output unit per phoneme, with a high desired output for the output unit corresponding to the target phoneme and a low desired output for the other units (see, e.g., Waibel *et al.*, 1989a). In these cases, one can interpret the output activations of the network as representing a degree of evidence. Using phonetic knowledge, coding schemes based on articulatory features have been considered. Examples of these features are horizontal and vertical place of articulation, voicing and nasality. Such a representation is in general more compact than the "one-output-per-phoneme" representation. Furthermore, this describes a more general space of phonetic characteristics, allowing a network trained with some phonemes to generalize to diphthongs (Cosi *et al.*, 1990) that were not part of the training set.

Another way to use prior knowledge for the design of output representations is to use "hint" output units. For example, in Cosi *et al.* (1990), in addition to the units representing each vowel, supervision was given to extra output units representing phonetic features. These additional constraints on the network guided it to take these phonetic features into account, with an improved generalization. In Yu and Simmons (1990), adding extra output units in order to improve generalization is also suggested. In Bengio *et al.* (1992a,b), context-dependent output units are used to impose additional constraints, resulting in improved performance.

Architecture and modularization

Network architecture design has two conflicting goals. First, the network has to be able to approximate the desired function as well as possible. Second, the size of the hypothesis space S, associated to the number of free parameters, has to be reduced. One way to reduce the number of parameters is to reduce the network connectivity. Another is to share weights among connections. In networks for sequence recognition, weights can be shared both in feature space and in time, i.e. weights that are associated with different (e.g., translated) input features may be shared, and weights that are associated with different (e.g., translated) times may be shared (see, e.g., LeCun (1989) and section 10.8.1).

A way to reduce connectivity is to partition the network into subnetworks or modules, where inter-module connectivity is low but intra-module connectivity is high. In practice, the best integration of all the modules together is the one for which the global error criterion or cost function is minimized. If such a global cost function is defined, then a *joint optimization* of all the parameters must be performed. A generic way to train such multimodular systems is described in Bottou (1991) and Bengio (1996), based on the computation, for each module, of input gradients and parameters gradients from output gradients. It is easy to imagine cases in which each module in a modular system is trained separately, which is suboptimal for the given complete architecture, even though each module may have reached a minimum of its local cost function (see Bengio (1996) for such a demonstration). In many instances, we would be able to train modules separately using prior knowledge of what each module should do. In that case, an initial, separate, *a priori* training should be followed by a global tuning with respect to a single global criterion function. A particular way to take advantage of modularization is to use specialized preprocessing for different modules acting in parallel. Another type of modularization is found in hybrids of ANNs and HMMs (see section 10.9).

10.5. RADIAL BASIS FUNCTION NETWORKS

Radial basis function (RBF) networks constitute another major class of models for application to problems of supervised learning. Unit activation is obtained in this case as a function of the distance between a prototype vector c and the input vector x. Each unit K_j corresponds to a basis function:

$$K_j(x) = \phi((x - c_j)' \Sigma_j (x - c_j)) \tag{10.35}$$

defined by the prototype (*center*) c_j in the input space R^{d_1}, by the $d_1 \times d_1$ positive definite matrix Σ_j which determines the shape of the unit receptive field, and by the kernel function $\phi : R^+ \to R$. Only one hidden layer of units is typically considered, and the network output is taken to be a linear combination of the basis functions K_j. It can be useful to include bias parameters and a linear term, which corresponds to adding a fixed kernel $K_0 \equiv 1$ and the identity $K_I(x) = x$ to the basis functions. In matrix notation, the following is a compact form for a general RBF map $f : R^{d_1} \to R^{d_2}$:

$$f(x) = HK(x) \tag{10.36}$$

where $K(x) \in R^{(n + d_1 + 1)}$ is the vector of kernel outputs, augmented by the bias and linear contributions, and H is the $d_2 \times (n + d_1 + 1)$ matrix of their coefficients. The basis function is *local* when it has a compact support or, at least, $\phi(r) \to 0$ for $r \to \infty$. However, localization is not strictly necessary: the K_j do not need to be kernels in the sense of continuous, bounded and symmetric functions which integrate to 1 (Härdle, 1990). Several forms of the functions ϕ may be used (Micchelli, 1986; Poggio and Girosi, 1990), and the more useful are namely the Gaussian (G), Hardy's multiquadric (H) and its inverse (IH):

$$(\text{Gaussian}) \quad \phi_G(r) = e^{-r}$$

$$(\text{Hardy}) \quad \phi_H(r) = (r+1)^{1/2}$$

$$(\text{InvHardy}) \quad \phi_{IH}(r) = (r+1)^{-1/2}$$

An important role is played by the Σ_j matrix, which defines a local distance about the centre c_j. When the matrix is diagonal, i.e. $\Sigma_j = \text{Diag}(\sigma_{j1}^{-2}, \ldots, \sigma_{jd_1}^{-2})$, the receptive field of the unit has constant values of activation on hyperellipsoids concentric around c_j, with axes parallel to the coordinate axes and axis lengths depending on the σ_{ji}. When $\Sigma_j = I\sigma_j^{-2}$, activation is constant on hyperspheres, i.e. $K_j(x)$ is radially symmetric around c_j, which gives the model its name; if the kernel is Gaussian, the unit activation is expected to be negligible for inputs at distance greater than $3\sigma_j$ from the centre.

Originating from a classical interpolation scheme (Powell, 1987), RBF networks have been shown to have the universal approximation property (Girosi and Poggio, 1990; Park and Sandberg, 1991, 1993). Results on the rate of approximation of smooth functions by RBF networks have been given in Girosi and Anzellotti (1993). Convergence rates have also been studied in terms of empirical risk minimization (see section 10.1.1) in Krzyzak *et al.* (1996) and in Niyogi and Girosi (1996), where a relationship between generalization error, sample complexity and hypothesis complexity has been demonstrated and verified on numerical examples for the RBF approximation scheme with spherical Gaussian units.

RBF networks are strongly related to non-parametric kernel regression (Härdle, 1990). In particular the *Nadaraya–Watson* estimator has been termed as *softmax* (Bridle, 1990b) in the neural network literature. A normalization factor is introduced such that the sum of the basis functions is identically equal to 1. The generic normalized basis function becomes (Moody and Darken, 1989):

$$U_j(x) = \frac{K_j(x)}{\sum_r K_r(x)} \tag{10.37}$$

a variant often considered in pattern recognition (Bishop, 1995; Ripley, 1996). The use of softmax activations for ANNs is discussed in general terms in section 10.6.

Training

The training of single-layer RBF networks defined as in equation (10.36) is usually performed by first estimating centres and scale parameters according to the probability density of the data, and then applying fast linear matrix inversion techniques to determine the coefficient matrix H (Broomhead and Lowe, 1988). For fixed K and training set $T = \{(x_i, y_i)\}_i$, minimization of the error function is reduced to solving a set of linear equations. Indicating with $\mathcal{K}^\dagger$ the Moore–Penrose pseudoinverse of the design matrix $(\mathcal{K})_{kj} = K_j(x_k)$, and $(Y)_{ik} = y_{ik}$, we get (Bishop, 1995):

$$H^t = \mathcal{K}^\dagger Y \tag{10.38}$$

To avoid problems of ill-conditioning due to numerical error or noise, the solution is found in practice by using the method of *singular value decomposition* (SVD); see Press *et al.* (1992) for introduction and suggested implementation.

Different methods are proposed to select optimal centres and scale parameters. Taking every input vector example as a centre as in kernel smoothing may lead to poor generalization or simply be unfeasible with large data sets. The basis functions centres c_j are thus usually chosen as representative vectors (prototypes) of the input data. In general, the *k-means clustering algorithm* is proposed for the initialization of a number of k network units (Moody and Darken, 1989). Once the locations of the centres have been chosen by the clustering procedure, the covariance matrices of the points within the clusters are used to initialize the scale parameters of the corresponding network units.

Alternative methods require the selection of a subset of input points: locations and scale parameters Σ_j (or σ_j, or a σ common to all centres) are usually chosen to give a smooth representation of the distribution of the training set. There are opposite views about the use of the error values in the allocation procedure. There are regression tasks in which the relevant variations of the unknown map take place in regions of the input space which are *not* correlated with higher density of the data. On the other hand, it is important to avoid fitting outlier points, which may correspond to significant errors without being representative of the data distribution. Stepwise regression procedures have been proposed to incrementally increase the number of basis functions and assign local parameters. An efficient procedure is *orthogonal least squares* (OLS) (Chen *et al.*, 1991), a Gram–Schmidt method in which the new basis function is chosen to originate a new column in the design matrix which is orthogonal to the previous columns. Regularized forward selection (Orr, 1995) has also been proposed to introduce allocation and removal of basis functions based on OLS. Regularization methods, which are not discussed here for the sake of simplicity, are designed to control the smoothness of the fitted function by adding a penalty term to the error function (Bishop, 1995; Ripley, 1996). It has been shown that a broad class of approximation schemes and neural network models, which include RBF networks, additive models and ridge regression models can be derived by regularization principles (Girosi *et al.*, 1995).

Another method for the recursive selection of basis functions is the resource-allocating RBF (RAN) procedure, originally proposed in Platt (1991) and modified by Kadirkamanathan and Niranjan (1993) and Furlanello *et al.*, 1995). Network parameters are adapted by on-line gradient descent (with the least mean squares or the extended Kalman filter approach) over the data sequence, unless novelty is detected in the data. If the current prediction error and the distance of the new input x_t from the nearest centre are respectively greater than a pair of critical values ε_c and δ_t, a new unit is added. Stability of the procedure in non-stationary environment has been recently investigated (Lowe and McLachlan, 1995).

Supervised gradient procedures allow for fine-tuning the parameters, and can be integrated with the two-stage training described above (Bishop, 1995), but user-defined thresholds and critical parameters have to be carefully controlled by model selection procedures. Model selection in RBF networks remains however an important issue with special regard to the number of basis functions and their scale parameters, if provided by the user. It is particularly critical to control these parameters in complex regression tasks in speech processing, which usually requires the use of a superposition of local neural network models (Furlanello *et al.*, 1997).

RBF and speech processing

RBF networks have been used in a variety of non-linear regression and classification tasks in speech processing. The advantages are fast two-stage training, possibly refined by gradient descent optimization, and a localized response to input signals. It is, however, important to use diagonal or full covariance matrices Σ_j for the scale parameters to limit the number of required units due to the high dimensionality typical of speech data. Thus adequate choice and preprocessing of input parameters is often advisable; the generalized RBF model called HyperBF (Poggio and Girosi, 1990) includes the use of a global input feature transformation trainable by gradient descent, also available within the generalized RAN training procedure of Furlanello *et al.* (1995). In Renals (1989) and Renals and Rowher (1989), RBFs are used for phoneme classification.

One attractive application of RBF networks for the development of speech synthesizers was presented in Schroeter and Sondhi (1994). The authors reviewed and compared different techniques available for estimating the shape of the vocal tract from the speech signal, addressing the acoustic-to-articulatory mapping problem. This is an ill-posed problem due to the non-uniqueness of the mapping, because more than one vocal tract shape y may correspond to the same acoustic representation. The acoustic space and the articulatory space were partitioned in clusters, obtaining a total of 64×4 subclusters of a training set of 125 000 pairs of corresponding acoustic and geometric vectors. Acoustic observation consisted of line spectral frequencies (LSFs), from tenth-order LPCs, observed in correspondence to log-area vectors (20 areas from glottis to lips). For each subcluster a specific RBF map was estimated. Gaussian multidimensional functions with diagonal covariance matrix were considered as the architecture, which included bias and linear terms. A dynamic programming algorithm was applied to search the centroid in the input space closest to a given acoustic vector. RBF maps were applied to produce four possible candidates, which were back-transformed into LSF vectors. Average spectral distortion for tenth-order LPC spectra was obtained with a best choice of 0.33 dB. The approach was compared with other neural networks, which estimated worse mappings according to the authors.

10.6. RELATION BETWEEN ANNs AND STATISTICAL MODELS

Statistical learning models are usually based on constraining assumptions on the form of the data distribution in the training set. In supervised training problems, these are assumptions on the form of the joint distribution $\Pr(X, Y)$ of the input X and output Y random variables.

For example, a Gaussian classifier assumes that $\Pr(X = x, Y = c) = \Pr(X = x | Y = c) \Pr(Y = c)$, where $\Pr(X = x | Y = c)$ is a normal distribution for class c, and $\Pr(Y = c)$ is the *a priori* probability for class c. Both $\Pr(X = x | Y = c)$ and $\Pr(Y = c)$ are independently estimated, and the parameters of each Gaussian are independently estimated for each class c. A nice feature of this approach is that a new class can be easily added, and that the model can provide useful information even when a new sample x does not belong to any of the observed classes (its likelihood $\Pr(X = x | Y = c)$ is low for all the classes c). Similarly, an HMM is used to compute $\Pr(X | W)$ ($X =$ sequence of acoustic features, $W =$ sequence of words), which can be multiplied by the language model $\Pr(W)$ to yield the full joint distribution of X and W.

A problem with this approach is that the model is essentially used to find a word sequence given an input (e.g., an acoustic description) x. For this purpose, it may not be necessary to learn the full joint distribution (which is difficult) but a suitable *decision function* $\hat{w}(x)$, which optimizes the criterion of interest, such as minimizing the number of classification errors.

Let us consider a particular classification problem, in which the decision function is represented by a decision surface in the space of the inputs. For the optimal decision function, the only values of X that really matter are those that are ambiguous, i.e., near the decision surface in X-space. Some learning algorithms (such as the perceptron learning rule (Rosenblatt, 1962), and the support vectors algorithm (Vapnik, 1995)) directly attempt to estimate an optimal decision surface. These algorithms are called *discriminant*. All their capacity is used to define in the best possible way the decision surface. On the other extreme, statistical models of the joint distribution of X and W, when used to take classification decisions, are *not discriminant*. They attempt to learn more than what is necessary to perform the recognition task, because they focus on the input distribution $\Pr(X)$. In many learning problems, X has a much higher dimensionality than W, and learning $\Pr(X)$ requires a lot of resources.

When used as classifiers, ANNs are often considered effective discriminators because they are trained to approximate the decision surface. The optimal decision surface in general is not found, because it would require minimizing a criterion, such as the frequency of classification errors, that is not continuous, and whose derivative is zero almost everywhere. Some highly discriminant algorithms have been proposed for ANNs trained to recognize phonemes (Hampshire and Waibel, 1990; Bottou, 1991) with a training criterion close to the objective of finding the optimal decision surface.

On the other hand, many popular ANN learning algorithms, in fact, optimize a criterion which has a probabilistic interpretation: estimating the conditional distribution $\Pr(Y|X, \theta)$, considering Y a generic type of output. This does not have the same discriminant power as (but is easier than) finding the optimal decision surface, but it has much more discrimination power than modelling the full joint distribution of X and Y. In particular, the mean squared error criterion (MSE) or squared loss, $Q(x, \theta) = 0.5(\hat{y}(x, \theta) - y)^2$, has a simple probabilistic interpretation. It corresponds to an assumption of Gaussian distribution for the conditional distribution of the output variable Y, when $X = x$ is given. Its conditional mean is given by the parameterized function $\hat{y}(x, \theta)$, and its covariance matrix is the identity matrix:

$$\operatorname*{argmin}_{\theta} \sum_p Q(x_p, \theta) = \operatorname*{argmin}_{\theta} -\log \prod_p \Pr(y_p|x_p, \theta)$$

$$= \operatorname*{argmin}_{\theta} -\sum_p \log \Pr(y_p|x_p, \theta)$$

$$= \operatorname*{argmin}_{\theta} \sum_p 0.5(y_p - \hat{y}(x, \theta))^2. \qquad (10.39)$$

In this context, it is not surprising to find in the literature proof (White, 1989) that an ANN trained to minimize the MSE criterion is in fact estimating the conditional expected value of the output variable Y, given the input variable $X = x$, i.e., performing a non-linear regression:

$$\hat{y}(x, \theta) = E[Y|X = x, \theta]. \qquad (10.40)$$

ANNs trained with this criterion can be interpreted as representing a (generally non-linear) model of the conditional expectation of Y given X (whereas linear regression does the same thing with a linear model of the expectation).

Another interesting probabilistic interpretation of ANNs is obtained considering the case in which Y is a Boolean variable (with values 0 or 1). In that case $E[Y|x] = 0 \times \Pr(Y = 0|x) + 1 \times \Pr(Y = 1|x)$, i.e., $E[Y|x] = \Pr(Y = 1|x)$. Therefore, with binary targets (desired outputs), the output of an ANN can be interpreted as probabilities of discrete events. Since the output units of ANNs often apply a sigmoid function $1/(1 + e^{-a})$ of their input a, the outputs of such ANNs range between 0 and 1, and can be used to represent a probability of a binary variable.

The probabilistic interpretation can be applied to other conditional output distributions, such as the binomial and the multinomial ones. In the binomial case the output variable is again binary (0 or 1), and the output of the network (a value between 0 and 1) is directly interpreted as $\Pr(Y = 1|X = x, \theta)$. In the maximum likelihood framework, the training criterion is:

$$C_{train}(\theta) = -\sum_p \log \Pr(Y = y_p|X = x_p, \theta) \tag{10.41}$$

which can be directly minimized by gradient descent. This is equivalent to the so-called cross-entropy criterion (Hinton, 1989) (when the desired "output" can be specified as a desired output distribution d_p):

$$C_{train}(\theta) = -\sum_p d_p \log(\Pr(Y = 1|X = x_p, \theta))$$

$$+ (1 - d_p) \log(1 - \Pr(Y = 1|X = x_p, \theta)). \tag{10.42}$$

The above is equivalent to the maximum likelihood criterion when $d_p = y_p$ is binary. Both the above criteria can be generalized to the multiclass case, i.e., the multinomial distribution. This requires computing a set of C probabilities $\Pr(Y = c|x)$ for $c = 1, 2, \ldots, C$. If the interpretation of those numbers does not need to be probabilistic (e.g., to pick $\text{argmax}_c \Pr(Y = c|x)$), then the usual sigmoid output for each output unit can be used. If, however, we require $\sum_c \Pr(Y = c|x) = 1$, then one of several normalization methods can be used. For example, the *softmax* activation function for ANNs has been proposed (Bridle, 1990a) for performing a kind of "soft" winner-take-all. The ith output $\hat{y}_i(x)$ of the ANN represents $\Pr(Y = i|x)$ and is computed as follows:

$$\hat{y}_i(x) = \frac{e^{a_i(x)}}{\sum_j e^{a_j(x)}} \tag{10.43}$$

where $a_j(x)$ is the weighted sum computed for each of the output units, in general a non-linear function of the ANN input x. A typical ANN unit computes a weighted sum of its inputs v_i from other units or from the input x, $a_i = \sum_j w_{ij} v_j$, with weights w_{ij} which are the free parameters of this unit.

However, a caveat should be made concerning the practical use of the interpretation of ANNs outputs as probabilities. If the ANN is directly trained to maximize the probability of the correct class given the input, or posterior class probability $\Pr(Y = y_p|x_p)$ over all the training samples (x_p, y_p), then the training algorithm will be driving the output units values towards 1 or 0 on the training data samples. To reach those extreme values of the activation function (a saturating non-linearity such as the sigmoid or the softmax), the weights of the ANN will be driven to very large values (since infinite activation values a_i are required to obtain output values $\hat{y}_i$ of 0 or 1). This is, however, highly undesirable for several reasons. The most important reason is that training will quickly get stuck because the sigmoid or softmax activation function will become close to a step function, whose derivative is close to zero almost everywhere. Learning algorithms for ANNs rely on the gradient of the training criterion with respect to the parameters. This gradient is scaled by the derivative of the activation function. When that derivative is close to zero, the gradients with respect to the parameters will also be very small, preventing effective training. Another reason for avoiding such large weights is that ANNs with large weights have more capacity than ANNs with small weights (so it is easier to overfit with large weights).

10.7. UNSUPERVISED LEARNING

Let us now consider the *training set* $T = \{x_k \mid k = 1, \ldots, N\}$, where N input unlabelled samples $x_1, \ldots, x_N$ have been collected. As no class labelling is available, the learning task is aimed at discovering, in an unsupervised manner, inherent properties of the data and the way they are distributed in the feature space. Although the problem of learning a classification scheme from an unlabelled training set is very difficult, statistical pattern recognition techniques for unsupervised parametric mixture estimation and data clustering have been successfully proposed and applied in the last decades. Recently, different connectionist approaches to the problem have been introduced, often strictly related to the statistical ones, but sometimes indeed novel. They usually rely on statistical and geometrical properties of the given data.

Some of the most popular unsupervised networks, namely self-supervised (auto-associative) nets and competitive networks, will be introduced in the following. Other unsupervised approaches to connectionist models are ART and ART2 (Carpenter and Grossberg, 1987, 1988), Kohonen's self-organizing map (SOM) and learning vector quantization (LVQ) (Kohonen, 1989, 1990), and Oja's and Sanger's networks (Oja, 1982; Oja and Karhunen, 1985; Oja, 1989; Sanger, 1989), which are capable of performing on-line projection of the input data along their principal components.

Good results of LVQ for speech coding were described in Kohonen *et al.* (1988). In Mäntysalo *et al.* (1992) LVQ is used for phoneme-level segmentation of a speech signal. Excellent examples of the application of LVQ in ASR can be found in McDermott and Katagiri (1989, 1991), where multicategory, shift-tolerant phoneme recognition experiments are reported.

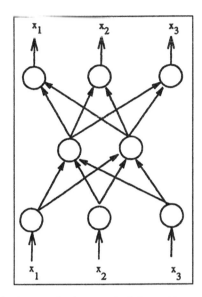

Figure 10.3 Self-supervised network: the same training pattern *x* is applied at the input as well as the output.

10.7.1. Self-Supervised Networks

Self-supervised networks (Cottrell *et al.*, 1987) are standard feedforward networks, such as MLPs, trained in a supervised way (for instance using the BP algorithm discussed in section 10.3) on the training set $T' = \{(x_k, x_k) \mid k = 1, \ldots, N\}$ obtained from the original training set T by pairing each pattern with itself. The major constraint on the topology of the network is that one of the hidden layers is built up of a number of hidden units that must be significantly lower than the dimensionality of the input space. An illustrative example is given in Figure 10.3, in which the same training pattern *x* is applied at the input as well as at the output.

Roughly speaking, the network is trained to reconstruct on its output units each input pattern which is fed into the input units, by forcing the pattern to be coded with a limited set of features through the low-dimensional hidden layer. This forces a low-dimensional representation of the information contained in the input data that is sufficient to reconstruct the original patterns. During the training step, the network learns low dimensional representations of the input vectors, preserving as much relevant information as possible. Once training is accomplished, the hidden layer can be used as an output layer to produce compressed patterns. This technique is an effective way to perform feature extraction and, more generally, dimensionality reduction of a given signal representation. In Elman and Zipser (1988) it is applied to the extraction of acoustic features from spectrograms. When there is only one linear hidden layer, this technique has been shown to be equivalent to the popular principal component analysis (Bourland and Kamp, 1988; Baldi and Hornik, 1989), which is the projection of the data along the space spanned by the principal eigenvectors (with the largest eigenvalues) of the data covariance matrix. The reconstruction error can be used as an indication of the similarity of the input pattern with the patterns of the training set. It has been successfully used in Gori *et al.* (1997) for a speaker verification task.

10.7.2. Competitive Neural Networks

Competitive neural networks (Hertz *et al.*, 1991) are one-layer feedforward models, dynamics of which forms the basis for several other unsupervised connectionist architectures (Grossberg, 1976; Lippmann, 1987; Winters and Rose, 1989). These models are called *competitive* because each unit competes with all the others for the classification of each input pattern: the latter is indeed assigned to the *winner unit*, which is the closest (according to a given distance measure) to the input itself, i.e. the most representative within a certain set of *prototypes*. This is strictly related to the concept of *clustering* (Duda and Hart, 1973), where each unit represents the centroid (or mean, or codeword) of one of the clusters. The propagation of the input vector through the network consists of a projection of the pattern onto the weights of the connections entering each output unit. Connection weights are assumed to represent the components of the corresponding centroid. The aim of the forward propagation is to establish the closest centroid to the input vector, i.e. the winner unit. During training, a simple weight update rule is used to move the winner centroid toward the novel pattern, so that the components of the centroid represent a sort of moving average of the input patterns belonging to the corresponding cluster. This is basically an on-line version of some partitioning clustering algorithms (Duda and Hart, 1973). In the following, we will derive it as a consequence of maximum likelihood estimation of the parameters of a mixture of Gaussians under certain assumptions. This simple, basic model can then be easily extended by introducing dynamic allocation of units, or combining it with various supervised techniques. A parallel implementation is also straightforward.

Let us consider again the training set $T = \{x_k \mid k = 1, \ldots, N\}$, where N input samples $x_1, \ldots, x_N$ are now supposed to be drawn from the *finite mixture* density

$$p(x \mid \Theta) = \sum_{i=1}^{C} \Pi_i p_i(x \mid \theta_i) \qquad (10.44)$$

where the parametric form of the component densities $p_i(), i = 1, \ldots, C$ is assumed to be known, as well as the *mixing parameters* $\Pi_1, \ldots, \Pi_C$ (*a priori* probabilities of the components) and $\Theta = (\theta_1, \ldots, \theta_C)$ is the vector of all parameters associated to each component density. In the present setup we want to use the unlabelled training samples to estimate the parameters Θ. In classical pattern recognition this is an unsupervised parametric estimation problem. The following discussion will introduce a connectionist approach to the same problem, leading to the formulation of an unsupervised learning rule for competitive neural networks that is consistent (under certain assumptions) with the above-mentioned statistical estimation.

Assuming the samples are independently drawn from $p(x \mid \Theta)$, the likelihood of the observed data T given a certain choice of parameters Θ can be written as:

$$p(T \mid \Theta) = \prod_{j=1}^{N} p(x_j \mid \Theta). \tag{10.45}$$

Maximum likelihood estimation techniques search for the parameters Θ that maximize expression (10.45), or equivalently the *log-likelihood*, as:

$$l(\Theta) = \log p(T \mid \Theta) = \sum_{j=1}^{N} \log p(x_j \mid \Theta). \tag{10.46}$$

Since the logarithm is a monotonic increasing function, parameters that maximize expressions (10.45) and (10.46) are the same. If a certain parameter vector Θ' maximizes $l(\Theta)$ then it has to satisfy the following necessary, but not sufficient, condition:

$$\nabla_{\theta_i'} l(\Theta') = \mathbf{0} \quad i = 1, \ldots, C \tag{10.47}$$

where the operator $\nabla_{\theta_i'}$ denotes the gradient vector computed with respect to the parameters θ_i', and $\mathbf{0}$ is the vector with all components equal to zero. In other words, we are looking for the zeros of the gradient of the log-likelihood. Substituting equation (10.44) into equation (10.46) and setting the latter equal to zero we can write:

$$\nabla_{\theta_i'} l(\Theta') = \sum_{j=1}^{N} \nabla_{\theta_i'} \log p(x_j \mid \Theta')$$

$$= \sum_{j=1}^{N} \nabla_{\theta_i'} \log \sum_{i=1}^{C} \Pi_i p_i(x_j \mid \theta_i')$$

$$= \sum_{j=1}^{N} \frac{1}{p(x_j \mid \Theta')} \nabla_{\theta_i'} \Pi_i p_i(x_j \mid \theta_i')$$

$$= \mathbf{0}. \tag{10.48}$$

Using Bayes' theorem we have:

$$\Pr(i \mid x_j, \theta_i') = \frac{\Pi_i p_i(x_j \mid \theta_i')}{p(x_j \mid \Theta)} \tag{10.49}$$

where $\Pr(i \mid x_j, \theta'_i)$ is the *a posteriori* probability of class i given the observation x_j and the parameters θ'_i. Equation (10.48) can thus be rewritten as:

$$\nabla_{\theta'_i} l(\Theta') = \sum_{j=1}^{N} \frac{\Pr(i \mid x_j, \theta'_i)}{\Pi_i p_i(x_j \mid \theta'_i)} \nabla_{\theta'_i} \Pi_i p_i(x_j \mid \theta'_i)$$

$$= \sum_{j=1}^{N} \Pr(i \mid x_j, \theta'_i) \nabla_{\theta'_i} \log \Pi_i p_i(x_j \mid \theta'_i)$$

$$= \mathbf{0}. \tag{10.50}$$

In the following, we will concentrate our attention on the case in which the component densities of the mixture are multivariate normal distributions. In this case

$$p_i(x_j \mid \theta_i) = (2\pi)^{-\frac{d}{2}} \mid \Sigma_i \mid^{-\frac{1}{2}} e^{\{-\frac{1}{2}(x_j - \mu_i)^T \Sigma_i^{-1} (x_j - \mu_i)\}} \tag{10.51}$$

where d is the dimension of the feature space, T denotes the transposition of a matrix, and the parameters to be estimated for the ith component density are its mean vector and its covariance matrix, that is to say:

$$\theta_i = (\mu_i, \Sigma_i). \tag{10.52}$$

Substituting equation (10.51) into equation (10.50) we can write the gradient of the log-likelihood for the case of normal component densities as:

$$\nabla_{\theta_i} l(\Theta) = \sum_{j=1}^{N} \Pr(i \mid x_j, \theta_i) \nabla_{\theta_i} \{\log \Pi_i (2\pi)^{-\frac{d}{2}} \mid \Sigma_i \mid^{-\frac{1}{2}}$$

$$- \tfrac{1}{2} (x_j - \mu_i)^T \Sigma_i^{-1} (x_j - \mu_i)\}. \tag{10.53}$$

Suppose now that the only unknown parameters to be estimated are the mean vectors of the Gaussian distributions, i.e. the covariances are known in advance. There are practical situations, for example in data clustering, in which the estimation of the means is sufficient; furthermore, this assumption simplifies the following mathematics, but the extension to the more general case of unknown covariances is rather simple. By setting $\Theta = (\mu_1, \ldots, \mu_C)$, equation (10.53) reduces to:

$$\nabla_{\theta_i} l(\Theta) = \sum_{i=1}^{N} \{\Pr(i \mid x_j, \mu_i) \nabla_{\mu_i} [-\tfrac{1}{2} (x_j - \mu_i)^T \Sigma_i^{-1} (x_j - \mu_i)]\}$$

$$= \sum_{j=1}^{N} \Pr(i \mid x_j, \mu_i) \Sigma_i^{-1} (x_j - \mu_i). \tag{10.54}$$

Again, we are looking for the parameters $\Theta' = (\mu'_1, \ldots, \mu'_C)$ that maximize the log-likelihood, i.e., that correspond to a zero of its gradient. From equation

(10.54), setting $\nabla_{\theta_i} l(\Theta') = 0$ allows us to write:

$$\sum_{j=1}^{N} \Pr(i \mid x_j, \mu_i') x_j = \sum_{j=1}^{N} \Pr(i \mid x_j, \mu_i') \mu_i' \tag{10.55}$$

which finally leads to the following central equation:

$$\mu_i' = \frac{\sum_{j=1}^{N} \Pr(i \mid x_j, \mu_i') x_j}{\sum_{j=1}^{N} \Pr(i \mid x_j, \mu_i')} \tag{10.56}$$

which shows that the maximum likelihood estimate for the ith mean vector is a weighted average of the samples of the training set, where each sample gives a contribution that is proportional to the *estimated* probability of the ith class given the sample itself. Equation (10.56) can not be explicitly solved, but it can be put in a quite interesting and practical iterative form by making explicit the dependence of the current estimate on the number t of iterative steps that have already been accomplished:

$$\mu_i'(t+1) = \frac{\sum_{j=1}^{N} \Pr(i \mid x_j, \mu_i'(t)) x_j}{\sum_{j=1}^{N} \Pr(i \mid x_j, \mu_i'(t))} \tag{10.57}$$

where $\mu_i'(t)$ denotes the estimate obtained at tth iterative step, and the corresponding value is actually used to compute the new estimate at $(t+1)$th step. This iterative algorithm is actually an instance of the EM algorithm, and it is guaranteed to converge superlinearly. Considering the fact that $\Pr(i \mid x_j, \mu_i'(t))$ is large when the Mahalanobis distance between x_j and $\mu_i'(t)$ is small, it is reasonable to estimate an approximation of $\Pr(i \mid x_j, \mu_i'(t))$ in the following way:

$$\Pr(i \mid x_j, \mu_i'(t)) \approx \begin{cases} 1 & \text{if } \text{dist}(x_j, \mu_i'(t)) = \min_{l=1,\dots,C} \text{dist}(x_j, \mu_l'(t)) \\ 0 & \text{otherwise} \end{cases} \tag{10.58}$$

for a given distance measure dist() (the Mahalanobis distance should be used, but the Euclidean distance is usually an effective choice), so expression (10.57) reduces to:

$$\mu_i'(t+1) = \frac{1}{n_i(t)} \sum_{k=1}^{n_i(t)} x_k^{(i)} \tag{10.59}$$

where $n_i(t)$ is the number of training patterns estimated to belong to class i at step t, i.e. the number of patterns for which $\Pr(i \mid x_j, \mu_i'(t)) = 1$ according to equation (10.58), and $x_k^{(i)}, k = 1, \dots, n_i(t)$ is the kth of these patterns. Note that equation (10.59) is the *k-means* clustering algorithm (Duda and Hart, 1973). To switch to an incremental form for equation (10.59), consider what happens when, after the ith mean vector has been calculated at step t over $n_i(t)$ patterns, a new pattern $x_{n_i(t)+1}^{(i)}$ has to be assigned to component i. This occurs when the quantity

$$\Pr(i \mid x_{n_i(t)+1}^{(i)}, \mu_i'(t))$$

given by relation (10.58) equals 1, while $\Pr(i \mid x^{(i)}_{n_i(t)+1}, \mu'_i(t-1))$ is 0. According to equation (10.59), the new mean vector is:

$$\mu'_i(t+1) = \frac{1}{n_i(t)+1} \left(\sum_{k=1}^{n_i(t)} x^{(i)}_k + x^{(i)}_{n_i(t)+1} \right)$$

$$= \frac{n_i(t)}{n_i(t)+1} \mu'_i(t) + \frac{1}{n_i(t)+1} x^{(i)}_{n_i(t)+1}$$

$$= \mu'_i(t) + \frac{1}{n_i(t)+1} (x^{(i)}_{n_i(t)+1} - \mu'_i(t)). \tag{10.60}$$

We can thus estimate the new mean vector after presentation of the $(n_i + 1)$th pattern in the following way:

$$\mu'_i(t+1) = \mu'_i(t) + \delta_{t+1}(x^{(i)}_{n_i(t)+1} - \mu'_i(t)) \tag{10.61}$$

where $\delta_{t+1} = 1/(n_i(t)+1)$ is a vanishing quantity. Using a fixed, small value η instead of δ_{t+1} and representing each component of the ith mean vector $\mu_i = (\mu_{i1}, \ldots, \mu_{id})$ with the weights $w_{i1}, \ldots, w_{id}$ of the corresponding connections in the competitive neural network model, the following weight update (learning) rule is obtained:

$$\Delta w_{ij} = \eta(x_j - w_{ij}) \tag{10.62}$$

where w_{ij} is the weight of the connection between input unit j and output unit i (the winner unit), η is the learning rate, and x_j is the jth component of the pattern, of class i, presented to the network. When a new pattern is fed into the network, its distance is computed with respect to all the output units – using the connection weights as components of the corresponding mean vectors – and, according to relation (10.58), it is assigned to the nearest unit (mixture component). The latter is referred to as the *winner* unit. Weight update, or *learning*, is then accomplished by modifying the connection weights of the winner unit by a direct application of equation (10.62). The weights of the other units are left unchanged. This is a typical *winner-take-all* approach, where the units are in competition for novel input patterns. This is the rationale for using the name *competitive neural networks*, and justifies why they have been successfully used for speech coding as it was mentioned in the introduction to this section. A detailed description of competitive learning and its relationships with statistical mixtures can be found in Nowlan (1991). The way used here to derive the learning rule makes it clear that competitive neural networks can be seen as an on-line version of the popular *k-means* clustering algorithm (Duda and Hart, 1973).

The same mathematical formulation can be extended to the case of unknown covariance matrices for the component densities of the mixture, and even for the case of unknown class prior probabilities (the mixing parameters). A very good review is presented in Duda and Hart (1973). The extension provides us iterative formulae similar to equation (10.57), for estimating the means and the other unknown parameters. This means that an on-line (incremental) connectionist version of these estimates could also be derived.

10.8. ANNs FOR TIME SEQUENCES

There are problems, especially in speech processing, in which samples are temporal sequences of patterns, instead of individual independent samples. To take these temporal dependencies into account, two major classes of neural networks have been proposed, namely *time-delay neural networks* and *recurrent neural networks*. While the former is still an MLP with units fed by an input value and a number of its predecessors, the latter generalizes the basic feedforward architecture of MLPs by allowing arbitrary connections between units, e.g. loops and backward connections.

10.8.1. Time-Delay Neural Networks

Time-delay neural networks (TDNNs), also known as *tapped delay lines*, represent an effective attempt to train a static MLP for time-sequence processing, by converting the temporal sequence into a spatial sequence over corresponding units. The idea is very simple, but useful in a variety of ASR applications, mostly for phoneme recognition (Waibel, 1989; Waibel *et al.*, 1989a; Bourlard and Morgan, 1994). An example of a TDNN is shown in Figure 10.4. The input layer has been enlarged to accept as many input patterns as the (fixed) sequence length to be processed at each time step. Input vectors enter the network from the leftmost set of input units. At each time step, inputs are shifted to the right through the unit delay line that links each set of input units to the right-adjacent one, and the next input pattern is fed into the leftmost position. The same extension can also be applied to subsequent layers, introducing a tapped-delay mechanism between hidden units (e.g. only the first block of units in the tapped line actually receives input from the previous layer), giving the ability to deal with more complicated time dependencies.

The BP algorithm can be used to train such a network. Relevant features are extracted from the original input, not based only on *a priori* knowledge, but on an automatic selection during the network training. The connections between adjacent layers can also be arranged in order to provide hidden units with selective inputs from groups of units in the previous layer (receptive fields). The resulting dynamic can be interpreted as a subsampling from the original temporal representation of the input data, with the effect of averaging over a specific time slice. In this way, different layers of the network provide the overall processing with representations of different temporal scales.

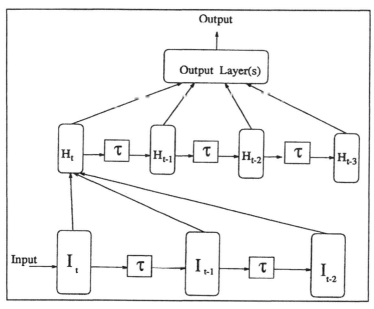

Figure 10.4 Time-delay neural network. Input is fed into the leftmost set of input units (I_t) at time t. Previous inputs (I_{t-1}, I_{t-2}) are shifted to the right, with unit delays represented by boxes labelled τ. A similar mechanism is present in the hidden layer $(H_t, \ldots)$. An integration over time of the input sequence is carried on by the leftmost set of hidden units, while the output layer of the net integrates over time the activations of the hidden units.

It should be noticed that the TDNN can be seen as a particular case of the *convolutional neural network* (Le Cun and Bengio, 1995) when used on "unidimensional" input (this is the case with sequences of acoustic vectors).

TDNNs have been successfully applied in ASR. Lang and Hinton (1988) obtained a 7.8% error rate in multi talker classification of the isolated letters "B, D, E, V", using acoustic material collected among 100 male speakers. Waibel *et al.* (1989b) were able to recognize isolated consonants uttered by a Japanese speaker with a low error rate (4.1%), using a combination of specialized TDNNs. A significant 1.4% error rate in vowel recognition was obtained in the same experiments.

10.8.2. Recurrent Neural Networks

Recurrent neural networks (RNN) provide a powerful extension of feedforward connectionist models by allowing connections between arbitrary pairs of units, independent of their position within the topology of the network. Self-recurrent loops of a unit onto itself, as well as backward connections to previous layers, or

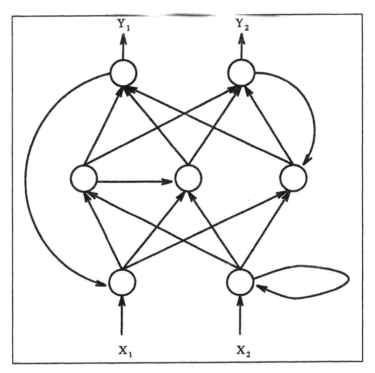

Figure 10.5 A recurrent neural network.

lateral links between units belonging to the same layer are all allowed. An example is given in Figure 10.5.

RNNs behave like dynamic systems. Once fed with an input, the recurrent connections are responsible for an evolution in time of the internal state of the network. RNNs are particularly suited for sequence processing, due to their ability to keep an internal trace, or memory, of the past. This memory is combined with the current input to provide a context-dependent output.

A first type of RNNs is applied to static patterns (i.e., the input is fixed) and its dynamic converges to specific attractors. For instance, in *Boltzmann machines* (Hinton *et al.*, 1984) the recurrent connections are symmetric (bidirectional propagation of signal is allowed along the connection, i.e. pairs of adjacent units have an influence on each other). An interpretation of Boltzmann machines in terms of statistical mechanics has been proposed, along with a learning algorithm based on *simulated annealing* (Kirkpatrick *et al.*, 1983). An important instance of Boltzmann machines is the Hopfield net (Hopfield, 1982; Hopfield and Tank, 1986), basically constituted of a single layer of fully and symmetrically connected linear units, able to act as an auto-associative memory. Limitations of Boltzmann machines reside in the requirement of symmetric (non-directional) recurrent connections, and in the

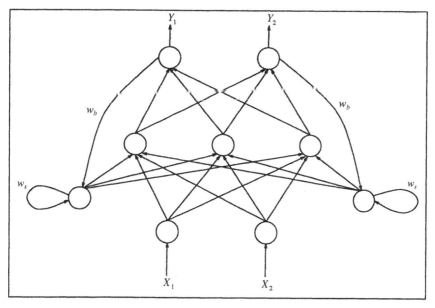

Figure 10.6 An example of a partially recurrent neural network, with two context units with backward connections from the output layer and self-connections. The weights w_s and w_b are constant.

considerable computation time required to perform the simulated annealing. In addition, although they are historically and conceptually relevant, they are practically not feasible for speech and sequence processing.

Another family of RNNs is sometimes referred to as *partially recurrent nets*. In this case the basic architecture is that of a standard MLP, with the addition of a set of recurrent connections from the units in a given layer to the corresponding units of a previous layer (or in the same layer). Recurrent connections propagate the signal back to the units of one of the layers of the MLP, or to an additional *context* or *state* layer. An example is shown in Figure 10.6. The units that receive signals from the recurrent connections act either as preprocessors, filtering the current (forward propagated) input with the previous signal, or as a register that keeps a memory of previous history. The weights of the recurrent connections are generally fixed and set equal to a constant, chosen in order to calibrate the amount of previous information to be taken into account. The standard BP algorithm is used to train the underlying MLP architecture, but without the computation of the full gradient on the parameters, since the effect of the past activities through recurrent connections is not taken into account. Partially recurrent nets were introduced in Jordan (1989), Elman (1990) and Mozer (1993) and resulted in a wide range of applications in sequence processing (both in recognition and in generation). Robinson and Fallside (1991) is a significant example of application of partially recurrent nets within a speaker-independent phoneme and word recognition system.

More generally, a recurrent neural network can have arbitrary directed connections, and all weights can be learned during the training. Different approaches to the problem of training recurrent connections have been proposed in the literature in recent years, mostly based on gradient descent techniques. Particularly remarkable are recurrent backpropagation (Pineda, 1989), backpropagation for sequences (BPS) (Gori *et al.*, 1989), real-time recurrent learning (Williams and Zipser, 1989a,b) and time-dependent recurrent backpropagation (Werbos, 1988; Pearlmutter, 1989; Sato, 1990).

A training method for general recurrent architectures is now briefly described. It can be easily derived from the standard BP algorithm for feedforward networks. In spite of its apparent simplicity, this technique is quite effective whenever the length of the sequences to be learned is not too large, and we are willing to wait for the end of a sequence before updating parameters. This is often the case when a whole training set with many sequences is available, i.e. when no on-line learning is required. The algorithm is called *backpropagation through time* (BPTT) or *unfolding in time* (Minsky and Papert, 1969; Rumelhart *et al.*, 1986a).

The general idea is the following. A discrete time sequence processing task is assumed. Suppose that the activity (state) of a given unit j at time t is given by:

$$\hat{y}_j(t) = f_j \left(\sum_{l \in L_j} w_{jl} \hat{y}_{s_l}(t - d_l) + x_j(t - 1) \right) \tag{10.63}$$

where we denote with w_{jl} the weight of the connection between s_lth and jth units, with d_l the delay (number of time steps) that affects the propagation of signal between these units, and with $x_j(t - 1)$ the external input to unit j at time $t - 1$ (it is assumed to be zero if no input is applied to unit j at that time). The sum over l is extended to all the links in L_j (whose destination unit is the jth unit). Each unit can receive an external input or produce output (or neither) at certain time steps during the processing. The network is then unfolded by turning it into a feedforward network, by introducing one copy of the original units for each time step. All forward connections present in the original net are replicated in the unfolded net. All recurrent connections are substituted by forward connections between a copy of the source unit at a given time step and the copy of the destination unit in the unfolded layer corresponding to the destination time step.

The unfolded net can then be trained using the BP algorithm, with the relevant constraint that all copies of a given connection w_{jk} are required to share the same weight value. This is accomplished by computing all the weight changes produced by BP at different layers, and then training using a common, unique weight change equal to the sum of the individual changes. It should be noticed that the above algorithm can deal with sequences of different

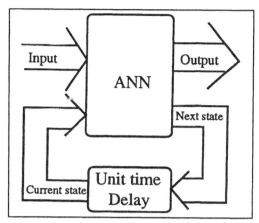

Figure 10.7 Scheme of Robinson's dynamic net.

lengths in the training set, by unfolding into a different number of layers for each case.

Recurrent nets have been applied in a variety of speech processing tasks. Particularly remarkable are the results obtained for phoneme recognition by Robinson *et al.* (Robinson and Fallside, 1988, 1991; Robinson, 1994), where RNNs are used as state-space machines, capable of computing an output and the next state, given the input and the current state. This results in a non-linear extension of linear control theory. A schematic representation of this RNN model is shown in Figure 10.7. The approach gave the best recognition performance on phoneme recognition with the TIMIT corpus and was also used for phone probability estimation. Recently, Robinson *et al.* (1993) have integrated RNNs into a hybrid HMM/ANN speech recognizer, where the networks are used to compute posterior state probabilities (see section 10.9.4). The system had slightly lower performance than some HMM-based systems in the *Wall Street Journal* dictation task, but it required far less model parameters to train.

Details of a recurrent network for plosive recognition (Bengio *et al.*, 1991; Flammia, 1991) are shown in Figure 10.8.

10.9. ANN/HMM HYBRID SYSTEMS

In order to combine the function approximation capabilities of ANNs with the modelling power of HMMs, hybrids of ANNs and HMMs have been introduced. These structures may have the advantage of adding the discriminative power of ANNs to HMM models, or to train ANNs to perform observation transformations for improving the quality of HMM models.

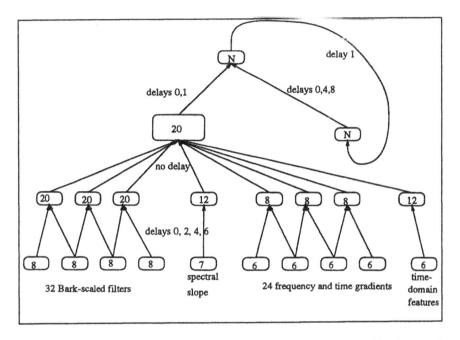

Figure 10.8 Architecture used for the recognition of plosives, nasals and fricatives on the TIMIT database. The first layer has a local connectivity in time and frequency. N is the number of outputs.

The majority of the proposed ANN/HMM hybrids are constructed by sending the output of an ANN into an HMM for ASR (Levin, 1990; Franzini *et al.*, 1990; Haffner *et al.*, 1991; Tebelskis *et al.*, 1991; Bengio *et al.*, 1992a). ANN architectures that emulate an HMM have also been proposed (Bridle, 1990a; Niles and Silverman, 1990). In some of them the dynamic programming algorithm is embedded in the ANN itself (Haffner *et al.*, 1991; Levin *et al.*, 1992). Alternatively, the ANN can be used to re-score the N-best hypotheses (phoneme by phoneme) produced with an HMM (Zavaliagkos *et al.*, 1993). In some cases (Bengio, 1996; Haffner *et al.*, 1991; Tebelskis *et al.*, 1991), the ANN outputs are not interpreted as probabilities, but are rather used as scores and generally combined with a dynamic programming algorithm akin to the Viterbi algorithm to perform alignment and segmentation. In particular, in Bengio (1996) and Bengio *et al.* (1992a), the ANN is used to transform a vector of acoustic features into more effective observations for HMMs. The models proposed by Bourlard *et al.* rely on a probabilistic interpretation of the ANN outputs (Bourlard and Morgan, 1994; Morgan *et al.*, 1995). Although the ANN and the HMM are sometimes trained separately, schemes have been proposed in which both are trained together, or at least the ANN is trained in a way that depends on the HMM.

10.9.1. The Viterbi Net

Lippmann and Gold (1987) proposed a recurrent neural network architecture, implemented in VLSI, able to mimic the decoding behaviour of the continuous-density Viterbi algorithm (see Chapter 5) for the recognition of isolated words. It was called the Viterbi net. Although the recognition performance did not represent any improvement with respect to what could be achieved with standard HMMs, this connectionist architecture is remarkable for historical reasons.

The structure of the Viterbi net has as many input units as the dimensionality of the acoustic vectors. Acoustic observations are fed into the network in sequence, one at a time. Inputs are propagated forward through a single, fully connected layer, and summed up before being passed to each one of a set of state units representing the states of a corresponding left-to-right HMM. A Viterbi network is built for each word model present in the HMM. The state units have a threshold-logic activation and a fixed delay on the output, and are laterally connected (each of them to the following one) in a way that resembles the topology of the left-to-right HMM. In addition to the summed inputs, each state unit also receives a feedback input from an associated subnetwork, able to select the maximum between the output from the state unit itself and the output from the adjacent state unit on the left.

There is no actual training procedure for the Viterbi net, and this is one of its major limitations. It is initialized using the parameters of the corresponding HMM, obtained using the Baum–Welch algorithm (see Chapter 5). After initialization, the recurrent dynamics of the net when fed with a sequence of input vectors result in a parallel version of Viterbi decoding, producing as the final output the logarithm of the likelihood of the input sequence (and most likely state path) given the model.

Experimental results on isolated word recognition tasks, performed using 12 mel cepstral coefficients and 13 differential mel cepstra as features, were satisfactory and comparable with those obtained with state-of-the-art HMMs.

10.9.2. The Alpha Net

Bridle (1990a) proposed a connectionist architecture able to behave like an HMM for ASR. The idea underlying his approach was to look at the forward and backward computation of probabilities in HMMs, and to give them an interpretation in terms of a neural network. In fact, the model was called *alpha net* because its architecture and its dynamics were calibrated to resemble the forward computation of the alphas in the Baum–Welch algorithm.

The alpha net is a recurrent neural network. As for the Viterbi net, its parameters are the same as those of the corresponding HMM, but in the present case a complete forward estimation of the likelihood of the observations given the models is accomplished, instead of a single best-path search as occurs with the Viterbi algorithm. Furthermore, a learning procedure, derived from the backward step of the Baum–Welch algorithm, is available. It is expressed as the backpropagation of the partial derivatives of a discriminant cost function (maximum mutual information). A recurrent architecture of the following kind is built for each unit (word) to be included in the model (and for which a corresponding HMM exists). Neurons are organized in order to represent states of the HMM. For instance, in the most common case of left-to-right HMMs, each unit (neuron) is connected with a recurrent connection to itself, and with a forward connection to the unit representing the following adjacent state in the HMM. The weights of these connections are equal to the state transition probabilities between the corresponding pairs of states. The likelihoods of the emission probabilities are fed into the recurrent loops from another, distinct part of the network, and are multiplied instead of summed. The units are linear, with a unit delay, thus resulting in the computation of the product of the joint probability of transition and emission for that state at each time step. In this way, the overall behaviour is consistent with the probabilistic framework of the HMM. The separate network that is responsible for computation of these likelihoods is supposed to rely, for example, on multipliers and exponentials in order to approximate as closely as possible the likelihoods generated by the Gaussian or mixture of Gaussians associated to the states of the corresponding HMM. The final output of such an architecture is the actual likelihood of the input acoustic sequence given the model, summed over all possible paths within the network.

10.9.3. A Non-linear Transformation for HMMs

Inspired from the alpha net is an ANN/HMM hybrid of which all the parameters can be simultaneously estimated in relation to a single criterion. Furthermore, the objective of learning is defined at the sequence level (e.g., word or sentence), rather than at the level of single phonemes or time steps. The ANN is basically used as a trained preprocessor for a continuous-density HMM: it transforms an input acoustic representation (which may be very high-dimensional and takes as input a window of the input sequence) into a concise low-dimensional representation that is easier to model for the HMM emission probability models, and improves the performance of the HMM recognition algorithm. Another way to apply the same idea views the ANN as an "object" spotter (e.g., for phonemes or characters), and the HMM as a post-processor that can align the sequence of outputs from the ANN with a higher-level (typically, linguistic and lexical) model of the temporal structure of the observed sequences. This model was introduced in Bengio *et al.* (1992b) and is also described in Bengio (1996).

The ANN transforms a raw input sequence u_1^L into an intermediate observation sequence x_1^L. For example, a Gaussian or Gaussian mixture model can be associated to each state i of the HMM in order to model the emission probabilities $\Pr(x_t \mid q_t = i)$. The basic idea is that the optimization criterion C used to train the HMM is a continuous and differentiable function of the intermediate observations x_t. Therefore, the gradients $\partial C / \partial x_t$ can be used to train the parameters w of the ANN (further backpropagation into the ANN yields the weight gradients $\partial C / \partial w$).

It turns out that the computation of $\partial C / \partial x_t$ is very simple to implement in practice, because the Baum–Welch algorithm implicitly computes the derivative of the HMM likelihood $\Pr(x_1^L \mid Y)$ (for a model constrained by the knowledge of the correct word sequence Y) with respect to the emission probabilities $b_{i,t} = \Pr(x_t \mid q_t = i)$.

In the forward pass, the Baum–Welch algorithm (an application of the EM algorithm) computes:

$$\alpha_{i,t} = b_{i,t} \sum_j a_{i,j} \alpha_{j,t-1} \tag{10.64}$$

where $\alpha_{i,t} = \Pr(q_t = i, x_1^t)$, and $a_{i,j}$ is the transition probability $\Pr(q_t = i \mid q_{t-1} = j)$. Finally the likelihood $\Pr(x_1^L)$ is obtained from the α's at the last time step, for the specially labelled "final" states:

$$\Pr(x_1^L) = \sum_{i \in \text{final states}} \alpha_{i,L} \tag{10.65}$$

The backward pass is initialized as follows:

$$\beta_{i,L} = \begin{cases} 1 & \text{if } i \in \text{final states} \\ 0 & \text{otherwise} \end{cases} \tag{10.66}$$

where $\beta_{i,t} = \Pr(x_{t+1}^L \mid q_t = i)$. These are computed recursively with:

$$\beta_{i,t} = \sum_j a_{j,i} \beta_{j,t+1} b_{j,t+1} \tag{10.67}$$

Note from equations (10.65) and (10.66) that $\partial \Pr(x_1^L) / \partial \alpha_{i,L} = \beta_{i,L}$. Inspecting equations (10.67) and (10.64) and proceeding by induction (and the chain rule) yields:

$$\frac{\partial \Pr(x_1^L)}{\partial \alpha_{i,t}} = \beta_{i,t} \tag{10.68}$$

Derivatives with respect to the emission probabilities can now be obtained from equation (10.64):

$$\frac{\partial \Pr(x_1^L)}{\partial b_{i,t}} = \frac{\alpha_{i,t} \beta_{i,t}}{b_{i,t}} \tag{10.69}$$

The simplest case is the one in which the training criterion C is the likelihood of the HMM observations (i.e., the product of the likelihoods $\Pr(x_1^L \mid Y)$ over the different training sequences). Using an HMM constrained by the correct word sequence Y, one obtains directly the gradient of the criterion C with respect to the emission probabilities, with equation (10.69). To obtain gradients with respect to the ANN outputs one needs only to be able to compute the derivatives of the emission density function with respect to the observations, $\partial \Pr(x_t \mid q_t = i)/\partial x_t$. See Bengio *et al.* (1992a) and Bengio (1996) for an example in the case of Gaussian or Gaussian-mixture emission models.

However, there is a potentially serious danger in training jointly the above ANN/HMM hybrid to maximize the likelihood of the *intermediate variables* x_1^L, rather than the raw acoustics u_1^L. An infinite value of the likelihood can be obtained by making the ANN produce a constant output: the Gaussian mixtures can then converge to zero variance, the emission probabilities also increase towards infinity, and $\Pr(x_1^L)$ increases towards infinity. In practice (Bengio *et al.*, 1992a; Bengio, 1996), this problem has not occurred, probably because the training converged to a (more interesting) local maximum of the likelihood. Note that similar problems can occur in training Gaussian mixtures to maximize the likelihood when a Gaussian concentrates on one point. This problem can be avoided when using a discriminant training criterion.

Although maximizing the maximum mutual likelihood training is a good starting point for the HMM, better performance can be obtained with the ANN/HMM hybrid when the training criterion is *discriminant*. For example, the system can be trained to maximize the maximum mutual information (MMI) criterion:

$$C_{MMI} = \log \frac{\Pr(x_1^L \mid Y = y)}{\Pr(x_1^L)} \qquad (10.70)$$

or (almost the same), the maximum *a posteriori* (MAP) criterion:

$$C_{MAP} = \Pr(Y = y \mid x_1^L) = \frac{\Pr(x_1^L \mid Y = y)\Pr(Y = y)}{\Pr(x_1^L)} \qquad (10.71)$$

In both cases one considers two HMM models: a *constrained model* $\Pr(x_1^L \mid Y = y)$, knowing the correct word sequence y, and a *recognition model* $\Pr(x_1^L) = \sum_y \Pr(x_1^L \mid Y = y)\Pr(Y = y)$, which allows all the possible word sequences Y. The reason why these criteria are discriminant is that training does not attempt to learn a good model of the distribution of x_1^t but instead to discriminate between the different word sequences Y: the likelihood of the correct model is raised, while the likelihoods of the other interpretations are pushed down.

The derivatives of the training criterion with respect to the ANN parameters can then be computed by considering separately the contributions to $\partial C/\partial x_t$ through the constrained model and through the recognition model. For

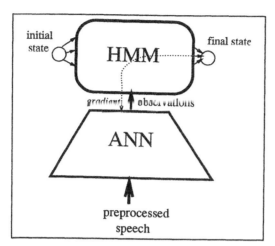

Figure 10.9 Global optimization of an hybrid system where the ANN performs feature extraction for the HMM.

example, for the MMI criterion, it holds that:

$$\frac{\partial C_{MMI}}{\partial x_t} = \frac{1}{\Pr(x_1^L | Y = y)} \frac{\partial \Pr(x_1^L | Y = y)}{\partial x_t} - \frac{1}{\Pr(x_1^L)} \frac{\partial \Pr(x_1^L)}{\partial x_t} \qquad (10.72)$$

It has been shown how to compute the individual likelihood gradients $\partial \Pr(x_1^L | Y = y)/\partial x_t$ and $\partial \Pr(x_1^L)/\partial x_t$ for the constrained $(Y = y)$ and unconstrained HMMs.

The basic hybrid system architecture is shown in Figure 10.9. Speech spectra or a transformation of them is the input of an ANN that performs a non-linear transformation of the input and produces new observations for the HMM integrated network.

The weights of the ANN specify the transformation it performs and are estimated by a joint optimization procedure with the HMM parameters in such a way that the recognition error is minimum. Thus the transformation is tailored in the specific time alignment and recognition method.

In practice the ANN is a combination of specialized ANNs, as shown in Figure 10.10, initialized to optimize recognition on a specific class of sounds (e.g. plosives) with a class-dependent set of acoustic features. A network that combines the outputs of specialized ANNs is initialized to perform principal component analysis.

It has been shown experimentally how training the ANN jointly with the HMM improves performance on a speech recognition problem (Bengio *et al.*, 1992a; Bengio, 1996), bringing down the error rate on a plosive recognition task from 19% to 14%. It has later been shown how using a discriminant training criterion (MMI) on a handwriting recognition problem (Bengio *et al.*, 1994) reduced the character error rate from 12.4%

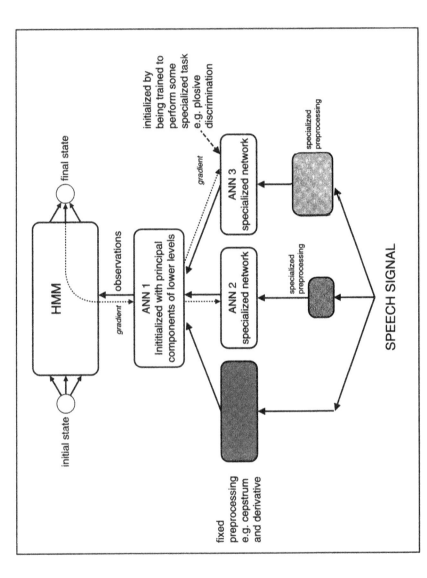

Figure 10.10 Feature extraction by combining specialized neural models into an hybrid ANN/HMM system with global optimization.

down to 8.2% (no dictionary), or from 2% down to 1.4% (with a 350-word dictionary).

10.9.4. ANNs to Compute State Posteriors

Bourlard and Morgan (1994) have proposed other HMM/ANN hybrids for continuous ASR. An MLP is trained to estimate posterior probabilities of HMM states, with the ultimate objective of maximizing the posterior probability of a given (left-to-right) Markov model M_i given an acoustic observation sequence X. Posterior probabilities can be written as:

$$\Pr(M_i \mid X) = \sum_{q_1^L} \Pr(q_1^L, M_i \mid X)$$

$$= \sum_{q_1^L} \Pr(q_1^L \mid X)\Pr(M_i \mid q_1^L, X)$$

$$= \sum_{q_1^L} \Pr(q_1^L \mid X)\Pr(M_i \mid q_1^L) \qquad (10.73)$$

where the model M_i is supposed to have Q states $q_1, \ldots, q_Q$, and the acoustic observation sequence $X = (x_1, \ldots, x_L)$ is assumed to be of length L. In equation (10.73) the sums are extended over all possible sequences q_1^L of states.

The quantity $\Pr(M_i \mid q_1^L)$ does not depend on the acoustics (observation sequence X), but only on higher-level choices made in the definition of the models, and can thus be computed separately.

Repeatedly applying the properties of joint probabilities, equation (10.73) can be rewritten as:

$$\Pr(M_i \mid X) = \sum_{q_1^L} \Pr(q_1 \mid X)\Pr(q_2 \mid X, q_1)\ldots$$

$$\ldots \Pr(q_L \mid X, q_1, \ldots, q_{L-1})\Pr(M_i \mid q_1^L)$$

$$= \sum_{q_1^L} \left(\prod_{\ell=1}^{L} \Pr(q_\ell \mid X, q_1^{\ell-1})\right)\Pr(M_i \mid q_1^L) \qquad (10.74)$$

Attempts to determine analytical developments for the present formulation, similar to those adopted in the maximization of the likelihood of the observations given the model (see Chapter 5) and that lead us to the *forward–backward* and the Viterbi algorithms, are not practicable. Bourlard's idea is then to use feedforward neural networks as estimators of the posterior probabilities of states given the observations and the previous state sequence. Actually, an approximate version of equation (10.75) is used, by taking:

$$\Pr(M_i \mid X) = P'(M_i \mid X)$$

$$\approx \sum_{q_1^L} \left(\prod_{\ell=1}^{L} \Pr(q_\ell \mid x_{\ell-k}, \dots, x_{\ell+k}, q_{\ell-1}) \right) \Pr(M_i \mid q_1^L) \quad (10.75)$$

that is to say, the network is trained to estimate the state posterior $\Pr(q_\ell \mid x_{\ell-k}, \dots, x_{\ell+k}, q_{\ell-1})$ given a fixed number $2k+1$ of acoustic vectors $x_{\ell-k}, \dots, x_{\ell+k}$ (a *window* or *context* of size k centred in the current acoustic observation x_ℓ) and the previous state. This is accomplished using the BP algorithm on a MLP, which has an output unit for each state (which represents the estimate of the state posterior probability). This is a particular case of what we called time-delay neural networks in section 10.8.1. Other attempts were made to use the MLP to estimate the posteriors in different ways, for example as a function of the current observation and of the previous state only, or as a function also of previous MLPs' outputs (previous states). In any case, the speech recognition performance of the resulting overall system was surprisingly poor in many experiments (Bourlard and Morgan, 1994). This was attributed to the fact that common HMMs (with all the practical tricks required to make them effective on real-world tasks) work well within the framework of likelihoods, but not with posterior probabilities, in spite of the theory sketched above. A step backward was then made by moving the system back to likelihoods. This issue was pursued by using a somewhat standard version of the HMM, in conjunction with neural networks. The latter were trained to perform exactly the same probability estimation as in equation (10.75), but with their outputs divided by the *a priori* probabilities of the corresponding states, in order to reduce probabilities to likelihoods normalized by the unconditional likelihood of each observation (using Bayes' theorem). Priors can be computed apart, from the training data or from statistical considerations on the constraints given by the specific task. This solution was effective and allowed the system to reach the recognition performance of state-of-the-art HMM recognizers on large-vocabulary continuous speech tasks, but at the expense of the original theoretical framework.

One central point raised with this approach concerns the training procedure. Indeed, networks are trained with BP, which would require knowledge of target values for the outputs in order to compute the gradient of the cost functional. With the exception of toy tasks, no supervised labelling of acoustic frames is actually available (labelling by hand in real-sized databases is not feasible). Bourlard *et al.* suggested an iterative training procedure that starts up with a linear segmentation of the acoustic observations, performs training of the networks according to the initial segmentation, then uses the Viterbi algorithm (in conjunction with the newly trained networks as estimators of the state-emission probabilities) in order to produce a new (more reliable) segmentation of the data, which in turn is used to train the networks again, and so on in an iterative fashion. Bourlard *et al.* argue that this is a particular instance of the expectation-maximization (EM) algorithm. This technique is interestingly effective, but it represents a divergence with respect to the theoretical developments that motivated the overall architecture of the system, as far as the networks are optimized over a cost function (squared differences between target and actual outputs) that is not the same one used to perform the segmentation (and the evaluation of the system performance), namely the word recognition error after Viterbi.

10.9.5. Input/Output HMMs

A promising new approach for combining ANNs and HMMs is the input/output HMM (IOHMM) (Bengio and Frasconi, 1995b; Bengio and Bengio, 1996). It is based on a posterior model of the output variable (e.g., correct word sequence) given the input variable (e.g., acoustic sequence), without involving, as an intermediate step, likelihood models of the input variable. An IOHMM represents the distribution of an output sequence given an input sequence (which may be of different lengths M and L, respectively). Using a discrete hidden state variable q_t for each time step, this conditional distribution $\Pr(Y_1^M \mid X_1^L)$ is expressed on the basis of conditional "emission" distributions $\Pr(Y_s \mid q_t = i, x_t)$ and transition distributions $\Pr(q_t = i \mid q_{t-1} = j, x_t)$. Both of these types of distributions can be modelled by an ANN, or by any other model. If a simple form of distribution (e.g., discrete) is used, then the EM algorithm can also be used to train the system. An IOHMM can also be interpreted as a recurrent mixture of experts (Jacobs *et al.*, 1991; Cacciatore and Nowlan, 1994), as well as a probabilistic transducer (Singer, 1996) with input and output variables which can be discrete as well as continuous-valued. IOHMMs are also related to the partially observable Markov decision processes (POMDPs) proposed in the control and reinforcement learning communities (Sondik, 1978)

In the first paper on IOHMMs (Bengio and Frasconi, 1995b), only the simpler synchronous case is considered: the output sequence has the same length as the input sequence, and $\Pr(Y_1^L \mid X_1^L)$ is modelled. In that case the mathematics of the model are very similar to those of HMMs, and a version of the Baum–Welch algorithm can be applied to train the system, with similar forward and backward recurrences. The equations are the same except that emission and transition probabilities are now conditioned on the input variable x_t, i.e., the transition probabilities change with time. However, the interpretation of variables is very different from HMMs: the variables that are modelled in the emission probabilities are now the word classes, not the acoustics. The acoustic sequence is only used to condition the emission probabilities and the transition probabilities.

Potential advantages of IOHMMs over HMMs are the following:

- The training criterion is discriminant (as already argued in previous sections, since the C_{MAP} criterion is used).
- The local models (emission and transitions) can be represented by ANNs, which are flexible non-linear models more powerful and yet more parsimonious than the Gaussian mixtures often used in HMMs. Furthermore, these ANNs can take into account a wide context (not just the acoustic information at time t but also a window of neighbouring acoustic frames). The ANN can even be recurrent (to take into account arbitrarily far past contexts).
- Transition probabilities and emission probabilities are generally better matched, thus reducing a problem observed in HMMs for ASR. Because outputs are in a much higher dimensional space than transitions in HMMs, the dynamic range of transition probabilities is much less than that of emission probabilities. Therefore in HMMs the choice between different paths (during recognition) is mostly influenced by emission rather than transition probabilities.
- Long-term dependencies are expected to be more easily learned in IOHMMs than in HMMs, because the transition probabilities are less ergodic. This issue is discussed in Bengio and Frasconi (1995a) together with an analysis of the difficulty of learning to represent long-term dependencies in Markovian models in general.

In a more recent paper on asynchronous HMMs (Bengio and Bengio, 1996), it is shown how to extend the formalism to the case of output sequences shorter than input sequences, which is normally the case in ASR (where the output sequence would typically be a phoneme sequence). For this purpose states can either emit or not emit an output at each time step, according to a certain probability (which can also be conditioned on the current input).

When conceived as a generative model of the output (given the input), an asynchronous IOHMM works as follows. At time $t = 0$, an initial state q_0 is chosen according to the distribution $\Pr(q_0)$, and the length of the output sequence s is initialized to 0. At other time steps $t > 0$, a state q_t is first picked according to the *transition distribution* $\Pr(q_t \mid q_{t-1}, x_t)$, using the state at the previous time step q_{t-1} and the current input x_t. A decision is then taken as to whether or not an output y_s will be produced at time t or not, according to the *emit-or-not distribution*. In the positive case, an output y_s is then produced according to the *emission distribution* $\Pr(y_s \mid q_t, x_t)$. The length of the output sequence is increased from $s - 1$ to s. The parameters of the model are thus the initial state probabilities, $\Pr(q_0 = i)$, and the parameters of the emit-or-not, emission and transition conditional distribution models, $\Pr(emit\text{-}or\text{-}not \mid q_t, x_t)$, $\Pr(y_s \mid q_t, x_t)$ and $\Pr(q_t \mid q_{t-1}, x_t)$. Since the input and output sequences are of different lengths, another hidden variable is introduced, τ_t, specifically to represent the alignment between inputs and outputs, with $\tau_t = s$ meaning that s outputs have been emitted at time t.

The conditional likelihood computation (given the correct output sequence y_1^M) proceeds in a recursive fashion similar to the forward pass of the Baum–Welch algorithm:

$$\alpha(i, s, t) = b(i, y_s, t)(1 - \varepsilon(i, t)) \sum_j a(i, j, t) \alpha(j, s - 1, t - 1)$$

$$+ \varepsilon(i, t) \sum_j a(i, j, t) \alpha(j, s, t - 1) \tag{10.76}$$

with $\alpha(i, s, t) = \Pr(q_t = i, \tau_t = s, y_1^s \mid x_1^t)$, transition probabilities $a(i, j, t) = \Pr(q_t = i \mid q_{t-1} = j, x_t)$, emission probabilities $b(i, y_s, t) = \Pr(y_s \mid q_t = i, x_t, \tau_t = s, \tau_{t-1} = s - 1)$, and emit-or-not-emit probabilities $\varepsilon(i, t) = \Pr(\tau_t = s \mid \tau_{t-1} = s, q_t = i, x_t)$. Finally, the conditional likelihood is computed as in HMMs, with $\Pr(y_1^M \mid x_1^L) = \sum_{i \in \text{final states}} \alpha(i, M, L)$.

The backward pass is computed in a similar way, since it corresponds to computing gradients of the conditional likelihood with respect to $\alpha(i, s, t)$. Unfortunately, these recurrences require storage and computation that are proportional to the product of the input and output lengths, times the number of transitions (whereas ordinary HMMs only require resources proportional to the product of the input length times the number of transitions). In practice, it has been found that much less memory and computation are necessary when a pruning algorithm (such as beam search) is used to explore the graph of α's (which is a standard practice in HMMs applied to large vocabularies), without hampering recognition performance. After the forward and backward passes have been performed, gradients with respect to the transition and emission probabilities can be used to update the parameters of these models (in a way that is very similar to what has already been explained in section 10.9.3).

A recognition algorithm (which looks for the most likely output sequence) can also be derived, similarly to the Viterbi algorithm for HMMs. Let us define $V(i, t)$ as the probability of the best state and output subsequence ending up in state i at time t:

$$V(i, t) = \max_{s, y_1^s, q_1^{t-1}} \Pr(y_1^s, q_1^{t-1}, q_t = i, \tau_t = s \mid x_1^t) \tag{10.77}$$

where the maximum is taken over all possible lengths s of output sequences y_1^s. This variable can be computed recursively by dynamic programming:

$$V(i, t) = \max(\varepsilon(i, t), (1 - \varepsilon(i, t)) \max_l b(i, l, t)))$$

$$\times \max_j (a(i, j, t) V(j, t - 1)). \tag{10.78}$$

At the end of the sequence, the best final state i^* which maximizes $V(i, L)$ is picked within the set of final states. If the argmax in the above recurrence is kept, then the best predecessor j and best output (y_s or the empty symbol) for each (i, t) can be used to trace back the optimal state and output sequence from i^*, like in the Viterbi algorithm. Luckily, this recognition algorithm has the same computational complexity as the recognition algorithm for ordinary HMMs, i.e., the number of transitions times the length of the input sequence.

10.10. CONCLUDING REMARKS

The idea of a formal neuron capable of performing a "logical" calculus in a way that resembles biological events (action potential of an actual cell in the nervous system, given the neurotransmitter coming from its synaptic junctions) was brought to the scientific community by McCulloch and Pitts (1943), and immediately had a wide resonance, although no computer simulations were possible at that time.

In 1949, Hebb introduced the physiological concept of synaptic modification and stated the learning rule which is named after him (see section 10.2). We have to wait until 1957 to find the novel model proposed by Rosenblatt, the *perceptron* (Rosenblatt, 1957). Described in the simple, linear form that we introduced at the beginning of section 10.2, the model was characterized by a well-defined learning rule and, above all, by a mathematical proof of its convergence properties. In 1960, Widrow and Hoff proposed another learning rule for a similar formalism, called *Adaline*. As has been shown in section 10.2, this algorithm is a direct consequence of gradient descent on a least mean squares problem. A comprehensive review of the learning models introduced so far and their ability to perform linear discrimination is due to Nilsson (1965), who published the milestone *Learning Machines*. Minsky and Papert (1969) marked an important, although twofold, point in the history of ANNs, with their book *Perceptrons*. They were able to prove some major limitations of one-layer perceptrons (they also argued that no better behaviour had to be expected from a multilayered network). A rigorous, realistic framework for research on ANNs was set. At the same time, a loss of interest in ANNs spread all over the scientific community, due to the apparently hopeless limitations of the model described therein.

Only during the 1970s did things begin to move again, but in a quite different direction, mainly thanks to the work by von der Malsburg and Willshaw (von der Malsburg, 1973; Willshaw and von der Malsburg, 1976) on *self-organizing maps*, that was carried on, after 1980, by Grossberg and Kohonen (see section 10.7).

Werbos (1974) presented the first formulation of a gradient descent optimization technique with "backpropagation", which could also be applied to layered networks. Surprisingly enough, the BP algorithm became popular, and caused enthusiastic reactions, only 12 years later, when it was described by Rumelhart *et al.* (1986a,b) (in 1985 the algorithm was also independently discovered by Le Cun).

The other major event of the 1980s occurred when Hopfield (1982) introduced a recurrent model that was described, in terms of mechanical statistics, as a dynamical system. The door to recurrent nets, Boltzmann machines and auto-associative memories was open.

The first work on RBF was published by Broomhead and Lowe (1988), and valuable theoretical developments of this model were proposed one year later (Poggio and Girosi, 1989).

Feedforward ANNs have been applied to acoustic feature extraction, phoneme recognition, letter-to-sound translation, mapping the acoustical properties of a speech signal to the vocal tract geometry, and the computation of observation posterior probabilities. Recurrent neural networks have been applied to phoneme recognition, feature transformation and probability computation. Recurrent ANNs should be, in principle, more powerful than just feedforward ANNs because they are able to model history. In practice, modelling history may turn out to be a difficult task.

A special issue of the *IEEE Transactions on Speech and Audio Processing* (January, 1994) describes some recent applications to speech processing.

ANN performance, when applied to ASR, was superior to HMMs in phoneme recognition, but slightly inferior when used in dictation systems.

As ANNs are theoretically superior to HMMs in modelling long-term dependencies, some interesting results may be obtained by using them, especially in transient analysis. New hybrids of ANNs and HMMs may offer an interesting direction for improving ASR.

Perhaps the use of ANNs will also find its place in one of the phases of progressive search.

11

Speaker Adaptation

Diego Giuliani[*] and Renato De Mori[†]

11.1. INTRODUCTION

Automatic speech recognition (ASR) technology has reached a sufficient level of maturity for industrial applications. An important factor that affects recognition performance in real-world applications is the mismatch between the acoustic conditions in training and operating environments, mostly concerning microphone, transmission channel, environmental noise and inter-speaker differences.

---

[*]Istituto per la Ricerca Scientifica e Tecnologica – 38050 Pantè di Povo, Trento, Italy.
[†]School of Computer Science, McGill University, Montreal, P.Q. H3A 2A7, Canada.

This chapter focuses on compensating inter speaker acoustic variations, which has a major impact on ASR performance. Robustness with respect to environmental noise will be discussed in Chapter 12. Although recent technology, based on hidden Markov models (HMMs) and on hybrid systems (artificial neural networks – HMMs), guarantees acceptable average performance for tasks with a vocabulary of more than 10 000 words, speaker-independent (SI) systems exhibit large performance fluctuations among speakers (Digalakis *et al.*, 1995; Leggetter and Woodland, 1995a; Waterhouse *et al.*, 1996). For example, experiments carried out with American English corpora show that the error rate for non-native speakers is tangibly higher than that obtained for native speakers when using systems trained for native speakers. Significant experiments have been carried out with the *Wall Street Journal* (*WSJ*) continuous speech database (see Appendix D). Concerning the 5000-word vocabulary (1994 evaluation) task of the *WSJ* corpus, in Leggetter and Woodland (1995a) it is reported that for a given SI baseline system, trained for native speakers, the word error rate (WER) for native and non-native speakers was of about 5% and 20%, respectively. This difference in performance is due to many sources of errors but the most important of them is the lack of modelling accuracy due to difference in phonetic characteristics.

SI systems are trained using a large amount of data collected from a number of speakers, and acoustic model parameters turn out to be a sort of average over speaker differences. This results in a limited modelling accuracy for each individual speaker. Furthermore, speakers having acoustic characteristics quite different from those of the training population are poorly represented by model parameter values. Acoustic differences among speakers are due to both physiological (e.g. vocal tract length, dimension of mouth and nasal cavities) and linguistic differences (e.g. accents, dialects). The simplest way to deal with inter-speaker variability is to train a speech recognizer for each new user. This leads to speaker-dependent (SD) recognition systems which, in general, given an adequate amount of speaker-specific data, perform better than SI systems (Huang and Lee, 1993; Digalakis *et al.*, 1995).

Collecting a sufficient amount of data for each single speaker, in order to properly train the acoustic models, is time consuming and unacceptable in many cases. As a compromise, speaker adaptation techniques attempt to "tune" the available recognition system to the voice of a new speaker in order to improve recognition performance. Thanks to recently introduced speaker adaptation techniques, requiring little speaker-specific acoustic data, adapted SI systems have shown comparable performance with respect to SD systems (Huang and Lee, 1993; Digalakis *et al.*, 1995). This justifies the increasing interest in speaker adaptation of SI systems.

Many techniques have been developed for speaker adaptation. They depend on many factors such as the nature of the speech models used by the recognizer (e.g. type of HMMs), the type of application for which the recognizer has been designed (e.g. automatic dictation, telephone dialogue), the cooperation required to the system user (e.g. for uttering prompt texts) and the application requirements (e.g. real-time). A broad distinction can be made between adaptation in the *model parameter space* (*model* adaptation approach) and adaptation in the *feature space* (*feature transformation* approach) (Leggetter and Woodland, 1995b; Sankar and Lee, 1995). Model adaptation deals with the modification of model parameters to better fit the new speaker acoustic data. Adaptation in the feature space attempts to reduce the inter-speaker acoustic differences by means of acoustic data transformations. Although this distinction is not exhaustive and in some sense weak, it may prove useful.

More precisely, model adaptation techniques use a pretrained set of HMMs and a limited amount of speech data (*adaptation* or training data) from a speaker, to *adapt* model parameters to that speaker. This can be achieved through model parameter re-estimation. Many model parameter re-estimation techniques are based on maximum *a posteriori* (MAP) parameter estimation (Lee *et al.*, 1991; Gauvain and Lee, 1994). A mathematical formulation for MAP adaptation of the different types of HMMs is proposed in Gauvain and Lee (1994) and Huo *et al.* (1995). Model parameter re-estimation techniques, while showing good capability to approximate SD performance when enough adaptation data are available, suffer from the fact that, with a small amount of adaptation data, only a part of model parameters are adapted. Various techniques have been investigated in order to ensure robustness to model parameter re-estimation and compensate for sparse adaptation data. They are mainly based on parameter tying/sharing strategies for decreasing the total number of parameters to be estimated (Zavaliagkos *et al.*, 1995b) and on *model parameter transformation* (Hao and Fang, 1994; Leggetter and Woodland, 1995b; Digalakis *et al.*, 1995). In particular, since *continuous density* HMMs (CDHMMs) are becoming a dominant solution in acoustic modelling, a lot of work has been devoted to the development of effective techniques for adapting Gaussian mixture densities. Adaptation of CDHMMs through parameter transformation has been recently proposed based on maximum likelihood (ML) linear transformations applied to the mean or to both mean and covariance of Gaussian mixture components (Leggetter and Woodland, 1995b; Gales *et al.*, 1996; Digalakis *et al.*, 1995).

Adaptation in the feature space makes use of an acoustic feature transformation that reduces acoustic differences between speakers. Generally speaking, a feature vector transformation is estimated between the acoustic feature space of a *new* speaker and that of a *reference* speaker for which a recognition system was previously trained. The feature vector transformation is estimated with a small amount of speech data from the new speaker and then applied to her/his acoustic data before recognition, so that reference's speaker speech models can still be used (Class *et al.*, 1990; Huang, 1992). Feature vector transformations of this type are often called *spectral transformations*. Linear, piecewise linear, and neural-network-based transformations have been widely investigated for this purpose (Choukri *et al.*, 1986; Montacié *et al.*, 1989; Class *et al.*, 1990; Matsukoto and Inoue, 1992; Huang, 1992). A variety of adaptation schemes have been developed, differing in the manner in which the acoustic feature transformations are estimated and applied. In some adaptation schemes, the application of these feature vector transformations results in model or code-book (for discrete HMMs) adaptation (Class *et al.*, 1990; Matsukoto and Inoue, 1992). In these cases, a transformation is estimated in order to reduce differences between reference speaker and new speaker acoustic data, and then applied to the speech models of the reference speaker rather than to the input speech. This avoids additional computation time during recognition for applying the estimated transformation to the input feature vectors.

Model selection based on *speaker clustering* and *speaker cluster selection* is another possible way to compensate for the lack in modelling accuracy (Lee, 1988b). In this case, speakers in the training set are first clustered in a small number of subsets. Speech data from training speakers belonging to the same cluster are used to train a set of models. Clustering of similar speakers should ensure, for each set of models, a better modelling accuracy in comparison with SI models. During recognition, the speaker is first assigned to a cluster of speakers whose models are then used for recognition.

This chapter is organized as follows. In section 11.2, adaptation modalities are reviewed. Section 11.3 mainly concerns ML-transformation-based approaches for adapting parameters of the Gaussian components of CDHMMs and model adaptation with MAP parameter re-estimation. Fast speaker adaptation based on vector field smoothing is then reviewed with significant techniques for adapting parameters of discrete HMMs. Section 11.4 discusses feature vector transformation techniques for speaker adaptation in the feature domain. Section 11.5 focuses on speaker clustering, training and selection of cluster-dependent acoustic models. Finally, section 11.6 contains some concluding remarks.

11.2. BATCH, INCREMENTAL AND INSTANTANEOUS SPEAKER ADAPTATION

From the point of view of execution modalities, which correspond to different applicative scenarios, speaker adaptation can be *batch*, *incremental*, or *instantaneous* (Zavaliagkos *et al.*, 1995a; Huo *et al.*, 1996). Furthermore, in analogy with other parameter estimation techniques, speaker adaptation can be *supervised* or *unsupervised* (Furui and Sondhi, 1991). Adaptation is supervised if the texts of the utterances it uses are known; otherwise, it is unsupervised. When a speaker is required to read a set of predetermined sentences, adaptation is *text-dependent*.

In batch (*off-line* or *static*) speaker adaptation, a sufficient amount of data from a given speaker is first collected, before performing adaptation. For

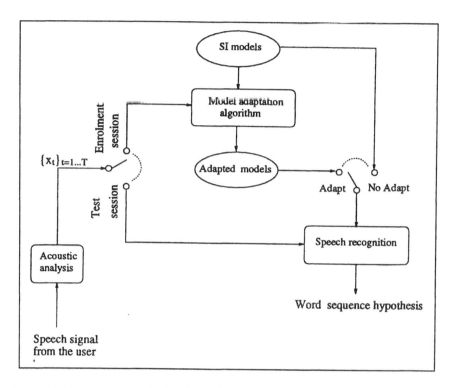

Figure 11.1 Block diagram for batch speaker adaptation.

some applications, such as automatic dictation, adaptation data can be collected during an *enrolment* session for a new speaker. In general, during the enrolment session, a new system user is required to read some tens of sentences whose text is carefully designed in order to have a balanced phonetic content. In this case adaptation is supervised. Figure 11.1 shows a block diagram for a speaker adaptive system with batch adaptation.

In incremental (*dynamic* or *sequential*) speaker adaptation (Matsuoka and Lee, 1993; Huang and Lee, 1993; Zavaliagkos *et al.*, 1995a; Huo *et al.*, 1996), the system is adapted *on-line* in a *transparent* continuous way, as soon as new data from the system user are obtained, without an explicit enrolment session. In this modality, speech models are updated after each utterance (or set of utterances) and used to recognize the next input utterance. With incremental adaptation, system performance improves while the user uses the system. However, it is important that the initial system setting has an acceptable initial recognition performance for the user, so that good recognition performance can be obtained with a small number of utterances. Adaptation "speed" is, in fact, another important factor in incremental adaptation. Figure 11.2 shows a block diagram for a speaker adaptive system with incremental adaptation.

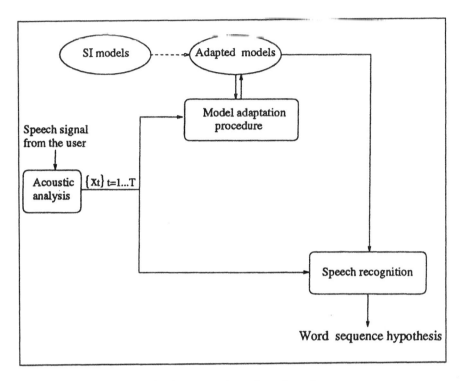

Figure 11.2 Block diagram for incremental speaker adaptation.

More generally, incremental adaptation deals with a challenging scenario in which the recognition system is dynamically and incrementally adapted to new acoustic conditions due to inter- and intra-speaker variations and changes in environmental conditions (Leggetter, 1995; Huo and Lee, 1996).

An open problem with incremental adaptation concerns how to deal with abrupt changes in acoustic conditions. When an abrupt change in acoustic conditions happens (e.g. changes in speaker or environmental acoustic condition) accumulated past data or statistics do not reflect the new acoustic conditions and this may result in very poor performance for the current system user. To deal with this problem, restoring of the initial system condition was proposed (Leggetter, 1995; Huo and Lee, 1996).

In most cases, incremental adaptation is unsupervised because it uses the response of the recognizer to determine the text uttered, with the risk that recognition errors have a negative effect on adaptation. In some applications (e.g. automatic dictation) the user can correct the recognized text before adaptation makes use of the data; in this case adaptation is supervised.

With incremental adaptation it is important that the computational cost and memory requirements of the adaptation algorithm are low as adaptation is interleaved with recognition.

In *self-adaptation* (Zavaliagkos, 1995; Zhao, 1996), unsupervised adaptation is carried out exploiting the test data. In applications such as automatic dictation, the user can record on tape the reports which are then transcribed *off-line* by the recognition system. In this case, test data for the same speaker and environment are available in a block. So, unsupervised batch adaptation can be accomplished exploiting the available test data. Utterance transcriptions for test data are available for adaptation through a preliminary recognition stage using the available set of models. An iterative batch adaptation procedure can then be obtained interleaving recognition (producing data transcriptions) and adaptation (updating the models) until convergence is achieved. A final recognition step, producing the answer, is performed after the adaptation procedure is completed (Woodland *et al.*, 1996; Homma *et al.*, 1996).

Self-adaptation can be formulated on an utterance-by-utterance basis, resulting in an on-line adaptation scheme. In this case it is called instantaneous speaker adaptation (Zavaliagkos *et al.*, 1995a; Matsui and Furui, 1996). Instantaneous adaptation is invisible to the user and is suitable when the interaction with the user is too short to perform effective incremental adaptation.

Figure 11.3 shows a block diagram for instantaneous speaker adaptation. This approach has also been proposed for channel compensation (Sankar and

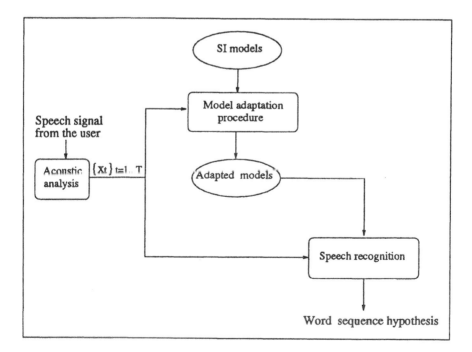

Figure 11.3 Block diagram for instantaneous adaptation.

Lee, 1995). However, instantaneous adaptation makes use of very few data so it is able to compensate only for broad acoustic differences between training and testing conditions.

11.3. ACOUSTIC-MODEL ADAPTATION

HMMs represent a widely adopted solution for acoustic modelling in modern recognition systems. In spite of recent advances in acoustic modelling, for speakers having voices with spectral characteristics quite different from those of the population used to train the HMMs, performance can be unsatisfactory (Digalakis *et al.*, 1995; Leggetter and Woodland, 1995a). In this section some approaches concerning HMM adaptation are reviewed.

Following the conventions and the notation introduced in Chapter 5, the parameter vector ϑ characterizing an HMM with a set $\mathcal{I}$ of S (N in Chapter 5) states is first defined. A model is characterized by an initial state probability vector $\pi^* = [\pi_1, \pi_2, \ldots, \pi_S]$, a transition probability matrix $A = [a_{ij}]$, with $i, j \in \mathcal{I}$ and a_{ij} denoting the transition probability from state i to state j, and the set B of parameters characterizing emission probability distributions. Here, it is assumed that vectors are column vectors (if not otherwise specified) and * denotes transposition.

Consider first a continuous-density HMM having each output distribution modelled with a mixture of multivariate Gaussian densities. The Gaussian mixture associated with the transition from state i to state j is specified as follows:

$$b_{ij}(x) = \sum_{k \in \mathcal{K}} w_{ijk} b_{ijk}(x) \tag{11.1}$$

where $b_{ijk}(x) = \mathcal{N}(x; \mu_{ijk}, \Sigma_{ijk})$ is the kth Gaussian density in the mixture characterized by the D-dimensional mean vector μ_{ijk} and the $D \times D$ covariance matrix Σ_{ijk}, and $\mathcal{K}$ is the set of mixture component indices. Non-negative mixture weights $w_{ij1}, \ldots, w_{ijK}$ satisfy the constraint $\sum_{k \in \mathcal{K}} w_{ijk} = 1$. For the sake of simplicity, it is assumed that each mixture in the HMM has the same number K of components. A CDHMM is then characterized by a parameter vector $\vartheta = [\pi, A, B]$, where $B = [B_{ij}]$, with $i, j \in \mathcal{I}$ and B_{ij} denoting parameters of the mixture associated to the model transition from state i to state j and characterized by the mixture weight vector $w_{ij}^* = [w_{ij1}, \ldots, w_{ijK}]$ and Gaussian component parameters $\{\mu_{ijk}, \Sigma_{ijk}\}_{k \in \mathcal{K}}$.

For a discrete HMM, π and A are defined as above, while $B_{ij} = [b_{ij}(1), b_{ij}(2), \ldots, b_{ij}(O)]$, with $b_{ij}(x)$ the discrete probability density associated to the model transition from state i to state j for which the following constraints hold:

$$b_{ij}(x) \geq 0, \quad 1 \leq x \leq O$$

$$\sum_{x=1}^{O} b_{ij}(x) = 1$$

where O is the number of discrete events (codebook size) on which the distribution is defined.

11.3.1. Parameter Transformation Approaches for CDHMM Adaptation

For continuous density HMMs with Gaussian mixtures, adaptation of probability distributions has been recently investigated by using a set of transformations applied to the Gaussian means alone, or to both means and covariances. The underlying idea is that the emission probability distributions for a new speaker can be obtained from those of the current available models by parameter transformation. Adaptation through Gaussian mean transformation can be interpreted as a relocation of the acoustic classes, from the original acoustic space, into the acoustic space of the new speaker.

First attempts to adapt SI models to a new speaker through Gaussian mean transformation were carried out by means of a global mean shift or an affine transformation (Cox and Bridle, 1990). The use of phone-dependent mean shift transformations, estimated in the Baum–Welch framework, was also investigated (Kenny *et al.*, 1990). Recently, more powerful ML transformation based approaches have been formulated for adapting Gaussian component of CDHMMs.

Leggetter and Woodland (1994b) proposed the use of a set of linear-regression-based transformations to modify Gaussian means and to obtain adapted models for a new speaker. In this case, a Gaussian mixture, associated to a transition from state i to state j, takes the form:

$$b_{ij}(x) = \sum_{k \in \mathcal{K}} w_{ijk} \mathcal{N}(x; U_{ijk}\mu_{ijk} + h_{ijk}, \Sigma_{ijk}) \tag{11.2}$$

where U_{ijk} is a $D \times D$ regression matrix, while h_{ijk} is a D-dimensional additive bias column vector. This approach is based on the assumption that the Gaussian means characterize the main acoustic differences between a new speaker and the available models. This assumption was recently confirmed by experimental evidence (Neumeyer *et al.*, 1995; Gales *et al.*, 1996). ML estimation of the transformation parameters has been proposed, in which the likelihood of the adaptation data, given the current set of models, has to be maximized with respect to U_{ijk} and h_{ijk}. When matrix U_{ijk} is forced to be the identity matrix a *mean shift* transformation is obtained.

Having a specific transformation for each Gaussian component of a mixture leads to a standard ML re-estimate of the Gaussian means with the problem that no adaptation occurs for Gaussian densities for which no adaptation data are observed. However, in general, the same transformation can be used for several distributions since Gaussian components representing similar acoustic phenomena should adapt similarly. For this purpose, Gaussian components can be grouped, according to their membership in a given mixture or phonetic class or by means of a clustering algorithm, obtaining *classes* of Gaussian components. Each class is formed by Gaussian components sharing a common transformation which is estimated using adaptation data available for each of the Gaussian components in the class. All members of a given class are then adapted by using the estimated transformation of the class which they belong to.

Digalakis *et al.* (1995) proposed a quite similar approach assuming a common transformation for all the Gaussian components of a mixture so that they are constrained to be jointly adapted. Furthermore, the transformation is applied to both the mean vector and the covariance matrix of each Gaussian component as follows:

$$b_{ij}(x) = \sum_{k \in \mathcal{K}} w_{ijk} \mathcal{N}(x; U_{ij}\mu_{ijk} + h_{ij}, U_{ij}\Sigma_{ijk}U_{ij}^*) \qquad (11.3)$$

In this approach, estimation of the transformation parameters is derived in the Baum–Welch framework, assuming diagonal covariance matrices and considering only diagonal transformation matrices (Digalakis *et al.*, 1995). To deal with sparse adaptation data, sharing of a given transformation among the mixture components of a group of mixtures was also investigated.

Other transformation-based approaches have been proposed for Gaussian component adaptation. A nonlinear transformation of Gaussian means was recently investigated by using multilayer perceptrons (Abrash *et al.*, 1996). A stochastic additive transformation approach was proposed for robust speech recognition and speaker adaptation (Sankar and Lee, 1994; Neumeyer *et al.*, 1995). Adaptation through linear transformation of the Gaussian means was recently formulated in the MAP framework (Zavaliagkos, 1995; Zavaliagkos *et al.*, 1995b).

The definition of the classes of Gaussian components plays an important role in the adaptation procedure and was investigated by different authors (Leggetter and Woodland, 1995a; Digalakis *et al.*, 1995; Zavaliagkos *et al.*, 1995b). This point will be discussed later after reviewing the maximum likelihood linear regression (MLLR) approach proposed by Leggetter and Woodland (Leggetter and Woodland, 1994b, 1995b).

Maximum likelihood linear regression

Let us consider the *k*th component of the Gaussian mixture $b_{ij}(x)$, specified by:

$$b_{ijk}(\boldsymbol{x}) = \frac{1}{\sqrt{(2\pi)^D \det(\boldsymbol{\Sigma}_{ijk})}} \exp\{-\tfrac{1}{2}(\boldsymbol{x} - \boldsymbol{\mu}_{ijk})^* \boldsymbol{\Sigma}_{ijk}^{-1}(\boldsymbol{x} - \boldsymbol{\mu}_{ijk})\} \qquad (11.4)$$

In the MLLR approach, Gaussian means of a pretrained HMM are adapted by using a set of affine transformations so that $b_{ijk}(\boldsymbol{x})$ takes the form:

$$b_{ijk}(\boldsymbol{x}) = \frac{1}{\sqrt{(2\pi)^D \det(\boldsymbol{\Sigma}_{ijk})}} \exp\{-\tfrac{1}{2}(\boldsymbol{x} - \boldsymbol{H}_{ijk}\boldsymbol{\eta}_{ijk})^* \boldsymbol{\Sigma}_{ijk}^{-1}(\boldsymbol{x} - \boldsymbol{H}_{ijk}\boldsymbol{\eta}_{ijk})\} \quad (11.5)$$

where $\boldsymbol{H}_{ijk}$ is a $D \times (D+1)$ transformation matrix, to be estimated, and $\boldsymbol{\eta}_{ijk}$ is the extended mean vector $\boldsymbol{\eta}_{ijk}^* = [1, \mu_{ijk1}, \mu_{ijk2}, \dots, \mu_{ijkD}]$. Mean vector extension allows the inclusion of an offset term directly in the transformation matrix $\boldsymbol{H}_{ijk}$. Once an estimate of $\boldsymbol{H}_{ijk}$ is obtained, let us say $\boldsymbol{H}_{ijk}'$, the adapted Gaussian mean $\boldsymbol{\mu}_{ijk}'$ is obtained as follows:

$$\boldsymbol{\mu}_{ijk}' = \boldsymbol{H}_{ijk}'\boldsymbol{\eta}_{ijk} \qquad (11.6)$$

To ensure computationally feasible closed-form solution even for a transformation matrix shared among a class of Gaussian components, all Gaussian densities are assumed to have a diagonal covariance matrix (Leggetter and Woodland, 1995b). Given an amount of adaptation data, Gaussian means are updated to maximize the likelihood of the adaptation data. Let us consider, for simplicity, the case of a single adaptation utterance.

Let $\boldsymbol{x}_1^T$ be an adaptation utterance formed by T D-dimensional observation vectors. Re-estimation of the current set of model parameters is accomplished through maximization of the objective function $\Pr(\boldsymbol{x}_1^T | \vartheta)$, which is the likelihood of the observation sequences $\boldsymbol{x}_1^T$ given the current set of model parameters ϑ and is specified as follows:

$$\Pr(\boldsymbol{x}_1^T | \vartheta) = \sum_{i_0^T \in \mathcal{I}^{T+1}, k_1^T \in \mathcal{K}^T} p(i_0^T, k_1^T, \vartheta) \qquad (11.7)$$

where $\mathcal{I}^{T+1}$ denotes all the possible state sequences of length $T+1$, $\mathcal{K}^T$ is the set of all the possible sequences of mixture component indices having length T and $p(i_0^T, k_1^T, \vartheta)$ is defined as follows:

$$p(i_0^T, k_1^T, \vartheta) \triangleq \pi_{i_0} \prod_{t=1}^{T} a_{i_{t-1}i_t} w_{i_{t-1}i_tk_t} b_{i_{t-1}i_tk_t}(\boldsymbol{x}_t) \qquad (11.8)$$

As discussed in Chapter 6, for ML parameter estimation it is convenient to specify an auxiliary function $Q(\vartheta, \vartheta')$ as follows:

$$Q(\vartheta, \vartheta') = \frac{1}{\Pr(\boldsymbol{x}_1^T | \vartheta)} \sum_{i_0^T \in \mathcal{I}^{T+1}, k_1^T \in \mathcal{K}^T} p(i_0^T, k_1^T, \vartheta) \log p(i_0^T, k_1^T, \vartheta') \qquad (11.9)$$

ML model parameter estimation is then carried out through iterative maximization of $Q(\vartheta, \vartheta')$. For this purpose, the auxiliary function $Q(\vartheta, \vartheta')$ is rewritten as:

$$Q(\vartheta, \vartheta') = \frac{1}{\Pr(x_1^T | \vartheta)} \sum_{i_0^T \in \mathcal{I}^{T+1}, k_1^T \in \mathcal{K}^T} p(i_0^T, k_1^T, \vartheta)$$

$$\times \left(\log \pi'_{i_0} + \sum_{t=1}^{T} \log a'_{i_{t-1}i_t} + \sum_{t=1}^{T} \log w'_{i_{t-1}i_tk_t} + \sum_{t-1}^{T} \log b'_{i_{t-1}i_tk_t}(x_t) \right)$$

$$(11.10)$$

The auxiliary function is therefore separated into different terms, each depending on a different component of the parameter set ϑ. For the estimation of the parameters of a specific transformation matrix, H_{ijk}, the auxiliary function can be conveniently rewritten as:

$$Q(\vartheta, \vartheta') = c - \frac{1}{2} \sum_{t=1}^{T} \gamma_t(i, j, k)\{(x_t - H'_{ijk}\eta_{ijk})^* \Sigma_{ijk}^{-1}(x_t - H'_{ijk}\eta_{ijk})\} \quad (11.11)$$

where c absorbs all the terms that do not depend on H'_{ijk} and $\gamma_t(i, j, k)$ is defined as follows:

$$\gamma_t(i, j, k) \triangleq \frac{w_{ijk}b_{ijk}(x_t)}{b_{ij}(x_t)} \gamma_t(i, j) \quad (11.12)$$

with

$$\gamma_t(i, j) \triangleq \frac{1}{\Pr(x_1^T | \vartheta)} \sum_{i_0^T \in \mathcal{I}^{T+1}} p(i_0^T, \vartheta)\delta(i_{t-1}, i)\delta(i_t, j) \quad (11.13)$$

and

$$p(i_0^T, \vartheta) \triangleq \pi_{i_0} \prod_{t=1}^{T} a_{i_{t-1}i_t} b_{i_{t-1}i_t}(x_t) \quad (11.14)$$

Efficient computation of the quantities $\gamma_t(i, j)$, in terms of forward and backward probabilities, can be found in Chapter 6.

Differentiating the auxiliary function with respect to matrix H'_{ijk}, and equating to zero the derivative in order to find the maximum, leads to:

$$\frac{\partial Q(\vartheta, \vartheta')}{\partial H'_{ijk}} = \sum_{t=1}^{T} \gamma_t(i, j, k) \Sigma_{ijk}^{-1}(x_t - H'_{ijk}\eta_{ijk})\eta_{ijk}^* = 0 \quad (11.15)$$

The solution of equation (11.15) gives the desired re-estimate for the matrix H_{ijk}. However, in order to compensate for sparse adaptation data, a given transformation matrix is, in general, shared among a class of Gaussian components. This ensures a more robust estimation of the transformation parameters and allows adaptation for Gaussian components for which no data have been observed in the adaptation set. Let us assume that Gaussian components in the models are partitioned into L classes. Then, denoting with C_l the set of Gaussian components forming the lth regression class with $1 \leq l \leq L$, the transformation matrix $H^{(l)}$, can be estimated considering contributions from all the Gaussian components in the class. For the transformation matrix $H'^{(l)}$ equation (11.15) can be rewritten as follows:

$$\frac{\partial \mathcal{Q}(\vartheta, \vartheta')}{\partial H'^{(l)}} = \sum_{t=1}^{T} \sum_{b_{ijk} \in C_l} \gamma_t(i,j,k) \Sigma_{ijk}^{-1} (x_t - H'^{(l)} \eta_{ijk}) \eta_{ijk}^* = 0 \qquad (11.16)$$

and

$$\sum_{t=1}^{T} \sum_{b_{ijk} \in C_l} \gamma_t(i,j,k) \Sigma_{ijk}^{-1} x_t \eta_{ijk}^* = \sum_{t=1}^{T} \sum_{b_{ijk} \in C_l} \gamma_t(i,j,k) \Sigma_{ijk}^{-1} H'^{(l)} \eta_{ijk} \eta_{ijk}^* \qquad (11.17)$$

which can be conveniently rewritten, isolating terms depending on time, as (Leggetter and Woodland, 1995a):

$$\sum_{b_{ijk} \in C_l} \Sigma_{ijk}^{-1} \left(\sum_{t=1}^{T} \gamma_t(i,j,k) x_t \right) \eta_{ijk}^* = \sum_{b_{ijk} \in C_l} \left(\sum_{t=1}^{T} \gamma_t(i,j,k) \right) \Sigma_{ijk}^{-1} H'^{(l)} \eta_{ijk} \eta_{ijk}^* \qquad (11.18)$$

Solving equation (11.18) leads to the desired re-estimate for matrix $H^{(l)}$. Let Z be the $D \times (D+1)$ matrix denoting the left-hand side of equation (11.18), which is independent on the transformation matrix:

$$Z = \sum_{b_{ijk} \in C_l} \Sigma_{ijk}^{-1} \left(\sum_{t=1}^{T} \gamma_t(i,j,k) x_t \right) \eta_{ijk}^* \qquad (11.19)$$

Then equation (11.18) is rewritten as follows:

$$Z = \sum_{b_{ijk} \in C_l} V^{(ijk)} H'^{(l)} \eta_{ijk} \eta_{ijk}^* \qquad (11.20)$$

where $V^{(ijk)}$ is a $D \times (D+1)$ diagonal matrix defined as:

$$V^{(ijk)} = \left(\sum_{t=1}^{T} \gamma_t(i,j,k) \right) \Sigma_{ijk}^{-1} \qquad (11.21)$$

In order to derive the re-estimation formula for $H'^{(l)}$, exploiting the fact that all covariance matrices are diagonal, a $(D+1) \times (D+1)$ symmetric matrix $G^{(q)}$ is defined as follows (Leggetter and Woodland, 1995b):

$$G^{(q)} = \sum_{b_{ijk} \in C_l} v_{qq}^{(ijk)} \eta_{ijk} \eta_{ijk}^* \qquad (11.22)$$

where $v_{qq}^{(ijk)}$ denotes qth diagonal element of matrix $V^{(ijk)}$.

Then, the transformation matrix $H'^{(l)}$ can be computed, row by row, as follows (Leggetter and Woodland, 1995b):

$$H_q'^{(l)} = Z_q G^{(q)-1} \qquad (11.23)$$

where Z_q and $H_q^{\prime(l)}$ denote the qth row vector of matrices Z and $H^{\prime(l)}$, respectively.

If only a few examples are available for the estimation of the transformation matrix of a given regression class, $G^{(q)}$ is likely to be a singular matrix. The use of a robust method for matrix inversion is thus recommended (Leggetter, 1995).

More iterations can be carried out in order to maximize the likelihood of the adaptation data. At each iteration, transformation matrices are initialized to identity transformations. Once transformation parameters are estimated, then Gaussian means are updated. If good initial models are available, convergence is achieved after very few iterations (Leggetter, 1995).

In a more realistic case, when multiple independent observation sequences are available, statistics are accumulated over all the observation sequences before performing estimation of the transformation matrices (Leggetter, 1995).

More recently, MLLR adaptation of the variances was proposed (Gales *et al.*, 1996). Basically, two distinct transformations are specified for the mean vector and covariance matrix of a Gaussian component. Means and variances are adapted in two separate steps. First, means are updated, as shown above, and then, given the new means, variances are adapted. In case, these two steps are repeated. Estimation of variance transformation parameters was also derived in the ML framework.

Batch and incremental MLLR adaptation

Both batch and incremental adaptation can be performed in the MLLR framework (Leggetter and Woodland, 1995a,b). An incremental adaptation scheme is obtained if transformation matrices are estimated and the model updated after each observation sequence (or set of observation sequences), while the required statistics are accumulated over time (see equation (11.18)), producing more and more accurate transformation matrix estimates. This can be done under the assumption that the alignment of each observation sequence against the corresponding models does not change too much as a consequence of model updates, so that the required statistics can be accumulated over time and used in future model updates.

Dynamic definition of regression classes

A sufficient amount of adaptation data is required for each regression class in order to ensure a robust estimate of the associated transformation matrix. Given a set of regression classes and an amount of adaptation data, it is possible that, for some classes, sufficient statistics are not available. For these classes, the corresponding transformation may be simply forced to be equal to the identity or to a global transformation associated to a class containing all the Gaussian mixture components in the system.

In order to deal with the trade-off between specificity and robust estimate, dynamic definition of regression classes has been proposed (Leggetter, 1995; Leggetter and Woodland, 1995a). In this approach, regression classes are organized in a tree, in which the leaves are associated to *base classes*, each formed, in principle, by a single Gaussian component. The tree root represents a single global class. Starting from base classes and using an agglomerative clustering procedure (Leggetter, 1995), regression classes, associated to internal nodes of the tree, are defined. Given the adaptation data, the required statistics are accumulated for each Gaussian component and then for each regression class using the statistics accumulated for the Gaussian component members of the class. Then, starting from the root, the class tree is inspected and a new regression class is defined at the lowest level for which sufficient statistics (according to a predefined empirical threshold) are accumulated. In this way, the definition of regression class is not fixed but depends on the available adaptation data. This approach is particularly suitable for incremental adaptation (where statistics are accumulated over time), allowing the definition of an increasing number of regression classes.

Parameter transformation issues

Adaptation through transformation of Gaussian component parameters has been widely investigated by using the *WSJ* NAB database (see Appendix D). The effectiveness of the unsupervised incremental MLLR adaptation of Gaussian means is motivated in Leggetter and Woodland (1995a). Batch MLLR adaptation of both means and variances is discussed in Gales *et al.* (1996). A comparison among different transformation-based approaches for batch adaptation is reported in Neumeyer *et al.* (1995).

The definition of Gaussian component classes is important for both batch and incremental adaptation (Leggetter and Woodland, 1995a; Neumeyer *et al.*, 1995; Gales *et al.*, 1996).

A transformation matrix can be full, diagonal (elements not in the main diagonal are forced to zero) or block diagonal (Leggetter and Woodland, 1995b; Neumeyer *et al.*, 1995; Gales *et al.*, 1996). The use of a block diagonal transformation matrix relies on the fact that the acoustic description accepted by a recognizer is in general formed by three distinct sets of features, namely a set of spectral features, their first-order time derivatives, and their second-order time derivatives. A separate transformation can be considered for each set of features, resulting in a block diagonal transformation matrix in which parameter correlation is considered only within the same set of features. The choice of the transformation matrix structure to be adopted is, in general, a trade-off between the number of parameters to be estimated and the amount of adaptation data.

11.3.2. Maximum *a posteriori* Estimation of HMM Parameters

MAP estimation has been proposed in speech recognition for model parameter estimation when training data are sparse (Gauvain and Lee, 1991, 1992, 1994).

MAP re-estimation of HMM parameters has been successfully applied for adjusting the parameters of a pretrained set of models exploiting the speaker-specific adaptation data and the available prior knowledge. This knowledge is represented by both the initial models and the information about the variability of HMM parameters among different speakers for which suitable prior distributions are assumed.

Model adaptation through MAP estimation was first introduced by Brown *et al.* (1983) for adapting output distributions of CDHMMs. Bayesian learning, described in Duda and Hart (1973), was proposed for adapting the prototype vectors of a codebook, to build a speaker-specific codebook for a discrete HMM-based recognition system (Ferretti and Scarci, 1989). A mathematical framework for estimating the means and the variances of CDHMMs was proposed by Lee *et al.* (1991). This work was then extended to MAP adaptation of HMM parameters in case of emission probability distributions modelled with mixtures of Gaussian densities (Gauvain and Lee, 1991, 1992, 1994). MAP adaptation has also been formulated for discrete and semicontinuous HMMs (Huo *et al.*, 1993, 1994, 1995). More recently, the MAP adaptation approach was extended in order to compensate the lack of adaptation data when adapting systems with a very large number of parameters (Zavaliagkos *et al.*, 1995b; Zavaliagkos, 1995).

Consider an HMM characterized by a parameter vector ϑ. MAP parameter estimation assumes that ϑ is a random vector and that a prior knowledge about ϑ is available. The prior knowledge is summarized by a prior *probability density function* (PDF) $g(\vartheta)$, whose parameters, also called *hyperparameters*, have to be assigned by the experimenter. This means that, before any data has been observed, it is known that ϑ is more likely to lie in certain regions of the parameter space than in others.

Assuming an "adaptation" utterance x_1^T, the MAP estimate of parameter vector ϑ is formulated as follows:

$$\tilde{\vartheta} = \operatorname*{argmax}_{\vartheta} \Pr(\vartheta|x_1^T) = \operatorname*{argmax}_{\vartheta} \Pr(x_1^T|\vartheta)g(\vartheta) \qquad (11.24)$$

where $\Pr(x_1^T|\vartheta)$ is the likelihood function.

When an uninformative prior distribution is assumed, i.e. $g(\vartheta)$ is uniform over the parameter space, then MAP estimation reduces to ML estimation.

In Chapter 6, the mathematical framework for MAP parameter estimation of HMM parameters has been presented and estimation formulae for the parameters of different types of HMMs have been derived. Three important issues are strictly connected with the MAP estimate formulation: the choice of the prior distribution family for the different type of model parameters, the

MAP evaluation and the estimation of the prior density parameters. In the following, these three aspects are considered for CDHMMs with Gaussian mixture components having diagonal covariance matrices.

Choice of the prior distribution families

In MAP estimation, it is important that the evaluation of the posterior density $\Pr(\vartheta \mid x_1^T)$ in equation (11.24) is computationally attractive. For this purpose, an important simplification is achieved if it is assumed that observations are drawn from a family of distributions for which there is a sufficient statistic of fixed dimension (Duda and Hart, 1973). In this case, the posterior PDF can be expressed in terms of a fixed number of parameters regardless of the size of the sample. Furthermore, under this assumption, it is always possible to select a prior distribution for the unknown parameter vector ϑ so that the posterior distribution is a member of the same family of distributions of the prior distribution regardless of the sample size and the values of the observations in the sample (DeGroot, 1970; Duda and Hart, 1973). Such a prior distribution is defined as a *conjugate* prior distribution for the parameter vector ϑ of the likelihood function.

For speaker adaptation, observations are drawn from a probabilistic function of a Markov chain, so no sufficient statistic of fixed dimension exists. However, a suitable choice of prior distributions has been suggested for the different components of the model parameter vector ϑ (Gauvain and Lee, 1994; Huo *et al.*, 1995). This choice exploits the fact that a sufficient statistic fixed dimension exists for model parameters if the *complete data* in the expectation step of the Baum–Welch estimation procedure (see Chapter 6) are considered. Thus, prior densities are chosen from a conjugate family for the complete-data density.

The Dirichlet density (see Chapter 6 for its definition) is a suitable candidate to represent prior knowledge about the parameter vector of a multinomial density (DeGroot, 1970). For the initial state probability vector π and the transition probability vectors $\{A_i\}_{i \in \mathcal{I}}$, the Dirichlet prior densities $g_\pi(\pi)$ and $g_{A_i}(A_i)$ satisfy the relations:

$$g_\pi(\pi) \propto \prod_{i \in \mathcal{I}} \pi_i^{\varepsilon_i - 1} \tag{1.25}$$

and

$$g_{A_i}(A_i) \propto \prod_{j \in \mathcal{I}} a_{ij}^{\xi_{ij} - 1} \tag{11.26}$$

where $\propto$ denotes proportionality, and ε and ξ_i are two vectors of positive hyperparameters characterizing the prior densities $g_\pi(\pi)$ and $g_{A_i}(A_i)$, respectively.

For CDHMMs, the main distribution is a Gaussian mixture. For the parameters of a Gaussian mixture no joint conjugate prior density can be specified (Gauvain and Lee, 1994). Assuming independence between mixture weights and the parameters of the individual mixture components, and also between the parameters of different mixture components, the prior density for the parameters of a mixture $b_{ij}(x)$ can be decomposed as follows (Gauvain and Lee, 1991, 1994):

$$g_{b_{ij}}(w_{ij}, \mu_{ij1}, \Sigma_{ij1}^{-1}, \ldots, \mu_{ijk}, \Sigma_{ijk}^{-1}) = g_{w_{ij}}(w_{ij}) \prod_{k \in \mathcal{K}} g_{b_{ijk}}(\mu_{ijk}, \Sigma_{ijk}^{-1}) \qquad (11.27)$$

where $g_{w_{ij}}(w_{ij})$ is a Dirichlet prior density for the multinomial density in the complete-data likelihood having parameter vector w_{ij} and $g_{b_{ijk}}(\mu_{ijk}, \Sigma_{ijk}^{-1})$ denotes the prior density for parameters of the kth Gaussian component in the mixture. The Dirichlet prior density $g_{w_{ij}}(w_{ij})$ is characterized by a vector ν_{ij} of positive hyperparameters such that:

$$g_{w_{ij}}(w_{ij}) \propto \prod_{k \in \mathcal{K}} w_{ijk}^{\nu_{ijk} - 1} \qquad (11.28)$$

Furthermore, exploiting the fact that each Gaussian mixture component has diagonal covariance matrix and therefore can be expressed as product of univariate Gaussians, for each mixture component one gets:

$$g_{b_{ijk}}(\mu_{ijk}, \Sigma_{ijk}^{-1}) \propto \prod_{d=1}^{D} g_{b_{ijkd}}(\mu_{ijkd}, r_{ijkd}) \qquad (11.29)$$

where $g_{b_{ijkd}}(\mu_{ijkd}, r_{ijkd})$ denotes the normal-gamma prior density for the mean μ_{ijkd} and the precision r_{ijkd} of the univariate Gaussian density $b_{ijkd}(x_d)$. The precision is defined as the reciprocal of the variance, therefore $r_{ijkd} = 1/\sigma_{ijkd}^2$, where σ_{ijkd}^2 is dth diagonal element of the covariance matrix Σ_{ijk}. In fact, a joint conjugate prior distribution for the mean μ and the precision r of a univariate normal distribution is the normal-gamma distribution (DeGroot, 1970). The conditional distribution of the mean, given the precision, is a normal distribution with mean m and precision τr with $\tau > 0$ and the marginal distribution of the precision is a gamma distribution with parameters $\alpha > 0$, and $\beta > 0$ (DeGroot, 1970) such that:

$$g(\mu, r) \propto (\tau r)^{\frac{1}{2}} e^{-\frac{\tau r}{2}(\mu - m)^2} r^{\alpha - 1} e^{-\beta r} \qquad (11.30)$$

A global prior density for model parameter vector ϑ can then be specified, assuming independence among different model parameter sets, as follows:

$$g(\vartheta) = g_{\pi}(\pi) \left(\prod_{i \in \mathcal{I}} g_{A_i}(A_i) \right) \prod_{i,j \in \mathcal{I}} \left(g_{w_{ij}}(w_{ij}) \prod_{k \in \mathcal{K}} g_{b_{ijk}}(\mu_{ijk}, \Sigma_{ijk}^{-1}) \right) \qquad (11.31)$$

Quite often, some parameters of the models are assumed to be fixed and known. This corresponds to having a deterministic knowledge about them and no prior distributions need to be specified for these parameters, thus reducing the number of prior parameters to estimate. In the following, initial state probabilities are assumed to be fixed and known.

MAP evaluation

For MAP estimation of HMM parameters, two algorithms have been proposed, namely the *Baum–Welch MAP* algorithm and the *segmental MAP* algorithm (Gauvain and Lee, 1994; Huo *et al.*, 1995). The latter can be seen as the counterpart of the *segmental k-means* training algorithm for ML parameter estimation (Lee *et al.*, 1991).

In the Baum–Welch MAP algorithm, given a training utterance x_1^T and an initial estimate of model parameters, a modified auxiliary function is introduced as follows:

$$Q_{MAP}(\vartheta, \vartheta') = Q(\vartheta, \vartheta') + \log g(\vartheta') \tag{11.32}$$

where $Q(\vartheta, \vartheta')$ denotes the auxiliary function for the Baum–Welch algorithm which, for the problem at hand, is defined by equation (11.10). As shown in Chapter 6, MAP parameter estimation can be carried out through iterative maximization of the auxiliary function $Q_{MAP}(\vartheta, \vartheta')$, by using the following re-estimation formulae:

$$d'_{ij} = \frac{\xi_{ij} - 1 + \gamma(i, j)}{\sum_{l \in \mathcal{I}} (\xi_{il} + \gamma(i, l)) - S} \tag{11.33}$$

$$w'_{ijk} = \frac{\nu_{ijk} - 1 + \gamma(i, j, k)}{\sum_{l \in \mathcal{K}} (\nu_{ijl} + \gamma(i, j, l)) - K} \tag{11.34}$$

$$\mu'_{ijkd} = \frac{\tau_{ijkd} m_{ijkd} + \gamma(i, j, k) \bar{x}_{ijkd}}{\tau_{ijkd} + \gamma(i, j, k)} \tag{11.35}$$

$$\sigma'^2_{ijkd} = \frac{2\beta_{ijkd} + \tau_{ijkd}(\mu'_{ijkd} - m_{ijkd})^2 + \sum_{t=1}^T \gamma_t(i, j, k)(x_{td} - \mu'_{ijkd})^2}{2\alpha_{ijkd} - 1 + \gamma(i, j, k)} \tag{11.36}$$

where:

$$\bar{x}_{ijkd} = \frac{1}{\gamma(i, j, k)} \sum_{t=1}^T \gamma_t(i, j, k) x_{td} \tag{11.37}$$

and

$$\gamma(i, j, k) \triangleq \sum_{t=1}^T \gamma_t(i, j, k) \tag{11.38}$$

$$\gamma(i, j) \triangleq \sum_{t=1}^T \gamma_t(i, j) \tag{11.39}$$

In analogy with ML parameter estimation, these results can be easily extended to the case in which more adaptation utterances are available (see Chapter 6).

The re-estimation formula for the mean, equation (11.35), is a weighted sum of the prior mean with the ML mean estimate. τ_{ijkd} is a balancing factor between prior knowledge and the adaptation data. When τ_{ijkd} is large, the variance of the prior distribution is small and the value of the mean μ_{ijkd} is assumed to be known with high certainty making the contribution of the prior bigger. When the amount of adaptation data is large, the MAP estimate approaches the ML estimate.

It can be shown that the posterior density of the parameters given the complete data has the same form of the prior global density $g(\vartheta)$, that is the product of Dirichlet, normal and gamma densities, with the following parameters (Gauvain and Lee, 1994; Zavaliagkos, 1995):

$$\hat{\xi}_{ij} = \xi_{ij} + \gamma(i, j) \tag{11.40}$$

$$\hat{\nu}_{ijk} = \nu_{ijk} + \gamma(i, j, k) \tag{11.41}$$

$$\hat{m}_{ijkd} = \frac{\tau_{ijkd} m_{ijkd} + \gamma(i, j, k)\bar{x}_{ijkd}}{\tau_{ijkd} + \gamma(i, j, k)} \tag{11.42}$$

$$\hat{\tau}_{ijkd} = \tau_{ijkd} + \gamma(i, j, k) \tag{11.43}$$

$$\hat{\alpha}_{ijkd} = \alpha_{ijkd} + \tfrac{1}{2}\gamma(i, j, k) \tag{11.44}$$

$$\hat{\beta}_{ijkd} = \beta_{ijkd} + \frac{1}{2}\sum_{t=1}^{T}\gamma_t(i, j, k)(x_{td} - \bar{x}_{ijkd})^2$$

$$+ \frac{\tau_{ijkd}\gamma(i, j, k)}{2(\tau_{ijkd} + \gamma(i, j, k))}(\bar{x}_{ijkd} - m_{ijkd})^2 \tag{11.45}$$

This justifies the choice of the prior density families for the different sets of model parameters. Furthermore, it is easy to show that the model parameter re-estimation formulae (11.33)–(11.36) can be obtained by considering the modes of the Dirichlet, normal and gamma posterior densities having hyper-parameters as specified in equations (11.40)–(11.45).

Parameter estimation for prior densities

In MAP estimation of HMM parameters, the parameter vector ϑ is assumed to be random. The parameter values of a set of models, trained with an SI set of data, is an example of estimate of ϑ. If more examples are available for ϑ, then they can be used for prior parameter estimation. For example, the SI training material can be partitioned on a speaker-by-speaker basis, and, for each SD subset of data, a set of models can be trained (Zavaliagkos, 1995). More generally, when not enough speaker-specific training data are available, training speakers can be grouped into clusters of speakers and a set of models can be trained for each cluster (Gauvain and Lee, 1994). Assuming that Q

sets of models were trained, then a set of parameter vectors, $\{\breve{\vartheta}_q\}_{q=1}^{Q}$, is obtained. The $\{\breve{\vartheta}_q\}_{q=1}^{Q}$ can be seen as a set of observation vectors drawn from a distribution having PDF $g(\vartheta)$. Finding ML estimates of the prior parameters is a difficult problem (Gauvain and Lee, 1994). Therefore, prior parameters can be conveniently estimated with the moment method (Huo *et al.*, 1995; Zavaliagkos, 1995; Ahadi-Sarkani, 1996). Basically, sample moments are first estimated for each parameter using the available samples $\{\breve{\vartheta}_q\}_{q=1}^{Q}$. These moments are then used to estimate the corresponding prior hyperparameters.

Simple *ad hoc* methods for prior parameter estimation have been also proposed (Gauvain and Lee, 1994; Huo *et al.*, 1995). For example, concerning with Gaussian mean estimation, prior parameter τ_{ijkd} can be empirically fixed to a constant value (typically a small integer such as 5 or 10) for all the Gaussian components and all the dimensions. The resulting adaptation scheme for the mean values, see equation (11.35), gives in practice good results.

Strictly related with prior parameter estimation is the initial estimate of parameters of the models used in the Baum–Welch MAP algorithm. Initial estimates of model parameters are important for minimizing the number of iterations in the Baum–Welch MAP algorithm and for finding good parameter estimates. The modes (and the means) of the prior distributions are suitable candidates as initial estimate of model parameters (Gauvain and Lee, 1994; Huo *et al.*, 1995). However, a practical approach uses a pretrained set of HMMs as initial models for the Baum–Welch MAP algorithm. These models are called *seed* or *initial* models. During prior parameter estimation with the moment method, constraints can be introduced so that the modes of the prior distributions become equal to the initial model parameters (Gauvain and Lee, 1994; Zavaliagkos, 1995). An adaptation scheme is therefore obtained in which a pretrained set of HMMs are adapted to a speaker using a small amount of speaker-specific data. In general, SI models are assumed as seed models.

Batch and incremental MAP adaptation

Batch and incremental adaptation have been formulated in the MAP parameter estimation framework (Gauvain and Lee, 1994; Zavaliagkos *et al.*, 1995a; Huo *et al.*, 1996; Huo and Lee, 1996).

For CDHMMs with Gaussian components having diagonal covariance matrices, batch model parameter adaptation can be performed using the above reported formulae.

In incremental adaptation, the models are dynamically and incrementally adapted while the user is using the system. As soon as a new utterance is obtained, MAP model parameter adaptation is performed using the current set of HMMs, the current set of prior densities and the current input utterance.

The current input utterance is used while the accumulated past knowledge about model parameters is represented by the prior distributions whose parameters are updated on an utterance-by-utterance basis. Adaptation is often unsupervised and the answer of the recognizer, using the current set of models, is used to supervise adaptation.

Incremental MAP adaptation of HMM parameters is an instance of recursive Bayesian inference (DeGroot, 1970). Due to the nature of the problem, however, approximations are introduced in order to overcome some computational difficulties (Zavaliagkos, 1995; Huo *et al.*, 1996; Huo and Lee, 1996). In case of CDHMMs with Gaussian components having diagonal covariance matrices, for each input utterance the above reported formulae could be, in principle, applied on an utterance-by-utterance basis for model parameters and prior parameters updating. However, in Zavaliagkos (1995) and Huo and Lee (1996), some simplifications and variations are introduced.

Robust MAP adaptation

In MAP parameter adaptation, parameters for which adaptation data are not observed are left unchanged. When the amount of adaptation data is very small and/or a recognition system has a large number of parameters (e.g. many thousands of Gaussian components), most of the parameters are left unchanged by the MAP adaptation algorithm, leading to a small performance improvement. A variety of techniques have been developed in order to overcome this problem and improve the adaptation speed.

Adaptation can be shared among the members of a class of Gaussian components, which are assumed to adapt similarly. Consider a Gaussian mixture $b_{ij}(\boldsymbol{x})$ having K components with a shared mean shift. For each Gaussian component the adapted Gaussian mean is obtained as follows:

$$\boldsymbol{\mu}'_{ijk} = \boldsymbol{\mu}_{ijk} + \boldsymbol{h}'_{ij}, \quad k = 1, 2, \ldots, K \tag{11.46}$$

where $\boldsymbol{h}'_{ij}$ is an estimated shift vector shared by all the mixture components. $\boldsymbol{h}'_{ij}$ is a sort of *average* mean shift that can be computed in the MAP framework (Zavaliagkos *et al.*, 1995b; Zavaliagkos, 1995). Similarly, precision scaling can be shared among the members of a class of Gaussian components (Zavaliagkos *et al.*, 1995b; Zavaliagkos, 1995).

A further step in this direction is represented by hierarchical class tying (Zavaliagkos *et al.*, 1995b; Zavaliagkos, 1995). In this case, Gaussian components are organized in a tree structure, in which each node represents a class of Gaussian components. The leaves of the tree are associated with classes formed by single Gaussian component, while non-terminal nodes are associated with classes of Gaussian components formed by merging classes in a lower level of the tree. Starting from the leaves, more general classes are formed moving toward the higher levels. A hierarchy of gradually broader classes is proposed such as classes formed by a single Gaussian component, Gaussian components of the same mixture, Gaussian components of mixtures modelling the same phoneme. Given an amount of adaptation data, MAP estimate is performed for each defined class of Gaussian components. For classes formed by a single Gaussian component, this results in the standard MAP estimation, while, for more general classes, a MAP formulation for estimating tied mean shift and variance scaling has been proposed (Zavaliagkos *et al.*, 1995b). Once MAP estimation has been carried out, starting from the upper level, shared mean shift and precision scaling are propagated from a parent node to its children nodes. Mean shift and precision scaling for a child node are obtained by interpolation of the obtained MAP estimates for the node itself and its parent node. A child node, associated to a class for which no data have been observed, simply inherits mean shift and variance scaling from its parent node. In this way, interpolation of the MAP estimates for a Gaussian component member of different classes, with varying degree of tying, is obtained.

Another interesting approach for accelerating adaptation speed is the extended MAP (EMAP) estimation (Zavaliagkos *et al.*, 1995b; Zavaliagkos, 1995). This approach considers *correlations* across various model parameters and has been formulated for re-estimation of Gaussian means of CDHMMs. In the MAP formulation, Gaussian means are assumed independent random vectors. In the EMAP estimation, given a set of Gaussian means, their full joint distribution is considered so that, thanks to the existing correlation among Gaussian mean parameters, adaptation data for a given Gaussian mean contribute to the adaptation of all the others. EMAP has also been extended to shared mean shift estimate and to hierarchical class tying (Zavaliagkos *et al.*, 1995b; Zavaliagkos, 1995).

Related techniques

A variety of approaches has been developed in which MAP adaptation is used in combination with other techniques as a preliminary or a refinement adaptation step.

ML-transformation-based adaptation techniques for CDHMMs provide faster adaptation with respect to the MAP adaptation approach which, in turn, has a better asymptotic behaviour. For this reason, it was proposed to use MAP adaptation in conjunction with ML-transformation-based adaptation (Digalakis and Neumeyer, 1995). In this case, a set of ML affine transformations are applied to Gaussian density parameters of a set of SI CDHMMs in order to obtain speaker-adapted models and an improved prior information for a MAP-based adaptation scheme (Digalakis and Neumeyer, 1995).

MAP adaptation has been used as a preliminary step for the vector field smoothing (VFS) method developed for fast speaker adaptation. VFS will be described in section 11.3.3. It was experimentally proven that the MAP/VFS method provides performance improvement over the pure MAP approach and accelerates the adaptation speed (Tonomura *et al.*, 1995; Takahashi and Sagayama, 1995a).

An approach, called regression-based model prediction, was proposed in which MAP adaptation of CDHMMs is a preliminary step (Ahadi and Woodland, 1995; Ahadi-Sarkani, 1996). After conventional MAP adaptation of Gaussian means, a pretrained set of linear regression relationships between Gaussian density mean parameters are used to predict suitable Gaussian mean values for poorly or not adapted Gaussian components. Experimental recognition results showed that, when few utterances were available for adaptation, the proposed approach significantly outperformed the pure MAP adaptation.

11.3.3. Vector Field Smoothing Method

The VFS method has been proposed for rapid speaker adaptation and channel-characteristic compensation (Ohkura *et al.*, 1992; Takahashi and Sagayama, 1994) when a very small amount of adaptation data (corresponding to few words) is available, and most of the models would remain untrained using a conventional intra-class Baum–Welch retraining. VFS can be viewed as an inter-class training for adapting models left untrained and a re-estimation error reduction procedure for trained models.

In VFS, intra-class training is first performed exploiting the available adaptation data by means of ML or MAP parameter estimation (Tonomura *et al.*, 1995; Takahashi and Sagayama, 1995a). With CDHMMs, due to the small amount of adaptation data, many Gaussian components are left unchanged and others are poorly re-estimated. Mean shift vectors, the so-called *transfer vectors*, obtained through model retraining, are considered a sample of the underlying transfer vector field. VFS is then performed by two procedures, namely *interpolation* and *smoothing* for untrained and trained Gaussian density mean vectors, respectively.

First, for the initial Gaussian mean vectors left untrained, estimation of the corresponding transfer vectors is obtained by interpolation of transfer vectors of trained Gaussian mean vectors. More precisely, for each mean vector left untrained, an adapted mean vector is obtained by interpolation of the estimated transfer vectors as follows:

$$\mu_i' = \mu_i + \frac{\sum_{j \in N(i)} \lambda_{ij} \Delta_{jj}}{\sum_{j \in N(i)} \lambda_{ij}} \tag{11.47}$$

with

$$\lambda_{ij} = \exp\left(\frac{-d_{ij}^2}{s}\right) \tag{11.48}$$

where $'$ applies to the adapted mean vectors. The second term in right-hand side of equation (11.47) represents the interpolated transfer vector for the initial mean vector μ_i obtained interpolating the transfer vectors of the group, denoted by $N(i)$, of M nearest-neighbour mean vectors of μ_i. λ_{ij} in equation (11.47) denotes the weighting coefficient for the transfer vector $\Delta_{jj} = (\hat{\mu}_j - \mu_j)$, with $\hat{}$ denoting the re-estimated mean vectors, involved in the interpolation. λ_{ij} is function of the distance measure d_{ij} (Euclidean distance) between the initial mean vectors μ_i and μ_j as specified in equation (11.48) where s is a weight control parameter.

Then, for already trained mean vectors, a smoothing procedure is carried out in order to ensure robustness to the obtained re-estimated mean vectors. Equation (11.47) is applied for initial mean vectors for which adaptation data have been observed. The ith mean vector, in equation (11.47), is contained in $N(i)$ (so that interpolation is performed considering other $M - 1$ neighbour mean vectors).

Both batch and incremental adaptation algorithms have been developed in the VFS framework (Tonomura *et al.*, 1995; Takahashi and Sagayama, 1995a).

11.3.4. Discrete HMM Adaptation

Discrete HMMs have been widely used for ASR and a number of effective techniques developed for the adaptation of their parameters and codebooks.

Model adaptation

The use of *probabilistic spectral mappings* between quantized spectral spaces of two speakers has been largely investigated for adapting discrete probability distributions of a pretrained set of SD HMMs (Schwartz *et al.*, 1987; Nishimura and Sugawara, 1988). Let $b_{ij}(x)$ be the discrete emission PDF associated with the transition from state i to state j of a given HMM. $b_{ij}(x)$ is defined over a set of O labels, corresponding to the output of a vector quantizer which uses the reference speaker codebook (formed by O vector prototypes), and its values are represented by the row vector B_{ij}.

Let $1 \leq l_R \leq O$ and $1 \leq l_N \leq O$ be the labels obtained by vector quantizing speech data from the reference speaker and the new speaker, respectively. Vector quantization can be performed by using reference speaker's prototype vectors for both the speakers, or using a speaker-specific codebook for each of the two speakers. The probability $\Pr(l_N|l_R)$, that the vector quantizer produces label l_N for the new speaker given that label l_R is observed for the reference speaker, has to be computed for each possible pair of labels l_N and l_R. An $O \times O$ probability transformation matrix P can then be defined, $P_{l_R l_N} = \Pr(l_N|l_R)$, and interpreted as the probabilistic spectral mapping between the quantized spectral spaces of the two speakers.

The required statistics for estimating the transformation matrix P are the relative frequencies of occurrence (in the adaptation set) of each new speaker label, given each reference speaker label. They are obtained by aligning the quantized adaptation data against the reference speaker's HMMs using the forward–backward algorithm (Schwartz *et al.*, 1987), or by time alignment (see section 11.4.2 for a brief description of the time alignment procedure) of adaptation sentences with corresponding sentences uttered by the reference speaker, to obtain aligned quantized spectra (Feng *et al.*, 1988). The matrix P is then applied to each emission discrete distribution in order to obtain a set of adapted models as follows:

$$B'_{ij} = B_{ij}P \qquad (11.49)$$

Improved time alignment algorithms of speech patterns, alignment of an adaptation utterance against multiple repetitions from the reference speakers, and phone-dependent transformation matrices lead to a tangible improvement with respect to the original adaptation technique (Feng *et al.*, 1989).

A parameter transformation approach was recently investigated, in which both output probability distributions and transition probabilities of a set of SD models are adapted by applying suitable transformation matrices (Hao and Fang, 1994). In this case, for each state of a model, two transformation matrices are defined, one for state transition probabilities and one for state emission distributions (being emission probability distributions associated to model states). An ML estimation algorithm is proposed for the estimation of the transformation matrices.

MAP adaptation for discrete HMM parameters is proposed in Huo *et al.* (1993, 1995).

Codebook adaptation

Another approach is *codebook adaptation*. In this case, the codebook used to quantize the input speech for a pretrained set of discrete SD HMMs, is adapted to a new speaker in order to obtain a speaker-specific codebook, while model parameters remain unchanged. The objective is to obtain an adapted codebook that, when used to quantize input speech of a new speaker, tends to produce the same codewords (labels) obtained using the original codebook for quantizing input speech of the reference speaker. Different techniques have been investigated for codebook adaptation.

Shikano *et al.* (1986) proposed various codebook mapping algorithms for vector-quantized template-based recognizers. An unsupervised, text-independent, codebook adaptation technique based on hierarchical clustering of adaptation data and reference speaker codebook prototypes is proposed in Furui (1989). Some techniques attempt to map the reference speaker codebook prototypes to the new speaker's prototypes by means of a feature vector transformation estimated to map the spectral space of the reference speaker to that of the new speaker (Class *et al.*, 1990). Bayesian adaptation of reference speaker prototypes was also investigated (Ferretti and Scarci, 1989; Ferretti and Mazza, 1991).

In Rtischev *et al.* (1994) codebook retraining in an ML framework is proposed. Basically, reference codebook centroids, represented by a set of Gaussian densities having diagonal covariance matrices, are used to initialize emission probability distributions of a set of tied-mixture continuous-parameter HMMs having suitable topologies. This set of models is trained by exploiting the available adaptation data and performing some iterations of the Baum–Welch algorithm. The new estimates for the Gaussian mixture components are used to update the original codebook into an adapted one. This supervised text-independent codebook adaptation technique was also investigated in conjunction with discrete HMM parameter adaptation, and shown to be effective even with a small amount of adaptation data.

Combined adaptation of model parameters and reference speaker's codebook centroids was also shown to be effective (Nishimura and Sugawara, 1988; Feng *et al.*, 1988; Hao and Fang, 1994).

Various techniques, namely speaker clustering and selection, co-occurrence smoothing, and deleted interpolation, for speaker adaptation of discrete HMMs were applied in the SPHINX system (Lee, 1988b).

Some of the above discrete HMM adaptation techniques were considered for adaptation of speaker-independent semicontinuous HMMs (Huang and Lee, 1993). HMM parameters and codebook adaptation experiments show that even with a small amount (few tens of utterances) of adaptation data, codebook adaptation leads to substantial performance improvement, while when a larger amount of adaptation data is available, adaptation of output distributions is more effective.

11.4. FEATURE VECTOR TRANSFORMATION APPROACH

The acoustic feature transformation approach attempts to compensate for inter-speaker acoustic variability by estimating feature mappings capable of reducing acoustic differences between speakers. Similar approaches were investigated for compensating acoustic mismatches among training and testing conditions, due to changes in the environment, acquisition channel or microphone (Acero, 1993; Neumeyer and Weintraub, 1994b; Sankar and Lee, 1995).

11.4.1. Problem Formulation

Assuming that a speech recognizer has been trained for a given speaker, namely the reference speaker, a feature vector transformation has to be estimated for any new system user such that, when applied to the input speech from the new speaker, it produces new features, with which better recognition performance is achieved.

Let $\varphi: R^{D_1} \rightarrow R^{D_2}$ be the feature vector transformation to be estimated, where D_1 and D_2 denote the dimensions of the acoustic spaces involved. For the sake of simplicity, let us assume that D_1 and D_2 are equal to D. The feature vector transformation $\varphi(x)$ is in general estimated using a set of vector pairs $\mathcal{L} = \{(x_n, y_n)\}_{n=1}^N$. For each vector pair $(x_n, y_n) \in \mathcal{L}$, $x_n, y_n \in R^D$ and x_n is a feature vector in the acoustic space of the new speaker, while y_n is the corresponding feature vector in the acoustic space of the reference speaker. The objective is to estimate $\varphi(x)$ in order to *map* the set of vectors $\{x_n\}$ in the corresponding set of vectors $\{y_n\}$. Once $\varphi(x)$ is estimated, it is applied to any input utterance, $x_1^T = x_1, \ldots, x_t, \ldots, x_T$, from the new speaker, in such a way that the transformed utterance, $y_1'^T = \varphi(x_1), \ldots, \varphi(x_t), \ldots, \varphi(x_T)$, better matches the acoustic space of the reference speaker, resulting in improved recognition performance.

The estimation of $\varphi(x)$ can be seen as a multiple regression problem. The functional relationship between the acoustic spaces of two speakers, represented by the two sets of vectors $\{x_n\}$ and $\{y_n\}$, is generally complex and highly nonlinear. A variety of linear, piecewise linear and neural-network-based techniques have been proposed in order to estimate suitable feature vector transformations (Choukri *et al.*, 1986; Class *et al.*, 1990; Matsukoto and Inoue, 1992; Huang, 1992). Figure 11.4 shows a block diagram for a speaker adaptation scheme based on acoustic feature transformation.

In general, a speech recognizer accepts acoustic observations formed by multiple sets of acoustic features, typically static features and dynamic features. Dynamic features can be first- and second-order time derivatives of static features, and prove to be more speaker invariant than static features (see Chapter 3). For this reason, feature vector transformations are often applied only to static features, while dynamic features are left unchanged or are computed from (static) transformed features (Huang, 1992; Furlanello *et al.*, 1995). This reduces the complexity of the transformation to estimate.

The speaker adaptation techniques in which a feature vector transformation is estimated and applied to the input feature vector of a speech recognizer are also called *speaker normalization* techniques, since their purpose is to reduce the acoustic difference between the reference and the new speaker by *normalizing* acoustic data of the new speaker.[1]

Proposed techniques not only differ in the way in which the transformation is estimated, but also in the way in which it is applied. In fact, the feature vector transformation $\varphi(x)$ can be estimated for different purposes and not only for

---

[1]In the literature, *speaker normalization* is also used to denote techniques that make use of a fixed normalization algorithm for processing speech from both training and test speakers. Broadly speaking, in this case, normalization consists of the *projection* of speech of any speaker into a normalized feature space in such a way that inter-speaker differences are minimized.

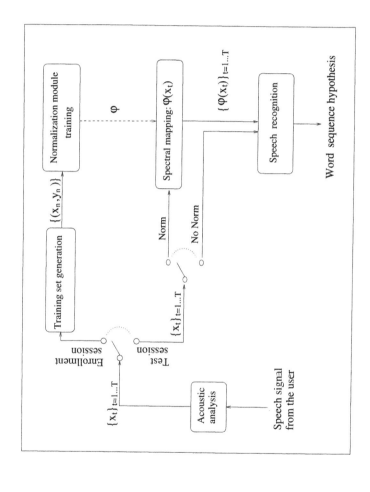

Figure 11.4 Block diagram for speaker adaptation with acoustic feature transformation.

mapping input speech. A variety of techniques based on feature vector transformations have been developed in which feature vector transformations are applied directly to speech models, in order to improve modelling accuracy for a new speaker, or both to input speech and speech models, or to reference speaker training data in order to create an enlarged set of speaker-dependent set of data. Some of these techniques will be recalled below.

11.4.2. Generation of the Training Set

The training set $\mathcal{L}$ is, in general, obtained by time alignment of speech patterns. The new speaker is required to read a set of utterances which are time aligned with the corresponding set of pre-registered utterances of the reference speaker.

Time alignment of speech patterns is performed with the well known dynamic time warping (DTW) algorithm (Sakoe and Chiba, 1978). Let $v_1^I = v_1, v_2, \ldots, v_I$ and $z_1^J = z_1, z_2, \ldots, z_J$ be the parametric representations of two utterances corresponding to the same text uttered by two speakers. The two feature vector sequences v_1^I and z_1^J have in general different lengths and are characterized by non-linear differences along the time axis. Moreover, they are subject to significant differences between corresponding spectra due to speaker characteristics. The DTW algorithm performs time alignment of acoustic sequences v_1^I and z_1^J yielding pairs, $c[q] = (i_q, j_q)$, $q = 1, \ldots, Q$, of indices of corresponding feature vectors in v_1^I and z_1^J, respectively. Figure 11.5 shows a graphical representation of time alignment between acoustic sequences v_1^I and z_1^J.

The resulting set of corresponding vector pair $\{(v_{i_q}, z_{j_q})\}$ can then be used to estimate a feature vector transformation allowing the acoustic difference between the two speakers to be reduced.

In general, more than two utterances are time aligned in order to obtain a representative set of feature vector pairs and the obtained vector pairs are arranged to form the training set $\mathcal{L}$. As the objective is also to minimize the amount of speech data required from a new speaker, an enlarged set of vector pairs can be obtained by aligning the set of utterances of the new speaker with multiple repetitions of the reference speaker (Class *et al.*, 1990).

Time alignment of speech patterns plays a crucial role in the estimate of the desired feature transformation. For this reason, improved time alignment procedures, based on iterative application of the DTW algorithm, have been proposed (Feng *et al.*, 1989; Gong *et al.*, 1992).

However, time alignment of speech patterns leads to a strictly text-dependent adaptation scheme. When the goal is to estimate a feature vector transformation to be applied to the feature vectors produced by the acoustic front end of a recognition system based on continuous density HMMs, a more flexible approach can be adopted. Each HMM transition, having associated a Gaussian mixture, is first expanded into a collection of parallel transitions, each one with a single Gaussian distribution. Each adaptation utterance is then aligned, with

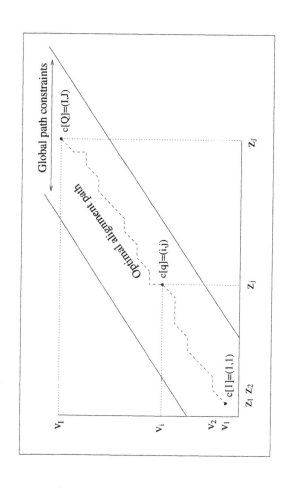

Figure 11.5 Time alignment path between speech patterns.

the Viterbi algorithm (see Chapter 9), against a concatenation of models corresponding to the utterance phonetic transcription (which can be found with a
preliminary recognition step). In this way, each input feature vector is associated with a Gaussian density whose mean vector becomes the corresponding
target vector (Furlanello *et al.*, 1997). Gaussian means play the role of synthetic
patterns in the acoustic space of the training data. Although the latter approach
may be less accurate, due to the limited number of Gaussian densities in the
system, it is text-independent and is suitable for both speaker-dependent and
speaker-independent recognition systems.

11.4.3. Linear and Non-linear Transformations

Given a feature vector from the new speaker, x_t, the goal is to estimate a
corresponding reference speaker's feature vector y'_t:

$$y'_t = \varphi(x_t) \tag{11.50}$$

Let us first assume a functional relationship between the acoustic spaces of
the new and the reference speaker expressed by the affine transformation:

$$y'_t = U^* x_t + h \tag{11.51}$$

where U is a $D \times D$ matrix, and h is a D-dimensional additive bias vector. Given
the training set $\mathcal{L} = \{(x_n, y_n)\}_{n=1}^{N}$, the estimation of the feature vector transformation reduces to a multiple linear regression problem. U and h can be
estimated minimizing the *mean squared error* defined as (Weisberg, 1980):

$$E = \frac{1}{N} \sum_{n=1}^{N} \|y_n - (U^* x_n + h)\|^2 \tag{11.52}$$

where $\| \ \|$ denotes the Euclidean distance. However, the adoption of the model
estimated by this simple solution does not lead, in many cases, to satisfactory
recognition results (Class *et al.*, 1990).

A different approach was proposed in Choukri *et al.* (1986). The reference
speaker's feature vectors $\{y_n\}$ and the new speaker's feature vectors $\{x_n\}$ are
projected into a *joint* feature space by means of two linear transformations:
$\hat{y} = U_R^* y$ and $\hat{x} = U_N^* x$. Assuming that the two sets of vectors $\{y_n\}$ and $\{x_n\}$
are mean centred (zero mean), the $D \times D$ transformation matrices U_N and
U_R are determined, minimizing the average *distance* between corresponding
projected vector pairs, that is:

$$E = \frac{1}{N} \sum_{n=1}^{N} \| U_R^* y_n - U_N^* x_n \|^2 \tag{11.53}$$

under the additional constraint that the components of the vectors in the two
transformed sets have unit variance. The minimization problem can then be

formulated, for each component $1 \leq d \leq D$, minimizing the expression:

$$E_d = \frac{1}{N} \sum_{n=1}^{N} (\hat{y}_{nd} - \hat{x}_{nd})^2 = 2 \left(1 - \frac{1}{N} \sum_{n=1}^{N} (\hat{y}_{nd} \hat{x}_{nd}) \right) \qquad (11.54)$$

E_d is minimum when the dth component of the transformed vectors $\{\hat{x}_n\}$ and $\{\hat{y}_n\}$ are maximally correlated. The problem solution is obtained with canonical correlation analysis (Choukri *et al.*, 1986).

Once matrices U_N and U_R have been estimated using the available adaptation data, speech recognition is performed in the joint feature space, transforming both the input speech from the new speaker and the reference speaker's speech data. Transforming reference speaker training data involves retraining the recognizer. In general, reference speaker's speech models are transformed, instead (e.g. speech templates or reference speaker's codebook centroids (Choukri *et al.*, 1986; Class *et al.*, 1990, 1992)). Furthermore, the combined application of U_N and U_R allows other different adaptation schemes, such as transforming just the input speech or the speech models (Class *et al.*, 1990).

A constrained estimation of the transformation matrix U was proposed in Class *et al.* (1990). The functional error E in equation (11.52) is minimized with the additional constraint that the variance for the components of new speaker's transformed vectors and the reference speaker's vector is equal. This approach has been proven effective for some sets of acoustic parameters.

Other interesting types of affine transformations have been investigated in Bellegarda *et al.* (1994) and Furlanello and Giuliani (1995).

However, since the functional relationship to estimate is complex, it can be just roughly approximated by an affine transformation. Exploiting the fact that neural networks are "universal" approximators (see Chapter 10), *multi-layer perceptrons* (MLP) have been proposed to learn the non-linear relationship between the acoustic spaces of two speakers (Montacié *et al.*, 1989; Nakamura and Shikano, 1990; Huang, 1992; Watrous, 1994). To exploit the temporal structure of speech patterns by using dynamic information to estimate network parameters, an MLP architecture was proposed that accepts as input the current feature vector together with its acoustic context (Huang, 1992). The acoustic context of the current input vector is formed by its preceding and following feature vectors in the utterance, resulting in multiple (namely three) input frames for the network.

The use of artificial neural networks with radial basis functions was also investigated for speaker normalization purposes (Furlanello *et al.*, 1995; Furlanello and Giuliani, 1995).

11.4.4. Combining Local Mappings

In general, it is convenient to assume that a non-linear functional relationship holds between the acoustic spaces represented by two sets of acoustic observations $\{x_n\}$ and $\{y_n\}$. In this case, the feature vector transformation $\varphi(x_t)$ has the following form:

$$y_t' = \sum_{k=1}^{C} p_k(x_t)\varphi_k(x_t; \theta_k) \qquad (11.55)$$

where $\varphi_k(x_t; \theta_k)$ denotes the kth *local* regression model characterized by the parameter vector θ_k, C is the total number of regression models used and $p_k(x_t)$ is a function of the observed vector x_t that represents the non-negative *weight* associated to model $\varphi_k(x_t)$, with $\sum_{k=1}^{C} p_k(x_t) = 1$. When notation $\varphi_k(\cdot)$ is used, dependence on model parameter is implicitly assumed. Given the current input feature vector x_t, the overall model response is expressed as the weighted sum of the responses of the local models $\{\varphi_k(x_t)\}$.

The basic idea is that a single regression model can hardly represent the existing functional relationship between the acoustic space of two speakers due to the inter-speaker spectra variation at the level of phonemes. Therefore, the use of *local* models, where each model is specialized for the functional relationship existing between a *subregion* of the input acoustic space and the target acoustic space, should be more appropriate. Furthermore, a suitable interpolation of the local model responses should ensure contiguity in the mapped space.

For linear local models, θ_k is formed by the parameters of the transformation matrix and of the offset term (see equation (11.51)) of the local model $\varphi_k(x_t)$. If local models are neural networks, then θ_k is formed by the network parameters of local model $\varphi_k(x_t)$. In the former case, the composed model defined by the (11.55) is reminiscent of the *piecewise linear spectral mapping* proposed for speaker adaptation (Matsukoto and Inoue, 1992) or can be viewed as a simplified realization of the *probabilistic optimum filtering* (Neumeyer and Weintraub, 1994b) proposed for robust speech recognition. When local models are neural networks, the composed model specified by equation (11.55) is defined to be a *linear opinion pool* model (Jordan and Jacobs, 1994; Waterhouse *et al.*, 1996).

To determine the combination weights $\{p_k(x_t)\}$, assume that the acoustic space of a given speaker can be modelled with a finite *mixture density* function $f(x_t)$ having C components expressed as:

$$f(x_t) = \sum_{k=1}^{C} w_k f_k(x_t) \qquad (11.56)$$

with component densities $\{f_k(x_t)\}$ and mixing parameters $\{w_k\}$. Here, $f_k(x_t)$ denotes the class-conditional probability density function of x_t given the kth of C *populations*, or *classes*. Gaussian mixture component densities with diagonal covariance matrices are a common choice. $w_1, w_2, \ldots, w_k$, denote prior class probabilities with $\sum_{k=1}^{C} w_k = 1$. When labelled data are available, i.e. for each training feature vector in $\{x_n\}$ the class to which it belongs is known, supervised Gaussian mixture parameter estimation can be performed on a class by class basis. For unlabelled data, parameter estimation can be performed by the expectation maximization algorithm (Dempster *et al.*, 1977). The components of the mixture density expressed in equation (11.56) are used in the computation of the weights for equation (11.55). Different weighting techniques can be considered. Two of them are outlined below.

Given the observation vector x_t, the first strategy consists in assigning weight 1 to the class associated to the dominant mixture component in equation (11.56), determined as follows:

$$k' = \max_k w_k f_k(x_t) \tag{11.57}$$

Once k' is determined, then $p_{k'}(x_t) = 1$ while a weight equal to 0 is assigned to all the other classes, i.e. $p_k(x_t) = 0$ if $k \neq k'$. Basically, given the observed vector x_t, the response of just a local model, selected according to equation (11.57), forms the overall model response. This weighting strategy leads to the well known piecewise linear and code-dependent neural network approaches (Matsukoto and Inoue, 1992; Huang, 1992), depending on the functional form chosen for the local models. For local model parameter estimation, first the training vectors $\{x_n\}$, and consequently the corresponding vector pairs $\{(x_n, y_n)\}$, are assigned to local models according to equation (11.57); then the parameters of each local model are estimated exploiting the specific available subset of vector pairs.

A more appropriate strategy is determining the weights $\{p_k(x_t)\}$ as follows:

$$p_k(x_t) = \frac{w_k f_k(x_t)}{\sum_{i=1}^C w_i f_i(x_t)} \tag{11.58}$$

In this case, all the local models concur to the overall model response according to their proper weights. Parameters of each local model are estimated this time using all the samples in the training set $\mathcal{L}$ but each pair (x_n, y_n) concurs to the estimation of the local model parameters according to the weights $\{p_k(x_n)\}$.

For linear local models, parameters can be estimated according to the *weighted* mean squared error criterion (Weisberg, 1980). For the kth model, parameters are determined minimizing the following error function (Neumeyer and Weintraub, 1994b; Furlanello *et al.*, 1997):

$$E^{(k)} = \sum_{n=1}^N p_k(x_n) \| y_n - (U_k^* x_n + h_k) \|^2 \tag{11.59}$$

where U_k is a $D \times D$ matrix and h_k is a D-dimensional offset vector forming the kth regression model.

In analogy, for neural network local models, a suitable cost function can be specified as follows:

$$E = \frac{1}{2} \sum_{n=1}^N \sum_{j=1}^D \left(y_{nj} - \sum_{k=1}^C p_k(x_n) o_{kj}(x_n) \right)^2 \tag{11.60}$$

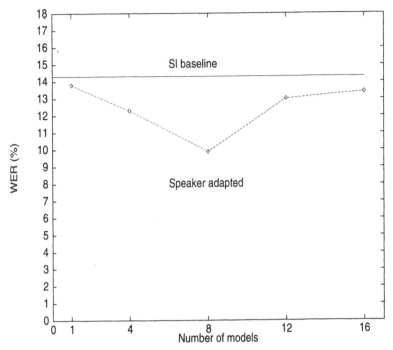

Figure 11.6 Rate (WER) as function of the number of local models.

where $o_{kj}(x_n)$ denotes the jth output of the kth network when fed with input x_n. Network parameters are estimated using the backpropagation algorithm by taking the partial derivatives of the defined cost function E, specified in equation (11.60), with respect to network weights (Furanello *et al.*, 1997).

It was experimentally shown that, if enough data are available for local model training, a mixture of local models ensures better recognition performance than a single global model when applied to transform the feature vectors produced by an acoustic front end for a continuous speech recognizer (Matsukoto and Inoue, 1992; Huang, 1992; Furanello *et al.*, 1997). From an applicative point of view, the number of local models has to be chosen considering different factors such as amount of available adaptation data and computational cost of the training.

As an example, Figure 11.6 depicts the word error rate (WER) as function of the number of local models. Performance is averaged over four test speakers (one female and three males), each speaker uttered 30 test sentences (about 600 words). Twenty adaptation utterances for each speaker were adopted to train the normalization module based on MLP local models (Furlanello *et al.*, 1997). The reported performance refers to an SI recognition system applied to a continuous speech task with a vocabulary of 10 000 words (Federico *et al.*, 1995). The system was based on 34 context-independent speech units modelled with CDHMMs. Each output distribution was modelled with a mixture having 16 Gaussian components with diagonal covariance matrices. The training set, for the normalization module, was generated by a suitable alignment procedure of the adaptation utterances against the concatenation of models corresponding to utterance phonetic transcriptions (as described in section 11.4.2). Only static features (8 mel-scaled cepstral coefficients plus log-energy) were transformed by the normalization module, while dynamic features (first- and second-order time derivatives of static features) were computed from transformed static features. For each test speaker the adaptation data were modelled with a Gaussian mixture used for computing local model weights. The second weighting strategy, described above, was adopted for both training and testing phases (so that all the local models concurred to the overall model response).

Figure 11.6 shows that enlarging the number of local models up to eight significantly improves recognition performance. However, given the amount of adaptation data, enlarging further the number of local models leads to a poor estimation of model parameters which results in a reduced effectiveness of the normalization module.

11.4.5. ML Estimate of Feature Vector Transformations

A feature vector transformation can be assumed for the input feature vectors to a recognizer and its estimate can be formulated in an ML framework. In analogy with the transformation-based approach for adapting CDHMM parameters, transformation parameters are not estimated to reduce differences among sets of data, but to increase the likelihood of the adaptation data given the current set of models.

Considering an affine transformation of the input data, the Gaussian mixture associated to the transition from state i to state j of a model takes the form:

$$b_{ij}(x) = \sum_{k=1}^{K} w_{ijk} \mathcal{N}(Ux + h; \mu_{ijk}, \Sigma_{ijk}) \qquad (11.61)$$

where U is a $D \times D$ transformation matrix and h is a D-dimensional additive bias vector. Transformation parameters (i.e. U and h) can be estimated to maximize the likelihood of the adaptation data (Leggetter, 1995).

A similar approach for channel compensation, in which separate spectral biases are estimated for *speech* and *silence* input frames on an utterance-by-utterance basis, was also proposed (Sankar and Lee, 1996).

These approaches are flexible as they are suitable for both speaker-dependent and speaker-independent recognition systems. In addition they are text-independent as they do not require time alignment of pairs of utterances.

11.4.6. Uses of Acoustic Feature Transformations

Feature vector transformations can be estimated for different purposes and applied in different manners.

In Class *et al.* (1990) a comparison on the use of different feature vector transformations, applied to the input feature vectors for template-based and discrete-HMM-based SD recognition systems, is reported. Only linear transformations are considered. Following the approach proposed in Choukri *et al.* (1986), recognition experiments were also carried out after projection in the joint feature space. Feature vector transformations were applied both to input feature vectors and to the speech models before recognition. For template-based recognition systems, the speech templates were transformed, for discrete HMM-based systems the codebook centroids were mapped. It was shown that performing recognition in the joint feature space gives better results in comparison with the use of a linear transformation applied either to input feature vectors or to speech models only.

The use of a piecewise linear approach was proposed for mapping acoustic data from one speaker to another, generating an augmented speaker-specific set of data (Bellegarda *et al.*, 1994, 1995). In this case, a set of transformations are estimated at phone level, although a different level can be chosen according to the available amount of data, following an approach called *metamorphic* transformation. Once a set of feature vector transformations are estimated with a small amount of adaptation data from a new speaker, the transformations are applied to the reference speaker's acoustic data in order to obtain an augmented speaker-specific set of data for the new speaker. The transformed data (obtained from one or more reference speakers), together with the adaptation data supplied by the new speaker, are then used to train a speaker-dependent recognition system for the new speaker.

With this data augmentation approach, starting with 100 adaptation sentences from the new speaker and generating 1500 additional sentences for system training from a pool of reference speakers, on a continuous speech large dictionary task, on the average, about the same WER was obtained as in the speaker-dependent case in which 600 sentences were used for system training (Bellegarda *et al.*, 1995).

An approach in which inter-speaker acoustic variability is modelled as a two-source problem was recently proposed (Zhao, 1994). Inter-speaker spectral variations are separated into two categories attributed to two different sources, namely the *acoustic source* and the *phone-specific* source. These two sources correspond to speaker's physical characteristics that cause acoustic variations independent of phone units and to speaker's individual articulations that cause phone-dependent spectral variations.

According to this model, acoustic and phone-specific variation sources are modelled as two separate linear transforms applied on the spectra of the reference speaker. In the logarithmic spectral domain, the composite effect of the two linear transformations introduces additive biases as follows:

$$x_{ph,t}^{(N)} = h^{(N)} + l_{ph}^{(N)} + x_{ph,t}^{(R)} \qquad (11.62)$$

where $x_{ph,t}^{(N)}$ and $x_{ph,t}^{(R)}$ denote the new and the reference speaker (logarithmic) spectra of phone *ph* at time *t*, respectively. $h^{(N)}$ denotes the spectral bias due to the acoustic source, while $l_{ph}^{(N)}$ is the phone-specific spectral bias. Analogously, this model holds for acoustic features linearly derived from the logarithmic spectra.

Starting from this model, a formulation for estimating $h^{(N)}$ and $l_{ph}^{(N)}$ was first derived; however, for practical reasons, some simplifications were introduced and a more pragmatic approach was proposed based on acoustic normalization and phone model adaptation.

Assuming the reference speaker is characterized by a set of phone CDHMMs trained with a speaker-independent set of data, then $h^{(N)}$ is estimated (for static features only) with unsupervised ML estimation exploiting the adaptation data, so that after the following normalization:

$$\hat{x}_t^{(N)} = x_t^{(N)} - \hat{h}^{(N)} \qquad (11.63)$$

where $\hat{h}^{(N)}$ denotes the estimated speaker-specific spectral bias, adaptation data better fit the reference speaker CDHMMs. It was also proposed to perform this acoustic normalization on both training and test data. Performing acoustic normalization, that is removing speaker-specific spectral biases, on the training data, increases the ability to capture statistical variation characterizing allophones during SI model training.

Then rather than directly estimating phone-specific spectral biases $\{l_{ph}^{(N)}\}$, phone-model adaptation is performed with Bayesian estimation of the Gaussian mixture component parameters of a set of SI models.

11.5. SPEAKER CLUSTERING AND MODEL SELECTION

A simple way to deal with the lack of modelling accuracy in an SI recognition system is clustering *similar* speakers available in the training set and training a separate set of models for each cluster of speakers (Lee, 1988b). Provided that enough training material is available for each speaker cluster, clustering of similar speakers should ensure, for each set of models, a better accuracy with respect to the SI models obtained using all the available training material. During recognition, a speaker is first classified as member of a cluster, and the corresponding set of models is selected and used for recognizing the incoming utterances from the speaker.

In Kosaka and Sagayama (1994) a hierarchical speaker model clustering algorithm is proposed. Basically, speaker clusters are associated with the nodes of a tree structure, where the tree root represents the cluster containing all the training population and lower levels of the tree are built using a suitable splitting clustering procedure. For each speaker cluster, associated to a node of the tree, a set of models is built starting from the SD models of the speakers in the cluster. The adaptation process inspects the tree and evaluates the likelihoods of the adaptation utterances at each node using the corresponding set of models. The most likely node is then selected and the corresponding set of models is used for recognition. Supervised and unsupervised adaptation have been recently compared (Kosaka *et al.*, 1996).

The speaker clustering approach suffers from several problems, mainly due to the limited amount of available training data and number of speakers. Enlarging the number of clusters ensures better modelling accuracy, but requires a large amount of training data. However, the acoustic variability among speakers in the same cluster may still be large. Furthermore, due to the limited number of training speakers, no speaker cluster may match well with a test speaker.

11.6. CONCLUSIONS

In the last few years, as speech technology became mature for practical applications, robust speech recognition has received increasing attention. Explicit modelling, during system training, of the various acoustic conditions in application environments is not feasible. Therefore, the development of recognition systems capable of adapting to environmental conditions is crucial to ensure acceptable recognition performance.

Speaker adaptive systems are able to compensate for the lack of model accuracy for a new user of the system. Batch, incremental and instantaneous adaptation techniques have been developed, according to the different applicative scenarios.

Two approaches have recently emerged for speaker adaptation: the transformation-based adaptation of CDHMM parameters (Digalakis *et al.*, 1995; Leggetter and Woodland, 1995b) and the MAP adaptation (Lee *et al.*, 1991; Gauvain and Lee, 1994). The former appears to be effective for recognition systems with a very large number of parameters or when a small amount of adaptation data is available as the number of transformations it uses can be made dependent on the amount of adaptation data (Leggetter and Woodland, 1995a). MAP adaptation suffers from the fact that models for which no adaptation data are observed are left unchanged. However, with recent strategies for model parameter tying/sharing and for exploiting model parameter correlations, MAP adaptation was also shown to be effective for adapting recognizers with a very large number of parameters (Zavaliagkos *et al.*, 1995b). Furthermore, due to its capability of optimally interpolating the available adaptation data with the prior knowledge about the parameters to estimate, MAP adaptation is used, as preliminary or refinement step, in many adaptation procedures (Ahadi and Woodland, 1995; Tonomura *et al.*, 1995; Digalakis and Neumeyer, 1995).

The effectiveness of many adaptation techniques, based on the two above approaches, is confirmed by the experimental results obtained on the *WSJ* corpus with large scale CDHMM based recognizers. Good error rate reduction was obtained for both native and non-native speakers with batch adaptation and a small amount of adaptation data (e.g. 40 utterances) (Neumeyer *et al.*, 1995; Sankar *et al.*, 1996; Zavaliagkos *et al.*, 1995b; Gales *et al.*, 1996). On the same corpus, incremental adaptation algorithms have also shown good capabilities of progressively adapting the system to the speaker (Leggetter, 1995; Leggetter and Woodland, 1995a; Zavaliagkos, 1995; Zavaliagkos *et al.*, 1995a). Instantaneous adaptation, due to its nature, has shown good performance with non-native speakers but little advantage for native speakers having spectral characteristics quite similar to the training population (Zavaliagkos, 1995; Zavaliagkos *et al.*, 1995a).

Artificial-neural-network-based speech recognizers are becoming more and more effective, even for large-vocabulary continuous speech tasks (Hochberg *et al.*, 1995). Increasing attention is devoted to the development of effective speaker adaptation techniques for these systems (Watrous, 1994; Neto *et al.*, 1995; Waterhouse *et al.*, 1996).

12

Robust Speech Recognition

Chafic Mokbel,[*] Denis Jouvet,[*] Jean Monné[*]
and Renato De Mori[†]

[*]France Télécom – CNET – DIH/RCP, 2 av. Pierre Marzin, 22300 Lannion, France.
[†]School of Computer Science, McGill University, Montréal, P.Q., H3A 2A7, Canada.

12.1. INTRODUCTION

Robustness is an important requirement for successful deployment of speech technologies in real-life applications (Juang, 1991; Gong, 1995). Unlike speech coding, speech enhancement or speech synthesis, automatic speech and speaker recognition cannot exploit the ability of the human auditory system to extract a selected voice in a mixture of acoustic signals. ASR systems have to be robust with respect to various types of additive noise, channel distortions, spurious noise sources and out-of-vocabulary words. Lack of robustness in any of these dimensions makes ASR unsuitable for real-life in spite of its potential in many areas such as voice dialling, information systems, reservation services and in some specific, generally adverse environments, such as a running car, a working factory or public places like airports and train stations. Furthermore, the rapid development of cellular networks, especially GSM (Global System for Mobile) and CDMA (Code Division Multiple Access), offers new opportunities for ASR applications.

First attempts to introduce speech recognition in real-life applications have made evident various robustness problems, stimulating a creative effort for the conception of new solutions. In order to improve robustness, attention was initially concentrated on endpoint detection for isolated word recognition, and on compensating for the alteration of speaker voices produced by environmental noise. A notable example of endpoint detection is proposed in Lamel *et al.* (1981) for low speech signal-to-noise ratio (SNR). Successive experiments have shown that ASR systems exhibiting good performance for clean speech, produced poor results in the presence of environmental noise or distortion introduced by the transmission channels. In Dautrich *et al.* (1983), experiments with an isolated-word ASR system trained with clean speech are described. The system achieves 95% word accuracy with test data of clean speech, but the error rate doubles when the same test is performed on signals with 18 dB SNR. At CNET–France Télécom it has been observed that the best performance in ASR with noise is obtained when no mismatch exists between training and testing conditions. In Das *et al.* (1993), it is mentioned that, while 1% word error rate was obtained in 20000 word-vocabulary, speaker-dependent isolated-word recognition, a 50% rate increase occurred in a cafeteria. In Mokbel and Chollet (1991), a speaker-dependent isolated word recognition system is described to achieve 100% word accuracy on a 43-word vocabulary in a car with the engine turned off. The performance of the same system drops to about 75% word accuracy when recognition is performed in a car running at 90 km/h. In Acero and Stern (1990), the effect of a mismatch between microphones in training and testing conditions is analysed showing a decrease in word accuracy, on average, from 80% to 30%. The two microphones used in this experiment were Sennheiser HMD224 and Crown PZM6fs. In Sorin *et al.* (1995), it is argued that, in telephone applications, most ASR errors are due to bad endpoint detection of speech segments and to wrong hypotheses for out-of-vocabulary (OOV) words. An energy-based endpoint detector is very sensitive to additive stationary noise. Furthermore, an error analysis for a real-world application is discussed in Bartkova *et al.* (1995) indicating that the presence of environmental noise may induce variation in the speaking style. This is known as the Lombard effect (Junqua, 1993). In Rajasekaran and Doddington (1986) it is suggested that changing the speaking style may strongly reduce recognition performance. An ML approach to acoustic mismatch compensation has been recently proposed in Afify *et al.* (1977b) for the recognition of noisy Lombard speech.

In order to identify the reasons for performance degradation in noisy conditions it is important to consider the various types of information conveyed by the speech signal, namely phonetic components, speaker-specific components, context-specific components, task-specific components and noise components. Robustness has to deal with all these types of variability. An ASR system is robust if no or little performance degradation is observed due to within- and inter-speaker variability, accent, Lombard effects, additive ambient noise, channel distortions and interference, echo and reverberation. While the previous chapter on speaker adaptation deals with speaker variability, this chapter mainly focuses on techniques for reducing the effects of stationary ambient noise, spurious noise, echo, reverberation, channel distortions and interference.

Techniques for improving robustness to variations in the acquisition environment (echo, ambient noise and channel distortion) include speech enhancement and echo cancelling with techniques in the area of microphone arrays, speech analysis and modelling. The purpose is to remove disturbing components in the observed signal or to increase the SNR in order to improve the performance of some ASR components such as endpoint detection. Echo cancelling makes anticipation possible in the dialogue between humans and machines, enabling the user to speak while the machine produces the output message. Moreover, robustness may also be improved by techniques like MAP, EM estimation or others available in more general domains such as signal processing, statistical modelling, information theory and communication. However, even if robustness has roots in speech processing or more general domains, ASR problems have inspired new aspects of basic algorithms in order to take into account the high complexity of a signal affected by many sources of variability. Notable examples are different filtering and channel equalization techniques, new spectral subtraction techniques, a combination of Wiener filtering and HMM modelling.

Section 12.2 is dedicated to the definition and the description of solution classes. Section 12.3 focuses on representations that may improve robustness, and on their distance measures. In fact, similarity between representations should be measurable by an appropriate distance. Section 12.4 describes the most popular techniques used to remove noisy components in the speech signal. The most important techniques for adapting ASR models to new specific recognition environments are introduced in section 12.5. Section 12.6 contains concluding remarks.

Important topics in the domain of robust speech recognition are not discussed here for the sake of brevity, namely OOV rejection and the compensation of the Lombard effect for which solutions are described in Rajasekarun and Doddington (1986), Van Summers *et al.* (1988), Chen (1988), Mokbel (1992), Junqua (1993) and Hansen and Cairns (1995).

12.2. PROBLEM DEFINITION AND SOLUTION CLASSES

Noise and distortions increase the probability of failure to separate speech and non-speech segments introducing new errors in ASR. The following four classes of solutions can be considered to increase system robustness:

- feature analysis, parametric and non-parametric spectral representations with the associated distance measures, and auditory modelling
- transformation of noisy speech features into the space of the corresponding clean speech features (includes preprocessing, speech enhancement and the use of microphone arrays)
- transformation of the acoustic space of speech reference patterns and/or speech reference models in order to properly model the particular noisy environment (e.g. in model parameter adaptation)
- techniques for transforming both clean speech features and noisy features into a common space where acoustic discrimination is better.

Various types of problems are now analysed in more detail.

12.2.1. Spurious Noise

Spurious noise refers to signal components that are not words in the application vocabulary, nor background stationary noise, nor frequency distortions slowly varying with time. In such a case, the observed signal $y(t)$ can be written as the sum of two components. The first one $y_1(t)$ corresponds to the noisy speech signal and the second one $y_2(t)$ represents segments of spurious noise:

$$y(t) = y_1(t) + y_2(t) \tag{12.1}$$

with:

$$y_2(t) \begin{cases} \neq 0 & \text{for } t \in \bigcup_k [t_{beg}(k), t_{end}(k)] \\ = 0 & \text{elsewhere} \end{cases} \tag{12.2}$$

$t_{beg}(k)$ and $t_{end}(k)$ are the extremes of the kth spurious noise segment.

It is worth distinguishing two cases. First, if the kth noise interval overlaps a word in the system vocabulary or a sentence, then a specific acoustic model should be provided or, at least, these situations should be detected and low confidence should be ascribed to hypotheses generated in these segments. Second, if the interval does not overlap with vocabulary words or sentences, then the system must exclude this part of the signal in the recognition process.

12.2.2. Echo Cancelling

Echo cancelling is very useful to improve the quality of dialogue between humans and machines. It allows the user of the system to speak while the machine broadcasts a message. For example, a user familiar with voice-activated services appreciates the possibility of speaking before the end of a system message. This problem is more critical for hands-free mobile telephones. Another useful application of echo cancelling techniques is the elimination of radio music in the signal to be recognized, if, for example, recognition is performed in a car.

Figure 12.1 shows a typical echo canceller scheme inspired by Messerschmitt (1982). The echo r_i of the reference signal x_i emitted at the point A is mixed with the signal itself. The main problem is due to the fact that the echo is a distorted version of the reference signal. The echo canceller generally approximates the echo by a filtered version of the reference signal $\hat{r}_i$; $\hat{r}_i$ is then subtracted from the observed signal to produce the echo-cancelled signal $\hat{e}_i$.

In order to perform reliable acoustic echo cancellation, long-term non-stationary impulse responses should be identified. This is quite a difficult problem. Moreover, implementation constraints make several solutions impractical. Typically, classical "recursive least squares" (RLS) algorithms,

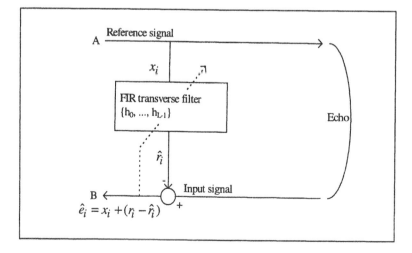

Figure 12.1 Principle of the echo canceller for one-way transmission.

introduced below, often have a prohibitive computational cost. Adaptive "Least Mean Squares" (LMS) algorithms (Haykin, 1991; Widrow and Stearns, 1985) are generally used to compute the values of the transversal filter parameters $\{h_i\}$ when the reference signal is active. Some of the problems, generally encountered when these algorithms are applied in practice, are voice activity detection and double speaking detection.

12.2.3. Least Mean Squares (LMS) Algorithms

Let the impulse response of length L of an adaptive transversal filter be represented by $\boldsymbol{h}(t)^T = [h_0(t); \ldots; h_{L-1}(t)]$. As the filter is adaptive, the impulse response varies with time t, which can be considered as a discrete variable. Let $s(t)$ be the filter input, and $r(t)$ the desired filter output. Assuming that the signals $s(t)$ and $x(t)$ are not correlated, the error sequence is given by:

$$\varepsilon(t) = r(t) - \hat{r}(t) = r(t) - \sum_{j=0}^{L-1} h_j(t)s(t-j) = r(t) - \boldsymbol{h}^T(t)s(t) \qquad (12.3)$$

The filter input and the desired output signals are supposed to be scalar (multichannel adaptive filtering is not considered here). The commonly used *minimum mean square error* (MMSE) criterion can be applied to compute the filter parameters in order to minimize $E[\varepsilon^2(t)]$. This yields the optimal filter:

$$\hat{\boldsymbol{h}}(t) = \Gamma_{ss}^{-1}(t)\Gamma_{sr}(t) \qquad (12.4)$$

where $\Gamma_{ss}(t) = E[s(t)s^T(t)]$ is the autocovariance matrix of the input signal and $\Gamma_{sr}(t) = E[s(t)r(t)]$ is the cross-covariance vector of the input and desired signal. The following adaptive solution for (12.4) with LMS algorithms gives:

$$\boldsymbol{h}(t+1) = \boldsymbol{h}(t) + \alpha M^{-1}(t)s(t)\varepsilon(t) \qquad (12.5)$$

where α is the adaptation step and $M(t)$ is the gradient normalization matrix.

The normalized LMS algorithm (NLMS) is used in applications where the input signal level exhibits wide fluctuations. In NLMS, the gradient normalization matrix depends on the power of the input signal; $M(t) = m(t)I_{L,L}$, where $I_{L,L}$ designates the identity matrix of dimension L, and:

$$m(t) = \mu m(t-1) + (1-\mu)s^2(t)$$

$m(t)$ is chosen equal to the following quantity:

$$m(t) = s^T(t)s(t)cte$$

The NLMS algorithm has the advantage of low computational cost (the complexity is of order $2L$ multiply–accumulate operations per iteration).

A more efficient computation is obtained with sign algorithms. These algorithms are especially used for high speed communication. In the signed error (SE) algorithm, the gradient normalization matrix factor is defined by:

$$m(t) = |\varepsilon(t)|$$

Clipped LMS or signed regressor (SR) uses a diagonal normalization matrix that has the following ith diagonal element:

$$M_{i,i}(t) = |s(t - i)|$$

In recent years, frequency-domain and block adaptive filters have been proposed. With these algorithms, the data are grouped into N-point blocks. The filter parameters are constant for the duration of a block. The parameters are updated at the end of each block. The structures of these methods allow pipeline and parallel computations. The computational cost can be greatly reduced by replacing time-domain convolution in (12.3) and (12.5) by fast transform-domain block convolution. However, these algorithms introduce a delay in the processing and have reduced stability when the input signal correlation increases. The normalized block LMS (NBLMS) is a good example of algorithms of this type. A good discussion of the implementation of these algorithms can be found in Shynk (1992). The direct use of frequency-domain adaptive filters (FDAF) for echo cancelling has a major drawback. Currently, for a data block of length B, the FDAF filter uses length-N FFTs with $N \geq B + L$. In practice, B and L may be very large. Thus, a direct implementation of FDAF introduces unacceptable transmission delays and poor performance. In Soo (1990), it is proposed to segment the impulse response into small blocks, resulting in a new algorithm called "multidelay adaptive filter" (MDF). Adapting the filter parameters to a higher rate than the block dimension yields to the "generalized multidelay adaptive filter" (GMDF) (Moulines and Laroche, 1995). Subband adaptive filters can be seen as a variant of FDAFs. These filters have also been successfully applied to echo cancelling (Gilloire, 1987).

12.2.4. Recursive Least Squares (RLS) Algorithms

In general, LMS algorithms exhibit non-uniform convergence and attempt to optimize a stochastic criterion on the basis of a local information. An alternative approach consists of estimating, at a time t, the parameters of the optimum filter using all the data available up to this time. The recursive least squares (RLS) algorithm approximates the MMSE criterion by recursively minimizing a quadratic error at time t:

$$J_t = \sum_{\tau=0}^{t} \varepsilon_\tau^2 = \sum_{\tau=0}^{t} [r(\tau) - h^T(\tau)s(\tau)]^2 \tag{12.6}$$

Differentiating (12.6) with respect to the filter parameters and equating it to zero leads to the set of normal equations (12.4). Generally, exponential windowing ($\lambda < 1$) of the error is introduced in the final optimization criterion:

$$\hat{h}(t) = \underset{h(t)}{\operatorname{argmin}} \left[\sum_{\tau=0}^{t} \lambda^{t-\tau} \varepsilon_{\tau}^2 \right] \tag{12.7}$$

This produces the following adaptive equations:

$$\Gamma^{-1}(t) = \frac{1}{\lambda} \left[\Gamma^{-1}(t-1) - \frac{\Gamma^{-1}(t-1)s(t)s^T(t)\Gamma^{-1}(t-1)}{\lambda + s^T(t)\Gamma^{-1}(t-1)s(t)} \right]$$

$$\varepsilon(t) = r(t) - h^T(t)s(t)$$

$$h(t+1) = h(t) + \alpha(t)\Gamma^{-1}(t)s(t)\varepsilon(t) \tag{12.8}$$

$$\alpha(t) = \frac{1}{\lambda + s^T(t)\Gamma^{-1}(t)s(t)}$$

This version has a time complexity $O(L^2)$. In fast RLS (FRLS) algorithms, the propagation of the inverse autocovariance matrix $\Gamma^{-1}(t)$ is performed using the Kalman gain within a prediction frame (Cioffi, 1984). The FRLS algorithms have a reduced complexity $O(L)$.

12.2.5. Design Considerations

The design of the system represented in Figure 12.1 assumes that the signal produced near the speaker whose utterance is to be recognized is uncorrelated with the speech signal. Unfortunately this assumption is often false, leading to convergence problems that can be alleviated by choosing a small adaptation step α with an increase in convergence time. Other practical considerations should be made for echo cancelling in the hands-free mobile communications environment where dealing with ambient noise and the detection of double-talk are relevant problems. For ambient noise, filtering structures are defined to combine speech enhancement and echo cancelling algorithms (Guelou *et al.*, 1996). A double-talk detector is described in Capman *et al.* (1995).

12.2.6. Endpoint Detection

Endpoint detection is very important for ASR, especially in the case of isolated words or short commands. Even if word boundary detection prior to recognition is not necessary in continuous speech, a decision module has to be introduced to determine when recognition should produce an output. Such a decision is generally made at the end of a group of words or at the end of a sentence.

Acoustic events are usually bound by changes in some acoustic parameters, like energy, describing the signal. Vocal-activity detectors generally determine these changes in the observed signal and interpret them. Detection of such changes is often based on speech processing techniques, while interpretation of change is generally based on the knowledge about the speech signal and the noise that may affect it. This knowledge is usually about temporal and spectral characteristics of the speech signal but may also involve environmental noise, spurious noise and frequency distortions that may be present in a given application.

Usually, endpoint detection is based on the computation of the signal energy as a function of time. The logarithm of the energy is computed for fixed-length signal windows that are generally shifted in time at a constant rate. A predefined threshold can be used to classify a signal frame as "speech" or "non-speech". Constraints on word and noise duration can be imposed in order to better classify a sequence of frames by a global automaton used for on-line detection of the beginning and ending points of an utterance. Several energy and duration thresholds may be used by a detection automaton. Energy-based detectors are very sensitive to variations in SNR. To improve their robustness, algorithms have been proposed to adapt the threshold according to the power of the ambient noise (Lamel *et al.*, 1981; Fissore, 1990; Mauuary, 1993). Energies in subbands can also be used in a feature vector in order to detect speech/non-speech boundaries (Mauuary, 1994).

12.2.7. Additive Noise and Frequency Distortions

In order to take into account additive noise and frequency distortions, an observed one-sensor speech signal $y(t)$ is expressed by the sum of the clean speech signal $s(t)$ and the additive noise signal $n(t)$, the whole convoluted with the frequency distortion impulse response $d(t)$:

$$y(t) = [s(t) + n(t)] * d(t) - x(t) * d(t) \qquad (12.9)$$

where $*$ designates the convolution operator.

Two disturbing components, one additive and the other convoluted, exist in $y(t)$. To better understand the effects of these components on the recognition performance, it is necessary to project (12.9) into the feature space where decoding is performed. The short-term spectrum energies of equation (12.9) have the following relation:

$$\Gamma_y(f) = \Gamma_x(f)|D(f)|^2 = [\Gamma_s(f) + \Gamma_n(f)]|D(f)|^2 \qquad (12.10)$$

where $\Gamma_u(f)$ and $|D(f)|^2$ designate the power spectral density of the signals $u(t)$ and of the transfer function of $d(t)$ respectively. Usually, energies are computed in frequency bins and f represents the central frequency of the bin.

Considering the logarithm of the functions in equation (12.10) one gets:

$$\Gamma_y^1(f) = \Gamma_x^1(f) + \log[|D(f)|^2]$$

$$= \left[\Gamma_s^1(f) + \log\left\{1 + \frac{\Gamma_n(f)}{\Gamma_s(f)}\right\}\right] + \log[|D(f)|^2] \tag{12.11}$$

$$\Gamma_y^1(f) = \left[\Gamma_s^1(f) + \log\left\{1 + \frac{1}{SNR(f)}\right\}\right] + \log[|D(f)|^2]$$

where $\Gamma_u^1(f)$ designates the logarithm of $\Gamma_u(f)$, and $SNR(f)$ is the signal-to-noise ratio in the frequency bin f.

It can be seen from (12.11) that, for simple cases where additive noise is stationary and the convoluted distortion is a linear time invariant (LTI) filter, the disturbing components in the log-spectral space are non-linear, since the additive noise introduces a non-linear effect.

In fact, the effect of the additive noise is expressed in terms of SNR in each frequency bin. This is the cause of additional complexity. This non-linearity remains when transforming (12.11) into the cepstral domain, since the inverse Fourier transform is linear (orthonormal), leading to:

$$C_y(\tau) = C_s(\tau) + C_{SNR}(\tau) + C(\tau) \tag{12.12}$$

where $C_u(t)$ designates the cepstral transformation of $u(t)$, τ is the "quefrency" index and $C_{SNR}(t)$ is the inverse Fourier transform of the term:

$$\log\left\{1 + \frac{1}{SNR(f)}\right\}$$

For signals with relatively high "signal-to-additive-noise ratio", only the transmission channel and the microphone introduce noisy components which can be considered as convoluted. In such a case and following equation (12.12), biases are introduced in the feature space. However, the problem remains complex, since even if we suppose that an LTI filter represents this convoluted component, its coefficients vary, for example, from one telephone call to another. It is therefore interesting to make the system robust to these effects, which often implies performing a blind equalization.

For signals with constant convoluted perturbations (fixed microphone and acquisition channel) and relatively low-signal-to-additive noise ratio, the problem is compensating for the effect of the additive noise. This may typically be done by using speech enhancement algorithms.

Several applications have both convoluted perturbations and additive noise affecting the signal. For example, recognition over mobile cellular networks should consider both convolved disturbing components and additive environmental noise. Moreover, in this specific environment, other noise components exist and are more difficult to compensate (channel fading, low coding rates).

A number of solutions are presented in the following that deal with additive noise and frequency distortions slowly varying with time.

12.3. ROBUST FEATURE ANALYSIS

In the presence of noise or other sources of distortion, recognition rates become poor when classical spectral representations are used because they fail to extract essential information in adverse environments. In recent years, new robust feature analysis techniques and the corresponding distance measures have been proposed.

In order to better understand and characterize the temporal evolution of the information carried out by the speech signal, time–frequency distributions (Cohen, 1989b), introduced in Chapter 3, have been considered. Several types of functions exist which satisfy some general characteristics that can be derived from their kernel functions. Nevertheless, time–frequency distributions mainly suffer from the propagation in time of the frequency characteristics. Spectrograms are usually obtained from windowed parts of the signal considered to be stationary. Although they do not correspond to a complete analytic function, they have become popular because of their computational simplicity. These representations have problems too, related to the use of short-time windows for consistency with the stationary hypothesis.

Even if other distributions, like wavelets and Wigner–Ville, have been proposed for spectral analysis on stationary windows (Lienard, 1987; Kronland-Martinet, 1988), only spectrogram-based representations are considered in this section. These spectral representations are generally based on the second-order moment. The use of higher order statistics-based (HOS) representations (Nikias and Mendel, 1993), which are robust to noise (Petropulu, 1990) is limited by their computational costs. Two classes of representations in the frequency domain are of particular importance:

- Spectral and model-based representations, which assume a parametric model of the signal frame: feature parameters are derived from the parameters of this model, and psycho-acoustical knowledge is generally included in these representations.
- Auditory-based representations: these are based on a model of the human auditory system.

12.3.1. Spectral- and Model-Based Representations

Let $s(k)$ be the sequence of samples of a random signal (e.g. the speech signal) where k is a discrete index. Assuming that its temporal evolution is described by a model, the model parameters are the representation of $s(k)$, where k represents the kth signal sample. In general, the model of the signal is a linear combination of functions which are the vectors of a given basis $\langle \Phi_p(k) \rangle$ (Cadzow, 1990):

$$s(k) = \sum_{p=1}^{P} a_p \Phi_p(k) \tag{12.13}$$

where P denotes the number of vectors in the basis.

Since it is impossible to process an infinite number of basis vectors unlimited in time, the basis dimension is generally limited to P and the temporal definition of the vectors (as well as $s(k)$) is limited to the analysis window size N. These practical constraints introduce an error frame into the modelling process, making it difficult to satisfy (12.13). The model produces a signal $\hat{s}(k)$ that must be close, following a given criterion, to the signal $s(k)$. The commonly used criterion to minimize is the least square error (LSE):

$$\sum_{k=1}^{N} (w_k[s(k) - \hat{s}(k)]^2) \tag{12.14}$$

where the $\{w_k\}$ are the samples of the analysis window (lifter).

The choice of the basis vectors characterizes the modelling type. For discrete Fourier transform (DFT), the basis vectors are a set of complex sinusoids and, in this specific case, there is no modelling error. In the case of autoregressive (AR) modelling, also known as "linear predictor coding" (LPC), the basis vector $\Phi_p(k)$ is the vector of the P preceding signal samples. In speech recognition, one can distinguish two main classes of analysis techniques, the first is based on filter bank modelling, the second on LPC modelling. These techniques are now reviewed from the point of view of robustness.

Filter bank-based spectral representations

As was described in Chapter 3, a filter bank defines a time-frequency distribution in which an energy is associated with the central frequency of each filter output. This can be obtained from the Page distribution (Cohen, 1989b). Figure 12.2 shows the block diagram of filter bank analysis.

A filter bank is generally characterized by the parameters described in the following.

• The distribution of the central frequencies of the band-pass filters and the corresponding bandwidths that were in the past uniformly distributed along the frequency scale. Following results of psycho-acoustic research, perceptually based filters were conceived to reproduce the critical bands of the ear, i.e. with central frequencies uniformly distributed on a perceptive scale (mel or bark scale). This scale is nearly linear below a frequency between 500 Hz and 1000 Hz and is logarithmic above 1000 Hz. A spectral analysis on a mel-type frequency scale increases the resolution at low frequencies. This

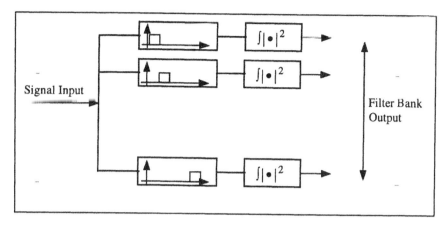

Figure 12.2 Block diagram of filter bank analysis.

agrees with the fact that the speech signal has most of its useful information at low frequencies.

- The number of filters, for the choice of which there is unfortunately no theory available. Generally, this parameter is empirically fixed to 24, corresponding to the number of critical bands in the ear.
- Filter types whose corresponding energies can be computed by multiplying the spectral density or amplitude by a band-pass filter frequency–energy template. Triangular, trapezoidal and sinusoidal templates are often used.

Taking the logarithm of the filter bank outputs gives an acceptable feature vector. In White and Neely (1976) it was shown that these parameters are more appropriate than the LPC parameters for speech recognition. Nevertheless, there are spectral representations that are more suitable for speech recognition. In Chollet (1982), it is shown that cepstrum parameters are more robust than filter bank parameters. In Hunt and Lefebvre (1988), experiments are described using an auditory model that produces more appropriate features for speech recognition than the classical filter bank. Even if more robust and effective parameters can be extracted, filter banks remain a widely used technique to estimate the spectral characteristics on the basis of which several other features can be extracted.

Mel frequency cepstral coefficients (MFCC)

Homomorphic analysis (Oppenheim *et al.*, 1968) of speech has been introduced in Chapter 3. The basic scheme is reproduced in Figure 12.3.

The resulting cepstrum $C_s(\tau)$ is defined in the frequency domain that is a temporal dimension. For voiced speech signals, the pitch has a rather low frequency

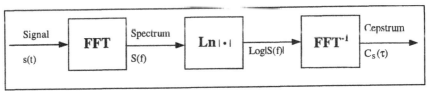

Figure 12.3 Basic scheme of homomorphic analysis.

with respect to the formants. Thus, the cepstrum of the vocal-tract transfer function is represented by low quefrency samples, while the cepstrum portion of the pitch has high quefrency indices. One can easily separate the pitch from the vocal-tract impulse responses in the cepstral domain by simply windowing in the quefrency domain.

Since the first cepstral coefficients represent the vocal-tract impulse response, which is generally speaker independent, these coefficients are commonly used for speech recognition. The fact that cepstral coefficients separate vocal-tract response and pitch impulse characteristics makes them very robust for speech recognition. Moreover, these parameters are not sensitive to the power of the input signal. If the analysed signal is multiplied by a gain factor, this introduces a bias in the log-spectral domain that is completely removed by the inverse Fourier transform for all indices different from 0. Besides, an easy to compute and effective Euclidean distance measure can be directly defined in the cepstral space, as will be described later.

As the filter bank outputs give a smoothed version of the spectral density of the analysis frame, the mel frequency cepstral coefficients (MFCC), introduced in Chapter 3, can be obtained by replacing the inverse FFT with the inverse cosine transform. This replacement is permissible because of the symmetry of the spectral density. These parameters are largely used in speech recognition and are often weighted by a given lifter.

Linear discriminant analysis

Linear discriminant analysis (LDA) is a statistical technique introduced in Chapter 4 and is considered here for robust feature extraction. Let us consider the following matrices:

- the global covariance matrix G of all the sample elements independent of their classes
- the within-class covariance matrix W that is the mean of the covariance matrices corresponding to each class
- the between-class covariance matrix B of the means of the different classes.

With Huygens' theorem it is proven that $G = W + B$.

In order to obtain good discrimination between different classes, the observation vectors may be projected on discriminant axes in such a way that the elements of a class are close to each other (small within-class variances) and the elements of different classes have sufficiently large between-class variances.

It can be shown that the first discriminant axis is the eigenvector corresponding to the highest eigenvalue of $G^{-1}B$, and that the eigenvalues of $G^{-1}B$ are positive with value less than 1. Once the first discriminant axis is determined, the second one is chosen as the eigenvector that corresponds to the remaining most significant eigenvalue or discriminant factor. All the eigenvectors corresponding to the significant eigenvalues can be considered and define the discriminant space where it is convenient to project the observations.

In general, LDA reduces the spectral representation space dimension and increases the discrimination in the reduced resulting space. In Hunt and Lefebvre (1988, 1989), LDA is used in a proposed representation called "Integrated representation on mel-scale using linear discriminant analysis" (IMELDA), with three variants. In IMELDA1, LDA is applied to the output of a large filter bank in order to produce a reduced feature vector discriminant in the Fisher sense. This is an automatic approach to compute MFCC equivalent features. In IMELDA2, discriminant analysis is performed on static and dynamic filter bank outputs. In IMELDA3, an auditory model is approximated by applying LDA on the logarithm of the sum of the energies of every pair made of a filter and its second successor (for example 5th and 7th). This simulates a notch stop-band filter that is part of the proposed auditory model. Reported experiments show that IMELDA3 produces better results than IMELDA1 and IMELDA2. Generally, IMELDA produces better results than both the auditory model and the MFCC representation, in the recognition of isolated words in quiet and noisy environments.

LPC-based spectral representations

In Fant (1970a), the production model shown in Figure 12.4 is proposed. An active component, the excitation or source, and a passive component, the glottis, are followed by the vocal and nasal tract models. The source generates a sequence of pulses regularly spaced in time for voiced sounds and a white noise for unvoiced sounds. The glottis acts as a low-pass filter with a cutoff frequency around 100 Hz for male speakers and 175 Hz for female speakers. The vocal tract can be approximated by an all-pole filter and the lip radiation by an all-zero filter or a moving-average (MA) model. The nasal tract has a fixed model connected to the vocal-tract one for producing nasalized sounds. Thus, an autoregressive moving-average (ARMA) model reliably approximates this speech production model. In general, the ARMA model is approximated by an autoregressive (AR) model that is simpler and has parameters that are easy to estimate. For the sake of simplicity, the source signal $e(t)$ can be white noise.

The LPC coefficients, introduced in Chapter 3, completely determine the frequency characteristics of a frame. The resulted spectral density is smoothed

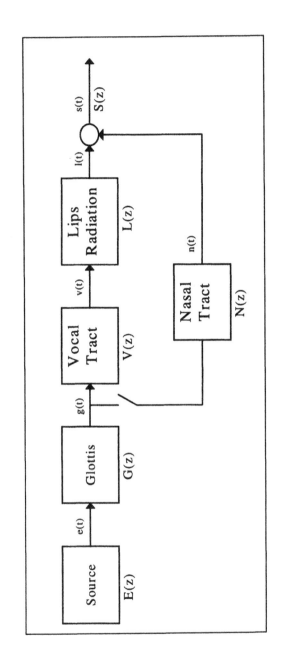

Figure 12.4 Speech production model.

by the AR model. This smoothed spectral density is adequate for speech recognition (Makhoul, 1975, 1977).

The presence of noise in the observed signal severely reduces the quality of the AR estimator. In Kay (1979), the effects of noise on the AR spectral estimator are described. Considering that the model of an AR signal, corrupted by additive noise, is an ARMA model, approximating this model by a finite-order AR model introduces confusion in the spectral estimation. A possible solution to this problem consists of increasing the order of the AR model. Nevertheless, attention should be paid to the fact that when the model order increases, the newly introduced poles come close to the poles of the clean signal AR model, making the global model very sensitive to the estimation of the autocovariance (or autocorrelation) matrix. Small estimation errors in the autocorrelation function may produce spurious peaks in the signal spectra. In Tierney (1980), it is shown that introducing a Hamming weighting window and a preprocessing preemphasis filter improves the spectral estimation of speech in presence of additive noise.

Cepstral parameters

Cepstral coefficients have been introduced in Chapter 3 and can be directly computed from AR coefficients using a recursive procedure. The use of their time derivative in robust ASR is discussed below.

Line spectrum pairs (LSP)

Line spectral pairs (LSP) (Itakura, 1975a), introduced in Chapter 3, have found extensive application in speech coding (Soong and Juang, 1984). The main idea is to extend a pth order AR model to the order $(p + 1)$ without additional information. This can be done by constraining $(p + 1)$th reflection coefficient K_{p+1} to be $+1$ or -1:

$$A_{p+1}(z) = A_p(z) \pm z^{-(p+1)} A_p(z^{-1}) \qquad (12.15)$$

Two polynomials, $P(z)$ (for $K_{p+1} = 1$) and $Q(z)$ (for $K_{p+1} = -1$), can be defined. It is obvious that $P(z)$ is symmetric and $Q(z)$ is anti-symmetric. Other important characteristics of these two polynomials are:

- Their zeros are on the unit circle.
- Their zeros are interlaced with each other.
- Minimum phase property of $A_p(z)$ is conserved after the quantization of their zeros.

The first two properties are very useful for simplifying the computation of the zeros. Several approaches have been proposed for the computation of these zeros. Among them, the use of Chebyshev polynomials is described in Kabal and Ramachundran (1986).

In Soong and Juang (1984), a spectral-based distance measure based on LSP parameters has been defined. It consists of first finding the spectral characteristics and then comparing the resulting spectra. This requires a high computational complexity. Several other distances based on LSP parameters measures have been experimented (Gurgen *et al.*, 1990). In Paliwal (1992b) it is shown that a good compromise for robust speech recognition is to use the LSP parameters combined with the first derivative of the cepstral coefficients.

Short-time modified coherence (SMC)

This technique is described in Mansour and Juang (1988, 1989a) and consists of the estimation of the AR parameters in the autocorrelation domain. The result has interesting properties for noise reduction (McGinn and Johnson, 1983). It has been shown that autocorrelation is a pole-preserving operation if the excitation is white noise or a pulse train. The autocorrelation of an all-pole sequence, with z-transform $\sigma/A(z)$, is an all-pole sequence with z-transform:

$$1/A(z)A(z^{-1})$$

with a proper gain term. So, using the autocorrelation function where the noise effects are reduced (the autocorrelation function of white noise is a Dirac function), the poles of $1/A(z)A(z^{-1})$ can be directly computed. This has two drawbacks:

- The increase in order from p to $2p$ increases the complexity of calculus of p double poles.
- The interaction between the pitch and the speech formants is more pronounced.

In order to overcome these problems, it was proposed to apply a spectral shaper (square-root function) that reduces by two the dynamic range in the log-spectral domain. The order of the AR model becomes p again and the interaction between pitch and formants is reduced. Figure 12.5 summarizes the SMC analysis principle. The Hamming window is useful to reduce the sidelobe effects enhanced by the increase of the spectral dynamic range.

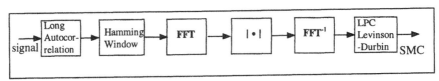

Figure 12.5 SMC analysis scheme.

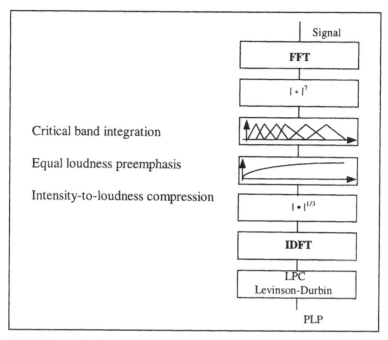

Figure 12.6 Scheme for the computation of PLP parameters.

From the SMC coefficients, the corresponding cepstral coefficients may be computed and used as feature vectors for robust speech recognition.

Perceptually based linear prediction (PLP)

Robust and discriminant representations of speech signal, are obtained with PLP that introduces psychoacoustical knowledge in the estimation of the AR model parameters (Hermansky, 1987; Hermansky and Junqua, 1988; Junqua and Wakita, 1989). Figure 12.6 shows the general scheme for the computation of PLP parameters.

Analytic critical band integration with the mel scale consists of performing linear prediction with a non-linear frequency scale. To improve spectral analysis, resolution must be increased in the low frequencies where a maximum of information exists. In Oppenheim *et al.* (1971), a computational method using FFT is proposed for spectra with non-uniform resolution on the frequency scale. A procedure for implementing a frequency warping all-pass transformation, known as bilinear transformation, estimates the AR parameters (of order p) using the outputs of p successive filters. These dephasing filters are preceded by a corrective filter in order to obtain an all-pass filter. The block diagram of the procedure is depicted in Figure 12.7.

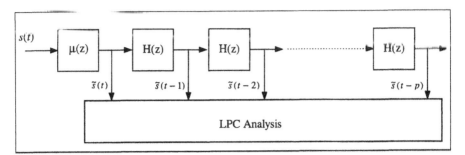

Figure 12.7 Scheme of bilinear transformation.

If first-order dephasing filters are considered with a z-transfer function $H(z)$ of the form:

$$H(z) = \frac{z^{-1} - \alpha}{1 - \alpha z^{-1}}, \quad \text{where } -1.0 \le \alpha \le 1.0 \tag{12.16}$$

then the frequency transformation is expressed by the following relation, where normalized frequencies are considered:

$$\omega' = 2\pi f' = \theta(2\pi f) = \tan^{-1} \left| \frac{(1 - \alpha^2)\sin(2\pi f)}{(1 - \alpha^2)\cos(2\pi f) - 2\alpha} \right| \tag{12.17}$$

and the corrective filter has a transfer function expressed by the following relation:

$$\mu(z) = \frac{1 - \alpha^2}{(1 - \alpha z^{-1})^2} \tag{12.18}$$

As this warping transformation corresponds to a good approximation of the mel scale it is of great interest for speech recognition, and has been integrated with SMC analysis, as described in Mokbel and Chollet (1995a).

Root homomorphic cepstral representation

In the computation of the real cepstrum, under the assumption that the signal phase is a minimum, the phase of the signal is neglected. This may introduce some discontinuities in the logarithmic spectrogram. These discontinuities can be seen as biases in spectral estimation. To overcome this problem, several approaches are proposed. In Lim (1979), the generalized cepstrum ("Spectral root deconvolution system", SRDS) is proposed as an alternative to the cepstrum where the logarithm function is replaced by the power function $(.)^\gamma$ in the computation module. Several methods for improving the estimation of the generalized cepstrum have been proposed (Kobayashi and Imai, 1984; Imai and Furuichi, 1988; Tokuda *et al.*, 1990). A simple root cepstral analysis approach is proposed in Alexandre and Lockwood (1993), where the classical computation of the autocorrelation sequence (by applying an inverse Fourier transform on the spectral density) is modified by changing the square of the short-time spectrum to the function $(.)^{\gamma}$.

Non-linear estimation of AR parameters

Following Lim and Oppenheim (1978), all-pole modelling of degraded speech is introduced hereafter. Let $x(t) = s(t) + n(t)$ be the observed signal where $n(t)$ denotes an additive noise. The prediction equation is given by:

$$a^T x_{p+1}(t) = e(t) + a^T n_{p+1}(t) \tag{12.19}$$

a being the parameters of the AR model of the clean speech signal.

Maximum *a posteriori* (MAP) estimation introduced in Chapter 6 is considered here for the maximization of $\Pr(a/x_N(t))$, which is dependent on the vector a. The maximization of this probability produces a set of non-linear equations. No simple solution exists for these equations.

Actually, this is a problem of incomplete data because the real AR sequence is not observed. Expectation-maximization (EM) algorithms offer an effective iterative solution for this kind of problem. Beginning with an assumed set of initial values for the vector a, the most likely estimate of the clean signal $s_N(t)$ can be computed. On the basis of the clean signal estimate, a new estimation of the AR parameters can be obtained, and this procedure can continue until convergence. Unfortunately, this converges to a *local* maximum of the joint probability density $p(a, s_N(t)/x_N(t), \sigma^2, \ldots)$. The initial values of the AR parameters determine whether or not the EM algorithm converges on the global optimum, or only on a local one. This procedure requires a great amount of computation for an estimate of the clean signal knowing some values for the AR vector parameters. If the window length increases, finding the estimate for the clean signal, knowing the AR model, has analogies with the design of a non-causal Wiener filter in the sense of minimum mean square error (MMSE). So, $s_N(t)$ can be computed by filtering $x_N(t)$ with a linear time invariant (LTI) Wiener filter. With this procedure a better spectral estimation of the speech signal in background additive noise can be obtained. It has also been shown that increasing the number of iterations, makes the clean signal converge to a perfect AR signal, which means that the formant bandwidths turn out to be very narrow. This makes it possible to perform just two or three iterations.

Other stochastic approaches have been proposed to improve spectral AR estimation in presence of additive noise (Preuss and Yarlagadda, 1984; Feder *et al.*, 1987). In Hansen and Clements (1987, 1991), inter-frame and within-frame constraints (expressed in the LSP domain) have been integrated into the algorithm. These constraints are relative to the formant bandwidths and to the continuity of the spectral peaks.

Some other techniques have been proposed to increase the robustness of linear prediction of speech. The main idea is to associate an appropriate non-uniform weighting function w_n with the residuals in the mean square error criterion (Lee, 1988a; Ma *et al.*, 1993) given by (12.14). These techniques take into account the non-Gaussian nature of the speech signal. In Kamp and Ma (1993), a relation between weighted LPC and high-order statistics for AR model estimation is established.

In order to determine a robust AR modelling in presence of noise, high-order Yule–Walker Equations (HOYWE) (Kay, 1980) can be used. As in the case of SMC techniques, autocorrelation exhibits interesting properties for noise processing, for example the autocorrelation function of a white Gaussian noise is a simple Dirac function. In HOYWE (similar to the classical Yule–Walker equations), the autocorrelation function at shift 0 is discarded from the covariance matrix. This provides more robustness to additive noise. However this method suffers from the sensitive estimation of the autocorrelation at high shifts. In Chan and Langford (1982), a "singular value decomposition" (SVD)-based (via pseudo-inverse) solution is proposed. In other work, Yule–Walker equations are used and robustness is increased by modifying the autocorrelation with a distortion function as shown in Jain and Xu (1987).

12.3.2. Dynamic Feature Vectors

The variation or the movement of the spectral information, such as the first and second derivatives of cepstral parameters with time, can be very useful for ASR (Furui, 1986; Aikawa and Furui, 1988) since it is more robust to variations of environments or speakers. Dynamic features were found to be robust and are often added to the cepstra vectors. These derivatives are usually computed over several frames as regression coefficients.

12.3.3. Auditory Model and Spectral Representations

The human auditory system is the best reference system capable of discriminating and interpreting sounds even under adverse conditions with a remarkable ability to adapt to the current environment. Major research effort has been made to understand the physiology of this system and the reasons for its high performance. Several cochlea and other auditory models have been derived from these studies (Schroeder and Hall, 1974; Allen, 1985, 1989).

Sounds are generally processed by the following four steps in the human auditory system.

- External and middle-ear signal processing to localize the sound source and to reduce the echo and reverberation effects: this processing can be modelled using linear band-pass (or low-pass) filters.

- Signal analysis by cochlea filtering performed by the basilar membrane and the organ of Corti: this filtering is similar to a filter bank defined on a non-linear frequency scale (mel scale). In Allen (1985), measures of cochlea impulse response are reported.
- Cochlea mechanical-to-electrical transduction performed at the output of the cochlea: this is a non-linear phenomenon characorized by a signal rectifier and a logarithmic compression coupled with a sort of automatic gain control (AGC) (Schroeder and Hall, 1974). A lateral inhibition in time and frequency domains is performed at this stage (Evans, 1985). This lateral inhibition is very important for spectral analysis as shown in Dang and Carre (1987).
- Neural transduction: a non-linear process transforming the output of the preceding stage into temporally coded binary pulses. No exact model of this process is known.

Several auditory models have been proposed for use in speech recognition. Some of the most popular models are reviewed in the following. These models have been used for ASR experiments showing that auditory models improve recognition performances especially in degraded conditions when compared to classical LPC parameters, filter bank outputs or MFCCs.

In Ghitza (1986), a computational auditory model is described based on temporal information in the auditory nerve fibre firing patterns. This model performs an analysis in two stages. In the first stage, a filter bank with N band-pass filters ($N = 85$ for a global frequency band 200–3200 Hz (Ghitza, 1987)), uniformly distributed on a bark scale, produces the cochlea outputs. In the second stage, each signal at a filter output is processed by an analysis block that computes the synchrony in the firing pattern of the individual nerve fibres. For this purpose, a multilevel (L) crossing detection is first performed ($L = 7$ level thresholds have been uniformly chosen on a log-scale). The interval histograms of the levels crossing are computed and summed over all the frequency bands to produce the resulting "ensemble interval histogram" (EIH). A EIH spectrum can be simply computed from the EIH parameters by inverting the temporal intervals into frequencies. Figure 12.8 shows the basic chain of the Ghitza model.

EIH representation has a large and precise spectral resolution (Ghitza, 1987). Formant peaks are amplified with this approach even in presence of additive noise. LPC coefficients computed on the basis of EIH seem to be more robust to noise than those corresponding to an FFT, as reported in Ghitza (1987) and Sreenivas *et al.* (1990).

A cochlear model has been introduced and tested for speech recognition (Lyon and Dyer, 1986; Loeb and Lyon, 1987). It has served as a basis for other auditory representations such as "reduced auditory representation" (RAR) (Beet *et al.*, 1988; Beet, 1990). The model has several components. First, the input signal is differentiated and low-pass filtered. Then, the signal is passed through a cascade of notch biquadratic filters (64 filters) that have

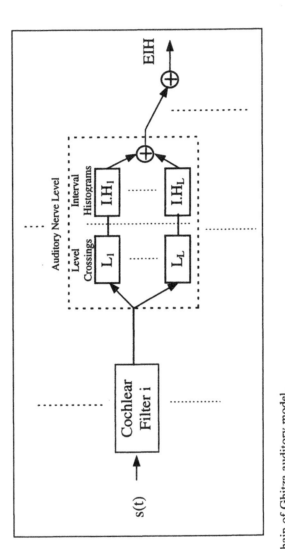

Figure 12.8 Basic chain of Ghitza auditory model.

their central frequencies distributed on a mel scale. The resulting signals are filtered by biquadratic resonant filters. The next stage of the model consists of three levels of dynamic range compression. Each compression level has a different adaptation speed, but an equal influence on the gain of its neighbours. The compressed signals are then rectified using a saturating soft half-wave rectifier. This produces a simulated version of the current flow in the hair cells. Finally, the obtained current flow causes neuron firing.

In Loeb and Lyon (1987), speech recognition experiments with this model are described. The results were encouraging. In RAR, three important parts of the model are considered:

- the filter bank
- the non-linear range compression
- the neural transduction that transforms the signal at the output of the preceding stage into time-coded impulses.

Three parameters are defined to characterize the basilar membrane displacements. Associating these parameters with Euclidean distance measures produces worse recognition performance than simple filter bank parameters. When using a discrimination measure called "position-tolerant", the RAR parameters outperform the classical filter bank even in the presence of additive noise.

In Seneff (1984), another auditory model was proposed that has since been used for speech recognition (Hunt and Lefebvre, 1986, 1988, 1989). This auditory model has three stages. The first one has a filter bank with 32 filters distributed on the critical bands between 200 Hz and 2700 Hz. At the output a non-linear compression of the signal envelope is performed with the following relation:

$$y(k) = \frac{x(k)}{D + ||x(k)||_\tau}$$

where $x(k)$, $y(k)$ and D denote the input, the output and a constant of the compression module, and $||x(k)||_\tau$ denotes the mean energy of the input signal over a period τ.

The compressed signal is then rectified before entering the next stage formed by a set of "generalized synchrony detectors" (GSD). The GSD compares the signal with its delayed version, the delay corresponds to the central frequency of the channel, and, in the case of synchrony, the GSD amplifies the signal. Thus GSD amplifies the formants. Finally, a pseudo-spectrogram can be computed when considering the outputs of the 32 channels as energies affected to the corresponding central frequencies.

Experiments with a modified version of this model are described in Hunt and Lefebvre (1986) for speaker dependent digits recognition in presence of additive noise and spectral tilt. Variants of this model outperform the classical MFCC, especially in noisy conditions.

12.3.4 Distance Measures

The definition of a spectral representation is not sufficient to completely characterize the observation space. A distance measure should be associated with the spectral representation in order to quantify similarity between representations. The choice of a spectral representation and a distance measure is an important robustness factor for an ASR system.

In general, a distance is called a metric if it satisfies the three properties:

- it is a similarity measure: $d(a, b) = 0 \Leftrightarrow a \equiv b$,
- it is symmetric: $d(a, b) = d(b, a)$,
- it satisfies the triangular inequality: $d(a, b) + d(b, c) \geq d(a, c)$.

Spectral distances are used for comparing representations, for clustering data and for transforming parameters.

A number of popular distance measures do not satisfy the metric properties, e.g. those between probability distributions and some of those used in speech processing for which triangular inequality or symmetry are not always satisfied. Nevertheless, in most of the cases, these distance measures are based on plausible physical motivations, on an optimality criterion, or on information theory (Basseville, 1989). In the following, the most commonly used distance measures for speech recognition are reviewed.

Log-spectral deviation

The distance between two spectral densities S_1 and S_2 can be measured as the Lq norm of their difference introduced in Chapter 4.

This distance is highly sensitive to variations in the measurement scale. To overcome this drawback, the log-spectral deviation measure is defined as the Lq norm of the difference of the logarithms of the spectra. This distance is invariant with respect to the measure scale. In general, computational efficiency suggests choosing value of 1 or 2 for q. It can be shown that $d_\infty \leq d_2 \leq d_1$. In Gray and Markel (1976), it is experimentally shown that, for speech spectra computed with the FFT, d_2 is equivalent to d_∞. In speech recognition, this distance is not directly computed on the spectral densities but on the filter bank outputs, which represent a smoothed version of the spectral densities. In Lee (1991), the log-spectral deviation distance is derived from the *generalized Kolmogorov variational distance* in the general framework of information theory.

Cepstral distance

The cepstral distance, defined in Chapter 4, is an approximation of the log-spectral deviation distance, and is the most commonly used distance in speech processing. In Lee (1991), it is shown that the cepstral distance, like the log-spectral deviation distance, can be derived from the *generalized Kolmogorov variational* distance.

Mahalanobis distance or weighted cepstral distance

In Lq-norm-based distance measures, the different dimensions of the observation space uniformly contribute to the global measure. However, the variances of the cepstral coefficients decrease exponentially with the cepstral index. This implies that, for simple cepstral distance, the first cepstral coefficients are the most relevant for discrimination. The Mahalanobis distance is a remedy to this problem and may be obtained by equating the weighting matrix to the inverse of the diagonal covariance matrix.

Global and within-class variances may be used to weight the cepstral dimensions in the weighted cepstral distance measure. In Tohkura (1986) several weighting lifters are considered for application to ASR. In a recognition system, the weighted cepstral distance measure appears to overcome the classical cepstral distance measure. In Hunt and Lefebvre (1989), it is shown that within-class variance weighting has better performance than global variance weighting for speech recognition in noise. In Lee (1991), it is shown that the weighted cepstral distance approximates the Kullback–Leibler divergence distance.

Kullback distance

The Kullback distance between two representations $f_1(y)$ and $f_2(y)$ is defined as follows:

$$\int_{\Omega_y} [f_1(y) - f_2(y)] \ln \frac{f_1(y)}{f_2(y)} \, dy$$

This distance is generally used to measure similarities between statistical distributions associated with HMMs.

Root-power sums (RPS)

This distance is also known as the "quefrency weighted cepstral distance measure" and is a special case of the weighted cepstral distance in which cepstral coefficients are weighted by their indices.

In Hansen (1986), it is shown that weighting the cepstral coefficients by their indices is equivalent to computing the distance between the spectral slopes that are much more invariant than the spectra. The relation is:

$$\sum_{i=-\infty}^{\infty} i^2 [C_1(i) - C_2(i)]^2 = \frac{1}{2\pi} \int_{-\pi}^{\pi} \left| \frac{\partial \ln |S_2(\omega)|}{\partial \omega} - \frac{\partial \ln |S_1(\omega)|}{\partial \omega} \right|^2 d\omega \quad (12.20)$$

A relation exists between the RPS distance and the weighted cepstral distance. Actually, an equivalence exists between the inverse of the variances and the indices up to a given order (Tohkura, 1986). The RPS distance has been largely used with the PLP spectral representation for ASR (Junqua and Wakita, 1989) and seems to produce better results than the cepstral distance. In Hunt and Lefebvre (1989), it is suggested that weighting with the inverse of the within-class variance in clustering patterns of the same word outperforms the RPS distance.

Band-pass liftering

Liftering was introduced in Juang *et al.* (1987) with the purpose of analytically defining a parametric function that approximates the inverse of the variances of the cepstral coefficients. For this purpose, the logarithm of the spectra is supposed to be ergodic, with constant mean and variance exponentially decreasing with frequency. Using these hypotheses, the optimal lifter in the cepstral domain is defined as:

$$w_k = 1 + h\sin(\pi k/P) \quad k = 1, -, p \qquad (12.21)$$

where P is the dimension of cepstral vectors. It has been empirically shown that an optimal value of h is $P/2$. Experiments have shown that combining the band-pass lifter with SMCC vectors produces large improvements, especially for ASR in noise. This lifter down-weights the first and last cepstral coefficients. It can be seen as an inverse variance lifter combined with a reduction of the cepstral coefficients of high order. This reduction is important because these cepstral coefficients are more sensitive to white noise or even low-frequency coloured noises.

Cepstral projection distance

In Mansour and Juang (1989a), the effect of white additive noise on the cepstral vectors is discussed. Two main effects have been made evident:

- a reduction of the amplitudes of the cepstral vectors
- a rotation of the cepstral vectors by an angle β, with $|\beta| < \pi/2$.

These effects can be equalized by using a projection operator:

$$d_\lambda(C_1, C_2) = (C_2 - \lambda C_1)^T (C_2 - \lambda C_1) \qquad (12.22)$$

Using the orthogonality principle, the parameter λ can be computed in order to minimize the distance independently of the sound segment. This implies that:

$$\lambda_{\text{opt}} = \frac{C_2^T C_1}{C_1^T C_1} \qquad (12.23)$$

and the optimal distance is given by:

$$d_{opt}(C_1, C_2) = |C_2|^2 (1 - \cos^2(\beta)) \tag{12.24}$$

where:

$$\cos(\beta) = \frac{C_2^T \cdot C_1}{|C_2| \cdot |C_1|}$$

By introducing a factor to compensate for the amplitude reduction of the cepstral vectors, the projection distance becomes:

$$d_{opt}(C_1, C_2) = |C_2|^\alpha (1 - \cos(\beta)), \quad \text{where } a = 0, 1, 2 \ldots$$

Recognition experiments show that an optimal value for the parameter α is one. These experiments also show that the cepstral projection distance outperforms the cepstral distance. Using this distance, SMC and LPC representations have been compared with the result that SMC is more robust than LPC for low SNR. However, LPC slightly outperforms SMC for high SNR. In Lee (1991), it is shown that this distance approximates the Battacharyya distance for $\alpha = 0$.

Itakura and weighted Itakura distances

The Itakura distance measure was introduced to compare LPC vectors without having to compute the cepstral parameters. In fact, an Euclidean distance on the AR vectors has no physical justification.

This distance has important asymptotic properties (Basseville, 1989). A modification of this distance was introduced in order to increase its robustness to scaling factors:

$$d_I(S_1, S_2) = \min_\alpha d_{IS}(S_1, \alpha \cdot S_2) \tag{12.25}$$

The statistical properties of the Itakura distance are discussed in De Souza (1977) and Tribolet *et al.* (1979). In Gray and Markel (1976), this distance has been compared to a symmetrized version and to the cepstral distance. As there is no distance that has proven to be superior to any other, the cepstral distance is still considered to be the most attractive for simplicity and efficiency.

Recently, some modifications have been proposed in order to increase the robustness of the Itakura distance in the presence of noise (Soong and Sondhi, 1988). These modifications consist of modifying the reference spectra by broadening the bandwidth of the estimated formants.

12.3.5. Concluding Remarks on Representations and Distances

The performance of a speech recognition system generally depends on the robustness of its speech analysis component. For the purpose of increasing robustness, spectral representations and auditory-model-based representations have been introduced with corresponding distance measures. Using LDA on the filter bank outputs produces robust spectral representations. The SMCC vectors seem to be robust to the presence of additive noise. Introducing psycho-acoustical knowledge with the PLP representation increases the reliability of spectral analysis. Several distance measures and lifters have been combined with these representations. Weighting the cepstral vectors with the inverse of the variances seems to improve ASR performance. The band-pass lifter is suitable for speech recognition in noise. Cepstral distance is computationally effective with good performance. Cepstral projection distance seems to be adequate for speech recognition in noise. Pairs of spectral representation–distance measures have been compared in Hunt and Lefebvre (1989), Mokbel and Chollet (1995a) and Junqua and Wakita (1989). In Hunt and Lefebvre (1989), the IMELDA representation is reported to outperform the auditory model representation and several weighted MFCC representations. In Junqua and Wakita (1989) comparatively better results are obtained with the PLP model. Encouraging results are obtained with SMCC and band-pass liftering and projection distance with respect to more classical representations. However, weighted MFCCs, together with their derivatives, seem to be a good choice for a computationally effective and robust analysis.

12.4. SPEECH ENHANCEMENT AND CHANNEL EQUALIZATION

Unfortunately, there is no spectral representation containing discriminant feature parameters that are not sensitive to the signal acquisition conditions or environment variations. Some degree of robustness can be achieved by pre-processing the speech signals or the derived representation vectors in order to reduce the effects of disturbing components. Knowledge about the way they affect the signal is necessary in this case. Multisensor systems and the related algorithms can be used in presence of ambient noise, reverberation and other distortions.

12.4.1. Microphone Arrays and Beamforming

In Chapter 2 it has been shown that a microphone array is formed by a set of spatially distinct sensor elements. Omnidirectional microphones are used in these arrays. The spatial organization of the sensors is a complex problem that is generally solved empirically. A microphone array is used for capturing the signal emitted by a given source and for discarding other signals. This is very interesting for acoustical echo cancellation, de-reverberation and speech enhancement. In order to focus on a given direction, beamformer techniques are generally used. A beamformer compensates for the delays of the signal emitted from the target point and then sums the signals gathered by each microphone. The useful components of the observed signals are placed in phase and enhanced, while the disturbing components that have incoherent phases are reduced by interference.

Microphone arrays have been experimentally evaluated in speech processing applications, such as teleconferencing and speaker tracking (Flanagan *et al.*, 1991), speech enhancement, especially in a reverberant space (Zelinski, 1988; Liu *et al.*, 1996; Omologo and Svaizer, 1993; Grenier, 1993), and speech recognition in a noisy environment (Grenier, 1993; Van Compernolle, 1990). Speech recognition results presented in Van Compernolle (1990) show encouraging improvements with SNRs in the 15–20 dB range, especially with the GSC beamformer. Poor performance is observed with low SNRs (12 dB). Similar conclusions are described in Grenier (1993).

12.4.2 Spectral Subtraction

Spectral subtraction is a widely used technique for speech enhancement, especially for single-sensor signals. It basically consists of estimating spectral characteristics of the environmental noise in the non-speech segments of the signal and to use these characteristics to "clean" the short-term spectra of the observed noisy signals. A block diagram of the basic spectral subtraction method is shown in Figure 12.9.

The input signal samples are grouped into frames. A speech/non-speech detector indicates if the spectral characteristics of a given frame can be used to update the noise mean spectral characteristics. The short-time spectrum of a frame is generally computed using an FFT.[1] Then the short-spectrum amplitude and phase are computed. The mean spectral noise amplitude is subtracted from each amplitude sample to produce a new short-term enhanced spectrum. The corresponding enhanced speech frame may be derived using an inverse FFT. Finally, the "overlap and add" (OLA) technique (Griffin and Lin, 1984) is used to recover the whole signal from the enhanced frames. This approach assumes that the noise signal is stationary and independent from the clean speech signal.

The following theoretical framework is proposed to describe spectral subtraction using second-order moments. An observed sampled signal $x(k)$ is considered to be the sum of a clean signal $s(k)$ and an independent stationary noise $n(k)$. The clean signal is considered to be locally stationary:

$$x(k) = s(k) + n(k) \tag{12.26}$$

---

[1] The short-time spectrum computed by the speech analysis module of the ASR system can be used for this purpose

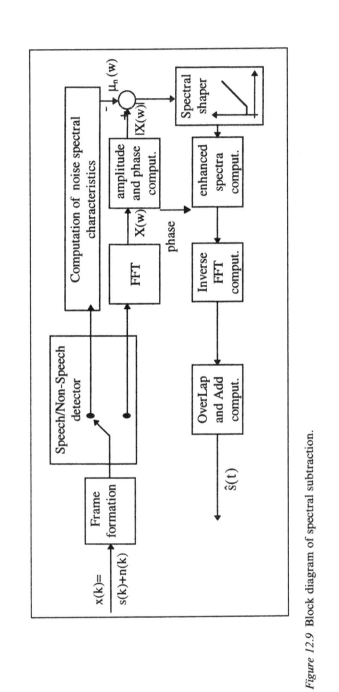

Figure 12.9 Block diagram of spectral subtraction.

Under the hypothesis that the clean signal and the additive noise are independent, the following relation holds between covariance matrices:

$$R_{xx} = R_{ss} + R_{nn} \tag{12.27}$$

where R_{uu} is the covariance matrix of the signal $u(k)$.

An estimate of the covariance matrix of the noisy signal can be obtained on a frame of length N: $\{x(1), x(2), \ldots, x(N)\}$. For this purpose, a circular matrix can be formed on the basis of the signal vector augmented by N zeros.

Using this circular matrix, an estimate of the covariance matrix can be obtained:

$$\hat{R}_{xx} = XX^{\#} \tag{12.28}$$

where $\#$ represents the conjugate transpose operator.

If F denotes the "discrete Fourier transform" (DFT) matrix, then (12.28) becomes:

$$\hat{R}_{xx} = F \operatorname{diag}(|\hat{X}(\omega)|)^2 F^{\#} \tag{12.29}$$

where $\hat{X}(\omega)$ designates the short-term spectrum of the signal frame extended by N zeros.

In order to obtain an estimate of the clean signal from the noisy signal, from (12.27) one gets:

$$\hat{R}_{ss} = \hat{R}_{xx} - \hat{R}_{nn} \tag{12.30}$$

where the estimate of the covariance matrix of the noisy signal is given by (12.29) and the estimate of the noise covariance matrix is computed using the non-speech segments. Using the definition of the Fourier transform matrix and of the circular signal matrix, (12.30) can be written as:

$$\hat{R}_{ss} = \hat{S}\hat{S}^{\#} = F \operatorname{Diag}(|\hat{X}(\omega)|^2 - |\hat{N}(\omega)|^2) F^{\#} \tag{12.31}$$

which, in turn, can be decomposed as following:

$$\hat{S}\hat{S}^{\#} = [F \operatorname{Diag}(\sqrt[2]{|\hat{X}(\omega)|^2 - |\hat{N}(\omega)|^2}) F^{\#}]$$
$$\times [F \operatorname{Diag}(\sqrt[2]{|\hat{X}(\omega)|^2 - |\hat{N}(\omega)|^2}) F^{\#}] \tag{12.32}$$

This equation ensures that a circular signal matrix is obtained, but does not ensure that the signal vector forming this matrix has N extending zeros. It would be interesting to try to solve this equation with the constraint that the final N elements of the clean signal vector are zeros. However, such a solution is not straightforward because it leads to non-linear equations, making the problem very difficult. Spectral subtraction suggests interesting solutions to this equation by fixing the clean signal phase to the phase of the noisy signal. The power spectral density estimates in (12.32) are used. Amplitude spectral subtraction is defined noticing that:

$$|\hat{X}(\omega)|^2 - |\hat{N}(\omega)|^2 = [|\hat{X}(\omega)| - |\hat{N}(\omega)|][|\hat{X}(\omega)| + |\hat{N}(\omega)|]$$

$$= [|\hat{X}(\omega)| - |\hat{N}(\omega)|]^2 + 2|\hat{N}(\omega)|[|\hat{X}(\omega)| - |\hat{N}(\omega)|]$$

$$\cong [|\hat{X}(\omega)| - |\hat{N}(\omega)|]^2 \qquad (12.33)$$

under the hypothesis:[2]

$$E[|N(\omega)|(|X(\omega)| - |N(\omega)|] = 0$$

Replacing (12.33) into (12.32), one gets:

$$\hat{S}\hat{S}^{\#} = [F\,\mathrm{Diag}(|\hat{X}(\omega)| - |\hat{N}(\omega)|)F^{\#}][F\,\mathrm{Diag}(|\hat{X}(\omega)| - |\hat{N}(\omega)|)F^{\#}) \qquad (12.34)$$

Both power spectral subtraction and spectral subtraction have the practical requirement that, at a given frequency bin, the spectral energy of the clean signal must be greater than the spectral energy of the noise. This may not be the case with spectral estimates. To overcome this problem, a minimum positive threshold is introduced in order to constrain the difference between the spectral energies of the observed signal and the noise to be positive.

In spectral subtraction, the phase of the estimated clean signal is forced to be equal to the phase of the noisy signal. This approximation is acceptable for speech since the influence of the phase of the signal is very weak on perception. However, this introduces distortions between successive frames. In order to reduce these distortions the OLA method is used, as shown in Figure 12.9.

Phase distortions caused by the inexact assumption of signal stationarity and the threshold introduced on the clean signal spectral energy increase the SNR but introduce a musical noise in the enhanced signal. This musical noise deteriorates the resulting signal quality.

Variants to spectral subtraction are proposed in the literature for reducing the effects of musical noise. In Berouti (1979), it is proposed to overestimate the noise mean spectrum by a factor α ($\alpha \geq 1$) to reduce the musical noise at the filter output. Several attempts have been proposed to optimize the factor α. In Lockwood and Boudy (1991), the overestimation factor is made dependent on the SNR in a given frequency bin. The proposed algorithm increases the overestimation factor when the SNR decreases. This is motivated by the fact that for spectral peaks, the signal has enough energy (high SNR) to mask the residual noise. Thus, for a specific frequency bin, the residual noise will not be perceived. This is not the case for spectral valleys (low SNR) where a residual noise can be perceived. Moreover, human perception is less sensitive to spectral valleys, allowing one to choose a large enough overestimation factor in these regions.

Another approach for spectral subtraction has been described in Mokbel and Chollet (1995a). The main idea is to constrain the enhanced frames at a fixed

---

[2]Valid for minimum phase signals (speech and noise).

distance from the corresponding clean signal (log-spectral deviation distance). This can be done by fixing the "signal to residual noise ratio" (SRNR) at the filter output which largely reduces the musical noise. This filter, unlike the filter proposed in Lockwood and Boudy (1991), overestimates the noise energy in frequency bands of high SNR and reduces the overestimation in frequency bands of low SNR. A modified spectral subtraction algorithm is proposed in Le Bouquin (1996). It performs an overestimation of noise which is in accordance with the filter developed in Mokbel (1995a).

The "minimum mean square error" (MMSE) criterion has also been used to improve the performance of spectral subtraction algorithms (Porter and Boll, 1984; Ephraim and Malah, 1984). In addition to the classical assumptions on stationarity and independence of noise and speech signals, in the MMSE framework, noise and signal are supposed to be Gaussian processes (with known or estimated parameters). In Ephraim and Malah (1984) a recursive estimation of these parameters is proposed.

In McAulay and Malpass (1980), a two-state model is proposed in order to improve the spectral subtraction performance. In the first state, the hypothesis $H_0(k)$ (no speech signal is present in the kth spectral component) is considered, while in the second state the hypothesis $H_1(k)$ (speech signal is present in the kth spectral component) is considered. Using this model, the optimal estimate of the clean signal amplitude is given by:

$$\hat{A}_s(k) = \Pr(H_0(k)/X(k))E[A_s(k)/X(k), H_0(k)]$$
$$+ \Pr(H_1(k)/X(k))E[A_s(k)/X(k), H_1(k)] \qquad (12.35)$$

Finally, it should be noted that spectral subtraction is an effective technique for reducing additive environmental noise in an observed speech signal, especially when a unique microphone is available to capture the signal. Unfortunately, this technique introduces musical noise in the enhanced signal. In order to reduce this musical noise, several approaches have been proposed, most of which are based on perceptual knowledge. An attempt to introduce a model of the clean speech signal in the enhancement scheme is made in the MMSE-based algorithms. Unfortunately, this model has limitations because it is generally based on a Gaussian distribution.

12.4.3. Channel Equalization Techniques

ASR over a telephone network is affected by disturbing components other than environmental noise. The telephone channel effects, the mismatch between the different microphones and coding or just quantization errors affect the quality of the speech signal and the performance of an ASR system operating in a telephone network. Some of the transmitting network effects are non-linear, and compensating for them is a very difficult problem. As an example, consider the problem of a spurious noise energy that suddenly appears in modern communications. The speech/non-speech detector often considers this kind of noise as speech. A possible solution is to explicitly model this noise within the HMM structure and to reject the corresponding acoustic signal when it appears.

Besides these non-linear disturbing components, there are some linear effects (or effects well approximated by linear convoluted filters). These effects are represented by the impulse response $d(t)$ in the general equation (12.9). If projected in the cepstral domain, these effects appear like a bias added to the cepstra of speech. As noted in Neumeyer *et al.* (1994), the integration of spectral energies within frequency bands makes the convoluted effect in (12.9) not exactly additive in the log-energies at the output of a filter bank (supposing the channel effects constant in a frequency band in order to get (12.11)) or in the final cepstral coefficients (same approximation to get (12.12)).

For telephone ASR, it has been observed that the channel effects introduce a bias in the cepstral domain that is almost constant for a given call but varies with the calls (Mokbel *et al.*, 1993, 1996). Several techniques have been proposed to compensate for the telephone channel effects, namely cepstral normalization (Mokbel *et al.*, 1993), high-pass filtering of cepstral or log-spectral trajectories (Hermansky *et al.*, 1991; Hirsch *et al.*, 1991) and "blind equalization using adaptive filtering" (Mokbel *et al.*, 1995c, 1996).

Cepstral normalization consists of estimating the mean of the observed cesptra for a given telephone call and subtracting it from these vectors. In Mokbel *et al.* (1996), it is shown that it is preferable to use the speech data alone (without non-speech segments) for estimating the cepstral mean (the channel effects). However, no problem occurs if few non-speech data are included to get an estimate of the channel effects. It has also been shown that 2–4 s of speech are sufficient to get a reliable estimate of the cepstral mean in order to perform cepstral normalization. In Neumeyer *et al.* (1994), it is proposed that a filter bank performs the normalization before integration in the spectral domain. Applying cepstral normalization on the training data increases the discrimination ability of the resulting acoustic models. However, some experiments conducted at CNET–France Télécom have shown that an increase[3] of the robustness is maintained even if the acoustic models are trained on non-normalized speech data and the recognition is performed on normalized data.

A suitable frame-synchronous approach to equalize the channel effects in the observed speech feature vectors consists of reducing the low-frequency energies in the cepstral (or log-spectral) trajectories (Hermansky *et al.*, 1991; Hirsch *et al.*, 1991). This can be performed with RASTA-like techniques where a first-order high-pass (band-pass) "infinite impulse response" (IIR) filter is applied to the observed cepstral (or log-spectral) trajectories. RASTA techniques are also

---

[3]Such an increase is smaller than the increase obtained if both training and testing are performed on equalized data.

used to increase the robustness to additive noise (Hermansky and Morgan, 1994).

With reference to equation (12.9), reducing the channel effects appears to be a blind deconvolution problem, since only the resulting signal $y(t)$ is observed at the input of the ASR system. Blind deconvolution has been widely studied in signal processing and in digital communication (Hilal, 1993). Adaptive filters are generally used to perform blind equalization. Based on the decision module and on some known statistical characteristics of the clean signal, an error criterion is used for adapting the filter parameters. In "blind equalization using adaptive filtering" (BEAF), described in (Mokbel *et al.*, 1996), the same principle is used. One can use fixed known statistics on the clean speech signal in order to adapt a LMS filter to blind equalization of the channel effects. The long-term spectrum of speech can be used to obtain simple statistics of the clean signal.[4] Since a filter bank (subband) analysis exists in the ASR system, a frequency implementation of the adaptive LMS filter is the most appropriate. Ignoring the phase of the speech signal, the "circular-convolution method" (Shynk, 1992) can be used to adapt the filter. This method is not optimal, since it corresponds to a circular convolution in the time domain. However, its computational simplicity compared to the well-known block-convolution-based frequency domain adaptive filters (overlap-add, overlap-save, . . .) motivates the choice.

The block diagram of this approach is shown in Figure 12.10.

For each input frame, a subband vector V_y (energies in the frequency bands) is computed by the feature analysis module of the ASR system. The subband energies are then multiplied by the filter parameters $W(i)$ to produce the equalized subband vector V_n. Comparing the long-term spectrum of the equalized vector V_n to a reference predefined long-term spectrum $R(f)$ allows computation of an error used to adapt the filter parameters $W(i)$. In the implemented version of the BEAF method, the long-term spectrum of the equalized subband vectors is not computed directly, but attention is paid to the choice of the adaptation parameters in order to guarantee a correct convergence of the filter. The convergence of the BEAF method is shown in Mokbel *et al.* (1996). A detailed study has been made on the choice of the adaptation procedure (e.g. NLMS, signed-LMS) as well as on the choice of the adaptation step. A description of this work is given in Mauuary (1996). The BEAF method has been tested on several telephone databases and has produced better performance than more classical techniques (Mokbel *et al.*, 1996).

Channel equalization and spectral subtraction techniques have been combined in order to reduce both additive noise and channel effects. For this purpose, it is shown in Mokbel and Jouvet (1995b) that spectral subtraction must be first applied followed by a channel equalization technique. This combination produces interesting results especially for ASR over mobile telephone

---

[4]More complex statistics (as the acoustic model of an ASR application) may be used.

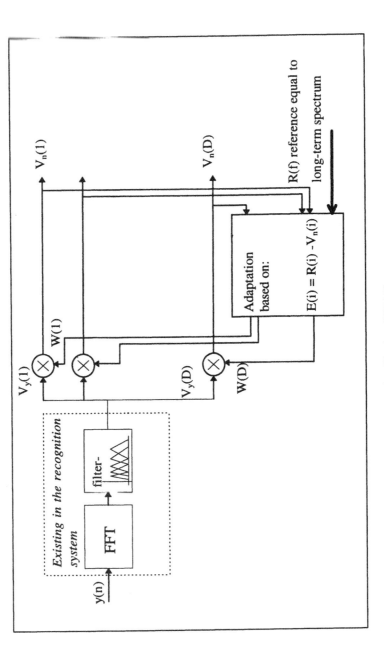

Figure 12.10 Block diagram of blind equalization using adaptive filtering (BEAF).

networks, like the GSM network, where the speaker environmental noise is high and where the channel effects cannot be neglected.

12.4.4 Use of Statistical Models in the Enhancement/Equalization Scheme

In the methods for speech enhancement and channel equalization described so far, either no or simple clean signal models are used. A simple statistical model is used in MMSE spectral subtraction and in the BEAF approach for channel equalization. Richer models of the clean speech signal in the enhancement/ equalization process are discussed in the following.

Model-based speech enhancement

The model-based speech enhancement (MBSE) approach has been proposed in Ephraim (1992a,b) in order to perform speech enhancement using joint statistics of the clean signal and noise. HMMs with Gaussian AR subsources are used to model both speech and noise processes. Let λ_u be the HMM of a signal u that represents either the speech s or the noise n. λ_u has Q_u states. Let the signal vectors sequence of length T be $u = \{u_t; t = 0, \ldots, T - 1\}$, the PDF of model λ_u is given by:

$$p_{\lambda_u}(u) = \sum_q \mathrm{Pr}_{\lambda_u}(q) p_{\lambda_u}(u/q) = \sum_q \mathrm{Pr}_{\lambda_u}(q) \prod_{t=0}^{T-1} b_u(u_t/q_t) \qquad (12.36)$$

where $q = \{q_t; t = 0, \ldots, T - 1\}$ is a possible sequence of states of length T, $\mathrm{Pr}(q)$ is its probability (computed as the product of the transition probabilities and the initial state probability, as described in Chapter 5), and $b_u(u_t/q_t)$ is the PDF of the subprocess associated with state q_t.

For HMMs with Gaussian AR subsources[5] the PDF $b_u(u_t/q_t)$ is given by:

$$b(s_t/q_t) = (2\pi)^{-k/2} ||\Gamma_{(u),q_t}||^{-1/2} \exp[-\tfrac{1}{2} u_t^{\#} \Gamma_{(u),q_t}^{-1} u_t] \qquad (12.37)$$

where $\Gamma_{(u),q_t}$ represents the covariance matrix associated with the state q_t which can be directly related to the parameters of the corresponding AR process, and k represents the length of a frame of the signal.

Based on the definition of the HMM of both the clean speech signal and the noise signal, the HMM Γ_x of the noisy signal x_t can be defined as a set of $Q_s Q_n$ states, where each element represents a couple of states from both speech and noise models. The probability of a state sequence (a path) in the noisy signal model is equal to the product of the probabilities of the corresponding paths in both λ_s and λ_n. The output distributions of the model are Gaussian but

---

[5]This modelling can be generalized to the case of HMMs with mixture of Gaussian AR subsources.

not AR, with zero mean and covariance:

$$\Gamma_{(x),q_t} = \Gamma_{(s),q_t} + \Gamma_{(n),q_t} \qquad (12.38)$$

This modelling technique can be used to reconstruct the clean speech signal given an observed noisy signal and the models of both the clean speech and the environmental noise. This estimation is based on two criteria, MMSE and MAP. Using the MMSE criterion, the best estimate of the clean speech vector at instant t, given the noisy vectors from 0 until time τ,[6] is:

$$\hat{s}_t = E[s_t/x_0, \ldots, x_\tau] = \sum_{q_t \in \lambda_x} \mathrm{Pr}_{\lambda_x}(q_t/x_0, \ldots, x_\tau) E[s_t/x_t, q_t] \qquad (12.39)$$

$\mathrm{Pr}_{\lambda_x}(q_t/x_0, \ldots, x_\tau)$ is the probability that the source is, at time t, in the state q_t of the noisy signal model given the observed noisy vectors. This quantity can be computed with the forward–backward algorithm. $E[s_t/x_t, q_t]$ is the expectation of the clean signal vector at instant t given the corresponding vector and the state q_t of the noisy model λ_x. This expectation is given by:[7]

$$\begin{aligned} E[s_t/x_t, q_t] &= \Gamma_{(s),q_t} \Gamma_{(x),q_t}^{-1} x_t \\ &= \Gamma_{(s),q_t} (\Gamma_{(s),q_t} + \Gamma_{(n),q_t})^{-1} x_t \\ &= W_{(x),q_t} x_t \qquad (12.40) \end{aligned}$$

Inspecting (12.39) and (12.40), the MBSE-MMSE filter appears to perform a soft-decision between a set of $Q_s Q_n$ Wiener filters ($W_{(x),q_t}$) corresponding to the pairs of clean and noisy signals. The contribution of each filter is defined by the probability of occupying the corresponding state in the noisy model λ_x based on the observed set of noisy vectors.

Another way to use the set of Wiener filters consists of choosing the filter corresponding to the most probable state. In Ephraim (1992b), it has been noted that the resulting hard-decision filter is not as good as the soft-decision one.

The MAP estimator of the clean signal given the models λ_s and λ_n and the observed set of noisy vectors, is obtained by maximizing:

$$\hat{s}_t = \underset{s_t}{\mathrm{argmax}}\ \mathrm{Pr}_{\lambda_x}(s_t/x_0, \ldots, x_\tau) \qquad (12.41)$$

This is a typical problem of incomplete data and no direct solution exists for (12.41). In order to locally maximize (12.41), the EM algorithm is generally used. Starting from an initial solution for the signal vector $s_t^{(0)}$, the EM algorithm proceeds iteratively by estimating the auxiliary function $Q(s_t', s_t)$ and by maximizing this function at the point $s_t = s_t^{(n)}$.

Experiments conducted with this method have shown (Ephraim, 1992b) that MBSE-MAP estimator behaves as hard-decision filter, since generally one state

---

[6] $\tau \geq t$ (equality corresponds to causal estimation).
[7] Equivalent to the Wiener filter knowing the covariance of the clean and noisy signal.

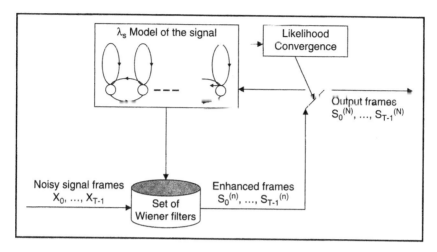

Figure 12.11 MBSE-MAP, Viterbi decoding and Wiener filtering enhancement.

has a predominant contribution in the auxiliary function to maximize. An extension of this approach consists of the estimation of the entire sequence of clean speech vectors $y_0, \ldots, y_\tau$ (Ephraim, 1992a). The main idea is to proceed, by iterations until convergence by aligning (using the Viterbi algorithm) the noisy vectors with the λ_x states, and estimating the clean signal vectors by using the Wiener filters of these aligned states, as shown in Figure 12.11.

This MBSE framework is interesting for speech enhancement. It has limitations in the fact that the noise is supposed to be stationary. In McKinley and Whipple (1996), a method is proposed for on-line adapting noise characteristics.

Stochastic matching techniques

MBSE is useful for dealing with environmental additive noise. This is interesting for speech recognition in noisy environments such as cars. For telephone ASR, one of the most disturbing components is due to convoluted effects introduced by the telephone network. This effect can be seen as an additive bias in the cepstral domain. Stochastic matching uses HMMs to estimate the bias to be removed from cepstral frames and to reduce channel perturbations (Sankar and Lee, 1995; Rahim and Juang, 1996; Zhao, 1996).

Let λ_s be the model (with Q states) of the clean signal defined in the feature space and $C_y = \{C_y(t); t = 0, \ldots, T - 1\}$ be the sequence of T feature vectors to be recognized (or equalized), let $T_\theta(C)$ be the equalization function depending on the parameter vector θ, and $q = \{q_t; t = 0, \ldots, T - 1\}$ be a sequence of T states (a path) in the HMM. The application of the equalization function produces a sequence of equalized feature vectors that corresponds to the clean signal:

$$\{C_{\hat{S}}(t)\} = \{T_{\hat{\theta}}[C_y(t)]\}, \quad t = 0, \ldots, T - 1 \tag{12.42}$$

Given the model of the clean signal λ_s, the model of the observed signal can be obtained by multiplying the output subprocesses density functions by the inverse of the determinant of the Jacobian matrix:

$$b_{\hat{\theta}, \lambda_y}(C_y(t)/q_t) = b_{\hat{\theta}, \lambda_y}(T_\vartheta[C_y(t)]/q_t)\|J[C_y(t)]\|^{-1}$$

where $J[C_y(t)]$ is the Jacobian matrix whose (k, l)th element is:

$$J_{k,l}[C_y(t)] = \frac{\partial C_y(t)_k}{\partial T_{\hat{\theta}}[C_y(t)]_l}$$

The parameter vector θ of the equalization function can be determined in order to satisfy:

$$\max_{\hat{\theta}} p_{\hat{\theta}, \lambda_s}(\{C_y(t)\}) = \max_{\theta} p_{\lambda_s}(\{T_{\hat{\theta}}[C_y(t)]\}) \prod_t \|J[C_y(t)]\|^{-1} \tag{12.43}$$

For HMM with Gaussian subsources, the likelihood of the observed vectors can be written as:

$$p_{\hat{\theta}, \lambda_s}(\{[C_y(t)]\}) = \sum_{q \in \lambda_s} \Pr(q/\lambda_s) p_{\vartheta, \lambda_s}(\{C_y(t)\}q)$$

$$= \sum_{q \in \lambda_s} \Pr(q/\lambda_s) \prod_{t=0}^{T-1} b_{\hat{\theta}, \lambda_s}(T_{\hat{\theta}}[C_y(t)]/q_t)\|J[C_y(t)]\|^{-1} \tag{12.44}$$

$$p_{\vartheta, \lambda_s}(\{T_\vartheta[C_y(t)]\}) = \sum_{q \in \lambda_s} \Pr(q/\lambda_s) \prod_{t=0}^{T-1} (2\pi)^{-p/2}\|\Gamma_{q_t}\|^{-\frac{1}{2}}\|J(C_y(t))\|^{-1}$$

$$\times \exp[-\tfrac{1}{2}(T_{\hat{\theta}}[C_y(t)] - \mu_{q_t})^T \Gamma_{q_t}^{-1}(T_{\hat{\theta}}[C_y(t)] - \mu_{q_t})]$$

where μ_{q_t} and γ_{q_t} are respectively the mean and covariance of the Gaussian associated with the state q_t.

No direct solution exists for (12.43) with the definition (12.44). Thus, the EM algorithm is used in the stochastic matching procedure. At each iteration of the EM algorithm, the auxiliary function is computed (estimation step):

$$Q(\theta, \theta^{(n)}) = E[\ln p_{\hat{\theta}, \lambda_s}(\{C_y(t)\}, q)/\{C_y(t)\}, \theta^{(n)}]$$

$$Q(\theta, \theta^{(n)}) = \sum_{q \in \lambda_s} p_{\hat{\theta}, \lambda_s}(\{C_y(t)\}, q) \ln p_{\hat{\theta}, \lambda_s}(\{C_y(t)\}, q) \tag{12.45}$$

Since the joint likelihood of $(C_y(t), q)$ introduces a product of Jacobian matrices that do not depend on q nor θ, defining $L_{\theta^{(n)}, \lambda_s}(q) = p_{\theta^{(n)}, \lambda_s}(\{T_{\theta^{(n)}}[C_y(t)]\}, q) =$

one gets:

$$\theta^{(n+1)} = \underset{\theta}{\text{argmax}} - \frac{1}{2} \sum_{q \in \lambda_s} L_{\theta^{(n)}, \lambda_s}(q)$$

$$\times \left\{ \sum_{t=0}^{T-1} (T_{\vartheta}[C_y(t)] - \mu_{q_t})^T \Gamma_{q_t}^{-1} (T_{\hat{\theta}}[C_y(t)] - \mu_{q_t}) + 2 \ln \|J(C_y(t))\| \right\}$$

If $\gamma_i(t)$ is the probability that the HMM is in state i at time t while generating the observed sequence using the current model parameters, the preceding auxiliary equation can be written as:

$$\theta^{(n+1)} = \underset{\theta}{\text{argmax}} - \sum_{i=1}^{Q} \sum_{t=0}^{T-1} \gamma_i(t) \left[(T_\theta[C_y(t)] - \mu_i)^T \Gamma_i^{-1} \right.$$

$$\left. \times (T_\theta[C_y(t)] - \mu_i) + 2 \ln \|J(C_y(t))\| \right] \tag{12.46}$$

The solution of the preceding equation can be obtained by differentiating with respect to all the elements of the parameter vector θ and equating the resulting vector to 0. In order to differentiate (12.46) with respect to θ, a derivative with respect to $(T_\theta[C_y(t)] - \mu_i)$ could be first performed, followed by the derivative of $(T_\theta[C_y(t)] - \mu_i)$ with respect to each element of θ. Finally, $\theta^{(n+1)}$ is obtained by solving the equation:

$$\sum_{i=1}^{Q} \sum_{t=0}^{T-1} \gamma_i(t) \left\{ (T_\theta[C_y(t)] - \mu_i)^T \Gamma_i^{-1} \left[\frac{\partial}{\partial \theta} T_\theta[C_y(t)] \right] + \left[\frac{\partial}{\partial \hat{\theta}} \ln \|J(C_y(t))\| \right] \right\} = 0_{1,p}$$

$$\tag{12.47}$$

where $\gamma_i(t)$ can be computed using the EM algorithm in the *estimate* step, $0_{1,p}$ is a zero line vector with dimension p equal to the vector dimension,

$$\frac{\partial}{\partial \theta} T_\theta[C_y(t)]$$

is a matrix with as many columns as the dimension of the parameter vector θ, each column representing the derivation of $T_\theta[C_y(t)]$ with respect to an element of the parameter vector, and

$$\left[\frac{\partial}{\partial \theta} \ln \|J(C_y(t))\| \right]$$

is a line vector whose ith element represents the derivation of the determinant of the Jacobian matrix with respect to the ith element of the θ vector.

Equation (12.47) is the general equation for computing the parameters of the equalization function within the EM algorithm. An asymptotic solution can also be obtained using the Viterbi algorithm instead of the EM. Using Viterbi algorithm is similar to MBSE-MAP with Viterbi algorithm.

The idea is to only consider the most likely path in the HMM in order to compute the parameters θ of the equalization function. This leads to the procedure

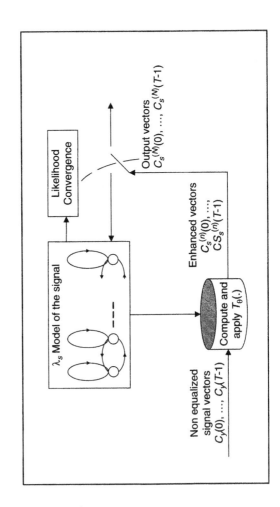

Figure 12.12 Block diagram of the stochastic matching (Viterbi) algorithm.

summarized in Figure 12.12. Comparing Figure 12.12 with Figure 12.11, it can be seen that stochastic matching is similar to the MBSE-MAP algorithm. Let us consider two particular cases of (12.47) where the equalization function consists of removing a bias as for linear multiple regression (LMR). In the first case, one can write:

$$T_\theta[C_y(t)] = C_y(t) - b \tag{12.48}$$

where b is the bias to be removed and $\theta = b$.

Replacing $T_\theta(\cdot)$ by its value in (12.48) one gets:

$$\sum_{i=0}^{Q} \sum_{t=0}^{T-1} \gamma_i(t)(C_y(t) - b - \mu_i)^T \Gamma_i^{-1} I_{p,p} = 0_{i,p}$$

where $I_{p,p}$ is the identity matrix. Solving this equation gives the values for the parameter vector b:

$$b^T = \left[\sum_{i=0}^{Q} \sum_{t=0}^{T-1} \gamma_i(t)(C_y(t) - \mu_i)^T \Gamma_i^{-1} \right] \left[\sum_{i=0}^{Q} \sum_{t=0}^{T-1} \gamma_i(t)\Gamma_i^{-1} \right]^{-1} \tag{12.49}$$

In (12.49), the bias estimated at the end of the maximize step of the EM algorithm is equal, as intuitively expected, to the weighted mean difference between the observed feature vectors and the corresponding means of the Gaussian distributions in the HMM for each possible path. For a given path, the contribution of a pair of vector/distribution is weighted by the inverse of the corresponding covariance matrix. The contribution of a given path is weighted by its likelihood estimated in the preceding estimate step. When using the Viterbi algorithm, only the most likely path is considered.

Let us consider the case where the equalization function is an LMR transformation, i.e.:

$$T_\theta[C_y(t)] = AC_y(t) - b \tag{12.50}$$

where $\theta = (A, b)$; A is the regression matrix and b the bias.

When replacing $T_\theta(\cdot)$ by its value in (12.47), and resolving for b (in a similar way as for $T_\theta(\cdot)$ corresponding to removing a bias) the following equation is obtained:

$$b^T = \left[\sum_{i=0}^{Q} \sum_{t=0}^{T-1} \gamma_i(t)(AC_y(t) - \mu_i)^T \Gamma_i^{-1} \right] \left[\sum_{i=0}^{Q} \sum_{t=0}^{T-1} \gamma_i(t)\Gamma_i^{-1} \right]^{-1} \tag{12.51}$$

Trying to resolve for A the determinant of the Jacobian matrix makes the equation very complex. In order for simplifying the resulting equation, diagonal regression and covariance matrices may be considered. This leads to the following equations to estimate (a, b) for each dimension l of the acoustical space:

$$b = \frac{\sum_{i=0}^{Q} \sum_{t=0}^{T-1} \gamma_i(t)(a\mathbf{C}_y(t)(l) - \mu_i(l))/\Gamma_i(l)}{\sum_{i=0}^{Q} \sum_{t=0}^{T-1} \gamma_i(t)/\Gamma_i(l)} \tag{12.52}$$

$$a^2 \left[\sum_{i=0}^{Q} \sum_{t=0}^{T-1} \gamma_i(t)C_y(t)(l)^2/\Gamma_i(l) \right.$$

$$\left. - \frac{\left(\sum_{i=0}^{Q} \sum_{t=0}^{T-1} \gamma_i(t)C_y(t)(l)/\Gamma_i(l) \right)\left(\sum_{j=0}^{Q} \sum_{t'=0}^{T-1} \gamma_j(t')C_y(t')(l)/\Gamma_j(l) \right)}{\left(\sum_{i=0}^{Q} \sum_{t=0}^{T-1} \gamma_i(t)/\Gamma_i(l) \right)} \right]$$

$$+ a \left[\frac{\left(\sum_{i=0}^{Q} \sum_{t=0}^{T-1} \gamma_i(t)C_y(t)(l)/\Gamma_i(l) \right)\left(\sum_{j=0}^{Q} \sum_{t'=0}^{T-1} \gamma_j(t')\mu_j(l)/\Gamma_j(l) \right)}{\left(\sum_{i=0}^{Q} \sum_{t=0}^{T-1} \gamma_i(t)/\Gamma_i(l) \right)} \right. \tag{12.53}$$

$$\left. - \sum_{i=0}^{Q} \sum_{t=0}^{T-1} \gamma_i(t)\mu_i(l)C_y(t)(l)/\Gamma_i(l) \right] - \sum_{i=0}^{Q} \sum_{t=0}^{T-1} \gamma_i(t) = 0$$

Even if MBSE and stochastic matching techniques have many positive aspects, they have problems too. First, these techniques are EM-based and cannot be easily applied in a time-synchronous way. Moreover, the choice of the clean signal model is crucial. In particular it is not clear whether or not it should be more general than the vocabulary model. The third problem is the high complexity of MBSE and the stochastic matching algorithms.

12.5. ADAPTATION OF MODEL PARAMETERS IN NEW CONDITIONS

A final important method for improving robustness of ASR systems is to work on model parameters. As noted earlier, the best recognition performance is obtained when training and testing (including practical use "in the field") are performed in the same conditions. Instead of using techniques for noise reduction, it may be useful to transform the model parameters in order to "adapt" the model to every new recognition condition. This requires knowledge about the new condition, and a transformation from the training (generally with clean speech) conditions to the new condition. For this purpose, some measurements have to be performed in the new condition. However, for practical reasons, the amount of adaptation data must be limited.

Adaptation of model parameters to a new environment has been widely studied in the last two decades. In early stages of ASR, speaker adaptation algorithms were introduced in order to adapt pattern references, VQ codebooks, or parameters of an acoustic-phonetic decoder, to the voice of a new speaker (Grenier, 1980). In Klatt (1976), a noise masking procedure is associated with the filter bank analysis. The main idea is to compute, for every frequency band, the maximum of noise energy (for training and testing condition) and to fix this maximum as a threshold. If the mismatch between training and testing conditions is limited, then satisfactory performance improvements can be obtained, while limitations appear when large mismatch in SNR exists between training and testing conditions.

In the following we will discuss three main classes of techniques used for the adaptation of HMM parameters to new environments, namely:

- model composition techniques,
- spectral transformation techniques,
- MAP or Bayesian techniques.

12.5.1. Model Composition Techniques

In Roe (1987), a procedure is defined to adapt codebook vectors to both the noise and the Lombard effect.[8] To adapt the codebook vectors to the Lombard effect, speech with and without Lombard effects is aligned. This alignment permits adapting the clean codebook vectors to the aligned Lombard vectors. For the effect of additive environmental noise the noise characteristics are added to the codebook vectors in the autocorrelation domain.

In Varga and Moore (1990), a technique based on HMM decomposition of speech and noise is defined. The principle is similar to that described above for the MBSE-MMSE approach, where two parallel models are defined in parallel, the model of the clean speech and the model of the noise. The model of the observed signal (clean speech and noise) is a combined model having as many states as the product of the numbers of states of both clean speech

---

[8]The Lombard effect designates the change in the speaking style in the presence of environmental noise. This effect has been largely investigated for speech recognition in adverse environment.

and noise models. As in the MBSE approach, each state in the model is equivalent to a couple of states in both clean speech and noise models: $q_x = (q_s, q_n)$. The difference between this approach and the MBSE-MMSE approach is that the combination of both components of the observed signal is not additive. Actually, the HMMs are defined in a log-spectral domain and for additive environmental noise, the combination is additive in the linear spectral domain. Thus, an observed noisy vector at instant t in the feature space is equal to:

$$\ln S_x(f) = \ln S_s(f) \otimes \ln S_n(f) = \ln[e^{\ln S_s(f)} + e^{\ln S_n(f)}] \quad \text{at time } t \quad (12.54)$$

The preceding operator $\otimes$ (expressing the combination between the feature vectors) is approximated by the operator maximum in order for simplifying the problem, leading to:

$$\ln S_x(f) = \ln S_s(f) \otimes \ln S_n(f) = \max[\ln S_s(f), \ln S_n(f)] \quad \text{at time } t \quad (12.55)$$

Using this approximation the combined output PDF of two subprocesses (of both clean speech (i) and noise (j) HMMs) is given by:

$$b_{s,i} \otimes b_{n,j}(\ln S_n(f)) = p[\max[\ln S_s(f), \ln S_n(f)]/q_s(i), q_n(j)]$$

which can be easily obtained from the Gaussian distributions relative to the states $q_s(i)$ and $q_n(j)$.

Parallel model combination (PMC) has been largely studied in recent years for robust speech recognition (Gales and Young, 1993). The basic idea is to adapt the set of output distributions of the clean speech HMM using the parameter of a Gaussian density modelling noise that is supposed to be additive in the spectral domain. As suggested in Varga (1990), the main problem is how to consider the complex relation involving the logarithm operator. In the PMC approach, the mean and covariance of a subprocess can be easily passed from the cepstral domain (μ_s^c, Γ_s^c) to the log-spectral domain (μ_s^l, Γ_s^l) using the cosine transform matrix C. These statistics are then transformed in the linear spectral domain (μ_s, Γ_s), where the distribution is log-normal. In Gales and Young (1993) it is shown that:

$$\mu_s(i) = \exp[\mu_s^l(i) + \Gamma_s^l(i, i)/2]$$
$$\Gamma_s(i, j) = \mu_s(i)\mu_s(j)[\exp(\Gamma_s^l(i, j)) - 1] \quad\quad (12.56)$$

The adapted mean and covariance matrices are then obtained, using the mean and covariance of the noise process (μ_n, Γ_n):

$$\hat{\mu}_x = g\mu_s + \mu_n$$
$$\hat{\Gamma}_x = g^2\Gamma_s + \Gamma_n \quad\quad (12.57)$$

g is a gain factor introduced to take into account possible differences between the energies of the clean speech used for training and noisy speech.

The adapted parameters in the log-spectral domain can then be easily found by inverting (12.56).

Reported experiments show that the PMC method does improve the robustness of an ASR system in the presence of additive environmental noise. Several variants of this technique have been described in the literature, in particular to consider the effect of a transmission channel (Minami, 1995).

In both methods, the main problem of HMM composition techniques concerns the simplification of the composition operator (additive in the linear domain). In Mokbel (1992) and Mokbel and Chollet (1995a), another approach for simplifying the transformation between the cepstral and the linear-spectral domain is proposed. Actually, a problem first arises when passing from the log-spectral to the cepstral domain, since a reduction in the space dimension is performed (the cosine transform matrix C is not a square one, thus it is singular). The proposed remedy to this problem is to also compute, during the training of the cepstral HMM, equivalent output distributions in the log-spectral domain. A solution with satisfactory results is proposed for passing from the log-spectral domain to the linear-spectral domain; it consists of approximating the logarithm function with its tangent at the mean of the considered distribution (Mokbel, 1992).

A method for the adaptation of just the noise model component is proposed in Logan and Robinson (1997). It consists of generating a new noise model by summing the expected values of the noise statistics given each observation at each HMM state, weighted by the likelihood of being in each state. Autoregressive HMMs are used to form Wiener filters to enhance speech. In this way, speech is segmented into clusters of signals with similar autocorrelation parameters.

In Matrouf and Gauvin (1997), data-driven model composition is considered for compensating noisy training data with the noise of the test data, assuming that training and test corpora have been recorded in different environmental conditions.

A Jacobian approach to fast acoustic model adaptation is proposed in Sagayama *et al.* (1997). Means and covariance matrices are adapted from a given to a new noisy condition using noise samples acquired in a pause between two successive messages of the system. The adaptation transformation is based on a Jacobian matrix containing derivative of cepstral coefficients obtained in the initial, given noisy condition.

12.5.2. Spectral Transformation for Model Adaptation

Given the HMMs for the words of an application vocabulary trained with data from specific conditions, it is practically important to adapt the model parameters, and more precisely the output distribution parameters, to one or more new conditions. In the previous subsections, adaptation methods have been proposed based on the knowledge of noise statistics, the models for clean speech, and especially on the combination of speech and noise components.

It would be interesting to consider an adaptation procedure based on a small amount of data collected in new recognition conditions. This avoids the need of a detailed knowledge of noise characteristics and the combination operator. A typical example of the problem considered now is the adaptation of PSN (public switch network) HMMs to GSM conditions. Spectral transformations can be used for this purpose. Similarly to the equalization function in the stochastic matching approach, the spectral transformation function can be denoted as $T_\theta(\cdot)$. The parameter vector θ of this transformation can be computed in two ways, namely, directly from data in both training and recognition conditions, or using the adaptation data and the "clean" HMMs.

In the first case, the estimation of the parameter vector θ in the feature space must be preceded by an alignment[9] between feature vectors from the training and the new conditions. This alignment is a source of errors since the only correspondence between training and adaptation data may be localized at the word level. This is a real problem related to the nature of the speech signal where spectral and temporal information are mixed in the observation. If the adaptation and the training data have several characteristics that exhibit substantial differences (different speakers, different conditions, etc.), then the alignment problem becomes very complex. Generally, dynamic time warping (DTW) is used for aligning vectors of identical words from two conditions.

In the second case, the estimation of the transformation parameters makes use of the "clean" model and of the small amount of adaptation data available. This is an elegant remedy to the alignment problem of the first case. Actually, in the "clean" model, the training conditions are mixed and the alignment between adaptation data and model parameters can be seen as a classical problem of incomplete data for which it has been shown that the EM algorithm is an effective solution. The transformation obtained in this way is directly applied to the model parameters for the new conditions.

As noted earlier in this section, the use of the "clean" model in the estimation process has several advantages. Actually this model integrates all the conditions of the training data, which is useful, for example, for the adaptation of a PSN speaker independent model to the GSM speaker independent corresponding model.[10] Moreover, with the use of the "clean" model, the EM algorithm can be directly applied to the alignment between training and adaptation data. Non-observed data are the association between the adaptation vectors and the subprocesses of the HMM.

---

[9]The unique transformation that does not need any alignment between feature vectors, does transform the global statistics of the two data sets.
[10]The training and adaptation data differ in both the speakers and the network used for the acquisition.

Unfortunately, there is no direct solution for finding the optimal value of a linear transformation. However, ASR systems generally use a diagonal covariance matrix for the sake of computational simplicity. Moreover, it has been shown (Mokbel, 1992) that a diagonal regression matrix is sufficient for obtaining reliable environment adaptation for ASR in adverse conditions such as in a car. With such a simplification, simple solutions can be obtained as in the case in which linear transformations are only applied on the mean vectors of the Gaussian densities by associating a linear transformation to a group of HMM subprocesses (Legetter and Woodland, 1994a,b). When linear regression transformation is applied on both mean and covariance matrices, with the hypotheses of diagonal covariance matrices and diagonal regression matrix, similar equations to (12.52) and (12.53) are obtained for each group of Gaussian densities in the model. Such techniques have been applied at CNET to adapt PSN models to the GSM environment and have produced satisfactory results.

Even if all the transformation parameters can be estimated, the problem of defining the classes of densities remains. This is equivalent to clustering HMM densities. At CNET–France Télécom, this is performed by building a binary tree going from the leaves to the root. At each step of the building procedure, the closest pair of densities[11] is grouped in a unique node to which the unique density representing the couple of densities is associated. To define the closest pair of densities, a distance measure is defined on the basis of the likelihood loss on the data that were used to estimate these densities.

12.5.3. Bayesian or MAP Adaptation of the Model Parameters

The classical approach to recognition introduced in Chapter 1 assumes that models and statistical parameters are correct, which is not the case in real situations. In fact, questions can be raised about the type of models, their statistical distributions and specification parameters, the type and size of the training set, and training conditions regarding microphone, channel, environment, task-dependent phonetic and linguistic facts, which are very often different from testing conditions.

Due to the fact that conditions may vary slowly during the recognition process, it is desirable to continuously adapt model parameters (and perhaps feature extraction or normalization) to an evolving environment. Unsupervised adaptation is preferable for such a task.

Robust ASR models can be obtained by retraining, with *maximum likelihood* (ML) estimation, the original models trained in a laboratory, using field adaptation data or by combining[12] field and laboratory data in a single training set. Another possibility consists of using a *Bayesian*, or *maximum a posteriori*

---

[11]Corresponding to the remaining free nodes.
[12]If sparse or insufficient amount of field data is available.

(MAP) estimation (Lee, 1991; Gauvain and Lee, 1992, 1994). The model, formerly trained with laboratory data, is adapted using field data. In order to perform this adaptation with MAP estimation, *a priori* densities are considered that describe how the model parameters[13] are distributed. These densities are used together with the new observed adaptation data for computing a new estimate of the model parameters that better correspond to the recognition conditions.

Estimation of the prior parameters

Since any physical knowledge about the prior parameters is not available, they are estimated from a large (hence, supposed condition-independent) database. This strategy is called *empirical Bayes* approach (Huo and Lee, 1995). Generally, in order to compute the prior parameters, several realizations of the model parameters should be considered. It is obvious that these realizations cannot be directly observed, and should be estimated with an EM algorithm (Huo and Lee, 1995; Miglietta *et al.*, 1996).

A well-known approach consists of estimating the prior parameters assuming that the components of each Gaussian mixture (associated with an HMM state) are different realizations of the *a priori* distribution associated with that mixture.

Another approach consists of splitting the large training database into several parts, each part corresponding to a specific condition or speaker. Then, each possible estimate of the model parameters, given a specified part of the database, can be considered by the EM algorithm as a realization of the *prior* distribution. For example, in Huo and Lee (1995) speaker classification is performed in order to create the different components for the estimation of the *priors*.

In Miglietta (1996) it is proposed to perform a vector quantization on the vectors associated with a given distribution in order to get sets of vectors corresponding to different realizations of the *prior* distribution.

Lack of adaptation data

As noted earlier, the adaptation data, collected in the field, are generally sparse. Even if a small amount of adaptation data may be used for adapting the model parameters, several distributions of the model cannot be adapted for lack of pertinent observations. This disparity in the adapted distributions may affect the adaptation results.

In order to increase the robustness of the adaptation procedure to the lack of adaptation data, in Zavaliagkos (1995), adaptation is defined for a phoneme

---

[13]The model parameters are considered to be the realization of a random process.

Gaussian and then propagated to the Gaussian densities of all the corresponding triphones. This allows a smooth adaptation of triphone Gaussian densities with a global procedure for a phoneme. Besides, the interdependence between the phonemes is ensured by the use of the extended MAP algorithm, where all the phonemes' Gaussian means are grouped in a unique vector to be globally adapted.

In Ahadı and Woodland (1995), a global regression model is defined, where each of the model parameters is related (using a regression transform) to another parameter. The parameters of these regressions are estimated on several pairs of parameters from different speaker-dependent models. In the adaptation procedure, the parameters for which adaptation data are available are adapted using the MAP algorithm. For the other parameters, the adapted value is obtained using the regression model and the adapted parameters.

In Tonomura *et al.* (1995) and Takahashi and Sagayama (1995a), an approach based on the fact that the adaptation function must be continuous in the feature space is proposed. Based on a distance measure between the densities, the densities for which there is a lack of adaptation data are adapted using the closest MAP-adapted densities. Moreover, MAP adaptation for the densities with enough observations are smoothed with the closest densities (vector field smoothing).

An approach similar to vector field smoothing is proposed in Miglietta (1996). The same binary tree described for spectral transformation is used. For densities without sufficient adaptation data, the tree is climbed gathering the adaptation vectors of the closest densities until sufficient adaptation data are obtained.

A combination of stochastic matching performed with MLLR, MAP and transfer vector interpolation (TVI) for adapting means of unseen units by interpolating the transfer vectors of seen units is proposed in Chien *et al.* (1997). MLLR is performed first to adapt all the Gaussians even if very few data are available and to obtain a prior distribution on which MAP adaptation is applied followed by a TVI post-processing.

12.5.4. Practical Considerations and Trends

Parallel model combination techniques for increasing the robustness of an ASR system to additive environmental noise have been discussed. The adaptation of the model parameters in order to match the new recognition conditions has also been discussed. Two classes of techniques have been considered, namely, spectral-transformation-based techniques and Bayesian-adaptation-based techniques. Work performed at CNET–France Télécom has shown that equivalent results may be obtained with LMR model transformation and Bayesian adaptation of a speaker independent model from laboratory to field conditions, and from PSN to GSM conditions. However, a combined spectral transformation and Bayesian adaptation has been proposed for speaker adaptation (Digalakis and Neumeyer, 1995).

In order to get more robust models for a specific task, adaptation data collected in a real task condition (e.g. users' calls to a vocal server) should be used to adapt the model parameters. A model prototype trained from laboratory utterances can be used to collect field data for training a more robust model. The main drawback is that field data are often *sparse*: because some words or sentences are seldom uttered, there may not be enough data to train some parts of the model, making it necessary to smooth the adaptation function on the basis of acoustical space clustering.

Once the estimation procedure and the density clustering technique are defined, some problems remain related to the number of classes (clusters), the required quantity of adaptation data, and the use of supervised or unsupervised adaptation. These problems are inter-dependent. The number of clusters may be chosen as a function of the amount of adaptation data available, and the adaptation data necessary to perform a reliable adaptation to the environment depends on the application, the supervised/unsupervised adaptation mode, and the number of classes. These practical problems exist for both spectral transformation-based techniques and Bayesian adaptation techniques. Experiments have shown that unsupervised adaptation may achieve high performances.

Incremental adaptation techniques are very interesting because the speech recognition model adapts its own parameters to new conditions (Zavaliagkos, 1995; Huo and Lee, 1997). However, on-line adaptation of speech recognition systems remains a major research topic with the previously discussed practical considerations.

Recent papers show a tendency to perform joint optimization of model and spectral transformations. In Hwang and Wang (1997) cepstral mean subtraction is proposed for performing a *static compensation* consisting of time-invariant mapping. A *dynamic compensation* is performed by a time-varying mapping based on HMM inversion. Speech feature vectors are estimated by the inversion process. In order to recover from misrecognized words, N-best inversions can be performed and temporal constraints can be imposed on the acoustic features obtained from the inversion process and used for a frame-by-frame normalization. Joint optimization allows one to obtain the inverted features and the model parameters in a single process.

A practically feasible and interesting algorithm for combining frequency warping and model parameter estimation is proposed in Potamianos and Rose (1997).

When adaptation appears to be difficult because not enough data are available for establishing reliable knowledge of a noisy environment, it may be interesting to represent several situations by a mixture of HMMs for each unit and let the recognition algorithm decide which HMM is better suited to provide recognition results. It is important to train each HMM of the mixture with parameter trajectories with a coherent time evolution and to define a distance between data of variable duration and an HMM. A solution to these problems with a new theory for mixtures of HMMs is proposed in Korkmazskiy *et al.* (1997).

In classical systems, acoustic features are combined in a single acoustic vector for each time frame. In order to take into account different temporal behaviours in different frequency bands, separate streams of features extracted in parallel channels can be considered. Each channel independently extracts features in a given frequency band and uses them as observation of channel-specific HMMs. The problem of when recombining the scores produced by the HMMs of different channels is discussed in Tibrewala and Hermansky (1977), Bourlard and Dupont (1997) and Tomlinson *et al.* (1997).

12.6. CONCLUSIONS

Robustness is essential in successful ASR systems. As has been discussed, all the modules of an ASR system may be affected by a global strategy to increase the robustness in real-life applications.

For the acquisition of the speech signal, microphone arrays may be used, when this is possible in practice, for increasing the SNR. Echo cancelling is very important in order to facilitate the dialogue between humans and machines, contributing to robust recognition when the user speaks while the system plays a message. Endpoint detection remains a crucial problem especially in adverse environments.

Robust feature analysis is a principal approach to increasing the robustness. The proposed representations, including auditory models, incorporate perceptual knowledge to increase the robustness. Autocorrelation features in presence of additive stationary noises are useful to define robust representations.

Preprocessing techniques may be used to reduce the disturbing components in the observed signal. It has been observed that, in order to gain a better understanding of the noise effects it is better to project the components of the signal in the feature space where decoding is performed. Spectral subtraction-based algorithms incorporating perceptual knowledge lead to improved quality features. For the equalization of channel effects (convoluted effects), of crucial importance for ASR over the telephone, classical techniques are based on the reduction of the low frequencies of the cepstral (or log-spectral) trajectories. Blind equalization approach may be used integrating statistical knowledge about the clean speech signal in the equalization process. Statistical models may also be used in a global equalization scheme. This is the case of the MBSE method where sets of Wiener filters are associated with the states of a combined speech and noise model. Stochastic matching techniques integrate the model of the clean signal in the equalization process. A general form of an equalization function has been discussed.

Finally, the adaptation of the model parameters to new conditions may be performed in order to increase the robustness. Several adaptation techniques have been described; using model combination, spectral transformation and Bayesian adaptation. For additive environmental noise, it was reported that adding the noise to the reference model parameters gives better results than the use of a preprocessing technique (Mokbel, 1992, 1995a). A lot of work remains to be done for developing better incremental on-line adaptation techniques.

13

On the Use of Formal Grammars

Anna Corazza[*] and Renato De Mori[†]

13.1. INTRODUCTION

The limit of n-grams is that they describe short-distance relations between words, ignoring long-distance ones. Furthermore, long-distance polygrams may not capture the presence of important structural constituents of a sentence.

[*]Istituto per la Ricerca Scientifica e Tecnologica – 38050 Pantè di Povo, Trento, Italy.
[†]School of Computer Science, McGill University, Montreal, P.Q. H3A 2A7, Canada.

In order to consider more general relations and categories of word groups, more sophisticated *formal grammars* can be used for describing phrase structures. In general, grammars generate sequences of words that are sentences of a language and can therefore be used to constrain ASR. The major practical problem with grammars is that they may not be capable of reproducing certain sentences in a natural language corpus. Unlike *n*-gram models, grammar-based models provide, in general, only a partial *coverage* of natural language. In spite of this problem, it may be useful to use grammars in conjunction with *n*-gram models, especially if grammars are stochastic ones and their application can produce a probability that the sentence belongs to a language. The use of a model combining *n*-gram and grammatical scores can result in a lower perplexity and more accurate recognition for a given corpus. Grammar knowledge can also be used to build syntactic constituents useful for sentence interpretation.

Recent work that will be described in this chapter has introduced algorithms for computing the upperbounds of probabilities that a stochastic grammar generates a sentence of which only chunks are known. This makes stochastic grammars suitable to be used in progressive search for expanding partial theories that are more likely than others to be completed with a high score. This concept follows a search paradigm known as *hypothesize and test*, widely used in ASU.

Sentence structures are of different types: active, passive, clauses, yes/no questions, WH-questions (e.g. "Where is John?"), infinitives (e.g. "She asked to leave"), prepositional and embedded. Sentence mood can be expressed by declarative, imperative and exclamatory forms. In general, sentences are made of smaller compounds called *phrases*. Of particular interest are verb phrases and noun–noun phrases (e.g. coffee table), agglutinated words (e.g. shareholder), complex noun groups (e.g. executive advisory board) and phrasal lexical entries (e.g. in and out).

The set of words of a language is the *terminal alphabet* (V_T) of a grammar. Abstract categories corresponding to types of word compounds are described by symbols of a *nonterminal alphabet* (V_N). One of these categories, usually indicated by the symbol S, represents *all* the sentences that a grammar can generate. Acceptable combinations of components can be described by a set P of *production rules* of a phrase structure grammar (PSG). In order to score phrases with probabilities, a probability can be associated with rules, making the grammar a stochastic one.

Section 13.2 reviews basic definitions of context-free grammars. Section 13.3 introduces stochastic context-free grammars. Section 13.4 discusses probability computation with stochastic grammars. Section 13.5 deals with the computation of probabilities of partial theories. Section 13.6 reports a few notes on the application of the theory discussed in the preceding sections. Section 13.7 reviews grammars and parsers for natural language processing (NLP). Section 13.8 reviews grammars and parsers for ASR and ASU.

13.2. CONTEXT-FREE GRAMMARS

Context-free grammars (CFGs) have been applied in different fields and are the most-used tools to describe programming languages. They are also used in other areas, e.g. for describing, among other things, biological phenomena and the syntactic structure of natural language sentences.

There are different types of strategies for natural language analysis with CFGs. A widely adopted classification is based on the analysis direction. For example, the analysis can be *left-to-right*, starting from the leftmost word in the sentence and progressing toward the rightmost one. On the contrary, *bidirectional* strategies select some words, in any position of the sentence, to be *seeds* that trigger further analysis steps. Seeds are then expanded into *islands*, that are sequences of adjacent words. Two or more islands can collapse into a unique island, and a process of this type can continue until all the words in the input string have been considered.

Note that bidirectional strategies are more general than the left-to-right ones (Stock *et al.*, 1989; Satta and Stock, 1994). The latter strategies, in fact, represent a special case of the former ones in which just one seed is considered, i.e. the first word in the string. The island is then expanded adding, at each step, the first non-analysed word at its right.

Bidirectional strategies are particularly useful when the recognizer outputs a word lattice or a word graph where the most probable word hypotheses can be used as seeds. Islands can be generated in spite of the errors introduced by the recognizer as a consequence of spontaneous speech phenomena. Input fragments containing low-probability words can be included into an analysis only if the expected compatibility with adjacent words is high.

Stochastic context-free grammars (SCFGs) (Salomaa, 1969) induce a probability distribution over language *sentences* generated by a CFG. They will be introduced in the next section.

13.2.1. Definitions

The definition of a CFG can be found, for example, in Aho and Ullman (1972) and is briefly recalled here.

A CFG is defined as a quadruple $G = (V_N, V_T, P, S)$, where:

- V_N is a finite set of *nonterminal* symbols, which, in natural language grammars correspond to syntactic classes.
- V_T is a finite set of *terminal* symbols disjoint from V_N, corresponding to the natural language vocabulary.
- S is a particular nonterminal symbol called *start symbol*.
- P is a finite set of *rewriting rules*.

The set of all and only the sequences of terminal words, which can be generated by rewriting the start symbol with rules in P and successively applying rewriting rules to the nonterminal symbols that progressively appear in the generation, is the *language* generated by the grammar.

In the following, H will denote a generic nonterminal; in particular, H_0 will denote the start symbol S. Non-terminal symbols will be denoted as $H_l, H_m, \ldots$, while terminal symbols will be denoted as $w_0, w_1, \ldots$. Given a set A, A^* will denote the set of all finite-length sequences of elements of A.

The grammar is context-free if the rules have the form $H \to \alpha$, where the symbol $\to$ does not belong to $V_T \cup V_N$ and indicates rewriting. $H \in V_N$ is also called the *left-hand side* of the rule and $\alpha \in (V_N \cup V_T)^*$ is the *right-hand side*. The intuitive meaning of each rule is that each nonterminal symbol can be rewritten by the right-hand side of one of the rules which has that symbol as left-hand side, independently from the context in which the symbol appears.

A rule having form $H \to \varepsilon$, with $H \in V_N$ and where ε corresponds to the empty string, is called *null rule*. Under the simple condition that the null string does not belong to the language generated by the grammar, it is always possible to find a grammar which is equivalent to the original one (i.e. that generates the same set of strings) and does not have null rules (Aho and Ullman, 1972). In the following, it is assumed that the considered grammars do not have null rules.

Given a CFG G and a terminal string $x \in V_T^*$, x can be derived in G if there exists a sequence of m rules r_i, $i = 0, \ldots, m-1$ and a sequence of strings $\alpha_i \in (V_N \cup V_T)^*$, $i = 0, \ldots, m$ fulfilling the following requirements: $\alpha_0 = S$; α_{i+1} can be obtained from α_i by substituting the left-hand side of r_i in α_i with its right-hand side; $\alpha_m = x$. The following notation will be used to describe derivations:

$$S \overset{r_1 \ldots r_m}{\Rightarrow} \alpha_m \quad \text{or} \quad S = \alpha_0 \overset{r_1}{\Rightarrow} \alpha_1 \overset{r_2}{\Rightarrow} \alpha_2 \overset{r_3}{\Rightarrow} \ldots \overset{r_{m-1}}{\Rightarrow} \alpha_{m-1} \overset{r_m}{\Rightarrow} \alpha_m = x \qquad (13.1)$$

where, for the sake of simplicity, the indication of rules r_i can be omitted.

A derivation represents the syntactic analysis of the sentence.

A *derivation tree* (or *parse tree*) can be associated with each derivation. This tree has a nonterminal symbol associated with each internal node and a terminal symbol associated with each leaf. The start symbol is associated with the root. The fact that $a_1 \ldots a_i$ (in this order) are the symbols associated with the children of a node, labelled by the nonterminal symbol H, implies that the rule $H \to a_1 \ldots a_i$ has been used to rewrite the symbol H.

Derivations that differ only in the order in which rules are applied are equivalent and correspond to the same derivation tree. Two different derivation trees for the sentence "I have seen a film with Paul Newman" are given in Figure 13.1. Note that they correspond to two different meanings of the sentence. The right parse tree in Figure 13.1 implies that Paul Newman is playing in the film, while, in the other case, the meaning is that the speaker and Paul Newman went to a cinema together. Grammars generating more

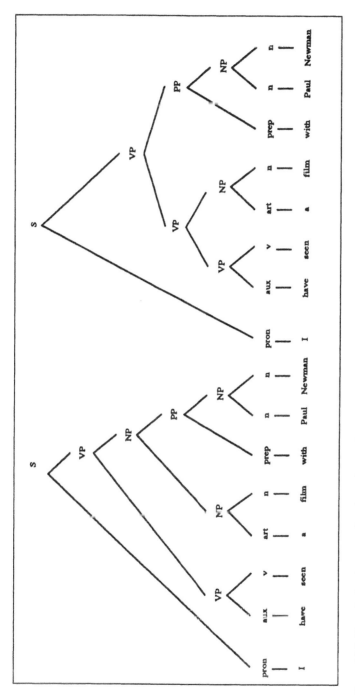

Figure 13.1 Two derivation trees for the string "I have seen a film with Paul Newman".

than one derivation tree for at least one sentence in the language are said to be
ambiguous. Since natural languages are ambiguous, the grammars generating
them are usually ambiguous.

For reasons discussed in Baker (1979), the algorithms presented in the
following are easier to explain if the grammar is in Chomsky normal form
(CNF). A CFG is in CNF if all the rules in P are either *nonterminal binary
rules,* i.e. in the form:

$$H_i \rightarrow H_j H_m, \quad H_i, H_j, H_m \in V_N \tag{13.2}$$

or *unary terminal rules* having the form:

$$H_i \rightarrow a, \quad H_i \in V_N, a \in V_T. \tag{13.3}$$

This is not a restriction, because every CFG (with no null rules) can be
converted into an equivalent one in CNF, by using an algorithm presented
in Aho and Ullman (1972). Note that the grammar used in the example depicted
in Figure 13.1 is in CNF.

13.3. STOCHASTIC CONTEXT-FREE GRAMMARS

Given a CFG, a probability distribution can be defined on the derivation trees
that can be obtained with the grammar. Such a distribution can be extended to
the set of all possible finite derivation trees by assigning null probability to all
the trees that cannot be derived by the grammar. The probability distribution
defined on the derivations is used to define a probability distribution on the
sentences of the language generated by the grammar. A more detailed
discussion on this subject can be found in Gonzales and Thomason (1978)
and in the two chapters by Jelinek (pp. 345–360) and Ney (pp. 319–344)
in De Mori and Laface (1992).

Given a CFG G and a derivation of string x in G, defined by the (13.1),
the sequence of rule applications can be considered as a sequence of
stochastic events $r_1 r_2 \ldots r_m$. The derivation probability $\Pr(r_1 r_2 \ldots r_m)$ can be
written as:

$$\Pr(S \overset{r_1 r_2 \ldots r_m}{\Rightarrow} x) = \Pr(r_1) \Pr(r_2 | r_1) \Pr(r_3 | r_1 r_2) \ldots \Pr(r_m | r_1 r_2 \ldots r_{m-1}) \tag{13.4}$$

where $\Pr(r_i | r_1 r_2 \ldots r_{i-1})$, with $1 < i \le m$, is the conditional probability that rule
r_i is applied under the condition that rules $r_1 r_2 \ldots r_{i-1}$ have been applied before.
The following approximation (Gonzales and Thomason, 1978) is widely
accepted:

$$\Pr(r_i | r_1 r_2 \ldots r_{i-1}) \simeq \Pr(r_i) \tag{13.5}$$

that is the probability of a rule application does not depend on previously
applied rules (the rule application history).

Under this hypothesis, equation (13.4) becomes:

$$\Pr(S \overset{r_1 r_2 \ldots r_m}{\Rightarrow} x) = \Pr(r_1) \Pr(r_2) \Pr(r_3) \ldots \Pr(r_m). \tag{13.6}$$

This is of course the simplest assumption, but not the only one. A different choice is made, for example, in Charniak and Carroll (1994), where the probability of a rule application depends also on the parent of its left-hand side nonterminal. Such an assumption increases the number of parameters to be estimated and can therefore be applied only when a sufficient quantity of training data is available. Bigram and trigram approximations of rule application histories can also be considered.

In conclusion, an SCFG is an extension of a CFG where a probability is associated with each rule. The probabilities of the rules rewriting a nonterminal symbol must satisfy the following constraint:

$$\sum_{\alpha \in (V_N \cup V_T)^*} \Pr(H \to \alpha) \leq 1, \quad \forall H \in V_N \tag{13.7}$$

If the equality holds, then the SCFG is said to be *proper*. Given an SCFG, its *characteristic grammar* is given by the CFG obtained disregarding all the probabilities associated with the rules. Notice that, while each SCFG has one and only one characteristic grammar, given a CFG there exists an infinite number of SCFGs which admit it as a characteristic grammar. Moreover, if an SCFG has a rule with null probability, this rule can be simply deleted from the grammar without affecting the language generated or the corresponding probability distribution.

An SCFG is usually obtained from a characteristic grammar by a data-driven estimation of the rule probabilities from a sufficiently large training corpus. A SCFG is a language model with a number of parameters to be estimated. If the grammar is proper, then the number of parameters to be estimated from data is equal to the difference between the number of rules and the number of nonterminal symbols. Often, a compromise has to be found between the quantity of available data and the dimension of the grammar.

13.3.1. SCFG Properties

In a proper grammar, every nonterminal symbol in a derivation is always rewritten and all the derivation trees produced by such a grammar are *terminal* ones, in the sense that all their leaves are terminal symbols.

Given the above definition of terminal tree, the set of all trees derived by the grammar can be partitioned into the subset of terminal trees and the one of "nonterminal trees", that is the subset of the trees in which at least one nonterminal symbol has not been rewritten. From each terminal tree with root S it is possible to obtain a sequence of terminal symbols considering the leaf labels from left to right. These strings are sentences of the language $\mathcal{L}_G$

generated by the grammar. Every sentence in the language is generated by at least one tree in the set and every tree in the set generates a sentence in the language. Therefore, the probability of the whole language is the probability of the set of all and only the terminal trees in the grammar having root S. In a non-proper grammar there exist nonterminal trees which have probability greater than zero; as a consequence, the language probability is lower than one. In this case, the SCFG is said to be *inconsistent*. On the contrary, whenever the following relation holds:

$$\sum_{\alpha \in \mathcal{L}_G} \Pr(S \Rightarrow \alpha) = \sum_{\alpha \in (V_N \cup V_T)^*} \Pr(S \Rightarrow \alpha) = 1, \quad \forall H \in V_N \qquad (13.8)$$

the grammar is said to be *consistent*. The above discussion shows that every non-proper grammar is inconsistent. However, it is also possible that a proper grammar is inconsistent. In this case, the probability of every nonterminal tree is null, but the probability that a tree is infinite is not null (Wetherell, 1980).

Every CFG which is cycle-free[1] and has no null rules can be put in CNF. Accordingly, every SCFG such that its characteristic grammar fulfills such requirements can be represented in CNF, while preserving the distribution of probabilities on the language. Furthermore, it can be shown that, even if, in general, the number of rules grows when a grammar is converted into CNF, the number of parameters to be estimated from a corpus does not change.

13.3.2. Sentence Probability

In the previous section, it has been mentioned that a probability distribution can be associated with the set of all the derivation trees generated by the grammar. If each sentence of the language had one and only one derivation tree, then the tree probability would be equal to the probability of the corresponding sentence of the language generated by the grammar. Unfortunately, this is not the case because CFGs can be ambiguous and generate sentences that can be derived with different trees (as shown in the example of Figure 13.1).

Thus, a sentence can be associated with the set of all its derivation trees and the sentence probability can be computed as the sum of the probabilities of the corresponding trees. Finding all the derivations of a sentence, computing the probability of each derivation and summing these probabilities may be computationally impractical. Fortunately, these probabilities can be factorized, resulting in an effective computational saving, as will be shown in section 13.4. The algorithm for this computation is called the *inside algorithm* (Baker, 1979; Jelinek *et al.*, 1992).

A different approach consists of associating with each sentence in the language the probability of its most probable derivation. This computation is

---

[1]A CFG is said to be *cycle-free* if it admits no derivation of the type $A \xRightarrow{r_1, r_2 \ldots r_m} A$ with $m > 0$.

performed by the Viterbi algorithm described in the next section. The Viterbi algorithm can easily generate also the most probable derivation of a given sentence in a given SCFG.

13.4. PROBABILITY COMPUTATION

In this section, some *dynamic programming* (Cormen *et al.*, 1990) algorithms for the computation of derivation probabilities are introduced after a brief description of the Cocke–Younger–Kasami (CYK) algorithm, on which probability computations are based.

13.4.1. The CYK Algorithm

Given a CFG G and a string u, a *recognizer* decides if u belongs to the language generated by the grammar. Furthermore, a *parser* finds all the derivations of the input string, which, in the applications considered here, is represented by a sentence. In the following, *tabular* algorithms are described in which computations are organized on the basis of an analysis table.

The most used tabular parsers are derived from the Earley algorithm (Earley, 1970; Graham and Harrison, 1976) and the Cocke–Younger–Kasami (CYK) (Younger, 1967; Graham and Harrison, 1976) algorithm. An intuitive description of the CYK algorithm is now proposed, because it will be used for probability computation later on. The CYK algorithm and all its extensions require that the grammar is in CNF. This does not restrict the set of languages that can be considered.

Recently, algorithms for probability computation have been formulated in the framework of Earley parsing (Stolcke, 1995).

Central to the CYK algorithm is a recognition phase based on the analysis table shown in Figure 13.2. This triangular table is made of half a square table of size $n \times n$, where n is the length of the input string, $w_1 \ldots w_n$. Each cell in the table corresponds to a substring of the input string: the cell (i, j) corresponds to the substring $w_i \ldots w_{i+j-1}$, starting from the ith word and having length equal to j words. Given the CFG in CNF, subsets of V_N are associated with each cell following the criterion that the nonterminal H_k is associated with the cell (i, j) if and only if a derivation tree exists having root H_k and yielding the substring of the cell: $w_i \ldots w_{i+j-1}$. Therefore, a necessary and sufficient condition for the string to belong to the language is that the grammar start symbol is associated with the cell $(1, n)$.

A dynamic programming algorithm fills the table in a bottom-up way, starting from the first row at the bottom, corresponding to unitary length substrings and going up with longer substrings. Let a parsing strategy be

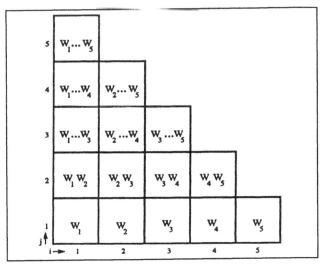

Figure 13.2 Analysis table for an input string $w_1 \ldots w_5$.

represented by a sequence of parsing steps in which a number is associated with a cell indicating at which step the cell is filled. In Figure 13.3, examples of the most popular strategies are reported. The strategies follow the fact that a non-terminal symbol H_k leads to a substring $w_i \ldots w_{i+j-1}$ if and only if at least one rule $H_k \rightarrow H_l H_m$ exists in P such that the substring $w_i \ldots w_{i+j-1}$ can be divided in two parts $w_i \ldots w_{i+h-1}$ and $w_{i+h} \ldots w_{i+j-1}$, respectively of length h and $j - h$ and two derivation trees exist for them having roots H_l and H_m respectively. A necessary and sufficient condition for this to happen is that H_l belongs to the cell (i, h) and H_m to the cell $(i + h, j - h)$ in the analysis table. Therefore, filling the cell (i, j) requires considering, for each rule in the grammar, all the pairs $(i, h), (i + h, j - h)$, for $h = 1, \ldots, j - 1$. In conclusion, each step corresponds

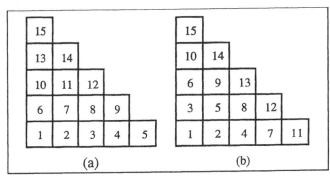

Figure 13.3 Table cells filling order in traditional bottom-up strategies (a) and in left-to-right strategies (b).

to building a new subtree (set) composed by a rule r and two previously built subtree sets τ_1 and τ_2.[2] This observation is important for the development of probabilistic algorithms.

A recognizer only needs to check, at the end of this bottom-up phase, if the start symbol belongs to the cell $(1, n)$ in the table. A parser, on the contrary, must perform a top-down pruning phase in which all partial derivations not leading to a complete tree are deleted from the table, leaving only the constituents of the complete derivation trees.

13.4.2. Probabilistic Parser

When an SCFG is considered, recognition involves computing the probability of the input string. This is performed by the so-called *inside algorithm* (Baker, 1979; Jelinek *et al.*, 1992), which computes the probability of the input string as the sum of the probabilities of each derivation. On the other hand, the Viterbi algorithm estimates the probability of the input string as the probability of its most probable derivation. In both cases, if derivations are required, a top-down phase must be added to the bottom-up one, similar to the original CYK algorithm. In the following, only the bottom-up phase will be considered, because the focus is on probability computation rather than on the construction of derivation trees.

13.4.3. Probability Estimation

Probability estimation of the rules in a SCFG from a sample set of sentences in the language is performed by the *inside–outside algorithm* (Baker, 1979), based on expectation-maximization (EM) techniques. The name was suggested to establish an analogy with the fact that it is a generalization of the *forward–backward algorithm* introduced in Chapter 5 for HMMs. For SCFGs, the probabilities are factorized in an "inside" part (containing the probabilities computed by the inside algorithm that a nonterminal generates a substring) and by an "outside" part (which can be intuitively seen as computing the probability of the remaining part of a derivation after the subtree used in the inside phase has been taken away).

The inside probability that a nonterminal H generates the substring $w_l \ldots w_{i+j}$ is denoted by $\Pr(H\langle w_i \ldots w_{l+j}\rangle)$. The outside probability corresponding to the same event in a tree generating the string $w_1 \ldots w_n$ starting from S is denoted by $\Pr(w_1 \ldots w_{i-1}\rangle H\langle w_{i+j+1} \ldots w_n)$.

---

[2] τ_1 and τ_2 are the sets of all the derivation trees rewriting the right-hand side of the rule into the two considered substrings.

If the sequence of rules used to generate a sentence is available, then estimation can be performed in a more direct way by simply evaluating the frequency of each rule.

13.4.4. The Inside Algorithm

The inside algorithm is analogous to CYK, except that a probability is associated, in each cell, with each nonterminal symbol, representing the probability that the symbol generates the substring associated with that cell. At the beginning, all these probabilities are set to zero. Each time a new possible derivation composed by a new rule r and two subtree sets τ_1 and τ_2 are found, the corresponding probability (given by the product of the probability of the rule and that of the two subtree sets) is added to the probability of what is at the left-hand side of the rule. In this way, the probability associated with the start symbol in cell $(1, n)$ gives the probability of the input sentence. The intuitive description given above can be formalized with the following relations:

$$\Pr(H_k\langle w_i\rangle) = \Pr(H_k \to w_i)$$

$$\Pr(H_k\langle w_i \ldots w_{i+j}\rangle) = \sum_{l,m}\sum_{h=1}^{j-1}\Pr(H_k \to H_l H_m)\Pr(H_l\langle w_i \ldots w_{i+h-1}\rangle)$$

$$\times \Pr(H_m\langle w_{i+h} \ldots w_{i+j-1}\rangle)$$

where $\Pr(H_k\langle w_i\rangle)$ is the probability associated with the nonterminal symbol H_k in cell $(i, 1)$ and $\Pr(H_k\langle w_i \ldots w_{i+j}\rangle)$ the one associated to symbol H_k in (i, j).

13.4.5. The Outside Algorithm

The *outside probabilities* are computed using a similar table, but in a reverse order with respect to the inside probabilities. The relation:

$$P_o(H_l, i, j) = \Pr(w_1 \ldots w_{i-1}\rangle H_l\langle w_{i+j} \ldots w_n) \tag{13.9}$$

refers to the probability that the string $w_1 \ldots w_n$ is generated given the subtree or the set $H_l\langle w_i \ldots w_{i+j+1}\rangle$. This probability is written in cell (i, j) and it is recursively computed starting from the following initial conditions, where the start symbol of the grammar is indicated by H_0, as introduced above:

$$P_o(H_0, 1, n) = 1$$

$$P_o(H_l, 1, n) = 0, \quad \text{for every } l \neq 0.$$

The other steps are then based on the following relation, for which an intuitive interpretation can be found by inspecting Figure 13.4:

$$P_o(H_m, i, j) = \sum_{k,l} \left\{ \sum_{h=1}^{i} \Pr(H_k \rightarrow H_l H_m) \Pr(H_l \langle w_{i-h} \ldots w_{i-1} \rangle) \right.$$

$$\times P_o(H_k, i - h, j) + \sum_{h=1}^{n-i-j} \Pr(H_k \rightarrow H_m H_l)$$

$$\left. \times \Pr(H_l \langle w_{i+j} \ldots w_{i+j+h-1} \rangle) P_o(H_k, i, j + h) \right\} \qquad (13.10)$$

13.4.6. The Viterbi Algorithm

The Viterbi algorithm computes the probability of the best derivation of the input string. When only the probability of the best derivation is associated with each string in the language, the probability of the language is in general less than one, because some derivation trees having non-zero probability may have been neglected in the sum. Therefore, probabilities defined in this way may not be elements of a probability distribution on the language. This can be corrected by introducing a normalization factor $\mathcal{N}$, defined by:

$$\mathcal{N} = \sum_{x \in \mathcal{L}} \max_{\tau : S \rightarrow^\tau x} \Pr \tau. \qquad (13.11)$$

No algorithm is known for an efficient computation of such factor. Fortunately, this is not necessary for optimization; in fact, it can be disregarded because only comparisons between competing candidates are performed. On the contrary, perplexity computation requires the knowledge of the value of $\mathcal{N}$.

The Viterbi algorithm is analogous to the inside algorithm, except that a maximum operator replaces the sum. The equations (13.9) are therefore modified as follows:

$$\Pr(H_k \langle w_i \rangle) = \Pr(H_k \rightarrow w_i)$$

$$\Pr(H_k \langle w_i \ldots w_{i+j} \rangle) = \max_{l, m, 1 \le h \le j-1} \Pr(H_k \rightarrow H_l H_m)$$

$$\times \Pr(H_l \langle w_i \ldots w_{i+h-1} \rangle) \Pr(H_m \langle w_{i+h} \ldots w_{i+j-1} \rangle).$$

13.4.7. Probability Estimation from Partially Bracketed Data

The inside–outside algorithm performs a re-estimation of probabilities based on a training corpus. In principle, these probabilities could be used to induce a grammar given only the nonterminal set. Indeed, it would suffice to start with a grammar where all possible rules have probability greater than zero. Successive iterations of the algorithm are expected to reduce to zero some of

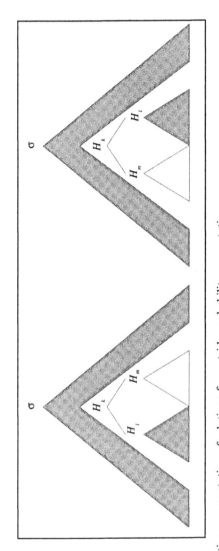

Figure 13.4 Intuitive representation of relations for outside probability computation.

these probabilities. Eventually, only rules with a probability greater than a threshold would be retained. Nevertheless, attempts (Lari and Young, 1990, 1991) to infer grammars in this way have failed in obtaining results with acceptable properties from a linguistic point of view.

On the other hand, the input data can be (partially) bracketed, like in the following example:

$$S[I/\text{pron VP}[\text{VP}[\text{VP}[have/\text{aux } seen/\text{v}] \text{ NP}[a/\text{det } film/\text{n}]]$$

$$PP[with/\text{prep NP}[Paul/\text{n } Newman/\text{n}]]]]$$

It can be seen that every terminal symbol is labelled with the corresponding preterminal; moreover, each bracket pair contains the bracketed version of the subtree generated by the nonterminal that precedes the left bracket. In this case, the probability estimation can be more accurate and produce a linguistically plausible grammar.

Bracketing can be only partial reflecting an abstention in decision making by the linguist who performed it. Even if several parse trees can be compatible with a partial bracketing, the exclusion of the less likely ones gives information that can be exploited to drive learning. Of course, variations exist from raw to fully bracketed texts with various degrees of partial bracketing.

In Pereira and Shabes (1992), a variation of the inside–outside algorithm is proposed, which takes advantage of partial bracketing in order to better focus probability re-estimation at every step. This is accomplished by letting only the parse trees which are compatible with the input bracketing contribute to the computation of inside and outside probabilities.

Experimental results show an improvement in the algorithm convergence rate and in the quality of the resulting grammar when some bracketing is available. Moreover, the actual complexity of computation of bracketed text is lower than that for raw text.

13.4.8. Computational Complexity

The asymptotic computational complexities of the three algorithms, CYK, Inside and Viterbi, are cubic in the length n of the input string. In fact, for each cell in the table (their number is proportional to n^2), all the $|P|$ rules have to be considered; for every rule, a number of cells proportional to n is considered. In total, the computational complexity of the algorithms is $O(n^3|P|)$. Note that in practical cases, $|P|$ is much greater than n.

13.5. PARTIAL ANALYSES

Recognition and interpretation strategies, especially in the case of progressive search, are an essential component of the A^* algorithm (Pearl, 1984) and may

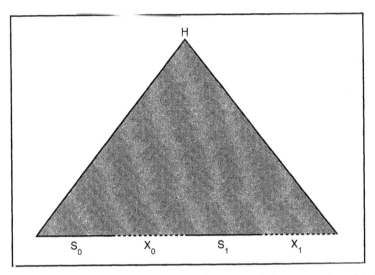

Figure 13.5 Scheme of a partial analysis derivation tree: solid segments (s_0, s_1) indicate parts of the input which has been recognized; dotted segments (x_0, x_1) correspond to parts of the input which still has to be analysed (gaps).

use SCFGs in many ways. Each partial interpretation, also called *theory*, is scored by the sum of two or more terms, one of them being an upperbound of the final score. This is required because search for an interpretation can be seen as a maximization problem in which a complete theory with maximum probability has to be found.

In many cases, the search strategy is left-to-right, following the order in which words are uttered. Bidirectional strategies (Stock *et al.*, 1989; Satta and Stock, 1994) have also been proposed, in particular, for dealing with errors at the beginning of the utterance. Moreover, an optimal bidirectional search strategy is very useful when the output of the recognizer is represented by a word lattice.

With a bidirectional strategy, possible partial theories are represented by any sequence of substrings (representing the already analysed parts of the input) and gaps, which represent an unknown sequence of words corresponding to the parts of the input not yet analysed (Figure 13.5). In the case of the inside probability, the best possible score which could be associated with partial theories would be the maximum of the probabilities of all the complete theories which could be obtained by expanding the partial theory. Unfortunately, no algorithm is known for computing such a score. However, it is possible to compute, for every partial theory, the sum of the probabilities of all the derivation trees of all the complete theories which can be derived by that partial theory (see Jelinek and Lafferty (1991) for the left-to-right case, and Corazza *et al.* (1991) for the bidirectional one). Even if such an upper bound is not optimal, there is evidence that it gradually approaches the optimal one with the progress of the analysis.

This computation has in general a practically unacceptable computational complexity. Nevertheless, whenever a distribution of probability can be defined on the number of words which can fill a gap, an algorithm with acceptable complexity can be applied to compute a tighter upper bound of the final probability.

On the other hand, if the Viterbi score is considered, it is possible to compute the tightest possible upper bound, that is the optimal score in an A^* strategy. Indeed, in this case, two properties whose proof can be found in Corazza *et al.* (1994) allow the general time complexity polynomial to be retained.

The first property is used to compute, for every nonterminal symbol, the maximum probability of all the trees which have that nonterminal as root node. In fact, it is shown that, when no constraint is imposed on the tree yield, an optimal derivation tree cannot have two nested subtrees having the same root as intuitively illustrated in Figure 13.6. As a consequence, a symbol cannot appear more than once in a path from the root node to any

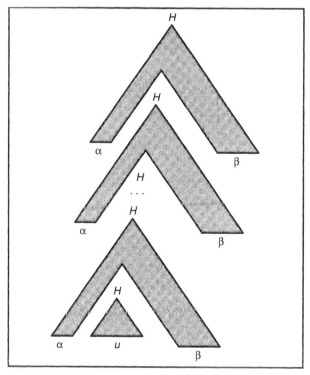

Figure 13.6 Nested trees having the same root lower the total probability and therefore are not allowed in the optimal tree.

leaf. Therefore, each optimal subtree has height[3] less than $|V_N|$. Since every subtree of an optimal tree must be optimal, the set of all optimal trees having for root any nonterminal can be built considering trees of increasing height in at most $|V_N|$ steps.

The second property, described in detail in Corazza *et al.* (1994) and not here for the sake of brevity, is used to restrict the tree set to be explored in order to find the best tree yielding a given partial analysis. The optimum of these trees belongs to a *ground* set, made of all and only the trees satisfying the property and such that none of their subtrees satisfies it.

These two facts can be effectively used to design an efficient algorithm to compute the Viterbi scores for partial theories given by a bidirectional parsing algorithm such as the one described in Satta and Stock (1994). In addition to that, all the computations which only depend on the grammar and not on the input sentence can be computed off-line, thus decreasing the on-line computation time.

13.6. APPLICATIONS

A problem which SCFGs share with other language models is that of limited coverage. Therefore, smoothing techniques can be used to avoid giving null probability to a rule which is not used in the training data.

From a slightly different point of view, this problem can be solved if SCFGs are not used alone, but are integrated with other models, such as bigrams or trigrams described in Chapter 7.

A way to combine different information sources has been proposed in Stolcke and Segal (1994) with a method to estimate bigram probabilities from an SCFG. This allows smoothing SCFG-derived bigrams with bigrams directly estimated from data. Experiments have shown an improvement on the overall ASR performance.

13.7. SOME MODELS FOR NATURAL LANGUAGE PROCESSING

Different points of view, such as linguistic plausibility or computational efficiency, have been taken in building models for natural language processing (NLP).

An important distinction is between general purpose language models with a broad coverage of human language and models limited to a restricted domain, a frequent choice for practical applications.

---

[3]The height of a tree is defined as the maximum length of all the paths connecting the root node to each leaf.

Another important distinction is between models mostly conceived by human experts and models built with machine learning from a corpus of spoken (or written) sentences. In order to assess the ability of the model to describing a corpus, *coverage* is evaluated as the percentage of sentences in the corpus correctly described by the model.

In the following, a few natural language models will be briefly introduced, which could be of interest for written and spoken language processing. An important difference between the two modalities is that for spoken languages, the words of the sentence to be analysed may be affected by recognition errors.

The main goal of syntactic analysis is to produce a parse tree of the input sentence. Natural language sentences are very often syntactically ambiguous, and their analysis may lead to more than one tree. So, a parsing algorithm should not only consider all the possible parse trees of the given sentence, but should also provide a ranking among them.

Probabilistic language models offer a natural ranking criterion based on parse tree probabilities, computed as discussed in section 13.4.6.

History-based grammars (HBG) (Black *et al.*, 1993) are based on the idea that the application of a rule should be decided in a bottom-up fashion and depend on the context of the rule itself. The context is represented by words and nonterminals surrounding the point where the rule should be used to expand a partial parse. Decision trees, described in Appendix B, can be used to extract only the parts of the context which are relevant for deciding which rule must be applied at a given point. Moreover, they can provide a probability distribution on the rule set.

Generalized phrase structure grammars (GPSG) (Gazdar *et al.*, 1985) have a CFG structure, where each nonterminal is represented by a *category*, described by a set of *features*. A unification mechanism is defined on these features. It is composed of a set of constraints regulating the "propagation" of features in the parse tree and of a set of propositions which must hold among the categories of a valid parse tree. In Fisher (1989), an efficient parsing algorithm is proposed for GPSG.

Head-driven phrase structure grammars (HPSG) (Pollard and Sag, 1994) are similar to GPSG, except that rules are more abstract and parsing is driven by specific constituents like verbs and nouns called *heads*.

In *case grammars*, a sentence representation is centred around the main verb and its cases, as will be described in Chapter 14.

Unification grammars associate to rules a unification mechanism based on theorem proving (Shieber, 1986) to impose the satisfaction of linguistic constraints such as number and gender agreement. These grammars have been applied to ASU as described in Chien *et al.* (1993).

Tree-adjoining grammars (TAGs) (TAGs, 1994) are context-sensitive and preserve all properties of CFGs, with rules for generating parse trees and semantic interpretations. In a *lexicalized* grammar, every elementary structure is associated with a lexical item (its *anchor*). *Lexicalized TAGs* used in NLP are the lexicalized version of TAGs.

Discontinuous grammars (Dahl, 1989) are able to "skip" unidentified strings of symbols and to relate specific non-contiguous constituents. This is useful to consider phenomena like movement and co-indexing.

A different approach with respect to phrase structure grammars is represented by *dependency grammars* (DGs) (Mel'cuk, 1988). These grammars describe links between words. The analysis of a sentence attempts to establish links between constituents that can be discontinuous, as described in Covington (1990).

With DG parsing, all words in a sentence must be connected by some link to other constituents. Links are oriented, from the word which "governs" the relation (*governor* or *head*) versus the *dependent* word. They can be represented as in the following example:

$$
\begin{bmatrix}
category : noun \\
gendre : masculin \\
number : singular \\
case : agentive
\end{bmatrix}
\leftarrow
\begin{bmatrix}
category : verb \\
person : third \\
number : singular
\end{bmatrix}
\tag{13.12}
$$

where a link is established from a *verb*, representing the head, and a *noun*. All the *dependency trees* of a sentence can be represented by a *syntactic graph* (SG) (Seo and Simmons, 1989). Figure 13.7 shows an example of an SG for the sentence: "I have seen a film with Paul Newman". Interestingly, dependency grammar is equivalent to a constrained version of a linguistic theory, called X-bar theory, where all terminal nodes are words and only one phrasal bar level is allowed (Covington, 1990).

If the additional condition is imposed that two links can never cross, then DGs are called *link grammars* (Sleator and Temperley, 1993). A probabilistic description of link grammars has been proposed (Lafferty *et al.*, 1992), together with a training algorithm for estimating link probabilities from a training corpus.

In *constraint-dependency grammars* (CDG) (Maruyama, 1990; Harper and Helzerman, 1995) each word is represented by a node with associated lexical roles. Each role is represented by a label and a link to another word that it can modify. In principle, all nodes are linked in a *constraint network* (CN), which can be seen as an *AND/OR graph*. Links are eliminated by a process of constraint satisfaction. Constraints are expressed in the form "*if antecedent then consequent*". CDGs are more expressive than CFGs and less than TAGs.

Slot grammars (Lappin and McCord, 1990) are similar to DGs. They are a lexicalized model in which a set of *slots* is associated to each word in the lexicon. Filling the slots associated to a special word, called the *head* of the sentence, generates dependent constituents.

Head-driven grammars (Chelba *et al.*, 1995) are lexicalized grammars, where head-words percolate upwards in the parse tree and replace nonterminal labels

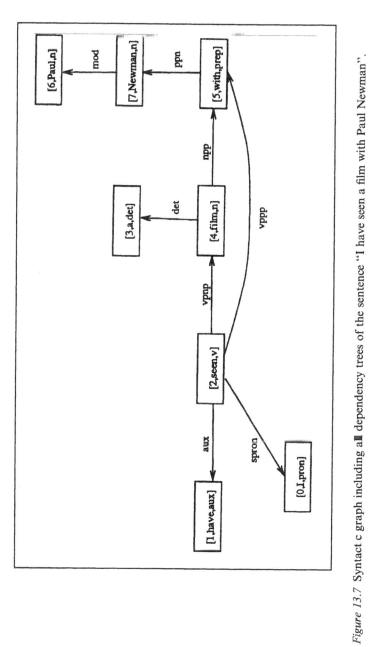

Figure 13.7 Syntactc graph including all dependency trees of the sentence "I have seen a film with Paul Newman".

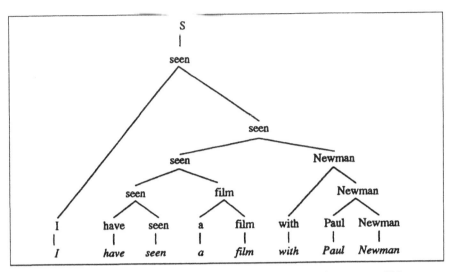

Figure 13.8 Example of a head-driven grammar derivation for the sentence "I have seen a film with Paul Newman".

(Figure 13.8). Probabilities are computed for each structure as the product of the probability of all the involved rules, considered with their multiplicity.

13.8. OVERVIEW OF GRAMMARS AND PARSERS FOR ASR AND ASU

Some of the concepts introduced in this chapter have been used in various ways for ASR and ASU. Parsing word hypotheses has two fundamental problems. First, some of the words may be wrong, so error correction may be necessary. Second, multiple, competing word hypotheses may be part of the input. Lattice parsers are proposed in Andry and Thornton (1991) and Rayner and Wyard (1995). In Seneff (1992b), a *robust parser* is described that handles certain types of errors by partial parsing the longest substring of the input with possibility of restarting after a fault has been encountered. The possibility of going back to a bigram LM when parsing fails is presented in Jurafsky *et al.* (1995). *Error correcting parsers* for ASR are proposed in Ward (1990), Okada *et al.* (1994) and Vidal *et al.* (1995). Relaxed grammar rules to be used if regular parsing fails are proposed in Bates *et al.* (1992). *Chunk recognition* can be performed by using hand-derived patterns of dependency links (Abney, 1993). Other techniques for sequence identification are proposed in Ries *et al.* (1995) and Wright *et al.* (1994). Of theoretical importance is the possibility of recognizing substrings of LR(k) languages in linear time (Bates and Lavie, 1994). Worth mentioning is also a partial parsing method for texts (McDonald,

1992). Chunks can be combined together with a bigram LM (Chien *et al.*, 1993), using a combination of a *constituent grammar* and a finite state *utterance grammar* (Meteer and Rohlicek, 1993).

Various problems arise when parsing with incompleteness and frequent ambiguities. Methods introduced for dealing with these problems generally increase time complexity. Practical solutions are based on the use of probabilistic grammars or probabilistic parsers and on the introduction of heuristics. Probabilistic LR parsers for ASR were proposed in Chitrao and Grishman (1990), Seneff *et al.* (1994), Goddeau (1994) and Jones and Eisner (1992). A review of parsing with stochastic grammars can be found in Kimura *et al.* (1994).

Other parsers for ASR were proposed in Kita and Ward (1991), Tsuboi and Takebayashi (1992), Wallerstein *et al.* (1994), Staab (1995). Of particular interest are those with *semantic constraints* for ASU proposed in Makino *et al.* (1991), Morimoto (1994) and Giachin (1992). An interpretation of syntax and semantics into a concept network is proposed in Pieraccini *et al.* (1992b), Ward and Issar (1994b) and Brown and Buntschuh (1994). Trees and trellises can be used to predict new words based on questions on what has already been parsed (Waegner and Young, 1994). Evidence that constraint dependency grammars are more powerful than CFG is provided in Zoltowski *et al.* (1992). Finite-state grammars that are simple and completely cover a given corpus, but generate much more sentences than the ones in the language to be modelled are discussed in Pereira and Shabes (1992). Dynamic generation of transition networks from LR parse tables appear to outperform finite-state models (Kita *et al.*, 1994).

Other heuristic-based CFG parsing algorithms are presented in Fred and Leitao (1993), a matrix parser is proposed in Singer and Sagayama (1993). New dynamic programming concepts are applied to parsing in Nagata (1994) and Ney (1991). A maximum-entropy model for parsing applied to history-based grammars is proposed in Ratnaparkhi *et al.* (1994). Connectionist parsers are proposed in Jain *et al.* (1992). Parsers based on Bayesian belief networks are proposed in Lucke (1995).

Various acoustic cues have been proposed as heuristics to be used for driving ASR parsers. Relative duration is proposed for syntactic disambiguation (Ostendorf *et al.*, 1990), recognition of prosodic phrases and the use of prosody for scoring candidates is proposed in Wightman and Ostendorf (1991), Bishop (1994), Veilleux *et al.* (1994), Fred and Leitao (1993). The use of prosody for predicting phrase boundaries is proposed in Kompe *et al.* (1994) and Ostendorf and Veilleux (1995).

13.9. CONCLUSIONS AND TRENDS

Syntactic information is very important for ASR and ASU and can be used in *explicit* form, in manually constructed grammars, or in *implicit* form, in corpora bracketed and labelled by experts. Each form has advantages and disadvantages, and the best solution is to combine the two.

Parsing can be seen as a search process involving all kinds of useful heuristics, including acoustic cues, interleaving syntactic/semantic interpretation taking into account grammar, repair, parse preference, and scoping. Moreover, automatic model learning can take advantage of clustering words into classes using mutual information. *Dynamic language adaptation* can increase the expectation of user preferences.

Some important facts and trends on the use of grammars for ASR and ASU are discussed in an interesting overview by Bates (1994), where important requirements of future systems are reported to be: *portability* to new domains, *scalability* from laboratory demonstrations to real applications, *robustness* and *feedback* that the system can give to the user to recover from errors.

Statistical models can help in ensuring coverage and performing robust recognition with phenomena typical in spoken language, like fragmentary utterances, after thoughts ("I'd like a return flight, ... morning flight"), repairs or self-corrections, metonymy ("I need info between Tampa and Montreal"), skips of tongue ("does Delta aircraft fly DC10?"), well-formed but odd sentences ("I need to return a flight from Denver to Boston") and ungrammatical sentences. Strategies may include the extension of linguistic rules, the separate use of constituent and utterance grammars and the use of general robust interpretation techniques.

14

Sentence Interpretation

Roland Kuhn[*] and Renato De Mori[†]

[*]Panasonic Speech Technology Laboratory, 3888 State Street #202, Santa Barbara, CA 93105, USA.
[†]School of Computer Science, McGill University, Montreal, P.Q. H3A 2A7, Canada.

14.1. INTRODUCTION

Semantics is the scientific study of the relations between signs or symbols and what they denote or mean. In programming languages, semantics specifies the operations a machine performs when an instruction is executed. In person–machine communication, the ultimate goal of understanding is the execution of an action. The result of understanding by a machine is represented by a data structure produced with an interpretation strategy using a semantic theory. For this purpose a semantic theory is usually based on a semantic representation describing relationships at three different levels, namely the meaning of individual words (relative to a vocabulary and structure of concepts), the meaning of a group of words in a syntactic structure, and the meaning of a sentence in its context.

Epistemology, the science of knowledge, considers a datum as the basic unit. A datum can have time and space coordinates, can have multiple aspects and qualities that make it different from others. A datum can be represented by an image or it can be abstract and be represented by a concept. A concept can be empirical, structural, or *a priori*. Computer epistemology deals with observable facts, their representation in a computer and rules permitting legitimate conclusions to be drawn from these facts (McCarty and Hayes, 1969).

In computers, a semantic representation treats data as *objects* respecting *logical adequacy* in order to precisely, formally and unambiguously represent any particular interpretation that a human may place on a sentence. The representation should be able to deal with *intension* (the essence of a concept) and *extension* (the set of all objects which are instances of a given concept).

There must be *algorithms* which make use of representations for subsequent inferences and actions.

Knowledge about the structure of the domain to be represented groups objects by their properties. The most important one is *type*. Types are organized into *hierarchies* of classes. Major classes suggested by Aristotle are substance, quantity, quality, relation, place, time, position, state, action and affection.

Judgement is expressed by *predicates* which describe relations between objects or classes. An example is the following representation for the question: "Does Air Canada fly from Toronto to Dallas?" which would be expressed in predicate calculus by the expression:

(TEST (CONNECT AC TORONTO DALLAS))

If a semantic interpretation of a sentence in a given language is obtained using the results of syntactic analysis, it is possible to make use of the information conveyed by the verb group, nouns, adjectives and classifiers, quantifiers and determiners, the preposition group, function and content words. A sentence may be described by *different syntactic structures* corresponding to different semantic interpretations. In this case, syntactic analysis can solve semantic ambiguities. Interpretation must account for *multiple meanings (ambiguities)* of words, phrases and sentences.

Language comprehension requires an *interpretation strategy* that attempts to match semantic representations with sentences expressed in natural language. The appropriate knowledge representation for effective comprehension by machine depends on the application

The most important criteria for judging machine comprehension are *precision* and *coverage*; they are relevant both for semantic representation and for the relation of semantic items to words and syntactic structures. Highly structured representations may be precise, but applicable to a limited number of cases. On the other hand, coverage of a great variety of sentences may be achieved through statistical methods relating the presence of certain words to the occurrence of a given concept. Such methods are often effective for simple concepts and in limited domains but not for complex structures of concepts. For speech understanding in limited domains, one can usually assume that the semantic representations encountered will be drawn from a small set of structures. In such cases, the interpretation strategy attempts to match the data to be interpreted to these structures and to produce instantiations of them.

Excellent references are Jackendoff (1990) for semantic structures, Allen (1987, chs 7 and 8) for semantic interpretation and Winograd (1983) for the characterization of information conveyed by syntactic structures.

This chapter reviews different types of knowledge representations and strategies employed in language comprehension. For a specific application, one must always try to find a compromise between accuracy and the complexity of the implementation. In many cases, rather than aiming at complete coverage, it may be more realistic to provide the system with dialogue capabilities that enable it to recover from comprehension errors. Other important design considerations are transportability, maintainability, cost, and processing time. To illustrate the decisions that must be made in designing a functioning speech understanding system, the knowledge representations and comprehension strategies employed by several different research groups for the Air Travel Information System (ATIS) task are described and discussed.

14.2. SEMANTIC REPRESENTATION IN COMPUTER SYSTEMS

14.2.1. Surface Representations

In analogy with syntactic analysis, semantic analysis can produce a *surface* or a *deep* representation of a sentence. A surface representation can be generated with knowledge associated to syntax rules and can be domain independent. This is the case of Montague grammars, in which each syntactic rule is associated with a semantic rule that turns the sentence into a formula (Partee, 1976).

Knowledge representation in computer systems is based on schemes for data structures. Knowledge about types of representation is often termed *meta-knowledge*. An interesting tutorial on the use of formal logic for semantic interpretation and communication between software agents can be found in Russell and Norvig (1995, ch. 22).

14.2.2. Case Structures

Many deep semantic representations are based on *deep-case n-ary relations* as proposed by Fillmore (1968). A *case* is the name of a particular *role* that a noun phrase or other component takes in the state or activity expressed by the *verb* of a sentence. There is a case structure for each main verb.

Deep-case systems have very few cases, each one representing a basic semantic constraint. Different *surface cases* can be mapped into a deep case that represents a sort of semantic invariant. The elements between which these relations are established can in turn be clustered into types structured into hierarchies.

Due to the nature of semantics, the *order* of constituents of a case is fixed or unimportant, thus suggesting the use of *logic* rather than grammars as an acceptable mathematical framework for formulating definitions of models and operations on their elements.

Case determination may depend on syntactic information (case signals) as well as feature checking (case conditions) and can be done by a case function. This function may return the *likelihood* that a given preposition term serves the case relationship to the main verb of the sentence.

It is possible to use a variable number of *preemptive levels*. A case function may return a value which preempts any previous use of that case.

Cases proposed in Fillmore (1968) are:

- agentive (A) – the animate instigator for an action
- instrumental (I) – inanimate force or object causally involved
- dative (D) – animate being affected
- factitive (F) – object or being resulted from an action
- locative (L) – location or spatial orientation
- objective (O) – determined by verb.

The verb determines a predicate P which has associated cases, as in "push $[O \{A\} \{I\}]$". The predicate means that push must have an object O; as $\{ \}$ means optional, push may have an agent A and a force I. The case structure of P is a set of sequences of cases. Cases which are properties of a verb are *inner* cases (in particular the obligatory ones).

A case condition is a *relation* establishing that a term in a set T may serve in a case with respect to a given predicate. A case condition is defined in terms of features. Features can be derived from lexical descriptions of words. A detailed presentation of case structures can be found in Bruce (1975).

14.2.3. Semantic Frames

Often, domain knowledge more specific than case structures is represented inside computers with data structures called *frames*. They are made of the name of an entity and relations represented by (ATTRIBUTE VALUE) pairs called *slots*. Section 14.6 discusses several frame-based systems for the ATIS task.

A frame expresses knowledge about a concept, a stereotypical situation, an exemplar, an individual. A frame is usually verb-centred. Acceptable frames to represent concepts in a domain can be characterized by *frame grammars* which generate acceptable data structures and have rules of the type:

⟨frame⟩:   ⟨frame-name⟩⟨slots⟩*
⟨slot⟩:   ⟨aspect-name⟩[⟨description⟩ "of potential slot fillers" : types]
⟨description⟩: ⟨description-indicator⟩⟨bridge-name⟩⟨frame-name⟩

Case structures can be represented by frames expressing a verb paradigm. For example, a case frame for a verb is:

[eat (animate-entity physical-object)]

following the general structure:

[verb (subject-object)]

Frames can represent semantic structures including attributes other than cases. Different frames may share slots with similarity links. Slots may contain expectations or replacements (to be considered if slots cannot be filled). Descriptions are attached to slots to specify constraints. Given a slot-filler for a slot, the attached description can be inferred. Descriptions can be instantiations of a concept carrier and can inherit its properties. Descriptions may have connectives, coreferential (descriptions attached to a slot are attached to another and *vice versa*), declarative conditions. Slots may contain slot-filling programs. There may be *necessary* and *optional* slots.

Fillers can be obtained by *attachment* of procedures, *inheritance*, default. Procedures of the type "when-needed" or "when-filled" can also be attached to slots. In the first case the procedure is executed when the value of the slot is needed, in the second case when the slot is filled.

Selectional restrictions describe how a word sense constrains the senses of the words near it. For example, the meaning of a verb can restrict the meaning of its arguments and *vice versa*. Scripts for propagating restrictions or for predictions can be added to frame structures.

A *frame system* is a network of frames. A good description of frame systems can be found in Winston (1992, chs 9 and 10).

14.2.4. Semantic Networks

Concepts and their relations can be organized into network representations often called *semantic networks*. Graph grammars can generate semantic networks.

Relations between frames and semantic networks are discussed in details in Woods (1975) and summarized in the following.

An asserted fact is a node in a semantic network and is represented by a frame, as in the following example:

{V1
  verb   give
  agent   George
  recipient   Leslie
  patient of action   pen   }

Relations or slot attributes are represented in a semantic network by links.

Links in the above example are *assertional* and correspond to predicates true for the node. There can be *structural links*.

In representing *functions* and *predicates*, there must be information about what kind of *entities* may fill arguments and how the values are computed. Furthermore, it is important to define *intensional entities* and in particular *definite entities*, *indefinite entities*, definite and indefinite *variable entities* which stand in some relation with other entities and whose instantiation will depend on the instantiation of those other entities. The following example gives a representation for the predicate INFORM corresponding to the eponymous verb, and shows information about entities which may fill the arguments. The form of an instance of it is shown below:

{INFORM
  agent   human
  recipient   human
}
{CONCEPT1
  verb   inform
  agent   Sue
  recipient   Victor
}

Quantified expressions can be represented by treating quantifiers as *higher predicates* which take as argument a variable name, a specification of the range of quantification, a possible restriction on the range and the proposition to be quantified. For example, the following expression:

$$(\forall a/\text{integer})(\exists b/\text{integer})(\text{SMALLER } a\ b)$$

can be represented by the following frames:

```
{CONCEPT2
    type                    quantifier
    quant-type              every
    variable                a
    class                   integer
    restriction             T
    proposition             PR1
}

{CONCEPT3
    type                    quantifier
    quant-type              some
    variable                b
    restriction             T
    proposition             PR2
}
```

Details of PR1 and PR2 are not given for the sake of brevity. Similar examples are shown below. Another possibility is to use "lambda-expressions", such as (FORALL INTEGER (LAMBDA (*a*) (FORSOME INTEGER (LAMBDA (*b*) (SMALLER (*a b*)))))), as in the following example:

```
{CONCEPT4
    type                    proposition
    verb                    FORALL (compute)
    class                   INTEGER
    predicate               PRED1
}

{PRED1
    type                    predicate
    arguments               a
    body                    PR3
}

{PR3
    type                    proposition
    verb                    FORSOME (compute)
    class                   INTEGER
    pred                    PRED2
}

{PRED2
    type                    predicate
    arguments               b
    body                    PR4
}
```

```
{PR4
    type                    proposition
    verb                    SMALLER
    arg1                    a
    arg2                    b
}
```

Word senses and selectional restrictions between senses can be represented by semantic networks. Nodes correspond to word senses and links represent semantic relations between senses.

Formal semantics can be provided for frame and semantic networks. Given the semantics it is possible to represent hierarchies of relations like *inheritance, part-of*, and others. Network hierarchies can also be conceived in which subnets are linked to the main net. Semantic networks, frames and associations are discussed in Hayes (1977).

Each semantic structure can be mapped into expressions in first-order logic (FOL). A discussion on this issue can be found in Levesque and Brachman (1985), a collection of most of the key papers on knowledge representation. This volume also offers a good historical view of the efforts in the field up to the early 1980s with a rich bibliography on the subject.

14.2.5. Conceptual Dependency

Other popular schemes are *conceptual structures*. These structures use *acts* such as transfer (of an information or a physical location), application of a physical force, movement, grasping, ingesting, expulsion, construction, speaking, focusing and *concept categories*, such as "conceptual nominal", physical object, state, location, time, modification of an act, values. A theory for knowledge representation called *conceptual dependency* with a limited number of act types called *primitives* has been developed (Shank and Colby, 1973); in this theory, many action verbs are described as combinations of primitives. A discussion on action representation and its relation to syntax can be found in Allen (1987, ch. 10). Conceptual dependency structures can be generated by dependency grammars.

14.3. USE OF KNOWLEDGE FOR LANGUAGE COMPREHENSION

Computer language comprehension produces a semantic representation of a sentence following an interpretation strategy that is used to control the interpretation process. An example of a strategy that would produce a representation in logical form of the sentence "a radio informed John" consists of the following steps:

1. generation by a parser of a bracketed representation:

$$[S[NP[\text{det a}][N \text{ radio}]][VP[V \text{ informed}][NP[N \text{ John}]]]]$$

2. rule-by-rule logic form (LF) computation:

$$[\langle\text{radio}\rangle\langle\text{past informed}\rangle\text{John}]$$

3. scoping:

$$[\text{past } (x : [x \text{ radio}][x \text{ inform John}])]$$

4. inference of other expressions.

A collection of fundamental papers on natural language processing giving a good historical perspective on the evolution of the field is Grosz *et al.* (1986).

14.3.1. Computation of Logical Forms

In Montague (1974) it is suggested that natural languages are susceptible to the same kind of semantic analysis as programming languages. Following Montague, in Gazdar *et al.* (1985, ch. 9) a function *Den* is introduced that associates with a syntactic category x the set of possible denotations associated with x in the semantic model for a language. Details and discussions about these associations and their use can be found in Partee (1976). The conciliation of conceptual dependency with Montague grammars is discussed in Jones and Warren (1982). The use of a lexicon with Montague grammars is discussed in Dowty (1979).

Along this line, categorial grammars were proposed allowing to obtain a surface semantic representation (Lambek, 1958). The syntax of a language is seen as an algebra, grammatical categories are seen as functions. Lexical representations have associated a syntactic pattern that suggests possible continuations of the syntactic analysis and the semantic expression to be generated, as shown in the following fragment of the lexicon:

eats	$(S\backslash NP)/NP$	$\lambda x \lambda y ((\text{EAT } x) y)$
Mary	$S/(S\backslash NP)$	$\lambda f (f \text{ Mary})$
an	NP/N	$\lambda x (\text{an } x)$
orange	N	

Elements are associated with a syntactic category which identifies them as functions and specifies the type and directionality of their arguments and the type of their results. So, in the example "Mary eats an orange", the lexical entry $\langle\text{eats } (S\backslash NP)/NP\rangle$ causes the fact that when "eats" in the data is matched with the lexical entry for "eat", the associated function $(S\backslash NP)/NP$ is applied.

The symbol / indicates a forward function application that looks for a match with an NP following "eats" and requires the evaluation of the function $(S \backslash NP)$. The word "an" has lexical entry $\langle$an $NP/N\rangle$. This causes the execution of another forward function application that looks for a noun following "an". As the noun is found ($\langle$orange $N\rangle$), the semantic function λx (an x) is executed, returning (an orange) which is associated to the assertion of NP that now matches the expectation of $(S \backslash NP)/NP$ with (an orange). The x of $\lambda x \lambda y$ ((EAT x) y), is bound to (an orange), leading to λy ((EAT an orange) y), as shown in example 14.1. Now the backward function $S \backslash NP$ has to be executed. The symbol \ means that the function will look backward for a match with a lexical entry with label NP which is found by performing the forward execution of the function associated with the lexical entry

$$\langle \text{Mary } S/(S \backslash NP) \rangle$$

The function considers the assertion of S if what follows is asserted. This is true because it is the backward expectation of the verb and NP is a rewriting for Mary. As a result of matching, y is bound to Mary, producing the semantic representation ((EAT an orange) Mary) and causing the assertion of the start symbol S with which the analysis of the sentence to be interpreted is successfully completed. Sometimes ambiguities in semantic interpretation can be resolved using intonation by associating prosodic patterns with rules (Steedman, 1989).

Following a slightly different approach, *procedural semantic* has rules for producing a semantic representation by binding variables in the matching of syntactic precondition structures (Woods, 1968).

Example 14.1

Mary	eats	an	orange	
$S/(S \backslash NP)$	$(S \backslash NP)/NP$	NP/N	N	
---	---	---	---	---
$S/(S \backslash NP)$	$(S \backslash NP)/NP$	NP		an orange
---	---	---	---	---
$S/(S \backslash NP)$	$(S \backslash NP)$			λy((EAT an orange) y)
---	---	---	---	---
S				((EAT an orange) Mary)

14.3.2. Semantic Syntax-Directed Translation

Semantic descriptions can be seen as phrases generated by a grammar. It is possible to see semantic interpretation as a translation of natural language sentences into semantic phrases. A syntax-directed translation schema (SDTS) is a five-tuple T: $[VN, VT1, VT2, R, S]$, where S is the start symbol,

VN is the set of non-terminal symbols, *VT*1 is the set of input words, *VT*2 is the set of semantic primitives, and *R* is the set of rules for rewriting non-terminal symbols, of the type:

$$A \rightarrow \alpha\beta, \quad \text{where } \alpha \in (VN \cup VT1)^*, \ A \in VN \text{ and } \beta \in (VN \cup VT2)^*$$

With these rules, sentences and the corresponding semantic descriptions can be generated. It is also possible to generate semantic descriptions during parsing of input sentences. Translations can be scored by probabilities in a stochastic SDTS. In this case, the syntax and semantic generating rules have associated probabilities with which it is possible to compute the probability that semantic rules generate the abstract tree of an interpretation given the abstract tree of the syntactic analysis of a sentence.

Rules for SDTS can be built manually, as in the examples given in section 14.6, or they can be learned with their probabilities by grammatical inference techniques from a corpus. As rules do not allow to generate all the possible observable sentences, the coverage of these grammars is only partial. Interpretation of sentences that cannot be generated by the rules is made possible by performing error-correcting parsing.

A good introduction of the formalism and its application to pattern recognition can be found in Fu (1982, ch. 2); an application to speech understanding of stochastic SDTS with learning capabilities is described in Vidal *et al.* (1993).

14.3.3. Frame Evocation

Frame instantiation may be triggered by evidence or by expectation. Evidence can be partial and may be confirmed by tests. Partial evidence may receive a contribution from knowledge about recently used structures, loci, or plausible subframes. Frames carry constraints; *goals* can be used to filter constraints. Usually, regular or context-free grammars are associated with slots. When one of these grammars recognizes a sentence in the data, the associated slot is considered filled (see the Phoenix system in section 14.6). Slot-filling activity should be transferable from one frame to another. It should be possible to use defaults, to suggest other alternatives when failure occurs, to perform partial filling and error correction. It should be possible to use *methods* for slot filling as well as for frame evocation and to reason about them with a *control strategy*.

14.3.4. Functional Structures in the Lexicon

The generation of semantic descriptions often starts with the semantic information associated with the words in the sentence to be interpreted. Thus, it is important to have lexical representations in which syntactic and semantic features are associated with each word. In order for a lexical representation to be useful, words should be represented by a structure containing syntactic, semantic, pragmatic and perceptual features. These structures should indicate the relationships between a word and other words in order to allow the interpretation program to compose entities or to disambiguate in the case of multiple word meanings. These forms of "reasoning with words and about words" are carried out by types of inference which operate on networks of relations between words (Miller, 1990). Word sense disambiguation is extensively discussed in McRoy (1991). Predictions can act as constraints for further interpretation or even for word detection in ASR.

For each lexical item, a procedure has to specify a translation into the appropriate type of logic. A frame can be associated with each word by means of pointers to a hierarchy of concepts. Syntactic functions and semantic roles (slots) can be linked by a *lexical functional grammar*. Frames can be generated from lexical items. An extensive discussion of lexical semantics can be found in Cruse (1986). In order to speed up lexical analysis, automata may be used for dictionary analysis.

Useful semantic information can be determined with statistical analysis of a lexical corpus. For instance, co-occurrence statistics can provide evidence of semantic information for *thematic role assignment* using a hierarchy of word patterns acquired from a corpus and transformed into *operational templates*. Lexical representations of the type [predicate, subject, object1, object2] can be acquired as proposed in Jacobs and Zernik (1988). Pairs of words appearing frequently within a sequence of words of a given length are likely to be semantically related and are called *collocations*. A measure for selecting these pairs is the *mutual information index of words* occurring within a fixed distance of each other (Church and Hanks, 1990):

$$MI(w_1 w_2) = \log \frac{f(w_1 w_2)}{f(w_1) f(w_2)} \tag{14.1}$$

where f denotes the frequency of occurrence.

Word sense disambiguation can be performed using word-nets (Miller, 1990) or various types of context probabilities, e.g. probabilities of parts of speech (POS) before and after a word, or probabilities involving collocational features (Bruce and Wiebe, 1994).

Unsupervised learning of lexical syntax can be applied to discover the syntactic phrases that can be used to represent the semantic arguments of verbs, and to discover the ability of verbs to take arguments that are infinitives, tense clauses, or noun phrases serving as direct or indirect objects (subcategorization frames, syntactic frames). Specific *cues* are considered for identifying argument phrases. Cues are used to identify frames and are applied to match the string of words immediately to the right of each verb. Statistics of occurrence with and without cues are obtained.

14.4. CONTROL STRATEGIES FOR INTERPRETATION

The most popular control strategies are now briefly reviewed.

14.4.1. Types of Strategies

Control strategies for interpretation determine how instances of semantic structures are built, how expectations are defined and how knowledge structures are matched with input data in the presence of constraints and imprecision.

There are two basic types of strategy. One is based on path extraction from a semantic or a frame network. The other adopts a constructionist approach that can use one or more of the following methods: inference, parsing, abduction, agenda-based formation and scoring of interpretation hypotheses called *theories*. In the constructionist approach, the meaning of a complex phrase is considered to be a function of the meanings of its constituent parts and the way in which these parts are syntactically combined. For example, in the sentence "the green tree", the meaning of the sentence can be obtained by composition of the meanings of each constituent word (compositional semantics).

14.4.2. Use of Syntax and Semantic Analysis

There are several ways of using syntactic and semantic analysis. In most systems, a semantic analyser has to work with a syntactic analyser and produce input for a logical deductive system.

Syntactic and semantic analyses can be carried out in cascade (Bobrow and Webber, 1980) or they can be integrated, as with Montague or categorial grammars. Tree adjoining grammars (TAG) also integrate syntax and logic form (LF) semantics. Links can be established between the two representations and operations carried out synchronously (Shabes and Joshi, 1990). With these TAG grammars, local representations are generated. An *interpretation* in a specific application domain can be obtained using a deep semantic representation which is usually domain dependent. Temporal representations can be made in higher-order logic with lambda abstraction (Crouch and Pulman, 1993).

Syntax and semantics are also integrated in a *race-based* parser in which the best parsing action "wins" a race. In a first stage, a limited number of words builds partial analyses called *packages*. In a second stage, an attachment processor incorporates a package into a structure. A case theory is used to predict new packages (McRoy and Hirst, 1990).

Classification-based parsing may use functional unification grammars (FUG), systemic grammars (SG), or head-driven phrase structure grammars (HDPSG), which are declarative representations of grammars with logical constraints stated in terms of *features* and *category structure*. Constraints on features are stated entirely in terms of sets of unifications that must be simultaneously satisfied whenever a grammatical rule is used. Parsing is characterized as an *inference* process called *incremental description refinement*. A description of an object may become increasingly more specific as additional features are learned from multiple knowledge sources. Simple grammars are used for detecting possible clauses, then classification-based parsing completes the analysis with inference (Kasper and Hovy, 1990).

Semantics may also drive the parser, causing it to make *attachments* in the parse tree. Semantics can resolve ambiguities and translate English words into semantic symbols using a *discriminant net* for disambiguation. Semantic parsing is discussed in Tait (1983). A semantic head-driven generator of natural language sentences is proposed in Shieber *et al.* (1990). A semantic first parser is described in Lytinen (1992).

The Delphi system (Bobrow *et al.*, 1990), developed at Bolt Beranek and Newman (BBN), contains a number of levels, namely, syntactic (using definite clause grammar, DCG), general semantics, domain semantics and action. Various translations are performed using links between representations at various levels. DCG rules have LHS and RHS elements with associated a functor (their major category) and zero or more features in a fixed a-rity positional order. Features are slots that can be filled by terms. Terms can be variables or functional terms. Semantic representation is based on frames. A grammatical relation has a component that triggers a translation relation. Binding operates on the semantic interpretation of the arguments to produce the semantic interpretation of a new phrase. In this way *semantic fragments* are built.

Integration of syntax, semantics and pragmatics in the KERNEL (Palmer *et al.*, 1993) text understanding system uses a *restriction grammar* to enforce well-formedness and prevent unnecessary structure building. *Meta rules* are used to include constraints (restrictions) and associated rules to obtain *Intermediate syntactic representation (ISR)* as in the following example:

$$((\text{OPS present}) (\text{VERB continue}) (\text{SUBJ}...)(\text{OBJ}...)).$$

Lexical conceptual clauses (LCC) are obtained by general or specific *mapping rules*. An *interpreter* based on control rules is used. Verbs generating clauses are represented by *lexical conceptual structures*. Clause analysis may trigger noun-phrase analysis.

Relations between lexical items and concepts are represented by (lexical, syntax, concept) triplets.

Rule-based inference with forward chaining is used for making implicit information explicit, recovering of essential thematic roles or elided syntactic constraints, instantiating situations and times.

Early work on inference driven semantic analysis with frame-activated inference can be found in Norvig (1983).

Because of the coverage problem, parsing may fail on sentences that are accepted by humans. Robust parsers to cope with this problem are introduced in section 14.6.

The results of semantic analysis can be used for *pragmatic analysis* whose key object is a *situation*. Its components are semantic relations, between a predicate and its arguments, and *temporal information* about when and how these relations have been asserted to occur. The goal of pragmatics is to instantiate *discourse* entities.

14.4.3. Agenda-Based Control

An approach can be called *constructive* if it gradually builds data structures using a basic queue called *agenda* where pointers to partial interpretations, called *theories*, are stored in an order dependent on the scores assigned to the theories.

The control program executes the basic algorithm of Table 14.1 in which "enter (item agenda)" stores *item* in the *agenda* in a position corresponding to an order that follows theory scores.

Extensions of a theory may be computed in different ways. A graph grammar may define a semantic network with attributes attached to nodes. Attributes are constraints. A theory is the instantiation of a partial path in the network. If constraints of a possible path extension are satisfied, they trigger rules that build and grow paths (chunks of semantic interpretations) to be placed into an agenda. This problem is NP-complete, but the process can be speeded up with heuristics. More on graphical representation of concepts can be found in Sowa (1984).

Constraints can be represented by *slot restrictions*. *Scripts* can be used for predictions. Semantic predictions can be ordered by *strength* (fewer word alternatives are better), and *urgency* (likelihood of success). A representation

Table 14.1 Agenda control algorithm

---

build and score seed theories;
for each theory enter (theory agenda);
remove (theory agenda);
continue := true;
repeat
    compute extensions (theory) using prediction, inference, abduction;
    new-theory := result of matching predicted extensions of actual theory with data
    enter (new-theory agenda);
    remove (theory agenda);
    if theory complete then continue := false;
until continue=false;

---

of what is understood is a path of a subnetwork of tokens which can be frame instantiations.

14.4.4. On the Use of Abduction

Abduction is the process of providing the best explanation of why logical expressions would be true. Given a schema $p(y)$ described by a *schema specification language*, and the rule $p(y) \supset q(y)$, if $q(A)$ is asserted to be true, then abduction would derive $p(A)$. New assertions increase the mutual belief of the speaker who made them and the hearer who performs abduction with them. This mode of inference does not have a completely valid theoretical ground. Nevertheless, it is made practically useful with heuristics represented by weights for consistency, simplicity and conciliance (Hobbs *et al.*, 1993).

14.4.5. Pattern Matching

In many cases, especially in limited-domain applications, a few types of information account for a very large proportion of utterances and the understanding process can be based on a *template matcher* that matches templates with the data.

Usually, templates have slots filled by short phrases with associated scores. By combining slot-filling scores, template scores can be obtained and the instantiation with the best score is considered to be the sentence interpretation. Systems of this type are SAM (Shank, 1975) and the template matcher described in section 14.6 (Jackson *et al.*, 1991).

Semantically driven parsers use templates to recognize items that match with the data. Matching may start with lexico-semantic patterns for instantiating initial lexical items. Interpretations are built by adding non-lexical items inferred by a search algorithm (Stallard and Bobrow, 1993).

The Phoenix system, described in section 14.6, uses a knowledge representation based on semantic grammars. This grammar generates frame structures in which slots are filled by language fragments recognized by a recursive transition network (RTN). Parsing of slots is order-independent, and possible interpretations are pursued in parallel (Young *et al.*, 1989).

Different types of matchers can be designed for different purposes. When the purpose is solely retrieval, a vector of features may adequately represent the content of a message.

Different structures are required if the purpose is that of obtaining a conceptual representation to be used for database access or for a dialogue whose goal is the execution of an action. Finite state pattern matchers, lexical pattern matchers, and sentence level pattern matchers are discussed in Hobbs and Israel (1994).

14.4.6. Marker Propagation

A semantic system can be constructed from a group of programs which are expert at looking at semantic structures. These programs activate memory structures by placing activation markers on them. Nodes in the memory structure are associated with input words. Prediction markers represent concept sequences which are in the process of being recognized; whenever a memory structure is activated, prediction markers are created for all concept sequences indexed by that structure through the concept lexicon. A prediction is altered by concept refinement and sequence advancement (Charniak, 1983; Waltz and Pollack, 1984).

As several markers can be propagated in parallel, a high degree of parallelism can be achieved with these models. Massive search of syntactic patterns and coarse semantic patterns following a *hierarchical network* is described in Kitano and Higuchi (1991).

14.5. SEMANTIC SCORES

Often semantic structures represent reality with a degree of imprecision. Furthermore, their relation to words and sentences is also imprecise and incomplete. Imprecision can be modelled by associating probabilities with items of knowledge. In particular, relations between slots in a frame-based representation and the possible natural language fillers can be probabilistic, and knowledge aggregation (concept composition) can be probabilistic. Furthermore, words mutually constrain each other. Constraints can be expressed by probabilities.

A general interpretation strategy can calculate probabilities resulting from the matching of various types of knowledge with the data; thus, theories can be ordered according to their probability scores.

Following relation (1.2) in Chapter 1, an interpretation can be made using probabilistic scores whose semantic component is $\Pr(CW)$ where C is a conceptual structure and W is the sequence of words expressing it. It is possible to express this probability in two ways, namely:

$$\Pr(CW) = \Pr(W|C)\Pr(C) \tag{14.2}$$

proposed by Pieraccini and Levin (1995b) or:

$$\Pr(CW) = \Pr(C|W)\Pr(W) \tag{14.3}$$

proposed in Corazza *et al.* (1991) and reviewed in Chapter 13.

$\Pr(W)$ is a language model (LM) probability. In semantic interpretation, it is possible that not all the words hypothesized by the recognizer are used. There are manual and automatic methods to find the "semantically useful" words.

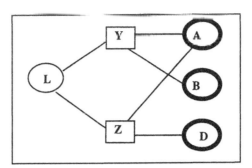

Figure 14.1 A simple semantic network.

In order to represent this fact, it is possible to write the sequence of words W in the following way:

$$W = x_1 w_1 x_2 w_2 \ldots x_n w_n \ldots x_N w_N \tag{14.4}$$

where x and w are sequences of words and the w contain the words used for semantic interpretation.

Figure 14.1 shows a semantic network represented by an AND/OR graph. OR nodes are represented by circles meaning that a semantic interpretation containing an instance of a node of this type must include at least one descendant of it. AND nodes are represented by squares. A semantic interpretation containing an instance of an AND node must include all the descendants of that node. Terminal nodes are thicker and become part of the representation of a sequence of words if a specific condition on the words is verified. A frame-based representation of this network can be easily obtained. Let $\Gamma(ABYL)$ be an interpretation structure obtained from the semantic knowledge shown in Figure 14.1.

Equation (14.3) can be written as:

$$\Pr(CW) = \Pr(C|W)\Pr(W) = \Pr(LYAB|W)\Pr(W) \tag{14.5}$$

where $\Pr(W)$ is given by the language model, $\Pr(LYAB/W)$ is the probability of having a conceptual structure with concepts A and B directly related to the surface structure of a sentence given the sequence of words W. This computation can use probabilities of pure semantic components like, for example, probabilities of semantic links (Bobrow *et al.*, 1990). If $\Gamma(LZAD)$ is another possible interpretation C', and concepts AD correspond to a word sequence W', obtained from another sequence of word hypotheses W' extracted from a word lattice, then:

$$\Pr(C'W') = \Pr(LZAD|W')\Pr(W')$$

If a syntactic analysis is available, then $\Pr(CW)$ can be expressed as:

$$\Pr(CW) = \Pr(C|(\tau(W))\Pr(S \to \tau(W))$$

where $\tau(W)$ is the parse tree generating the string of words W and S is the start symbol of the language grammar.

The probability $\Pr(S \rightarrow \tau(W))$ can be computed as follows:

$$\Pr(S \rightarrow \tau(W)) = \Pr(S \rightarrow \tau(g(W)))\Pr(W|g(W))$$

where $g(W)$ is the sequence of parts of speech (POS) of the words in W.

An upper bound of this probability can be obtained even if W is made of words which are semantically significant and "glue" words, that may be unknown, using the algorithms presented in Corazza *et al.* (1994).

All the pertinent conceptual structures C of a given task can be seen as phrases generated by a *semantic grammar*. The terminal symbols $\{c_1, c_2, \ldots, c_j, \ldots, c_J\}$ of this grammars are elementary concepts and the non-terminal symbols $\{C_1, C_2, \ldots, C_k, \ldots, C_K\}$ are conceptual categories. For example, a conceptual category "trip" may be a structure containing the elementary concepts "origin" and "destination". A conceptual structure can be seen as a parse tree representing the generation with the semantic network of a set of elementary concepts triggered by the detection of word patterns.

Semantic grammars can be stochastic context-free grammars. Competing interpretations due, among other things, to the detection of competing words and elementary concepts, can be ranked using a combination of acoustic, linguistic and semantic scores, the latter being obtained by parsing with a stochastic context-free semantic grammar (SCFSG).

Recent results (Corazza *et al.*, 1994) on scoring partial parses of a SCFSG show how to score a partial semantic interpretation and to find the most probable completion of it. The dialogue strategy may propose the semantic completion as an information intended but not expressed by the speaker or expressed but not detected by the recognizer and ask, for example, for a simple confirmation.

In the example of Figure 14.1, semantic completion may lead to the assumption that the conceptual structure expressed in the speaker sentence is $\Gamma(LYAB)$ even if the recognized words provide evidence only of the concept A and not of B nor of D.

$\Pr(C|W)$ and $\Pr(W)$ can be dynamically adapted taking the dialogue history into account. History h of previous interpretations, coming, for example, from previously exchanged sentences in a person–machine dialogue can be taken into account in a dynamic model as follows:

$$\Pr(CW|h) = \Pr(C|Wh)\Pr(W|h) = \Pr(LYAB|Wh)\Pr(W|h) \tag{14.6}$$

Semantic expectations can be adapted to the evolution of the dialogue. $\Pr(W|h)$ is obtained by a dynamic language model.

In a dialogue framework, both types of adaptation can be made dependent on a dialogue state. LM can be made dependent on a dialogue state if dialogue is represented by a finite state automaton. Unfortunately this is not always the case. A dialogue can be described by logical formulae and, in theory, a dialogue state is defined by the set of values to which all the variables are bound. The number of states defined in this way can be prohibitively high. A good clustering of dialogue states into "dialogue situations" can be performed by considering the predicates used in the formula for generating an output message and selecting the one which is more likely to condition the answer.

If there are K situations of this type, let $Q(W)$ be the static LM probability and $P_k(W)$ be the probability for the kth situation, then the dynamic probability can be expressed as:

$$P(W) = d_s Q(W) + \sum_{k=1}^{K} d_k P_k(W)$$

(14.7)

$$d_s + \sum_{k=1}^{K} d_k = 1$$

In the case of *LM adaptation* the coefficients d_k are "modulated" by the situations. If the dialogue strategy can assess that the system is in a specific situation k, then one can write:

$$P(W) = d_s Q(W) + d_k P_k(W)$$

$$d_k = 1 - d_s$$

(14.8)

14.6. SEMANTICS IN ASU: THE EXPERIENCE OF THE ATIS SYSTEM

The ATIS project is based on a corpus described in Appendix D. The purpose of the project was to develop technologies for ASU and to evaluate them systematically.

It is relatively easy to define quantitative measures for speech recognition performance (SPREC): one simply chooses some function of the number of insertions, substitutions, and deletions separating the recognized word sequence from the correct word sequence. ATIS's natural language (NL) and spoken language system (SLS) benchmarks pose a much harder question: how do we define a quantitative measure for understanding? Even for the severely constrained domain of ATIS, the ambiguity of natural language gave rise to considerable debate.

When someone wants to know about flights *around* 7 p.m., how wide is the window around the given time – e.g., should an 8 p.m. flight be shown or not? if someone wants to see "flights with meals", should flights that only serve snacks be included or not? if someone says, "show me flights between A and B", should we show only flights from A to B or flights in both directions? if a request begins, "how many flights..." must it be answered by a number (the literal interpretation) or by a display of flights meeting the constraints (the pragmatic interpretation). To keep debate about such issues within reasonable bounds, each release of ATIS training data was accompanied by a document called "Principles of Interpretation". Some examples of rules found in this document: "around" means within a window of 15 minutes before and 15 minutes after; a snack counts as a meal; "between" means "from", not "from or to"; a request beginning "how many..." may be answered by a number or by a display.

The inclusion of "D" sentences making reference to previous sentences further complicates matters. Consider the following sequence of requests: "flights from A to B please", "now the cheapest ones", "OK, now all the ones that serve dinner". If there is more than one cheapest flight, the last request can be interpreted two ways: as "show me, among the cheapest flights from A to B, those that serve dinner" or "show me the flights from A to B that serve dinner" (if the "OK, now" is interpreted as annulling the previous request).

Many of these questions of interpretation arose because the original ATIS scenario did not allow the system to engage in dialogue – the system's only permissible outputs were the results of database queries, i.e., it could display on the screen rows of the database or numbers derived from those rows (such as row counts or maxima, minima, or averages of numerical attributes). This prevented the system from asking the user what was meant, e.g.: "are you interested in flights with snacks?" There were other negative results. For instance, users tried to cram linguistically unnatural amounts of information into a single sentence, because they knew the system could not ask follow-up questions.

Overall, the decision to avoid evaluating dialogue made sense. With dialogue permitted during data collection, the users' utterances would inevitably have been dependent on the questions posed to the users. Such utterances would have been much less useful for training and testing – instead of being tested on utterances sent to them on CD-ROM, systems would have had to be tested by users who were physically present.

This decision also ensured that the speed of the recognition algorithms would not become a criterion. Dialogue capabilities make evaluation of a semantic module even more subjective: effectiveness and user-friendliness are notoriously slippery concepts. Finally, user testing is quite expensive. All these considerations ensured that though there was discussion in the ATIS community about "end-to-end" evaluations in which dialogue capabilities would be measured, they never really got off the ground. Several groups built good ATIS related dialogue systems that, however, could not be benchmarked against each other (different purposes, interfaces, etc.)

ATIS succeeded brilliantly in accelerating the development of spoken language understanding systems by focusing on a database access task that was not too far removed from plausible real-life scenarios. As we will see, system developers showed a healthy tendency to borrow each others' best ideas, which is a precondition for technological progress. In our opinion, the various articles on ATIS systems remain among the best sources in the entire field of computational linguistics for practical descriptions of how to build natural language understanding systems.

We will now describe the semantic modules in the following order:

1. those which were almost entirely hand-coded (i.e. those for which machine learning techniques played a small role)
2. those which depended heavily on machine learning techniques.

For instance, the DELPHI system (mostly hand-coded) is described separately from the HUM system that relies on machine learning techniques. Both systems were developed at BBN.

14.6.1. The Gemini and the "Template-Matcher-Based" Systems

The system developed at Stanford Research Institute (SRI) consists of two semantic modules yoked together: a unification-grammar-based module called (in recent evaluations) "Gemini", and the "Template Matcher" which acts as a fallback if Gemini cannot produce an acceptable database query (Appelt, 1996).

The Template Matcher

The input to the Template Matcher (TM) is the top word sequence hypothesis generated by the speech recognition component, which uses a bigram language model. The TM simply tries to fill slots in frame-like templates. An early version had just eight templates dealing with flights, fares, ground transportation, meanings of codes and headings, aircraft, cities, airlines and airports. The different templates compete with each other on each utterance; all are scored, and the template with the best score generates the database query (provided its score is greater than a certain *cutoff*). Slots are filled by looking through the utterance for certain phrases and words.

Here is a typical example, adapted from Jackson *et al.* (1991). For the utterance "Show me all the Delta flights Denver to Atlanta nonstop on the twelfth of April leaving after ten in the morning", the following flight template would be generated:

```
[flight, [stops, nonstop],
    [airline, DL],
    [origin, DENVER],
    [destination, ATLANTA],
    [departing_after,[1000]],
    [date, [april,12,current_ year]]
].
```

Words in the utterance may contribute to selection and filling of a template in various ways:

- They may help to identify the template – the occurrence of the word "downtown" is a good indicator of the *ground transportation* template.
- They may fill a slot – like "Denver" and "Atlanta" in the example,
- They may help to indicate what slot a phrase goes in – like "from" or "to" preceding a slot-filling phrase.

However, many words are irrelevant: "please", "show me", "would you", and so on. The TM simply skips over these.

The score for a template is basically the percentage of words in the utterance that contribute to filling the template. However, certain keywords that are strongly correlated with a particular template will strongly boost the score of that template, if they occur in the utterance. For instance, the occurrence of *how much*, *fare*, or *price* boosts the score of the *fare* template; the occurrence of *what is*, *explain*, or *define* boosts the score of the meaning template. However, if the template has no slots filled, it is assigned a score of zero; or if the system has tried to assign two or more values to the same slot in the template, the template is aborted.

If the best score does not exceed a certain numerical *cutoff*, the system responds with *no answer* rather than with the template that yielded the best score. Recall that ATIS scoring penalizes wrong answers rather harshly, so that *no answer* is often a preferable response; to optimize the performance of their system on tests, the SRI researchers set the cutoff to the value that yielded the best results on training data.

In a later version of the ASU system, the conventional parser was scrapped and the TM was kept (Appelt and Jackson, 1992). Several improvements were made in the TM. The early version could only fill slots with fixed words or phrases – it had no ability to deal with general phrase categories like numbers, dates and times. In the second version, phrases falling into these categories in the incoming utterance were parsed by special grammars, and were then put into slots by the matcher. Slots were filled by matching regular expressions – for instance, *from* followed by a city or airport name would cause the name to be put into the origin slot of the *flight* template.

The major difference between the two versions of the TM is that the latter contained a context handling mechanism for class "D" (context-dependent) queries; the early version was only designed to work with class "A" (context-independent, acceptable) queries. The context handling mechanism allowed slots to be inherited from previous utterances by the same user. Note that if the user's first utterance is wrongly interpreted, his subsequent context-dependent utterances may all be correctly recognized yet misunderstood: this might be called the "getting off on the wrong foot" problem.

If systems were allowed to ask users for confirmation from time to time, this problem would be relatively unimportant. However, the ATIS evaluations did not permit dialogue, so several ingenious mechanisms were devised for preventing the problem. For instance, when the system gave *no answer* to a query, subsequent context-dependent queries also yielded *no answer*, until a query that sets a completely new context arrived. In data collection mode, on the other hand, the system generated an answer when possible, on the ground that users prefer slightly incorrect answers to "I don't understand".

Recent papers have not emphasized the Template Matcher, focusing on the Gemini component instead (Moore *et al.*, 1994, 1995). Nevertheless, the TM acted as a backup to Gemini in later versions. In Dowding (1996) it is reported that, in the latest version of the system, the TM yielded about 5–10% improvement in the error rate over Gemini alone.

Gemini

Gemini is a unification-based natural-language parser that combines general syntactic and semantic rules for English with an ATIS-specific lexicon and sortal/selectional restrictions. A simplified example of a Gemini syntactic rule is (Dowding *et al.*, 1993):

```
syn(whq_ ynq_slash_np,
   [s:[sentence_type=whq, form=tnsd, gapsin=G, gapsout=G],
    np:[wh=ynq, pers_num=N],
     s:[sentence_type=ynq, form=tnsd, gapsin=np:[pers_num=N],
       gapsout=null]]).
```

This rule, named *whq_ynq_slash_np*, says that a sentence (category *s*) can be made up of a noun phrase (category *np*) followed by a sentence, where the *np* has the value *ynq* for its *wh* feature and value *N* for its *pers_num* feature, and where the daughter sentence has a category value for its gaps in feature (an *np*) whose *pers_num* value is the same as the *pers_num* value of the *wh* phrase. The rule means that a gapless sentence with *sentence_type whq* can be built by finding a *wh* phrase followed by a sentence with a noun-phrase gap in it that has the same person number as the *wh* phrase (Dowding *et al.*, 1993).

Semantic rules look similar, except that each of the constituents mentioned in the phrase-structure skeleton is associated with a logical form. The semantics for the syntactic rule just given is:

```
sem(whq_ ynq_slash_np,
   [([whq,S],s:[ ]),
    (Np,np:[ ]),
    (S,s:[gapsin=np:[gapsem=Np]])]).
```

The semantics of the mother *s* is the semantics of the daughter *s* with the illocutionary force marker *whq* wrapped around it. Also the semantics of the *s* gap's *np*'s *gapsem* has been unified with the semantics of the *wh* phrase.

With a succession of unifications, the *wh* phrase's semantics is assigned to the gap position in the argument structure of the *s* (Dowding *et al.*, 1993).

For a single syntactic rule, any number of semantic rules may be written. At the end of 1992, Gemini contained 243 syntactic rules and 315 semantic rules (Dowding *et al.*, 1993). Gemini's domain-specific ATIS lexicon at this time contained 1315 entries, which could be expanded to 2019 entries by the system's morphological rules. Gemini's sortal/selectional restrictions include both highly domain-specific predicate-argument information (e.g., the object of the verb "to depart" must be an airport or a city) and very general predicate restrictions (e.g., the adjective "further" applies to distances).

An important component of Gemini handles repairs. Repairs occur when the speaker intends the hearer to delete one or more words.

To find constituents, Gemini uses an all-paths, bottom-up chart parser, which identifies all possible edges admissible by the grammar. The parser is "on-line", meaning that all edges that end at position i are constructed before those that end at position $i + 1$. Syntactic and semantic processing are interleaved: when a syntactic rule has been satisfied for a word span, semantic rules and sortal checking take place. The syntactic edge is only added to the chart if it is determined to be semantically/sortally well-formed. Once all constituents have been found, Gemini uses an utterance parser (with a different set of syntactic and semantic rules) to build an analysis for the entire utterance from them.

In the attempt to use natural-language constraints to improve recognition, a parser analyses the N-best hypotheses output by the recognizer; the preferred hypothesis is the one closest to the top that can be parsed completely. The problem is that grammars seldom model spontaneous speech accurately.

Gemini deals with this by separating *constituent* parsing from *utterance* parsing. Thus, Gemini can often identify possible syntactic constituents of an utterance, even though it has been unable to parse the utterance as a whole. This fact was exploited to devise a heuristic for scoring the N-best hypotheses output by their recognizer. Underlying this heuristic was the assumption that a small number of constituents is better than a large number. Thus, the final score for a hypothesis combined the recognition score, the number of constituents, a bonus for a complete analysis of the utterance, and penalties for using unusual grammar rules. This approach yielded a modest improvement on the output of the recognizer alone (SNL, 1994).

In the 1994 ATIS evaluations, it was shown that the application of natural-language constraints could yield recognition performance improvement relative to a state-of-the-art recognizer (SLS, 1995). This achievement – a first among NL groups participating in ATIS – was brought about by means of a new kind of language model that drew on rules in Gemini. After analysing the N-best hypotheses as sequences of fragments, N-gram statistics are used to calculate the probability of the hypothesis under that analysis.

This N-gram model has two levels (SLS, 1995). At the top level, we have fragments of the following types: sentence, noun phrase, modifier phrase,

filler (e.g. "please") and skipped word sequences. Transitions between these
fragments are modelled by means of trigrams Within each fragment, the units
are words and word classes, with transitions modelled as quadrigrams – this
is the lower level. The same quadrigram statistics are used for each
fragment type, but each fragment is taken to begin with a characteristic token
(e.g. *begin_nominal_phrase*). The probability of the first few words of each
fragment is conditioned on what type of fragment it is, but once several
words of context are available, the probability estimate is based on these
words instead (Moore *et al.*, 1995). A word class is defined for each group of
items in the lexicon that share the same syntactic and semantic features and
semantic class (e.g., city names); multiword sequences that are fixed entries in
the lexicon (e.g., *D C 10*) are treated as single words.

Sections of the hypothesis that Gemini has analysed as repair portions are
treated as a special kind of fragment that can be inserted within another
fragment, and whose presence is indicated by the markers *begin_repair* and
end_repair. The lower-level word-sequence *N*-gram model incorporates
estimates of the probability of beginning a repair at any point within another
fragment type; once *begin_repair* has appeared, the probability of *end_repair*
is greater than zero. After *end_repair* has appeared, the probability of the
following word sequence is conditioned on the words preceding *begin_repair*.
For instance, in the hypothesis "I want to fly *begin_repair* to san *end_repair*
to los angeles" the probability estimate for "to los angeles" is conditioned on
"I want to fly".

By rescoring the output of the recognizer with this Gemini-based language
model, it was possible to obtain a reduction in word errors by 13.1% and in
the number of utterances misrecognized by 12.7% .

14.6.2. The DELPHI System

DELPHI is a linguistic analyser that generates the *N*-best hypotheses using a
fast, simple algorithm (Ostendorf *et al.*, 1991; Schwartz *et al.*, 1992), then
repeatedly rescores these hypotheses by means of more complex, slower
algorithms. In this manner, several different knowledge sources can contribute
to the final result without complicating the control structure or significantly
slowing down derivation of the final result.

The first version of DELPHI consisted of a chart-based unification parser
(Austin *et al.*, 1991a). An important and useful feature of this parser, which
has been retained in all subsequent versions, was the incorporation of probabilities for different senses of a word and for application of grammatical rules.
These probabilities are estimated from data and used to reduce the search
space for parsing (Bates *et al.*, 1993, 1994).

A robust fallback module has been incorporated in successive versions (Bates
et al., 1994). The fallback understanding module within DELPHI was called if

the unification chart parser failed (Stallard and Bobrow, 1993; Bates *et al.*, 1993). Rather than employing the semantic module to assign an explicit natural-language score to hypotheses, DELPHI tried to parse the first $N = 10$ hypotheses completely, stopping when a complete interpretation could be generated. If that did not work, another pass through these 10 hypotheses would be made with the fallback module, which tried to generate a robust interpretation from parsed fragments left over from the first, failed parse.

The fallback module was itself made up of two parts: the Syntactic Combiner and the Frame Combiner. The Syntactic Combiner used extended grammatical rules that skipped over intervening material in an attempt to generate a complete parse. If the attempt failed, the Frame Combiner tried to fill slots in frames in a manner similar to that of SRI's Template Matcher. The Frame Combiner used many pragmatic rules obtained through study of training data which could not be defended on abstract grounds. For instance, interpretations which combine flight and ground transportation information are ruled out because they are never observed in the data, even though a query like "Show flights to airports with limousine service" is theoretically possible.

Surprisingly, the fallback module worked better if only the Frame Combiner – but not the Syntactic Combiner – was included.

In order to increase robustness and reduce reliance on the fallback module (Bates *et al.*, 1994), a *semantic graph* data structure was introduced and syntactic evidence was considered only one way of determining the *semantic links* out of which the graph is built (Bates *et al.*, 1994). A semantic graph is a directed acyclic graph in which nodes correspond to meanings of head words (e.g. *arrival, flight, Boston*) and the arcs are binary semantic relations. The basic parsing operation is that of linking two disconnected graphs with a new arc.

If the chart parser does not succeed in connecting such disconnected graphs, the Semantic Linker is invoked. This component can ignore fragment order, skip over unanalysable material, and even "hallucinate" a new node if that is the only way to link fragments. For instance, the utterance "Boston noon first-class to Denver" causes the Linker to hypothesize a FLIGHT node from which the fragments are hung.

14.6.3. The Phoenix System

In many respects, the Phoenix system of Carnegie Mellon University (CMU) is very similar to SRI's Template Matcher (Issar and Ward, 1994; Ward, 1990, 1991; Ward *et al.*, 1992). To analyse an utterance, the system considers different frames in parallel via a dynamic programming beam search. As slot-filling semantic phrases are recognized, they are added to the frames for which they are relevant. There is no global grammar – instead, each possible slot (there are about 70) has a grammar of its own, represented by a top-down Recursive Transition Network with the possibility of activating a chart parser for each.

The score for a frame is simply the number of words in an utterance it accounts for, though certain non-content words are ignored.

In early versions of the system, the input to Phoenix was the top hypothesis of the speech recognition component. Subsequently (Ward and Issar, 1994a), a search algorithm was implemented in which information from the RTN slot parsers was employed during the A* portion of the recognizer. Adopting the more conventional approach, in which the natural language component rescores a set N-best hypotheses generated with standard N-gram language models, did not yield better recognition performance. On the other hand, it did yield significant improvement in understanding performance.

The breakdown of the system's errors in this evaluation is quite interesting (Ward and Issar, 1995). Five classes of error were defined, in the following order of frequency:

- Grammar – the system did not provide a correct parse (42% of errors).
- Context – the system had a correct parse, but handled correct context from previous utterances incorrectly (28% of errors).
- Backend – the parser and the context mechanism did everything correctly, but an error occurred during SQL generation (14% of errors).
- Propagated error – the current utterance was handled correctly, but incorrect context was inherited from a previous utterance (9% of errors).
- Semantics – the meaning of the current utterance was not even imagined when the SQL-generating mechanism was built (7% of errors).

14.6.4. The TINA System

The linguistic analyser TINA, developed at the Massachusetts Institute of Technology (MIT), went through the same evolution as other linguistic analysers: originally it consisted of a global syntactic parser, but, subsequently, a robust matcher was added as backup when the global parser fails (Zue *et al.*, 1992; Seneff, 1992a). TINA's grammar is written as a set of probabilistic context free rewrite rules with constraints, which is converted automatically at run-time to a network form in which each node represents a syntactic or semantic category (Seneff, 1989). The probabilities associated with rules are calculated from training data, and serve to constrain search during recognition (without them, all possible parses would have to be considered).

The robust matcher was obtained by modifying the grammar to allow partial parses (Seneff, 1992a, c). In robust mode, the parser proceeds left-to-right as usual, but an exhaustive set of possible parses is generated starting at each word of the utterance. As in DELPHI, the matcher then fills slots in frames with these phrases, ultimately choosing the best frame. The unusual aspect of this robust matcher is that it exploits features of the history mechanism built to make dialogue possible. During dialogue, this history mechanism allows slots to be inherited from previous utterances. Similarly, the robust matcher "remembers" slots filled earlier in the same utterance. Only one adjustment was needed to make the history mechanism suitable for sentence-internal parsing: overwriting of slots was forbidden (it occurs between utterances in the dialogue version).

After the creation of the robust matcher, there were few changes in the structure of the natural language component. New context-free rules were added to increase coverage, including rules that handle false starts (Zue *et al.*, 1993). In the most recent versions of the system, the parser tried out the *N*-best hypotheses in order; if none of them could be parsed, the robust matcher was applied to hypothesis #1 (Glass *et al.*, 1995; Zue *et al.*, 1994). A variant of the system employed TINA to rescore the top five hypotheses produced by the recognizer, but this gave no performance advantage (Glass *et al.*, 1995).

Most of the recent efforts went into software engineering – the entire system was rewritten to make it more modular, efficient and portable – and into the development of a dialogue system (Glass *et al.*, 1995). In fact, two dialogue systems were developed. The first allowed users to talk to a screen which displayed information relevant to the dialogue; for instance, a user "ordering" an airline ticket could watch as the fields of the ticket (origin, destination, date, etc.) were filled in by the system, and thus visualize and correct misunderstandings as they occurred. The second, "displayless" version was designed to operate over the telephone. This is a much harder system to build. For instance, if 25 flights satisfy a request, it's reasonable to display them on a screen, but unreasonable for the system to read them out. Thus, the displayless system must take a very active role in narrowing user requests by posing appropriate questions.

14.6.5. The CHANEL System

The CHANEL system is the result of research conducted at McGill University, in the program of the Institute of Robotics and Intelligent Systems (IRIS), a Canadian Network of Centers of Excellence. It was successively improved and integrated with an ASR system at the Centre de Recherche en Informatique de Montréal (CRIM).

Among systems participating in the ATIS benchmarks in November 1992, only CHANEL and AT&T's Chronus embodied a strong emphasis on machine learning. CHANEL learns semantic interpretation rules by means of a forest of specialized decision trees called *semantic classification trees* (SCTs).

There is an SCT for every elementary concept. An SCT is a binary tree with a question associated to each node. Each node has two successors, one is reached if the answer to the node question is YES, the other node is reached if the answer is NO. Questions are about sentence patterns made of words and wildcard symbols (+). If the node pattern matches with the sentence to be interpreted,

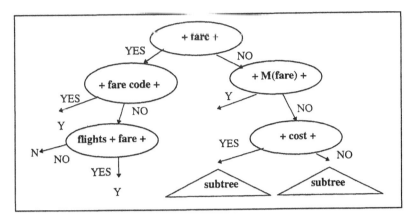

Figure 14.2 Example of an SCT.

then the answer to the node question is YES and the successor node pointed by the arc labeled YES is considered, otherwise the answer is NO and the corresponding successor node is considered. Figure 14.2 shows an example of a tree for the concept *fare*. An example of question pattern is $\langle +M(fare)+\rangle$, which matches with a sentence containing any word member of the member set $M(fare)$ of words expressing the same meaning as fare.

The nature of the questions in the SCTs is such that the rules learnt are robust to grammatical and lexical errors in the input from the recognizer (Kuhn and De Mori, 1995). In fact, these questions are generated in a manner that tends to minimize the number of words that must be correct for understanding to take place. Question generation involves "gaps": words and groups of words that can be ignored. Thus, each leaf of an SCT corresponds to a regular expression containing gaps, words, and syntactic units (e.g., times, dates, airplane types). Most SCTs in CHANEL decide whether a given concept is present or absent from the semantic representation for an utterance; for such SCTs, the label Y or N in a leaf denotes the presence or absence of the corresponding concept.

If one generalizes away from the domain-specific details of CHANEL (which are given in Kuhn and De Mori (1995)), one can give the following recipe for building a CHANEL-like system.

1. Collect a corpus of utterances in which each utterance is accompanied by its semantic representation.
2. Write a local parser that recognizes semantically important noun phrases that encode variables in the semantic representation (e.g., times, locations) and replaces such phrases with a generic code (while retaining a value for each variable). For instance, a time might be replaced by the symbol TIME, and a city name by the symbol CITY. Thus, the utterance "give me all uh ten at night flights out of Boston" might become "give me all uh TIME[22:00] flights out of CITY[Bos]".

3. Devise a way of mapping the rest of the semantic representation (i.e., the part that does not consist of the variables just mentioned) into a vector of N bits. For example, CHANEL had "fare" bit that was set to 1 if the user wanted to know the cost of a flight, and to 0 otherwise. Some bits are allocated to deciding the role of variables – e.g., to deciding whether the CITY in "give me all uh TIME flights out of CITY" should be an origin or a destination.

4. Grow N SCTs, one for each position in the bit vector. The training data for each SCT are the whole training corpus of utterances after processing by the local parser (with variable values stripped out); the label for each utterance is the value of the appropriate bit. For instance, for CHANEL two typical training utterances for the *fare* SCT might be:
"give me all uh TIME flights out of CITY"$\Rightarrow 0$
"how much are flights to CITY these days"$\Rightarrow 1$.

5. Given a new utterance, one can generate a semantic representation from the resulting system as follows:
   - Pass the utterance through the local parser.
   - Temporarily strip out variable values (saving them for later use) and submit the resulting string to the N SCTs (each SCT receives a complete copy).
   - The resulting vector of bits, together with saved variable values, gives a unique semantic representation for the utterance.

The hand-coding of a local parser, sounds like cheating: isn't hand-coding exactly what one is trying to avoid in adopting an approach based on machine learning? The answer is that, practically speaking, good parsers for semantically important noun phrases can be hand-coded quite quickly; implementing machine learning of the rules in these parsers would have been more trouble than it was worth. Without exception, all other teams working on ATIS made the same design decision.

The following is an example of the semantic representation generated by CHANEL:

DISPLAYED_ATTRIBUTES (flights, fares)
CONSTRAINTS (flight_from_airport   ←BBOS
                flight_to_airport   ←DDEN
                flight_departure_time   ←10.00AM).

A scheme of the CHANEL system architecture is shown in Figure 14.3. Elementary concepts are detected by SCTs, then they are composed by rules into a knowledge representation language (KRL) description and translated into a query to a database in the SQL language.

The most interesting aspect of CHANEL is that the inference carried out by the SCTs explicitly models *don't care* words, allowing the system to tolerate a high degree of misrecognition in semantically unimportant words. The

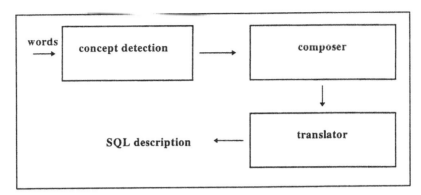

Figure 14.3 CHANEL architecture.

literature on grammatical inference (Fu, 1982) focuses on production rather than comprehension, and thus implicitly assumes that the goal is to learn rules that account for all the symbols in a given string. SCTs instead try to discover rules involving as few words or syntactic units as possible.

There is another important difference between CHANEL and systems such as AT&T's Chronus (described later). Chronus carries out a one-to-one mapping between sentence segments and concepts, while each of the SCTs in CHANEL builds part of the semantic representation, and looks at the entire utterance in order to do so. This permits a given word or phrase to contribute to more than one *concept*, and also permits words or phrases that are far apart from each other to contribute to the same concept.

14.6.6. The Chronus System

Chronus is a hybrid system: its core is a stochastic model whose parameters are learned from a corpus, but all the other components are hand-coded (Pieraccini and Levin, 1995b; Levin and Pieraccini, 1995; Pieraccini *et al.*, 1991, 1992a, b). The *conceptual decoder* at the core of Chronus is based on a view of utterances as generated by an HMM-like process whose hidden states correspond to meaning units called *concepts*. Thus, understanding is a decoding of these concepts hidden in an utterance.

A version of Chronus obtained the best score on the 1994 natural language (NL) benchmark. It was based on the following principles (Pieraccini and Levin, 1995b):

- Locality – the analysis of the entire sentence is delayed as long as possible.
- Learnability – everything that can be learned automatically from data should be.
- Patchability – it should be easy to introduce new knowledge into the system.

- Separation – among algorithms, and between general and specific knowledge.
- Habitability – the focus should be on robustness to unexpected non-linguistic phenomena and recognizer mistakes, rather than on dealing with rare, complex linguistic events.

The success of this system is in some respects surprising, given that the conceptual decoder chops an utterance up into non-overlapping segments, which to a first approximation are considered to contribute to the meaning independently of each other (interactions are handled by the "interpreter", a small hand-coded module, at a later stage of processing).

A later version of Chronus has four main modules: the lexical analyser, the conceptual decoder, the template generator, and the interpreter. The input to the lexical analyser is the top hypothesis generated by the recognizer. The lexical analyser recognizes predefined semantic categories, which group together all possible idiomatic variants of the same word or fixed phrase: for instance, "JFK", "Kennedy Airport", "Kennedy International Airport", "New York City International Airport" are all assigned to the same semantic category. The lexical analyser also groups together singular and plural forms of a word, and inflectional variants of a verb, thus achieving robustness to minor speech recognition errors.

As mentioned earlier, the conceptual decoder views the modified word sequences emerging from the lexical analyser as conceptual hidden Markov models (conceptual HMMs), with the words being the observations and the concepts being the states. Concept sequences are currently modelled via a bigram language model, and the sequence of words within a concept is modelled as a concept-dependent N-gram language model.

The function of the conceptual decoder is to segment an utterance into phrases, each representing a concept. This is equivalent to finding the most likely sequence of states in the conceptual HMM, given the sequence produced by the lexical analyser.

The choice of conceptual units is a domain-dependent design decision. For ATIS, some concepts relate directly to database entities (e.g., "destination", "origin", "aircraft_type") and others are more linguistic (e.g., "question", "dummy" – for irrelevant words, and "subject" – what the user wants to know). Once these units have been defined, the parameters of the conceptual HMM must be estimated from a training corpus of segmented, labelled word sequences by means of the Viterbi training algorithm for HMMs.

This process can be bootstrapped (Pieraccini and Levin, 1995a). Initially, about 500 sentences were segmented by hand, and the conceptual HMM was trained on these.

A typical output from the conceptual decoder might look like this (Levin and Pieraccini, 1995):

| wish | : I WOULD LIKE TO GO |
| origin | : FROM NEW YORK |

destin	: TO SAN FRANCISCO
day	: SATURDAY
time	: MORNING
aircraft	: PREFERABLY ON A BOEING SEVEN FORTY SEVEN

The template generator turns the output of the conceptual decoder into an unordered set of keyword/value pairs, most of which map directly onto the database. The rules in the template generator were hand-written, but in most cases were simple enough that they could also have been learned automatically. Only a few concepts, such as *time*, require complicated rules. After processing by the template generator, the example above yields a template like this:

ORIGIN_CITY	: NNYC
DESTINATION_CITY	: SSFO
WEEKDAY	: SATURDAY
ORIGIN_TIME	: 0<1200
AIRCRAFT	: 74M

Finally, the interpreter exists in order to resolve possible ambiguities in the template. In particular, non-locality of information is handled here: only at this late stage of processing does Chronus depart from a "flat" approach. The interpreter also deals with dialogue phenomena, such as inheritance of information from previous utterances. Most of the hand-coded rules in Chronus are in the interpreter.

The problem that usually arises with hand-coded rules in computational linguistics is that after a certain point, new rules tend to interfere with old rules in unpredictable ways. A clever method of evaluating the impact of new rules was developed: every time new rules were introduced, the performance of the system was re-evaluated on about 5000 ATIS sentences. This made it possible to detect and repair new problems before it was too late (Pieraccini and Levin, 1995b).

14.6.7. The HUM System

The hidden understanding model (HUM) system, developed at BBN, is based on an entirely different approach inspired by (but not formally equivalent to) hidden Markov models (Miller *et al.*, 1994, 1995). Let M be the meaning of an utterance, and let W be the sequence of words that convey this meaning. By Bayes's rule, we can write:

$$\Pr(M|W) = \Pr(W|M)\Pr(M)/\Pr(W) \tag{14.9}$$

For given W, we wish to find the M that maximizes $\Pr(M|W)$; this can be done by maximizing $\Pr(W|M)\Pr(M)$, since $\Pr(W)$ is fixed. $\Pr(M)$ can be estimated from a *semantic language model* that specifies how meaning expressions are generated stochastically; $\Pr(W|M)$ can be estimated from a *lexical realization model* that specifies how words are generated, given a meaning.

The semantic language model employs *tree-structured meaning representations*: concepts are represented as nodes in a tree, with subconcepts represented as child nodes.

Each terminal node is the parent of a word or of a sequence of words. Note that unlike Chronus, HUM allows arbitrary nesting of concepts.

For instance, the concept FLIGHT has as possible subconcepts AIRLINE, FLIGHT_NUMBER, ORIGIN, and DESTINATION. ORIGIN and DESTINATION have as possible children the terminal nodes (respectively) ORIGIN_IND and CITY, and DEST_IND and CITY. In this tree structured representation, the phrase "United flight 203 from Dallas to Atlanta" could be analysed as:

```
FLIGHT   [AIRLINE[United]
              FLIGHT_IND[flight]
              FLT_NUM[203]
              ORIGIN[ORIGIN_IND[from] CITY[Dallas]]
              DESTINATION[DEST_IND[to] CITY[Atlanta]] ]
```

This is a slightly modified version of an example in Miller *et al.* (1994). Probabilities in the semantic language model are of the form $\Pr(\text{state}\{i\}|\text{state}\{i-1\},\text{context})$ where *context* is the parent concept, and are estimated from data. For instance, since in the ATIS corpora people usually mention an origin before a destination, almost always mention the destination if they mention either, but sometimes omit the origin:

$$\Pr(\text{DESTINATION}|\text{ORIGIN, FLIGHT})$$

will be higher than:

$$\Pr(\text{ORIGIN}|\text{DESTINATION, FLIGHT})$$

The lexical realization model is a bigram language model augmented with information about the current parent concept: $\Pr(\text{word}\{i\}|\text{word}\{i-1\},\text{concept})$. Two pseudo-words *begin and *end mark the beginning and end of a phrase, where a phrase is defined as a sequence of words produced by a terminal. Thus, $\Pr(\text{leaving}|\text{*begin*, ORIGIN\_IND})$ is the probability that "leaving" is the first word of an ORIGIN_IND phrase.

We saw that finding the meaning M for a word string W is equivalent to finding the M that maximizes $\Pr(W|M)\Pr(M)$. In practice, this is done by finding the maximum-probability path through the network made up of the two combined models (semantic language model and lexical realization model), which in theory could require exponential time with respect to sentence length. Fortunately, as for search problem in ASR, the Viterbi algorithm can be combined with a judicious amount of pruning to keep computational requirements within reasonable bounds (Miller *et al.*, 1994, 1995).

In a first version, HUM was trained on 6000 sentences whose semantic representation had been produced by the DELPHI system, which also handled discourse and backend processing. The NL class A error rate was 16%, the NL class D error rate (context-dependent) was 31%.

In a successive version, 10 000 training sentences were annotated by hand by four undergraduate students with no previous training (Miller *et al.*, 1995).

Each sentence was annotated by at least two annotators, to ensure accuracy and consistency. The discourse component was still hand-coded. This time, the NL error rate was about 10%.

14.6.8. Other Systems

Other systems were developed which did not participate in an ATIS evaluation. Based on extensive research on statistical machine translation (Brown *et al.*, 1993), a system for understanding only class A (context-independent) ATIS sentences was developed at IBM (Koppelman *et al.*, 1995; Epstein *et al.*, 1996) based on the following concepts.

Let E be the sequence of English-language words in an ATIS utterance, and let F be the semantic content of the utterance as represented in an appropriate formal language. We are interested in the joint distribution $\Pr(F, E) = \Pr(F)\Pr(E|F)$. In particular, for a given E, we want to find its most probable translation:

$$\mathrm{argmax}[\Pr(F|E)] = \mathrm{argmax}[\Pr(F, E)] = \mathrm{argmax}[\Pr(F)\Pr(E|F)] \quad (14.10)$$

Thus, one needs a language model $\Pr(F)$ for the semantic content of ATIS requests, and a translation model $\Pr(E|F)$.

Other systems for ATIS-like tasks were developed in French (Bonneau *et al.*, 1993) and Italian.

14.7. CONCLUDING REMARKS

The first conclusion to be drawn from the history of the ATIS evaluations is that considerable attention must be paid to spontaneous speech phenomena.

In Template Matcher and Phoenix, syntax is applied locally, and semantics and pragmatics globally. Among other advantages, this approach permits partial understanding of an utterance when global understanding proves impossible; such partial understanding is a good basis for user–system dialogue. By the end of ATIS, all participating systems possessed modes of functioning that resembled that of the Template Matcher and Phoenix, no matter what their creators claimed to be doing theoretically.

Of course, when utterances requiring complex global syntactic analysis do occur, it is important that one's system possess the capability to carry out such an analysis. If the ATIS corpus is any indication of the problems that will be encountered by dialogue systems, however, such complex but well-formed utterances are much less frequent than simple, "flat", syntactically ill-formed utterances that can be disambiguated by means of semantics and pragmatics. This represents a genuine linguistic discovery: spoken utterances are often made up of islands of syntactically correct phrases separated by verbal "noise", with weak or non-existent global syntactic constraints (Kuhn and De Mori, 1995).

What about the relative advantages of hand-coded systems, versus those that rely on machine learning? Note that all the ATIS systems in the latter category, without exception, contain hand-coded rules for recognizing important noun phrases, such as times, dates, locations, and types of airplanes. Presumably such rules could be learned automatically from a sufficiently large database, but no such database is available. Furthermore, the rules for these types of noun phrases are fairly easy to write down. Thus, even strong advocates of machine learning are willing to hand-code rules when it is clearly more convenient. On the other hand, at least one system that leans more towards manually coded rules (TINA) employs probabilities during search.

The question is therefore not "which is better, hand-coding or machine learning?" but which elements of the speech understanding system should be hand-coded, and which trained on data? It is clear that human beings should define the semantics of the system, and define the syntax and semantic interpretation rules for important types of noun phrases. On the other hand, machine learning techniques may be helpful in putting together a semantic interpretation for the whole utterance, since human experts seem to do a poor job in guessing how such noun phrases are strung together in spontaneous speech. Some results show that aspects of the semantic module of the system can be incorporated into the probabilistic language model, yielding considerable performance improvement.

There might seem to be an economic advantage in using only hand-coded rules: systems that rely heavily on machine learning techniques require large training corpora. One can imagine an opponent of machine learning techniques arguing that since the ATIS data were free to system developers, the evaluations contained a concealed bias in favour of machine learning. For a new, real-life application for which training data were unavailable, it might be cheaper to hand-code a system from scratch rather than be forced to collect these data. The flaw in this argument is that even hand-coded systems must be tested on large quantities of data; furthermore, such systems will be rewritten whenever new data become available (because new phenomena will be seen in the new data). The history of ATIS suggests that whether one favours hand-coded rules or machine learning techniques, large amounts of data will be required to design a functional speech understanding system.

One interesting issue is still open. Can machine learning techniques be applied to interpretation of discourse-dependent utterances? In principle the answer is surely "yes". However, note that for a system to learn rules for interpreting such utterances from training data, the training data must be annotated in an unusual way.

An example will make this clear. Let U indicate the user's utterances, and S the system's responses:

1. U: show me US Air flights from Washington to Boston serving lunch
   S: ⟨displays flights⟩
2. U: any flights from Boston to Washington
   S: ⟨displays flights⟩
3. U: can I get a cab in Boston
   S: ⟨displays ground transport information⟩
4. U: now, just those US Air flights you showed me under $700

The semantic annotation for the last user utterance should contain at least the following elements:

1. its literal interpretation (US Air flights costing less than $700)
2. its context-dependent interpretation (probably, US Air flights from Washington to Boston serving lunch and costing less than $700)
3. a pointer to the most recent previous utterance from which information was inherited (user utterance 1)

Clearly, machine learning of discourse-dependent rules will require careful planning of, and substantial investment in, the creation of training corpora.

The most important conclusion from ATIS is that it is possible to build a speech understanding system with good performance on a realistic task in a reasonable amount of time.

15

Dialogue Systems

David Sadek[*] and Renato De Mori[†]

[*]France Télécom – Centre National d'Etudes de Télécommunications (CNET) – DIH/RCP, Technopole Anticipa – 2, avenue Pierre Marzin, 22307 Lannion Cedex, France.
[†]School of Computer Science, McGill University, Montréal, P.Q. H3A 2A7, Canada.

15.1. INTRODUCTION

The emerging perspective of accessing information through the World Wide Web by a large, international, heterogeneous population brings the problem of the quality of interaction to the forefront. This makes it necessary to consider natural language as an appropriate, if not the most, media for interaction. Furthermore, the possibility of using spoken language is attractive for many reasons, the main reason being that speech is the natural and fundamental communication vehicle and is the only modality available to most telephone users. Recent efforts show a growing industrial interest along this direction (see, e.g., Wildfire, 1994; Osprey, 1995; Martin and Kehler, 1994; Vysotsky, 1994; Asadi *et al.*, 1995).

Interaction should be *user-friendly*. Obviously, the user-friendliness (or conviviality) criteria vary not only according to the application context but also according to the category of the potential user population. The reluctance of a user to use a system often depends on a particular non-satisfactory behaviour of the system. Conviviality should be viewed and handled as a global feature of a system, and should "emerge" from its *intelligence*; it should not be handled as a set of specific features identified one by one by the system's or the interface's designer. Let us call a *dialogue system*, a (more or less) *convivial* interactive system that is capable of managing elaborate contextual exchanges with the user (see section 15.3 for the definition of some significant criteria for convivial interaction). The machine component of person–machine communication (PMC) is an *intelligent agent* whose dialogue abilities are based on its primitive capacities of rational, cooperative behaviour.

In the general case, it is unlikely that a user can access the desired information with just a single query. The query might be imprecise, incomplete, intrinsically inconsistent, or incoherent with respect to the dialogue history. It might not be completely understood by the system, especially in a context of spoken interaction, given that ASR and NL understanding technologies are known to be imperfect. Furthermore, even if the request is well formed, unambiguous, perfectly recognized and understood, it is possible that the size of the answer is so big that the system has to consult the user in order to reach an agreement on the responses (e.g., the documents) the user is really interested in.

Clarification, completion and negotiation dialogues are underlain by plans (or strategies) that should guide the user to provide the necessary elements of a "task" description that the system knows and considers practically and economically feasible. The final objective of the dialogue would be that of accomplishing the required "task" by performing the appropriate (communicative and/or non-communicative) actions.

Simple human–computer spoken dialogues usually implement rigid strategies. This makes ASR robust because rigidity requires the speaker to respond to a proposed menu with a small active vocabulary at each dialogue step. On the contrary, casual users do not like rigid systems and are inclined to get frustrated and refuse to use them.

As technology progresses, it becomes possible to reduce rigidity by allowing the user to speak with more freedom. This requires a more sophisticated dialogue component, with more detailed knowledge about the content and structure of the information repository, and a more elaborate capability of reasoning about the user's utterances (or messages, in general). In this view, *interface ergonomy* is largely based on *agent's intelligence* and *knowledge* (see Sadek (1996) for more details on this consideration).

In user-friendly interaction, the system's intelligence is made complex by the need to interpret (in context) and handle a very large variety of utterances (and, more generally, multimedia messages), and by the need to generate a large variety of (possibly multimedia) answers. This is due, in particular, to the fact that the granularity or the degree of completeness of the user's requests can vary significantly. Modern and useful telephone services, even without ASR but just using the telephone keyboard, should require a certain degree of "intelligence" to produce an answer like: "I do not have any subscriber by the last name of André either in Antibes or in the closest surrounding area, but I have ten in Nice, one of them being a woman. If you want to select one of them press the two first letters of the name; if you want to select the woman subscriber press 1; if you want the whole list press #; and if your are not interested in any of them press *".

Note that even if communication in natural language, especially with speech, has obvious (and non-obvious) advantages compared to other media (such as direct manipulation; see, e.g., Cohen, 1992), one can easily think of intelligent, convivial interaction with mouse input and image output.[1] The phenomena, problems and interaction mechanisms introduced in this chapter are illustrated with examples from natural language interaction, but they can be easily transposed to interaction contexts that involve other communication media, possibly used jointly with natural language.

In this view, designing a service should not be approached as a twofold operation: (1) the definition of the service content or functionalities and (2) the designing of its user interface. Rather, a dialogue system should *embody* the service, and it is the system's intelligence that will guarantee a "good" ergonomy of the service.

Section 15.2 introduces simple and "rigid" dialogue systems. Section 15.3 discusses some basic dialogue phenomena that need to be taken into account to design more "intelligent" dialogue systems. Section 15.4 is about the computational models of advanced dialogue systems. Section 15.5 introduces the

---

[1]For instance, a "lodging" server that offers an access to an image database can allow the user to select in various menus a set of search criteria. If the selected criteria have not allowed to identify the sought lodging precisely, the system will propose to the user images considered close to what is sought; the user can modify her/his request by clicking on the part of the image she/he wants to modify.

principles of *rational interaction* to design dialogue agents. Section 15.6 deals
with domain-independent constraints. Section 15.7 discusses some aspects of
the use of natural language in advanced dialogues and provides examples of
real human–computer telephone dialogues that a system can handle. Some
remarks conclude the chapter.

15.2. SIMPLE DIALOGUE MODELS

Simple dialogue models reflect a dialogue strategy based on *finite-state diagrams*
(FSD). FSD can be viewed as a specification formalism for dialogue models that
has well-known advantages in terms of soundness (the underlying theory
provides methods for evaluating correctness and completeness) and under-
standability (the formalism is widely known by computer scientists). Extensions
of FSD for specifying dialogue models are formal grammars, especially CFGs,
which maintain the above-mentioned advantages. CFGs can be converted into
AND/OR graphs (Larson, 1992) allowing one to view dialogues as problem-
solving activities and to use various heuristics to optimize system responses.

A simple example of an FSD for a dialogue is shown in Figure 15.1. In a state,
the dialogue system prepares the system message (SM) to be sent to the user and
the LM that represents the system expectation about what the user can say.
With this LM, the ASR component decodes the user message, which is then
interpreted by the semantic interpretation component. This is represented in
Figure 15.1 by the expression $INTi = ASU(LMi\ UMi)$, meaning that the
interpretation $INTi$ of the ith user message UMi is obtained by the ASU
system using the language model LMi. Based on the interpretation results,
the conditions associated with the arcs following the state are evaluated. If
the conditions are set in such a way that one and only one of them is satisfied,
then the dialogue strategy will simply transfer control to the state that
corresponds to the destination of the arc whose condition has been satisfied.
Generation and recognition procedures associated with this arc will then be
executed.

Various methods are available for structuring, factorizing, grouping,
parallelizing portions of FSD and also for parsing dialogue grammars
(Larson, 1992).

In regard to spoken dialogue, the interesting aspect is that a LM can be
designed for each dialogue state. If the dialogue is very rigid, this LM can be
just a set of isolated words. In a more flexible system, the state-dependent
LM can be a finite-state automaton (FSA) or a stochastic FSA with words
associated with arcs. For less constrained systems, state-dependent LMs can
be integrated bigram or trigram networks. What would make the LMs state-
dependent are the bigram or trigram probabilities. If it is not possible to collect
a large enough corpus for each state and properly estimate the corresponding

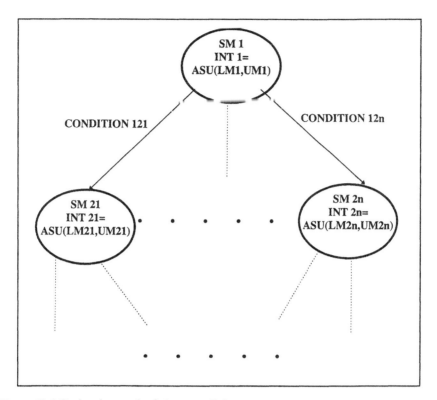

Figure 15.1 Basic scheme of a finite-state dialogue system.

probabilities, it is possible to cluster states into *situations*, build a LM for each situation and have a general model that is a mixture of these LMs as discussed in section 14.5. Only mixture coefficients can then be made state-dependent. Various degrees of state clustering may be considered for this purpose, depending on the amount and quality of data available.

15.3. BASIC DIALOGUE PHENOMENA

A number of laboratory prototypes for human–computer dialogue systems have been developed in the past.[2] The most ancient of them is probably Eliza (Weizenbaum, 1966). Most of these systems show the capability to concatenate simple exchanges with a human user following a stereotypical structure and a

---

[2]See, for example Asadi *et al.* (1995), Ferrieux and Sadek (1994), Osprey (1995), Pieraccini and Levin (1995) and Wildfire (1994).

limited application framework. In general, their ability to generate cooperative
answers does not create the conditions of an interaction perceived as *natural* by
humans, even for highly constrained and limited application frameworks. There
are reasons for this. The first reason is the difficulty of integrating methodologies for artificial *intelligent* agents and human *natural* communication.
This difficulty increases in the context of spoken dialogue because, in this
case, communication is strongly affected by ASR errors (Sorin, 1996).

Another reason for the limitations of dialogue systems for PMC is that most
of the approaches consider dialogue as an isolated phenomenon, in which
external manifestations have to be identified and reproduced by machines.
This ignores the *cognitive* aspects of dialogue, i.e. the link between external
manifestations and the internal *"intelligence"* of the machine.

A possible software architecture for a multimedia dialogue system that allows
cognitive aspects of dialogue to be implemented is shown in Figure 15.2. Here, a
reaction unit consists of an *inference engine* that operationalizes behaviour
principles coded in a *behaviour knowledge base*, thus creating and maintaining
a *dialogue history*. The reaction unit interacts with various resource managers
via a *resource manager interface*, such as an *application knowledge base* (e.g., a
semantic network describing the domain knowledge), a (possibly remote)
database manager and an *input/output manager*. The input/output manager in
turn handles message interpretation and generation and controls the graphic
and audio interfaces and their synchronization. The *audio interface* controls
speech recognition (*ASR unit*) and speech generation (*audio output*).

The reaction unit performs inferences about the user's beliefs and intentions,
based on the results provided by the input/output manager, and about the
actions to be taken (communicative act planning, database access, display or
sound generation). Inference is based on the behaviour principles, the dialogue
history, and the different available knowledge resources.

Among the features of an interactive system that make the user view it as a
user-friendly human–computer dialogue system, the most significant are:
negotiation ability, contextual interpretation, flexibility of the input language,
flexibility of interaction, capability to produce cooperative responses, and the
adequacy of the response style. These features are now introduced and
discussed.

15.3.1. Negotiation Ability

Negotiation between the user and the dialogue system is made necessary by the
fact that the ultimate objective of the enterprise is *user satisfaction*. In fact, the
most obvious reaction may not correspond to what has been apparently
requested by the user (even if all the words uttered by the user were perfectly
recognized). For instance, the user might have deliberately formulated an
incomplete request, such as "I am looking for a job around here", or "I

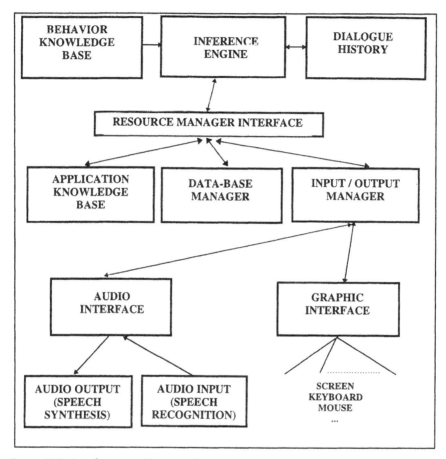

Figure 15.2 A software architecture for a multimedia dialogue system with reasoning
capabilities.

would like to know the departure time of a flight to Paris", waiting for the
system to assist her/him in formulating more specific requirements.

The user's request may contain sufficient information to access a database
and provide an answer, but the number of possible answers might be too
large. In this case the dialogue strategy is to negotiate with the user more
constraints on her/his request, by signalling that the list of possible answers
would be too long.

Another possibility is that there is no answer available for the user's request.
In this case, the system has to advise the user and guide her/him to formulate a
request that is compatible with the system's knowledge.

The user may also wish to negotiate new requests (on the basis of the answers
given by the system), especially once she/he has a better understanding of what
the system can provide.

All these cases may intertwine, thus increasing the complexity of the negotiation process. Sophisticated negotiation capabilities usually make the dialogue system more user-friendly.

15.3.2. Context Interpretation and Language Flexibility

An interactive system that expects the user to formulate her/his message in such a way that it can be understood independently from the context can in no way be viewed as a convivial system. *A fortiori*, a "question–answer" system (i.e., a system which can only react to completely specified requests, as was roughly the case with the ATIS systems (e.g., Bonneau *et al.*, 1993), cannot be considered as a dialogue system.[3]

An effective dialogue system has to be able to interpret a user's utterance with respect to the previously exchanged utterances. This capability is a necessary requirement for real systems because users frequently use *ellipses* (e.g., once a list of flights for Paris has been required and obtained, the user might then ask: "And for New York"), *anaphoras* (e.g. "Give me the cheapest flight") or questions of the type "Is a server of this type available from here?".

Note that in natural communication, contextual interpretation is the general case rather than the exception, because as noted in Kayser (1984), the communicated message is always *differential*: a person does not describe a (whole) situation; she/he tends to express the difference between the situation she/he wants to describe and what she/he believes that her/his interlocutor already knows. More specifically, during a dialogue, the interlocutors tend to make reference to an existing *situation* in order to modify it, rather than making frequent initializations of new situations.

For a speech-based system to handle complex context dependencies, it must be able to deal with spontaneous speech and hence very large vocabularies. Whether or not its ASR component has to correctly recognize all the words might be debatable, but, certainly, the system should be able to properly identify all the semantically relevant words embedded in a very large variety of sentences.

In a multimedia system, the flexibility of the input language would involve, for example, that no constraint (such as specific order) be imposed on the way media can be combined, or that a medium be not only reserved for a certain type of action.

---

[3]Actually, the capability of interpreting a user utterance contextually is present to a very limited extent in the ATIS systems. Anyway, if such a capability were "fully" present there, it would not have been easy to deal with it in the ATIS "contest" (for the comparison of speech-based interactive systems), because of the difficulty to evaluate system performance when complex dialogue histories can be taken into account.

15.3.3. Interaction Flexibility

There are certainly situations where the user might find it useful to be closely guided by the system. However, not being constrained to follow a pre-established structure, as is the case of navigating with a hypertext system, notably increases the comfort of a dialogue system. It should be possible for the user to change topic or dialogue objectives even before the completion of a (seemingly) mutually agreed dialogue task.

More importantly, the need for a non-pre-established structure of interaction clearly appears whenever communication troubles arise. Indeed, while it is acceptable that during a "consensual" proceeding of the dialogue, the user need not take the initiative to express her/his requests, she/he should be allowed to deviate from the "regular" course of interaction whenever she/he has identified a communication problem. Note that the possibility of distortion between the message sent and the message received is common in communication. The problems of erroneous perception or interpretation should be treated as the general case rather that the exception. It is therefore natural that the user can rectify a misunderstanding of the system, or correct her/himself. The more the possibility to contest is independent from the dialogue state, the less the user feels afraid to be engaged in one-way paths that she/he has not chosen. Only a system that allows for flexible interaction (i.e., without any pre-established interaction structure) can offer this possibility in a generic way (i.e., independently from the dialogue state).

In the general case, the possibility to contest is directly related to the global capability of a system to revise its beliefs. So far, there are only a few systems that provide it. The reason for that is the difficulty to implement it in the approaches where dialogue is constrained to follow pre-established structures.

15.3.4. Cooperative Reactions

Let us consider the following question that could be asked at a booth of a railway station: "What is the departure time of the next train to Paris?". It is not unnatural to get an answer such as the following: "At 3:30 PM, track number 21". Consider also the following question "Do you know what time it is?" to which one can answer "Yes! I do know", but for which it is natural to expect an answer like "It is 2:30". The common aspect of these examples is that the answer extends beyond the question in a pertinent way. When this happens, the answer is said to be *cooperative*.

In human–human dialogue, cooperative responses are the general case rather than the exception. A friendly dialogue system should attempt to produce them too. There is a large variety of cooperative answers. Major types of *cooperative answers* are introduced in the following (see also Siroux *et al.* (1989) for other types of cooperative answers).

Completion answers

Completion answers (sometimes called over-informative answers) contain more information than has been explicitly requested by the user (see in the example above the answer to the request about "the departure time of the next train to Paris"). The need to provide additional information and its content have been *inferred* from user requests and dialogue history.

Corrective answers

Corrective answers are given when questions imply certain things to be true, while, in reality, they are not. For example the question: "At what time does the flight from Montreal to Tucson stop in Chicago?" implies that there is a flight from Montreal to Tucson (which is not true) and that it stops in Chicago (which, consequently, is also not true). Obviously, the answer to a question like this has to be a corrective one, like: "There are no flights from Montreal to Tucson".

Suggestive answers

There are questions for which the answer should be "negative", but from which it is possible to infer that the user might be interested in the answer of another question of a related topic even if she/he did not mention this topic explicitly. This is the case of answers of the type "No, there is no train to Grenoble today, *but there is a train to Lyon and from there you can take a shuttle bus to Grenoble*". In certain cases, a reasoning process may infer that the answer to a question related to the one the user has effectively asked may be more informative and appreciated by the user.

Conditional answers

There are questions for which there may be positive answers under conditions that constrain the user request beyond her/his intention. For example: "Give me the flights to Detroit before 7:00 AM" may receive a conditional answer of the type: "There is a flight at 6:50 AM on weekdays only".

Intensional answers

There are cases in which providing a "factorized" answer not only makes it more presentable and understandable to the user (especially in the context of spoken communication) but can also inform her/him about the genericity of its semantic. For example, the question: "Give me the list of all the non-smoking flights between Canada and the Netherlands", for which an intensional answer would be: "All KLM flights".

It is worth noting that calculating the intensional form of an answer on the basis of an extensional set of solutions may require a relatively complex inference process.

15.3.5. Adequacy of Response Style

For a dialogue system, not only must it determine the right reaction, but it must also determine the appropriate way to present it to the user. In particular, it is important for the system to be able to choose the medium, or some combination, for the answer as well as the appropriate level of verbosity. For example, if the answer to a question is a list of 30 flights, it is better to display it on a screen, if this is possible, rather than using spoken output. If this is not possible, it may be necessary to negotiate with the user in order to arrive at an answer of an acceptable size. In the case of graphic output, colours, font type and size, and layout of the answer may affect user satisfaction.

More generally, "formatting" the answer, "factorizing" it according to semantic criteria, choosing the best verbosity level and the right medium (or combination) are operations which contribute to the quality of a dialogue system reaction.

15.3.6. Impact of User-Friendly Requirements on System Design

Even though setting a list of conviviality criteria such as those introduced above may be crucial for external specification and for evaluation of dialogue systems, this cannot be taken as a methodological basis for system design.

The first reason is that the impact on system design of such a list of criteria is limited by the fact that it is potentially open to extensions, such as the need for responses in real time, and/or customization, and may depend on the application domain.

But more importantly, most of these criteria are interdependent, and it is only when they are satisfied jointly and generically (i.e., independently from dialogue state) that they can significantly affect the degree of system conviviality.

Even if their external manifestations are different, these criteria rely on the same basic mechanisms. Therefore, aiming at satisfying them one by one is neither an optimal nor a generic approach. Thus, the designer should attempt to meet most of them with a global view. Importantly, the way that the satisfaction of these criteria is handled, namely extensionally or as a consequence of a deeper "intelligence" of the system determines a fundamental division in the approaches of dialogue system design.

15.4. COMPUTATIONAL MODELS FOR DIALOGUE SYSTEMS

15.4.1. Structural Approaches

Structural approaches based on FSDs or dialogue grammars were introduced in section 15.2. They can be anchored by a computer science background (see, e.g. Winograd and Flores, 1986; Dahlbäck and Jönsson, 1992) or by a linguistic background (see, e.g. Clarke, 1979; Moeschler, 1989; Bilange, 1992) and attempt to model regularities in human–computer or human–human dialogues. Structural approaches are based on the assumption that there exists a regular structure in dialogue, and that this structure can be represented "finitely" (for example by an FSA or a CFG). They consider that dialogue coherence is residing in its structure and are therefore descriptive: they are based on descriptions of observed sequencing of utterances, not on explanations of what is observed. Although effective practical systems can be built with these approaches, these systems tend to appear rigid to the user and limit her/his degree of satisfaction.

The structural approaches concentrate on the *co-text* (i.e., the text that "comes with"), leaving away the *contextual* nature of communication. These limitations rule out these approaches as a basis for computational models of *intelligent interaction*. Other approaches (such as described below) are required. The implementation of these approaches is more complex as is their specification. Recent progress has shown that prototypes of these systems can be built and tested. These systems have inference engines and knowledge representations with which real-time implementations is now possible. This motivates a great interest in their study.

15.4.2. Classical Plan-Oriented Approaches

Classical plan-based or differential approaches (Cohen and Perrault, 1979; Allen and Perrault, 1980; Perrault and Allen, 1980; Bruce, 1975; Appelt, 1985; Litman and Allen, 1987, 1990; Carberry, 1990; Guyomard *et al.*, 1993; Chu-Carol and Carberry, 1994) consider an utterance not only as a collection of *signs* (e.g., a sequence of words), but also as a realization of observable communicative actions, also called *speech acts* or *dialogue acts*, such as *inform, request, confirm, commit*, etc. Language is viewed as a means for identifying and instantiating a common context within dialogue partners.

These approaches follow the philosophical principle that "communicating is acting" (Austin, 1962). They rely on the idea that communicative actions, similarly to (physical) non-communicative actions are oriented toward goal achievement, and are planned with this motivation. In this view, the objective of communication is to change the *mental state* (including beliefs, intentions, etc.) of the interlocutor. Thus, communicative actions can be planned and recognized, as regular actions, on the basis of mental states. Dialogue analysis is considered in the framework of explaining actions based on mental states, relying on general models of actions and mental attitudes.

In practice, it is assumed that persons generally have *goals* and *plans* in mind when they interact with other persons or machines. The purpose of a dialogue is to recognize such goals and plans, and to produce effects corresponding to the *purpose* of the plans.

To some extent, the recognition problem can be viewed as that of classifying an *end event* that generates a set of *observed events*. For this purpose, an *event hierarchy* can be considered. It can be formalized by a collection of restricted forms of first-order axioms used to define the abstraction, specialization and functional relationships between various kinds of events. Events used in discourse analysis follow communicative act event types and their specialization and utterance types. Event types have associated *function roles*. Recognition of a plan *P*, based on observation of events produced by an action set *A* can be viewed as a kind of *hypothetical reasoning* to infer *P* such that, if an agent had the objective to achieve *P*, then he would do the observed actions in *A*.

The plan-based approaches can be enriched with heuristics and structural models of discourse (Grosz and Sidner, 1990).

15.4.3. Speech Acts

Speech act theory was first proposed by Austin (1962) and then further developed by Searle (1969). The theory considers that there are statements, like "I declare the session open", that should not be judged for their truth, because they state the accomplishment of the event they describe and they should be considered as actions, called *performatives*. A generalization of this leads to a formulation for which a communication activity accomplishes three basic speech acts. The first act is a *locutionary* act, consisting of producing a set of signs (e.g., phonemes, words). The second act is an *illocutionary* act, which is accomplished in producing the signs in a context of social relation, and which consists of expressing an intention. The third act is a *perlocutionary* act, which is accomplished by producing the sequence of signs. Inform, request, threaten, etc., are examples of illocutionary acts; convince, incite, fear, etc. are examples of perlocutionary acts. Illocutionary acts are taken to be the essence of communication. Perlocutionary acts are characterized in terms of perlocutionary effects because they appear as effects of illocutionary acts and may not be performed intentionally.

In addition to these three types of acts, Searle added propositional acts, namely *predication* and *reference* acts, which are the acts for referring to objects and for describing properties of the world (such as relations between objects). Searle also proposed semi-formal conditions of successful performance accomplishment of illocutory acts. This account is detailed and formalized in Searle and Vanderveken (1985).

Locutionary acts can be considered to be physical, while illocutionary and perlocutionary acts are mental. An illocutionary act is defined by its *illocutionary force* and its *propositional* (or *semantic*) *content*. A taxonomy of illocutionary acts, initially proposed by Austin and refined by Searle, consists of five act types: *assertive acts* (e.g., assert, inform, confirm), *directive acts* (e.g., request, commend), *commissive acts* (e.g., promise, commit), *declarative acts* (e.g., open a session, mary) and *expressive acts* (e.g., apologize, express regret). For more details see Austin (1962), Searle (1969, 1979) and Strawson (1971).

Independently from this characterization and taxonomy of "speech acts", a *communicative act* can be defined as an act that is produced to be observed by (at least) one other agent, thus aiming at causing a change in her/his mental state (Sadek, 1991a,b). An agent uses this behaviour to communicate an intention. If the term "speech" in "speech act theory" is taken to mean "instrument of communication", then the notions of communicative act and of speech act are identical. Notice that non-linguistic acts, such as actions of referring by pointing at objects, are communicative acts.

A conversational system is a set of human or artificial agents, each one of which is capable of accomplishing communication acts and of interpreting communication acts of other agents.

For each act of a communication system, three agent types are considered, namely *the author*, the *recipient* and the *observer*. The author as well as the recipient are also observers. The accomplishment of the act also modifies the mental state of the author who, among other things, has to add to her/his *belief system*, the fact that the act has been just been performed (Sadek, 1991a).

15.4.4. Comments on the Classical Plan-Based Approach

Fundamental work about the differential (or plan-based) approach to natural communication (Cohen and Perrault, 1979; Allen and Perrault, 1980; Perrault and Allen, 1980; Bruce, 1975) has shown that the philosophical theory of speech acts can have a formal foundation in the theory of action. In spite of the large popularity gained by the plan-based approach, it is still difficult to formulate, within this framework, a "coherent", global solution to the problem of user-friendly, "natural" PMC.

One reason is that the use of logical formulation for mental attitudes is weak (if not hazardous) if the interpretation of the formalism remains intuitive. For example, the concepts of *belief* and *intention* which are fundamental components in communication and cooperation philosophy (Grice, 1957), cannot be properly used without an adequate model of their semantics. Note that analysing these concepts is not interesting for the study of communication (and cooperation) only, but more generally for modelling the background common to the so-called intelligent behaviours. In fact, the more general problem is the maintenance of the *rational balance* existing between the different mental attitudes of an agent, and also existing between the agent's attitudes and plans and actions. In the classical plan-based approaches, the relation between mental attitudes (in particular intention) and action, is purely operational. The lack of explicit rationality principles and their (logical) links with action models is an important limitation, not only of this approach, but more generally of the work related to the concept of intelligent agency.

A second reason is that since a communicative act is, in principle, an action, its modelling has to cope with the problems, well-known in AI, related to characterizing action effects and preconditions (such as the frame problem (McCarthy, 1980), the qualification problem (McCarthy and Hayes, 1969), or the ramification problem (Ginsberg and Smith, 1988)). In particular, the effect of a communication act on its recipient (and also on its author) depends on her/his mental state before the act is performed. A more general problem underlying this phenomenon is that of *belief reconstruction* (Sadek, 1991a, 1994c) following the observation of a communicative act (or, more generally, an event). Belief revision (and its counterpart, consistency preserving) following the "consummation" of an event is an aspect of this problem. Thus, characterizing the effect of an act as a function of the mental context in which the act has been performed turns out to be a difficult issue.

The third reason is that the differential approach has, somehow, neglected the question of the criteria for determining the act *types* to model, and, for a given act, the question of the specification of the mental attitudes it encapsulates (more details can be found in Sadek (1991b) and Cohen and Levesque (1990b)).

15.5. PRINCIPLES OF THE RATIONAL INTERACTION APPROACH

15.5.1. Motivations

The rational interaction approach to understanding person–machine dialogue can be viewed as a recasting, in a comprehensive formal framework, of the plan-based approach, and as adopting a "radical" view of communication as a special case of intelligent behaviour. It is thus based on the assumption that a system capable of carrying on an 'intelligent" dialogue has to be an *intelligent system*, in which the communication ability is not primitive, but is grounded on a more general competence that characterizes *rational behaviour*.[4]

In a simplified way, for an agent to behave rationally is to be permanently driven, at a certain *representation level*, by principles which optimally select actions leading to those future in conformity with a given set of motivations and desires (see, e.g., Cohen and Levesque, 1990b; Sadek, 1991a, 1994b). It is at this (hypothesized) *knowledge level* (Newell, 1982) that the concepts of mental attitude and intentional action are relevant.

The first most significant contribution to the rational interaction approach is Cohen and Levesque's work (see, in particular, Cohen and Levesque, 1990a, b), which provided a robust methodological framework for expressing formal theories of intention and communication. Even though their account suffered from a certain number of theoretical modelization problems (see Sadek, 1991a, 1992) and handled only some aspects of rational behaviour and (cooperative) interaction, it had been the first rigorous, formal analysis of intentional action and communication.[5]

In regard to the formal framework to couch this approach, the logic representation is adequate for various reasons: its homogeneity, its generic structure (due to its large coverage), its ability to properly describe mental states (which makes it easy to maintain), and its potential usability as a tool for both modelling and implementation.

A delicate problem concerning the implementation of these systems is the need of methods and procedures for *automated inference* (or *theorem proving*), the heart of the reasoning system, with acceptable time (and space) complexity. Some interesting solutions have been proposed in some of the above-mentioned systems.

The rational interaction approach leads to a new paradigm for designing dialogue systems, that of *dialoguing rational agent*. The ARTIMIS technology developed at France Télécom–CNET is an effective implementation of this paradigm.

As a framework to dialogue system design, the logical model of rational interaction relies on two basic ideas. The first one is that a dialogue process can be completely justified by rational behaviour principles (which are more basic that discourse rules), and does not require, in principle, any structural model; instances of dialogue structure will dynamically emerge from the dynamics of rationality principles. The second one is that the same logical

---

[4]The most consensual achievement of intelligent behaviour is *rationality*. An overview of different aspects of the notion of rationality can be found in Russell (1995). See also Doyle (1990), for example, for an approach to *economic rationality*.

[5]Other work more specific to intelligent agent modelling and implementation comes within the same spirit as this approach (see, e.g., Rao and Georgeff, 1992; Shoham, 1993; Konolige and Pollack, 1993; Wooldrige and Jennings, 1994).

theory can account for different aspects of rational behaviour, in particular in situations of cooperative dialogue.

Due to the generic structure of its principles, this approach achieves the *robustness* required by a(n intelligent) dialogue system: to soundly react to complex situations, possibly incompletely specified when the system has been designed.

15.5.2. Mental Attitudes

Two basic notions are at the centre of the intelligent behaviour modelling, namely mental attitude (or more generally intentionality (Searle, 1983)) and action. The approach aiming at designing computational models of communication, which comes within the more general framework of rational action, consequently relies on these two notions.

Mental attitude can be intuitively viewed as the relation between an agent and a situation (identifiable to a proposition) or an object (in a general sense). A detailed discussion of this notion can be found in Searle (1983) and Barwise and Perry (1983).

In logical terms, a proposition is a *belief* of an agent if the agent considers that the proposition is true. Belief is the mental attitude whereby an agent has a model of the world. An agent's belief system is the mean that allows the agent to maintain and update its representation of the external world.

Uncertainty is a way of representing an approximate perception of the world. In the formal framework for rational interaction (Sadek, 1991a, b), uncertainty is not represented by any type of degree, not even qualitative; it is handled in a global way and expresses the fact that the agent believes that a proposition is not true, but it is more likely than its negation. (See also Rabin and Halpern (1987) for a logic of likelihood.)

Intention is strongly related to action. It is the mental attitude whereby an agent can determine and control his evolution. It is a composite concept, which cannot be analysed independently from the other mental attitudes (Cohen and Levesque 1990a). Formally, an agent has the intention to bring about a proposition if and only if:[6]

- The agent believes that the proposition is false.
- The agent *chooses* to evolve toward a future in which the proposition is true and to act coherently with this choice.
- The agent commits himself to maintain this choice until the agent comes to believe that the proposition holds or he comes to believe that the proposition is impossible.[7]

---

[6]Note that while the object of belief or uncertainty is necessarily a proposition, intention might have an action (that is a term in the logical sense) as object.

[7]See Cohen and Levesque (1990a) and Sadek (1991a, 1992) for formal theories of intention relying on the bases just introduced.

It may be debatable to ascribe mental attitudes to machines. Whether or not a
machine can have mental attitudes is probably undecidable. What is relevant is
the possibility of considering a machine *as if* it has such or such mental attitude,
through the causal role this mental attitude plays in its behaviour. As analysed by
Dennett (1987), the problem is not to know whether a system is really
intentional or not, but to know whether it can be considered as such coherently.
As McCarthy (1979) pointed out, it is legitimate to consider a machine as having
mental attitudes if this is useful.

15.5.3. Elements of the Theoretical Framework

Concepts of mental attitude (belief, uncertainty, intention) and action are
formalized in the framework of first-order modal logic described in detail in
Sadek (1991a, 1992). For the sake of brevity, only the aspects of the formalism
used in this chapter will be introduced in the following.

Symbols $\neg$, $\wedge$, $\vee$ and $\Rightarrow$ represent classical logical connectives of negation,
conjunction, disjunction and implication, while $\forall$ and $\exists$, are respectively the
universal and existential quantifiers.

Symbol p represents a closed formula denoting a proposition.

ϕ, ψ and δ are formula schema, i, j and h are variable schema denoting
agents.

Notation $\models \phi$ means that formula ϕ is valid.

Mental attitudes considered as semantic primitives, i.e., belief, uncertainty
and choice (or preference, or, to some extent, goal) are formalized by the
modal operators B, U and C respectively.

Formulae of the type $B(i, p)$, $U(i, p)$, and $C(i, p)$ can be respectively read as: "*i*
believes that p is true", "*i* is uncertain about the truth of p", and "*i* desires that p
be currently true".

The logical model for operator B accounts for interesting properties of a
rational agent, such as consistency of beliefs, and introspection capacity,
formally characterized by the validity of logical schema such as:

$$B(i, \phi) \Rightarrow \neg B(i, \neg\phi)$$

$$B(i, \phi) \Rightarrow B(i, B(i, \phi)) \tag{15.1}$$

$$\neg B(i, \phi) \Rightarrow B(i, \neg B(i, \phi))$$

As regards uncertainty, the logical model ensures the validity of suitable
properties such as, for example, the fact that an agent cannot be uncertain of
its mental attitudes:

$$\models \neg U(i, M(i, \phi)) \tag{15.2}$$

with M representing any modality, and therefore belonging to
$\{B, \neg B, C, \neg C, U, \neg U, \text{etc.}\}$.

The logical model for choice has properties such that an agent chooses the logical consequences of its choices:

$$\models (C(i, \phi) \wedge B(i, \phi \Rightarrow \psi)) \Rightarrow C(i, \psi) \tag{15.3}$$

or that an agent must choose the event courses it believes it is already in:[8]

$$\models B(i, \phi) \Rightarrow C(i, \phi) \tag{15.4}$$

Intention, which is not a semantic primitive, is formalized by operator I that is defined in a complex way using operators C and K. A formula like $I(i, p)$ can be read as: "i has the intention to bring about p".

The definition of intention implies that an agent cannot bring about a situation if the agent believes that it already holds:

$$\models I(i, \phi) \Rightarrow (i, \neg\phi) \tag{15.5}$$

It also ensures that an agent does not intend to bring about the "side effects" of its intentions.

In order to enable reasoning about actions, the universe of discourse includes, in addition to the individual objects and agents, event sequences. The language includes terms (in particular variables like $e, e_1, \ldots$) that range over the set of event sequences. A sequence may be formed with a single event that can be the *void* event. Events (or actions) can be combined in various ways to form action expressions such as sequences $a_1; a_2$, or nondeterministic choices $a_1 | a_2$. Schematic variables $a, a_1, a_2, \ldots$ denote action expressions. The following operators are also introduced: *Feasible, Done* and *Agent*. Formulae like *Feasible*(a, p), *Done*(a, p) and *Agent*(i, a), mean respectively that action a can take place after which p will become true, a has just taken place and p was true before, and i denotes the only agent of the events appearing in a.

A fundamental property of the just introduced logic is that agents are in perfect agreement with themselves about their own mental attitudes. Formally, the following property holds:

$$\vdash \phi \leftrightarrow B(i, \phi) \tag{15.6}$$

where ϕ is governed by a modal operator formalizing a mental attitude of agent i (Sadek, 1991a, 1992).

For semantic interpretation, belief is characterized by a possible-worlds structure (Hintikka, 1962; Kripke, 1963), of type *KD45* (Halpern and Moses, 1985), with a principle of uniform domain (Garson, 1984). This structure is also the framework for the interpretation of uncertainty, the set of possible worlds being viewed as a probability space. The concept of choice is also interpreted in terms of possible worlds, characterized by a specific accessibility relation. Similar considerations hold for the notion of event (feasibility).

---

[8]This property, called *the realism constraint*, was introduced by Cohen and Levesque (1990a).

The following abbreviations are used, *True* being the propositional constant always true:

$$Feasible(a) \equiv Feasible(a, True)$$
$$Done(a) \equiv Done(a, True)$$
$$Possible(\phi) \equiv (\exists e)Feasible(e, \phi)$$
$$Bif(i, \phi) \equiv B(i, \phi) \vee B(i, \neg\phi)$$
$$Bref(i, \iota x\, \delta(x)) \equiv (\exists y)B(i, \iota x\, \delta(x) = y)$$
$$Uif(i, \phi) \equiv U(i, \phi) \vee U(i, \neg\phi)$$
$$Uref(i, \iota x\, \delta(x)) \equiv (\exists y)U(i, \iota x\, \delta(x) = y)$$
$$AB_{n,i,j}\phi \equiv B_i B_j B_i \ldots \phi$$

In the fifth and seventh abbreviations, ι is the operator for definite description, defined as a term producer as follows:

$$\phi(\iota x\, \delta(x)) \equiv \exists y\, \phi(y) \wedge \delta(y) \wedge \forall z(\delta(z) \Rightarrow z = y)$$

$\iota x\delta(x)$ is read "the (x which is) δ". $Bref_i\delta(x)$ means that agent i (thinks that it) knows the (x which is) δ. agent i knows δ.[9] $Uif_i\phi$ means that either agent i is uncertain about ϕ (in the sense defined above) or that it is uncertain about $\neg\phi$. $Uref_i\delta(x)$ has the same meaning as $Bref_i\delta(x)$, except that agent i has an uncertainty attitude with respect to $\delta(x)$ instead of a belief (or a knowledge) attitude. In the last abbreviation, which introduces the concept of *alternate beliefs*, n is a positive integer representing the number of B operators alternating between i and j.

Rationality principles and action model

The components of an action model, in particular, a communicative act (CA) model, that are involved in a planning process characterize both the reasons for which the action is selected and the conditions that have to be satisfied for the action to be planned. For a given action, the former is referred to as the *rational effect* (RE),[10] and the latter as the *feasibility preconditions* (FP), or the qualifications of the action.

Two rationality principles relate an agent's intention to its plans and actions. The first principle gives an agent the capability of planning an act whenever the agent intends to achieve its RE. It states that an agent's intention to achieve a given goal generates its intention to do one of the acts known to the agent, whose rational effect (RE) corresponds to the agent's goal, and that the agent

---

[9] Formula $Bref(i, \iota x\delta(x))$ can be used for $(\exists x)\, B(i, \delta(x))$. In such a case, the operator ι produces an *indefinite description*, meaning that the uniqueness constraint, corresponding to the component $\forall z(\delta(z) \Rightarrow z = y)$ in the defintion of $\phi(\iota x\delta(x))$, is abandoned.

[10] This effect is also referred to as the *perlocutionary effect* in some of Sadek's previous work, in analogy with the use of the term in speech acts theory.

has no reason for not doing them. Formally, this is expressed by the following property:

$$\models I(i,p) \Rightarrow I(Done(a_1|\dots|a_n)) \tag{15.7}$$

where a_k, k ranging from 1 to n, are all the actions such that:

- p is the rational effect of a_k (i.e., the reason for which a_k is planned).
- Agent i knows action a_k: $Bref(i, a_k)$.
- $\neg C(i, \neg Possible(Done(a_k)))$.

The second principle imposes on an agent, whenever the agent selects an action (by virtue of the first rationality principle), to seek the satisfiability of its FPs.[11] It states that an agent, having the intention that some action be done, adopts the intention that the action be feasible, unless the agent believes that it is already feasible. This is formally expressed as follows:

$$\models I(i, Done(a)) \Rightarrow B(i, Feasible(a)) \vee I(i, B(i, Feasible(a))) \tag{15.8}$$

If an agent has the intention that (the illocutionary component of) a communicative act be performed, it necessarily has the intention to bring about the act's RE. The following property formalizes this idea:

$$\models I(i, Done(a)) \Rightarrow I(i, RE(a)) \tag{15.9}$$

where $RE(a)$ is the rational effect of act a.

Consider now the opposite aspect of CA planning: the consummation of CAs. When an agent observes a CA, it has to come to believe that the agent performing the act has the intention (to make public its intention) to achieve the act RE. This kind of act effect is called the *intentional effect*. The following property captures this consideration:[12]

$$\models B(i, Done(a) \wedge Agent(j, a) \Rightarrow I(j, RE(a))) \tag{15.10}$$

Some FPs persist after the correponding act has been performed. For the particular case of CAs, this property is valid for all the FPs which do not refer to time. Then, when an agent observes a CA, it has to come to believe that the persistent FPs hold:

$$\models B(i, Done(a) \Rightarrow FP(a)) \tag{15.11}$$

A communicative act model will be presented as follows:

$$\langle i, Act(j, \phi)\rangle$$

$$\text{FP:} \quad \psi_1$$

$$\text{RE:} \quad \phi_2$$

---

[11] See Sadek (1991b) for a generalized version of this property.
[12] Precisely, this property is as follows: $\models B(i, Done(a) \wedge Agent(j, a) \Rightarrow I(j, B(i, I(j, RE(a)))))$.

where i is the agent of the act, j the addressee, Act the name of the act, ϕ its semantic content (SC) (or propositional content[13]), ϕ_1 and ϕ_2 propositions.

A model of rational action should specify feasibility preconditions and the rationale of the action. The expression of such a model is, in general, complex for two main reasons. The first is that the set of action qualifications is potentially infinite (see Sadek (1991b) for the case of communicative acts). The second reason is that the effect of an action on the world is strongly context-dependent and cannot be formulated in general terms (Perrault, 1990; Sadek, 1994c); furthermore, it is difficult to "summarize" what an action should leave unchanged.

A solution that goes round the problem of effect specification is directly related to the expression of the rationality principles. In fact, if it is not possible to specify the actual effects of an action, it is still possible to state (in a logically valid way) what is expected from an action, that is, the reasons for which the action has been selected. This is exactly what is expressed by the first rationality principle. This semantics for action effect, within the framework of a model of rational behaviour, allows one to overcome the problem of effect unpredictability.

The set of feasibility preconditions for a CA can be split into two subsets: the *ability preconditions* and the *context-relevance preconditions*. The ability preconditions characterize the intrinsic ability of an agent to perform a given CA. For instance, to *sincerely assert* some proposition p, an agent has to believe that p. The context-relevance preconditions characterize the relevance of the act with respect to the context in which it is to be performed. For instance, an agent can be intrinsically able to make a promise while believing that the promised action is not needed by the addressee. The context-relevance preconditions may correspond to the Gricean quantity and relation maxims (Grice, 1957).

As an example, a simplified model (as far as the expression of the preconditions) is proposed below of the communication act of *informing* about the truth of a proposition:

$$\langle i, Inform(j, \phi)\rangle$$

$$FP: B(i, \phi) \wedge \neg B(i, B(j, \phi))$$

$$RE: B(j, \phi)$$

This model is directly axiomatized within the logical theory through the above mentioned rationality principles and the following scheme:

$$B(h, Feasible(\langle i, Inform(j, \phi)\rangle)) \Leftrightarrow B(i, \phi) \wedge \neg B(i, B(j, \phi))) \qquad (15.12)$$

Notice that actions are not handled by a planning process as data structures, as in the case of the classical plan-based approach, but have a logical semantics within the theory itself.

---

[13] See Searle (1969) for the notion(s) of *propositional content* (and *illocutionary force*) of an *illocutionary act*.

Notice also that the two first rationality principles specify by themselves, without any non-logic artifact, a planning algorithm that deductively generates plans of actions, by allowing the inference of causal chains of intentions.

Cooperative behaviour

Cooperative answers are a significant manifestation of cooperative behaviour. However, their role must be made relative with respect to this behaviour taken in a generic way.[14] Firstly, they must not be implemented as response schema to be instantiated systematically: their production totally depends on the context. For example, it is wrong to write a specific rule in a dialogue system, stating that if there is a request of the departure time of a train, the answer should also specify the number of the track. Such a rule would appear inadequate every time the context would allow one to infer that the user does not intend to take that train, but she/he just wants to check on the validity of the schedule in her/his possession.

Analogously, an agent should not be blindly cooperative: for example, the agent has to take into account the degree of confidentiality of the information it is handling. In conclusion, providing cooperative answers should appear as a global predisposition of an agent to behave cooperatively, which materializes in a way depending on the context of interaction and still governed by the principles of rational behaviour.

Informally, an agent *i* (for example, the system) can be qualified as cooperative toward an agent *j* (for example, the user) if *i* attempts to help *j* to achieve *j*'s objectives if they do not contradict *i*'s objectives, and if *i* does not limit itself to satisfy *j*'s objectives, but tries to infer the ultimate goals of *j* with the intention of helping it to achieve them (Sadek, 1994c).[15]

This definition assumes that an agent accepts the following minimal commitments:

- Participate actively in a conversation, in particular by paying continuous attention to its partners (and more generally to the environment).
- Attempt to understand partners' concerns.
- Generate answers to these concerns.
- Express the answers in such a way that they account optimally (regarding conversation rules) for the intentions they achieve.

Beyond these aspects, an agent should:

- not abandon the partners to retain erroneous beliefs, and prevent them, as much as possible, from getting wrongly oriented in the dialogue

---

[14]Grice's cooperation principle and maxims (Grice, 1957, 1975), though stated informally, are a reference point for characterizing cooperative (and "efficient") contribution to a dialogue.
[15]The notion of cooperative agent has to be distinguished from the notion of collaborative agent as in the case of most existing multiagent systems (Ferber, 1995) which just share their knowledge.

- bring them, as much as possible, information required for achieving their objectives, and, in particular, anticipate the needs that they have not (yet) explicitly mentioned.

In fact, interaction is impossible without a minimum of cooperation. As may be noted through the commitments mentioned, the predisposition to cooperation appears at the different processing levels of a communicating system, namely, understanding, reaction determination and answer formulation. At all these levels, these commitments aim at adopting and satisfying the partner's intentions, and therefore, firstly at recognizing them.

Intention recognition includes the complex operation of reconstructing communicative acts from linguistic forms. This reconstruction is, at a first step, literal, and reveals the *communicated meaning* only following the inference of causal chains of intentions. This inference process allows, in particular, an understanding of *indirect speech acts* (Bretier, 1995). The literal meaning of an indirect speech act reveals a "weaker" intention compared to the real intention of the speaker. This may indicate the speaker's lack of information about the information the system can provide. For example, the question "Do you know the telephone number of the City Hall?" may express the request of getting such a phone number if available. It can also be just a matter of politeness, as in "It is warm in here", meaning in reality "Please open the window". A non-literal reaction to indirect speech acts illustrates an elementary form of cooperation in situation of communication.

The above-mentioned commitments can be expressed in terms of more primitive principles of cooperative interaction such as intention adoption, sincerity and pertinence (Sadek, 1994a). These principles can be expressed in terms of mental attitudes of belief and intention, and, therefore, be formalized in the theory of rational interaction sketched above (Sadek, 1991a, 1994a).

Adoption of intention or minimal principle of cooperation

A minimal degree of cooperation is required for communication to be possible. For example, suppose that an agent i asks an agent j if proposition p is true; if both agents respect the semantics of the communication language, j knows that i intends to know if p is true. But, without a minimal degree of cooperation, j is in no way constrained to react to i's request.

Informally, the *minimal principle of cooperation* states that agents must not only react when they are addressed but, more than that, they must adopt the interlocutor's intention whenever they recognize it, and if there have no objection to adopt it. In other words, *if an agent i believes that an agent j intends to achieve property p, and that itself does not have an opposite intention, then i will adopt the intention that j will (sometime) come to believe that p holds.*

Formally, such a principle translates into the validity of the following scheme (Sadek, 1991a):

$$(B(i, I(j, \phi)) \wedge \neg I(i, \neg\phi)) \Rightarrow I(i, B(j, \phi)) \qquad (15.13)$$

In particular, if an agent i thinks that an agent j is expecting something from it (and it has no objections to doing it), then it adopts the intention that j will realize that i has done what was expected. Thus, from the point of view of j, agent i is cooperating.

It is worth noting that the minimal principle of cooperation has a wide range of application: it may lead to cooperative behaviours which are much more complex than merely answering questions, such as making an agent forward a request to a competent agent if it cannot answer the request by itself.

Sincerity

The previous property does not ensure that agent i really believes what it will make j believe. Sincerity is an integral part of cooperation commitments. In terms of mental attitudes, sincerity can be expressed as follows.

An agent i cannot have the intention that agent j to believe that a proposition p is true without believing p itself or without having the intention to come to believe p.

This property, which accounts for the Grice's quality maxim (Grice, 1975) formally translates into the validity of the following formula scheme:

$$I(i, B(j, \phi)) \Rightarrow B(i, \phi) \vee I(i, B(i, \phi)) \qquad (15.14)$$

This property, taken together with the previous one, ensures that an agent will act sincerely, and therefore will cooperate. They account for the fact that whenever an agent is aware of the objectives of another agent, then, as far as possible, it will help it to achieve them.

Pertinence

Most of the cooperative answers are characterized by the fact that they provide supplementary information with respect to what has been explicitly asked. Nevertheless, the amount of additional information provided depends on the interests assumed in the dialogue partner and, in particular, on her/his recognized intentions. The notion of interest is highly context-dependent and very difficult to characterize in general. On the contrary, it is easier to establish what is the information the dialogue partner does not need, in particular, that (supposed to be already) known to her/him. Avoiding redundancy is an aspect of cooperative behaviour. This can be expressed as follows: *if an agent i intends to let an agent j believe a proposition p, then i has to know that j does not know p yet.* This property is formally captured by the validity of the following formula scheme:

$$I(i, D(j, \phi)) \implies B(i, \neg B(j, \phi)) \tag{15.15}$$

Belief adjustment

A corrective answer is produced with the intention of correcting a belief that is considered wrong. Such a belief is usually a presupposition inferred (by *implication* (Grice, 1975)) from the recognized communication act. A corrective intention arises in an agent when its belief concerning a proposition, about which it is competent,[16] is in contradiction with that of its interlocutor. Formally, this property is expressed by the validity of the following schema:

$$B(i, \phi \wedge B(j, \neg\phi) \wedge Comp(i, \phi)) \Rightarrow I(i, B(j, \phi)) \tag{15.16}$$

Agent reaction when solicited

The fact that an agent reacts when solicited by other agents (and more generally by its environment) is a prerequisite for cooperative behaviour. This is formalized following two considerations. First, if an agent perceives a phenomenon to which it cannot associate any intelligible event or if it considers unacceptable, with respect to its beliefs, any event that it can associate to this phenomenon, then the agent will adopt the intention to know what the event is that has just occurred, typically by requesting for repetition. Second, if the agent cannot accept, regarding its mental state, any rational event corresponding to what it has observed, it will adopt the intention to let the author of the event (e.g., communicative act) know its disagreement about what it has understood; this may be manifested by telling the author of the event what prevents the agent from accepting the act in question. Formally, this is expressed by the validity of the two following schema. The predicates $Observe(i, o)$ and $Realize(o, e)$ respectively mean that agent i has just observed the observable entity o (e.g., an utterance) and that o is a way of realizing the event e:

(i) $(\exists e) Done(e) \wedge \neg Bref(i, Done(e_1)) \Rightarrow I(i, Bref(i, Done(e_2)))$

(ii) $(\forall o)(\forall e)[Observe(i, o)$ and $Realize(o, e) \wedge Agent(j, e)$ and

$\qquad \neg Bref(i, Done(e_1)) \Rightarrow I(i, B(j, \neg B(i, Done(e)))) \tag{15.17}$

Harmony between agents

In a multiagent context, the behaviour an agent adopts with respect to other agents has to be basically a generalization of the behaviour of the agent with

---

[16]Competence is formally defined as follows: $Comp(i, \phi) \equiv B(i, \phi) \Rightarrow \phi \wedge B(i, \neg\phi) \Rightarrow \neg\phi$.

respect to itself. (For example, it must be valid that an agent is sincere, coherent and "cooperative" with respect to itself.) A cooperative agent should not cause a loss of information to other agents. In particular, it does not have to bring about uncertainty for other agents, unless it considers that this is the "right" attitude with respect to a proposition; this supposes that it is adopting this attitude too. This is formally captured by the following property;

$$C(i, Possible(U(j, \phi))) \Rightarrow \Gamma_1 \qquad (15.18)$$

where Γ_1 can, for example, account for the fact that the choice for another agent of a future where it is uncertain about a proposition, implies that this future is only a transient step toward a situation of certainty. Formally Γ_1 can be:

$$C(i, (\forall e)(Feasible(e, U(j, \phi)) \Rightarrow (\exists e') Feasible(e; e', Bif(j, \phi))) \lor U(i, \phi) \quad (15.19)$$

A similar property can be established about not seeking ignorance for other agents. For example, an agent i who desires that another agent j should no longer believe (or not be uncertain of) a proposition p, must not believe (or not be uncertain of) p itself and desires that j adopts the same attitude as it. This can be formalized by the validity of the following schemas:

(i) $C(i, Possible(\neg B(j, \phi))) \Rightarrow \Gamma_2$

(ii) $C(i, Possible(\neg U(j, \phi))) \Rightarrow \Gamma_3$ $\qquad (15.20)$

where conditions Γ_2 and Γ_3 are similar to Γ_1. These conditions are intentionally left incompletely specified because their precise expression depends on the behaviour to be ascribed to the modelled agent. They may be simply reduced to *False*. Anyway, they do not have an impact on the rest of the theory.

Depending on the content of conditions Γ_k, it is possible to validate schemas such as:

(i) $\neg I(i, \neg Bif(j, \phi))$

(ii) $\neg I(i, \neg Bref(j, \iota x \phi(x)))$

(iii) $I(i, \neg Uif(j, \phi)) \Rightarrow I(i, Bif(j, \phi))$

(vi) $I(i, \neg Uref(j, \phi(x))) \Rightarrow I(i, Bref(j, \iota x \phi(x)))$ $\qquad (15.21)$

15.6. DOMAIN-DEPENDENT CONSTRAINTS

Usually, two levels of cooperative behaviour in dialogue are identified, namely the *communication* and the *domain* levels, and therefore, two types of intentions to be recognized. Recognition of intentions at the first level is the basis for the detection of indirect speech acts, while the intentions recognized at the second level, which underlie domain plan recognition, are the starting point for the production of the over-informative, corrective or suggestive components of cooperative answers. Indeed, an over-informative answer can be produced to remove an obstacle in the (recognized) plan of the dialogue partner (Allen and Perrault, 1980). A corrective answer may signal the reason for the failure of the partner's plan (Quilici *et al.*, 1988; Nerzic, 1993). A suggestive answer may propose an alternate plan to satisfy the partner's intentions.

In practice, the process of plan recognition can be complex and expensive (Bretier, 1995; Kautz, 1991), particularly when the application domain is rich. This requires one to have a model of all the domain-dependent actions that may be implicitly or explicitly referred to in the communication, which is relatively a heavy task. In the framework of informative dialogues, in particular for database query, it is possible to emulate the plan recognition process by introducing specific functions. These ·functions consider the "domain" component of a speaker message as a set of constraints which, in a default situation, have to be augmented, reduced or substituted. Thus, they can perform the following types of operations:

- Find the reasons for the failure of a request, when, for example, the answer is empty or negative.
- Compute a solution to a request *close* (according to a given distance criterion) to the request that was asked.
- Find information to add to what was strictly made explicit by the request.
- Find the appropriate information to be negotiated to constraint a request for which the set of possible answers is too large.

These procedures can be generic with respect to the computation they perform (Sadek *et al.*, 1996a; Sadek, 1996; Ferrieux and Sadek, 1994) but, in general, they "freeze" schema for plan recognition. In relation to the global process of rational interaction, these functions are *black boxes*, which do not affect the overall logical integrity. They produce intentions as a "regular" plan recognition process, and, especially, they can be integrated, in a natural way (as meta-predicates) into the global logic model.

For example, the production of an intention leading to "over-information" (i.e., richer information than what was initially required) may result from the following property: *if an agent i has the intention that an agent j believes proposition p and i thinks (through its function of "over-information") that q is pertinent in the "stream" of p, then i will adopt the intention that j comes to be aware of (i.e., to believe) that q.*

The black-box functions for domain-dependent constraint management are directly accessible from the logical framework characterizing the behaviour of a rational agent (Bretier, 1995). As an example, the access to the *over-information* procedure is made by the following scheme, where *SURINF* is a meta-predicate:

$$B(i, (I(i, B(j, p))) \wedge SURINF(p, q)) \Rightarrow I(i, B(j, q)) \qquad (15.22)$$

This formula expresses the following property: *if an agent i has the intention that an agent j believes a proposition p and i thinks (because of its over-information function) that proposition q can be a pertinent over-information of p, then i adopts the intention that j comes to be aware of (i.e., to believe) that q.*

15.7. DIALOGUE AND NATURAL LANGUAGE

The understanding and reaction determination process of a dialogue system (and therefore of a rational agent) functions on formal representations of semantic-pragmatic information, such as dialogue acts. Mental states are reconstructed, through inference processes, on the basis of observing and "admitting" dialogue acts. Such acts are obtained by sentence interpretation and formally represented as logical formulae.

Going from language to these representations implies that the system has, in addition to its language perception and production components (e.g., speech recognition and speech synthesis systems), interpretation and generation capabilities for the language(s) used by its interlocutor(s). More than for other media, in the case of natural language, the design and implementation of such mechanisms is a whole issue.

As mentioned above, the flexibility of the input language is a requirement for cooperative dialogue. Obviously, the more flexible the input is, the more sophisticated are the required mechanisms that have to be implemented for the extraction of the semantic information relevant for dialogue procedure. This problem of utterance analysis and interpretation is particularly salient in the context of oral interaction. Indeed, in such a context, not only is it difficult to constrain the user to a speech mode which may be in between a command language and spontaneous speech, but the inescapable presence of speech recognition errors makes it more difficult to find robust cues to anchor meaning extraction.

Similarly, natural language generation starting from formal representations is an issue *per se*. In a dialogue context, the difficulty is increased by the fact that the linguistic realization of a given dialogue act strongly depends on the dialogue state. There is no two-way relation between communicative acts and utterances: an act sequence can be realized by a single sentence, and a single act may be verbalized by a complex utterance. Moreover, the naturalness of the produced utterances depends on the system's capability to generate typical linguistic phenomena such as ellipsis and anaphora, and to take into account the linguistic behaviour of the interlocutor (Panaget, 1994, 1996).

For both interpretation and generation, the efficiency of the implemented mechanisms is generally a function of the degree of genericity of the relationships set up between natural language and "mental" representation (Bretier *et al.*, 1995).

Techniques and methods for the extraction of semantic representations from naturally spoken sentences, and for natural language generation, are described in Chapters 14 and 16, respectively.

16.7.1. The ARTIMIS/AGS System

ARTIMIS[17] is an agent technology developed at France Télécom–CNET, which provides a generic framework to instantiate *intelligent dialoguing agents*. These agents can interact with human users as well as with other software agents. When instantiated in a human–agent interaction context, ARTIMIS-like agents can engage in mixed-initiative cooperative interaction in natural language with human users. The resulting systems are able to display advanced dialogue functionality, such as negotiating the user's requests, producing cooperative answers, etc.

ARTIMIS is a stand-alone software package, currently integrated in a speech–telephony–computer platform (i.e., speech recognition software, speech synthesis software and ISDN board/software). ARTIMIS currently works in the lab version of a real application, AGS,[18] a directory of voice servers hosted by France Télécom (Audiotel servers). The resulting system, ARTIMIS/AGS (Sadek *et al.*, 1995, 1996a), is a prototype of a cooperative spoken dialogue system, applied to the areas of "employment" and "weather forecasting" of the Audiotel servers directory.

Global architecture

The system has a global architecture following the general scheme of Figure 1.4. The main components are:

- an ISDN interface for input and output over the telephone
- the CNET' software package, PHIL/DIANE (Jouvet *et al.*, 1991; Dupont, 1993), for speaker-independent, continuous speech analysis and recognition, using HMMs and a bigram LM
- a sentence analyser/interpreter (i.e., understanding), which produces, in terms of dialogue acts (represented in a logical form, in a language called ARCOL[19]), the best coherent interpretation from the most likely word sequence output by the recognizer
- the rational unit, the kernel of the dialogue system, which produces a plan (e.g., a sequence) of dialogue acts, as a reaction to the "understood" input
- a natural language generation subsystem, which verbalizes the dialogue act plan produced by the rational unit, by producing an utterance (a sequence of words) relevant to the current linguistic context, as an answer to the user

---

[17] ARTIMIS is a French acronym for *Agent Rationnel à base d'une Théorie de l'Interaction mise en oeuvre par un Moteur d'Inférence Syntaxique*.
[18] AGS is a French acronym for Audiotel – Guide des Services.
[19] ARCOL is an acronym for ARtimis COmmunication Language.

- the speech synthesizer CNETVOX/PSOLA (Bigorgne *et al.*, 1993), which generates the spoken signal corresponding to the computed answer. This signal is sent to the telephone line through the ISDN interface.

Analysis/interpretation process

Roughly speaking, the ARTIMIS software consists of three main components (Sadek *et al.*, 1996a): a rational unit (which constitutes the heart of the technology), and two front-end components for natural language processing: understanding (analysis and interpretation) and generation.

The recognized word sequence is handled by an analysis/interpretation process, the goal being to reconstruct, as far as possible, in a logical form, the dialogue act realized by the input utterance. The utterance analysis is based on detecting "small" syntactic structures which potentially activate semantic entities. This corresponds to one of the processes described in Chapter 14 in which semantically relevant words are extracted from the recognized words.

Example 15.1. Consider the utterance: *"Je voudrais connaître le numéro d'un serveur météo pour la région de Lannion"* (*"I'd like to know the number of a server for weather forecasts in the Lannion area"*) recognized by the speech recognition component as *"Je voudrais X météo pour X Lannion"* (*"I'd like X weather forecast for X Lannion"*), which in turn, activates the concepts of *intention of the user*, *weather server*, and *Lannion* (a city in Brittany, North-West of France).

Starting from the set of the activated concepts (which can be a list of possibilities in the case of nondeterminism due to syntactic overlapping), a *semantic completion process* finds other possible "ingredients" to be added to the detected concepts to build a well-formed logical formula that represents the semantic content of the dialogue act. This process is based on the hypothesis of *semantic connectivity* in the user's utterance. This assumes that the utterance corresponds to a path in a semantic network describing the application domain knowledge.

Example 15.2. In the previous example, the inferred semantic complements are that the question deals with a *telephone number* of a *server* about a *topic* that is weather forecast and whose *geographic domain* is Lannion.

Formally, this leads to the production of the following dialogue act:

$$\langle u, Inform(s, I(u, Bref(u, \iota x \, numtel(x) \wedge \exists y \, server(y) \wedge number(x, y)$$
$$\wedge \, topic(y, weather\text{-}forecast) \wedge domain(y, lannion)))\rangle$$

meaning that the user (*u*) informs the system (*s*) that she/he wants ($I(u, \ldots)$) to know ($Bref(u, \iota x \ldots)$) the telephone number of a weather forecast server for Lannion.

It is worth noting that semantic-island-driven analysis and semantic completion ensure a syntactic and semantic robustness to the analysis/interpretation process, particularly required in the context of spontaneous speech.

15.7.2. The Rational Unit

The rational unit is the kernel of an intelligent agent. It is based on a set of logical axioms which formalizes basic principles for rational behaviour and introspection, communication, and cooperation (Sadek, 1991a, 1994a,b; Bretier and Sadek, 1995). They can be summarized as follows. (See section 15.3.3 for more details, in particular concerning the formal model.)

- *Rationality principles* characterize the agent's planning capabilities and reasoning about observed actions. They specify necessary conditions for planning and performing actions (in particular communicative acts) and allow the agent to infer the intentions that have (presumably) motivated the performance of observed actions (in particular communicative acts).
- *Cooperation principles* express the motivations for the agent to behave in a cooperative manner.
- *Coherence relations*, such as the consistency of an agent's beliefs and the relations between intentions and beliefs, together with rationality (and cooperation) principles, assess a sound framework for the *rational balance* between the different mental attitudes of an agent on one side, and between mental attitudes and action plans on another side.

In such a framework, planning derives from rationality principles and is totally deductive: a plan is generated by inference of causal intention chains.

The *inference engine* which supports the rational unit is a theorem prover for first-order modal logic, based on a "syntactic" approach (extended modal resolution and schema instantiation by subformulae unification) (Bretier, 1995; Bretier and Sadek, 1995).

Example 15.3. Assume that, after utterance analysis/interpretation, the recognized communicative act is that *the user wants to inform the server that she/he wants to know if p (e.g., if the server 36-68-02-22 is operated by Météo-France)*. On the basis of the rationality principles, the system infers *the intention of the user to know if p*. The cooperation principles allow the system to adopt *the intention that the user eventually comes to know if p*. Again based on the rationality principles, the system adopts *the intention of informing the user that p or informing her/him that not p*. The system then selects which one of these two actions is currently *feasible* (for example, if the system believes *p*, *the action of informing the user that p*) and transmits the selected action (i.e., communicative act) to the natural language generator.

The constraint relaxation engine

The rational unit has access to the data-base, which is represented here as a semantic network describing the application knowledge, through a "black-box" engine that finds satisfactory "approximate" solutions when there is no "exact" solution to the user's request. This is implemented by "compiling" the semantic network into a product metric space where the dimensions are the application relations (topic, domain, specialty, etc.). A function $d(a, b)$ is assigned to each dimension in order to quantify the approximation made when relaxing a into b. Constraint relaxation is viewed as the operation of finding the nearest neighbours in the metric space.

The same technique is used to solve the "opposite" problem, namely to introduce additional constraints when the request is too "weak" and further constraints have to be added in order to reduce the number of possible solutions. The constraint to be instantiated (by the user) is the one corresponding to the dimension with the longest diameter.

15.7.3. Natural Language Generation

Natural language generation follows two highly coupled phases (Panaget, 1994, 1996). The first one determines the surface acts (that specify, in particular, declarative, imperative, interrogative modes) and reference acts (that specify, in particular, the designation modes: nominal groups, pronouns, proper nouns, etc.), which achieves the dialogue act(s) to be sent to the user. In the second phase, the best formulation of the acts specified in the first phase is found, depending on the linguistic available resources (e.g., language, lexicon, grammatical structures) and on the current linguistic context (dialogue state, vocabulary and syntax used by the user in the previous dialogue turn, preferences of the user group, etc.).

Example 15.4. If the system wants to inform the user that there is a relation of the type *provider* between the "Côtes d'Armor" weather forecast server and "Météo-France", the system would send the following message to the generator:

$$\langle s, Inform(u, provider(\iota y(server(y) \land topic(y, weather\text{-}forecast)$$
$$\land domain(y, cotes\text{-}d\text{-}armor)), meteo\text{-}france)\rangle$$

The generator will produce (in natural language: French, English or Russian), depending on the context, a declarative sentence with a proper noun and a nominal group, or a positive answer with a pronoun and a proper noun, or an elliptic sentence with a proper noun:

"Le fournisseur du serveur de météo générale pour les Côtes d'Armor est Météo France"
The server provider for general weather forecast for the Côtes d'Armor area is Météo France

"Oui, il est fourni par Météo-France".
Yes, it is provided by Météo-France
"Météo-France".
Météo-France.
etc.

The natural language generator integrated to the ARTIMIS/AGS system is based on generic mechanisms which make it easily portable to other applications but also to other languages. For instance, the system has been easily ported from French into English (with the possibility to switch from one language to another one during the same dialogue) with a very moderate effort (about half an engineer-month).

Example 15.5. A sample dialogue carried by the ARTIMIS/AGS system is given in the following. S stands for the system, U for the user, and R for the output of the ASR component. XXX represents one or more words that are semantically irrelevant.

S: **Welcome to the ARTIMIS/AGS server. How can I help you?**
   Bienvenue sur le serveur ARTIMIS/AGS. Que puis-je pour vous?

U: **I'm looking for a job in the Calais area. Are there any servers?**
   Je recherche un emploi à Calais. Est ce que il y a des serveurs?
R: *je XXX emploi a calais est ce que il y a XXX*

S: **No, there aren't any employment servers for Calais. However, there is an employment server for Pas-de-Calais and an employment server for Lille. Are you interested in one of these?**
   Non, il n'y a pas de serveurs d'emploi pour Calais. Par contre, il y a un serveur d'emploi pour le Pas-de-Calais et un serveur d'emploi pour Lille. L'un d'eux vous convient-il?

U: **For Nord, not for Calais.**
   Pour le Nord pas Calais.
R: *XXX nord pas calais.*

S: **The phone number of the server of employment advertisements for Nord is 36 68 74 44. Do you want any other information?**
   Le numéro du serveur de petites annonces d'emploi pour le Nord est le 36 68 74 44. Désirez-vous un autre renseignement?

U: **Is it accessible from Calais?**
   Est-ce qu'il est accessible de Calais?
R: *est ce que XXX accessible de calais*

S: **Yes, it is accessible from Calais. Do you want any other information?**
   Oui, il est accessible de Calais. Désirez-vous un autre renseignement?

U: **I also want the weather forecasts.**
   Je veux aussi la météo.
R: *XXX XXX meteo*

S: **Are you interested in general weather forecasts or in specialized weather forecasts?**
   Êtes-vous intéressé par la météo générale ou par la météo spécialisée?

U: **Specialized weather forecasts.**
   La météo specialisée.
R: *XXX meteo specialisee*

S: **A server for which specialized weather forecasts?**
   Un serveur de quelle météo spécialisée?

U: **What can you suggest?**
   Que me proposez vous?
R: *XXX proposez XXX*

S: **There are eight kinds of specialized weather forecasts. The two first are atmospheric weather forecasts and coastal weather forecasts. Which specialized weather forecasts are you interested in?**
   Il y a huit types de météo spécialisées. Les deux premières sont la météo aérienne et la météo côtière. Vous recherchez un serveur de quelle météo spécialisée?

U: **Coastal, for the Nord-Pas-de-Calais area.**
   Cotière pour le Nord-Pas-de-Calais.
R: *cotiere XXX nord pas calais.*

S: **There aren't any servers of coastal weather forecasts for the Nord-Pas-de-Calais region. However, there are two servers of coastal weather forecasts for the departments of Nord-Pas-de-Calais and a server of general weather forecasts for the region of Nord-Pas-de-Calais. Are you interested in one of these?**
   Il n'y a pas de serveurs de météo côtière pour la region Nord-Pas-de-Calais. Par contre, il y a deux serveurs de météo côtières pour les départements du Nord-Pas-de-Calais et un serveur de météo générale pour la region Nord-Pas-de-Calais. L'un d'eux vous convient-il?

U: **Yes, the latter.**
   Oui le second.
R: *oui le second*

S: **The phone number of the second one is 36 68 00 00. Do you want any other information?**
   Le numéro du second est le 36 68 00 00. Désirez-vous un autre renseignement?

U: **Who is its provider?**
   Quel est son fournisseur?
R: *quel XXX fournisseur*

S: **The provider of 36 68 00 00 is Météo-France. Do you want any other information?**
   Le fournisseur du 36 68 00 00 est Météo-France. Désirez-vous un autre renseignement?

U: **No.**
   Non.
R: *non*

S: **Goodbye.**
   Au revoir.

Example 15.6. What follows is an example of a dialogue with a hypothetical, less cooperative system.

S: **Welcome to the NON-AGS system. Which topic are you interested in: weather forecast or employment?**

U: **Weather forecast.**
   météo.
R: *météo*

S: **Weather forecast. For which area?**
   météo. Pour quelle région?

U: **Finistère.**
   finistère.
R: *finistère*

S: **The weather forecast for Finistère. Which specialty?**

U: **Coastal weather forecast.**
   météo côtière.
R: *météo côtière*

S: **Weather forecast for Finistère, specialty Coastal weather forecast. There are no servers with this specialty. But there are some for general weather forecast. Is that acceptable?**
   Un serveur météo pour le Finistère, spécialité météo côtière. Il n'y a pas de serveurs ayant cette spécialité, mais il y en a avec la spécialité météo générale. Cela vous convient-il?

U: **No, I want the coastal weather forecast.**
   non je veux la météo côtière.
R: *non X météo côtière*

S: **Weather forecast for Finistère, specialty Coastal weather forecast. There are no servers with this specialty. But there are some for general weather forecast. Is that acceptable?**
   la météo pour le Finistère, spécialité météo côtière. Il n'y a pas de serveurs ayant cette spécialité, mais il y en a avec la spécialité météo générale. Cela vous convient-il?

U: **No.**
   non.
R: *non*

S: **The weather forecast for Finistère. Which specialty?**
la météo pour le Finistère. Pour quelle spécialité?

U: **Correction.**
correction.
R: *correction*

S: **The weather forecast. For which area?**
la météo. Pour quelle région?

U: **In Brittany.**
en Bretagne.
R: *bretagne*

S: **The weather forecast for Brittany. Which specialty?**
la météo pour la bretagne. Pour quelle spécialité?

U: **Coastal weather.**
côtière.
R: *côtière*

S: **Weather forecast for Brittany, specialty Coastal weather forecast. There are no coastal weather forecast servers for this area. But there are some for the Channel and the Atlantic. Is that acceptable?**
la météo pour la Bretagne, spécialité météo côtière. Il n'y a pas de serveurs de météo côtière.pour cette région, mais il y en a pour la Manche et pour l'Atlantique. Cela vous convient-il?

U: **Yes.**
oui.
R: *oui*

S: **The weather forecast for Brittany, specialty Coastal weather forecast. There are no coastal weather forecast servers for this area, but there are some for the Channel and the Atlantic. Is one of these acceptable?**
La météo pour la Bretagne, spécialité météo côtière. Il n'y a pas de serveurs de météo marine pour cette région, mais il y en a pour la Manche et pour l'Atlantique. Cela vous convient-il?

U: **The Channel.**
la Manche.
R: *la manche*

S: **The weather forecast for the Channel. Specialty Coastal weather forecast. There two servers: 36 70 12 34 and 36 68 08 08. Would you like more information about these servers?**
la météo pour la Manche, spécialité météo côtière. Il y a deux serveurs: le 36 70 12 34 et le 36 68 08 08. Désirez-vous des informations complémentaires sur ces serveurs?

U: **Yes.**
oui

R: *oui*

S: **36 70 12 34 is provided by ZZZ, located at 99 AAA street at BBB. 36 68 08 08 is provided by Météo France, located at 88 CCC street at DDD. Would like more information?**
Le 36 70 12 34 est fourni par ZZZ, sis au 99 rue AAA a BBB. Le 36 68 08 08 est fourni par Météo France, sis au 88 rue CCC a DDD. Désirez-vous un autre renseignement?

U: **No, that's it.**
non ca suffit !!!

R: *non X*

S: **Bye.**
Au revoir.

15.8. CONCLUSIONS

It is widely accepted that, alone, (spoken or written) natural language processing, or mere integration of communication media, is not sufficient for building systems that can engage in a truly cooperative dialogue with humans. Moreover, improving system ergonomy can only be a placeholder for the fundamental requirement, which is system intelligence.

Many of the prototypes that have been developed so far, especially those based on simple finite-state diagrams, are too rigid and do not exhibit the degree of "intelligence" that makes them appear as cooperative as a normal user would expect. An important question that needs to be addressed is "What should be the basis for system intelligence?".

A new paradigm, that of *dialoguing rational agent*, for designing and implementing convivial dialogue systems has been introduced in this chapter. An associated formal framework (based on a first-order modal logic) for representing behaviour principles (rationality, communication, cooperation, etc.) and for reasoning about mental attitudes (belief, uncertainty, intention) and communicative acts (and actions, in general) has been provided.

Some of the important issues that need to be explored in the future with rigorous experimentation are the following:

- effective procedures for default reasoning; in particular, defining methods for establishing priorities between inference alternatives in interpretation and planning
- tractable belief revision models that are compatible with the formal framework introduced in this chapter, in particular for managing the dialogue history in a generic way

- tractable, relevant-for-communication formal models of plan recognition
- formal models for complex planning methods (conjunctive goals, hierarchical planning, etc.)
- more sophisticated logical systems for handling uncertainty as a mental attitude, and dealing with plausible inference
- building application models (e.g., semantic networks) automatically, starting from non-structured data
- computational methods that enable rational agents (and therefore dialogue systems) to learn users' profiles and behaviours
- techniques for learning from examples how some components of communicative acts can be determined from utterances (and, more generally, multimedia messages)
- heuristics and decision procedures for determining when to attempt to infer new information from the current dialogue state or when it is more convenient to switch to a question/answering interaction
- methodologies and techniques for the testing, evaluation, and validation of advanced dialogue system.

16

Sentence Generation

Christel Sorin[*] and Renato De Mori[†]

16.1. INTRODUCTION

Sentence generation generally involves two main steps, namely, the retrieval or composition of one or more sentences to be sent by a machine to a user and the transformation of this message into a speech signal.

If the number of possible messages is not very high and the messages are all previously known, it is possible to store a sampled version of the corresponding waveforms or a *coded* version of them. Techniques for achieving low bit rates and acceptable memory storage while maintaining a high quality of the reconstructed speech are discussed in many papers, and, in particular for the applications discussed here, in Kroon and Atal (1988). The messages can be either

[*]TSS-RCP-LAA, Centre National d'Etudes de Télécommunications, France Télécom, 2, Avenue Pierre Marzin, 22307 Lannion, France.
[†]School of Computer Science, McGill University, Montréal, P.Q. H3A 2A7, Canada.

recorded and stored as a whole, or composed using *fixed* and *variable* pre-recorded speech elements.

Special attention should be paid when units are chosen in the case of *automatic message composition* in order to avoid discontinuities in the generated signal, which can have an unpleasant perceptual effect. In particular, it is possible that the same word or set of words need to be recorded with different pitch contours and stored as different units. The choice among these units may depend on the syntactic or semantic structure which the unit will be part of. Dynamic programming has recently been used (Lamel *et al.*, 1993) to optimize the automatic composition of prerecorded units. The "best" sequence of units is selected among the possible ones by taking into account the phonetic and/or word context, the pitch of successive units and punctuation marks.

These *store-and-forward* systems are well adapted to application classes in which the structure of all the units can be specified in advance and there is no need to frequently update the units or insert new ones. This is a difficult and expensive operation, since at every update, the original speaker must be available and recorded under the same acoustic conditions, otherwise, the entire database of units must be recorded again.

With the increasing and growing popularity of *interactive voice response* (IVR) systems, the above-mentioned difficulties and the need to develop more and more complex systems, capable of evolving in time, makes the use of *text-to-speech* (TTS) systems more appealing. In particular, TTS systems are more and more requested for applications containing variable and frequently updated items to be embedded into natural speech sentences. An example of these systems is a catalogue sale service already in place at France Télécom (Gagnoulet and Sorin, 1993). However, the preparation of speech messages has to be done by professional experts using flexible *editing tools* for the phonetic and prosodic descriptions.

Oral access to any written information such as fax, e-mail and textual databases, is another domain in which TTS is the technology preferred with respect to others. Systems for this purpose should have perfect *intelligibility*, *text-processing* capabilities and *maximum degree of naturalness* with different (at least two, one for commands and one for the content) types of voices. TTS systems should be able to operate in different languages.

Speech synthesis systems are those which can convert a string of phonemes and pauses into a speech signal. Figure 16.1 shows a scheme of the two most popular types of speech synthesizers.

One scheme generates the speech signal by composition of units that are concatenated to produce a waveform or a stream of vectors of parameters capable of driving a computer model of waveform generation. In this scheme, units are retrieved from a collection, based on the input phoneme strings. Units are then modified by concatenation procedures in order to produce a smooth and natural sound.

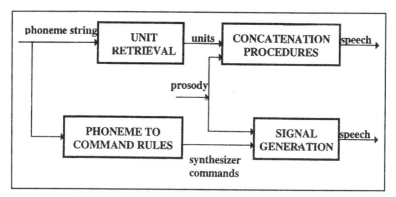

Figure 16.1 Two schemes for speech synthesizers.

The second scheme *generates* the stream of parameters for driving a model for speech production. Generation is usually controlled by rules that represent speech production knowledge especially tailored for the type of speech production model to which the commands are sent. Recent progress in speech synthesis is described in van Santen *et al.* (1996).

Concatenation procedures and the speech production model also take into account prosodic information, consisting of duration values, intensity and pitch contours produced by a prosody generation module shown in Figure 16.2.

Prosody generation uses syntactic and lexical knowledge for the analysis of the message to be synthesized. Syntactic and lexical analysis also influence the generation of phoneme strings from character strings. This is performed by the module labelled *grapheme-to-phoneme* conversion in Figure 16.2. The message to be generated, in orthographic form, can be directly retrieved from a database or a file system or can be produced by a text generation module driven by a conceptual representation as shown in Figure 16.2. This is the case of dialogue, in which a dialogue reasoning system decides the content of the message to be sent to the user after performing an inference producing one or more logical formulae. Sentence generation has to transform a set of logical formulae into a sentence in natural language whose meaning can be represented by the formulae.

16.2. TEXT GENERATION FROM CONCEPTUAL REPRESENTATIONS

16.2.1. Architectures for Sentence Generation

Sentence generation is based on two major components, each component being characterized by its knowledge sources (KSs) and decision strategies.

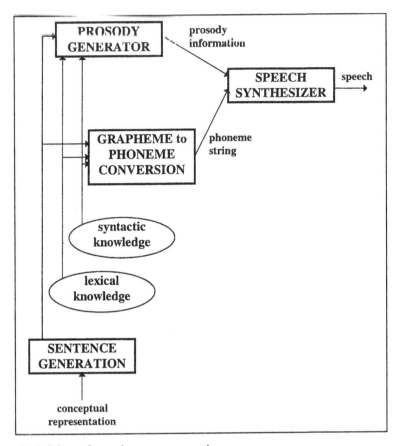

Figure 16.2 Scheme for oral reponse generation.

The first component is a *concept generator* and produces a logical representation of "what to say". Its KSs may represent domain knowledge and general communication knowledge. Its decision strategy is based on inference algorithms that produce conceptual representations. The concept generator is usually part of a dialogue system, it reasons about dialogue history and messages from the human user to decide what the next message has to be in order to achieve a communication goal.

The second component is a *sentence or text generator* that uses linguistic knowledge and whose goal is the production of a text in natural language. Its strategies are mainly compositional, and the goal is "how to express" in natural language a set of concepts.

There are three types of architectures for text generation schematically represented in Figure 16.3. The first architecture consists of a *pipeline* of the two generators. It is strictly sequential, and the output of the concept generator is the input of the text generator. The second architecture is based on *interleaving*

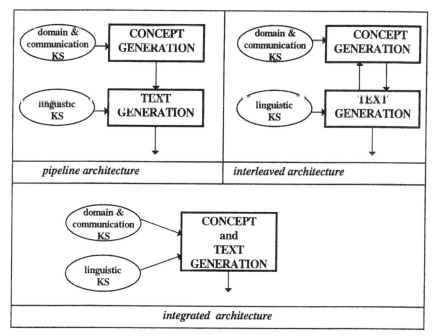

Figure 16.3 Language generation architectures.

the two generators in such a way that the partial results of one of them can be used by the other one.

The third type consists of *integrating* the two generators in such a way that a common strategy is used for concept as well as for text generation.

The pipeline architecture is the most widely used in spoken dialogue systems in which dialogue does not produce a long text, but one or few sentences at a time.

Domain knowledge is usually represented by semantic and conceptual ontologies. Main semantic categories are objects, events and qualities (e.g. manner, property). Hierarchies of semantic categories to be used for sentence generation are inspired by Halliday (1985) and discussed in Bateman (1992), Bateman *et al.* (1990) and Meteer (1992).

Linguistic knowledge usually contains a detailed description of the linguistic resources, mainly lexical and syntactic ones and a set of criteria for selecting a resource. The two types of knowledge can be represented in a declarative or in a procedural way. The choice depends, among other things, on the way the following problems are approached.

Synonym choice is the problem of choosing among the many possible expressions of the same semantic content.

Lexical gap is the problem of deciding how to say things when the lexicon does not provide any resource for expressing a semantic content.

The choice between more or less specific resources is a third problem.

Selection is based on two types of criteria according to Steede (1993), namely *constraints* and *preferences*. The first are essential, while the second ones are optional. Syntactic constraints impose that the generated text is syntactically correct, semantic constraints require that the generated text is semantically sound. Other criteria are *colocation constraints* for selecting a resource taking into account the selection of other resources, *focus constraints* that select resources based on specific element of the message and *pragmatic preferences* dealing with style, connotations, rhetoric objectives and stylistical features.

16.2.2. Theories for Language Generation

Most language generation systems are based on a philosophical theory of language (Austin, 1962; Searle, 1969) for which a speaker accomplishes at least three types of distinct *language acts*, namely:

- *locutory* acts for the enunciation of a sequence of morphemes
- *illocutory* acts to express an intention like an order
- *perlocutory* acts representing the result of the enunciation, like convincing or impressing.

It is important to distinguish *utterance* generation with respect to *text* generation. The first case is the most frequent in person–machine dialogues in which the machine usually produces just one sentence or few sentences at a time. In this case the most difficult problem is to ensure contextual coherence.

Utterance generation is driven by a conceptual representation consisting of a sequence of *dialogue acts*. Following the principle that communication is action, utterances are produced by *planning* linguistic actions.

In Allen and Perrault (1980), two types of illocutory acts are considered, namely INFORM that usually generates declarative statements, and REQUEST that usually generates questions. Acts are defined based on a representation of mental attitudes such as *believe, know* and *want*.

Illocutory acts are defined by *preconditions PRE*, expressing the fact that a speaker has certain beliefs about the external world and wants to change it. A necessary condition for making real an illocutory act is that the listener recognizes that the speaker intends to produce the act. Such a recognition is expressed as the *body BD* ("BO" is a slang term in North America!) of the act which induces the goal of message planning. Propositions that the speaker intends to make true represent the *effect EF* of the act.

As an example, INFORM is defined as follows:

$$\text{INFORM}(i, j, \Phi)$$

PRE: $know_i \Phi \wedge want_i(\text{INFORM}(i, j, \Phi))$

EF: $know_j \Phi$

BD: $bel_j want_i know_j \Phi$

The meaning is that the precondition for subject i to inform subject j about content Φ is that subject i knows Φ and wants to inform subject j about Φ. The effect is that subject j will know Φ and the body is that subject j believes that subject i wants subject j to know Φ.

A good example of a planning system for sentence generation is TENDUM (Bunt, 1987), based on theoretical work described in Allen and Perrault (1980). In this system, every dialogue act is a pair made of a communication function and a semantic content expressed in a proper language in which constants correspond to domain objects. Definitions of acts set goals for the planning system, which produce a plan made of dialogue actions.

An example of a plan is the following:

⟨YNANSWER, NOT(Country(Departureplace(ac871)) = canada)⟩
⟨WHANSWER, Country(Departureplace(ac871))) = france)⟩
⟨WHANSWER, Departureplace(ac871) = paris⟩

The plan is made of three dialogue actions, each one described by one line in the above example. The first act is for answering a YES/NO question and states that the country of departure city of flight AC871 is not Canada. The second and the third acts answer open questions stating that the country of departure is France and the city is Paris.

The first step towards generation consists of transforming the plans into another representation, described by a frame language in which constants have a one-to-one correspondence with lexical items. Translation rules between the two languages associate a constant in the lexicon with lambda-expressions containing variables. These expressions match with elements of plan descriptions causing a binding of variables in the expressions with constants in the plan description.

An example of translation rule is:

$$\text{COMEFROM } \lambda x : \text{Departure}(\text{elem}_1(x)) = \text{elem}_2(x)$$

$$\lambda x : \text{Country}(\text{Departure}(\text{elem}_1(x)) = \text{elem}_2(x)$$

which allows translation of the expression:

Country(Departureplace(ac871))) = canada)

into:

COMEFROM (⟨AC871, CANADA⟩)

This will be further transformed into the following expression:

(COMEFROM (⟨AC871, CANADA⟩), [mood : declar, concord : neg])⟩

This statement can drive generation using a generalized phrase structure grammar (GPSG) (Gazder *et al.*, 1985) producing the sentence:

"AC871 does not come from Canada".

Another example of a planning system for sentence generation is the Knowledge and Modality Planner (KAMP) (Moore, 1980) This planner produces a procedural network represented by a two-dimensional data structure. Along the temporal dimension, actions are represented by a partial order of execution. The other dimension corresponds to a hierarchical ordering. At the lower levels of the hierarchies, linguistic constraints and utterance actions become predominant. An elegant component for planning is a unification grammar called TELEological GRAMmar (TELEGRAM) (Appelt, 1983). This grammar associates a functional description to an act and detects if it is incomplete. If the description is incomplete, the language generator component requires the planner to provide elements for completion.

There are interesting systems for text generation. Their description is beyond the scope of this book. Some popular ones are EPICURE (Dale, 1990), TEXT (McKeown, 1985), KPML (Teich and Bateman, 1994) based on the theory of functional grammars (Halliday, 1985), RST based on rhetoric operators (Hovy, 1990), and Explainable Expert System (Moore and Paris, 1991).

16.2.3. An Example of Natural Language Generation for a Dialogue System

The system, introduced in Chapter 15, called Audiotel – Guide des Services (AGS), developed at CNET–France Télécom for telephone applications is described as an example (Panaget, 1996). The system is designed taking into account that most of the information to be communicated to the user is *a priori* determined, that it has to be adaptable to other telephone applications and has to operate in many languages (Sadek *et al.*, 1995).

Lexical and syntactic resources are represented by a unique abstract organization, called linguistic ontology, while semantic ontology supports the computation of system reaction based on the theory of *rational interaction* (Sadek, 1991). Knowledge is represented with a logic of mental attitudes (belief, uncertainty and intention) and rational action. The representation formalism is in first order modal logic in which modalities are belief, uncertainty and intention respectively represented as $K_i\Phi$, $U_i\Phi$ and $I_i\Phi$, where i is an agent and Φ is a well-formed formula in modal logic.

This knowledge is used to produce a sequence of dialogue acts of the type:

$$\langle i, \text{ACT-TYPE}(j, PC)\rangle \tag{16.1}$$

where j is the recipient and PC is a well-formed formula in modal logic with constants, unary predicates, binary predicates and quantifiers as shown in the following example:

$$\langle s, \text{INFORM}(u, (\forall x)\, \text{server}(x) \Rightarrow ((\exists y)\, \text{telephone-number}(y) \wedge \text{number}(x, y))))\rangle$$

This act means that there is an agent s (the system) which informs the agent u (the user) that each server x has a telephone number y and that y is the number of x.

Domain semantics are represented by a class hierarchy including surface type of the sentence (e.g. question, declaration, order), types of quantifiers, types of objects (e.g. physical, mental), type of process (e.g. mental, verbal), quality. From this hierarchy, the description of an object (e.g. a telephone server) is obtained as a well-formed formula.

Textual semantics are also represented by a class hierarchy including items like clause, group, modifier.

Selection of abstract linguistic resources is made by a semantic head-driven algorithm (Shieber *et al.*, 1990).

Syntax is represented by a tree adjoining grammar (TAG) (Joshi, 1987) because it separates syntax from semantics and makes efficient use of lexical knowledge.

Utterance generation follows the scheme of Figure 16.4 in which the *surface and reference* act planner interacts with a language generator. The *act planner* issues a request, in terms of the conceptual representation and facts present in its memory, to the language generator for producing an utterance. The language generator returns a logic formula Φ to the act planner and can ask the act planner whether Φ is true. A *macro-planner* translates the conceptual representation which is in a form convenient for performing automatic reasoning (cc-expr) into another logical form (id-expr) with a finer granularity and whose terms are closer to lexical or syntactic items. Furthermore, the *macro-planner* selects the rhetoric structure of the message to be generated. Translation is performed

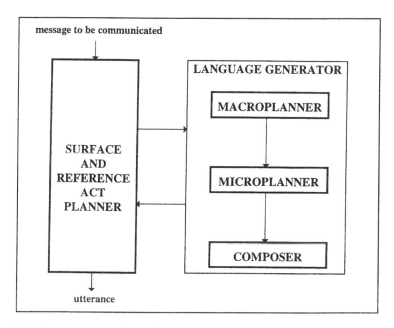

Figure 16.4 Utterance generation scheme.

by *rules* of the type.

$$\text{cc-expr} \rightarrow \text{id-expr} \, [\Phi] \tag{16.2}$$

where Φ is a condition to be verified on the facts provided by the act planner.

An example of translation rule is the following, expressing the specification of a service provider:

$$\text{cc}(\text{service}(x,y)) \rightarrow [\text{provide}(e), \text{provider}(e, \text{cc}(x)), \text{specification}(e, \text{cc}(y))] \; [\text{true}]$$

or

$$\text{cc}(\text{service}(x,y)) \rightarrow \text{use-property-ascription}(\text{cc}(x), \text{cc}(y)) \quad [\text{true}]$$

by which the cc expression:

$$\text{cc}((\exists x) \, \text{server}(x) \wedge (\exists y) \, \text{air-travel-information}(y) \wedge \text{service}(x,y))$$

is translated, using the second option for service, into:

[existence(e),range(e, *term*([sample], o1, [server(o1), use-property-ascription (o1, *term*([unique], o2, air-travel-information (o2)))])])]

which has predicates for quantifiers and is more suitable for producing a sentence.

Considering only surface acts, for the sake of brevity each is defined by a frame structure containing the type of act, a precondition of pertinence in the context (PP), a precondition of ability (PA) referring to the ability of the agent to perform the required action and an expression of the direct effect (DE).

For example, the declaration that a statement Φ was not the object of a YES/ NO question, is represented by the following surface act:

$\langle i, \text{DECLARE}(j, x, \Phi) \rangle$

PP $(\forall e)\neg\text{pres}(((\langle j, \text{YNQUESTION}(i, \Phi)\rangle \vee \langle j, \text{YNQUESTION}(i, \neg\Phi)\rangle)); e)$:

PA: *can-be-converted*$(i, j, x, \text{declare}(\text{cc}(\Phi)))$

DE: *converted*$(x, \text{INFORM}(j, \Phi))$

can-be-converted is a predicate, true if, for a speaker i and a listener j, the linguistic object x is the conversion of the id-expr that follows; *converted* is a predicate expressing the effect of the conversion. PP is a condition on the fact that there are no YES/NO question asked about proposition Φ nor its negation.

A *micro-planner* determines the best textual representation of the message by selecting the appropriate linguistic resources that satisfy various constraints and preferences. It transforms id-expressions into *textual* structures. They are tree structures in which each node contains information about the id-expression, the semantic instance, the corresponding linguistic class, surface properties and restrictions, relations with father and children nodes. Tree structures are built by replacing logical components with linguistic resources. Decomposition of expressions causes the addition of branches in a tree.

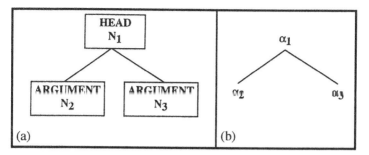

Figure 16.5 (a) Textual structure; (b) TAG structure.

Final linguistic details are set by the *utterance composer*, which produces the final version of the utterance by transforming textual structures into TAG trees, taking into account all syntactic constraints.

For example, the textual structure shown in Figure 16.5(a) is transformed into the TAG structure of Figure 16.5(b) in which each node symbol α_i ($i = 1, 2, 3$) can be rewritten by TAG rules into partial trees. Descriptions in terms of textual semantic classes are attached to nodes of TAG trees.

The system has been evaluated on its capability of generating text for different applications and different languages (French and English).

In Panaget (1996) a theory is proposed for an integrated architecture as shown in Figure 16.3, in which linguistic resources are used for the analysis of an incoming message and the formulation of an output message based on an *intensional object representation*. These objects are processed by an understanding component or are produced by a verbalizing component acting on *mental representations*. These representations are identified at the end of the understanding process and constructed as a result of the reaction of an agent to input facts. This theory is still under development. A practical application of it will have to deal with the complexity of inference derived by chaining reasoning processes at various levels and the imprecision of actually available identification methods which have to recognize more abstract entities from less abstract ones.

16.3. TEXT-TO-SOUND CONVERSION

Following the scheme for describing system architectures introduced in chapter 1, text to sound conversion is performed by a system whose main function is to produce a sequence of phonemes, given a text. The system data structures are, in this case, complex knowledge sources introduced in Figure 16.3 and represented with a more detailed decomposition in Figure 16.6.

Linguistic preprocessing transforms chains of numbers, acronyms and abbreviations into a full string of characters representing letters and numbers

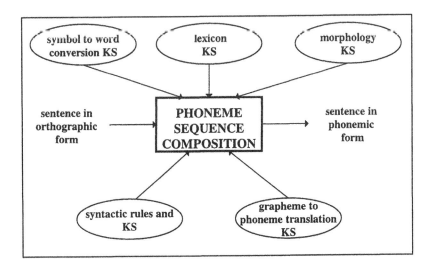

Figure 16.6 Knowledge sources for grapheme-to-phoneme conversion.

as if they were words. So, for example, 1 is translated into "one", L is translated into "el" and also "." is translated into "point".

Words belonging to a lexicon are used to obtain a *lexeme*, which becomes a key to retrieving a lexical entry containing the syntactic class and a phoneme string representing the pronunciation of a word. If, for example, a noun is plural, the corresponding lexeme will be the singular version. The phoneme string of the plural version is obtained by applying rules.

In many languages there are various problems at this level. The first one is that a word may belong to more that one syntactic category. In English, for example, "show" may be a noun or a verb. In French, more than 70% of the words are *homographs* having the same orthography but with the possibility of belonging to more than one syntactic class (Moulines and Cappé, 1996).

The phonetic transcriptions have symbols from a phonetic alphabet, which, for example, for French, contains 16 vocalic sounds, 17 consonants and three semivowels.

There are *eterophone homographs* that are words having the same ortho-graphy but different phonemic transcriptions depending on their syntactic class. There are 150 such cases in French (Moulines and Cappé, 1996). French also contains a number of *eterographic homophones* that are words with different orthography bus with the same phonemic transcription.

Morphological analysis allows decomposition of a word into *morphs* that are lexical components like prefix, suffix, root, termination. In French, there are about 100 000 morphs with which 1 million words can be created.

Morpho-syntactic analysis is performed after decomposition of words into morphs and, for those morphs for which a lexeme exists, the corresponding phonemic transcription is found in the lexicon. Morpho-syntactic analysis based on rules or statistical taggers attempts to assign a unique syntactic class to each morph in such a way that ambiguities in phonemic transcriptions are resolved.

Syntactic knowledge expresses constraints among classes of words in a sentence. Ambiguities often produce sequences of syntactic classes which do not satisfy some syntactic constraint. If syntactic knowledge is rich enough, then only one sequence is found which satisfies all the applicable constraints. An interesting approach to automatically training statistical taggers that assign syntactic classes to words by resolving ambiguities is described in Merialdo (1994). Automatic rule-based tagging has roots in Klein and Simmons (1963). Neural network taggers are proposed in Benello *et al.* (1989).

Statistical taggers are based on an algorithm that finds the optimal sequence of tags T^* given a sequence of words W with a probabilistic decision:

$$T^* = \underset{T}{\operatorname{argmax}} \, \Pr(T|W) = \underset{T}{\operatorname{argmax}} \, \Pr(W, T) \qquad (16.3)$$

where $\Pr(W, T)$ is computed with the following approximation:

$$\Pr(W, T) = \prod_{i=1}^{I} \Pr(w_i | w_1 t_1, w_2 t_2, \ldots, w_{i-1} t_{i-1}) \Pr(t_i | w_1 t_1, w_2 t_2, \ldots, w_{i-1} t_{i-1})$$

$$= \Pr(w_i | t_i) \Pr(t_i | t_{i-1}, t_{i-2})$$

Trigram and word-given tag probabilities can be estimated with methods introduced in Chapter 7. Optimal tagging can be obtained with the Viterbi algorithm.

Words in orthographic form for which there are no phonemic transcriptions in the lexicon are transformed into a phonemic form by grapheme-to-phoneme translation rules. For languages like Spanish, translation can be performed with less than 100 rules. For French, more than 500 rules are required. These rules can be derived manually or obtained by machine learning algorithms, including those based on neural networks mentioned in Chapter 10 (Sejnowski and Rosenberg, 1986).

Word boundary phonemic modifications due to coarticulation effects are described by phonological rules, which are applied to make sure that the phoneme sequence generated by lexical knowledge also satisfies the phonological constraints.

16.4. USE OF PROSODY FOR SPEECH SYNTHESIS

Prosody deals with models of the time evolution of the fundamental frequency, acoustic correlation of vocal-cord vibration frequency and also with models of phoneme and syllable duration, pause insertion and their duration, and of intensity contours.

The study of prosody is very important for speech synthesis because there is experimental evidence that the quality of the synthesized version of a sentence improves when it is resynthesized with the prosody contour extracted from a human utterance of the same sentence (Moulines and Cappé, 1996).

Prosodic parameters are assigned based on the segmentation of a sentence into *prosodic groups* obtained by detecting *prosodic boundaries* in a sentence. Prosodic groups may correspond to syntactic groups obtained by syntactic analysis of the orthographic form of the sentence to be generated. Simple systems make this assumption when crude heuristic rules cannot find prosodic boundaries. Although the definition of prosodic groups is still the object of research, there exist in languages like English and French sets of complex rules that take into account syntactic analysis as well as other factors to determine more precisely prosodic groups based on which a better quality synthesized speech can be obtained compared to the one obtained with simple and crude rules.

Prosodic groups are organized in a hierarchy. The role and position of a prosodic group in a sentence as well as its functional relation with other groups, the sentence meaning and the speaker intention determine pitch and intensity contour patterns, phoneme and segment durations.

Decomposing a sentence into prosodic groups may turn out to be ambiguous. Disambiguation can be performed taking into account the conceptual representation of the sentence and the user intention. Classification trees have been proposed for the prediction of prosodic boundaries (Wang and Hirshberg, 1992). Intonational characteristics in discourse structures are described in Grosz and Hirscberg (1992). The problem of automatically labelling prosodic patterns is discussed in Wightman and Ostendorf (1994). In general, the use of prosody for syntactic disambiguation is described in Price *et al.* (1991). Parse scoring with prosodic information with the purpose of ranking alternatives when ambiguities arise is presented in Ostendorf *et al.* (1993).

Pauses are silence segments that are usually inserted at the end of a syntactic or a prosodic group, like a phrase, a clause, a noun or a verb group.

An average duration and pitch value are provided for each phoneme. With these values, a *neutral* version of the sentence is produced. This version is then modified by altering durations based on phoneme and syllable contexts and positions. For example, in French, the last syllable of a word is very often stressed and its duration is made longer. Predictive models of duration are used for this purpose.

An average pitch value is also available for each phoneme. Modifications of these values are performed based on pitch patterns for syllables and sentences. Phoneme pitch values are modified according to its position in a syllable (*micromelody*) and pitch in a sentence is modified according to global pitch patterns (*macromelody*). For example a query is usually made with a sentence having

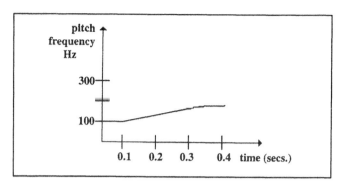

Figure 16.7 Pitch contour for a final syllable of a query.

pitch frequency rising in the last syllable. Figure 16.7 shows the pitch contour for the last syllable of a query. In general, specific rules exist for the first and last syllable of a prosodic group.

A recent thesis by Kompe (1996) describes the effective use of prosodic phrase models in a speech dialogue system. Other applications of prosody to ASR and ASU are: pitch-based mel-cepstrum normalization (Singer and Sagayama, 1992), explicit pitch and duration models (Dumouchel and O'Shaughnessy, 1995), lexical access with prosodic information (Waibel, 1988b), *n*-best rescoring with the use of prosody (Anastasakos *et al.*, 1995; Nöth, 1991). More details on prosody can be found in Olive *et al.* (1996), Hardcastle and Marchal (1990) and Moulines and Laroche (1995).

16.5. SPEECH SYNTHESIZERS

As it has been mentioned at the beginning of this chapter, there are two major approaches to speech synthesis, one is based on a model of the vocal tract and the other on concatenation of units.

16.5.1. Synthesizers Based on Vocal-Tract Models

Various types of vocal-tract models have been proposed, based on seminal work by Fant (1959, 1970a). Models taking into account physical details of human speech generation are studied in Schroeder (1967) and Schroeter and Sondhi (1994). A vocal-tract model based on a transversal all-pole digital filter, whose coefficients are computed with linear prediction, is described in Atal and Hanauer (1971). Neural networks for approximating vocal-tract functions are described in Rahim (1994).

Early and still-popular systems are based on a model requiring a small number of specification parameters. Synthesizers using these models have two basic components. The first determines time sequences of specification parameter vectors using conversion rules from phoneme strings and prosodic descriptions to sequences of vectors. The second component generates samples of synthetic speech depending on the sequence of parameter vectors it receives. Early systems used analogue components that could be specified by commands in digital form.

Human speech is generated by the modification in the vocal tract of various types of signals produced by constrictions in the tract itself or by vocal-cord vibration. The most popular models use one or more source generation models feeding a vocal-tract model. Both models have specification parameters provided by a *rule*-based system.

The vocal tract and, to some extent, the nasal tract, can be modelled by cavities whose resonant frequencies depend on the tract geometry. The two tracts are coupled by a velum that can be open (for nasal sounds) or closed. These cavities are modelled, with good approximation, by digital filters. Variations of the geometry of the cavities correspond to variations of the filter coefficients.

Because of the inertia of the articulators, coefficients are stable for time intervals ranging from 10 to 50 ms and should exhibit time variations between target values in such a way that dynamic constraints representing articulation inertia are respected. In practice, time evolutions of these coefficients can be sampled every 10–20 ms.

Rules determine the time evolution of specification parameters between two target values, usually taken in the central frame of vowels or stable consonant intervals. Interpolation between these values has to respect coarticulation constraints of the vocal tract motion.

Constraints model minimum physical effort of articulation. Popular synthesizers use coefficients determined as function of the first three or four formant frequencies, whose values and transitions have been widely investigated and can be well modelled by rules. Excellent reviews on text-to-speech conversion and formant synthesizers are in Klatt (1987) and O'Shaughnessy (1987). Deriving rules is a long and delicate process that may take as much as 10 years (Moulines and Cappé, 1996). A good example of rules for English can be found in Holmes *et al.* (1964).

The excitation signal has an asymmetric waveform that represents a slow opening phase of the vocal cords followed by a rapid intensity decrease in the closing phase. The repetition period of these waveforms is the *pitch period*. Opening and closing phases are described by two coefficients describing linear evolutions in the two phases. Unvoiced sounds have frication noise as a source. This noise is generated by air flow going from the lungs through distributed constrictions in the vocal tract. This is modelled by noise generators. Voiced fricatives and plosives have both type of sources active at the same time with a main resonance at low frequency.

16.5.2. Synthesis by Concatenation of Units

Synthesis by concatenation of units was first proposed in Harris (1953) and does not make explicit reference to a speech production model, the main process being retrieving and concatenation of prerecorded speech segments.

Of fundamental importance for this approach is the choice of units, which is a compromise between quality and memory requirements. Phonemes are definitely too short for this purpose. Concatenation of phoneme segments does not produce good-quality speech. The minimal choice for obtaining acceptable synthetic speech is to have *diphones* as units (Moulines and Charpantier, 1990). Diphones are segments starting at a stable frame of a phoneme and ending at the stable frame of the successive phoneme. There are about 2000 such diphones in a language like French requiring a memory occupation of close to 10 Mbytes. Intelligibility tests have shown that diphone concatenation produces speech in which liquids and semivowels are often confused, at least in French (Moulines and Cappé, 1996).

A better choice seems to be *pseudo-syllabic segments* defined by sequences of phonemes made of every valid sequence of consonants between two vowels. In French, there are 15 000 segments of this type. If concatenation is made using *sequences with a variable number of phonemes*, then concatenation can be performed where it is known how to smooth easily the boundaries between adjacent segments. Vowels seem to be the best phonemes on which smoothing can be effectively performed. The approach does not exclude using even longer segments like words or frequent phrases or sentences.

Segments are obtained from spoken sentences that contain all the required units perhaps concatenated in sentences without any meaning. Segmentation is performed after alignment obtained with ASR techniques.

Elementary fragments are obtained from each segment, by multiplying the segment signal $x(nT)$ $(n = 1, 2, \ldots, N)$ by a window $wn[(n_a + k)T]$ centred at the analysis sample n_a. In theory, k varies between $-\infty$ and $+\infty$. In practice, the window function has a peak for $k = 0$ and decreases to zero as $|k|$ grows beyond a value corresponding to a pitch period. For the sake of simplicity, the signals will be referred to the sample index rather than to time, so the window will simply be indicated as $wn(n_a + k)$, and the signal as $x(n)$. For every pitch period of a segment obtained by the analysis there is a fragment whose index is n_a, which varies between 1 and the number N_a of pitch periods in the analysed signal. The n_ath fragment $v(n_a, n)$ is defined as follows:

$$v(n_a, n) = x(n)wn(n_a + k) \tag{16.4}$$

which is practically non-zero only in an interval around n_a.

An association function $F(n_a)$ associates with each time reference in the analysis signal a new time reference n_s for the signal to be synthesized. In this way, durations can be adjusted by repeating or removing fragments in a segment; also, the pitch period can be varied by properly selecting n_s values.

Synthesis fragments $y(n_s, n)$ can be obtained from analysis fragments as follows:

$$y(n_s, n) = \nu(F(n_a), n) \tag{16.5}$$

and the corresponding signal is obtained by summing the synthesis fragments over n_s, and normalizing by dividing this sum for the sum of the pure window contributions at each n supposing a window is placed corresponding to each value of n_s.

The synthesized waveform is thus the result of concatenating segments with smoothing at the segment boundaries with pitch and duration selected by the prosody component (Moulines and Laroche, 1995). This concatenation technique is known as *pitch synchronous overlap-add (PSOLA)* in the time domain and is the object of a patent hold by CNET–France Télécom.

16.6. STATE OF THE ART AND SPEECH SYNTHESIS SYSTEMS

The rule-based approach to speech generation has been considered for long time the best method for generating good-quality synthetic speech. Recently, concatenation methods, especially the PSOLA one, have been the basis for very-high-quality systems as shown in a recent comparative evaluation described in Fellbaum *et al.* (1994).

PSOLA-based operational systems are CNETVOX-PSOLA for French (Moulines and Charpantier, 1990), ALLVOC and HISPAVOC-PSOLA for German and Spanish respectively (Bigorgne *et al.*, 1993), Plain Talk for English (Lee, 1993) and Eloquens for Italian (Balestri *et al.*, 1993). Other systems based on concatenation of units are ORATOR for English from Bellcore, which has a very accurate component for dealing with abbreviations, acronyms and proper nouns, and MONOLOGUE from Creative Labs also for English. Multilingual systems are ProVerbe from Elan Informatique and the one from Lernout & Hauspie.

The concatenation-based approach is more attractive than others for industrial applications because it gives an impressive performance with PC technology. Nevertheless, improving quality may probably require a combination of rule-based and concatenation methods.

Rule-based systems have rules that are difficult to induce from examples and are language-dependent. Furthermore, poor-quality speech is generated by systems without a sophisticated model of the source. The difficulty is partially alleviated with a detailed modelling of the glottal signal with the possibility of parametrizing opening duration, speed of closure, breathy nature and degree of frication with the inclusion of aspiration noise and aperiodicities. More difficult and computationally complex is the use of detailed models of the vocal tract (Stevens, 1992). An interesting rule-based multilingual system is the one from Infovox derived from research at the Royal Institute of

Technology (KTH) in Stockholm. Excellent systems for English are DECTalk, derived from work by D. H. Klatt at MIT, and TrueTalk from Entropic, derived from research at AT&T. The latter system has nine different voices. Most of the systems are available in different implementation forms, including the pure software ones for UNIX and Microsoft Windows environments.

Concatenation-based systems can be effectively implemented and produce very-good-quality speech if *polyphones* are used. In practice, from 1000 to 4000 polyphones provide good quality in the above-mentioned systems. The number and type of phonemes appearing in polyphones is determined by humans, although research is in progress towards the identification and selection of effective speech units (Iwahashi *et al.*, 1992). The use of sequences of vectors of LP coefficients for polyphone segments instead of speech samples was considered but discarded because the quality of the synthesized speech was not as good as the one obtained by concatenating sampled waveforms (Sorin, 1994).

The lexicon of the best synthesis systems available today contain between 30 000 and 60 000 word entries with orthographic, phonemic and syntactic representations. Additional tables are used for this purpose and text normalization. Letter-to-sound rules are used for the words not present in the dictionary or tables, especially for expanding acronyms and abbreviations. Obtaining an accurate pronunciation for proper nouns is still a difficult problem. The 5000 most common names in the US cover 59.1% of the 1.5 million most common name list considering the proper frequency of each item. The most frequent 200 000 names cover only 93% of such a list (Rabiner, 1994). The current trend is to augment a dictionary of fully phonetically transcribed names with a good set of rules. The European project ONOMASTICA has this objective for nine European languages (Schmidt *et al.*, 1993).

Characterization of prosody has two main still open problems, namely *prosodic segmentation* and association of adequate *prosodic contours* to each segment. For the first problem, machine learning procedures based on HMMs (Ljolje and Fallside, 1986) and ANNs (Traber, 1992) have been proposed. These techniques require a preliminary definition of units to be used as an alphabet to describe a segment. The availability of standard prosodic segmentations and transcriptions, as in the English ToBi (Barbosa and Bailly, 1994) will certainly help in this task. Prosodic contours are described by languages and generated by rules. Pilot work in rule compilers is described in Carlson and Granstrom (1975). The integration of contour generation and message generation seems to be a promising approach.

Trends for the future are in the design of personalized systems. Two main factors are essential for this purpose, namely the capability of specifying *speaking styles* that mainly depend on size and type of intonation contour, rhythm, relative segmental duration, intensity levels, and *voice timbres* that result from physiological properties of the speech organs, like glottal source and vocal tract. Both problems are still open for research.

16.7. CONCLUDING REMARKS

A number of speech synthesis systems are now integrated into commercial products for the telephone network. Promising applications are information and reservation services, sales by telephone services and others.

Interesting perspectives are in e-mail automatic reading, person–machine dialogue systems and replacing human operators for simple tasks in which input can be by voice or by touch-tone telephone keyboards.

Another area of great importance is the aid to handicapped persons. Of special interest are reading machines for blind people.

17

System Architectures and Applications

Giuliano Antoniol,[*] Roberto Fiutem,[*] Gianni Lazzari[*] and Renato De Mori[†]

17.1. INTRODUCTION AND PROBLEM STATEMENT

Very-large-vocabulary ASR and ASU systems as well as systems for language generation and speech synthesis can be implemented as pure software solutions in modern workstations with fast central processing units (CPUs) and large central memories. The complexity and time requirements of pure software systems introduce a new class of design problems, in addition to the ones of conceiving algorithms and data structures, involving the overall system structure.

[*]Istituto per la Ricerca Scientifica e Tecnologica – 38050 Pantè di Provo, Trento, Italy.
[†]School of Computer Science, McGill University, Montreal, P.Q. H3A 2A7, Canada.

A discussion on architecture would be similar for ASR, ASU, synthesis and dialogue. This chapter will focus on ASR architectures for the sake of brevity. ASR is the activity that has the most stringent time constraints related to real-time requirements.

Issues such as global organization, communication protocols, synchronization, data access, assignment of functionality to elements, composition of design elements, physical distribution, in other words, *software architecture* design (Garlan and Shaw, 1993) emerge as key elements for the success of application.

Many software architectures have been developed, becoming part of core software engineering vocabulary. *Client–server, pipeline and object oriented approaches* are just examples of current widely applied software architectural patterns or styles.

Architectures for user interface (UI) are also discussed with reference to the design issues implied by embedding ASR into a UI. Human factor analysis plays a central role in understanding user needs and prevents user rejection of the application.

Section 17.2 introduces software architecture definitions and problems of data acquisition and processing. Section 17.3 discusses ASR applications in relation to a general software operating environment with particular emphasis on client–server structures. Section 17.4 deals with user interface design and implementation constraints. Section 17.5 addresses the problem of human–computer interaction involving speech modality. Section 17.6 concludes the chapter with a review of applications.

17.2. SOFTWARE ARCHITECTURES

17.2.1. Definitions

Following the general architectural concepts introduced in Chapter 1 and focusing on data exchanged between computational units, an architectural representation based on a graph of *interacting components* is introduced (Garlan and Shaw, 1993; Garlan and Perry, 1995). *Components* represent computational elements, and correspond to nodes in the graph, while *connectors*, the arcs, represent the interactions between *components*. Components of an ASR system are identified by the following blocks, which can be organized in a *pipe-and-filter* style (Garlan and Shaw, 1993):

1. signal acquisition
2. transformation and feature extraction
3. search, performed by a recognition engine.

Figure 17.1 is an example of such classic and simple architecture for ASR.

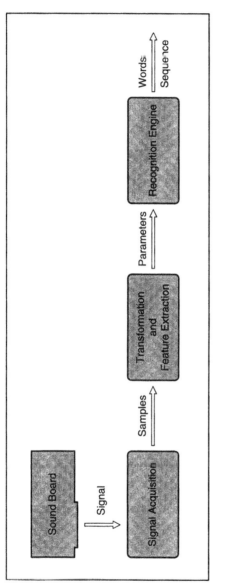

Figure 17.1 Pipe-and-filter style architecture.

In the pipe-and-filter style, each component has a set of inputs and outputs; a component reads streams of data at its inputs and produces streams of data at the outputs. Outputs are usually obtained by applying a local transformation to the input streams. Usually, the generation of output data begins before the input of data ends. Connectors act as "pipes" and components as "filters". By restricting the topology to a linear sequence of filters a *pipeline* is obtained.

Operating systems like Unix[RT],[1] Microsoft Windows NT[RT], Windows 95[RT] and Microsoft Disk Operating System (MS-DOS[RT])[2] supply mechanisms for organizing programs in pipelines. However, while the first three provide a run-time mechanism for implementing pipes in a multitasking environment, so that filters (programs) are separated tasks executed in parallel, MS-DOS pipes are simulated via files and filters are applied sequentially because concurrency is not allowed.

The *pipe-and-filter* style of Figure 17.1 abstracts the domain- and user-specific components (the language model and the acoustic models). Since the amount of time spent in recognizing a particular signal fragment cannot be predicted, it is possible that recognition results are produced after several utterances are acquired. Thus, buffers must be introduced with dimensions dependent upon the system host resources, the goal of the application (command and control or dictation), the presence or absence of other buffers in the operating system or the acquisition hardware.

The *pipe-and-filter* style is a conceptual model of an interactive modality in which the signal samples are directly sent to the recognizer, while the user is speaking, and the generated text is immediately available in the user environment. Applications requiring these modalities are command and control (e.g., menu-driven systems) or dictation in which time constraints are severe (e.g., hospital emergency reporting).

More complex ASR architectures offer alternative interaction modes that better exploit system resources. Whenever time constraints could be relaxed, a *batch* modality suffices to fulfil system requirements. This is inspired by early operating systems where jobs were enqueued and executed when system loads made resources available. Speech fragments corresponding to words, sentences or entire texts, saved for later recognition, feed a pool of recognizers acting as a centralized transcription system. Different policies could be adopted to administrate system resources and recognizer input: first-in first-out, priority-based or a mixture of the two, depending on the required system flexibility and complexity.

Other ASR software architectures presented in the literature are based on the *object-oriented* or the *client–server* (Angelini *et al.*, 1994a) paradigms. In the object-oriented model, style components (recognition engines, signals sources, grammars, etc.) are objects which interact through messages, functions and

---

[1]Unix is a registered trademark of AT&T.
[2]Windows 95, Windows NT and MS-DOS are registered trademarks of Microsoft Corporation.

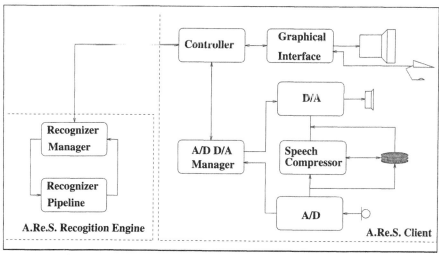

Figure 17.2 A.Re.S: an example of domain-specific architecture.

procedure invocations. Nevertheless, the recognition engine could be shared among many application programs, which could be regarded as ASR clients.

The A.Re.S system, developed at the Istituto per la Ricerca Scientifica e Tecnologica (IRST) in Trento, Italy (Angelini *et al.*, 1994a), is an example of the client–server approach. A.Re.S has a distributed software architecture whose scheme is shown in Figure 17.2. Here, many clients (that may be physically distributed) share an ASR.

The A.Re.S recognition engine has the layered structure shown in Figure 17.3 with a *recognizer manager* supervising the data flow between the application and

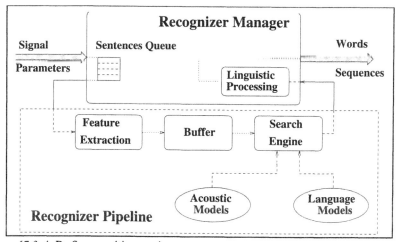

Figure 17.3 A.Re.S recognition engine.

the *recognizer pipeline* and performing *linguistic processing*, which puts the Search Engine output into an appropriate form for the user. The *recognizer pipeline* follows the *pipe-and-filter* configuration and it is composed of three processes:

- feature extraction for computing the acoustic parameters needed by the search engine
- buffer, to account for different speeds
- search engine, which decodes the signal representation into a sequence of words.

Both *interactive* and *batch* modalities are allowed. The last one is implemented with the *recognizer manager* "first-in first-out" queue. In the interactive mode, the priorities of other ASR systems competing with the one in use are lowered. A specific recognition engine is created with a limited queue and this engine has the highest priority in the system. The number of interactive connections depends on the system resources. Because of time constraints, user requirements must be met in the worst case. By adopting a start–endpoint detector, the amount of data processed during recognition is reduced at the expense of delaying interactive mode at most by one sentence.

The Microsoft object-oriented model and A.Re.S are good examples of how software architectures for ASR systems can be adapted from pure forms (e.g., the pipe and filter) to specialized styles that meet the needs of the application domain. In other words, they are *domain-specific* architectures.

17.2.2. Data Acquisition and Processing

ASR customers have the following requirements:

- real-time response
- high recognition rate
- overall system cost proportional to application benefits.

Performance and costs of available systems are highly dependent on the architecture which could range form pure software (apart from microphone and loudspeaker) to a customized hardware one.

Four different hardware configurations have been considered and will be discussed:

- a workstation with an integrated AD/DA
- similar to the previous one, but with an AD/DA board (e.g., a PC with a sound card)
- a mixed solution including a DSP board for signal acquisition and some computation (e.g., feature extraction, probability distribution evaluation)
- a dedicated hardware (e.g., a DSP board) performing all processing.

Table 17.1 Features of various hardware platform configurations

Configuration	Dedicated hardware	AD/DA	Feature extraction	Recognition engine
1	None	Internal	Software	Software
2	AD/DA board	On board	Software	Software
3	DSP board	On board	On board	Software
4	DSP board	On board	On board	On board

Notice that DSP on commercial PC sound cards cannot be programmed by end-users even if microcode is downloaded during the startup phase. The main purpose of these components is to increase sound quality and more generally board functionalities. Therefore, the second configuration substantially differs from the third one in which computation in the DSP board decreases the load of the hosting CPU.

Table 17.1 summarizes the characteristics of different configurations. The first configuration has the advantage of being almost completely portable on different hardware platforms (only the AD/DA driver has to be rewritten). Workstations offer good development environments, they are open to possible hardware enhancements, architectural modifications are not problematic and finally there is no further cost for AD/DA.

The BBN Hark[RT 3] 40 000-word continuous speech recognition system and A.Re.S. are examples of a domain architecture evolved from the mixed structure (configuration 3) to pure software systems (configuration 1). DragonDictate[RT 4] is a large-vocabulary (up to 60 000 active words) isolated-word recognizer with continuous command capability that evolved in a similar way: while early releases were based on a DSP board, the actual system is a pure software one.

An early version of the Hark system used DSP boards to speed up computation (Austin *et al.*, 1991b). In 1992 the first pure software release of Hark was announced. A 20 000-word system was demonstrated as described in BBN (1993) (see also http://www.bbn.com).

The 1991 A.Re.S release was based on a reduced instruction set computer (RISC) workstation with a DSP 32 C board to perform signal acquisition and feature extraction (Antoniol *et al.*, 1991) in 1994 the first pure software, real-time, 10 000 words continuous speech recognition system was demonstrated (Angelini *et al.*, 1994a). In Fall 1996 the A.Re.S software architecture was ported on Windows NT and Windows 95 platforms. The first PC version of A.Re.S was released in both configurations: client–server or stand-alone system. In the last configuration at least a Pentium 133 with 16 Mbytes of memory is required to guarantee an acceptable response time.

---

[3] Hark is a registered trademark of BBN Corporation.
[4] DragonDictate is a registered trademark of Dragon System Inc.

The second configuration is a mandatory choice for PCs that do not have incorporated AD/DA on motherboards; dealers quite often offer PCs with configurations including sound cards because the cost of good-quality sound boards is only a fraction of the hardware cost and does not influence the system price nor the user choice. The power of today's PCs (e.g., Pentium- or Pentium-Pro-based) makes this configuration appealing for continuous speech, real-time, small-vocabulary (such as menu-driven applications) ASR or dictation systems with no severe time constraints. Examples of the latter application in which real-time is not required and a delay of few minutes is not considered as a penalty, are batch ASR word processing systems (Angelini *et al.*, 1994a).

Pure software solutions have the drawback that handling the AD/DA directly by the operating system may cause loss of data. Assuming a sampling rate for the input signal of 16 kHz, an interrupt is generated by the AD/DA unit every $62.5 \mu s$. This means that, in the worst case, the AD/DA driver must take over the CPU control, to correctly process the input sample, 16 000 times per second. To reduce CPU overload, almost all available sound cards adopt direct memory access (DMA). With DMA chips on board, data are transferred in and out of the PC memory or disks directly. In this way, the board driver is less time critical and the CPU is freed from a considerable amount of input/output operation.

The main advantage of the third configuration is that the CPU avoids performing a remarkable amount of number crunching. The DSP and the CPU can proceed in pipeline, thus enhancing system performance. However, a full exploitation of the DSP power can be obtained only with a careful optimization of the DSP code, which, quite often, requires assembler programming and deep understanding of the underlying DSP architecture. Although new tools and development environments have reduced the performance gap between DSP assembler code and compiler-generated code, the hardware cost and the time spent in recoding (a commonly adopted practice is to optimize by hand the assembler code generated by a compiler) frequently executed code fragments (e.g., distribution evaluation, Viterbi computation) is not negligible.

An example of configuration 3 is the Philips dictation system (Steinbiss *et al.*, 1993) (see also http://www.philips.com/), which is based on a PC and uses an accelerator board.

In the last configuration, the previously outlined problems are extended to the entire system. Moreover, the available memory on dedicated hardware is quite often limited by cost, which requires an optimization of the algorithms both in the time and space domains, making this solution suitable for ASR systems produced on a large scale.

Table 17.2 summarizes the comparison of the configurations in terms of portability, development environment, AD/DA driver constraints and cost.

Table 17.2 Comparison of configuration types

Configuration	Portability	Development environment	AD/DA driver constraints
1	High	Good	High
2	High	Good	High
3	Medium	Medium	Low
4	Low	Poor	Low

17.2.3. Real-Time Software Issues for ASR Data Acquisition

In this subsection, software implications of the previously presented configurations are analysed. The first and second configurations are pure software: all the processing, apart from AD/DA conversion, is performed by the main computer and speech tasks concurrently run within the environment with other applications. Two critical components can be identified:

- *input signal acquisition and feature extraction*, in which the loss of data may compromise all the remaining processing (thus correct behaviour of the AD/DA driver is of fundamental importance)
- *recognition engine*, for which the speed is not critical (although it is a bottleneck which may lower the response time of the whole system).

To handle signal acquisition and feature extraction, three different policies are possible, depending on the hardware and the operating system:

- The AD/DA driver has a higher priority in the system. This is obviously possible in a real-time operating system, where the response time to asynchronous events can be guaranteed within a predictable time, or in other operating systems (for example Hp Unix) where it is possible to set real-time priority of execution for a process (using the *rtprio* command).
- The operating system (kernel) has enough resources to ensure a correct handling of the AD/DA; this usually requires a tuning of the AD/DA driver.
- In a *multiprocessor* system, the AD/DA could be handled by an always active thread.

Common aspects of these policies are the presence of an intermediate buffering level, as shown in Figure 17.4, and the adoption of start–endpoint detectors which may be embedded in the AD/DA driver. These detectors (Rabiner and Juang, 1993) isolate the useful part of the signal avoiding unnecessary overhead for the whole system. Operating system buffer and user-defined buffer size depend on the sampling rate, machine speed and the load of the system. Large buffers are required on slow machines, with recording/playing high-quality audio or when there are other processes running on the same system. Recording to hard disk is also likely to require large buffers.

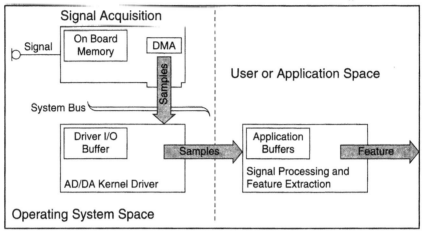

Figure 17.4 System buffering levels in ASR data acquisition.

However, large buffers will not only produce a response delay proportional to the sampling rate, but also result in a waste of valuable physical memory. The right buffer size can be easily determined by making some experiments with different machine load situations to find a compromise between resource use and relative delay.

In the authors' experience, a kernel buffer ranging from 4 Kbytes to 8 Kbytes and an application buffer from 32 to 64 Kbytes suffice for both in line and batch modalities. The larger configuration (8 Kbytes of kernel buffer and 64 Kbytes of application buffers) was used on a 486 PC machine, while on Sun Sparc Station or Hp workstation no kernel buffer is required, and 32 Kbytes suffice for the application buffer.

Even though configurations with a DSP board do not suffer from the problems outlined before, a not-too-complex driver for the board is still required. In this case, the board can temporarily store the input samples and the extracted features or intermediate computations in its memory.

Systems implemented entirely on a DSP board or on dedicated hardware are designed to fulfil user requirements like real-time response. However, actually available systems, almost in every case, are mainly limited in the dictionary size.

17.3. ASR APPLICATION ARCHITECTURES AND THEIR ENVIRONMENT

Some of the available PCs and workstations have enough computing power for real-time execution of pure-software, large-vocabulary continuous speech recognition as well as speech synthesis. However, since speech recognition is a highly computational intensive task, increasing the vocabulary size or the language model complexity pushes to the limits the performance of affordable workstations.

For this reason, it is very important to study how the algorithms described in this book can be programmed in the framework of known software environments and how the resulting systems can be executed under the control of popular operating systems.

While pipeline software architecture seems to be the most appropriate for achieving real-time requirements, it is possible to combine pipeline with object-oriented architectures that can be allocated in client–server machine configurations.

As architectural considerations are similar for synthesis and recognition, examples for the latter task will be considered in detail for the sake of brevity and because recognition actually appears to have more complex requirements.

In a client–server architecture, the most computationally demanding task can be delegated to a centralized host. In this case, the operating system must support multimodal interactions and ensure data integrity, while other tasks or user applications may run concurrently on the machine. Data acquisition and the required graphical interface, as well as other user interactions can be performed by client machines, including presentation and editing capabilities for the ASR results. Widely diffused operating systems such as Windows NT, Windows 95 and Unix enable tasks to run concurrently and offer different primitives and application program interfaces (API) to simplify multitasking and multimodal interactions.

Future operating systems for network-centric, low cost, computers will maintain multimodal capabilities, with the possibility of retrieving and executing software components in the network. Network centric machines are different from simple terminals or X-terminals,[5] in that, once a component is downloaded from the network, it is executed locally. The network not only provides software components and connectivity capabilities but also additional power for applications overwhelming local processors. Unconstrained or very-large-vocabulary continuous speech recognition will benefit from the network centric model because clients will be able to execute massive computation in the network servers.

In the A.Re.S distributed architecture, many clients (low-end PCs) communicate with a high-end workstation. The number of clients is mainly limited by the required time to allow physicians to revise the recognized text with a delay of a few minutes. The A.Re.S suggested configuration is limited to five clients for an Hp 715/790 or a SPARCstation 10 machine.

---

[5]X-terminals are diskless workstations dedicated to running the MIT X Window System server.

17.3.1. Client–Server Model and Formalism

A process corresponds to the execution of a software module; clients and servers are processes which cooperate to perform a task. In the case of ASR programming the task is recognition.

A *server* is a process waiting to be contacted by a *client* process to do something for it. A typical scenario is as follows:

- The server process is started on some computer system, it initializes itself, then is suspended, waiting for a client process to contact it requesting some service.
- A client process sends a request to the server for a service of some form.
- When the server process has finished providing its service to the client, the server is suspended again, waiting for the next request from a client.

The server process acts according to two basic strategies:

- Whenever the client request can be handled in a known, short, amount of time, the server process handles the requests sequentially.
- When the amount of time of the service depends upon the request itself, the server usually handles it in a *concurrent* fashion.

As speech recognition response time cannot be foreseen, a server process, which handles the requests for performing recognition, usually acts according to the second policy. It creates, for every request, another concurrent process to execute the requested service. In this way, there is a request handler concurrent with other processes, one for each request.

Operating systems allowing multiple processes to run concurrently (multi-tasking), with inter-process communication, resource allocation policies and locking/unlocking primitives are particularly useful for ASR.

Locking/unlocking primitives are essential since every concurrent process requests some shared resource and it is essential that resources are treated as *critical regions* accessible only with mutual exclusion so that only one process at a time can access the resource. Simple examples of such critical resources are: RAM, the CPU, or the voice input/output device. In order to properly produce a dictated report in an acceptable time, a recognition process requires a certain amount of memory and CPU time which could be guaranteed by limiting the number of recognizers concurrently running and by locking the memory used by each process. This can be implemented by the server maintaining a table of active processes and allocated resources; locking and unlocking is used to assure the consistency of the operation on the table.

Commonly available locking policies are based on *advisory locking* which means that the operating system maintains knowledge of which files have been locked by which process, but it does not prevent some process from writing to a file that is locked by another process. Cooperating processes could assume that no one intentionally violates the locking mechanism; thus, advisory locking is sufficient. On the contrary, with *mandatory locking* provided by some systems, the operating system checks, for every read and write request, whether the operation interferes with an already present lock held by the same or another process. All versions of the Unix operating system provide at least advisory locking, other operating systems have a locking policy exploiting basic inter-process communication facilities (e.g., semaphores in Windows 95).

Systems based on cooperative processes require considerable development effort, a formal description of processes, and inter-process communications. In general, a good description of system behaviour is useful for designing, coding, testing and maintaining interactive systems. Appendix D briefly introduces description methods (Milner, 1989) and summarizes a formal description of ASR systems in terms of cooperating processes.

17.3.2. Speech API

Client–server interactions are generally implemented on top of APIs which allow a client to "see" the server, negotiate resources and services, exchange data and results. Furthermore, APIs hide implementation details, allowing a server to be shared with other applications. APIs should be industrial standards, platform and vendor independent, allowing a "speech-aware" application to exploit transparently speech components of different vendors on different platforms. Figure 17.5 shows a conceptual representation of the various software/ hardware components involved in speech applications.

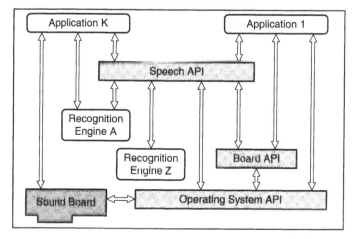

Figure 17.5 Speech API and applications.

APIs provided by the operating system vendor allow access to machine resources (e.g., a device like an audio board). Sound board vendors provide APIs to acquire, store and play speech or sound data. Speech recognizers APIs could be used to build dictation systems. In Figure 17.5, APIs hide at different levels software and hardware details. An application has to rely on them to perform useful tasks. An application can include a program for an audio device to read the samples, send the data to a recognizer and present the results to the user. Nevertheless, the same application considered at a higher level of abstraction, relying for example on a speech API, can be portable across hardware or software platforms and exploit multiple recognizers not tied to a particular interface.

At present, several companies (e.g., Microsoft Corporation, AT&T) and consortia (SRAPI, ECTF) have already proposed APIs for general-purpose speech applications and for the telephone (TAPI) market. APIs have in common the support of:

- voice commands
- speech recognition
- text-to-speech
- multimedia.

With the Microsoft (http://www.microsoft.com) Speech API (SAPI), applications can be developed with the ability to incorporate speech recognition (command and control or dictation) or text-to-speech, using either C/C++ or Visual Basic. SAPI follows the OLE Component Object Model architecture.

The Speech Recognition API (SRAPI) provides support for speech recognition, text-to-speech and other media playback. (More details on it can be found at http://www.srapi.com/.) SRAPI is based on a call-back model and supports recognition engines managing simultaneous sessions. Under a distributed client–server model, SRAPI assumes that all the interactions between applications and the recognition server are managed by a single entity on the client machine.

Telephone APIs, for example the Microsoft TAPI, allow applications to support telephone communication. Facilities include:

- connecting to a telephone network
- phone dialling
- data transmission
- voice mail
- access to data.

Enterprise Computer Telephony Forum (ECTF) is an industry organization formed to foster an open, competitive market for computer telephony integration technology. ECTS supports the S.100 specification (available at http://www.ectf.org/) which includes an automatic speech recognition API.

17.4. USER INTERFACE

17.4.1. Architectural Design Models

A functional architecture model for interactive applications is shown in Figure 17.6. Functional components of the model are organized in a hierarchy of abstract machines (Bass and Coutaz, 1991). The lower layers handle acquisition and transduction of user-generated events and the virtualization of input and output devices.

The two lower layers are usually shared among different applications and represent a framework to build interactive applications. The remaining layers are more application specific: the *presentation* layer is the supervisor of interaction objects through which the user interacts with an application, while the *application functions* layer performs computations specific to the application. The latter needs the functions of the presentation layer to obtain user input and to present application outputs. However, the application functions layer does not use these services directly. Rather, an intermediate layer, called *dialogue control* (or *script*) layer, controls the sequence of information exchange

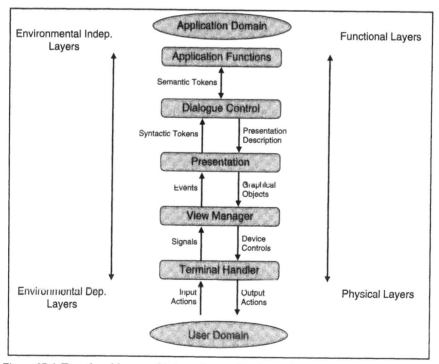

Figure 17.6 Functional layers of interactive application software.

between the user and the application. Its main functions include maintaining a correspondence between *semantic* and *interaction objects*, translating syntactic tokens generated by interaction objects into *semantic tokens* and *vice versa* and maintaining a dynamic representation of the state of the dialogue (e.g. deciding when an interaction object is accessible to the user). A detailed introduction of these concepts can be found in Larson (1992).

The functional decomposition in Figure 17.6 is an abstract model. A number of system architectures have been proposed in the literature to implement the functional model (Green, 1983; Krasner and Pope, 1988). These architectures adopt different ways of partitioning the components of the functional model into real components, sometimes grouping them into a single real component or further decomposing them into more detailed components. There is no best architecture for all situations; however, each choice can be evaluated according to software engineering principles such as re-usability of components, interface simplicity, minimal redundancy and so on (Ghezzi *et al.*, 1992).

The spectrum of the possible different architectural organizations ranges from a *monolithic architecture*, in which all the functional, dialogue and user presentation aspects are implemented in a single component, to a *multiagent* architecture, where an interactive application is decomposed into a collection of entities called *agents*, each one implementing a different application functionality, owning a separate state and possibly having a separate thread of execution. Clearly, going from a monolithic organization towards a multi-agent one corresponds to increasing separation of concerns among components, component re-usability and simplicity, while augmenting redundancy.

In the intermediate organizations, the number of functional components that are separately implemented increases: in the *client–server* organization, only the presentation layer is implemented separately. In the *Seeheim* (Green, 1983) or *model view controller* (MVC) (Krasner and Pope, 1988) organizations, all the functional components are implemented separately (Larson, 1992).

Figure 17.7 shows the role of speech recognition in the functional architecture.

Speech is one of the input/output modalities within a multimodal user interface and would naturally fit into the terminal functional layer. The events generated by this component could be treated as logical events and handled by the user interface in the same way as mouse clicks or keystrokes.

The architecture of Figure 17.7 is appropriate for simple command and control applications in which speech is used to activate and select menu options. The speech channel generates *events* to be handled by the presentation layer and translated into *syntactic tokens* for the dialogue control layer.

However, when the task to be performed becomes more complex, involving, for example, robot commands, an interpretation phase is necessary to translate ASR results into valid actions for the application. Spontaneous speech phenomena like breath, coughs and all other sounds that could cause a wrong interpretation of user input have also to be detected and excluded.

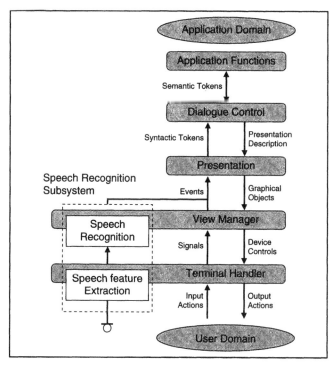

Figure 17.7 Role of speech recognition subsystem within the functional architecture of interactive applications where speech is used as an alternative to mouse and keyboard.

Figure 17.8 shows the role of the speech recognition subsystem for the considered interactive applications.

When the user interface is no longer multimodal but voice is the only channel available, e.g. in telephone-based remote applications, or when voice is the main input channel because end users are not trained computer users (for example in database query by voice), an understanding component has to drive the dialogue with the user, assuming the functionalities of the dialogue control layer and interacting directly with the application. The architecture of Figure 17.8 evolves into the one of Figure 17.9.

In the case of dictation, voice is not another input/output channel for a multimodal user interface. In this case, the user interacts with usual devices (mouse, keyboard) but the functional core of the application is speech to text translation. Spoken sentences are not commands but data.

In the A.Re.S system, for example, the user interface is designed to control the whole process of radiological report production involving activation of speech acquisition, saving the signal, activation of the speech recognizer, editing the text produced, storing the reports and so on. All these activities are accomplished using only mouse and keyboard (although speech could also be used for interface commands). Speech transcription is the main functionality

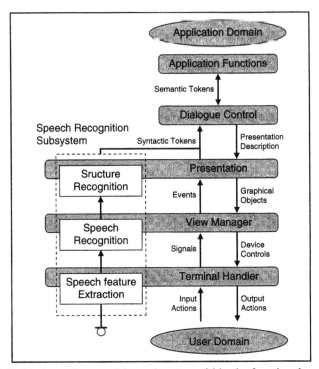

Figure 17.8 Role of speech recognition subsystem within the functional architecture of interactive applications in the case of spoken language understanding systems.

of the system and speech recognition has to be considered as the functional core of the application. Figure 17.10 shows the functional architecture for dictation systems.

In conclusion, the generic functional architecture model of interactive software is still applicable with the addition of the speech channel, provided that there is a proper *virtual terminal* and possibly an *interaction object* handling the speech channel or that the speech channel itself represents the functional core of the application.

17.4.2. Implementation constraints

While, from a functional and conceptual point of view, the addition of a speech recognition subsystem does not affect the overall system organization, implementation should take some specific constraints into account.

Furthermore, the communication mechanisms used to exchange information tokens among the components of the implementation models have a great impact on system performance. In fact, some constraints may force a choice of a specific communication mean. Basic communication means are: subroutine

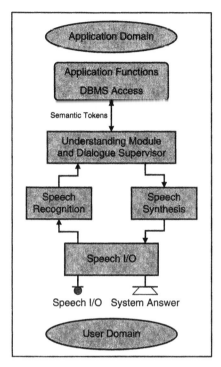

Figure 17.9 A database query by voice system architecture: the understanding module drives user dialogue.

calls, shared memory and message passing. In general, the means are independent of the user interface models, but in practice, some models require different communication paradigms. For example, a monolithic architecture will naturally be implemented using subroutine calls, while an MVC or a multiagent architecture will use shared memory or message passing within a multithreading or multiprocessing environment, to exploit the intrinsic concurrency present in the model and give a single thread to each component, object or set of objects.

Among the implementation models described in the previous section, the monolithic architecture model cannot be used for speech recognition, because of real-time requirements that would prevent any other activity during recognition. A client–server architecture is an acceptable solution, in which the speech recognition subsystem is implemented as a separate process or thread. The communication mechanism has to be inter-process and, in order to guarantee that voice input samples are not missed, the speech recognition subsystem must have its own thread of execution with a proper priority.

This is true for all kinds of speech-based applications, from command and control to dictation systems. A speech recognition subsystem contains at least the speech acquisition and feature extraction components and the speech recognition engine.

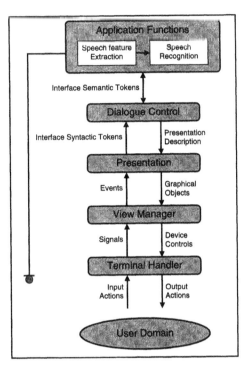

Figure 17.10 Role of speech recognition subsystem within the functional architecture of interactive applications in speech-based dictation systems.

In the case of dictation, there is a further simple reason to implement the speech recognition subsystem as a process separated from the rest of the application. As speech recognition is a computationally intensive task, if the user interface were implemented within the same process, the user would have to wait for the completion of the transcription before being able to perform any other type of interaction including corrections with mouse and keyboard.

Another constraint, common to all applications having a graphical user interface, derives from the *external control model*. Graphical user interfaces are mostly event driven and the interface program is structured as a main loop that responds to events generated by the user through input devices. The interface programmer associates application actions in response to user interaction events. In a client–server architecture, events are delivered by the window system. The interface program has no control over it and can only respond to events. The programming paradigm is *event based*. On the contrary, a speech recognizer is a sequential process that receives input signals and produces the corresponding (hypothesized) transcriptions. Implementing a speech recognizer within the external control model of the interface would be much more complicated and the real-time constraints might not be satisfied.

Finally, other practical considerations are in favour of the separation of the speech recognition subsystem from the rest of the application. These include the possibility of using different languages, different environments and toolkits to implement different components, or even, by using graphical user interface builders, to interactively design the user interface and automatically generate its code.

Removing the monolithic architectures from the set of the possible choices, the remaining architectures are not constrained by the presence of speech recognition. Adopting architectural models with a higher degree of user inter-face functionality decomposition (such as MVC or multiagent) makes it easier to follow software engineering principles of modularity, information hiding, re-usability and independence, obtaining better performance. For example, a multiagent architecture may be convenient because it has the advantage of decomposing the application functionalities into different objects that can possibly be executed in parallel, exploiting the intrinsic concurrency within user tasks.

For example, in the A.Re.S system implementation, a multiprocess architec-ture has been adopted. A scheme of it is shown in Figure 17.11, where all the boxes represent concurrent processes. Being a dictation system, all the speech recognition modules (signal acquisition, feature extraction, speech recognition) can be grouped and considered as the functional core component of the appli-cation. The controller process is logically the part of the functional core, which interfaces with the graphical interface process. It translates user requests coming

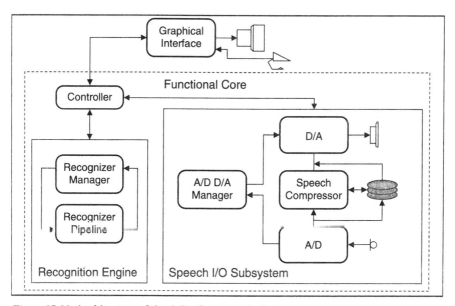

Figure 17.11 Architecture of the A.Re.S system: the boxes represent concurrent processes.

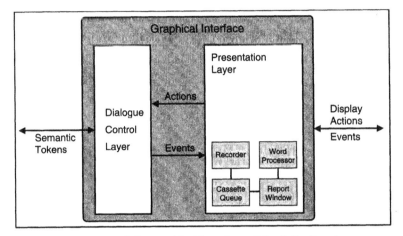

Figure 17.12 Architecture of the graphical interface of the A.Re.S system.

from it into commands for the speech input/output or the recognition engine subsystems and coordinates their activity; it receives back messages from them and translates these messages into semantic tokens for the graphical interface process.

Within the graphical interface process, shown in detail in Figure 17.12, two functional layers can be identified: the first one implements the *presentation* component, where each interaction object is implemented as a separate object with its own state. It consists of four main objects, the digital voice recorder (recorder object), the queue of recorded cassettes (cassette queue), the window of completed reports (report window object) and the word processor object. The cassette queue object contains a set of cassette objects representing the stored signal, that still have to be transcribed by the speech recognition engine. The window of the completed reports contains a set of reports, representing the already transcribed reports, that can be checked for correctness by a human inspector.

The second layer implements the *dialogue control*: it collects the events coming from the *interaction objects* of the *presentation* layer and translates them into *semantic tokens* for the *functional core*. It receives semantic tokens from the *functional core* and translates them into actions to be performed by the *interaction objects*.

17.4.3. User Configuration

Nowadays, software is often delivered with setup procedures which analyse system hardware and software, install software components and configure the application, following the so-called *plug-and-play* model.

For a speech-based system, this means that different user configurations must be provided. They include sets of data structures like language-dependent acoustics models (e.g., English, Spanish, Italian) and applications (e.g., command and control, dictation, database query) with a language model for each application or application domain (e.g., medical, legal, business). Since the space required to store acoustic and linguistic information is relevant, it is convenient that baseline configurations be shared among users in a centralized repository.

Performance of recognition engines, especially for large vocabulary continuous speech applications, can be improved with a user dependent configuration. It is well known, that in most cases, retraining acoustic models or performing speaker adaptation increases recognition accuracy. Language model adaptation may be obtained by allowing users to add new words or to define keywords to the baseline. In a speech based interface, users may prefer, for example, spoken interaction for certain dialogues rather then manual/visual interaction (Bradford, 1995).

User customization is commonly supported in commercial systems. For example, Microsoft Corporation defines objects called *speaker profiles* which contain, among other information (Microsoft Corporation, 1995):

- the language for training
- the known patterns of speech and the language model
- the phonetic training for the speaker
- the speaker identifier
- the speaker's preferences.

In the A.Re.S system, a similar organization was adopted, although in a domain-specific application with language models currently tailored for radiological reporting. Each user shares phonetic models, domain-specific language models, and a set of predefined texts. User customization is possible and newly defined user configurations are stored in users' private repositories.

Generally speaking, systems ought to supply customization and configuration procedures to add or delete users in the system and to modify, store and retrieve user configurations. Whenever a recognition service is required by a user, her/his user configuration may be considered for negotiating services provided by the system. In fact, available recognition engines could supply the desired recognition service, thus minimizing the use of computer resources.

17.5. ASR-BASED SYSTEM USABILITY

Early studies have considered the value of using speech input in human–computer interfaces, making empirical evaluations of performance differences when speech input replaces traditional keyboard input in restricted applications. Such performance measures were usually *speed of task completion* and *error rates* within data-entry applications using isolated-word, small-vocabulary ASR systems. Results were contradictory. They were essentially negative for the use of speech input alone. Nevertheless, advantages for using speech appeared evident in situations of concurrent, secondary tasking and high cognitive workload (Welch, 1977; Nye, 1982; Poock, 1982). These studies indicated hands-busy, eyes-busy tasks as situations in which speech offers an advantage by providing an additional, non-manual input channel. Another reported advantage of using speech input in conjunction with a keyboard over using a keyboard alone was the achievement of function separation by modality (Morrison *et al.*, 1984), but limited to users not trained to the specific task. Applications for the handicapped (Damper, 1984) were identified as a further area in which speech input technology has a great potential.

More recent studies indicate that automatic dictation by discrete-word, large-vocabulary recognition systems is feasible and useful (Wylegala, 1989). Speech input has also been shown useful for dictation of prerecorded texts (Joseph, 1989) and for providing remote information services by telephone (Noyes and Frankish, 1989). Other studies have focused on the utility of speech input as an additional modality in multimodal interfaces: psychological research supports the view that people are more efficient in performing multiple tasks if activities are distributed across different perceptual channels, since interference of tasks in the same modality decreases (Martin, 1989).

Research is in progress to evaluate the utility of speech input in several different tasks compared to traditional input devices. A study on the utility of using speech input to control window navigation in a window system shows no significant difference in speed between speech input and mouse input to navigate between exposed windows but also shows that speech is superior in controlling obscured windows (Schmandt *et al.*, 1990). Other studies investigated speech input utility compared to mouse and keyboard in graphical editing (Paush and Leatherby, 1991), word processing (Karl *et al.*, 1993) and command and control applications (Damper and Wood, 1995). The first two studies reported faster task completion times when using speech input, most of the benefits stemming from the reduction of cursor motion by replacing mouse-based activation with speech-based activation. The third study shows, on the contrary, that speech is slightly slower than keying but much more error-prone.

All these studies, although somewhat contradictory, provide insight into using speech input within an application, leading to the following considerations.

1. Comparing different input media is often difficult. In command and control applications, for example, performance obtained using speech can be directly compared with that obtained with a mouse or keyboards. These comparisons are meaningful, since speech is used as an alternate input medium. However, for dictation, speech must be used for the main activity

while the other input channels can be used to control the transcription process and to correct the recognition results. Mixed systems (Joseph, 1989), that combine predefined text with dictation, may not be flexible enough from a linguistic point of view and may be perceived as unnatural by end users. Moreover, continuous speech ASR with medium-large vocabulary is now feasible with general purpose hardware. Thus, there is no longer a need to constrain the user to a structured, template-based approach for document production.

2. The user profile is another important variable to take into account. A study on the effects of input modality in text editing (Morrison *et al.*, 1984) reported that typists preferred keyboard instead of speech, while non-typists began with a preference for speech input, shifting later from speech to keyboard.

In the A.Re.S system, when functioning in the *batch* modality, two different user roles are considered, namely physicians and verification personnel. Physicians dictate reports, mainly using speech input, with limited interaction through the graphical user interface (mouse and keyboard are only used to activate/deactivate a digital tape recorder implemented in software in the system). Verification personnel correct possible recognizer errors without using speech input. Speech output is used to listen to dictated reports, for the purpose of text correction. The reason for having two user profiles is obvious. Verification personnel consist of professional typists and computer users, who can take advantage of the full power of the graphical user interface. Physicians, on the other hand, are often not trained computer users. They may not accept the work of typing. Without ASR, reports would be manually transcribed by listening to tape cassettes. The transcription time is obviously shorter with ASR. On the contrary, physicians have no particular advantage. The decision to switch to automated reporting, however, is usually taken by physicians, thus the user interface of such an application must be adapted to the physician's way of working.

A useful human–computer interaction design technique that can help reduce the risk that the system is refused by end users is based on *metaphors* (Carrol and Mack, 1995). Metaphors describe a new model in terms of a known model. Metaphors allow the creation of interaction objects that correspond to user conceptual models.

Example. The A.Re.S system graphical user interface, shown in Figure 17.13, has been designed with a direct manipulation dialogue style that mimics the traditional, non-automated way of radiological report production. For example, in the system batch modality, reports are dictated using a simulated digital tape recorder and are represented by tape cassette icons. After dictation completion, cassettes are transferred to a waiting queue of cassettes, which represents the set of the reports to be transcribed by the speech recognizer. Once the recognition phase has been completed, the cassette on the top of the

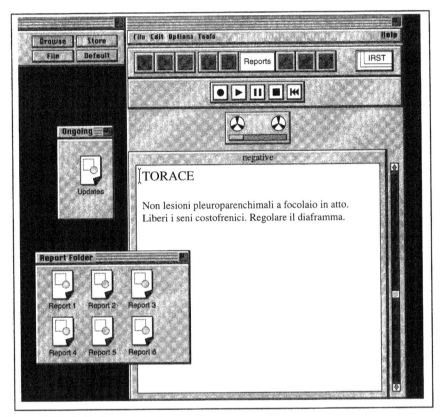

Figure 17.13 A.Re.S user interface.

queue is transformed into a text report represented by an appropriate icon. By interacting with this icon, the text can be verified, corrected and finally printed. The direct electronic simulation of the traditional reporting method helps physicians and verification personnel accept the reporting automation process, letting them feel more comfortable and guiding them to accomplish the task.

Other important factors for the acceptance of a speech-based system by end users are dictation modality, i.e. isolated-word *vs.* continuous speech, and ASR accuracy. While isolated-word ASR is suitable for command and control applications that usually require short voice interactions, the possibility of continuous speech is preferred by users. In the case of medical reporting systems, for example, there have been cases in which physicians found isolated-word dictation unnatural and used the language model adaptation features to concatenate words into a word sequence to be recognized as a single word, thus using the isolated-word ASR as a continuous speech one (Antoniol *et al.*, 1993). In the long run, physicians tended to refuse isolated-word ASR systems, switching back to non-automated reporting. ASR accuracy, or recognition rate, is critical for command and control applications, where other competing media (mouse, keyboard) can perform equally fast or even faster, but above all, without errors. For dictation, ASR accuracy is less critical but it should not fall below a certain threshold, otherwise the additional time required for correction eliminates the benefits of dictation over typing, and could frustrate the user.

17.6. CONCLUDING REMARKS

Applications for ASR and speech synthesis are receiving considerable attention in Industry. The technology, although imperfect, has acceptable performance for certain practical sectors.

ASR applications, in particular, are now used in practice in many countries, for example for the dictation of medical reports, for information retrieval by telephone and for data entry. Nevertheless, there are still some problems preventing further diffusion of ASR applications. They are partly related to the cost and to technical limitations, particularly concerns of robustness, especially when there is a background noise, the speaker is not very close to the microphone or makes hesitations, false starts, corrections and other actions which are not yet properly modelled.

The ASR market can be subdivided into four fundamental segments, namely telephone services, computer interfaces, industrial control, and home systems.

While the first two segments are in great expansion, for the other two the technology does not seem to be ready yet at a cost acceptable to the other two segments.

A great industrial effort is made nowadays in the fourth sector, especially for the use of low-cost ASR devices in cars and in cellular telephones.

ASR telephone applications are facing now the problem of improving performance in spite of poor transducers, limited bandwidth and channel noise. Some of these problems will be alleviated by the progressive extension of the telephone network bandwidth to carrying digital information.

With rigid and simple dialogue systems, it is possible to achieve acceptable performance in applications such as collect-call management, directory assistance, limited information retrieval, and voice-driven switching, to contact a person in a company by pronouncing her/his name.

Decreasing cost, increasing robustness, capturing speech with microphone arrays (thus giving speakers more freedom) and improving models so that more natural speech can be properly recognized are some of the major challenges for the future.

Appendix A

Signal Processing

Daniele Falauigna,[*] Maurizio Omologi,[*] Piergiorgio Suaizer[*]
and Renato De Mori[†]

This appendix is intended to provide some basic concepts of digital signal processing. The reader is advised to refer to fundamental books such as Rabiner and Gold (1975), Rabiner and Schafer (1978), Marple (1987), Oppenheim and Schafer (1989) and Haykin (1995) for further details on the items introduced here.

In order to be processed by a computer, the continuous time speech signal needs to be transformed into a discrete time sequence. This operation is carried out by means of a *sampling* step (Oppenheim and Schafer, 1989) and of a subsequent *analogue to digital* conversion. To avoid distortions, known as *aliasing*, on the resulting discrete signal, the sampling frequency F_s must be equal or greater than twice the bandwidth of the continuous signal.[1] Furthermore, in the analogue-to-digital conversion a *quantization error* (Rabiner and Gold, 1975) is also introduced that depends on the number of bits of the converter. Although in the following we will only consider discrete time real sequences, $[s(n)]_{n=0}^{N-1}$ of length N, the extension to infinite-length sequences is straightforward.

A sequence $s(n)$ can be conveniently represented and analysed by means of its *z-transform* $S(z)$, defined as:

$$S(z) = \sum_{n=0}^{N-1} s(n) z^{-n} \qquad (A.1)$$

[*]Istituto per la Ricerca Scientifica e Tecnologica – 38050 Pantè di Povo, Trento, Italy.
[†]School of Computer Science, McGill University, Montréal, P.Q. H3A 2A7, Canada.
[1]As stated by the sampling theorem (Oppenheim and Schafer, 1989), the band of the sampled signal corresponds to the frequency interval $[0, F_s/2]$, where $F_s/2$ is often called the *Nyquist* frequency.

where z is a complex variable. Generally, the properties of a discrete sequence can be studied in terms of poles and zeros of the corresponding z-transform. If the complex variable z is restricted to vary on the unitary circle, i.e. $z = e^{j\omega}$ $0 \leq \omega \leq 2\pi$, then (A.1) can be written as:

$$S(e^{j\omega}) = \sum_{n=0}^{N-1} s(n)e^{-j\omega n} \tag{A.2}$$

The equation above defines the *Fourier transform* of $s(n)$.

Since it is necessary to use discrete samples of the Fourier transform, a *discrete Fourier transform* (DFT) is introduced as follows (Oppenheim and Schafer, 1989):

$$S(k) = \sum_{n=0}^{N-1} s(n)e^{-j2\pi(kn/N)}, \quad 0 \leq k \leq N-1 \tag{A.3}$$

The sequence $[S(k)]_{k=0}^{N-1}$ is obtained by sampling[2] the Fourier transform $S(e^{j\omega})$ at points $\omega_k = 2\pi(kn/N)$. Efficient methods based on the *fast Fourier transform* (FFT) algorithm, for the evaluation of the DFT, are described in Rabiner and Gold (1975) and Oppenheim and Schafer (1989). An important property of the DFT of a real sequence $s(n)$ is *symmetry*. It can be expressed as follows:

$$R_e(S(k)) = R_e(S(N-k)) \tag{A.4}$$

$$I_m(S(k)) = -I_m(S(N-k)) \tag{A.5}$$

where $R_e(S(k))$ and $I_m(S(k))$ indicate real and imaginary parts of $S(k)$, respectively. Since in speech applications only the module of the DFT is generally used, it is sufficient to consider the sequence $[\|S(k)\|]_{k=0}^{N-1}$ only in the interval $[0, (N-1)/2]$. The inverse discrete Fourier transform (IDFT) has the following form:

$$s(n) = \frac{1}{N} \sum_{k=0}^{N-1} S(k)e^{j2\pi(kn/N)} \quad 0 \leq n \leq N-1 \tag{A.6}$$

Many speech applications require the use of digital filters for processing the input signal $s(n)$. For the purpose of this book, it is sufficient to consider only causal *linear time invariant* (LTI) filters (Oppenheim and Schafer, 1989), described by the following time domain relation:

$$y(n) = \sum_{k=0}^{N-1} s(k)h(n-k) = \sum_{k=0}^{N-1} s(n-k)h(k) \tag{A.7}$$

where $y(n)$ is the filter output and $h(n)$ is called *impulse response* of the filter. The summation defined by (A.7) is also called *convolution sum* (Oppenheim and

---

[2]Note that the sampling of the Fourier transform corresponds to the time periodic repetition (with period N) of the sequence $s(n)$. Hence, particular care must be taken in order to avoid time aliasing effects, as explained in Oppenheim and Schafer (1989).

Schafer, 1989); it has the equivalent representation:

$$Y(z) = S(z)H(z) \tag{A.8}$$

in terms of z-transform. The z-transform, $H(z)$, of the impulse response is called the *transfer function* of the filter. The filter properties can be selected by properly placing poles and zeros of the transfer function on the z-plane. As an example, if the poles of $H(z)$ are all inside the unitary circle, the filter is *stable* (i.e. it provides limited outputs for limited inputs). The Fourier transform of the impulse response is called *frequency response* of the filter and, in general, it is designed to attenuate some frequency components of the input signal. According to the type of frequency response, the filters can be distinguished into *low pass*, *high pass* and *band pass*. According to the length of the impulse response, filters can be divided into *finite impulse response* (FIR) filters and *infinite impulse response* (IIR) filters. FIR and IIR filters have different properties that make them suitable for different applications. Well-known techniques for their design and realization are reported in Rabiner and Gold (1975), Crochiere and Rabinen (1983) and Oppenheim and Schafer (1989).

The *autocorrelation function* of $s(n)$ is defined as:

$$R_s(m) = \sum_{n=0}^{N-|m|-1} s(n)s(n+|m|), \quad -(N-1) \leq m \leq N-1 \tag{A.9}$$

The autocorrelation[3] is an even function, i.e. $R_s(m) = R_s(-m)$, with maximum value at $m = 0$. Note that $R_s(0)$ is also equal to the energy E_s of the given signal:

$$E_s = \sum_{n=0}^{N-1} s^2(n) \tag{A.10}$$

The *power spectrum* $P_s(e^{j\omega})$ of a signal $s(n)$ is defined as the Fourier transform (or the DFT) of the corresponding autocorrelation sequence:

$$P_s(e^{j\omega}) = \sum_{n=-(N-1)}^{N-1} R_s(n)e^{-j\omega n} \tag{A.11}$$

It can be shown that the power spectrum of a real signal is a real even function and that:

$$P_s(e^{j\omega}) = S(e^{j\omega})S^*(e^{j\omega}) = |S(e^{j\omega})|^2 \tag{A.12}$$

where $S(e^{j\omega})$ is the Fourier transform of the signal $s(n)$ and $*$ denotes complex conjugate. Equations (A.11) and (A.12) suggest an efficient method for obtaining the autocorrelation function (Markel and Gray, 1976). It consists of the

---

[3]When dealing with random processes (Papoulis, 1991), the autocorrelation function of finite length sequences is often defined by multiplying (A.9) for either $1/N$ or $1/(N-|m|)$.

following steps:

- Apply the FFT to the given signal.
- Evaluate the squares of the FFT samples.
- Compute the autocorrelation sequence with an inverse FFT.

A sort of energy conservation principle between the time and frequency domains is stated by the following relation, known as *Parseval theorem*:

$$E_s = \sum_{n=0}^{N-1} s^2(n) = \frac{1}{2\pi} \int_0^{2\pi} |S(e^{j\omega})|^2 d\omega \qquad (A.13)$$

A useful parameter in speech processing is the *zero crossing rate* (ZCR), defined as the number of zero crossing per unit of time in the signal $s(n)$. A formal definition is the following (Rabiner and Schafer, 1978):

$$\text{ZCR}_s = \frac{1}{2N} \sum_{n=1}^{N-1} |\text{sign}(s(n)) - \text{sign}(s(n-1))| \qquad (A.14)$$

where:

$$\text{sign}(s(n)) = 1, \qquad s(n) \geq 0 \qquad (A.15)$$

$$\text{sign}(s(n)) = -1, \quad s(n) < 0 \qquad (A.16)$$

The ZCR assumes high values if the signal has energy concentrations at high frequencies, such as in the case of unvoiced sounds (see Chapter 3). On the contrary, the ZCR is small in voiced speech segments. As a consequence, the ZCR is an effective parameter for voiced/unvoiced discrimination.

A *cross-correlation function* $R_{s_1 s_2}(m)$ between two sequences $s_1(n)$ and $s_2(n)$ can be defined as follows:

$$R_{s_1 s_2}(m) = \sum_{n=0}^{N-m-1} s_2(n) s_1(n+m), \quad 0 \leq m \leq N-1$$

$$\qquad (A.17)$$

$$R_{s_1 s_2}(m) = \sum_{n=0}^{N-|m|-1} s_2(n+|m|) s_1(n), \quad -(N-1) \leq m < 0$$

Unlike the autocorrelation, the cross-correlation is not an even function and therefore the values for positive and negative lag indexes must be computed separately.

The *cross-power spectrum* is defined as the Fourier transform of the cross-correlation function:

$$P_{s_1 s_2}(e^{j\omega}) = \sum_{n=-(N-1)}^{N-1} R_{s_1 s_2}(n) e^{-j\omega n} \qquad (A.18)$$

The cross-spectrum is not an even function and it can be easily shown that:

$$P_{s_1 s_2}(e^{j\omega}) = S_1(e^{j\omega}) S_2^*(e^{j\omega}) \tag{A.19}$$

where $S_1(e^{j\omega})$ and $S_2(e^{j\omega})$ are the Fourier transforms of the sequences $s_1(n)$ and $s_2(n)$ respectively.

It is interesting to derive the relation between the power spectra of the input and output sequences of a linear filter. From equations (A.7) and (A.9), it can be shown that:

$$R_y(m) = \sum_{k=-(N-1)}^{N-1} R_s(m-k) R_h(k), \quad -2(N-1) \leq m \leq 2(N-1) \tag{A.20}$$

and from (A.8) and (A.12):

$$P_y(e^{j\omega}) = |H(e^{j\omega})|^2 P_s(e^{j\omega}) \tag{A.21}$$

which is the power spectrum of the output signal is equal to the power spectrum of the input signal multiplied by the power spectrum of the filter impulse response.

In speech processing, an important role is played by *orthogonal linear transforms*, which can be applied directly to signal samples or to feature vectors derived from them (see Chapters 3 and 4). The DFT itself is an example of such a transform where the *basis vectors* are the exponential functions of equation (A.3). Other transforms are represented by the *Karhunen–Loeve transform*, the *discrete Walsh–Hadamard transform*, the *discrete cosine transform*. For a review of transforms and for their use the reader should refer to Jayant and Noll (1984).

In ASR, as well as in many other applications, an important problem, which can cause intolerable performance degradation, is represented by *noise*. Noise can be seen as a random signal (Papoulis, 1991) (e.g. environmental noise, electrical noise of circuits and transmission systems, quantization noise, etc.) which is added to clean speech. Noise should be distinguished from *distortion*, which has convolutive effects on the clean speech (as in the case of reverberation) and therefore can be modelled by means of linear filtering. In practical applications, the speech signal is subjected to noise and distortion at the same time so that the term *convolutive noise* is often used.

If noise is considered to be only additive, a *signal-to-noise ratio* (SNR) is defined to quantify the noise level with respect to the signal level:

$$\text{SNR} = 10 \log_{10}\left(\frac{E_s}{E_n}\right) \tag{A.22}$$

where E_s and E_n are the signal energy and the noise energy respectively. Generally, the noise energy is estimated on a signal interval where speech is not present.

Appendix B

Classification Trees

Roland Kuhn[*] and Renato De Mori[†]

A binary classification tree contains internal nodes that each consist of a yes/no question that can be applied to data items, a YES subtree and a NO subtree; each leaf node of the tree is labelled with a category. To label a new data item, the question at the root is applied to it and it is then sent to either the YES or the NO subtree, depending on the answer to the question. The same procedure is followed recursively at the data item's current node until the item arrives at a leaf node, whose label it receives. In the last few years efficient algorithms for growing binary classification trees from training data have been devised.

Some of these derive from Breiman *et al.* (1984), and some from Quinlan (1990); the notation proposed in Breiman *et al.* (1984) will be employed here. Classification trees can be applied to a wide variety of problems. They should be considered when the data have some of the following characteristics (Breiman *et al.*, 1984, p. 7):

- high dimensionality
- a mixture of data types
- non-standard data structure
- non-homogeneity, i.e., different relationships hold between variables in different parts of the measurement space.

A recent survey comparing results obtained by means of decision trees with those obtained by other machine learning methods is (Langley and Simon, 1995).

To illustrate the concept, we reproduce in Figure B.1 the classification tree of Figure 14.2. A corpus of data was used to grow the tree.

---

[*]Panasonic, Speech Technology Laboratory, 3888 State Street #202, Santa Barbara, CA 93105, USA.
[†]School of Computer Science, McGill University, Montreal, P.Q. H3A 2A7, Canada.

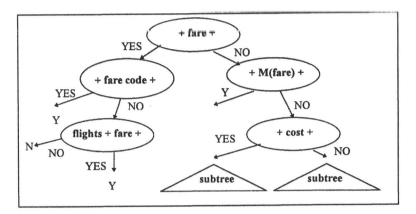

Figure B.1 Example of a classification tree.

To grow a decision tree, one must supply three elements:

- a set of possible yes/no questions that can be applied to data items
- a rule for selecting the best question at a node, or deciding that it should be a
  leaf node, on the basis of training data
- a method for pruning trees to prevent over-training.

The set of questions one supplies to the tree-growing algorithm is always
larger than the set of questions ultimately assigned to nodes of the tree.

Any question that yields a YES or NO answer when applied to the type of data
one is studying is permissible in principle; the algorithm discards most of the
possible questions and determines the placement in the tree of the remaining questions on the basis of training data. Thus, if one thinks a certain feature or combination of features in the data might conceivably be relevant to classification,
one should supply a question reflecting this aspect of the data to the algorithm
– if the aspect has little predictive value, the corresponding question will presumably not be chosen. In this way, one can go beyond the primary purpose of classification tree methodology – to generate from training data a set of rules for
predicting the category for new data items – by allowing the choice of question
for the trees to suggest which features of the data have the most predictive value.

The rule for selecting the best question at a node should always try to separate
as much as possible data items with different class labels. For the case where
there are only two labels represented in a node, the rule should always choose
the question that comes closest to putting all training data items with one
label in one child – say, the YES child – and all the items with the other label
in the other (NO) child. In Breiman *et al.* (1984), it is suggested to define a
measure of the *impurity* of a node with the following properties:

- The impurity is always non-negative.

- A node containing equal proportions of all possible categories has maximum impurity.
- A node containing only one of the possible categories has impurity of 0.0 (the minimum possible impurity).

One always chooses the question with the purest YES and NO children. More precisely, given a node τ, the question is chosen that maximizes the *drop of impurity* defined by the following relation:

$$\Delta\psi = \psi(\tau) - p(y)\psi(\text{YES}) - p(n)\psi(\text{NO}) \tag{B.1}$$

where $p(y)$ is the proportion of items at τ that the question will send to the YES node, $\psi(\text{YES})$ is the resulting impurity at that node, $p(n)$ is the proportion of items at τ that the question will send to the NO node, and $\psi(\text{NO})$ is the resulting impurity at that node.

There are several impurity functions, all of which depend only on the counts of each category within a node. In Breiman *et al.* (1984), several of these measures are considered. It was found that the performance of the tree is quite insensitive to the measure chosen, as long as it satisfies the properties listed above. This conclusion is confirmed by more recent studies (Murthy and Salzberg, 1995a,b; Murthy, 1995). Impurity functions can be grouped into classes, the most popular ones are based on information or entropy, on distance and dependency measures.

Let a training set have y and n elements assigned respectively to subtrees YES and NO of node τ. The *amount of information* of this classification $I(y, n)$ is expressed by:

$$I(y, n) = -\frac{y}{y+n} \log\left(\frac{y}{y+n}\right) - \frac{n}{y+n} \log\left(\frac{n}{y+n}\right) \tag{B.2}$$

Assuming that the question at node τ is about the value a_i $(i = 1, \ldots, N)$ of a feature A, let y_i and n_i be the numbers of objects in the training set having value a_i and assigned to YES and NO subtrees respectively, the expected information contributed by feature A is:

$$E(A) = \sum_{i=1}^{N} \frac{y_i + n_i}{y+n} I(y_i, n_i) \tag{B.3}$$

If the information gained by node τ asking a question about the value of feature A is the corresponding drop of impurity, then it can be expressed as follows:

$$\Delta\psi(A) = I(y, n) - E(A) \tag{B.4}$$

A distance-based impurity function is the Gini impurity defined as follows:

$$\psi(\tau) = \sum_{i \neq j} p(i|\tau)p(j|\tau) \tag{B.5}$$

where $p(i|\tau)$ is the probability that a sample in the training set has the answer YES to a question about feature i at node τ.

Clearly, the children of a given node will be less impure than their parent. If this process is carried out recursively to generate grandchildren, great-grand-children, and so on of the original root node, some of the descendants of the root may have impurity of 0. These nodes will be designated leaf nodes, and labelled with the name of the single category they contain. Other leaf nodes will be designated as such because there is no way of reducing the impurity any further, or because the best possible drop in impurity from the node to YES and NO children is too small, or because there are too few training data items in the node, or for some other reason. These leaf nodes will be labelled with the name of the most common category they contain; ties are broken arbitrarily. The criteria used to determine when a node should be prevented from splitting further by declaring it a leaf node are called the *stopping rules*. In Breiman *et al.* (1984), experiments are reported with a variety of stopping rules to obtain the best-sized tree. None of them achieved the desired goal of obtaining a tree with strong predictive power. Thus, a tree-growing strategy with two stages was ultimately adopted: first grow a tree that is much too large using a simple stopping rule, then prune the tree upwards from the leaves using an independent data set. The simple adopted stopping rule was to keep splitting nodes until, for each terminal node, either there are fewer than N items (N close to 1), or no improvement in impurity from a node to its children is possible. The tree obtained in this way is over-trained – it will pre-dict the training data perfectly, but perform poorly on new data. Hence, the tree must be pruned on new data. This growing–pruning strategy yielded better results than most sophisticated stopping rules, and is followed by most research-ers who use decision trees today.

However, the CART cross-validation pruning method described in Breiman *et al.* (1984) is not necessarily the best. In Kuhn and De Mori (1995) is suggested instead the iterative expansion pruning algorithm proposed by Gelfand *et al.* (1991). This algorithm is elegant, computationally cheap, simple to implement, and guaranteed to perform as well as or better than cross-validation pruning.

Finally, note that decision-tree growing is a greedy heuristic; there is no guar-antee whatsoever that the performance of a tree will be close to that of the opti-mal tree for the training data. It seems intuitively obvious that if enough computing power is available, questions for the internal nodes of a tree should be chosen so as to minimize the misclassification rate of the whole tree on the training data. Failing that, one might think it desirable to employ a look-ahead version of the algorithm in which the criterion is the impurity of the grandchildren or great-grandchildren of the current node, rather than the impurity of the children. Some fascinating recent work (Quinlan and Cameron-Jones, 1995; Murthy and Salzberg, 1995a,b; Murthy, 1995) shows that intuition is misleading in this case. Decision trees obtained by means of one-level greedy search frequently perform better on new data than look-ahead trees, or even than trees that are optimal for the training data. In other words, it is quite hard to improve on the simple greedy algorithm originally described in Breiman *et al.* (1984).

Appendix C

Speech Corpora

Renato De Mori[*] and Roland Kuhn[†]

Speech recognition technology has made rapid strides in the last two decades partly because the major US sponsor of research in this area, the Advanced Research Project Agency (ARPA), made funding for US speech recognition groups contingent on regular quantitative evaluations of their systems.

These evaluations involve two similar but disjoint data sets: the training set and the test set. The training set is released to system designers some time before the evaluation, and gives them a chance to fine-tune their systems. The test set is not released until the time of the evaluation; only results on this set are considered valid indicators of system performance.

As the performance of the technology improved, ARPA periodically defined new, more ambitious, benchmarks. At various times ARPA has tested digit recognition in continuous speech with the TIDIGIT corpus (see Normandin *et al.* (1994) for an overview of the corpus and recent results), read speech with a 1000-word vocabulary (the *Resource Management Task* (Price *et al.*, 1988)), and more recently, large-vocabulary read speech (the *Continuous*

---

[*]School of Computer Science, McGill University, Montreal, P.Q. H3A 2A7, Canada.
[†]Panasonic, Speech Technology Laboratory, 3888 State Street #202, Santa Barbara, CA 93105, USA.

Speech Recognition or *Wall Street Journal* evaluation), ATIS (Price *et al.*, 1991) and the SWITCHBOARD (Godfrey *et al.*, 1992).

These corpora are distributed by the Linguistic Data Consortium (LDC) in the US. The European Language Resources Association (ELRA) provide services for distributing corpora collected in Europe.

C.1. TIMIT

This corpus, developed at Texas Instruments and MIT (TIMIT), is a collection of continuous speech sentences fully segmented and labelled with phoneme symbols (Fisher *et al.*, 1987). It contains 6300 sentences, 10 sentences spoken by each of 630 speakers from eight major dialect regions of the US. The set contains dialect sentences, labelled *sa*, phonetically compact sentences, labelled *sx*, and phonetically diverse sentences, labelled *si*.

A training set is made of 3696 sentences. A test set is made of 1344 sentences.

C.2. RESOURCE MANAGEMENT

The Resource Management (RM) corpus consists of 3990 sentences, 2830 of which are pronounced by 78 male speakers and 1160 by 31 female speakers. There are four different test sets and a portion of the corpus for speaker-dependent experiments.

A word-pair grammar (bigrams without probabilities) is provided. It is constructed from the finite-state network used to construct the sentences of the corpus.

C.3. *WALL STREET JOURNAL*

The *Wall Street Journal* (*WSJ*) corpus contains passages read from the popular American financial newspaper. The corpus was collected using desktop and close-talking head microphones.

Part of the corpus contains verbalized punctuation. The WSJ0 section is for training and was collected asking the speaker to read the given prompts exactly as written. The WSJ1 portion was collected by letting the speakers use their normal speaking style. The two corpora contain more than 60 hours of speech.

C.4. NORTH AMERICAN BUSINESS

The North American Business (NAB) corpus is an extension of the *WSJ* corpus to include texts from other North American business publications. The total corpus contains close to 300 million words.

Various test sets were conceived for different purposes. They are described in SLS (1995).

C.5. ATIS

The importance of the ATIS (Air Travel Information System) test is that it evaluates not only speech recognition, but also speech understanding. A corpus of spoken questions about air travel, their written form, and their "translations" into the SQL database language was obtained, and then split into training and test corpora.

Systems were evaluated according to three benchmarks: SPREC (speech recognition performance), NL (natural language understanding of written transcriptions of the spoken sentences) and SLS (spoken language understanding). Note that even if the semantic module of each system operated on the output of the same recognizer, the semantic module with the best NL results might not be the same as the semantic module with the best SPREC results – errors introduced by the recognizer may be more easily overcome by some approaches than by others.

The first official ATIS evaluation took place in February 1991, after a dry run in June 1990. The database for the evaluation was extracted from the Official Airline Guide (OAG) database for airlines operating in North America by retaining only information about 11 cities. The metric penalized false answers more heavily than the response "No answer" by weighting the former twice as heavily as the latter. In the November 1992 evaluation, test utterances were classified as A (semantically independent of earlier sentences), D (semantically dependent on earlier sentences), or X (unevaluatable); both A and D utterances were evaluated. Furthermore, since people may have different ideas about exactly how much information should be given in response to a query, the November 1992 evaluation introduced the min-max criterion, in which all answers giving at least as much information as in ARPA's minimal answer and no more information than in ARPA's weighted error metric seemed to favour systems that yielded the unhelpful "No answer" response; when in doubt, this metric was dropped for the December 1993 evaluation and replaced by a metric in which false answers and "No answer" were penalized equally. The December 1993 evaluation was the first that used the expanded, 46-city, ATIS-3 database. This expansion increased the number of flights in the database by a factor of over 30.

C.6. SWITCHBOARD

This is a telephone corpus, which includes more than 2000 conversations carried on by about 500 volunteers of both sexes for major American dialects. The corpus contains time-aligned transcriptions at the word level and can be used for speaker verification as well.

C.7. EUROPEAN CORPORA

Interesting corpora have or are in development for various European languages. Among them, EUROM1 contains more than 60 speakers per language recorded in the same conditions in eight European languages. Worth noting are the POLYPHONE databases in various languages and the corpora containing phonetically rich sentences, namely BREF for French, PhonDat for German, Groningen for Dutch and APASCI for Italian.

Corpora for newspaper dictation are the British version of *WSJ*, the German *Frankfurter Rundschau*, the French *Le Monde* and the Italian *Il Sole 24 Ore*. Worth noting is the Spanish geographic corpus. A multilanguage pronunciation dictionary, called ONOMASTICA, is also available.

Appendix D

Formal Equations of Agent Behaviour

Giuliano Antoniol,[*] Roberto Fiutem[*] and Renato De Mori[†]

Complex systems are composed of several parts, each acting concurrently with and independently of other parts. Coordination among parts is achieved through communication. The central idea to describe these systems is that parts whose identity persists through time, could be identified and called *agents*. Each action of an agent is either an interaction with its neighbouring agents (i.e., a communication) or an independent activity. Part of the communication theory is a notion of *behaviour* defined as the entire capability of communicating. It may be argued that behaviour is exactly what is observable and observing a system corresponds to communicating with it.

A formal specification of a client–server ASR system in term of agents and their behaviour is presented here. It is expressed with a formal language called Calculus of Communicating Systems (CCS) a general theory of processes described in Milner (1989).

Let an agent A be a single cell, which may hold a single data item. The agent reads a data input and copies it on its output. This is represented formally by the following equations:

$$A \stackrel{\text{def}}{=} in(x) \, . \, A'(x) \tag{D.1}$$

$$A'(x) \stackrel{\text{def}}{=} \overline{out}(x) \, . \, A \tag{D.2}$$

[*]Istituto per la Ricerca Scientifica e Tecnologica – 38050 Pantè di Povo, Trento, Italy.
[†]School of Computer Science, McGill University, Montréal, P.Q. H3A 2A7, Canada.

Figure D.1 Agents forming a buffer.

These equations recursively define two agents A and A', one in terms of the other. A' has an internal variable x. $in(x)$ represents a *handshake* in which a value is received at the input port *in*. This value binds variable x.

$in(x) . A'(x)$ is an agent expression, whose behaviour is to perform the handshake and proceed according to the definition of $A'(x)$. Analogously, $\overline{out}(x)$ means that the value x is output at port $\overline{out}$ of agent A'. There are two ways in which a variable is given a scope:

- by its occurrence in an input prefix like $in(x)$ (in such a case the scope is the agent expression beginning with $in(x)$)
- by its occurrence as a formal parameter on the left side of a defining equation as in $A'(x) \stackrel{\text{def}}{=} \overline{out}(x) . A$ and its scope is the whole equation:

$$A \stackrel{\text{def}}{=} in(x) . A'(x) \tag{D.3}$$

$$A'(y) \stackrel{\text{def}}{=} \overline{out}(y) . A \tag{D.4}$$

or in a more concise way:

$$A \stackrel{\text{def}}{=} in(x) . \overline{out}(x) . A$$

Systems can also be represented graphically by *flow graphs*, where agents are represented as circles, containing the agent name; small blobs are the input/ output ports and arrows stand for communication actions. An agent can be connected with other agents forming a more complex system: for example, in Figure D.1 a buffer with capacity of n tokens is represented as the concatenation of n elementary cells C resulting in a more complex agent described by the equations:

$$Buff_n\langle \varepsilon \rangle \stackrel{\text{def}}{=} in(s) . Buff_n\langle s \rangle \tag{D.5}$$

$$Buff_n\langle s_1, \ldots, s_m \rangle \stackrel{\text{def}}{=} in(y) . Buff_n\langle y, s_1, \ldots, s_m \rangle$$
$$+ \overline{out(s_m)} . Buff_n\langle s_1, \ldots, s_{m-1} \rangle, \quad 1 < m < n \tag{D.6}$$

$$Buff_n\langle s_1, \ldots, s_n \rangle \stackrel{\text{def}}{=} \overline{out(s_n)} . Buff_n\langle s_1, \ldots, s_{n-1} \rangle \tag{D.7}$$

The operator "$+$" means that $P + Q$ behaves like agent P or Q, i.e., as soon as one performs its action, the other is discarded. Generally speaking, $P + Q$ is a non-deterministic choice resulting in the behaviour of P in one occasion and of Q in others.

D.1. SERVER EQUATIONS

The previous equations represent a high-level abstraction of a recognition engine. Sentences, to be recognized, are represented by items s_j belonging to a sequence $\langle s_1, \ldots, s_m \rangle$ and $Buff_n\langle \varepsilon \rangle$ is the empty *recognizer*. As far as there are sentences to be recognized, i.e., buffer items, the recognizer could produce a recognized sentence, $out(s)$, decreasing the buffer occupation. Alternatively, the system could enqueue (up to the buffer limit) new input data. The non-deterministic behaviour accounts for the inability to predict the amount of time spent in recognizing a particular signal fragment (several utterances can occur before recognition results are returned). Therefore, there must be a buffer and its dimension depends upon the host resources, the application task (command and control or dictation), the presence or absence of other buffers in the system, etc.

To describe a system composed of two subsystems running concurrently, the operator | is used to represent *composition*. $P|Q$ is a system in which P and Q may proceed independently but may also interact through complementary ports. The composition operator can be used to formalize systems where the number of agents increases, up to a limit or indefinitely:

$$S(k) \stackrel{\text{def}}{=} port(r) . getl(x) . P(x, r, k+1) \tag{D.8}$$

$$P(x, r, k) \stackrel{\text{def}}{=} \overline{putl(x - g(r))} . (A(r, k) | S(k+1)), \quad 0 < k < MAX \tag{D.9}$$

$$P_{x,r,MAX} \stackrel{\text{def}}{=} \overline{putl(x)} . S(MAX - 1), \quad k = MAX - 1 \tag{D.10}$$

A supervisor is a server $S(k)$ with k recognizers already active, $A(r, k)$. Its behaviour, formalized by equations (D.8)–(D.10), is described as follows. Read from *port* the required service (r), input the available amount of system resources $getl(x)$, decrease system resources by a function $g(\ )$ of the client request r, create a new agent $A(r, k)$ to provide the service and proceed concurrently with it; if the maximum number of agents is already active, then the supervisor does not create new processes. Resource locking and critical regions are assured by a resource manager which forces the correct sequence of $getl$, $putl$ operations:

$$Res(x) \stackrel{\text{def}}{=} \overline{putl(x)} . getl(z) . Res(z)$$

To complete the example, it is realistic to imagine that, once some actions are performed, $A(r, k)$ resources are released with notification of the conclusion of the work to the server. This is formally represented as:

$$A(r, k) \stackrel{\text{def}}{=} \overline{actions} . A(r, k) + E(r, k)$$

$$E(r, k) \stackrel{\text{def}}{=} \overline{done} . STOP$$

$$S(k) \stackrel{\text{def}}{=} port(r) . getl(x) . P(x, r, k+1)$$
$$+ done . getl(x) . \overline{putl(x + g(r))} . S(k - 1)$$

Equation (D.8) was rewritten to accommodate the presence of a variable number of servers in the system. Details can be added like process handshaking, resource negotiation and error management.

In the following, a more realistic example derived from the A.Re.S system design will be presented. A client starts a recognition session with a handshake on a port of a supervisor, S in which it communicates its request r. The corresponding supervisor specification does not change from equation (D.8). However, since resources, x, are finite, the supervisor can accept or refuse client requests. Furthermore, having knowledge of the current system configuration, the supervisor can return to the client the address of an already existing recognizer matching the client's request, to be shared among other applications, or decide to create a new recognition server, *SRec*, with an amount of resources which is a function *rec( )* of the service:

$$P(x,r,k) \overset{\text{def}}{=} \overline{putl(x - g(s) - rec(s))} \cdot \overline{out(p(s))} \cdot (SRec(s,p(s))|S(k+1))$$
$$+ \overline{putl(x - g(s))} \cdot \overline{out(p(s))} \cdot S(k)$$

In both cases, s represents the actually offered service which may or may not coincide with r, the requested one. The environment resources are decreased by the amount $g(s)$, assigned to the client and $p(s)$ represents a port where the service s is supplied.

To avoid deadlock or to maintain an adequate service level, the server could refuse the connection, for example, when resources reach a minimum level or the maximum number of processes are already active:

$$P(MIN,r,k) \overset{\text{def}}{=} \overline{putl(MIN)} \cdot \overline{refuse} \cdot S(k)$$

$$P(x,r,MAX) \overset{\text{def}}{=} \overline{putl(x)} \cdot \overline{refuse} \cdot S(MAX)$$

The recognition server *SRec* represents a sleeping recognizer waiting for clients: once the first client acknowledges the offered service, it starts the active recognizer, *Rec*, on port p (subscripts p specify that the communication action is referred to the pth recognizer), and recognition engine buffer $B_{n,s,p,1}$ (a buffer with capacity n on the port p corresponding to s resources and one connected client):

$$SRec(s,p) \overset{\text{def}}{=} listen_p \cdot \overline{service_p(s)} \cdot accepted_p \cdot (B_{n,s,p,1}\langle \varepsilon \rangle | Rec(s,p))$$
$$+ listen_p \cdot \overline{service_p(s)} \cdot rejected_p \cdot getl(x) \cdot \overline{putl(x + g(s))} \cdot SRec(s,p)$$
$$+ killrec(s) \cdot Release(s,p)$$

The system supervisor, S, may decide to close some service by killing recognizer processes or recognition servers broadcasting a specific signal. Therefore, both recognizers and recognition servers are aware of the *killrec(s)* signal which causes processes to release resources and stop according to the following equation:

$$Release(s,p) \stackrel{\text{def}}{=} getl(x) . \overline{putl(x + rec(s))} . STOP$$

A recognizer *Rec* waits for its clients, informs them of the services it can perform and, if the service is accepted, connects them to the buffer $B_{n,s,p,c}$ (modelled with the handshake $connect_p$). The offered service could differ in terms of speech sampling rate, type of signal processing, acoustic or language model used, etc. The application could accept or reject a request as shown by the following equation:

$$Rec(s,p) \stackrel{\text{def}}{=} listen_p . \overline{service_p(s)} . accepted_p . \overline{connect_p} Rec(s,p)$$

$$+ listen_p . \overline{service_p(s)} . reject_p . getl(x) . \overline{putl(x + rec(s))} . Rec(s,p)$$

$$+ endrec_p . V(s,p) + killrec(s) . Release(s,p)$$

Whenever a buffer is empty with no connected clients, $B_{n,r,p,0}\langle\varepsilon\rangle$, it issues an $endrec_p$ signal to inform the recognizer. As a result, the recognizer will ask the supervisor whether or not it should let the system behave like the agent $V(s,p)$:

$$V(s,p) \stackrel{\text{def}}{=} \overline{exit(s)} . killrec(s) . Release(s,p) + \overline{exit(s)} . stay(s) . SRec(s,p)$$

The $B_{n,r,p,0}\langle\varepsilon\rangle$ agent releases resources and stops:

$$B_{n,r,p,0}\langle\varepsilon\rangle \stackrel{\text{def}}{=} \overline{endrec_p(s)} . STOP$$

The supervisor must maintain knowledge of system configuration and consistency, administering recognition engines according to its own policy. This is formally represented by rewriting equation (D.8) as follows:

$$S(k) \stackrel{\text{def}}{=} port(r) . getl(x) . \overline{P(x,r,k + 1)} + exit(s) . \overline{killrec(s)} . S(k - 1)$$

$$+ exit(s) . \overline{stay(s)} . S(k) + \overline{killrec(s)} . S(k - 1)$$

Buffer $B_{n,s,p,c}\langle \ldots \rangle$ is somewhat complex. In fact, being used with a recognition engine, it sends a speech fragment to its internal recognizer and waits in a nonblocking fashion (agent $W_{n,s,p,c}\langle \ldots \rangle$) until the recognition ends. Both $B_{n,s,p,c}\langle \ldots \rangle$ and $W_{n,s,p,c}\langle \ldots \rangle$ allow clients to connect and to enqueue sentences. Both manage communication errors or client crashes (represented as err_p) as well as the normal end of recognition sessions, $close_p$, by decreasing the active application number c:

$$B_{n,s,p,c}\langle s_1, \ldots, s_m \rangle \stackrel{\text{def}}{=} in(y) . B_{n,s,p,c}\langle y, s_1, \ldots, s_m \rangle$$

$$+ \overline{outrec_p(s_m)} . W_{n,s,p,c}\langle s_1, \ldots, s_{m-1} \rangle$$

$$+ err_p . getl(x) . \overline{putl(x + g(s))} . B_{n,s,p,c}\langle s_1, \ldots, s_m \rangle$$

$$+ close_p . getl(x) . \overline{putl(x + g(s))} . B_{n,s,p,c-1}\langle s_1, \ldots, s_m \rangle$$

$$+ connect_p . B_{n,s,p,c+1}\langle s_1, \ldots, s_m \rangle$$

$$W_{n,s,p,c}\langle s_1, \ldots, s_m \rangle \stackrel{\text{def}}{=} in(y) . W_{n,s,p,c}\langle y, s_1, \ldots, s_m \rangle$$

$$| \ err_p . getl(x) . \overline{putl(x + g(s))} . W_{n,s,p,c}\langle s_1, \ldots, s_m \rangle$$

$$+ close_p . getl(x) . \overline{putl(x + g(s))} . W_{n,s,p,c-1}\langle s_1, \ldots, s_m \rangle$$

$$+ connect_p . W_{n,s,p,c+1}\langle s_1, \ldots, s_m \rangle$$

$$+ inrec_p(ph_j) . \overline{phrase_p(ph_j)} . B_{n,s,p,c}\langle s_1, \ldots, s_m \rangle$$

Once a sentence is recognized, a notification $\overline{phrase_p(ph_n)}$ is issued to the client. Whenever the buffer reaches its capacity limit, it follows equation (D.7). Batch recognition processes require that, for a certain amount of time, some sentences are recognized without the presence of connected clients as represented by the following equation:

$$B_{n,r,p,0}\langle s_1, \ldots, s_m \rangle \stackrel{\text{def}}{=} \overline{outrec_p(s_m)} . inrec_p(ph_m) . \overline{store(ph_m)} . B_{n,r,p,0}\langle s_1, \ldots, s_{m-1} \rangle$$

$\overline{store(ph_j)}$ represents the act of storing the recognized sentence in a centralized repository for future processing. In the A.Re.S system, buffer $B_{n,r,p,c}\langle \ldots \rangle$ (and $W_{n,r,p,c}\langle \ldots \rangle$) are not aware of the *killrec* signal, therefore all the enqueued speech fragments are recognized and saved.

D.2. CLIENT EQUATIONS

Equations describing client behaviour must be in agreement with the supervisor, recognizer and buffer behaviours. For example, a service recognition session is started by a handshaking corresponding to the negotiation:

$$Client \stackrel{\text{def}}{=} \overline{port(r)} . out(p) . IsOk(r,p) + refuse . Client$$

$$IsOk(r,p) \stackrel{\text{def}}{=} \overline{listen_p} . service(s) . \overline{accepted_p} . Appl(r,p,s)$$

$$+ \overline{listen_p} . service(s) . \overline{rejected_p} . Client$$

Once the application, $Appl(r,p,s)$, has successfully obtained a recognizer address with resources s, which may or may not coincide with the requested r, it sends sentences to be recognized and reads results from the system:

$$Appl(r,p,s) \stackrel{\text{def}}{=} \overline{in_p(y)} . Appl(r,p,s) + \overline{close_p(s)} . Client$$

$$+ \overline{err_p} . Client + phrase_p(ph_j) . Appl(r,p,s)$$

Once again, the non-deterministic behaviour implied by the "+" operator corresponds to the application inability to predict when the next recognized sentence will be received.

Bibliography

Abney, S. (1993) Measures and models for phrase recognition. In *Arpa Human Language Technologies Workshop*. Morgan Kaufmann Publishers, San Mateo, California.

Abrash, V., Sankar, A., Franco, H. and Cohen, M. (1996) Acoustic adaptation using non-linear transformations of HMM parameters. In *Proceedings of the IEEE International Conference on Acoustics, Speech and Signal Processing*, II: 729–732, Atlanta, Georgia, USA.

Abu-Mostafa, Y. S. (1990) Learning from hints in neural networks. *Journal of Complexity*, 6: 192–198.

Acero, A. (1993) *Acoustical and Environmental Robustness in Automatic Speech Recognition*. Kluwer Academic Publishers, Boston, USA.

Acero, A. and Stern, R. (1990) Environmental robustness in automatic speech recognition. In *Proceedings of the IEEE International Conference on Acoustics, Speech and Signal Processing*, 849–852, Albuquerque, New Mexico, USA.

Adams, J. (1991) A new optimal window. *IEEE Transactions on Signal Processing*, 39(8): 1753–1769.

Adcock, J. E., Gotoh, Y., Mashao, D. and Silverman, H. (1996) Microphone-array speech recognition via incremental MAP training. In *Proceedings of the IEEE International Conference on Acoustics, Speech and Signal Processing*, II: 897–900, Atlanta, Georgia, USA.

Afify, M., Gong, Y. and Haton, J. P. (1996) A unified approach to acoustic mismatch compensation: application to Lombard speech recognition. In *International Conference on Acoustics, Speech and Signal Processing*, 839–842, Munich, Germany.

Afify, M., Gong, Y. and Haton, J. P. (1997a) Estimation of mixtures of stochastic dynamic trajectories: application to continuous speech recognition. *Computer Speech and Language*, 10(1): 23–36.

Ahadi, S. M. and Woodland, P. C. (1995) Rapid speaker adaptation using model prediction. In *Proceedings of the IEEE International Conference on Acoustics, Speech and Signal Processing*, I: 684–687, Detroit, Michigan, USA.

Ahadi-Sarkani, S. M. (1996) Bayesian and predictive techniques for speaker adaptation. Ph.D. thesis, Cambridge University, Cambridge, UK.

Aho, A., Hopcroft, J. and Ullman, J. (1974) *The Design and Analysis of Computer Algorithms*. Addison-Wesley, Reading, Massachusetts, USA.

Aho, A. V. and Ullman, J. D. (1972) *The Theory of Parsing, Translation and Compiling*. Prentice-Hall, Englewood Cliffs, New Jersey, USA.

Aikawa, K. and Furui, S. (1988). Spectral movement function and its application to speech recognition. In *Proceedings of the IEEE International Conference on Acoustics, Speech and Signal Processing*, 223–226, New York, USA.

Aikawa, K., Singer, H., Kawahara, H. and Tohkura, Y. (1993) A dynamic cepstrum incorporating time-frequency masking and its application to continuous speech recognition. In *Proceedings of the IEEE International Conference on Acoustics, Speech and Signal Processing*, 2: 668–671, Minneapolis, Minnesota, USA.

Alexandre, P. and Lockwood, P. (1993) Root cepstral analysis: a unified view, application to speech processing in car noise environments. *Speech Communication*, 12(3): 277–288.

Algazi, V. R., Brown, K. L., Ready, M. J., Irvine, D. H., Cadwell, C. L. and Chung, S. (1993) Transform representation of the spectra of acoustic speech segments with applications – General approach and application to speech recognition. *IEEE Transactions on Speech and Audio Processing*, 1(2): 180–195.

Allen, J. (1985) Cochlear modeling. *IEEE ASSP Magazine*, 2(1): 3–29.

Allen, J. (1987) *Natural Language Understanding*. The Benjamin/Cummings Publishing Company, Menlo Park, California, USA.

Allen, J. (1989) On the application of hearing models to digital signal processing problems. In *IEEE ASSP Workshop on Applications of Signal Processing to Audio and Acoustics*, Arden House, New York, USA.

Allen, J., Hunnicutt, M. and Klatt, D. (1987) *From Text to Speech: the MITalk System*. University Press, Cambridge, UK.

Allen, J. and Perrault, C. (1980) Analyzing intentions in utterances. *Artificial Intelligence*, 15(3): 143–178.

Allen, J. B. (1994) How do humans process and recognize speech? *IEEE Transactions on Speech and Audio Processing*, 2(4): 567–577.

Allen, J. B. (1996) Harvey Fletcher's role in the creation of communication acoustics. *Journal of the Acoustical Society of America*, 4(1): 1825–1839.

Allen, J. B. and Berkley, D. A. (1979) Image method for efficiently simulating small-room acoustics. *Journal of the Acoustical Society of America*, 65(4): 943–950.

Alleva, F., Huang, X. and Hwang, M.-Y. (1993) An improved search algorithm using incremental knowledge for continuous speech recognition. In *Proceedings of the IEEE International Conference on Acoustics, Speech and Signal Processing*, II: 307–310, Minneapolis, Minnesota, USA.

Alleva, F., Huang, X. and Hwang, M.-Y. (1996) Improvements on the pronunciation prefix tree search organization. In *Proceedings of the IEEE International Conference on Acoustics, Speech and Signal Processing*, 133–136, Atlanta, Georgia, USA.

Alvarado, V. M. (1990) Talker localization and optimal placement of microphones with a linear microphone array using stochastic region contraction. Ph.D. thesis, Brown University, Rhode Island, USA.

Anastasakos, A., Kubala, F., Makhoul, J. and Schwartz, R. (1994) Adaptation to new microphones using tied-mixture normalization. In *Proceedings of the IEEE International Conference on Acoustics, Speech and Signal Processing*, I: 433–436, Adelaide, Australia.

Anastasakos, A., Schwartz, R. and Sun, H. (1995) Duration modeling in large vocabulary speech recognition. In *Proceedings of the IEEE International Conference on Acoustics, Speech and Signal Processing*, 1: 628–631, Detroit, Michigan, USA.

Andre-Obrecht, R. (1988) A new statistical approach for the automatic segmentation of continuous speech signals. *IEEE Transactions on Acoustics, Speech and Signal Processing*, 36(1): 29–40.

Andry, F. and Thornton, S. (1991) A parser for speech lattices using a UCG grammar. In *Proceedings of the European Conference on Speech Communication and Technology*, 219–222, Genova, Italy.

Angelini, B., Antoniol, G., Brugnara, F., Cettolo, M., Federico, M., Fiutem, R. and Lazzari, G. (1994a) Radiological reporting by speech recognition: the A.Re.S. system. In *Proceedings of the International Conference on Spoken Language Processing*, 1267–1270, Yokohama, Japan.

Angelini, B., Brugnara, F., Falavigna, D., Giuliani, D., Gretter, R. and Omologo, M. (1994b) Speaker independent continuous speech recognition using an acoustic-phonetic Italian corpus. In *Proceedings of the International Conference on Spoken Language Processing*, 1391–1394, Yokohama, Japan.

Antoniol, G., Brugnara, F., Dalla Palma, F., Lazzari, G. and Moser, E. (1991) Gore, S. An interface for automating reporting by speech. In *Proceedings of the European Conference on Speech Communication and Technology*, Genova, Italy.

Antoniol, G., Fiutem, R., Flor, R. and Lazzari, G. (1993) Radiological reporting based on voice recognition, *Proceedings of East–West International Conference on Human–Computer Interaction* [EW-HCI93] Lecture Notes in Computer Science, Vol. 753, L. Bass, J. Gornostaer and C. Unger (Eds), Springer-Verlag, 1993.

Appelt, D. (1983) TELEGRAM: a grammar formalism for language planning. In *Proceedings of the International Joint Conference on Artificial Intelligence*, 595–599, Karlsruhe, Germany.

Appelt, D. (1992) *Planning English Sentences*. Cambridge University Press.

Appelt, D. (1996) Personal communication to R. Kuhn.

Appelt, D. and Jackson, E. (1992) SRI international February, 1992 ATIS benchmark test results. In *Proceedings of the 1992 DARPA Speech and Natural Language Workshop*, Palo Alto, California, USA.

Asadi, A., Lubensky, D., Mandhavrao, L., Naik, J., Raman, V. and Vysotsky, G. (1995) Combining speech algorithms into a natural language application of speech technology for telephone network services. In *Proceedings of the European Conference on Speech Communication and Technology*, 273–276, Madrid, Spain.

Asadi, A., Schwartz, R. and Makhoul, J. (1990) Automatic detection of new words in a large vocabulary continuous speech recognition system. In *Proceedings of the IEEE International Conference on Acoustics, Speech and Signal Processing*, 125–128, Albuquerque, New Mexico, USA.

Asadi, A., Schwartz, R. and Makhoul, J. (1991) Automatic modeling for adding new words to a large-vocabulary continuous speech recognition system. In *Proceedings of the IEEE International Conference on Acoustics, Speech and Signal Processing*, 305–308, Toronto, Canada.

Atal, B. S., Cuperman, V. and Gersho, A. (eds) (1993) *Speech and Audio Coding for Wireless and Network Applications*. Kluwer Academic Publishers, Norwell, Massachusetts, USA.

Atal, B. S. and Hanauer, L. (1971) Speech analysis and synthesis by linear prediction of the speech wave. *Journal of the Acoustical Society of America*, **50**: 637–655.

Atal, B. S. (1970a) Determination of the vocal tract shape directly from the speech wave. *Journal of the Acoustical Society of America*, **A47**(64).

Atal, B. S. (1970b) Speech analysis and synthesis by linear prediction of the speech wave. *Journal of the Acoustical Society of America*, **A47**(63).

Atal, B. (1974a) Effectiveness of linear prediction characteristics of the speech wave for automatic speaker identification and verification. *Journal of the Acoustical Society of America*, **55**(6): 1304–1312.

Atal, B. S. (1974b) Influence of pitch on formant frequencies and bandwidths obtained by linear prediction analysis. *Journal of the Acoustical Society of America*, **55**. Paper NN2, 87th Meeting ASA.

Aubert, X., Dugast, C., Ney, H. and Steinbiss, V. (1994) Large vocabulary continuous speech recognition of Wall Street journal data. In *Proceedings of the IEEE International Conference on Acoustics, Speech and Signal Processing*, **II**: 129–132, Adelaide, Australia.

Aubert, X., Haeb Umbach, R. and Ney, H. (1993) Continuous mixture densities and linear discriminant analysis for improved context-dependent acoustic models. In *Proceedings of the IEEE International Conference on Acoustics, Speech and Signal Processing*, **II**: 648–651, Minneapolis, Minnesota, USA.

Aubert, X. and Ney, H. (1995) Large vocabulary continuous speech recognition using word graphs. In *Proceedings of the IEEE International Conference on Acoustics, Speech and Signal Processing*, 49–52, Detroit, Michigan, USA.

Austin, J. (1962) *How To Do Things with Words*. Oxford University Press, Oxford, UK.

Austin, S., Ayuso, D. *et al.* (1991a) BBN HARC and DELPHI results on the ATIS benchmarks   February 1991. In *Proceedings of the DARPA Speech and Natural Language Workshop*, Morgan Kaufmann Publishers, Palo Alto, California, USA.

Austin, S., Schwartz, R. and Placeway, P. (1991b) The forward-backward search algorithm. In *Proceedings of the IEEE International Conference on Acoustics, Speech and Signal Processing*, 697–700, Toronto, Canada.

Bahl, L. and Jelinek, F. (1975) Decoding for channels with insertions, deletions and substitutions with applications to speech recognition. *IEEE Transactions on Information Theory*, **IT-21**: 404–411.

Bahl, L., Baker, J., Cohen, P., Cole, A., Jelinek, F., Lewis, B. and Mercer, R. (1978) Automatic recognition of continuously spoken sentences from a finite state grammar. In *IEEE International Conference on Acoustics, Speech and Signal Processing*, 418–421, Tulsa, Oklahoma, USA.

Bahl, L. R., Bellegarda, J. R., de Souza, P. V., Gopalakrishnan, P. S., Nahamoo, D. and Picheny, M. A. (1993b) Multonic Markov word models for large vocabulary continuous speech recognition. *IEEE Transactions on Speech and Audio Processing*, **1**(3): 334–344.

Bahl, L. R., Brown, P. F., de Souza, P. V. and Mercer, R. L. (1987) Speech recognition with continuous-parameter hidden Markov models. *Computer Speech and Language*, **2**(2): 219–234.

Bahl, L. R., Brown, P. F., de Souza, P. V. and Mercer, R. L. (1993c) Estimating hidden Markov model parameters so as to maximize speech recognition accuracy. *IEEE Transactions on Speech and Audio Processing*, **1**(1): 77–83.

Bahl, L. R., Brown, P. F., de Souza, P. V., Mercer, R. L. and Picheny, M. A. (1988) Acoustic Markov models used in the Tangora speech recognition system. In *Proceedings of the IEEE International Conference on Acoustics, Speech and Signal Processing*, 497–500, New York, USA.

Bahl, L. R., Brown, P. F., de Souza, P. V., Mercer, R. L. and Picheny, M. A. (1993d) A method for the construction of acoustic Markov models for words. *IEEE Transactions on Speech and Audio Processing*, **1**(4): 443–452.

Bahl, L. R., Brown, P. F., Souza, P. and Mercer, R. (1989a) A tree-based statistical language model for natural language speech recognition. *IEEE Transactions on Acoustics, Speech and Signal Processing*, **37**(7): 1001–1008.

Bahl, L. R., Das, S., de Souza, P. V., Epstein, M., Mercer, R. L., Merialdo, B., Nahamoo, D., Picheny, M. A. and Powell, J. (1991a) Automatic phonetic baseform determination. In *Proceedings of the IEEE International Conference on Acoustics, Speech and Signal Processing*, 173–176, Toronto, Canada.

Bahl, L. R., De Gennaro, S. V., Gopalakrishnan, P. S. and Mercer, R. L. (1993e) A fast approximate acoustic match for large vocabulary speech recognition. *IEEE Transactions on Speech and Audio Processing*, **1**(1): 59–67.

Bahl, L. R., de Souza, P. V., Gopalakrishnan, P. S., Nahamoo, D. and Picheny, M. (1991b) Decision trees for phonological rules in continuous speech. In *Proceedings of the IEEE International Conference on Acoustics, Speech and Signal Processing*, 185–188, Toronto, Canada.

Bahl, L., de Souza, P. V., Gopalakrishnan, P. S. and Picheny, M. A. (1993a) Context dependent vector quantization for continuous speech recognition. In *Proceedings of the IEEE International Conference on Acoustics, Speech and Signal Processing*, **II**: 632–635, Minneapolis, Minnesota, USA.

Bahl, L. R., de Souza, P. V., Gopalakrishnan, P. S., Kanevsky, D. S. and Nahamoo, D. (1992) Constructing candidate word lists using acoustically similar word groups. *IEEE Transactions on Signal Processing*, **40**(11): 2814–2816.

Bahl, L. R., Gopalakrishnan, P. S., Kanevsky, D. S. and Nahamoo, D. (1989b) Matrix fast match: a fast method for identifying a short list of candidate words for decoding. In *Proceedings of the IEEE International Conference on Acoustics, Speech and Signal Processing*, 345–347, Glasgow, Scotland, UK.

Bahl, L. R. and Jelinek, F. (1988) Apparatus and method for determining a likely word sequence from labels generated by an acoustic processor. *US Patent 4,748,670.*

Bahl, L. R., Jelinek, F. and Mercer, R. L. (1983) A maximum likelihood approach to continuous speech recognition. *IEEE Transactions on Pattern Analysis and Machine Intelligence*, **5**(2): 179–190.

Baker, J. (1975) The DRAGON system. An overview. *IEEE Transactions on Acoustics, Speech and Signal Processing*, **23**: 24–29.

Baker, J. K. (1979) Trainable grammars for speech recognition (Klatt, D. H. and Wolf, J. eds). In *Proceedings of the Spring Conference of the Acoustical Society of America*, 547–550, MIT, Cambridge, Massachusetts, USA.

Bakis, R. (1976) Continuous speech recognition via centiseconds acoustic states. In *Meeting of the Acoustical Society of America*, Washington, DC, April.

Baldi, P. and Hornik, K. (1989) Neural networks and principal component analysis: learning from examples without local minima. *Neural Networks*, **2**: 53–58.

Balestri, M., Lazzaretto, S., Salza, P. and Sandri, S. (1993) The CSELT system for Italian text-to-speech synthesis. In *Proceedings of the European Conference on Speech Communication and Technology*, **3**: 2091–2094, Berlin, Germany.

Barbosa, P. and Bailly, G. (1994) Characterization of rhythmic patterns for text-to-speech synthesis. *Speech Communication*, **15**: 127–138.

Bar-Shalom, Y. and Fortmann, T. E. (1988) *Tracking and Data Association*. Academic Press, London, UK.

Bartkova, K., Dubois, D., Jouvet, D. and Monne, J. (1995) Error analysis on field data and improved garbage HMM. In *Proceedings of the European Conference on Speech Communication and Technology*, 1275–1278, Madrid, Spain.

Barwise, J. and Perry, J. (1983) *Situations and Attitudes*. MIT Press, Cambridge, Massachusetts, USA.

Bass, L. and Coutaz, J. (1991) *Developing Software for the User Interface*. Addison-Wesley Publishing Company, Reading, Massachusetts, USA.

Basseville, M. (1989) Distance measures for signal processing and pattern recognition. *Signal Processing*, **18**: 349–369.

Bateman, J. (1992) The theoretical status of ontologies in natural language processing. In *KIT-FAST Workshop on Text Representation and Domain Modelling – Ideas from Linguistics and AI*, 50–99, Technical University of Berlin, Germany.

Bateman, J., Kasper, R., Moore, J. and Whitney, R. (1990) A general organization of the knowledge for natural language processing: the Penman upper model. Technical report, Information Sciences Institute of the University of Southern California, Marina del Rey, California, USA.

Bates, J. and Lavie, A. (1994) Recognizing substrings of LR(κ) languages in linear time. *ACM Transactions on Programming Languages and Systems*, **16**(3): 1051–1077.

Bates, M. (1994) Models of natural language understanding. In Roe, D. and Wilpon, J., (eds), *Voice Communication between Humans and Machine*, 238–253, National Academy of Sciences, Washington, DC, USA.

Bates, M., Bobrow, R., Fung, P., Ingria, R., Kubula, F., Makhoul, J., Nguyen, L., Schwartz, R. and Stallard, D. (1992) Design and performance of HARC, the BBN spoken language understanding system. In *Proceedings of the International Conference on Spoken Language Processing*, **1**: 241–244, Banff, Canada.

Bates, M., Bobrow, R. *et al.* (1993) The BBN/HARC spoken language understanding system. In *Proceedings of the IEEE International Conference on Acoustics, Speech and Signal Processing*, **II**: 111–114, Minneapolis, Minnesota, USA.

Bates, M., Bobrow, R. *et al.* (1994) Advances in BBN's spoken language system. In *Proceedings of the Spoken Language Technology Workshop*, 43–47, Plainsboro, Jersey, Morgan Kaufmann Publishers, Palo Alto, California, USA.

Bates, M. and Lavie, A. (1994) Recognizing substrings of LRS(k)s languages in linear time. *ACM Transaction on Programming Languages and Systems*, **16**(3): 1051–1077.

Batteau, D. W. (1967) The role of the pinna in human localization. *Proceedings of the Royal Society of London*, **B168**: 158–180.

Battiti, R. (1989) Accelerated backpropagation learning: Two optimization methods. *Complex Systems*, **3**: 331–342.

Baum, L. E. (1972) An inequality and associated maximization technique in statistical estimation for probabilistic functions of Markov process. *Inequalities*, **3**: 1–8.

Baum, L. E. and Eagon, J. A. (1967) An inequality with applications to statistical estimation for probabilistic functions of Markov processes and to a model for ecology. *Bulletin of American Mathematical Society*, **73**: 360–363.

Baum, L. E., Petrie, T., Soules, G. and Weiss, N. (1970) A maximization technique occurring in the statistical analysis of probabilistic functions of Markov chains. *Annals of Mathematical Statistics*, **41**(1): 164–171.

Baum, L. E. and Sell, G. R. (1968) Growth transformations for functions on manifolds. *Pacific Journal of Mathematics*, **27**(2): 211–227.

BBN (1993) BBN demos real-time, large vocabulary, speaker-independent continuous recognition. ASRNews.

Beet, S. (1990) Automatic speech recognition using a reduced auditory representation and position-tolerant discrimination. *Computer Speech and Language*, **4**: 17–33.

Beet, S., Powrie, H., Moore, R. and Tomlinson, R. (1988) Improved speech recognition using a reduced auditory representation. In *Proceedings of the IEEE International Conference on Acoustics, Speech and Signal Processing*, 75–78, New York, USA.

Bellegarda, J. R. and Nahamoo, D. (1990) Tied mixture continuous parameter modeling for speech recognition. *IEEE Transactions on Acoustics, Speech and Signal Processing*, **38**(12): 2033–2045.

Bellegarda, J. R., de Souza, P. V., Nádas, A. J., Nahamoo, D., Picheny, M. A. and Bahl, L. R. (1994) The metamorphic algorithm: A speaker mapping approach to data augmentation. *IEEE Transactions on Speech and Audio Processing*, **2**(3): 413–419.

Bellegarda, J. R., de Souza, P. V., Nahamoo, D., Padmanabhan, M., Picheny, M. A. and Bahl, L. R. (1995) Experiments using data augmentation for speaker adaptation. In *Proceedings of the IEEE International Conference on Acoustics, Speech and Signal Processing*, **I**: 692–695, Detroit, Michigan, USA.

Belrhali, R., Aubergé, V. and Boë, L.-J. (1992) From lexicon to rules: toward a descriptive method of French text-to-phonetics transcription. In *Proceedings of the International Conference on Spoken Language Processing*, 1183–1186, Banff, Canada.

Benello, J., Mackie, A. and Anderson, J. (1989) Syntactic category disambiguation with neural networks. *Computer Speech and Language*, **3**: 207–217.

Bengio, S. and Bengio, Y. (1996) An EM algorithm for asynchronous input/output hidden Markov models. In Xu, L. (ed.) *International Conference on Neural Information Processing*, Hong Kong.

Bengio, Y. (1996) *Neural Networks for Speech and Sequence Recognition*. International Thomson Computer Press, London, UK.

Bengio, Y. and Frasconi, P. (1995a) Diffusion of context and credit information in Markovian models. *Journal of Artificial Intelligence Research*, **3**: 223–244.

Bengio, Y. and Frasconi, P. (1995b) An input/output HMM architecture. In Tesauro, G., Touretzky, D. and Leen, T. (eds) *Advances in Neural Information Processing Systems 7*, 427–434, MIT Press, Cambridge, Massachusetts, USA.

Bengio, Y., De Mori, R., Flammia, G. and Kompe, R. (1991) Phonetically motivated acoustic parameters for continuous speech recognition using artificial neural networks. In *Proceedings of the European Conference on Speech Communication and Technology*, Genova, Italy, 1007–1010.

Bengio, Y., De Mori, R., Flammia, G. and Kompe, R. (1992a) Global optimization of a neural network-hidden Markov model hybrid. *IEEE Transactions on Neural Networks*, 3(2): 252–259.

Bengio, Y., De Mori, R., Flammia, G. and Kompe, R. (1992b) Phonetically motivated acoustic parameters for continuous speech recognition using artificial neural networks. *Speech Communication*, 11(2–3): 261–271.

Bengio, Y., LeCun, Y. and Henderson, D. (1994) Globally trained handwritten word recognizer using spatial representation, space displacement neural networks and hidden Markov models. In Cowan, J., Tesauro, G. and Alspectro, J. (eds) *Advances in Neural Information Processing Systems 6*, 937–944.

Beppu, T. and Aikawa, K. (1995) Spontaneous speech recognition using dynamic cepstra incorporating forward and backward masking effect. In *Proceedings of the European Conference on Speech Communication and Technology*, 1: 511–514, Madrid, Spain.

Berkhout, A. J., de Vries, D. and Boone, M. M. (1980) A new method to acquire impulse responses in concert halls. *Journal of the Acoustical Society of America*, 68(1): 179–183.

Berouti, M., Schwartz, R. and Makhoul, J. (1979) Enhancement of speech corrupted by acoustic noise. In *Proceedings of the IEEE International Conference on Acoustics, Speech and Signal Processing*, 208–211, Washington, DC, USA.

Besling, S. and Meier, H. (1995) Language model speaker adaptation. In *Proceedings of the European Conference on Speech Communication and Technology*, 3: 1755–1758, Madrid, Spain.

Beulen, K., Welling, L. and Ney, H. (1995) Experiments with linear feature extraction in speech recognition. In *Proceedings of the European Conference on Speech Communication and Technology*, 1415–1418, Madrid, Spain.

Bienvenu, J. and Kopp, L. (1980) Adaptivity to background noise spatial coherence for high resolution passive methods. In *Proceedings of the IEEE International Conference on Acoustics, Speech and Signal Processing*, 307–310, Denver, Colorado, USA.

Bigorgne, D., Boeffard, O., Cherbonnel, B., Emerard, F., Larreur, D., Saint-Milon, J. L., Metayer, I., Sorin, C. and White, S. (1993) Multilingual PSOLA text-to-speech system. In *Proceedings of the IEEE International Conference on Acoustics, Speech and Signal Processing*, 2: 187–190, Minneapolis, Minnesota, USA.

Bilange, E. (1992) *Dialogue Personne-Machine: Modelisation et Realisation Informatique*. Hermes, Paris, France.

Bird, S. and Ellison, T. M. (1994) One-level phonology: autosegmental representations and rules as finite automata. *Computational Linguistics*, 20(1). 55–90.

Bishop, C. M. (1995) *Neural Networks for Pattern Recognition*. Oxford University Press, Oxford, UK.

Bishop, K. (1994) Modeling sentential stress in the context of a large vocabulary continuous speech recognizer. In *Proceedings of the International Conference on Spoken Language Processing*, 437–440, Banff, Canada.

Black, E., Jelinek, F., Lafferty, J., Magerman, D. M., Mercer, R. and Roukos, S. (1993) Towards history-based grammars: using richer models for probabilistic parsing. In *Proceedings of the Annual Meeting of the Association for Computational Linguistics*, 31–37, Ohio State University, Columbus, Ohio, USA.

Blauert, J. (1983) *Spatial Hearing*. MIT Press, Cambridge, Massachusetts, USA.

Blomberg, M., Carlson, R., Elenius, K., Granstrom, B., Gustafson, J., Hunnicutt, S., Lindell, R. and Neovius, L. (1993) An experimental dialogue system: WAXHOLM. In *Proceedings of the European Conference on Speech Communication and Technology*, 1867–1870, Berlin, Germany.

Bobrow, R. and Webber, B. (1980) Knowledge representation for syntactic/semantic processing. In *Proceedings of National Conference on Artificial Intelligence*, 99–107, Washington D.C., USA.

Bobrow, R., Ingria, R. and Stallard, D. (1990) Syntactic and semantic knowledge in the DELPHI unification grammar. In *Proceedings of Speech and Natural Language Workshop*, 230–236, Hidden Valley, Pennsylvania, Morgan Kaufmann Publishers, Palo Alto, California, USA.

Bocchieri, E. L. and Wilpon, J. G. (1993) Discriminative feature selection for speech recognition. *Computer Speech and Language*, 7: 229–246.

Bodden, M. (1993) Modeling human sound-source localization and the cocktail-party-effect. *Acta Acustica*, 1: 43–55.

Boiteau, D. and Haffner, P. (1993) Connectionist segmental post-processing of the n-best solutions in isolated and connected word recognition task. In *Proceedings of the European Conference on Speech Communication and Technology*, 1933–1936, Berlin, Germany.

Bondarko, L., Zagoruiko, N., Kozhevnikov, V., Molchanov, A. and Chistovich, L. (1968) *The Model of Speech Perception By Humans*. Nauka, Novisibirsk, USSR (in Russian).

Bonneau-Mightnard, H., Gauvain, J.-L., Goodine, D., Lamel, L., Polifroni, J. and Seneff, S. (1993) A French version of the MIT-ATIS system: portability issues. In *Proceedings of Eurospeech '93*, Berlin, Germany.

Bottou, L. (1991) Une approche théorique de l'apprentissage connexioniste; applications à la reconnaissance de la parole. Ph.D. thesis, Université de Paris XI, France.

Bourlard, H., D'hoore, B. and Boite, J. (1994) Optimizing recognition and rejection performance in wordspotting systems. In *Proceedings of the IEEE International Conference on Acoustics, Speech and Signal Processing*, I: 373–376, Adelaide, Australia.

Bourlard, H. and Dupont, S. (1997) Sub-band based speech recognition. In *International Conference on Acoustics, Speech and Signal Processing*, 1251–1254, Munich, Germany.

Bourlard, H., Hermansky, H. and Morgan, N. (1996) Towards increasing speech recognition error rates. *Speech Communication*, 18: 205–231.

Bourlard, H. and Kamp, Y. (1988) Auto-association by multilayer perceptrons and singular value decomposition. *Biological Cybernetics*, 59: 291–294.

Bourlard, H. and Morgan, N. (1994) *Connectionist Speech Recognition. A Hybrid Approach*, volume 247 of The Kluwer International Series in Engineering and Computer Science. Kluwer Academic Publishers, Boston, Massachusetts, USA.

Bradford, J. H. (1995) The human factors of speech-based interfaces. *SIGCHI Bulletin*, 27(2): 61–67.

Brandstein, M. S. (1995) A framework for speech source localization using sensor arrays. Ph.D. thesis, Brown University, Rhode Island, USA.

Brandstein, M. S., Adcock, J. E. and Silverman, H. F. (1995) A practical time-delay estimator for localizing speech sources with a microphone array. *Computer Speech and Language*, 9(2): 153–169.

Brandstein, M. S., Adcock, J. E. and Silverman, H. F. (1996) Microphone array localization error estimation with application to sensor placement. *Journal of the Acoustical Society of America*, 99(6): 3807–3816.

Brandstein, M. S., Adcock, J. E. and Silverman, H. F. (1997) A closed-form location estimator for use with room environment microphone arrays. *IEEE Transactions on Speech and Audio Processing*, 5(1): 45–50.

Breiman, L., Friedman, J., Olshen, R. and Stone, C. (1984) *Classification and Regression Trees*. Wadsworth, Pacific Grove, California, USA.

Bretier, P. (1995) La communication orale coopérative: contribution à la modélisation logique et à la mise en oeuvre d'un agent rationnel dialoguant. Ph.D. thesis, Universite de Paris XIII, France.

Bretier, P., Panaget, F. and Sadek, M. D. (1995) Integrating linguistic capabilities in the formal model of a rational agent: application to cooperative spoken dialogue. In *Proceedings of the AAAI '95, Fall Symposium on Rational Agency*, Cambridge, Massachusetts, USA.

Bretier, P. and Sadek, M. (1995) Designing and implementing a theory of rational interaction to be the kernel of a cooperative spoken dialogue system. In *Proceedings of the AAAI '95, Fall Symposium on Rational Agency*, Cambridge, Massachusetts, USA.

Bridle, J. S. (1973) An efficient elastic template method for detecting keywords in running speech. In *British Acoustical Society Meeting*, April, 1–4.

Bridle, J. S. (1990a) Alphanets: a recurrent 'neural' network architecture with a hidden Markov model interpretation. *Speech Communication*, 9(1): 83–92.

Bridle, J. S. (1990b) Training stochastic model recognition algorithms as networks can lead to maximum mutual information estimation of parameters. In Touretzky, D. (ed.) *Advances in Neural Information Processing Systems 2*, 211–217, Morgan Kaufmann Publishers, San Mateo, California, USA.

Bridle, J. S. and Brown, M. D. (1974) An experimental automatic word recognition system. *JSRU Research Report*, No. 1003, Malvern, UK.

Broomhead, D. and Lowe, D. (1988) Multivariable functional interpolation and adaptive networks. *Complex Systems*, 2: 321–355.

Brown, K. L. and Algazi, V. R. (1991) Speech recognition using dynamic features of acoustic subword spectra. In *Proceedings of the IEEE International Conference on Acoustics, Speech and Signal Processing*, 1: 293–296, Toronto, Canada.

Brown, M. K. and Buntschuh, B. M. (1994) A context-free grammar compiler for speech understanding systems. In *Proceedings of the International Conference on Spoken Language Processing*, 21–24, Yokohama, Japan.

Brown, P., Della Pietra, S., Della Pietro, V. J. and Mercer, R. L. (1993) The mathematics of statistical machine translation: parameter estimation. *Computational Linguistics*, 19(2): 263–311.

Brown, P., Lee, C.-H. and Spohrer, J. (1983) Bayesian adaptation in speech recognition. In *Proceedings of the IEEE International Conference on Acoustics, Speech and Signal Processing*, II: 761–764, Boston, Massachusetts, USA.

Brown, P., Pietra, A. D., Della Pietra, V. and Mercer, R. (1995) The mathematics of statistical machine translation: parameter estimation. *Computational Linguistics*, 19(2): 263–312.

Brown, P. F. (1987) *The acoustic-modeling problem in automatic speech recognition*. Ph.D. dissertation, Carnegie Mellon University, Pittsburg, Pennsylvania, USA.

Brown, P. F., Della Pietra, V. J., de Souza, P. V., Lai, J. C. and Mercer, R. L. (1992a) Class-based *n*-gram models of natural language. *Computational Linguistics*, 18(4): 467–479.

Brown, P. F., Della Pietra, V. J., Mercer, R. L., Della Pietra, S. A. and Lai, J. C. (1992b). An estimate of an upper bound of the entropy of English. *Computational Linguistics*, 18(1): 31–40.

Bruce, B. (1975). Case systems for natural language. *Artificial Intelligence*, 6: 327–360.

Bruce, R. and Wiebe, J. (1994) A new approach to word sense disambiguation. In *Proceedings of the Human Technology Workshop*, 244–249, Plaisboro, New Jersey, Morgan Kaufmann, Publishers, Palo Alto, California, USA.

Brugnara, F. and Cettolo, M. (1995) Improvements in tree-based language model representation. In *Proceedings of the European Conference on Speech Communication and Technology*, 1797–1800, Madrid, Spain.

Brugnara, F., Falavigna, D. and Omologo, M. (1993) Automatic segmentation and labeling of speech based on hidden Markov models. *Speech Communication*, 12: 357–370.

Brugnara, F. and Federico, M (1996) Techniques for approximating a trigram language model. In *Proceedings of the International Conference on Spoken Language Processing*, 2075–2078, Philadelphia, Pennsylvania, USA.

Brugnara, F., De Mori, R., Giuliani, D. and Omologo, M. (1992a) A family of parallel hidden Markov models. In *Proceedings of the IEEE International Conference on Acoustics, Speech and Signal Processing*, 377–380, San Francisco, California, USA.

Brugnara, F., De Mori, R., Giuliani, D. and Omologo, M. (1992b) Improved connected digit recognition using spectral variation functions. In *Proceedings of the International Conference on Spoken Language Processing*, 1: 627–630, Banff, Canada.

Brunelli, R. and Falavigna, D. (1995) Person identification using multiple cues. *IEEE Transactions on Pattern Analysis and Machine Intelligence*, 17(10): 955–966.

Bunt, H. (1987) Utterance generation from semantic representations augmented with pragmatic information. In K. G. (ed.) *Natural Language Generation: New Results in Artificial Intelligence, Psychology and Linguistics*, 333–348, Nijhoff, Boston, Massachusetts, USA.

Buzo, A., Gray, A. H., Gray, R. M. and Markel, J. D. (1980) Speech coding based upon vector quantization. *IEEE Transactions on Acoustics, Speech and Signal Processing*, 28(5): 562–574.

Cacciatore, T. W. and Nowlan, S. (1994) Mixtures of controllers for jump linear and non-linear plants. In Cowan, J. D., Tesauro, G. and Alspector, J. (eds) *Advances in Neural Information Processing Systems*, 6: 719–726, Morgan Kaufmann Publishers, San Mateo, California, USA.

Cadzow, J. (1990) Signal processing via least squares error modeling. *IEEE ASSP Magazine*, 7(4): 12–31.

Capman, F., Boudy, J. and Lockwood, P. (1995) Acoustic echo cancellation using a fast QR-RLS algorithm and multirate schemes. In *Proceedings of the IEEE International Conference on Acoustics, Speech and Signal Processing*, 969–972, Detroit, Michigan, USA.

Carberry, S. (1990) *Plan Recognition in Natural Language*. The MIT Press.

Carlson, R. (1994) Models of speech synthesis. In Roe, D. and Wilpon J. (eds) *Voice Communications Between Humans and Machines*, National Academy of Sciences, Washington D.C., USA.

Carlson, R. and Granstrom, B. (1975) A phonetically oriented programming language for rule description of speech. In Fant, G. (ed.) *Speech Communication*, 2: 2095–2098, Almvquist, Stockholm, Sweden.

Carpenter, G. and Grossberg, S. (1987) ART2: self-organization of stable category recognition codes for analog input patterns. *Applied Optics*, 26: 4919–4930.

Carpenter, G. and Grossberg, S. (1988) The ART of adaptive pattern recognition by a self-organizing neural network. *Computer*, 22: 77–88.

Carrol, J. and Mack, R. (1995) Metaphor, computing systems and active learning. *International Journal of Man-Machine Studies*, 22(1): 39–57.

Casacuberta, F., Vidal, E., Mas, B. and Rulot, H. (1990) Learning the structure of HMM's through grammatical inference techniques. In *Proceedings of the IEEE International Conference on Acoustics, Speech and Signal Processing*, 717–720, Albuquerque, New Mexico, USA.

Cerf, P. L., Ma, W. and Compernolle, D. V. (1994) Multilayer perceptrons as labelers for hidden Markov models. *IEEE Transactions on Speech and Audio Processing*, 2(1, pt II): 185–193.

Cerf-Danon, H. and El-Bèze, M. (1991) Three different probabilistic language models: comparison and combination. In *Proceedings of the IEEE International Conference on Acoustics, Speech and Signal Processing*, 1: 297–300, Toronto, Canada.

Champagne, B., Bedard, S. and Stephenne, A. (1996) Performance of time-delay estimation in the presence of room reverberation. *IEEE Transactions on Speech and Audio Processing*, 4(2): 148–152.

Chan, Y. and Langford (1982) Spectral estimation via the higher-order Yule Walker equations. *IEEE Transactions on Acoustics, Speech and Signal Processing*, **30**: 689–698.

Chan, Y. T. and Ho, K. C. (1994) A simple and efficient estimator for hyperbolic location. *IEEE Transactions on Signal Processing*, **42**(8): 1905–1915.

Chang, J. and Zue, V. (1994) A study of speech recognition system robustness to microphone variations: experiments in phonetic classification. In *Proceedings of the International Conference on Spoken Language Processing*, 995–998.

Charniak, E. (1983) Passing markers: a theory of contextual inference in language comprehension. *Cognitive Science*, **7**(3): 171–190.

Charniak, E. and Carroll, G. (1994) Context-sensitive statistics for improved grammatical language models. In *Proceedings of Twelfth National Conference on Artificial Intelligence*, 728–733, AAAI Press/MIT Press, Seattle, Washington.

Charpantier, F. and Moulines, E. (1990) Pitch-synchronous waveform processing techniques for text-to-speech synthesis using diphones. *Speech Communication*, **9**(5): 453–467.

Che, C., Lin, Q., Pearson, J., Devries, B. and Flanagan, J. (1994) Microphone arrays and neural networks for robust speech recognition. In *Proceedings of ARPA HLT Workshop*, 342–347, New Jersey, USA.

Chelba, C., Corazza, A. and Jelinek, F. (1995) A context free headword language model. In *Proceedings of IEEE Automatic Speech Recognition Workshop*, 89–90, Snowbird, Utah, USA.

Chen, F. R. (1990) Identification of contextual factors for pronunciation networks. In *Proceedings of the IEEE International Conference on Acoustics, Speech and Signal Processing*, 753–756, Albuquerque, New Mexico, USA.

Chen, S. (1996) Building probabilistic models for natural language. Ph.D. thesis, Center for research in computing technology, Harvard University, Cambridge, Massachusetts, USA.

Chen, S., Cowan, C. and Grant, P. M. (1991) Orthogonal least squares learning algorithm for radial basis function networks. *IEEE Transactions on Neural Networks*, **2**(2): 302–309.

Chen, Y. (1988) Cepstral domain talker stress compensation for robust speech recognition. *IEEE Transactions on Acoustics, Speech and Signal Processing*, **36**(4): 433–439.

Chevalier, H., Ingold, C., Kunz, C., Moore, C., Roven, C., Yamron, J., Baker, B., Bamberg, P., Bridle, S., Bruce, T. and Weader, A. (1995) Large-vocabulary speech recognition in specialized domains. In *Proceedings of the IEEE International Conference on Acoustics, Speech and Signal Processing*, **1**: 217–220, Detroit, Michigan, USA.

Chien, J. T., Lee, C. H. and Wang, H. C. (1997) Improved bayesian learning of hidden Markov models for speaker adaptation. In *International Conference on Acoustics, Speech and Signal Processing*, 1027–1030, Munich, Germany.

Chien, L., Chen, K. and Lee, L. (1993) A best-first language processing model integrating the unification grammar and Markov language model for speech recognition applications. *IEEE Transactions on Speech and Audio Processing*, **1**(2): 221–240, Minneapolis, Minnesota, USA.

Chitrao, M. and Grishman, R. (1990) Statistical parsing of messages. In *Proceedings of the DARPA Speech and Natural Language Workshop*, 263–266, Hidden Valley, Pennsylvania, USA.

Chollet, G. and Gagnoulet, C. (1982) On the evaluation of speech recognizers and databases using a reference system. In *Proceedings of the IEEE International Conference on Acoustics, Speech and Signal Processing*, 2026–2029, Paris, France.

Chomsky, N. and Halle, M. (1968) *The Sound Pattern of English*. Harper & Row, New York, USA.

Chou, T. (1995) Frequency-independent beamformer with low response error. In *Proceedings of the IEEE International Conference on Acoustics, Speech and Signal Processing*, 2995–2998, Detroit, Michigan, USA.

Chou, W., Lee, C.-H. and Juang, B.-H. (1994) Minimum error rate training of inter-word context dependent acoustic model units in speech recognition. In *Proceedings of the International Conference on Spoken Language Processing*, 439–442, Yokohama, Japan.

Choukri, K., Chollet, G. and Grenier, Y. (1986) Spectral transformations through canonical correlation analysis in ASR. In *Proceedings of the IEEE International Conference on Acoustics, Speech and Signal Processing*, 2659–2662, Tokyo, Japan.

Chu, P. (1995) Desktop mic array for teleconferencing. In *Proceedings of the IEEE International Conference on Acoustics, Speech and Signal Processing*, 2999–3002, Detroit, Michigan, USA.

Chu-Carrol, J. and Carberry, S. (1994) A plan-based model for response generation in collaborative task-oriented dialogues. In *Proceedings of AAAI'94*, Seattle, Washington, USA.

Church, K. (1988) A stochastic parts program and noun phrase parser for unrestricted text. In *Proceedings of the Second Conference on Applied Natural Language Processing*, 136–143, Austin, Texas, USA.

Church, K. and Gale, W. (1991) A comparison of the enhanced Good-Turing and deleted estimation methods for estimating probabilities of English bigrams. *Computer Speech and Language*, 5: 19–54.

Church, K. and Hanks, P. (1990) Word association norms, mutual information and lexicography. *Computational Linguistics*, 16(1): 22–29.

Church, K. and Mercer, R. (1993) Introduction to the special issue on computational linguistics using large corpora. *Computational Linguistics*, 19: 1–24.

Cioffi, J. and Kkailath, T. (1984) Fast RLS transversal filters for adaptive filtering. In *IEEE Transactions on Acoustics, Speech and Signal Processing*, 32(2): 304–337.

Clarke, D. (1979) The linguistic analogy or when is a speech act like a morpheme? In Ginsborg, G. P. (ed.) *Emerging Strategies in Social Psychological Research*, John Wiley, Chichester.

Class, F., Kaltenmeier, A., Regel, P. and Troller, K. (1990) Fast speaker adaptation for speech recognition system. In *Proceedings of the IEEE International Conference on Acoustics, Speech and Signal Processing*, I: 133–136, Albuquerque, New Mexico, USA.

Class, F., Kaltenmeier, A. and Regel-Brietzmann, P. (1992) Fast speaker adaptation combined with soft vector quantization in an HMM speech recognition system. In *Proceedings of the IEEE International Conference on Acoustics, Speech and Signal Processing*, I: 461–464, San Francisco, California, USA.

Class, F., Kaltenmeier, A. and Regel-Brietzmann, P. (1993) Optimization of an HMM-based continuous speech recognizer. In *Proceedings of the European Conference on Speech Communication and Technology*, 803–806, Berlin, Germany.

Clifford, M. (1986) *Microphones*. TAB BOOKS Inc. – Blue Ridge Summit, Pennsylvania, USA, third edition.

Cohen, A. and Kovacevic, J. (1996) Wavelets: the mathematical background. *Proceedings of the IEEE*, 84(4): 514–522.

Cohen, J. R. (1989a) Application of an auditory model to speech recognition. *Journal of the Acoustical Society of America*, 85: 2623–2629.

Cohen, L. (1989b) Time-frequency distributions – a review. *Proceedings of the IEEE*, 77(7): 941–981.

Cohen, L. and Posch, T. (1985) Positive time-frequency distribution functions. *IEEE Transactions on Acoustics, Speech and Signal Processing*, 33(1): 31–38.

Cohen, P. (1992) The role of natural language in a multimodal interface. In *Proceedings of the 2nd FRIEND'21, International Symposium on Next Generation Human Interface Technology*, Tokyo, Japan.

Cohen, P. and Levesque, H. (1990a) Intention is choice with commitment. *Artificial Intelligence*, 42(2–3): 213–262.

Cohen, P. R. and Levesque, H. J. (1990b) Rational interaction as the basis for communication. In *Intentions in Communication*, MIT Press, Cambridge, Massachusetts, USA.

Cohen, P., Morgan, J. and Pollack, M. (eds) (1990) *Intentions in Communication*. MIT Press.

Cohen, P. and Perrault, C. (1979) Elements of a plan-based theory of speech acts. *Cognitive Science*, **3**(3): 177–212.

Coker, C. H. (1967) Synthesis by rule from articulatory parameters. *IEEE Conference on Speech Communication and Processing*. Cambridge, Massachusetts, USA.

Colburn, H. S. and Durlach, N. I. (1978) *Models of Binaural Interaction*, volume 4 of *Handbook of Perception*, E. C. Carterette and M. P. Friedman (eds). Academic Press, London, UK.

Compton, R. T. (1988) *Adaptive antennas: concepts and performance*. Prentice Hall, Englewood Cliffs, New Jersey, USA.

Corazza, A., De Mori, R., Gretter, R. and Satta, G. (1991) Computation of probabilities for an island-driven parser. *IEEE Transactions on Pattern Analysis and Machine Intelligence*, **13**(9): 936–950.

Corazza, A., De Mori, R., Gretter, R. and Satta, G. (1994) Optimal probabilistic evaluation functions for search controlled by stochastic context-free grammars. *IEEE Transactions on Pattern Analysis and Machine Intelligence*, **16**(10): 1018–1027.

Cormen, T. H., Leiserson, C. E. and Rivest, R. L. (1990) *Introduction to Algorithms*. MIT Press, Cambridge, Massachusetts, USA.

Cosi, P., Bengio, Y. and De Mori, R. (1990) Phonetically-based multi-layered networks for acoustic property extraction and automatic speech recognition. *Speech Communication*, **9**(1): 15–30.

Cosi, P., Dellana, L., Mian, G. and Omologo, M. (1991) Auditory model implementation on a DSP32C board. In *Proceedings of GRETSI*, Juan Les Pins, France.

Cottrell, G., Munro, P. and Zipser, D. (1987) Learning internal representations from gray-scale images: An example of extensional programming. In *Ninth Annual Conference of the Cognitive Science Society*, 462–473, Lawrence Erlbaum, Hillsdale, Seattle, Washington, USA.

Cover, T. and Thomas, J. (1991) *Elements of Information Theory*. Wiley Series in Telecommunications, John Wiley & Sons, New York, USA.

Covington, M. (1990) Parsing discontinuous constituents in dependency grammar. *Computational Linguistics*, **16**(4): 234–236.

Cox, S. J. and Bridle, J. S. (1990) Simultaneous speaker normalization and utterance labeling using bayesian/neural net techniques. In *Proceedings of the IEEE International Conference on Acoustics, Speech and Signal Processing*, I: 161–164, Albuquerque, New Mexico, USA.

Cremelie, N. and Martens, J.-P. (1995) On the use of pronunciation rules for improved word recognition. In *Proceedings of the European Conference on Speech Communication and Technology*, 1747–1750, Madrid, Spain.

Crochiere, R. E. and Rabiner, L. R. (1983) *Multirate Digital Signal Processing*. Prentice-Hall, Englewood Cliffs, New Jersey, USA.

Crouch, R. and Pulman, S. (1993) Time and modality in a natural language interface to a planning system. *Artificial Intelligence*, **3**: 265–304.

Cruse, D. (1986) *Lexical Semantics*. Cambridge University Press, Cambridge, UK.

Cutting, D., Kupiec, J., Pedersen, J. and Sibun, P. (1992) A practical part-of-speech tagger. In *Proceedings of the 3rd Conference on Applied Natural Language Processing*, 133–140, Trento, Italy.

Dahl, V. (1989) Discontinuous grammars. *Computational Intelligence*, **5**: 161–179.

Dahlbäck, N. and Jönsson, A. (1992) An empirically based computationally tractable dialogue model. In *Proceedings of the 14th Conference of the Cognitive Science Society (COGSCI'92)*, Bloomington, Indiana, USA.

DalDegan, N. and Prati, C. (1988) Acoustic noise analysis and speech enhancement techniques for mobile radio applications. *Signal Processing*, **15**: 43–56.

Dale, R. (1990) Generating recipes: an overview of EPICURE. In Dale, R. C. M. and Zock, M. (eds) *Current Research in Natural Language Generation*, 229–255, Academic Press, London, UK.

Damper, R. (1984) Voice-input aids for the physically handicapped. *International Journal of Man-Machine Studies*, **21**: 541–553.

Damper, R. and Wood, S. (1995) Speech versus keying in command and control applications. *International Journal of Man-Machine Studies*, **42**: 289–305.

Dang, V. and Carre, R. (1987) Lateral inhibition and speech signal processing. In *Proceedings of ICPhs*, 251–254, Tallinn, Estonia, USSR.

Darroch, J. N. and Ratcliff, D. (1972) Generalized iterative scaling for log-linear models. *The Annals of Mathematical Statistics*, **43**(5): 1470–1480.

Das, S., Bakis, R., Nadas, A., Nahamoo, D. and Picheny, M. (1993) Influence of background noise and microphone on the performance of the IBM TANGORA speech recognition system. In *Proceedings of the IEEE International Conference on Acoustics, Speech and Signal Processing*, **II**: 71–74.

Dautrich, B., Rabiner, L. and Martin, T. (1983) On the effects of varying filter bank parameters on isolated word recognition. *IEEE Transactions on Acoustics, Speech and Signal Processing*, **31**(4): 793–807.

Davis, D. and Davis, C. (1989) *Sound System Engineering*. Howard W. Sams & Co., second edition.

Davis, S. and Mermelstein, P. (1980) Comparison of parametric representation for monosyllable word recognition in continuously spoken sentences. *IEEE Transactions on Acoustics, Speech and Signal Processing*, **28**(4): 357–366.

DeGroot, M. H. (1970) *Optimal Statistical Decisions*. McGraw-Hill, New York, USA.

Delattre, P., Liberman, A. and Cooper, F. (1955) Acoustic loci and transitional cues for consonants. *Journal of the Acoustical Society of America*, **27**: 769–773.

Della Pietra, S. and Della Pietra, V. (1994) Statistical modeling using maximum entropy. Research report, IBM Watson Center, Yorktown Heights, New York, USA.

Della Pietra, S., Della Pietra, V., Mercer, R. and Roukos, S. (1992) Adaptive language model estimation using minimum discrimination estimation. In *Proceedings of the IEEE International Conference on Acoustics, Speech and Signal Processing*, **I**: 633–636, San Francisco, California, USA.

Delosme, J. M., Morf, M. and Friedlander, B. (1980) Source location from time-difference-of-arrival measurements. In *Proceedings of the IEEE International Conference on Acoustics, Speech and Signal Processing*, 818–824, Denver, Colorado, USA.

De Mori, R. (1979) Recent advances in automatic speech recognition. *Signal Processing*, **1**(2): 95–124.

De Mori, R. and Galler, M. (1996) The use of syllable phonotactics for word hypothesization. In *Proceedings of the IEEE International Conference on Acoustics, Speech and Signal Processing*, 877–880, Atlanta, Georgia, USA.

De Mori, R., Galler, M. and Brugnara, F. (1995a) Search and learning strategies for improving hidden Markov models. *Computer Speech and Language*, **9**(2): 107–121.

De Mori, R., Gilli, L. and Meo, A. (1970) A flexible real-time recognizer of spoken words for man-machine communication. *International Journal of Man-Machine Studies*, **2**(4): 317–326.

De Mori, R., Giuliani, D. and Gretter, R. (1994) Phone-based prefiltering for continuous speech recognition. In *Proceedings of the International Conference on Spoken Language Processing*, 2203–2206, Yokohama, Japan.

De Mori, R. and Laface, P. (eds) (1992) *Speech Recognition and Understanding: Recent Advances, Trends and Applications*. Springer-Verlag, Berlin and Heidelberg, Germany.

De Mori, R. and Omologo, M. (1993) Normalized correlation features for speech analysis and pitch extraction. In Cooke, M., Beet, S. and Crawford, M. (eds) *Visual Representation of Speech Signals*, 299–306, Wiley, New York, USA.

De Mori, R., Snow, C. and Galler, M. (1995b) On the use of stochastic inference networks for representing multiple word pronunciations. In *Proceedings of the IEEE International Conference on Acoustics, Speech and Signal Processing*, 568–571, Detroit, Michigan, USA.

Dempster, A. P., Laird, N. M. and Rubin, D. B. (1977) Maximum-likelihood from incomplete data via the EM algorithm. *Journal of the Royal Statistical Society ser. B*, **39**: 1–38.

Deng, L., Aksmanovic, M., Sun, X. and Wu, C. F. J. (1994) Speech recognition using hidden Markov models with polynomial regression functions as nonstationary states. *IEEE Transactions on Speech and Audio Processing*, **2**(4): 507–520.

Deng, L. and Erler, K. (1991) Microstructural speech units and their HMM representation for discrete utterance speech recognition. In *Proceedings of the IEEE International Conference on Acoustics, Speech and Signal Processing*, 193–196, Toronto, Canada.

Deng, L., Wu, J. and Sameti, H. (1995) Improved speech modeling and recognition using multi-dimensional articulatory states as primitive speech units. In *Proceedings of the IEEE International Conference on Acoustics, Speech and Signal Processing*, 385–388, Detroit, Michigan, USA.

Dennett, D. (1987) *The Intentional Stance*. The MIT Press, Cambridge, Massachusetts, USA.

DeRose, S. (1988) Grammatical category disambiguation by statistical optimization. *Computational Linguistics*, **14**(1): 31–39.

Derouault, A. and Merialdo, B. (1986) Natural language modeling for phoneme-to-text transcription. *IEEE Transactions on Pattern Analysis and Machine Intelligence*, **8**(6): 742–749.

DeSouza, P. (1977) Statistical tests and distance measures for LPC coefficients. *IEEE Transactions on Acoustics, Speech and Signal Processing*, **25**(6): 554–559.

Digalakis, V. and Murveit, H. (1994) Genones: optimizing the degree of mixture tying in a large vocabulary hidden Markov model based speech recognizer. In *Proceedings of the IEEE International Conference on Acoustics, Speech and Signal Processing*, **I**: 537–540, Adelaide, Australia.

Digalakis, V. and Neumeyer, L. (1995) Speaker adaptation using combined transformation and bayesian methods. In *Proceedings of the IEEE International Conference on Acoustics, Speech and Signal Processing*, **I**: 680–683, Detroit, Michigan, USA.

Digalakis, V., Rtischev, D. and Neumeyer, L. G. (1995) Speaker adaptation using constrained estimation of Gaussian mixtures. *IEEE Transactions on Speech and Audio Processing*, **3**(5): 357–366.

Dowding, J. (1996) Personal communication to R. Kuhn.

Dowding, J., Gawron, J. *et al.* (1993) Gemini: a natural language system for spoken-language understanding. In *Proceedings of the Spoken Language Systems Technology Workshop*, MIT Press, Cambridge, Massachusetts, USA.

Dowty, D. (1979) *Word Meaning and Montague Grammar*. Reidel, Dordrecht, The Netherlands.

Doyle, J. (1990) Rationality and its role in reasoning. In *Proceedings of AAAI'90*, 1093–1100, Boston, Massachusetts, USA.

Duda, R. O. and Hart, P. E. (1973) *Pattern Classification and Scene Analysis*. Wiley, New York, USA.

Dudley, H. (1939) Remaking speech. *Journal of the Acoustical Society of America*, **11**.

Dudley, H. and Balashek, S. (1958) Automatic recognition of phonetic patterns in speech. *Journal of the Acoustical Society of America*, **30**(8): 721–732.

Dugast, C., Aubert, X. and Kneser, R. (1995) The Philips large-vocabulary recognition system for American English, French and German. In *Proceedings of the European Conference on Speech Communication and Technology*, 197–200, Madrid, Spain.

Dumouchel, P. and O'Shaughnessy, D. (1995) Segmental duration and HMM modeling. In *Proceedings of European Conference on Speech Processing (EUROSPEECH)*, 2: 803–806, Madrid, Spain.

Dupont, P. (1993) Dynamic use of syntactical knowledge in continuous speech recognition. In *Proceedings of the European Conference on Speech Communication and Technology*, 1959–1962, Berlin, Germany.

Earley, J. (1970) An efficient context-free parsing algorithm. *Communications of the Association for Computing Machinery*, 13(2): 94–102.

Eisele, T., Haeb-Umbach, R. and Langmann, D. (1996) A comparative study of linear feature transformation techniques for automatic speech recognition. In *Proceedings of the International Conference on Spoken Language Processing*, 252–255, Philadelphia, Pennsylvania, USA.

El-Bèze, M. and Derouault, A.-M. (1990) A morphological model for large vocabulary speech recognition. In *Proceedings of the IEEE International Conference on Acoustics, Speech and Signal Processing*, 1: 577–580, Albuquerque, New Mexico, USA.

El-Jaroudi, A. and Makhoul, J. (1991) Discrete all-pole modeling. *IEEE Transactions on Signal Processing*, 39(2): 411–423.

Elman, J. (1990) Finding structure in time. *Cognitive Science*, 14: 179–211.

Elman, J. and Zipser, D. (1988) Learning the hidden structure of speech. *Journal of the Acoustical Society of America*, 83: 1615–1626.

Ephraim, Y. (1992a) A bayesian estimation approach for speech enhancement using hidden Markov models. *IEEE Transactions on Signal Processing*, 40(4): 725–735.

Ephraim, Y. (1992b) Speech enhancement using state dependent dynamical system model. In *Proceedings of the IEEE International Conference on Acoustics, Speech and Signal Processing*, 289–292, San Francisco, California, USA.

Ephraim, Y. and Malah, D. (1984) Speech enhancement using minimum mean square error short time spectral amplitude estimator. *IEEE Transactions on Acoustics, Speech and Signal Processing*, 32(6): 1109–1121.

Ephraim, Y. and Rabiner, L. R. (1990) On the relations between modeling approaches for speech recognition. *IEEE Transactions on Information Theory*, 36(2): 372–380.

Epstein, M., Pepineni, K., Roukos, S., Ward, T. and Della Pietra, S. (1996) Statistical natural language understanding using hidden clumpsing. In *Proceedings of the IEEE International Conference on Acoustics, Speech and Signal Processing*, 176–179, Detroit, Michigan, USA.

Erell, A. and Weintraub, M. (1991) Pitch-aided spectral estimation for noise-robust speech recognition. In *Proceedings of the IEEE International Conference on Acoustics, Speech and Signal Processing*, 1: 909–912, Toronto, Canada.

Erell, A. and Weintraub, M. (1994) Estimation of noise-corrupted speech DFT-spectrum using the pitch period. *IEEE Transactions on Speech and Audio Processing*, 2(1): 1–8.

Erman, L., Hayes-Roth, F., Lesser, V. and Reddy, D. (1980) The Hearsay II speech understanding system: integrating knowledge to resolve uncertainty. *Association for Computing Machinery Computing Surveys*, 12(2): 213–253.

Evans, E. (1985) Aspects of neural coding of time in the mammalian peripheral auditory system relevant to time resolution. In Michelson, A. (ed.) *Time Resolution in Auditory Systems*, 74–95, Springer-Verlag, Berlin, Germany.

Fang, B. T. (1990) Simple solutions for hyperbolic and related position fixes. *IEEE Transactions on Aerospace and Electronic Systems*, 26(5): 748–753.

Fant, G. (1959) Acoustic analysis and synthesis of speech with application to Swedish. *Ericsson Techniques*, **15**: 3–1089.

Fant, G. (1970a) *Acoustic Theory of Speech Production.* Mouton, The Hague, The Netherlands.

Fant, G. (1970b) Automatic recognition and speech research. Technical report 1/1970, Speech Transmission Lab., Stockholm, Sweden.

Feder, M., Oppenheim, A. and Weinstein, E. (1987) Methods for noise cancellation based on the EM algorithm. In *Proceedings of the IEEE International Conference on Acoustics, Speech and Signal Processing*, 201–204, Tulsa, Dallas, Texas, USA.

Federico, M. (1996a) Bayesian estimation methods for *n*-gram language model adaptation. In *Proceedings of the International Conference on Spoken Language Processing*, Philadelphia, Pennsylvania, USA.

Federico, M. (1996b) Language modeling for the Sole-24-Ore task. Technical report, IRST, Trento, Italy.

Federico, M., Cettolo, M., Brugnara, F. and Antoniol, G. (1995) Language modeling for efficient beam-search. *Computer Speech and Language*, **9**: 353–379.

Fellbaum, K., Klaus, H. and Sotscheck, J. (1994) Höversuche zur beurteilung der sprachqualität von sprachsynthessesystemen für die deutsche sprache. In *Proceedings of the DAGA Vorkolloquium*, Dresden, Germany.

Feng, M.-W., Kubala, F., Schwartz, R. and Makhoul, J. (1988) Improved speaker adaptation using text dependent spectral mappings. In *Proceedings of the IEEE International Conference on Acoustics, Speech and Signal Processing*, **I**: 131–134, New York, USA.

Feng, M.-W., Schwartz, R., Kubala, F. and Makhoul, J. (1989) Interactive normalization for speaker-adaptive training in continuous speech recognition. In *Proceedings of the IEEE International Conference on Acoustics, Speech and Signal Processing*, **I**: 612–615, Glasgow, UK.

Ferber, J. (1995) Les systèmes multi-agents. *Vers une intelligence collective.* InterEditions, Paris, France.

Ferguson, J. D. (1980) Variable duration models for speech. In Ferguson, J. D. (ed.) *Proceedings of the Symposium on the Application of Hidden Markov Models to Text and Speech*, 143–179, Princeton, New Jersey, USA.

Ferretti, M. and Mazza, A. M. (1991) Fast speaker adaptation: some experiments on different techniques for codebook and HMM parameter estimation. In *Proceedings of the IEEE International Conference on Acoustics, Speech and Signal Processing*, **II**: 849–852, Toronto, Canada.

Ferretti, M. and Scarci, S. (1989) Large-vocabulary speech recognition with speaker-adapted codebook and HMM parameters. In *Proceedings of the European Conference on Speech Communication and Technology*, 154–156, Paris, France.

Ferrieux, A. and Sadek, M. (1994) An efficient data-driven model for cooperation spoken dialogue. In *Proceedings of the International Conference on Spoken Language Processing*, 979–982, Yokohama, Japan.

Fillmore, C. (1968) The case for case. In Bach, E. and Harms, R. (eds) *Universals in Linguistic Theory.* Holt, Rinehart and Winston, New York, USA.

Fischer, S. and Simmer, K. U. (1995) An adaptive microphone array for hands-free communication. In *Proceedings of 4th International Workshop on Acoustic Echo and Noise Control*, Røros, Norway, 44–47.

Fischer, S. and Simmer, K. U. (1996) Beamforming microphone arrays for speech acquisition in noisy environments. *Speech Communication*, **20**: 215–227.

Fisher, A. (1989) Practical parsing of generalized phrase structure grammar. *Computational Linguistics*, **15**(3): 139–148.

Fisher, W. M., Zue, V., Bernstein, J. and Pallett, D. (1987) An acoustic-phonetic data base. In *Meeting of the Acoustical Society of America*, Philadelphia, Pennsylvania, USA.

Fissore, L., Giachin, E., Laface, P., Micca, G., Pieraccini, R. and Rullent, C. (1988) Experimental results in large-vocabulary continuous speech recognition and understanding. In *Proceedings of the IEEE International Conference on Acoustics, Speech and Signal Processing*, 414–417, New York, USA.

Fissore, L., Laface, P., Codogno, M. and Venuti, G. (1990) HMM modelling for voice activated mobile-radio system. In *Proceedings of International Conference on Spoken Language Processing*, 1137–1140, Kobe, Japan.

Flach, G. (1995) Modeling pronunciation variability for special domains. In *Proceedings of the European Conference on Speech Communication and Technology*, 1743–1746, Madrid, Spain.

Flammia, G. (1991) Speaker independent consonant recognition in continuous speech with distinctive phonetic features. Master's thesis, McGill University, School of Computer Science, Montreal, Canada.

Flanagan, J. L. (1972a) *Speech Analysis Synthesis and Perception*. Springer-Verlag, Berlin, Germany.

Flanagan, J. L. (1972b) Voices of men and machines. *Journal of the Acoustical Society of America*, **51**: 1375–1387.

Flanagan, J., Berkley, D., Elko, G., West, J. and Sondhi, M. (1991) Autodirective Microphone Systems. *Acustica*, **75**: 58–71.

Flanagan, J. L. (1985) Use of acoustic filtering to control the beamwidth of steered microphone arrays. *Journal of the Acoustical Society of America*, **78**(2): 423–428.

Flanagan, J. L. (1987) Three-dimensional microphone arrays. *Journal of the Acoustical Society of America*, **82**: S.39.

Flanagan, J. L., Johnston, J. D., Zahn, R. and Elko, G. W. (1985) Computer-steered microphone arrays for sound transduction in large rooms. *Journal of the Acoustical Society of America*, **78**(5): 1508–1518.

Flanagan, J. L., Surendran, A. C. and Jan, E. E. (1993) Spatially selective sound capture for speech and audio processing. *Speech Communication*, **13**: 207–222.

Foote, J. T., Jones, G. J. F., Jones, K. S. and Young, S. J. (1995) Talker-independent keyword spotting for information retrieval. In *Proceedings of the European Conference on Speech Communication and Technology*, 2145–2148, Madrid, Spain.

Forney, G. D. Jr. (1973) The Viterbi algorithm. *Proceedings of the IEEE*, **61**(3): 268–278.

Foy, W. H. (1976) Position-location solutions by Taylor-series estimation. *IEEE Transactions on Aerospace and Electronic Systems*, **12**(2): 187–194.

Franzini, M., Lee, K. and Waibel, A. (1990) Connectionist Viterbi training: a new hybrid method for continuous speech recognition. In *Proceedings of the IEEE International Conference on Acoustics, Speech and Signal Processing*, 425–428, Albuquerque, New Mexico, USA.

Fred, A. and Leitao, J. (1993) An heuristic-based context-free parsing algorithm. In *Proceedings of the IEEE International Conference on Acoustics, Speech and Signal Processing*, **II**: 67–70, Minneapolis, Minnesota, USA.

Friedlander, B. (1987) A passive localization algorithm and its accuracy analysis. *IEEE Journal on Oceanic Engineering*, **12**: 234–245.

Frost, O. L. (1972) An algorithm for linearly constrained adaptive array processing. *Proceedings of the IEEE*, **60**(8): 926–935.

Fry, D. (1976) *Acoustic Phonetics: a Course of Basic Readings*. Cambridge University Press, Cambridge, UK.

Fu, K. (1982) *Syntactic Pattern Recognition and Applications*. Prentice Hall, Englewood Cliffs, New Jersey, USA.

Fujimura, O. (1962) Analysis of nasal consonants. *Journal of the Acoustical Society of America*, **34**: 1865–1875.

Fukunaga, K. (1990) *Introduction to Statistical Pattern Recognition*. Academic Press, 2nd edition, London, UK.

Furlanello, C. and Giuliani, D. (1995) Combining local PCA and radial basis function networks for speaker normalization. In *Proceedings of the 1995 IEEE Workshop on Neural Networks for Signal Processing V*, 233–242, Cambridge, Massachusetts, USA.

Furlanello, C., Giuliani, D. and Trentin, E. (1995) Connectionist speaker normalization with Generalized Resource Allocating Networks. In Tesauro, G. D., Touretzky, S. T. and Leen, T. K. (eds) *Advances in Neural Information Processing Systems 7, 1994*, 1704–1707, MIT Press, Cambridge, Massachusetts, USA.

Furlanello, C., Giuliani, D., Trentin, E. and Merler, S. (1997) Speaker normalization and model selection of combined neural nets. *Connection Science*, **9**(1): 31–50.

Furui, S. (1981) Cepstral analysis techniques for automatic speaker verification. *IEEE Transactions on Acoustics, Speech and Signal Processing*, **29**(2): 254–272.

Furui, S. (1986) Speaker-independent isolated word recognition using dynamic features of speech spectrum. *IEEE Transactions on Acoustics, Speech and Signal Processing*, **34**: 52–59.

Furui, S. (1989) Unsupervised speaker adaptation method based on hierarchical spectral clustering. In *Proceedings of the IEEE International Conference on Acoustics, Speech and Signal Processing*, **I**: 286–289, Glasgow, UK.

Furui, S. and Sondhi, M. M. (eds) (1991) *Advances in Speech Signal Processing*. Marcel Dekker, New York, USA.

Gagnoulet, C. and Sorin, C. (1993) Speech recognition and text-to-speech for tele-communication applications. In *Proceedings of the ESCA/NATO RSG10 Workshop on Applications of Speech Technology*, 31–34, Lautrach, Germany.

Gaik, W. (1993) Combined evaluation of interaural time and intensity differences: psychoacoustical results and computer modeling. *Journal of the Acoustical Society of America*, **94**: 98–110.

Gales, M. and Young, S. (1993) Cepstral parameter compensation for HMM recognition in noise. *Speech Communication*, **12**: 231–239.

Gales, M. J. F., Pye, D. and Woodland, P. (1996) Variance compensation within the MLLR framework for robust speech recognition and speaker adaptation. In *Proceedings of the International Conference on Spoken Language Processing*, 1828–1931, Philadelphia, Pennsylvania, USA.

Gales, M. J. F. and Young, S. J. (1996) Robust continuous speech recognition using parallel model combination. *IEEE Transactions on Speech and Audio Processing*, **4**(5): 352–359.

Garlan, D. and Perry, D. E. (1995) Introduction to the special issue on software architecture. *IEEE Transactions on Software Engineering*, **21**(4): 269–274.

Garlan, D. and Shaw, M. (1993) An introduction to software architecture. In *Advances in Software Engineering and Knowledge Engineering*, Vol. 1, World Scientific Publishing Co., New York, USA.

Garside, R., Leech, G. and Sampson, G. (eds) (1987) *The Computational Analysis of English: A Corpus Based Approach*. Longman, London, UK.

Garson, G. (1984) Quantification in modal logic. In Gabbay, D. and Guentner, F. (eds) *Handbook of Philosophical Logic, Volume II: Extensions of Classical Logic*, 249–307, Reidel Publishing Company.

Gauvain, J. L., Lamel, L. and Adda-Decker, M. (1995) Developments in continuous speech dictation using the ARPA WSJ task. In *Proceedings of the IEEE International Conference on Acoustics, Speech and Signal Processing*, 65–68, Detroit, Michigan, USA.

Gauvain, J. L. and Lee, C.-H. (1991) Bayesian learning of Gaussian mixture densities for hidden Markov models. In *Proceedings of the DARPA Speech and Natural Language Workshop*, 272–277, Palo Alto, California, USA.

Gauvain, J. L. and Lee, C.-H. (1992) Bayesian learning for hidden Markov model with Gaussian mixture state observation densities. *Speech Communication*, **11**(2-3): 205–213.

Gauvain, J. L. and Lee, C. H. (1994) Maximum *a posteriori* estimation for multivariate Gaussian mixture observations of Markov chains. *IEEE Transactions on Speech and Audio Processing*, **2**(2). 291–298.

Gazdar, G., Klein, E., Pullum, G. and Sag, I. (1985) *Generalized Phrase Structure Grammars*. Harvard University Press, Cambridge, Massachusetts, USA.

Gelfand, S., Ravishankar, C. and Delp, E. (1991) An iterative growing and pruning algorithm for classification tree design. *IEEE Transactions on Pattern Analysis and Machine Intelligence*, **13**(6): 163–174.

Geutner, P. (1995) Using morphology towards better large vocabulary speech recognition. In *Proceedings of the IEEE International Conference on Acoustics, Speech and Signal Processing*, 445–448, Detroit, Michigan, USA.

Ghezzi, C., Jazayeri, M. and Mandrioli, D. (1992) *Fundamentals of Software Engineering*. Prentice-Hall, Englewood Cliffs, New Jersey, USA.

Ghitza, O. (1986) Auditory nerve representation as a front-end for speech recognition in noisy environment. *Computer Speech and Language*, **1**(1): 109–130.

Ghitza, O. (1987) Robustness against noise: The role of timing-synchrony measurement. In *Proceedings of the IEEE International Conference on Acoustics, Speech and Signal Processing*, 2372–2375, Dallas, Texas, USA.

Ghitza, O. (1988) Temporal non-place information in the auditory-nerve firing patterns as a front-end for speech recognition in a noisy environment. *Journal of Phonetics*, **16**(1): 109–124.

Ghitza, O. and Sondhi, M. M. (1993) Hidden Markov models with templates as non-stationary states: an application to speech recognition. *Computer Speech and Language*, **7**(2): 101–120.

Giachin, E. (1992) Automatic training of stochastic finite-state language models for speech understanding. In *Proceedings of the IEEE International Conference on Acoustics, Speech and Signal Processing*, 173–175, San Francisco, California, USA.

Giachin, E. (1995) Phrase bigrams for continuous speech recognition. In *Proceedings of the IEEE International Conference on Acoustics, Speech and Signal Processing*, **I**: 225–228, Detroit, Michigan, USA.

Giachin, E., Lee, C.-H., Rabiner, L. B., Rosenberg, A. and Pieraccini, R. (1992) On the use of inter-word context-dependent units for word juncture modeling. *Computer Speech and Language*, **6**(3): 197–213.

Giachin, E. P., Rosenberg, A. E. and Lee, C.-H. (1991) Word juncture modeling using phonological rules for HMM-based continuous speech recognition. *Computer Speech and Language*, **5**(2): 155–168.

Gill, P., Murray, W. and Wright, M. (1981) *Practical Optimization*. Academic Press, London, UK.

Gilloire, A. (1987) Experiments with sub-band acoustic echo cancellers for teleconferencing. In *Proceedings of the IEEE International Conference on Acoustics, Speech and Signal Processing*, 2141–2144, Dallas, Texas, USA.

Ginsberg, M. and Smith, D. (1988) Reasoning about action I: a possible world approach. *Artificial Intelligence*, **35**: 165–195.

Girosi, F. and Anzellotti, G. (1993) Rates of convergence for radial basis functions and neural networks. In Mammone, R. J. (ed.) *Artificial Neural Networks for Speech and Vision*, 97–114, Chapman and Hall, London, UK.

Girosi, F., Jones, M. and Poggio, T. (1995) Regularization theory and neural network architectures. *Neural Computation*, **7**: 1219–1269.

Girosi, F. and Poggio, T. (1990) Networks and the best approximation property. *Biological Cybernetics*, **63**: 169–176.

Giuliani, D., Matassoni, M., Omologo, M. and Svaizer, P. (1995) Robust continuous speech recognition using a microphone array. In *Proceedings of the European Conference on Speech Communication and Technology*, 2021–2024, Madrid, Spain.

Giuliani, D., Omologo, M. and Svaizer, P. (1996) Experiments of speech recognition in a noisy and reverberant environment using a microphone array and HMM adaptation. In *Proceedings of the International Conference on Spoken Language Processing*, 1329–1332, Philadelphia, Pennsylvania, USA.

Glass, J., Goddeau, D., Hetherington, L., McCandless, M., Pao, C., Phillips, M., Polifroni, J., Seneff, S. and Zue, V. (1995) The MIT ATIS System: December 1994 Progress Report. In *Proceedings of the ARPA Spoken Language Technology Workshop*, Austin, Texas, USA.

Glass, J. R. and Zue, V. W. (1989) Multi level acoustic segmentation of speech signals. In *Proceedings of the IEEE International Conference on Acoustics, Speech and Signal Processing*, 429–432, Glasgow, UK.

Goddeau, D. (1994) Using probabilistic shift-reduce parsing in speech recognition systems. In *Proceedings of the International Conference on Spoken Language Processing*, 321–324, Banff, Canada.

Godfrey, J.J., Holliman, E. C. and McDaniel, J. (1992) SWITCHBOARD: telephone speech corpus for research and development. In *Proceedings of the IEEE International Conference on Acoustics, Speech and Signal Processing*, I: 517–520, San Francisco, California, USA.

Gold, B. and Rabiner, L. R. (1969) Parallel processing techniques for estimating pitch periods of speech in the time domain. *Journal of the Acoustical Society of America*, **46**: 422–448.

Gong, Y. (1995) Speech recognition in noisy environments: a survey. *Speech Communication*, **16**: 261–291.

Gong, Y., Siohan, O. and Haton, J.-P. (1992) Minimization of speech alignment error by iterative transformation for speaker adaptation. In *Proceedings of the International Conference on Spoken Language Processing*, 377–379, Banff, Canada.

Gonzales, R. C. and Thomason, M. G. (1978) *Syntactic Patter Recognition*. Addison-Wesley Publishing Company, Reading, Massachusetts, USA.

Good, I. J. (1953) The population frequencies of species and the estimation of population parameters. *Biometrika*, **40**: 237–264.

Goodwin, M. M. and Elko, G. W. (1993) Constant beamwidth beamforming. In *Proceedings of the IEEE International Conference on Acoustics, Speech and Signal Processing*, I: 169–172, Minneapolis, Minnesota, USA.

Gopalakrishnan, P. S., Bahl, L. R. and Mercer, R. L. (1995) A tree search strategy for large-vocabulary continuous speech recognition. In *Proceedings of the IEEE International Conference on Acoustics, Speech and Signal Processing*, 572–575, Detroit, Michigan, USA.

Gopalakrishnan, P. S., Kanevsky, D., Nádas, A. and Nahamoo, D. (1991) An inequality for rational functions with applications to some statistical estimation problems. *IEEE Transactions on Information Theory*, **37**(1): 107–113.

Gopalakrishnan, P. S., Nahamoo, D., Padmanabhan, M. and Picheny, M. A. (1994) A channel-bank-based phone detection strategy. In *Proceedings of the IEEE International Conference on Acoustics, Speech and Signal Processing*, II: 161–164, Adelaide, Australia.

Gori, M., Bengio, Y. and De Mori, R. (1989) BPS: A learning algorithm for capturing the dynamical nature of speech. In *Proceedings of the International Joint Conference on Neural Networks*, 643–644, Washington D.C. IEEE, New York, USA.

Gori, M., Lastrucci, L. and Soda, G. (1995) Autoassociator-based models for speaker verification. *Pattern Recognition Letters*, **7**: 241–250.

Gori, M. and Tesi, A. (1992) On the problem of local minima in backpropagation. *IEEE Transactions on Pattern Analysis and Machine Intelligence*, **14**(1): 76–86.

Gottfried, T. and Strange, W. (1980) Identification of coarticulated vowels. *Journal of the Acoustical Society of America*, **68**: 1626–1635.

Graham, S. L. and Harrison, M. A. (1976) Parsing of general context free languages. In *Advances in Computers*, **14**: 77–185, Academic Press, London, UK.

Gray, A. H. and Markel, J. D. (1976) Distance measures for speech processing. *IEEE Transaction on Acoustics, Speech and Signal Processing*, **24**(5): 380–391.

Gray, R. M. (1984) Vector quantization. *IEEE ASSP Magazine*, 4–28.

Gray, R. M., Buzo, A., Gray, A. H. and Matsuyama, Y. (1980) Distortion measures for speech processing. *IEEE Transactions on Acoustics, Speech and Signal Processing*, **28**(4): 367–376.

Green, M. (1983) Report on dialogue specification, user interface management systems. In Pfaff, G. (ed.) *Proceedings of the Workshop on User Interface Management Systems*, 9–20, Springer-Verlag, Berlin, Germany.

Greenberg, J. E. and Zurek, P. M. (1992) Evaluation of an adaptive beamforming method for hearing aids. *Journal of the Acoustical Society of America*, **91**: 1662–1676.

Greenberg, S. (1988) The ear as a speech analyzer. *Journal of Phonetics*, **15**(4): 139–149.

Grenier, Y. (1980) Speaker adaptation through canonical correlation analysis. In *Proceedings of the IEEE International Conference on Acoustics, Speech and Signal Processing*, 888–891, Denver, Colorado, USA.

Grenier, Y. (1992) A microphone array for car environments. In *Proceedings of the IEEE International Conference on Acoustics, Speech and Signal Processing*, 305–308, San Francisco, California, USA.

Grenier, Y. (1993) A microphone array for car environments. *Speech Communication*, **12**: 25–39.

Gretter, R. (1996) Word spotting – work in progress. Technical Report 9601-13, IRST, Trento, Italy.

Gretter, R., Mian, G. A., Rinaldo, R. and Salmasi, M. (1990) Linguistic processing for an Italian text-to-speech system. In *Verba 90*, 334–342, Roma, Italy.

Grice, H. (1957) Meaning. *Philosophical Review*, **66**: 377–388.

Grice, H. (1975) Logic and conversation. In *Syntax and Semantics: Speech Acts*, **3**: 41–48, Academic Press, London, UK.

Griffin, D. and Lim, J. (1984) Signal estimation from modified short-time Fourier Transform. *IEEE Transactions on Acoustics, Speech and Signal Processing*, **32**(2): 236–243.

Griffiths, L. J. and Jim, C. W. (1982) An alternative approach to linearly constrained adaptive beamforming. *IEEE Transactions on Antennas and Propagation*, **30**(1): 27–34.

Grossberg, S. (1976) Adaptive pattern classification and universal recording: I. Parallel development and coding of neural feature detectors. *Biological Cybernetics*, **23**: 121–134.

Grosz, B. and Hirscberg, J. (1992) Some intonational characteristics of discourse structure. In *Proceedings of the International Conference on Spoken Language Processing*, **1**: 429–432, Banff, Canada.

Grosz, B., Jones, F. S. and Webber, B. (eds) (1986) *Readings in Natural Language Processing*. Morgan Kaufmann Publishers, Los Altos, California, USA.

Grosz, B. and Sidner, C. (1990) Plans for discourse. In *Intentions in Communication*, Cohen, P., Morgan, J. and Pollack, M. (eds). MIT Press, Cambridge, Massachusetts, USA.

Guelou, Y., Benamar, A. and Scalart, P. (1996) Analysis of two structures for combined acoustic echo cancellation and noise reduction. In *Proceedings of the IEEE International Conference on Acoustics, Speech and Signal Processing*, 637–640, Atlanta, Georgia, USA.

Gulikers, L. and Willemse, R. (1992) A lexicon for a text-to-speech system. In *Proceedings of the International Conference on Spoken Language Processing*, 101–104, Banff, Canada.

Gupta, S. K., Soong, F. and Haimi-Cohen, R. (1996) High-accuracy connected digit recognition for mobile applications. In *Proceedings of the IEEE International Conference on Acoustics, Speech and Signal Processing*, **I**: 57–60, Atlanta, Georgia, USA.

Gupta, V. N., Lenning, M. and Melmerstein, P. (1987) Integration of acoustic information in a large vocabulary word recognizer. In *Proceedings of the IEEE International Conference on Acoustics, Speech and Signal Processing*, 697–700, Dallas, Texas, USA.

Gurgen, F., Bagayama, G. and Furui, S. (1990) Line spectrum pair frequency-based distance measures for speech recognition. In *Proceedings of the International Conference on Spoken Language Processing*, 521–524, Kobe, Japan.

Gutman, M. (1989) Asymptotically optimal classification for multiple test with empirically observed statistics. *IEEE Transactions on Information Theory*, **IT-35**(2): 401–408.

Guyomard, M., Nerzic, P. and Siroux, J. (1993) Plans, metaplans et dialogue. In *Actes de la 4ème ecole d'été sur les Traitement des langues naturelles*, Lannion, France.

Haeb-Umbach, R., Beyerlein, P. and Thelen, E. (1995) Automatic transcription of unknown words in a speech recognition system. In *Proceedings of the IEEE International Conference on Acoustics, Speech and Signal Processing*, 840–843, Detroit, Michigan, USA.

Haeb-Umbach, R., Geller, D. and Ney, H. (1993) Improvements in connected digit recognition using linear discriminant analysis and mixture densities. In *Proceedings of the IEEE International Conference on Acoustics, Speech and Signal Processing*, **II**: 239–242, Minneapolis, Minnesota, USA.

Haeb-Umbach, R. and Ney, H. (1991) A look-ahead search technique for large vocabulary continuous speech recognition. In *Proceedings of the European Conference on Speech Communication and Technology*, 495–498, Genova, Italy.

Haeb-Umbach, R. and Ney, H. (1992) Linear discriminant analysis for improved large vocabulary continuous speech recognition. In *Proceedings of the IEEE International Conference on Acoustics, Speech and Signal Processing*, **I**: 13–16, San Francisco, California, USA.

Haeb-Umbach, R. and Ney, H. (1994) Improvements in time-synchronous beam-search for 10 000-word continuous speech recognition. *IEEE Transactions on Speech and Audio Processing*, **2**(4): 353–365.

Haffner, P., Franzini, M. and Waibel, A. (1991) Integrating time alignment and neural networks for high performance continuous speech recognition. In *Proceedings of the IEEE International Conference on Acoustics, Speech and Signal Processing*, 105–108, Toronto, Canada.

Halliday, M. (1985) *Introduction to Functional Grammars*. Edward Arnold.

Halpern, J. and Moses, Y. (1985) A guide to the modal logics of knowledge and belief: a preliminary draft. In *Proceedings of the International Joint Conference on Artificial Intelligence*, Los Angeles, California, USA.

Hampshire, J. B. and Waibel, A. H. (1990) A novel objective function for improved phoneme recognition using time-delay neural networks. *IEEE Transactions on Neural Networks*, **1**(2): 216–228.

Han, N., Kim, H., Hwang, K., Ahn, Y. and Ryoo, J. (1995) Continuous speech recognition system using finite-state network and viterbi beam-search for the automatic interpretation. In *Proceedings of the IEEE International Conference on Acoustics, Speech and Signal Processing*, 117–120, Detroit, Michigan, USA.

Hansen, J. and Cairns, D. (1995) ICARUS: source generator based real-time recognition of speech in noisy stressful and Lombard effect environments. *Speech Communication*, **16**: 391–422.

Hansen, J. and Clements, M. (1987) Iterative speech enhancement with spectral constraints. In *Proceedings of the IEEE International Conference on Acoustics, Speech and Signal Processing*, 189–192, Dallas, Texas, USA.

Hansen, J. and Clements, M. (1991) Iterative speech enhancement with spectral constraints. *IEEE Transactions on Signal Processing*, 39(4): 195–805.

Hao, Y. and Fang, D. (1994) Speech recognition using speaker adaptation by system parameter transformation. *IEEE Transactions on Speech and Audio Processing*, 2(1, Pt I): 63–68.

Hardcastle, W. and Laver, J. (eds) (1997) *The Handbook of Phonetic Sciences*. Blackwell Publishers, Cambridge, Massachusetts, USA.

Hardcastle, W. and Marchal, A. (1990) *Speech Production and Speech Modeling*. Kluwer Academic Publishers, Norwell, Massachusetts, USA.

Härdle, W. (1990) *Applied Nonparametric Regression*, vol. 19 of Economics Society Monographs. Cambridge University Press, Cambridge, UK.

Harper, M. and Helzerman, R. (1995) Extensions to constraint dependency parsing for spoken language processing. *Computer Speech and Language*, 9(3): 187–234.

Harris, L. (1953) A Study of building blocks in speech. *Journal of the Acoustical Society of America*, 25: 962–969.

Hassab, J. C. (1990) *Underwater Signal and Data Processing*. CRC Press Incorporation, 2nd edition, Boca Raton, Florida, USA.

Hayes, P. (1977) On semantic nets, frames and associations. In *Proceedings of the International Joint Conference on Artificial Intelligence*, 99–107, Cambridge, Massachusetts, USA.

Haykin, S. (1991) *Adaptive Filter Theory*, 2nd edition. Prentice-Hall, Englewood Cliffs, New Jersey, USA.

Haykin, S. (ed.) (1995) *Advances in Spectrum Analysis and Array Processing*. Prentice Hall, Englewood Cliffs, New Jersey, USA.

Hemert, J. P. V. (1991) Automatic segmentation of speech. *IEEE Transactions on Signal Processing*, 39(6): 1008–1012.

Hermansky, H. (1987) An efficient speaker independent automatic speech recognition by simulation of some properties of human auditory perception. In *Proceedings of the IEEE International Conference on Acoustics, Speech and Signal Processing*, 1159–1162, Dallas, Texas, USA.

Hermansky, H. (1990) Perceptual linear predictive (PLP) analysis of speech. *Journal of the Acoustical Society of America*, 87(4): 1738–1752.

Hermansky, H. and Junqua, J. (1988) Optimization of perceptually-based ASR front-end. In *Proceedings of the IEEE International Conference on Acoustics, Speech and Signal Processing*, 219–222, New York, USA.

Hermansky, H. and Morgan, N. (1994) RASTA processing of speech. *IEEE Transactions on Speech and Audio Processing*, 2(4): 578–589.

Hermansky, H., Morgan, N., Bayya, A. and Kohn, P. (1991) Compensation for the effect of the communication channel in auditory-like analysis of speech (RASTA-PLP). In *Proceedings of the European Conference on Speech Communication and Technology*, 1367–1371, Genova, Italy.

Hertz, J., Krogh, A. and Palmer, R. G. (1991) *Introduction to the Theory of Neural Computation*. Addison Wesley, Reading, Massachusetts, USA.

Hess, W. (1983) *Pitch Determination of Speech Signals*. Springer-Verlag, New York, USA.

Hetherington, I. L., Phillips, M. S., Glass, J. R. and Zue, V. W. (1993) A* word network search for continuous speech recognition. In *Proceedings of the European Conference on Speech Communication and Technology*, 1533–1536, Berlin, Germany.

Higgins, A. L. and Wohlford, R. E. (1985) Keyword recognition using template concatenation. In *Proceedings of the IEEE International Conference on Acoustics, Speech and Signal Processing*, 1233–1236, Tampa, Florida, USA.

Hikichi, T. and Itakura, F. (1994) Compensation of the time variation of the acoustic transfer function using linear time warping of the impulse response. *Proceedings of the Acoustical Society of Japan*, 455–456.

Hilal, K. (1993) *Algorithmes accelerés d'égalisation adaptative autodidacte.* Ph.D. thesis, ENST, Telecom Paris 93 E 018, Paris, France.

Hintikka, J. (1962) *Knowledge and Belief.* Cornell University Press, Ithaca, New York, USA.

Hinton, G. E. and Galland, C. C. (1989) Deterministic learning in networks with asymmetric connectivity. *Technical Report CRG-TR-89-6,* Department of Computer Science, University of Toronto, Toronto, Ontario, Canada.

Hinton, G., Williams, C. and Revow, M. (1992) Adaptive elastic models for hand-printed character recognition. In Moody, J., Hanson, S. and Lippmann, R. (eds) *Advances in Neural Information Processing Systems 4,* 512–519, Morgan Kaufmann Publishers, San Mateo, California, USA.

Hinton, G. E., Sejnowski, T. J. and Ackley, D. H. (1984) Boltzmann machines: constraint satisfaction networks that learn. Technical Report TR-CMU-CS-84-119, Carnegie-Mellon University, Department of Computer Science, Pittsburg, Pennsylvania, USA.

Hirahara, T. (1991) Internal speech spectrum representation by spatio-temporal masking pattern. *Journal of the Acoustical Society of America,* **12**(2): 57–68.

Hirsch, H., Meyer, P. and Ruehl, H. (1991) Improved speech recognition using high-pass filtering of subband envelopes. In *Proceedings of the European Conference on Speech Communication and Technology,* 413–416, Genova, Italy.

Ho, T., Wang, H., Chien, L., Chien, K. and Lee, L. (1995) Fast and accurate continuous speech recognition for Chinese language with very large vocabulary. In *Proceedings of the European Conference on Speech Communication and Technology,* Madrid, Spain.

Hobbs, J. and Israel, D. (1994) Principles of template design. In *Proceedings of the Human Language Technology Workshop,* 177–178, Plaisboro, New Jersey; Morgan Kaufmann, Los Altos, California, USA.

Hobbs, J., Stickel, M., Appelt, D. and Martin, P. (1993) Interpretation as abduction. *Artificial Intelligence,* **3**: 69–142.

Hochberg, J., Mniszewski, S. M., Calleja, T. and Papcun, G. J. (1991) A default hierarchy for pronouncing English. *IEEE Transactions on Pattern Analysis and Machine Intelligence,* **13**(9): 957–964.

Hochberg, M. M., Renals, S. J., Robinson, A. J. and Cook, G. D. (1995) Recent improvements to the ABBOT large vocabulary CSR system. In *Proceedings of the IEEE International Conference on Acoustics, Speech and Signal Processing,* I: 69–72, Detroit, Michigan, USA.

Hoffman, M. W. and Buckley, K. M. (1995) Robust time-domain processing of broadband microphone array data. *IEEE Transactions on Speech and Audio Processing,* **3**(3): 193–203.

Hofstetter, E. M. and Rose, R. C. (1992) Techniques for task independent word spotting in continuous speech messages. In *Proceedings of the IEEE International Conference on Acoustics, Speech and Signal Processing,* II: 101–104, San Francisco, California.

Holmes, J., Mattingly, I. and Shearme, J. (1964) Speech synthesis by rule. *Language and Speech,* **7**(3): 127–143.

Homma, S., Takahashi, J. and Sagayama, S. (1996) Iterative unsupervised speaker adaptation for batch dictation. In *Proceedings of the International Conference on Spoken Language Processing,* 1137–1140, Philadelphia, Pennsylvania, USA.

Honig, M. and Messerschmidt, D. (1984) *Adaptive Filters: Structures, Algorithms, and Applications.* Kluwer Academic Publishers, Norwell, Massachusetts, USA.

Hopfield, J. (1982) Neural networks and physical systems with emergent collective computational abilities. *Proceedings of the National Academy of Sciences, USA,* **79**: 2554–2558.

Hopfield, J. and Tank, D. (1986) Computing with neural circuits: a model. *Science,* **233**: 625–633.

Houtgast, T. and Steeneken, H. J. M. (1985) A review of the MTF concept in room acoustics and its use for estimating speech intelligibility in auditoria. *Journal of the Acoustical Society of America*, 77(3): 1069–1077.

Hovy, E. (1990) Pragmatics and natural language generation. *Artificial Intelligence*, 43(2): 153–197.

Huang, X. D. (1992) Speaker normalization for speech recognition. In *Proceedings of the IEEE International Conference on Acoustics, Speech and Signal Processing*, I: 465–468, San Francisco, California, USA.

Huang, C. B., Son-Bell, M. A. and Baggett, D. M. (1994) Generation of pronunciations from orthographies using transformation-based error-driven learning. In *Proceedings of the International Conference on Spoken Language Processing*, 411–414, Yokohama, Japan.

Huang, X., Alleva, F., Hwang, H.-W. H. M.-Y., Lee, K.-F. and Rosenfeld, R. (1993) The SPHINX-II speech recognition system: an overview. *Computer Speech and Language*, 2: 137–148.

Huang, X. and Jack, M. (1989a) Unified technique for vector quantization and hidden Markov modeling using semicontinuous models. In *Proceedings of the IEEE International Conference on Acoustics, Speech and Signal Processing*, I: 639–642, Glasgow, UK.

Huang, X. D. and Jack, M. A. (1989b) Semi-continuous hidden Markov models for speech signals. *Computer Speech and Language*, 3(3): 239–252.

Huang, X. and Lee, K.-F. (1993) On speaker-independent, speaker-dependent, and speaker-adaptive speech recognition. *IEEE Transactions on Speech and Audio Processing*, 1(2): 150–157.

Huang, X., Lee, K. F., Hon, H. W. and Hwang, M. Y. (1991) Improved acoustic modeling with the SPHINX speech recognition system. In *Proceedings of the IEEE International Conference on Acoustics, Speech and Signal Processing*, 1: 345–348, Toronto, Canada.

Hunt, J. M., Lennig, M. and Mermelstein, P. (1980) Experiments in syllable-based recognition of continuous speech. In *Proceedings of the IEEE International Conference on Acoustics, Speech and Signal Processing*, 880–883, Denver, Colorado, USA.

Hunt, M. and Lefebvre, C. (1986) Speech recognition using a Cochlear model. In *Proceedings of the IEEE International Conference on Acoustics, Speech and Signal Processing*, 1979–1982, Tokyo, Japan.

Hunt, M. and Lefebvre, C. (1988) Speaker dependent and independent recognition experiments with an auditory model. In *Proceedings of the IEEE International Conference on Acoustics, Speech and Signal Processing*, 215–218, New York, USA.

Hunt, M. and Lefebvre, C. (1989) A comparison of several acoustic representations for speech recognition with degraded and undegraded speech. In *Proceedings of the IEEE International Conference on Acoustics, Speech and Signal Processing*, 262–265, Glasgow, UK.

Hunt, M. J., Richardson, S. M., Bateman, D. C. and Piau, A. (1991) An investigation of PLP and IMELDA acoustic representations and of their potential for combination. In *Proceedings of the IEEE International Conference on Acoustics, Speech and Signal Processing*, II: 881–884, Toronto, Canada.

Huo, Q., Chan, C. and Lee, C.-H. (1993) Bayesian learning of the parameters of discrete and tied mixture HMM's for speech recognition. In *Proceedings of the European Conference on Speech Communication and Technology*, 1567–1570, Berlin, Germany.

Huo, Q., Chan, C. and Lee, C.-H. (1994) Bayesian learning of the SCHMM parameters for speech recognition. In *Proceedings of the IEEE International Conference on Acoustics, Speech and Signal Processing*, I: 221–224, Adelaide, Australia.

Huo, Q., Chan, C. and Lee, C.-H. (1995) Bayesian adaptive learning of the parameters of hidden Markov models for speech recognition. *IEEE Transactions on Speech and Audio Processing*, 3(5): 334–345.

Huo, Q., Chan, C. and Lee, C.-H. (1996) On-line adaptation of the SCHMM parameters based on the segmental quasi-Bayes learning for speech recognition. *IEEE Transactions on Speech and Audio Processing*, **4**(2): 141–144.

Huo, Q. and Lee, C.-H. (1996) A study of on-line quasi-Bayes adaptation for CDHMM-based speech recognition. In *Proceedings of the IEEE International Conference on Acoustics, Speech and Signal Processing*, **II**: 705–708, Atlanta, USA.

Huo, Q. and Lee, C. H. (1997) On-line adaptive learning of continuous density hidden Markov models based on approximate recursive bayesian estimate. *IEEE Transactions on Audio and Speech Processing*, **5**(2): 161–162.

Hwang, J. and Wang, C. (1997) Joint model and feature space optimization for robust speech recognition. In *International Conference on Acoustics, Speech and Signal Processing*, 855–858, Munich, Germany.

Hwang, M. Y., Huang, X. and Alleva, F. (1993) Predicting unseen triphones with senones. In *Proceedings of the IEEE International Conference on Acoustics, Speech and Signal Processing*, **II**: 311–314, Minneapolis, Minnesota, USA.

Hyde, S. (1972) Automatic speech recognition: literature, survey, and discussion. In David, E. and Denes, P. B. (eds) *Human Communication, A Unified Approach*, McGraw-Hill, New York, USA.

ICASSP (1997) *Proceedings of the IEEE International Conference on Acoustics, Speech and Signal Processing*, Munich, Germany.

Imai, S. and Furuichi, C. (1988) Unbiased estimator of log spectrum and its application to speech signal processing. In *Proceedings of EUSIPCO Conference*, 203–206.

Isotani, R. and Matsunaga, S. (1994) A stochastic language model for speech recognition integrating local and global constraints. In *Proceedings of the IEEE International Conference on Acoustics, Speech and Signal Processing*, **2**: 5–8, Adelaide, Australia.

Issar, S. and Ward, W. (1994) Flexible parsing: CMU's approach to spoken language understanding. In *Proceedings of the Spoken Language Technology Workshop*, 53–58, Plainsboro, New Jersey; Morgan Kaufmann Publishers, Los Altos, California, USA.

Itahashi, S. and Kido, K. (1971) Spoken word recognition using dictionary and phonological rules. *Journal of the Acoustical Society of Japan*, **27**: 473–482.

Itakura, F. (1975a) Line spectrum representation of linear predictive coefficients. *Journal of the Acoustical Society of America*, **57**(4): 535.

Itakura, F. (1975b) Minimum prediction residual principle applied to speech recognition. *IEEE Transactions on Acoustics, Speech and Signal Processing*, **23**: 67–72.

Itakura, F. and Saito, S. (1968) Analysis synthesis telephony based on the maximum likelihood method. In *Proceedings of 6th International Congress on Acoustics*, C-17–C-20, Tokyo, Japan.

Iwahashi, N., Kaiki, N. and Sagisaka, Y. (1992) Concatenation speech synthesis by minimum distortion criteria. In *Proceedings of the IEEE International Conference on Acoustics, Speech and Signal Processing*, **2**: 65–68, San Francisco, California, USA.

Iyer, R., Ostendorf, M. and Rohlicek, J. R. (1994) Language modeling with sentence-level mixtures. In *Proceedings of the ARPA Human Language Technology Workshop*, 82–86, Plainsboro, New Jersey; Morgan Kaufmann, Los Altos, California, USA.

Jackendoff, R. (1990) *Semantic Structures*. The MIT Press, Cambridge, Massachusetts, USA.

Jackson, E., Appelt, D., Bear, J., Moore, R. and Podlozny, A. (1991) A template matcher for robust natural language interpretation. In *Proceedings of the Speech and Natural Language Workshop*, 190–194, Asilomar, California; Morgan Kaufmann Publishers, Los Altos, California, USA.

Jacobs, P. and Zernik, U. (1988) Acquiring lexical knowledge from text: a case study. In *Proceedings of the National Conference on Artificial Intelligence*, 739–744, St. Paul, Minnesota, USA.

Jacobs, R. A., Jordan, M. I., Nowlan, S. J. and Hinton, G. E. (1991) Adaptive mixture of local experts. *Neural Computation*, **3**: 79–87.

Jain, A., Waibel, A. and Touretzly, D. (1992) PARSEC: a structured connectionist parsing system for spoken language. In *Proceedings of the IEEE International Conference on Acoustics, Speech and Signal Processing*, 205–208, San Francisco, California, USA.

Jain, V. and Xu, B. (1987) Autocorrelation distortion function for improved AR modeling. In *Proceedings of the IEEE International Conference on Acoustics, Speech and Signal Processing*, 356–359, Dallas, Texas, USA.

James, D. A. and Young, S. J. (1994) A fast lattice-based approach to vocabulary independent wordspotting. In *Proceedings of the IEEE International Conference on Acoustics, Speech and Signal Processing*, **I**: 377–380, Adelaide, Australia.

Jan, E. E. (1995) Parallel processing of large scale microphone arrays for sound capture. Ph.D. thesis, Rutgers University, New Jersey, USA.

Jan, E. E. and Flanagan, J. L. (1996) Sound capture from spatial volumes: matched-filter processing of microphone arrays having randomly-distributed sensors. In *Proceedings of the IEEE International Conference on Acoustics, Speech and Signal Processing*, 917–920, Atlanta, Georgia, USA.

Jan, E. E., Svaizer, P. and Flanagan, J. L. (1995) Matched-filter processing of microphone array for spatial volume selectivity. In *Proceedings of IEEE ISCAS '95*, 1460–1463.

Jankowski, C. R., Vo, H.-D. and Lippmann, R. P. (1995) A comparison of signal processing front ends for automatic word recognition. *IEEE Transactions on Speech and Audio Processing*, **3**(4): 286–293.

Jardino, M. (1996) Multilingual stochastic *n*-gram class language models. In *Proceedings of the IEEE International Conference on Acoustics, Speech and Signal Processing*, **1**: 161–163, Atlanta, Georgia, USA.

Jardino, M. and Adda, G. (1993) Automatic word classification using simulated annealing. In *Proceedings of the IEEE International Conference on Acoustics, Speech and Signal Processing*, **2**: 41–44, Minneapolis, Minnesota, USA.

Jayant, N. S. and Noll, P. (1984) *Digital Coding of Waveforms*. Prentice-Hall, Englewood Cliffs, New Jersey, USA.

Jaynes, E. T. (1957) Information theory and statistical mechanics. *Physics Reviews*, **106**: 620–630.

Jeanrenaud, P., Ng, K., Siu, M.-H., Rohlicek, J. R. and Gish, H. (1993) Phonetic-based word spotter: various configurations and application to event spotting. In *Proceedings of the European Conference on Speech Communication and Technology*, 1057–1060, Berlin, Germany.

Jeanrenaud, P., Siu, M.-H., Rohlicek, J. R., Meteer, M. and Gish, H. (1994) Spotting events in continuous speech. In *Proceedings of the IEEE International Conference on Acoustics, Speech and Signal Processing*, **I**: 381–384, Adelaide, Australia.

Jelinek, F. (1969) A fast sequential decoding algorithm using a stack. *IBM Journal of Research Development*, **13**: 675–685.

Jelinek, F. (1976) Continuous speech recognition by statistical methods. *Proceedings of the IEEE*, **64**(4): 532–556.

Jelinek, F. (1990) Self-organized language modeling for speech recognition. In Waibel, A. and Lee, K. (eds) *Readings in Speech Recognition*, 450–505. Morgan Kaufmann Publishers, Los Altos, California, USA.

Jelinek, F. (1991) Up from trigrams! The struggle for improved language models. In *Proceedings of the European Conference on Speech Communication and Technology*, 1037–1040, Genova, Italy.

Jelinek, F., Bahl, L. R. and Mercer, R. L. (1975) Design of a linguistic statistical decoder for the recognition of continuous speech. *IEEE Transactions on Information Theory*, **21**(3): 250–256.

Jelinek, F. and Lafferty, J. D. (1991) Computation of the probability of initial substring generation by stochastic context free grammars. *Computational Linguistics*, **17**(3): 315–323.

Jelinek, F., Lafferty, J. D. and Mercer, R. L. (1992) Basic methods of probabilistic context free grammars. In De Mori, R. and Laface, P. (eds) *NATO ASI Speech Recognition and Understanding: Recent Advances, Trends and Applications*, 345–360, Springer Verlag, Berlin and Heidelberg, Germany.

Jelinek, F. and Mercer, R. L. (1980) Interpolated estimation of Markov source parameters from sparse data. In *Pattern Recognition in Practice*, 381–397, Amsterdam, Holland.

Jelinek, F., Merialdo, B., Roukos, S. and Strauss, M. (1991) A dynamic language model for speech recognition. In *Proceedings of the DARPA Speech and Natural Language Workshop*, 293–296, Asilomar, California, USA.

Johnson, D. H. and Dudgeon, D. E. (1993) *Array Signal Processing: Concepts and Techniques*. Prentice Hall, Englewood Cliffs, New Jersey, USA.

Jones, A. and Eisner, J. (1992) A probabilistic parser applied to software testing documents. In *Proceedings of the Tenth National Conference on Artificial Intelligence*, 322–328, San Jose, California, AAAI Press, Menlo Park/MIT Press, Cambridge, USA.

Jones, G. J. F., Foote, J. T., Jones, K. S. and Young, S. J. (1995) Video mail retrieval: the effect of word spotting accuracy on precision. In *Proceedings of the IEEE International Conference on Acoustics, Speech and Signal Processing*, 309–312, Detroit, Michigan, USA.

Jones, G. J. F., Wright, J. H. and Wrigley, E. N. (1992) The HMM interface with hybrid grammar-bigram language models for speech recognition. In *Proceedings of the International Conference on Spoken Language Processing*, 253–256, Banff, Canada.

Jones, M. and Warren, D. (1982) Conceptual dependency and Montague grammar: a step towards reconciliation. In *Proceedings of the National Conference on Artificial Intelligence*, 79–83, Pittsburg, Pennsylvania, USA.

Jordan, M. (1989) Serial order: a parallel, distributed approach. In Elman, J. and Rumelhart, D. (eds) *Advances in Connectionist Theory: Speech*, Lawrence Erlbaum, Hillsdale, Michigan, USA.

Jordan, M. I. and Jacobs, R. A. (1994) Hierarchical mixtures of experts and the EM algorithm. *Neural Computation*, **6**: 181–214.

Joseph, R. (1989) Large vocabulary voice-to-text systems for medical reporting. *Speech Technology*, April–May, 49–51.

Joshi, A. (1987) An introduction to tree-adjoining grammars. In Manaster-Ramer, A. (ed.) *Mathematics of Language*, John Benjamins, Amsterdam, The Netherlands.

Jouvet, D., Bartkova, K. and Monne, J. (1991) On the modelization of allophones in an HMM-based speech recognition system. In *Proceedings of the European Conference on Speech Communication and Technology*, 923–926, Genova, Italy.

Juang, B. (1991) Speech recognition in adverse environments. *Computer Speech and Language*, **5**: 275–294.

Juang, B., Rabiner, L. and Wilpon, J. (1987) On the use of bandpass liftering in speech recognition. *IEEE Transactions on Acoustics, Speech and Signal Processing*, **35**(7): 947–954.

Juang, B. H., Chou, W. and Lee, C. H. (1995) Statistical and discriminative training for speech recognition. In Ayuso, A. J. R. and Soler, J. M. L. (eds) *Speech Recognition and Coding. New Advances and Trends*, 41–55, Springer-Verlag, Berlin, Germany.

Junqua, J. (1993) The Lombard reflex and its role on human listeners and automatic speech recognition. *Journal of the Acoustical Society of America*, **93**(1): 510–524.

Junqua, J. and Wakita, H. (1989) A comparative study of cepstral lifters and distance measures for all-pole models of speech in noise. In *Proceedings of the IEEE International Conference on Acoustics, Speech and Signal Processing*, 476–479, Glasgow, UK.

Junqua, J. C., Mak, B. and Reaves, B. (1994) A robust algorithm for word boundary detection in the presence of noise. *IEEE Transactions on Speech and Audio Processing*, 2(3): 406–412.

Jurafsky, D., Wooters, C., Segal, J., Stolcke, A., Fosler, E., Tajchman, G. and Morgan, N. (1995) Using a stochastic context-free grammar as a language model for speech recognition. In *Proceedings of the IEEE International Conference on Acoustics, Speech and Signal Processing*, 189–192, Detroit, Michigan, USA.

Kabal, P. and Ramachandran, R. P. (1986) The computation of line spectral frequencies using Chebyshev polynomials. *IEEE Transactions on Acoustics, Speech and Signal Processing*, 34(6): 1419–1426.

Kadirkamanathan, V. and Niranjan, M. (1993) A function estimation approach to sequential learning with neural networks. *Neural Computation*, 5(6): 954–975.

Kamp, Y. and Ma, C. (1993) Connection between weighted LPC and high-order statistics for AR model estimation. In *Proceedings of the European Conference on Speech Communication and Technology*, 345–348, Berlin, Germany.

Kaneda, Y. and Ohga, J. (1986) Adaptive microphone-array system for noise reduction. *IEEE Transactions on Acoustics, Speech and Signal Processing*, 34(6): 1391–1400.

Karl, L., Pettey, M. and Shneiderman, B. (1993) Speech versus mouse commands for word processing: an empirical evaluation. *International Journal of Man-Machine Studies*, 39: 667–687.

Kasper, R. and Hovy, E. (1990) Performing integrated syntactic and semantic parsing using classification. In *Proceedings of Speech and National Language Workshop*, 54–59, Hidden Valley, Pennsylvania; Morgan Kaufmann Publishers, Los Altos, California, USA.

Katz, S. M. (1987) Estimation of probabilities from sparse data for the language model component of a speech recognizer. *IEEE Transactions on Acoustics, Speech and Signal Processing*, 35(3): 400–401.

Kautz, H. (1991) *A Formal Theory of Plan Recognition and Its Implementation*. Morgan Kaufmann Publishers, San Mateo, California, USA.

Kawabata, T. and Tamoto, M. (1996) Back-off method for *n*-gram smoothing based on binomial posteriori distribution. In *Proceedings of the IEEE International Conference on Acoustics, Speech and Signal Processing*, 1: 192–195, Atlanta, Georgia, USA.

Kay, S. (1979) The effects of noise on the autoregressive spectral estimator. *IEEE Transactions on Acoustics, Speech and Signal Processing*, 27(5): 478–485.

Kay, S. (1980) Noise compensation for autoregressive spectral estimates. *IEEE Transactions on Acoustics, Speech and Signal Processing*, 28: 292–303.

Kay, S. (1993) *Fundamentals of Statistical Signal Processing: Estimation Theory*, 1st edition. Prentice Hall, Englewood Cliffs, New Jersey, USA.

Kayser, D. (1984) Representer les connaissances: pourquoi? Comment? In *Actes du seminaire GRECO Dialogue homme-machine a composante orale*, Nancy, France.

Kelly, J. and Gerstman, L. (1961) An artificial talker driven from phonetic input. *Journal of the Acoustical Society of America*, 33: 835(A).

Kenne, P. E., O'Kane, M. and Pearcy, H. G. (1995) Language modeling of spontaneous speech in a court context. In *Proceedings of the European Conference on Speech Communication and Technology*, 3: 1801–1804, Madrid, Spain.

Kennedy, R. A., Abhayapala, T., Ward, D. B. and Williamson, R. C. (1996) Nearfield broadband frequency invariant beamforming. In *Proceedings of the IEEE International Conference on Acoustics, Speech and Signal Processing*, 905–908, Atlanta, Georgia, USA.

Kenny, P., Hollan, R., Gupta, V. N., Lennig, M., Mermelstein, P. and O'Shaughnessy, D. (1993) A*-admissible heuristics for rapid lexical access. *IEEE Transactions on Speech and Audio Processing*, 1(1): 49–58.

Kenny, P., Lennig, M. and Mermelstein, P. (1990) Speaker adaptation in a large-vocabulary Gaussian HMM recognizer. *IEEE Transactions on Pattern Analysis and Machine Intelligence*, 12(9): 917–920.

Kent, R. and Read, C. (1992) *The Acoustic Analysis of Speech*. Singular Publishing Group, San Diego, California.

Khalil, F., Jullien, J. P. and Gilloire, A. (1994) Microphone array for sound pickup in teleconference systems. *Journal of the Audio Engineering Society*, **42**(9): 691–700.

Kimura, S. (1990) 100,000-word recognition using acoustic-segment networks. In *Proceedings of the IEEE International Conference on Acoustics, Speech and Signal Processing*, 61–64, Albuquerque, New Mexico, USA.

Kimura, S., Iwamida, H. and Sanada, T. (1989) Extraction and evaluation of phonetic acoustic rules for continuous speech recognition. In *Proceedings of the IEEE International Conference on Acoustics, Speech and Signal Processing*, 338–341, Glasgow, Scotland, UK.

Kimura, T., Endo, M., Hiraoka, S. and Xiyada, K. (1994) Speaker independent word recognition using continuous matching of parameters in time-spectral form based on statistical measure. In *Proceedings of the International Conference on Spoken Language Processing*, 169–172, Banff, Canada.

Kinsler, L. E., Frey, A. R., Coppens, A. B. and Sanders, J. V. (1982) *Fundamentals of Acoustics*, 3rd edition. John Wiley & Sons, New York, USA.

Kirkpatrick, S., Jr., Gelatt, C. D. and Vecchi, M. (1983) Optimization by simulated annealing. *Science*, **220**: 621–680.

Kita, K. and Ward, W. (1991) Incorporating LR parsing into SPHINX. In *Proceedings of the IEEE International Conference on Acoustics, Speech and Signal Processing*, 269–272, Toronto, Canada.

Kita, K., Yano, Y. and Morimoto, T. (1994) One-pass continuous speech recognition directed by generalized LR parsing. In *Proceedings of the International Conference on Spoken Language Processing*, 13–16, Yokohama, Japan.

Kitano, H. and Higuchi, T. (1991) Massively parallel memory based parsing. In *Proceedings of the International Joint Conference on Artificial Intelligence*, 918–924, Sydney, Australia.

Klatt, D. (1976) A digital filter bank for spectral matching. In *Proceedings of the IEEE International Conference on Acoustics, Speech and Signal Processing*, 573–576, Philadelphia, Pennsylvania, USA.

Klatt, D. (1977) Review of the ARPA speech understanding project. *Journal of the Acoustical Society of America*, **62**(6): 1324–1366.

Klatt, D. (1979) Speech perception: a model of acoustic-phonetic analysis and lexical access. *Journal of Phonetics*, **7**: 279–312.

Klatt, D. (1980) Software for a cascade/parallel formant synthesizer. *Journal of the Acoustical Society of America*, **67**: 971–995.

Klatt, D. (1987) Review of text to speech conversion for English. *Journal of the Acoustical Society of America*, **82**: 737–793.

Klein, S. and Simmons, R. (1963) A grammatical approach to grammatical coding of English words. *Journal of the Association for Computing Machinery*, **10**: 334–347.

Klein, W. and Paliwal, K. (eds) (1995) *Speech Coding and Synthesis*. Elsevier, Amsterdam, The Netherlands.

Knapp, C. H. and Carter, G. C. (1976) The generalized correlation method for estimation of time delay. *IEEE Transactions on Acoustics, Speech and Signal Processing*, **24**(4): 320–327.

Kneser, R. (1996) Statistical language modeling using a variable context. In *Proceedings of the International Conference on Spoken Language Processing*, 494–497, Philadelphia, Pennsylvania, USA.

Kneser, R. and Ney, H. (1991) Forming word classes by statistical clustering for statistical language modelling. In Köhler, R. and Rieger, B. B. (eds) *Proceedings of the First International Conference on Quantitative Linguistics*, 221–226, Kluwer Academic Publishers, Norwell, Massachusetts, USA.

Kneser, R. and Ney, H. (1993) Improved clustering technique for class-based statistical language modeling. In *Proceedings of the European Conference on Speech Communication and Technology*, 973–976, Berlin, Germany.

Kneser, R. and Ney, H. (1995) Improved backing-off for *n*-gram language modeling. In *Proceedings of the IEEE International Conference on Acoustics, Speech and Signal Processing*, 1: 181–184, Detroit, Michigan, USA.

Kneser, R. and Steinbiss, V. (1993) On the dynamic adaptation of stochastic language models. In *Proceedings of the IEEE International Conference on Acoustics, Speech and Signal Processing*, II: 586–588, Minneapolis, Minnesota, USA.

Kobayashi, T. and Imai, S. (1984) Spectral analysis using generalized cepstrum. *IEEE Transactions on Acoustics, Speech and Signal Processing*, 32(5).

Koenig, R., Dunn, H. K. and Lacy, L. Y. (1946) The sound spectrograph. *Journal of the Acoustical Society of America*, 18: 19–49.

Kohda, M., Hascimoto, S. and Saito, S. (1970) Spoken digit recognition system with the learning function of reference patterns. In *Fall Meeting Acoustical Society of Japan*, 155–156.

Kohonen, T. (1989) *Self-Organization and Associative Memory*, 3rd edition. Springer-Verlag, Berlin, Germany.

Kohonen, T. (1990) The self-organizing map. *Proceedings of the IEEE*, 78(9): 1464–1480.

Kohonen, T., Barna, G. and Chrisley, R. (1988) Statistical pattern recognition with neural networks: benchmarking studies. In *IEEE International Conference on Neural Networks*, 1: 61–68, San Diego, California; IEEE, New York, USA.

Kompe, R. (1996) Prosody in speech understanding systems. Ph.D. thesis, University of Erlangen, Germany.

Kompe, R., Batliner, A., Kiessling, A., Kilian, U., Niemann, H., Noeth, E. and Regel-Brietzmann, P. (1994) Automatic classification of prosodically marked phrase boundaries in German. In *Proceedings of the IEEE International Conference on Acoustics, Speech and Signal Processing*, II: 173–176, Adelaide, Australia.

Konolige, K. and Pollack, M. (1993) A representationalist theory of intention. In *Proceedings of the International Joint Conference on Artificial Intelligence*, 390–395, Chambery, France.

Konst, E. M. and Boves, L. (1994) Automatic grapheme-to-phoneme conversion of Dutch names. In *Proceedings of the International Conference on Spoken Language Processing*, 735–738, Yokohama, Japan.

Kopec, G. E. (1986) Formant tracking using hidden Markov models and vector quantization. *IEEE Transactions on Acoustics, Speech and Signal Processing*, 34(4): 709–729.

Koppelman, J., Pietra, S. D., Epstein, M., Roukos, S. and Ward, T. (1995) A statistical approach to language modelling for the ATIS task. In *Proceedings of the European Conference on Speech Communication and Technology*, 1785–1788, Madrid, Spain.

Korkmazskiy, F., Juang, B. and Soong, F. (1997) Generalized mixtures of HMMs for continuous speech recognition. In *International Conference on Acoustics, Speech and Signal Processing*, 1443–1446, Munich, Germany.

Kosaka, T., Matsunaga, S. and Sagayama, S. (1996) Speaker-independent speech recognition based on tree-structured speaker clustering. *Computer Speech and Language*, 10(1): 55–74.

Kosaka, T. and Sagayama, S. (1994) Tree-structured speaker clustering for fast speaker adaptation. In *Proceedings of the IEEE International Conference on Acoustics, Speech and Signal Processing*, 245–248, Adelaide, Australia.

Krasner, G. and Pope, S. (1988) A cookbook for using the model-view-controller user interface paradigm in Smalltalk-80. *Journal of Object-Oriented Programming*, 26–49.

Krause, L. O. (1987) A direct solution to GPS-type navigation equations. *IEEE Transactions on Aerospace and Electronic Systems*, 23(2): 225–232.

Kripke, S. (1963) Semantical considerations on modal logic. *Acta Philosophica Fennica*, **16**: 83–94.

Kronland-Martinet, R. (1988) The wavelet transform for analysis, synthesis and processing of speech and music sounds. *Computer Music Journal*, **1**(4): 11–20.

Kroon, P. and Atal, B. (1988) Strategies for improving the performance of CELP coders at low bit rates. In *Proceedings of the IEEE International Conference on Acoustics, Speech and Signal Processing*, 151–154, New York, USA.

Krzyzak, A., Linder, T. and Lugosi, G. (1996) Nonparametric estimation and classification using radial basis functions nets and empirical risk minimization. *IEEE Transactions on Information Theory*, **38**(4): 1323–1338.

Kuhn, R. (1988) Speech recognition and the frequency of recently used words: a modified Markov model for natural language. In *Proceedings of COLING*, 348–350, Budapest, Hungary.

Kuhn, R. and De Mori, R. (1990) A cache-based natural language method for speech recognition. *IEEE Transactions on Pattern Analysis and Machine Intelligence*, **12**(6): 570–582.

Kuhn, R. and De Mori, R. (1995) The application of semantic classification trees to natural language understanding. *IEEE Transactions on Pattern Analysis and Machine Intelligence*, **17**(7): 449–460.

Kukich, K. (1992) Techniques for automatically correcting words in text. *ACM Computing Surveys*, **24**(4): 377–439.

Kupiec, J. (1989) Probabilistic models of short and long distance word dependencies in running text. In *Proceedings of the DARPA Speech and Natural Language Workshop*, 290–295, Morgan Kaufmann Publishers, San Mateo, California, USA.

Kurematsu, A., Takeda, M. and Inoue, S. (1971) A method of pattern recognition using rewriting rules. In *Proceedings of the International Joint Conference on Artificial Intelligence*, 287–297, London, UK.

Kuttruff, H. (1991) *Room Acoustics*, 3rd edition. Elsevier Applied Science, Amsterdam, The Netherlands.

Kuttruff, H. (1994) On the acoustics of auditoria. *Journal of Building Acoustics*, **1**(1): 27–48.

Lacouture, R. and De Mori, R. (1991) Lexical tree compression. In *Proceedings of the European Conference on Speech Communication and Technology*, 581–584, Genova, Italy.

Lacouture, R. and Normandin, Y. (1993) Efficient lexical access strategies. In *Proceedings of the European Conference on Speech Communication and Technology*, 1537–1540, Berlin, Germany.

Ladefoged, P. and Maddieson, J. (1990) Vowels of the world's languages. *Journal of Phonetics*, **80**: 93–122.

Ladefoged, P. and Maddieson, J. (1996) *The Sounds of the World's Languages*. Blackwell Publishers, Cambridge, Massachusetts, USA.

Laface, P., Fissore, L. and Ravera, F. (1994) Automatic generation of words toward flexible vocabulary isolated word recognition. In *Proceedings of the International Conference on Spoken Language Processing*, 2215–2218, Yokohama, Japan.

Lafferty, J., Sleator, D. and Temperley, D. (1992) Grammatical trigrams: a probabilistic model of link grammar. In *Proceedings of the AAAI Conference on Probabilistic Approaches to Natural Language*.

Lafferty, J. D. and Suhm, B. (1995) Cluster expansions and iterative scaling for maximum entropy language models. In Hanson, K. and Silver, R. (eds) *Maximum Entropy and Bayesian Methods*. Kluwer Academic Publishers, Norwell, Massachusetts, USA.

Lambek, J. (1958) The mathematics of sentence structure. *American Mathematical Monthly*, **5**: 154–170.

Lamel, L., Adda-Decker, M. and Gauvain, J. L. (1995) Issues in large vocabulary, multilingual speech recognition. *Eurospeech*, 185–189, Madrid, Spain.

Lamel, L. and De Mori, R. (1995) Speech recognition of European languages. In *Proceedings of the IEEE Automatic Speech Recognition Workshop*, 51–54, Snowbird, Utah, USA.

Lamel, L., Gauvain, J., Prouts, B., Bouhier, C. and Boesch, R. (1993) Generation and synthesis of broadcast messages. In *Proceedings of the ESCA/NATO RSG10 Workshop on Applications of Speech Technology*, 207–210, Lautrach, Germany.

Lamel, L. F. and Gauvain, J. L. (1993) High performance speaker-independent phone recognition using CDHMM. In *Proceedings of the European Conference on Speech Communication and Technology*, 121–124, Berlin, Germany.

Lamel, L. F., Kessel, R. H. and Seneff, S. (1986) Speech database development: design and analysis of the acoustic-phonetic corpus. In Baumann, L. S. (ed.) *Proceedings of the DARPA Workshop on Speech Recognition*, 100–109.

Lamel, L. F., Rabiner, L. R., Rosenberg, A. E. and Wilpon, J. G. (1981) An improved endpoint detector for isolated word recognition. *IEEE Transactions on Acoustics, Speech and Signal Processing*, **29**: 777–785.

Lang, K. J. and Hinton, G. E. (1988) The development of the time-delay neural network architecture for speech recognition. Technical Report CMU-CS-88-152, Carnegie-Mellon University, Pittsburg, Pennsylvania, USA.

Langley, P. and Simon, H. (1995) Applications of machine learning and rule induction. *Communications of the ACM*, **38**(11): 55–64.

Lappin, S. and McCord, M. (1990) Anaphora resolution in slot grammars. *Computational Linguistics*, **16**(4): 197–212.

Lari, K. and Young, S. J. (1990) The estimation of stochastic context-free grammars using the inside-outside algorithm. *Computer Speech and Language*, **4**(1): 35–56.

Lari, K. and Young, S. J. (1991) Applications of stochastic context-free grammars using the inside-outside algorithm. *Computer Speech and Language*, **5**(3): 237–257.

Larson, J. (1992) *Interactive software: tools for building interactive user interfaces.* Prentice-Hall, Englewood Cliffs, New Jersey, USA.

Laver, J. (1994) *Principles of Phonetics.* Cambridge University Press, Cambridge, UK.

Lea, W. (1980) *Trends in Speech Recognition.* Prentice-Hall, Englewood Cliffs, New Jersey, USA.

Le Bouquin, R. (1996) Enhancement of noisy speech signals: application to mobile radio communications. *Speech Communication,* **18**: 3–19.

LeCun, Y. (1986) Learning processes in an asymmetric threshold network. In Soulie, F. F., Bienenstock, E. and Weisbuch, G. (eds) *Disordered Systems and Biological Organization*, 233–240, Springer-Verlag, Berlin, Germany.

LeCun, Y. (1989) Generalization and network design strategies. In Pfeifer, R., Schreter, Z., Soulié F. F. and Steels, L. (eds) *Connectionism in Perspective*, 143–155, Elsevier Publishers, Amsterdam, The Netherlands.

LeCun, Y. and Bengio, Y. (1995) Convolutional networks for images, speech, and time-series. In Arbib, M. A. (ed.) *The Handbook of Brain Theory and Neural Networks*, 255–257, MIT Press.

Lee, C.-H. (1988) On robust linear prediction of speech. In *IEEE Transactions and Signal Processing*, **36**(5).

Lee, C.-H., Rabiner, L. R., Pieraccini, R. and Wilpon, J. (1990) Acoustic modeling for large vocabulary speech recognition. *Computer Speech and Language*, **4**: 127–165.

Lee, C.-H. and Rabiner, L. R. (1989) A frame-synchronous network search algorithm for connected word recognition. *IEEE Transactions on Acoustics, Speech and Signal Processing*, **37**(11): 1649–1658.

Lee, C.-H., Giachin, E., Rabiner, L. R., Pieraccini, R. and Rosenberg, A. E. (1992) Improved acoustic modeling for large vocabulary continuous speech recognition. *Computer Speech and Language*, **6**(2): 103–127.

Lee, C.-H., Lin, C.-H. and Juang, B.-H. (1991) A study on speaker adaptation of the parameters of continuous density hidden Markov models. *IEEE Transactions on Signal Processing*, **39**(4): 806–814.

Lee, K. (1993) The conversational computer: an APPLE perspective. In *Proceedings of the European Conference on Speech Communication and Technology*, **3**: 1377–1380, Berlin, Germany.

Lee, K. and Waibel, A. (1990) *Readings in Speech Recognition*. Morgan Kaufmann Publishers, San Mateo, California, USA.

Lee, K. F. (1988b) Large-vocabulary speaker-independent continuous speech recognition: The SPHINX System. Ph.D. thesis, Carnegie-Mellon University, Pittsburg, Pennsylvania, USA.

Lee, K. F. and Hon, H. W. (1989b) Speaker-independent phone recognition using hidden Markov models. *IEEE Transactions on Acoustics, Speech and Signal Processing*, **37**(11): 1641–1648.

Lee, K. F., Hon, H.-W., Hwang, M.-Y. and Mahajan, S. (1990b) Recent progress and future outlook of the SPHINX speech recognition system. *Computer Speech and Language*, **4**(1): 57–69.

Lee, K. F., Hon, H.-W. and Reddy, R. (1990c) An overview of the SPHINX speech recognition system. *IEEE Transactions on Acoustics, Speech and Signal Processing*, **38**(1): 35–45.

Lee, T., Ching, P. C., Chan, L. W., Cheng, Y. H. and Mak, B. (1995) Tone recognition of isolated Cantonese syllables. *IEEE Transactions on Speech and Audio Processing*, **3**(3): 204–209.

Lee, Y. (1991) Information-theoretic distortion measures for speech recognition. *IEEE Transactions on Signal Processing*, **39**(2): 330–335.

Leggetter, C. J. (1995) Improved acoustic modeling for HMMs using linear transformations. Ph.D. thesis, Cambridge University, Cambridge.

Leggetter, C. and Woodland, P. (1994a) Speaker adaptation of HMMs using linear regression. CUED/F-INFENG 181, Cambridge University, UK.

Leggetter, C. J. and Woodland, P. C. (1994b) Speaker adaptation of continuous density HMMs using multivariate linear regressing. In *Proceedings of the International Conference on Spoken Language Processing*, 451–454, Yokohama, Japan.

Leggetter, C. J. and Woodland, P. C. (1995a) Flexible speaker adaptation for large vocabulary speech recognition. In *Proceedings of the European Conference on Speech Communication and Technology*, 1155–1158, Madrid, Spain.

Leggetter, C. J. and Woodland, P. C. (1995b) Maximum likelihood linear regression for speaker adaptation of continuous density hidden Markov models. *Computer Speech and Language*, **9**: 171–185.

Lennig, M., Sharp, D., Kenny, P., Gupta, V. and Precoda, K. (1992) Flexible vocabulary recognition of speech. In *Proceedings of the International Conference on Spoken Language Processing*, 93–96, Banff, Canada.

Leonard, R. G. (1984) A database for speaker independent digit recognition. In *Proceedings of the IEEE International Conference on Acoustics, Speech and Signal Processing*, **1**: 42.11.1–42.11.4, San Diego, California, USA.

Lepschy, A., Mian, G. and Viaro, U. (1988) A note on line spectral frequencies. *IEEE Transactions on Acoustics, Speech and Signal Processing*, **36**(8): 1355–1357.

Levesque, H. and Brachman, R. (1985) A fundamental tradeoff in knowledge representation and reasoning. In Levesque, H. and Brachman, R. (eds) *Readings in Knowledge Representation*, 42–70, Morgan Kaufmann Publishers, Los Altos, California, USA.

Levin, E. (1990) Word recognition using hidden control neural architecture. In *Proceedings of the IEEE International Conference on Acoustics, Speech and Signal Processing*, 433–436, Albuquerque, New Mexico, USA.

Levin, E. and Pieraccini, R. (1995) Concept-based spontaneous speech understanding system. In *Proceedings of the European Conference on Speech Communication and Technology*, 555–558, Madrid, Spain.

Levin, E., Pieraccini, R. and Bocchieri, E. (1992) Time-warping network: a hybrid framework for speech recognition. In Moody, J., Hanson, S. and Lippmann, R. (eds) *Advances in Neural Information Processing Systems 4*, 151–158, Denver, Colorado, USA.

Levinson, S. E. (1986) Continuously variable duration hidden Markov models for automatic speech recognition. *Computer Speech and Language*, 1(1): 29–45.

Levinson, S. E., Rabiner, L. R. and Sondhi, M. M. (1983) An introduction to the application of the theory of probabilistic functions of a Markov process to automatic speech recognition. *The Bell System Technical Journal*, 62(4): 1035–1074.

Li, T. H. and Gibson, J. D. (1996) Speech analysis and segmentation by parametric filtering. *IEEE Transactions on Speech and Audio Processing*, 4(3): 203–213.

Lieberman, P. and Blumstein, S. (1988) *Speech Physiology, Speech Perception and Acoustic Phonetics*. Cambridge University Press, Cambridge, UK.

Lienard, J.-S. (1987) Speech analysis and reconstruction using short-time elementary waveforms. In *Proceedings of the IEEE International Conference on Acoustics, Speech and Signal Processing*, 948–951, Austin, Texas, USA.

Liljencrants, J. (1968) The OVE-III speech synthesizer. *IEEE Transactions on Audio and Electroacoustics*, 16(1): 137–140.

Lim, J. (1979) Spectral root homomorphic deconvolution system. *IEEE Transactions on Acoustics, Speech and Signal Processing*, 27(3): 223–233.

Lim, J. and Oppenheim, A. (1978) All-pole modeling of degraded speech. *IEEE Transactions on Acoustics, Speech and Signal Processing*, 26(3): 197–210.

Lin, Q., Che, C., Yuk, D., Jin, L., de Vries, B., Pearson, J. and Flanagan, J. L. (1996) Robust distant talking speech recognition. In *Proceedings of the IEEE International Conference on Acoustics, Speech and Signal Processing*, I: 21–24, Atlanta, Georgia, USA.

Linde, Y., Buzo, A. and Gray, R. (1980) An algorithm for vector quantizer design. *IEEE Transactions on Communications*, 28(1): 84–95.

Lindemann, W. (1986) Extension of a binaural cross-correlation model by contralateral inhibition I and II. *Journal of the Acoustical Society of America*, 80: 1608–1630.

Linz, P. (1990) *An Introduction to Formal Languages and Automata*. D.C. Heat and Company, Lexington, MA.

Lippmann, R. (1987) An introduction to computing with neural nets. *IEEE ASSP Magazine*, 4–22.

Lippmann, R. P. and Gold, B. (1987) Neural classifiers useful for speech recognition. In *IEEE Proceedings in First International Conference on Neural Networks*, IV: 417–422, San Diego, California, USA.

Litman, D. and Allen, J. (1987) A plan recognition model for subdialogues in conversations. *Cognitive Science*, 11(2): 163–200.

Litman, D. and Allen, J. (1990) Discourse processing and commonsense plans. In Cohen, P., Morgan, J. and Pollack, M. (eds) *Intentions in Communication*, 365–388, MIT Press, Cambridge, Massachusetts, USA.

Liu, F. H., Moreno, P. J., Stern, R. M. and Acero, A. (1994) Signal processing for robust speech recognition. In *Proceedings of the Spoken Language Technology Workshop*, 309–314. Morgan Kaufmann Publishers, San Mateo, California, USA.

Liu, Q., Champagne, B. and Kabal, P. (1996) A microphone array processing technique for speech enhancement in reverberant space. *Speech Communication*, 18: 317–334.

Ljolje, A. (1994) The importance of cepstral parameter correlations in speech recognition. *Computer Speech and Language*, 8: 223–232.

Ljolje, A. and Fallside, F. (1986) Synthesis of natural sounding pitch contours in isolated utterances. *IEEE Transactions on Acoustics, Speech and Signal Processing*, 34: 1074–1079.

Lockwood, P. and Blanchet, M. (1993) An algorithm for the dynamic inference of hidden Markov models (DIHMM). In *Proceedings of the IEEE International Conference on Acoustics, Speech and Signal Processing*, **II**: 251–254, Minneapolis, Minnesota, USA.

Lockwood, P. and Boudy, J. (1991) Experiments with non-linear spectral subtraction (NSS), hidden Markov models and the projection, for robust speech recognition in cars. In *Proceedings of the European Conference on Speech Communication and Technology*, **1**: 79–82, Genova, Italy.

Loeb, E. and Lyon, R. (1987) Experiments in isolated digit recognition with a Cochlear model. In *Proceedings of the IEEE International Conference on Acoustics, Speech and Signal Processing*, 1131–1134, Dallas, Texas, USA.

Logan, B. T. and Robinson, A. J. (1997) Enhancement and recognition of noisy speech within an autoregressive hidden Markov model framework using noise estimates from the noisy signal. In *International Conference of Acoustics on Speech and Signal Processing*, 843–846, Munich, Germany.

Lokbani, M. N., Jouvet, D. and Monné, J. (1993) Segmental post-processing of the *n*-best solutions in a speech recognition system. In *Proceedings of the European Conference on Speech Communication and Technology*, 811–814, Berlin, Germany.

Lowe, D. and McLachlan, A. (1995) Modeling of non-stationary processes using radial basis function networks. In *Fourth IEE International Conference on Artificial Neural Networks*, 300–305.

Lowerre, B. (1976) A comparative performance analysis of speech understanding systems. Ph.D. thesis, Carnegie-Mellon University, Pittsburgh, Pennsylvania, USA.

Lucassen, J. M. and Mercer, R. L. (1984) An information-theoretic approach to the automatic determination of phonemic baseforms. In *Proceedings of the IEEE International Conference on Acoustics, Speech and Signal Processing*, 42.5.1–42.5.4, San Diego, California, USA.

Lucke, H. (1995) Bayesian belief networks as a tool for stochastic parsing. *Speech Communication*, **16**: 89–118.

Luk, R. W. P. and Damper, R. I. (1991) A novel approach to inferring letter-phoneme correspondences. In *Proceedings of the IEEE International Conference on Acoustics, Speech and Signal Processing*, 741–744, Toronto, Canada.

Lyon, R. and Dyer, L. (1986) Experiments with a computational model of the Cochlea. In *Proceedings of the IEEE International Conference on Acoustics, Speech and Signal Processing*, 1975–1978, Tokyo, Japan.

Lyon, R. and Mead, C. (1988) An analog electronic Cochlea. *IEEE Transactions on Acoustics, Speech and Signal Processing*, **36**(7): 1119–1134.

Lytinen, S. (1992) Semantic-first natural language processing. In *Proceedings of the National Conference on Artificial Intelligence*, 111–116, San Jose, California, USA.

Lyu, R., Chen, L., Hwang, S., Hsieh, H., Yang, R., Bai, B., Weng, J., Yang, Y., Lin, S., Chen, K., Tseng, C. and Lee, L. (1995) Golden Mandarin (III) – a user-adaptive prosodic segment-based Mandarin dictation machine for Chinese language with very large vocabulary. In *Proceedings of the IEEE International Conference on Acoustics, Speech and Signal Processing*, 57–60, Detroit, Michigan, USA.

Ma, C., Kamp, Y. and Willems, L. (1993) Robust signal selection for linear prediction analysis of voiced speech. *Speech Communication*, **12**(1): 69–81.

MacWilliams, F. J. and Sloane, N. J. A. (1976) Pseudo-random sequences and arrays. *Proceedings of the IEEE*, **64**(12): 1715–1729.

Maddieson, J. (1987) *Patterns of Sounds*, 2nd edition. Cambridge studies in speech science and communication. Cambridge University Press, Cambridge, UK.

Maeda, S. (1982) A digital simulation method of the vocal tract system. *Speech Communication*, **1**: 199–229.

Makhoul, J. (1973) Spectral analysis of speech by linear prediction. *IEEE Transactions on Acoustics, Speech and Signal Processing*, **21**(3): 140–148.

Makhoul, J. (1975) Linear prediction: a tutorial review. In *Proceedings of the Institute of Electrical and Electronic Engineering (IEEE)*, **63**(4): 561–580, April.

Makhoul, J. (1977) Stable and efficient lattice methods for linear prediction. In *IEEE Transactions on Acoustics, Speech and Signal Processing*, **25**(5): 423–433, October.

Makhoul, J., Roukos, S. and Gish, H. (1985) Vector quantization in speech coding. *Proceedings of the IEEE*, **73**(11): 1551–1588.

Makino, S., Ito, A., Endo, M. and Kido, K. (1991) A Japanese text dictation system based on phoneme recognition and a dependency grammar. In *Proceedings of the IEEE International Conference on Acoustics, Speech and Signal Processing*, 273–276, Toronto, Canada.

Maltese, G. and Mancini, F. (1992) An automatic technique to include grammatical and morphological information in a trigram-based statistical language model. In *Proceedings of the IEEE International Conference on Acoustics, Speech and Signal Processing*, I: 157–160, San Francisco, California, USA.

Mansour, D. and Juang, B. (1988) The short-time modified coherence representation and its application for noisy speech recognition. In *Proceedings of the IEEE International Conference on Acoustics, Speech and Signal Processing*, 525–528, New York, USA.

Mansour, D. and Juang, B. (1989a) A family of distorsion measures based upon projection operation for robust speech recognition. *IEEE Transactions on Acoustics, Speech and Signal Processing*, **37**(11): 1659–1671.

Mansour, D. and Juang, B. (1989b) The short-time modified coherence representation and noisy speech recognition. *IEEE Transactions on Acoustics, Speech and Signal Processing*, **37**(6): 795–804.

Mäntysalo, J., Torkkola, K. and Kohonen, T. (1992) Experiments on the use of LVQ in phoneme-level segmentation of speech. In *Proceedings of the Second Workshop on Neural Networks for Speech Processing*, 39–52, Firenze, Italy.

Mari, J. F. and Haton, J. P. (1994) Automatic word recognition based on second-order hidden Markov models. In *Proceedings of the International Conference on Spoken Language Processing*, 274–277, Yokohama, Japan.

Markel, J. D. (1972) The SIFT algorithm for fundamental frequency estimation. *IEEE Transactions on AU*, **20**: 367–377.

Markel, J. D. and Gray, A. H. (1976) *Linear Prediction of Speech*. Springer-Verlag, Berlin, Germany.

Markov, A. A. (1913) An example of statistical investigation in the text of 'Eugene Onyegin', illustrating coupling of tests in chains. *Proceedings of the Academy of Sciences of St. Petersburg*, **7**: 153–162, Russia.

Marple, S. L. (1987) *Digital Spectral Analysis with Applications*. Prentice-Hall, Englewood Cliffs, New Jersey, USA.

Martin, G. (1989) The utility of speech input in user-computer interfaces. *International Journal of Man-Machine Studies*, **30**: 355–375.

Martin, P. and Kehler, A. (1994) Speech acts: a test bed for continuous speech applications. In *Proceedings of the AAAI'94, Workshop on Integration of Natural Language and Speech Processing*, Seattle, Washington, USA.

Martin, S., Liermann, J. and Ney, H. (1995) Algorithms for bigram and trigram word clustering. In *Proceedings of the European Conference on Speech Communication and Technology*, **2**: 1253–1256, Madrid, Spain.

Maruyama, H. (1990) Constraint dependency grammar and its weak generative capacity. *Computer Software*.

Marzal, A. and Vidal, E. (1990) A review and new approaches for automatic segmentation of speech signals. In *Proceedings of EUSIPCO*, 43–55, Barcelona, Spain.

Matrouf, D. and Gauvin, J. L. (1997) Model compensation for noises in training and test data. In *International Conference on Acoustics, Speech and Signal Processing*, 831–834, Munich, Germany.

Matsui, T. and Furui, S. (1996) *N*-best-based instantaneous speaker adaptation method for speech recognition. In *Proceedings of the International Conference on Spoken Language Processing*, 969–972, Philadelphia, Pennsylvania, USA.

Matsui, T., Matsuoka, T. and Furui, S. (1997) Smoothed *n*-best based speaker adaptation for speech recognition. In *International Conference on Acoustics, Speech and Signal Processing*, 1015–1018, Munich, Germany.

Matsukoto, H. and Inoue, H. (1992) A piecewise linear spectral mapping for supervised speaker adaptation. In *Proceedings of the IEEE International Conference on Acoustics, Speech and Signal Processing*, I: 449–452, San Francisco, California, USA.

Matsunaga, S., Kosaka, T. and Shimizu, T. (1995) Speaking-style and speaker adaptation for the recognition of spontaneous dialogue speech. In *Proceedings of the European Conference on Speech Communication and Technology*, 1135–1139, Madrid, Spain.

Matsuoka, T. and Lee, C.-H. (1993) A study of on-line bayesian adaptation for HMM-based speech recognition. In *Proceedings of the European Conference on Speech Communication and Technology*, 815–818, Berlin, Germany.

Mauuary, L. (1994) Amelioration des performances des serveurs vocaux interactifs. Ph.D. thesis, University of Rennes, Rennes, France.

Mauuary, L. (1996) Blind equalization for robust telephone based speech recognition. In *Proceedings EUSIPCO*, 125–128, Trieste, Italy.

Mauuary, L. and Monné, J. (1993) Speech/non-speech detection for voice response systems. *Proceedings of Eurospeech*, 1097–1100, Berlin, Germany.

McAulay, R. and Malpass, M. (1980) Speech enhancement using a soft-decision noise suppression filter. *IEEE Transactions on Acoustics, Speech and Signal Processing*, **28**(2): 137–145.

McCandless, M. and Glass, J. (1994) Empirical acquisition of language models for speech recognition. In *Proceedings of the International Conference on Spoken Language Processing*, **2**: 835–838, Yokohama, Japan.

McCarthy, J. (1979) Ascribing mental qualities to machines. Technical report TR stan-CS-79,-725, AIM-326, Stanford University, California, USA.

McCarthy, J. (1980) Circumscription – a form of non-monotic reasoning. *Artificial Intelligence*, **13**: 27–39.

McCarthy, J. and Hayes, P. (1969) Some philosophical problems from the stand point of artificial intelligence. *Machine Intelligence*, **4**: 463–502.

McCulloch, W. and Pitts, W. (1943) A logical calculus of ideas immanent in nervous activity. *Bulletin of Mathematical Biophysics*, **5**: 115–133.

McDermott, E. and Katagiri, S. (1989) Shift-invariant, multi-category phoneme recognition using Kohonen's LVQ2. In *Proceedings of the IEEE International Conference on Acoustics, Speech and Signal Processing*, **1**: 81–84, Glasgow, UK.

McDermott, E. and Katagiri, S. (1991) LVQ-based shift-tolerant phoneme recognition. *IEEE Transactions on Signal Processing*, **39**(6): 1398–1411.

McDonald, D. (1992) An efficient chart-based algorithm for partial-parsing of unrestricted texts. In *Proceedings of the Third Conference on Applied Natural Language Processing*, 193–200, Trento, Italy.

McDonough, J., Anastasakos, T., Zavaliagkos, G. and Gish, H. (1997) Speaker-adapted training on the switchboard corpus. In *International Conference on Acoustics, Speech and Signal Processing*, 1059–1062, Munich, Germany.

McGinn, D. and Johnson, D. (1983) Reduction of all-pole parameter estimation bias by successive autocorrelation. In *Proceedings of the IEEE International Conference on Acoustics, Speech and Signal Processing*, 713–716, Boston, Massachusetts, USA.

McKeown, K. (1985) Discourse strategies for generating natural-language texts. *Artificial Intelligence*, **27**(1): 1–41.

McKinley, B. L. and Whipple, G. H. (1996) Noise model adaptation in model based speech enhancement. In *Proceedings of the IEEE International Conference on Acoustics, Speech and Signal Processing*, 633–636, Atlanta, Georgia, USA.

McLachlan, G. (1992) *Discriminant Analysis and Statistical Pattern Recognition*. Wiley Series in Probability and Mathematical Statistics, John Wiley & Sons.

McRoy, S. (1991) Using multiple knowledge sources for word sense disambiguation. *Computational Linguistics*, **18**(1): 1–30.

McRoy, S. and Hirst, G. (1990) Race-based syntactic attachment. *Cognitive Science*, **14**(3): 313–354.

Medan, Y. and Yair, E. (1989) Pitch synchronous analysis scheme for voiced speech. *IEEE Transactions on Acoustics, Speech and Signal Processing*, **37**(9): 1321–1328.

Medan, Y., Yair, E. and Chazan, D. (1991) Super resolution pitch determination of speech signals. *IEEE Transaction on Signal Processing*, **39**(1): 40–48.

Mel'cuk, I. (1988) *Dependency Syntax: Theory and Practice*. SUNY Press, Albany.

Meng, H. M., Seneff, S. and Zue, V. W. (1994) Phonological parsing for reversible letter-to-sound/sound-to-letter generation. In *Proceedings of the IEEE International Conference on Acoustics, Speech and Signal Processing*, **II**: 1–4, Adelaide, Australia.

Merhav, N. and Ephraim, Y. (1991) Hidden Markov modeling using a dominant state sequence with application to speech recognition. *Computer Speech and Language*, **5**(5): 327–339.

Merialdo, B. (1994) Tagging English text with a probabilistic model. *Computational Linguistics*, **20**(2): 155–172.

Messerschmitt, C. (1982) Echo cancellation in speech and data transmission. *IEEE Journal of Selected Areas in Communications*, **2**(2): 283–297.

Meteer, M. (1992) *Expressibility and the Problem of Efficient Text Planning*. Pinter.

Meteer, M. and Rohlicek, J. (1993) Statistical language modeling combining *n*-gram and context-free grammars. In *Proceedings of the IEEE International Conference on Acoustics, Speech and Signal Processing*, **II**: 37–40, Minneapolis, Minnesota, USA.

Micchelli, C. A. (1986) Interpolation of scattered data: distance matrices and conditionally positive definite functions. *Constrained Approximation*, **2**: 11–22.

Microsoft Corporation (1995) *Speech API Specification*. Microsoft Press, USA.

Miglietta, C., Mokbel, C., Jouvet, D. and Monne, J. (1996) Bayesian adaptation of speech recognizers to field speech data. In *Proceedings of the International Conference on Spoken Language Processing*, 917–920, Philadelphia, Pennsylvania, USA.

Miller, G. (1990) Wordnets. *International Journal of Lexicography*, **4**(3).

Miller, S., Bates, M. *et al.* (1995) Recent progress in hidden understanding models. In *Proceedings of the ARPA Spoken Language Systems Technology Workshop*, 22–25, Austin, Texas. Morgan Kaufmann Publishers, Palo Altos, California, USA.

Miller, S., Bobrow, R., Schwartz, R. and Ingria, R. (1994) Statistical language processing using hidden understanding models. In *Proceedings of the Spoken Language Technology Workshop*, 48–52, Plainsboro, New Jersey; Morgan Kaufmann Publishing, Los Altos, California, USA.

Milner, R. (1989) *Communications and Concurrency*. Prentice-Hall, Englewood Cliffs, New Jersey, USA.

Minami, Y. and Furui, S. (1995) A maximum likelihood procedure for universal adaptation method based on HMM composition. *Proceedings of the IEEE International Conference on Acoustics, Speech and Signal Processing*, 129–132, Detroit, Michigan, USA.

Minsky, M. and Papert, S. (1969) *Perceptrons*. MIT Press, Cambridge, Massachusetts, USA.

Miyoshi, M. and Kaneda, Y. (1988) Inverse filtering of room acoustics. *IEEE Transactions on Acoustics, Speech and Signal Processing*, **36**(2): 145–152.

Moeschler, J. (1989) *Modelisation du Dialogue*. Hermes, Paris, France.

Moisa, L. and Giachin, E. (1995) Automatic clustering of words for probabilistic language models. In *Proceedings of the European Conference on Speech Communication and Technology*, **2**: 1249–1252, Madrid, Spain.

Mokbel, C. (1992) Reconnaissance de la parole dans le bruit: bruitage debruitage. Ph.D. thesis, ENST, TELECOM Paris 92 E 008, France.

Mokbel, C. and Chollet, C. (1991) Word recognition in the car: speech enhancement/ spectral transformation. In *Proceedings of the IEEE International Conference on Acoustics, Speech and Signal Processing*, 925–928, Toronto, Canada.

Mokbel, C. and Chollet, C. (1995) Automatic word recognition in cars. *IEEE Transactions on Speech and Audio Processing*, **3**(5): 346–356.

Mokbel, C. and Jouvet, D. (1995) Recognition of digits over PSN & GSM networks. In *Proceedings of IEEE Workshop on ASR*, 167–168, Snowbird, Utah, USA.

Mokbel, C., Jouvet, D. and Monne, J. (1995) Blind equalization using adaptive filtering for improving speech recognition over telephone. In *Proceedings of Eurospeech*, 1987–1990, Madrid, Spain.

Mokbel, C., Jouvet, D. and Monne, J. (1996) Deconvolution of telephone line effects for speech recognition. *Speech Communication*, **19**(3): 185–196.

Mokbel, C., Monne, J. and Jouvet, D. (1993) On-line adaptation of a speech recognizer to variations in telephone line conditions. In *Proceedings of the European Conference on Speech Communication and Technology*, 1247–1250, Berlin, Germany.

Mokbel, C., Pachès-Leal, P., Jouvet, D. and Monnè, J. (1994) Compensation of telephone line effects for robust speech recognition. In *Proceedings of the International Conference on Spoken Language Processing*, **3**: 987–990, Yokohama, Japan.

Moller, M. (1992) Supervised learning on large redundant training sets. In *Neural Networks for Signal Processing 2*, IEEE Press.

Montacié, C., Choukri, K. and Chollet, G. (1989) Speech recognition using temporal decomposition and multi-layer feed-forward automata. In *Proceedings of the IEEE International Conference on Acoustics, Speech and Signal Processing*, **I**: 409–412, Glasgow, UK.

Montague, R. (1974) *Formal Philosophy*. Yale University Press, New Haven, Connecticut, USA.

Monzingo, R. and Miller, T. (1980) *Introduction to Adaptive Arrays*. John Wiley & Sons, New York, USA.

Mood, A., Graybill, F. and Boes, D. (1974) *Introduction to the Theory of Statistics*. McGraw-Hill, New York, USA.

Moody, J. and Darken, C. (1989) Fast learning in networks of locally-tuned processing units. *Neural Computation*, **1**: 281–294.

Moore, J. and Paris, C. (1991) Requirements for an expert system explanation facility. *Computational Intelligence*, **7**(4): 367–370.

Moore, R. (1980) Reasoning about knowledge and actions. Ph.D. thesis, Mass. Institute of Technology, Cambridge, Massachusetts, USA.

Moore, R., Appelt, D. *et al.* (1995) Combining linguistic and statistical knowledge sources in natural-language processing for ATIS. In *Proceedings of the ARPA Spoken Language Systems Technology Workshop*, Austin, Texas; Morgan Kaufmann Publishers, Los Altos, California, USA.

Moore, R., Cohen, M. *et al.* (1994) SRI's recent progress on the ATIS task. In *Proceedings of the Spoken Language Technology Workshop*, 72–75, Plainsboro, New Jersey; Morgan Kaufmann Publishers, Los Altos, California, USA.

Morgan, N., Konig, Y., Wu, S. and Bourlard, H. (1995) Transition-based statistical training for ASR. In *Proceedings of IEEE Automatic Speech Recognition Workshop*, 133–134, Snowbird, Utah, USA.

Morimoto, T. (1994) Continuous speech recognition using a combination of syntactic constraints and dependency relationship. In *Proceedings of the International Conference on Spoken Language Processing*, 401–404, Banff, Canada.

Morrison, D., Green, T., Shaw, A. and Payne, S. (1984) Speech controlled text editing: effects of input modality and command structure. *International Journal of Man-Machine Studies*, **21**: 49–63.

Morse, P. M. and Ingard, K. U. (1986) *Theoretical Acoustics*. Princeton University Press, Princeton, New Jersey, USA.

Moulines, C. and Charpantier, F. (1990) Pitch-synchronous waveform processing techniques for text-to-speech synthesis using dyphones. *Speech Communication*, **9**: 453–467.

Moulines, E. and Cappé, O. (1996) Synthèse de la Parole à Partir du Texte. *Techniques de l'Ingénieur, traité informatique.*

Moulines, E. and Laroche, J. (1995) Non-parametric techniques for pitch-scale and time-scale modification of speech. *Speech Communication*, **6**: 175–206.

Mourjopoulos, J. N. (1994) Digital equalization of room acoustics. *Journal of the Audio Engineering Society*, **42**(11): 884–900.

Mozer, M. C. (1993) Neural net architectures for temporal sequence processing. In Weigend, A. and Gershenfeld, N. (eds) *Predicting the Future and Understanding the Past*, 243–264, Addison-Wesley, Reading, Massachusetts, USA.

Murthy, S. (1995) On growing better decision trees from data. Ph.D. thesis, Johns Hopkins University, Baltimore, Maryland, USA.

Murthy, S. and Salzberg, S. (1995a) Decision tree induction: how effective is the greedy heuristic? In *Proceedings of the First International Conference on Knowledge Discovery and Data Mining (KDD-95)*, 222–227, Montreal, Canada.

Murthy, S. and Salzberg, S. (1995b) Lookahead and pathology in decision tree induction. In *Proceedings of the International Joint Conference on Artificial Intelligence*, **2**: 1019–1024, Montreal, Canada.

Murveit, H., Butzberger, J., Digalakis, V. and Weintraub, M. (1993) Large vocabulary dictation using SRI's DECIPHER® speech recognition system: progressive search techniques. In *Proceedings of the IEEE International Conference on Acoustics, Speech and Signal Processing*, **II**: 319–322, Minneapolis, Minnesota, USA.

Murveit, H., Monaco, P., Digalakis, V. and Butzberger, J. (1994) Techniques to achieve an accurate real-time large-vocabulary speech recognition system. In *Proceedings of the ARPA Human Language Technology Workshop*, 368–373, Plainsboro, New Jersey, USA.

Musicant, A. D. and Butler, R. A. (1984) The influence of pinnae-based spectral cues on sound localization. *Journal of the Acoustical Society of America*, **75**: 1195–1200.

Nadas, A. (1985) On Turing's formula for word probabilities. *IEEE Transactions on Acoustics, Speech and Signal Processing*, **32**: 1414–1416.

Nagai, A., Takami, J. and Sagayama, S. (1992) The SSS-LR continuous speech recognition system: integrating SSS-derived allophone models and a phoneme-context-dependent TR-parser. In *Proceedings of the International Conference on Spoken Language Processing*, 1511–1514, Banff, Canada.

Nagata, M. (1994) A stochastic morphological analyzer for spontaneously spoken languages. In *Proceedings of the International Conference on Spoken Language Processing*, 795–798, Yokohama, Japan.

Nakamura, S. and Shikano, K. (1990) A comparative study of spectral mapping for speaker adaptation. In *Proceedings of the IEEE International Conference on Acoustics, Speech and Signal Processing*, **I**: 157–160, Albuquerque, New Mexico, USA.

Nathan, K. S., Lee, Y. and Silverman, H. F. (1991) A time-varying analysis method for rapid transitions in speech. *IEEE Transactions on Acoustics, Speech and Signal Processing*, **39**(4): 815–824.

Neely, S. T. and Allen, J. B. (1979) Invertibility of a room impulse response. *Journal of the Acoustical Society of America*, **66**(1): 165–169.

Nerzic, P. (1993) Erreurs et échec dans le dialogue oral homme-machine: détection et réparation. Ph.D. thesis, Universite de Rennes I, France.

Neto, J., Almeida, L., Hochberg, M., Martins, C., Nunes, L., Renals, S. and Robinson, T. (1995) Speaker-adaptation for hybrid HMM-ANN continuous speech recognition system. In *Proceedings of the European Conference on Speech Communication and Technology*, 2171–2174, Madrid, Spain.

Neumeyer, L., Diagalakis, V. and M., M. W. (1994) Training issues and channel equalization techniques for the construction of telephone acoustic models using a high-quality speech corpus. *IEEE Transactions on Speech and Audio Processing*, 2(4): 590–597.

Neumeyer, L., Sankar, A. and Digalakis, V. (1995) A comparative study of speaker adaptation techniques. In *Proceedings of the European Conference on Speech Communication and Technology*, 1127–1130, Madrid, Spain.

Neumeyer, L. and Weintraub, M. (1994a) Microphone-independent robust signal processing using probabilistic optimum filtering. In *Proceedings of Spoken Language Technology Workshop*, 315–320, Morgan Kaufmann Publishers, San Mateo, California, USA.

Neumeyer, L. and Weintraub, M. (1994b) Probabilistic optimum filtering for robust speech recognition. In *Proceedings of the IEEE International Conference on Acoustics, Speech and Signal Processing*, I: 417–420, Adelaide, Australia.

Newell, A. (1982) The knowledge level. *Artificial Intelligence*, 18: 87–128.

Ney, H. (1981) An optimization algorithm for determining the endpoints of isolated utterances. In *Proceedings of the IEEE International Conference on Acoustics, Speech and Signal Processing*, 720–723, Atlanta, Georgia, USA.

Ney, H. (1982) Connected utterance recognition using dynamic programming. In *Proceedings 3rd FASE Conference, DAGA*, 1119–1125, Goettingen, Germany.

Ney, H. (1991) Dynamic programming parsing for context-free grammars in continuous-speech recognition. *IEEE Transactions on Signal Processing*, 39(2): 336–340.

Ney, H. (1992) A comparative study of two search strategies for connected word recognition: dynamic programming and heuristic search. *IEEE Transactions on Pattern Analysis and Machine Intelligence*, 14(5): 586–595.

Ney, H. (1995) Architecture and search strategies for large-vocabulary continuous speech recognition. In Rubio Ayuso, A. and Soler, J. L. (eds) *Speech Recognition and Coding: New Advances and Trends*, vol. 147 of *NATO-ASI Series F*, Springer-Verlag, Berlin, Germany.

Ney, H. and Aubert, X. (1994) A word graph algorithm for large vocabulary, continuous speech recognition. In *Proceedings of the International Conference on Spoken Language Processing*, 1355–1358, Yokohama, Japan.

Ney, H. and Essen, U. (1991) On smoothing techniques for bigram-based natural language modeling. In *Proceedings of the IEEE International Conference on Acoustics, Speech and Signal Processing*, S12.11: 825–828, Toronto, Canada.

Ney, H., Essen, U. and Kneser, R. (1994) On structuring probabilistic dependences in stochastic language modeling. *Computer Speech and Language*, 8: 1 38.

Ney, H., Haeb-Umbach, R., Tran, B.-H. and Oerder, M. (1992a) Improvements in beam search for 10 000-word continuous speech recognition. In *Proceedings of the IEEE International Conference on Acoustics, Speech and Signal Processing*, I: 9–12, San Francisco, California, USA.

Ney, H., Mergel, D., Noll, A. and Paeseler, A. (1992b) Data driven search organization for continuous speech recognition. *IEEE Transactions on Signal Processing*, 40(2): 272–281.

Ney, H. and Noll, A. (1994) Acoustic-phonetic modeling in the SPICOS system. *IEEE Transactions on Speech and Audio Processing*, 2(2): 312–319.

Nguyen, L., Schwartz, R., Zhao, Y. and Zavaliagkos, G. (1994) Is *n*-best dead? In *Proceedings of the ARPA Human Language Technology Workshop*, 386–389, Plainsboro, New Jersey, USA.

Nielsen, N. H. and Wickerhausek, M. (1996) Wavelets and time-frequency analysis. *Proceedings of the IEEE*, 84(4): 523–540.

Nikias, C. L. and Mendel, J. M. (1993) Signal processing with higher-order spectra. *IEEE Signal Processing Magazine*, 10–35.

Niles, L. and Silverman, H. (1990) Combining hidden Markov models and neural network classifiers. In *Proceedings of the IEEE International Conference on Acoustics, Speech and Signal Processing*, 417–420, Albuquerque, New Mexico, USA.

Nilsson, N. J. (1965) *Learning Machines*. McGraw-Hill, New York, USA.

Nilsson, N. J. (1982) *Principles of Artificial Intelligence*. Springer-Verlag, Berlin, Germany.

Nishimura, M. and Sugawara, K. (1988) Speaker adaptation method for HMM-based speech recognition. In *Proceedings of the IEEE International Conference on Acoustics, Speech and Signal Processing*, I: 207–210, New York, USA.

Niyogi, P. and Girosi, F. (1996) On the relationship between generalization error, hypothesis complexity, and sample complexity for radial basis functions. *Neural Computation*, 819–842.

Noll, A. M. (1964) Short time spectrum and cepstrum techniques for vocal pitch detection. *Journal of the Acoustical Society of America*, **36**: 296–302.

Noll, A. M. (1967) Cepstrum pitch determination. *Journal of the Acoustical Society of America*, **41**: 293–309.

Normandin, Y. (1991) Hidden Markov models, maximum mutual information estimation, and the speech recognition problem. Ph.D. thesis, McGill University, Montreal, Quebec, Canada.

Normandin, Y., Cardin, R. and De Mori, R. (1994) High-performance connected digit recognition using maximum mutual information estimation. *IEEE Transactions on Speech and Audio Processing*, **2**(2): 299–311.

Norvig, P. (1983) Frame activated inferences in a story understanding program. In *Proceedings of the International Joint Conference on Artificial Intelligence*, 624–626, Karlsruhe, Germany.

Nöth, E. (1991) *Prosodische Information in der automatischen spracherkennung – berechnung und anwendung*. Nyemeyer, Germany.

Nowlan, S. J. (1991) Soft competitive adaptation: neural network learning algorithms based on fitting statistical mixtures, Ph.D. thesis CMU-CS-91-126, School of Computer Science, Carnegie-Mellon University, Pittsburgh, Pennsylvania, USA.

Noyes, M. and Frankish, C. (1989) A review of speech recognition applications in the office. *Behavior and Technology*, **8**: 475–486.

Nye, J. (1982) Human factor analysis of speech recognition systems. *Speech Technology*, **1**: 50–57.

Odell, J. J., Valtchev, V., Woodland, P. C. and Young, S. J. (1994) A one pass decoder design for large vocabulary recognition. In *Proceedings of the ARPA Human Language Technology Workshop*, 380–385, Plainsboro, New Jersey, USA.

Oerder, M. and Ney, H. (1993) Word graphs: an efficient interface between continuous speech recognition and language understanding. In *Proceedings of the IEEE International Conference on Acoustics, Speech and Signal Processing*, II: 119–122, Minneapolis, Minnesota, USA.

Oh, S. and Viswanathan, V. (1992) Hands-free voice communication in an automobile with a microphone array. In *Proceedings of the IEEE International Conference on Acoustics, Speech and Signal Processing*, I: 281–284, San Francisco, California, USA.

Ohkura, K., Sugiyama, M. and Sagayama, S. (1992) Speaker adaptation based on transfer vector field smoothing with continuous mixture density HMMs. In *Proceedings of the International Conference on Spoken Language Processing*, 369–372, Banff, Canada.

Oja, E. (1982) A simplified neuron model as a principal component analyzer. *Journal of Mathematical Biology*, **15**: 267–273.

Oja, E. (1989) Neural networks, principal components, and subspaces. *International Journal of Neural Systems*, **1**: 61–68.

Oja, E. and Karhunen, J. (1985) On stochastic approximation of the Eigenvectors and Eigenvalues of the expectation of a random matrix. *Journal of Mathematical Analysis and Applications*, **106**: 69–84.

Okada, M., Kurihara, S. and Nakatsu, R. (1994) Incremental elaboration in generating and interpreting spontaneous speech. In *Proceedings of the International Conference on Spoken Language Processing*, 103–106, Yokohama, Japan.

Olive, J., Greenwood, A. and Coleman, J. (1996) *Acoustics of American English Speech.* Springer-Verlag, Berlin and Heidelberg, Germany.

Omologo, M. and Svaizer, P. (1993) Talker localization and speech enhancement in a noisy environment using a microphone array based acquisition system. In *Proceedings of the European Conference on Speech Communication and Technology*, 605–608, Berlin, Germany.

Omologo, M. and Svaizer, P. (1994) Acoustic event localization using a crosspower-spectrum phase based technique. In *Proceedings of the IEEE International Conference on Acoustics, Speech and Signal Processing*, **II**: 273–276, Adelaide, Australia.

Omologo, M. and Svaizer, P. (1996) Acoustic source location in noisy and reverberant environment using CSP analysis. In *Proceedings of the IEEE International Conference on Acoustics, Speech and Signal Processing*, **II**: 921–924, Atlanta, Georgia, USA.

Omologo, M. and Svaizer, P. (1997) Use of the cross-power-spectrum phase in acoustic event location. *IEEE Transactions on Speech and Audio Processing*, **5**(3): 288–292.

Oppenheim, A., Johnson, D. and Steiglitz, S. (1971) Computation of spectra with unequal resolution using fast Fourier transform. *Proceedings of the IEEE*, **59**: 299–301.

Oppenheim, A., Schafer, R. and Stockham, T. (1968) Nonlinear filtering of multiplied and convolved signals. *Proceedings of the IEEE*, **56**: 1264–1291.

Oppenheim, A. V. and Schafer, R. W. (1989) *Discrete-Time Signal Processing.* Prentice-Hall, Englewood Cliffs, New Jersey, USA.

Orr, M. (1995) Regularisation in the selection of radial basis centres. *Neural Computation*, **7**(3): 606–623.

O'Shaughnessy, D. (1987) *Speech Communication – Human and Machine.* Addison-Wesley, Reading, Massachusetts, USA.

Ostendorf, M., Digalakis, V. V. and Kimball, O. A. (1996) From HMM's to segment models: a unified view of stochastic modeling for speech recognition. *IEEE Transactions on Speech and Audio Processing*, **4**(5): 360–378.

Ostendorf, M., Kannan, A. *et al.* (1991) Integration of diverse recognition methodologies through reevaluation of *n*-best sentence hypothesis. In *Proceedings of the 1991 Speech and Natural Language Workshop*, 83–87, Morgan Kaufmann Publishers, Los Altos, California, USA.

Ostendorf, M., Price, P., Bear, J. and Wightman, C. (1990) The use of relative duration in syntactic disambiguation. In *Proceedings of the DARPA Speech and Natural Language Workshop*, 26–31, Hidden Valley, Pennsylvania, USA.

Ostendorf, M. and Roukos, S. (1989) A stochastic segment model for phoneme-based continuous speech recognition. *IEEE Transactions on Acoustics, Speech and Signal Processing*, **37**: 1857–1869.

Ostendorf, M. and Veilleux, N. (1995) A hierarchical stochastic model for automatic prediction of prosodic boundary location. *Computational Linguistics*, **20**(1): 27–54.

Ostendorf, M., Wightman, C. and Veilleux, M. (1993) Parse scoring with prosodic information. *Computer Speech and Language*, **8**: 193–210.

Pachunke, T., Mertineit, O., Wothke, K. and Schmidt, R. (1994) The linguistic knowledge in a morphological segmentation procedure for German. *Computer Speech and Language*, **8**(3): 233–245.

Paliwal, K. K. (1984) Performance of the weighted Burg methods of AR spectral estimation for pitch-synchronous analysis of voiced speech. *Speech Communication*, **3**: 221–231.

Paliwal, K. K. and Atal, B. (1993) Efficient vector quantization of LPC parameters at 24 bits/frame. *IEEE Transactions on Speech and Audio Processing*, **1**(1): 3–14.

Paliwal, K. K. (1988) A study of line spectrum pair frequencies for speech recognition. In *Proceedings of the IEEE International Conference on Acoustics, Speech and Signal Processing*, **1**: 485–488, New York, USA.

Paliwal, K. K. (1990) Lexicon-building methods for an acoustic sub-word based speech recognizer. In *Proceedings of the IEEE International Conference on Acoustics, Speech and Signal Processing*, 729–732, Albuquerque, New Mexico, USA.

Paliwal, K. K. (1992a) Dimensionality reduction of the enhanced feature set for the HMM-based speech recognizer. *Digital Signal Processing*, **2**: 157–173.

Paliwal, K. K. (1992b) On the use of line spectral frequency parameters for speech recognition. *Digital Signal Processing*, **2**: 80–87.

Pallett, D., Fiscus, J., Fisher, W., Garofolo, J., Lund, B. and Pryzbocki, M. (1994) The 1993 benchmark tests for the ARPA spoken language program. In *Proceedings of the ARPA Human Language Technology Workshop*, 51–73, Plainsboro, New Jersey, USA.

Pallett, D. S., Fiscus, J. G., Fisher, W. M., Garofolo, J. S., Lund, B. A. and Pryzbocki, M. A. (1995) The 1994 benchmark tests for the ARPA spoken language program. In *Proceedings of the ARPA Spoken Language Technology Workshop*, 5–38, Austin, Texas, USA.

Palmer, M., Passonneau, R., Weir, C. and Finin, T. (1993) The KERNEL text understanding system. *Artificial Intelligence*, **63**: 17–68.

Panaget, F. (1994) Using a textual representational level component in the context of discourse or dialogue generation. In *Proceedings of the Seventh International Workshop on Natural Language Generation (IWNLG)*, Kennebunkport, Maine, USA.

Panaget, F. (1996) D'un système générique de génération d'énoncés en contexte de dialogue oral à la formalisation logique des capacités linguistiques d'un agent rationnel dialoguant. PhD thesis, University of Rennes, France.

Papoulis, A. (1991) *Probability, Random Variables, and Stochastic Processes*. 3rd edition. McGraw-Hill, New York, USA.

Park, J. and Sandberg, I. W. (1991) Universal approximation using radial-basis-function networks. *Neural Computation*, **3**(2): 246–257.

Park, J. and Sandberg, I. W. (1993) Approximation and radial basis function networks. *Neural Computation*, **5**(2): 305–316.

Partee, B. (1976) *Montague Grammar*. Academic Press, London, UK.

Paul, D. B. (1991a) Algorithms for an optimal A* search and linearizing the search in the stack decoder. In *Proceedings of the IEEE International Conference on Acoustics, Speech and Signal Processing*, 693–696, Toronto, Canada.

Paul, D. B. (1991b) The Lincoln tied-mixture HMM continuous speech recognizer. In *Proceedings of the IEEE International Conference on Acoustics, Speech and Signal Processing*, 329–332, Toronto, Canada.

Paul, D. B. (1992) An efficient A* stack decoder algorithm for continuous speech recognition with a stochastic language model. In *Proceedings of the IEEE International Conference on Acoustics, Speech and Signal Processing*, **I**: 25–28, San Francisco, California, USA.

Paul, D. B. (1995) New developments in the Lincoln stack-decoder based large-vocabulary CSR system. In *Proceedings of the IEEE International Conference on Acoustics, Speech and Signal Processing*, 45–48, Detroit, Michigan, USA.

Paush, R. and Leatherby, J. (1991) A study comparing mouse-only input vs. mouse-plus-voice input for a graphical editor. *Journal of the American Voice Input/Output Society*, **9**(2).

Pearl, J. (1984) *Heuristics: Intelligent Search Strategies for Computer Problem Solving*. Addison-Wesley Publishing Company, Reading, Massachusetts, USA.

Pearlmutter, B. (1989) Learning state space trajectories in recurrent neural networks. *Neural Computation*, 1: 263–269.

Peinado, A., Segura, J., Rubio, A., Garcia, P. and Perez, J. (1996) Discriminative codebook design using multiple vector quantization in HMM-based speech recognizers. *IEEE Transactions on Speech and Audio Processing*, 4(2): 89–95.

Pereira, F., Riley, M. and Sproat, R. (1994) Weighted rational transductions and their application to human language processing. In *Proceedings of the ARPA Human Language Technology Workshop*, 249–254, Plainsboro, New Jersey, USA.

Pereira, F. and Shabes, Y. (1992) Inside-outside reestimation from partially bracketed corpora. In *Proceedings of the Annual Meeting of the Association for Computational Linguistics*, 128–135.

Pereira, F. and Singer, Y. (1995) Beyond word *n*-grams. In *Proceedings of the 3rd Workshop on Very Large Corpora*, MIT, Cambridge, Massachusetts, USA.

Perrault, C. (1990) An application of default logic to speech act theory. In Cohen, P., Morgan, J. and Pollack, M. (eds) *Intentions in Communication*, MIT Press, Cambridge, Massachusetts, USA.

Perrault, C. and Allen, J. (1980) A plan based analysis of indirect speech acts. *American Journal of Computational Linguistics*, 6(3): 167–182.

Peterson, P. M. (1986) Simulating the response of multiple microphones to a single acoustic source in a reverberant room. *Journal of the Acoustical Society of America*, 80(5): 1527–1529.

Petropulu, A. P. and Nikias, C. L. (1990) The complex cepstrum and bicepstrum analytic performance evaluation in the presence of Gaussian noise. *IEEE Transactions on Acoustics, Speech and Signal Processing*, 38(7): 1246–1256.

Phillips, M., Glass, J. and Zue, V. (1991) Modeling context dependency in acoustic-phonetic and lexical representations. In *Proceedings of the Speech and Natural Language Workshop*, 71–76, Asilomar, California, USA.

Phillips, M. and Goddeau, D. (1994) Fast match for segment-based large vocabulary continuous speech recognition. In *Proceedings of the International Conference on Spoken Language Processing*, 1359–1362, Yokohama, Japan.

Pickles, J. O. (1982) *An Introduction to the Physiology of Hearing*. Academic Press, London, UK.

Pieraccini, R. and Levin, E. (1995a) A learning approach to natural language understanding. In Rubio Ayuso, A. and Soler, J. L. (eds) *New Advances and Trends in Speech Recognition and Coding*, NATO meeting/ASI Series volume, Springer-Verlag, Berlin, Germany.

Pieraccini, R. and Levin, E. (1995b) A Spontaneous-speech understanding system for database query applications. In *ESCA Workshop on Spoken Dialogue Systems – Theories and Applications*, Vigso, Denmark.

Pieraccini, R., Levin, E. and Lee, C. (1991) Stochastic representation of conceptual structure in the ATIS task. In *Proceedings of the DARPA Speech and Natural Language Workshop*, 121–124, Morgan Kaufmann Publishers, Los Altos, California, USA.

Pieraccini, R., Tzoukermann, E. *et al.* (1992a) Progress report on the chronus system: ATIS benchmark results. In *Proceedings of the DARPA Speech and Natural Language Workshop*, Morgan Kaufmann Publishers, Los Altos, California, USA.

Pieraccini, R., Tzoukermann, E., Gorelov, Z., Gauvain, J., Levin, E., Lee, C. and Wilpon, J. (1992b) A speech understanding system based on statistical representation of semantics. In *Proceedings of the IEEE International Conference on Acoustics, Speech and Signal Processing*, 193–196, San Francisco, California, USA.

Pineda, F. (1989) Recurrent back-propagation and the dynamical approach to adaptive neural computation. *Neural Computation*, 1: 161–172.

Pinter, I. (1996) Perceptual wavelet-representation of speech signals and its application to speech enhancement. *Computer Speech and Language*, 10(1): 1–22.

Pitton, J. W., Atlas, L. E. and Loughlin, P. J. (1994) Applications of positive time-frequency distributions to speech processing. *IEEE Transactions on Speech and Audio Processing*, **2**(4): 554 566.

Placeway, P., Schwartz, R., Fung, P. and Nguyen, L. (1993) The estimation of powerful language models from small and large corpora. In *Proceedings of the IEEE International Conference on Acoustics, Speech and Signal Processing*, **II**: 33–36, Minneapolis, Minnesota, USA.

Platt, J. (1991) A resource-allocating network for function interpolation. *Neural Computation*, **3**(2): 213–225.

Poggio, T. and Girosi, F. (1989) A theory of networks for approximation and learning. Technical Report 1140, MIT AI Laboratory, Cambridge, Massachusetts, USA.

Poggio, T. and Girosi, F. (1990) Networks for approximation and learning. *Proceedings of the IEEE*, **78**(9): 1481–1497.

Pollard, C. and Sag, I. A. (1994) *Head-Driven Phrase Structure Grammar*. University of Chicago Press, Chicago, USA.

Pols, L. (1971) Real-time recognition of spoken words. *IEEE Transactions on Computers*, **20**(9): 972–978.

Ponting, K. M. and Peeling, S. M. (1991) The use of variable frame rate analysis in speech recognition. *Computer Speech and Language*, **5**(2): 169–180.

Poock, G. (1982) Voice recognition boosts command terminal throughput. *Speech Technology*, **1**: 36–39.

Porter, J. and Boll, S. (1984) Optimal estimators for spectral restoration of noisy speech. In *Proceedings of the IEEE International Conference on Acoustics, Speech and Signal Processing*, 18A2.1–18A2.4, San Diego, California, USA.

Potamianos, A. and Rose, R. C. (1997) On combining frequency warping and spectral shaping in HMM based speech recognition. In *International Conference on Acoustics, Speech and Signal Processing*, 1775–1778, Munich, Germany.

Powell, M. J. D. (1987) Radial basis functions for multivariable interpolation: a review. In Mason, J. C. and Cox, M. G. (eds) *Algorithms for Approximation: IMA-1985 Conference*, Clarendon Press, Oxford, UK.

Pratt, L. and Kamm, C. (1991) Improving a phoneme classification neural network through problem decomposition. In *International Joint Conference on Neural Networks*, **2**: 821–826, Seattle, Washington, IEEE Press.

Press, W. H., Teukolsky, S. A., Vetterling, W. T. and Flannery, B. F. (1992) *Numerical Recipes in C: the Art of Scientific Computing*, 2nd edition. Cambridge University Press.

Preuss, R. and Yarlagadda, R. (1984) Autoregressive spectral estimation in noise with application to speech analysis. In *Proceedings of the IEEE International Conference on Acoustics, Speech and Signal Processing*, **1**: 6.6.1–6.6.4, San Diego, California, USA.

Price, P. (1990) Evaluation of spoken language systems: the ATIS domain. In *Proceedings of the DARPA Speech and Natural Language Workshop*, 91–95, Morgan Kaufmann Publishers, Los Altos, California, USA.

Price, P., Fisher, W., Bernstein, J. and Pallet, D. (1988) The DARPA 1000-word resource management database for continuous speech recognition. In *Proceedings of the IEEE International Conference on Acoustics, Speech and Signal Processing*, 651–654, New York, USA.

Price, P., Ostendorf, M., Shattuch-Hufnagel, S. and Fong, C. (1991) The use of prosody in syntactic disambiguation. *Journal of the Acoustical Society of America*, **90**(6): 2956–2970.

Putnam, W., Rocchesso, D. and Smith, J. (1995) A numerical investigation of the invertibility of room transfer functions. In *Proceedings of IEEE Workshop on Application of Signal Processing to Audio and Acoustics*, Mohonk Mountain House, New Paltz, New York, USA.

Pye, D. and Woodland, P. C. (1997) Experiments in speaker normalization and adaptation for large vocabulary speech recognition. In *International Conference on Acoustics, Speech and Signal Processing*, 1047–1050, Munich, Germany.

Pye, D., Young, S. and Woodland, P. (1995) Large vocabulary multilingual speech recognition using HTK. In *Proceedings of the European Conference on Speech Communication and Technology*, 181–184, Madrid, Spain.

Quilici, A., Dyers, M. and Flowers, M. (1988) Recognizing and responding to plan-oriented misconceptions. *Computational Linguistics*, 14(3). 38–51.

Quinlan, J. (1990) Learning logical definitions from relations. *Machine Learning*, 5: 239–266.

Quinlan, J. and Cameron-Jones, R. (1995) Oversearching and layered search in empirical learning. In *Proceedings of the International Joint Conference on Artificial Intelligence*, 2: 1019–1024, Montreal, Canada.

Rabin, M. and Halpern, J. (1987) A logic to reason about likelihood. *Artificial Intelligence*, 32(3): 379–406.

Rabiner, L. R. (1994) Applications of voice processing to telecommunications. *IEEE Transactions on Speech and Audio Processing*, 2: 199–230.

Rabiner, L. R. and Levinson, S. (1981) Isolated and connected word recognition-theory and selected applications. *IEEE Transactions on Communications*, 29: 621–659.

Rabiner, L. R. and Sambur, M. (1975) An algorithm for determining the endpoints of isolated utterances. *Bell Systems Technical Journal*, 54(2): 297–315.

Rabiner, L. R. (1977) On the use of autocorrelation analysis for pitch detection. *IEEE Transactions on Acoustics, Speech and Signal Processing*, 25: 24–33.

Rabiner, L. R. and Gold, B. (1975) *Theory and Application of Digital Signal Processing*. Prentice-Hall, Englewood Cliffs, New Jersey, USA.

Rabiner, L. R. and Juang, B. H. (1993) *Fundamentals of Speech Recognition*. Prentice-Hall, Englewood Cliffs, New Jersey, USA.

Rabiner, L. R. and Schafer, R. W. (1978) *Digital Processing of Speech Signals*. Prentice-Hall, Englewood Cliffs, New Jersey, USA.

Rabiner, L. R., Wilpon, J. G. and Juang, B. H. (1986) A segmental κ-means training procedure for connected word recognition. *AT&T Technical Journal*, 64(3): 21–40.

Rabiner, L. R., Wilpon, J. G. and Soong, F. K. (1989) High performance connected digit recognition using hidden Markov models. *IEEE Transactions on Acoustics, Speech and Signal Processing*, 37(8): 1214–1225.

Rabinkin, D. V., Renomeron, R. J., Dahl, A., French, J. C., Flanagan, J. L. and Bianchi, M. H. (1996) A DSP implementation of source location using microphone arrays. In *Proceedings of the SPIE '96*, 2846, 88–99, Denver, Colorado, USA.

Rahim, M. (1994) *Artificial Neural Networks for Speech Analysis/Synthesis*. Chapman & Hall, London, UK.

Rahim, M. and Juang, B. (1996) Signal bias removal by maximum likelihood estimation for robust telephone speech recognition. *IEEE Transactions on Speech and Audio Processing*, 4(1): 19–30.

Rajasekaran, P. and Doddington, G. (1986) Recognition of speech under stress and in noise. In *Proceedings of IEEE International Conference on Acoustics, Speech and Signal Processing*, 733–736, Tokyo, Japan.

Ramachandran, P. R. and Kabal, P. (1989) Pitch prediction filters in speech coding. *IEEE Transactions on Acoustics, Speech and Signal Processing*, 37(4): 467–478.

Rao, A. and Georgeff, M. (1992) An abstract architecture for rational agents. In *Proceedings of KR'92*, Cambridge, Massachusetts, USA.

Rao, P. (1993) VOICE: An integrated speech recognition synthesis system for the Hindi language. *Speech Communication*, 13: 197–205.

Ratnaparkhi, A., Roukos, S. and Ward, R. T. (1994) A maximum entropy model for parsing. In *Proceedings of the International Conference on Spoken Language Processing*, 803–806, Yokohama, Japan.

Rayleigh, L. (1907) On our perception of sound direction. *Philosophical Magazine*, 13(6th series): 214–232.

Rayner, M., Carter, D., Digalakis, V. and Price, P. (1994) Combining knowledge sources to reorder *n*-best speech hypothesis lists. In *Proceedings of the ARPA Human Language Technology Workshop*, 212–217, Plainsboro, New Jersey, USA.

Rayner, M. and Wyard, P. (1995) Robust parsing of *n*-best speech hypothesis list using a general grammar-based language model. In *Proceedings of the European Conference on Speech Communication and Technology*, 1793–1796, Madrid, Spain.

Reddy, D. (ed.) (1974) *Speech Recognition*. Academic Press, London, UK.

Reddy, D. (1976) Speech recognition by machine: a review. *Proceedings of the IEEE*, 64(4): 502–531.

Renals, S. (1989) Radial basis function network for speech pattern classification. *Electronics Letters*, 25: 437–439.

Renals, S. and Hochberg, M. (1995) Efficient search using posterior phone probability estimates. In *Proceedings of the IEEE International Conference on Acoustics, Speech and Signal Processing*, 596–599, Detroit, Michigan, USA.

Renals, S. and Rowher, R. (1989) Phoneme classification experiments using radial basis functions. In *International Joint Conference on Neural Networks*, 1: 461–467, Washington D.C., USA.

Rentzepopoulos, P. A. and Kokkinakis, G. K. (1992) Multilingual phoneme to grapheme conversion system based on HMM. In *Proceedings of the International Conference on Spoken Language Processing*, 1191–1194, Banff, Canada.

Ries, K., Buo, F. and Wang, Y. (1995) Improved language modeling by unsupervised acquisition of structure. In *Proceedings of the IEEE International Conference on Acoustics, Speech and Signal Processing*, 193–196, Detroit, Michigan, USA.

Rigoll, G. (1992) Unsupervised information theory-based training algorithms for multi-layer neural networks. In *Proceedings of the IEEE International Conference on Acoustics, Speech and Signal Processing*, I: 393–396, San Francisco, California, USA.

Riley, M., Ljolje, A., Hindle, D. and Pereira, F. (1995) The AT&T 60,000 word speech-to-text system. In *Proceedings of the European Conference on Speech Communication and Technology*, 207–210, Madrid, Spain.

Riley, M. D. (1991) A statistical model for generating pronunciation networks. In *Proceedings of the IEEE International Conference on Acoustics, Speech and Signal Processing*, 737–740, Toronto, Canada.

Rioul, O. and Vetterli, M. (1991) Wavelets and signal processing. *IEEE Signal Processing Magazine*, 14–38.

Ripley, B. (1996) *Pattern Recognition and Neural Networks*. Cambridge University Press, Cambridge, UK.

Robinson, A. J., Almeida, L., Boite, J. M., Bourlard, H., Fallside, F., Hochberg, M., Kershaw, D., Kohn, P., Konig, Y., Morgan, N., Neto, J. P., Renals, S., Saerens, M. and Wooters, C. (1993) A neural network based, speaker independent, large vocabulary, continuous speech recognition system: The WERNICKE project. In *Proceedings of the European Conference on Speech Communication and Technology*, 1941–1944, Berlin, Germany.

Robinson, A. J. and Fallside, F. (1988) Static and dynamic error propagation networks with application to speech coding. In Anderson, D. (ed.) *Neural Information Processing Systems*, 632–641, Denver, CO; American Institute of Physics, New York, USA.

Robinson, A. J. (1994) An application of recurrent nets to phone probability estimation. *IEEE Transactions on Neural Networks*, 5(2): 298–305.

Robinson, A. J. and Fallside, F. (1991) A recurrent error propagation network speech recognition system. *Computer Speech and Language*, 5(3): 259–274.

Roe, D. (1987) Speech recognition with a noise-adapting codebook. In *Proceedings of the IEEE International Conference on Acoustics, Speech and Signal Processing*, 1139–1142, Austin, Texas, USA.

Roe, D. B. and Riley, M. D. (1994) Prediction of word confusabilities for speech recognition. In *Proceedings of the International Conference on Spoken Language Processing*, 227–230, Yokohama, Japan.

Rohlicek, J. R., Jeanrenaud, P., Ng, K., Gish, H., Musicus, B. and Siu, M. (1993) Phonetic training and language modeling for word spotting. In *Proceedings of the IEEE International Conference on Acoustics, Speech and Signal Processing*, II: 459–462, Minneapolis, Minnesota, USA.

Rohlicek, J. R., Russel, W., Roukos, S. and Gish, H. (1989) Continuous hidden Markov modeling for speaker-independent word spotting. In *Proceedings of the IEEE International Conference on Acoustics, Speech and Signal Processing*, 627–630, Glasgow, UK.

Rose, R. C. (1992) Discriminant wordspotting techniques for rejecting non-vocabulary utterances in unconstrained speech. In *Proceedings of the IEEE International Conference on Acoustics, Speech and Signal Processing*, 105–108, San Francisco, California, USA.

Rose, R. C. (1993) Definition of subword acoustic units for wordspotting. In *Proceedings of the European Conference on Speech Communication and Technology*, 1049–1052, Berlin, Germany.

Rose, R. C. and Paul, D. B. (1990) A hidden Markov model based keyword recognition system. In *Proceedings of the IEEE International Conference on Acoustics, Speech and Signal Processing*, 129–132, Albuquerque, New Mexico, USA.

Rosenberg, A. E. and Soong, F. K. (1987) Evaluation of a vector quantization talker recognition system in text independent and text dependent modes. *Computer Speech and Language*, 2: 143–157.

Rosenblatt, F. (1957) The perceptron – a perceiving and recognizing automaton. Technical Report 85-460-1, Cornell Aeronautical Laboratory, Ithaca, New York, USA.

Rosenblatt, F. (1962) *Principles of Neurodynamics*. Spartan, New York, USA.

Rosenfeld, R. (1994) Adaptive statistical language modeling: a maximum entropy approach. Ph.D. thesis, School of Computer Science, Carnegie Mellon University, Pittsburgh, Pennsylvania, USA.

Rosenfeld, R. (1995) Optimizing lexical and *n*-gram coverage via judicious use of linguistic data. In *Proceedings of the European Conference on Speech Communication and Technology*, 3: 1763–1766, Madrid, Spain.

Rosenfeld, R. (1996) A maximum entropy approach to adaptive statistical language modeling. *Computer Speech and Language*, 10: 187–228.

Rosenfeld, R. and Huang, X. (1992) Improvements in stochastic language modeling. In *Proceedings of the DARPA Speech and Natural Language Workshop*, Morgan Kaufmann Publishers, San Mateo, California.

Ross, K., Ostendorf, M. and Shattuck-Hufnagel, S. (1992) Factors affecting pitch accent placement. In *Proceedings of the International Conference on Spoken Language Processing*, 365–368, Banff, Canada.

Rossen, M. L. (1989) Speech syllable recognition with a neural network. Ph.D. thesis, Brown University, Rhode Island, USA.

Rtischev, D., Nahamoo, D. and Picheny, M. (1994) Speaker adaptation via VQ prototype modification. *IEEE Transactions on Speech and Audio Processing*, 2(1, Pt I). 94–97.

Rumelhart, D., Hinton, G. and Williams, R. (1986a) Learning internal representations by error propagation. In Rumelhart, D. and McClelland, J. (eds) *Parallel Distributed Processing*, 1: 318–362, MIT Press, Cambridge, Massachusetts, USA.

Rumelhart, D., Hinton, G. and Williams, R. (1986b) Learning representations by back-propagating errors. *Nature*, 323: 533–536.

Ruske, G. and Schotola, T. (1981) The efficiency of demisyllable segmentation in the recognition of spoken words. In *Proceedings of the IEEE International Conference on Acoustics, Speech and Signal Processing*, 971–974, Atlanta, Georgia, USA.

Russel, M. J. and Moore, R. K. (1985) Explicit modeling of state occupancy in hidden Markov models for automatic speech recognition. In *Proceedings of the IEEE International Conference on Acoustics, Speech and Signal Processing*, 5–8, Tampa, Florida, USA.

Russell, S. and Norvig, P. (1995) *Artificial Intelligence. A Modern Approach*. Hall, Englewood Cliffs, New Jersey, USA.

Sadek, D. M. (1991) Attitudes mentales et interaction rationnelle: vers une theorie formelle de la communication. Ph.D. thesis, Universite de Rennes I, France.

Sadek, D. M. (1992) A study of the logic of intention. In *Proceedings of the 3rd Conference on Principles of Knowledge Representation and Reasoning (KR'92)*, 462–473, Cambridge, Massachusetts, USA.

Sadek, D. M. (1994a) Attitudes mentales et fondement du comportement coopératif. In Pavard, B. (ed.) *Systemes coopératifs: de la modélisation à la conception*, 93–117, Octares Eds.

Sadek, D. M. (1994b) Towards a theory of belief reconstruction: application to communication. *Speech Communication Journal*, **15**(3–4): 251–263. (Special issue on Spoken Dialogue from the International Symposium on Spoken Dialogue, Tokyo, Japan, 1993.)

Sadek, D. M. (1996) Le dialogue homme-machine: de l'ergonomie des interfaces, l'agent intelligent dialoguant. In *Nouvelles Interfaces Homme-Machine*, volume Sirie ARAGO no. 18, 277–321, Lavoisier Editeur, Paris, France.

Sadek, D. M., Bretier, P., Cadoret, V., Cozannet, A., Dupont, P., Ferrieux, A. and Panaget, F. (1995) A cooperative spoken dialogue system based on a rational agent model. A first implementation on the AGS application. In *Proceedings of the Conference on Dialogue Systems*, Hanstholm, Denmark.

Sadek, D. M., Ferrieux, A., Cozannet, A., Bretier, P., Panaget, F., Dupont, P., Simonin, J., Calvary, N. and Tourpin, S. (1996a) Le démonstrateur AGS de système du dialogue oral: principes, implémentation et évaluation. *Note Technique CNET*.

Sadek, D. M., Ferrieux, A., Cozannet, A., Bretier, P., Panaget, F. and Simonin, J. (1996b) Effective human-computer cooperative spoken dialogue: the AGS demonstrator. In *Proceedings of the International Conference on Spoken Language Processing*, 546–549, Philadelphia, Pennsylvania, USA.

Sagayama, S., Yamaguchi, Y., Takahashi, S. and Takahashi, J. (1997) Jacobian approach to fast acoustic model adaptation. In *International Conference on Acoustic, Speech and Signal Processing*, 835–838, Munich, Germany.

Sagisaka, Y. (1990) Speech synthesis from text. *IEEE Communication Magazine* (1).

Sagisaka, Y. and Lee, L. (1995) Speech recognition of Asian languages. In *Proceedings of the IEEE Automatic Speech Recognition Workshop*, 55–57, Snowbird, Utah, USA.

Saito, S. and Itakura, F. (1966) The theoretical consideration of statistically optimum methods for speech spectral density. Electrical Communication Laboratory, NTT, Report (3107), Musashimo, Japan.

Sakai, T. and Doshita, S. (1962) The phonetic typewriter. In *Proceedings of the Conference of the International Federation for Information Processing*, IFIP Munich, Germany.

Sakoe, H. and Chiba, S. (1971) Recognition of continuously spoken words based on time-normalization by dynamic programming. *Journal of the Acoustical Society of Japan*, **27**: 483–490.

Sakoe, H. and Chiba, S. (1978) Dynamic programming algorithm optimization for spoken word recognition. *IEEE Transactions on Acoustics, Speech and Signal Processing*, **26**(1): 43–49.

Salomaa, A. (1969) Probabilistic and weighted grammars. *Information and Control*, **15**: 529–544.

Sanger, T. (1989) An optimality principle for unsupervised learning. In Touretzky, D. (ed.) *Advances in Neural Information Processing Systems* **1**: 11–19, Denver, Colorado; Morgan Kaufmann Publishers, San Mateo, California, USA.

Sankar, A., Beaufays, F. and Digalakis, V. (1995) Training data clustering for improved speech recognition. In *Proceedings of the European Conference on Speech Communication and Technology*, 503–506, Madrid, Spain.

Sankar, A. and Lee, C.-H. (1994) Stochastic matching for robust speech recognition. *Signal Processing Letters*, **1**(8): 124–125.

Sankar, A. and Lee, C.-H. (1995) Robust speech recognition based on stochastic matching. In *Proceedings of the IEEE International Conference on Acoustics, Speech and Signal Processing*, **I**: 121–124, Detroit, Michigan, USA.

Sankar, A. and Lee, C.-H. (1996) A maximum-likelihood approach to stochastic matching for robust speech recognition. *IEEE Transactions on Speech and Audio Processing*, **4**(3): 190–202.

Sankar, A., Neumeyer, L. and Weintraub, M. (1996) An experimental study of acoustic adaptation algorithms. In *Proceedings of the IEEE International Conference on Acoustics, Speech and Signal Processing*, **II**: 713–716, Atlanta, Georgia, USA.

Sato, M. (1990) A real time learning algorithm for recurrent analog neural networks. *Biological Cybernetics*, **62**: 237–241.

Satta, G. and Stock, O. (1994) Bi-directional context-free grammar parsing for natural language processing. *Artificial Intelligence*, **69**(1–2): 123–164.

Schafer, R. W. and Rabiner, L. R. (1970) System for automatic formant analysis of voiced speech. *Journal of the Acoustical Society of America*, **47**: 634–678.

Schau, H. C. and Robinson, A. Z. (1987) Passive source localization employing spherical surfaces from time-of-arrival differences. *IEEE Transactions on Acoustics, Speech and Signal Processing*, **35**: 1223–1225.

Schmandt, C., Ackerman, M. and Hindus, D. (1990) Augmenting a Window system with speech input. *IEEE Computer*, 50–56.

Schmidt, M., Fitt, S., Scott, C. and Jack, M. (1993) Phonetic transcription standards for European names (ONOMASTICA). In *Proceedings of the European Conference on Speech Communication and Technology*, **1**: 279–283, Berlin, Germany.

Schmidt, R. O. (1979) Multiple emitter location and signal parameter estimation. In *Proceedings of the RADC Spectrum Estimation Workshop*, 243–258.

Schroeter, J. and Sondhi, M. M. (1994) Techniques for estimating vocal-tract shapes from the speech signals. *IEEE Transactions on Speech and Audio Processing*, **2**(1): 133–150.

Schroeder, M. R. (1967) Determination of the geometry of the human vocal tract by acoustic measurements. *Journal of the Acoustical Society of America*, **41**(4, Pt 2): 1002–1010.

Schroeder, M. R. and Hall, J. L. (1974) A model for mechanical to neural transduction in the auditory receptor. *Journal of the Acoustical Society of America*, **55**: 1486–1498.

Schroeder, M. R. (1979) Integrated-impulse method measuring sound decay without using impulses. *Journal of the Acoustical Society of America*, **66**(2): 497–500.

Schroeter, J. and Sondhi, M. M. (1994) Techniques for estimating vocal-tract shapes from the speech signal. *IEEE Transactions on Acoustics, Speech and Signal Processing*, **2**(1): 133–150.

Schukat-Talamazzini, E., Kuhn, T. and Niemann, H. (1994) Speech recognition for spoken dialogue systems. In Nieman, H., De Mori, R. and Haurieder, G. (eds) *Progress and Prospects of Speech Research and Technology*, Infix, Munchen, Germany.

Schukat-Talamazzini, E. G., Hendrych, R., Kompe, R. and Niemann, H. (1995) Permugram language models. In *Proceedings of the European Conference on Speech Communication and Technology*, 1773–1776, Madrid, Spain.

Schwartz, R. and Austin, S. (1991) A comparison of several approximate algorithms for finding multiple (*n*-best) sentence hypotheses. In *Proceedings of the IEEE International Conference on Acoustics, Speech and Signal Processing*, 701–704, Toronto, Canada.

Schwartz, R., Austin, S., Kubala, F., Makhoul, J., Nguyen, L., Placeway, P. and Zavaliagkos, G. (1992) New uses for the *n*-best sentence hypotheses within the Byblos speech recognition system. In *Proceedings of the IEEE International Conference on Acoustics, Speech and Signal Processing*, I: 1–4, San Francisco, California, USA.

Schwartz, R. and Chow, Y. L. (1990) The *n*-best algorithm: an efficient and exact procedure for finding the *n* most likely sentence hypothesis. In *Proceedings of the IEEE International Conference on Acoustics, Speech and Signal Processing*, 81–84, Albuquerque, New Mexico, USA.

Schwartz, R., Chow, Y., Kimball, O., Roucos, S., Krasner, M. and Makhoul, J. (1985) Context-dependent modeling for acoustic-phonetic recognition of speech signals. In *Proceedings of the IEEE International Conference on Acoustics, Speech and Signal Processing*, 1205–1208, Tampa, Florida, USA.

Schwartz, R., Chow, Y. and Kubala, F. (1987) Rapid speaker adaptation using a probabilistic spectral mapping. In *Proceedings of the IEEE International Conference on Acoustics, Speech and Signal Processing*, I: 633–636, Dallas, Texas, USA.

Schwartz, R., Nguyen, L., Kubala, F., Chou, G., Zavaliagkos, G. and Makhoul, J. (1994) On using written language training data for spoken language modeling. In *Proceedings of the ARPA Human Language Technology Workshop*, 93–96, Plainsboro, New Jersey, USA.

Searle, J. (1969) *Speech Acts*. Cambridge University Press, UK.

Searle, J. (1979) *Expression and Meaning*. Cambridge University Press, UK.

Searle, J. (1983) *Intentionality: An Essay of Philosophy of Mind*. Cambridge University Press, UK.

Searle, J. and Vanderveken, D. (1985) *Foundations of Illocutionary Logic*. Cambridge University Press, UK.

Sejnowski, T. and Rosenberg, C. C. (1986) NETtalk: A parallel network that learns to read aloud. Technical report 86-01, Department of Electrical Engineering and Computer Science, Johns Hopkins University, Baltimore, Maryland, USA.

Sejnowski, T. and Rosenberg, C. (1987) Parallel networks that learn to pronounce English text. *Complex Systems*, 1(1): 145–168.

Seneff, S. (1984) Pitch and spectral estimation of speech based on an auditory synchrony model. *In Proceedings of the IEEE International Conference on Acoustics, Speech and Signal Processing*, San Diego, California, USA.

Seneff, S. (1988) A joint synchrony/mean-rate model of auditory speech processing. *Journal of Phonetics*, 16(1): 55–76.

Seneff, S. (1989) TINA: a probabilistic syntactic parser for speech understanding systems. *Proceedings of IEEE International Conference on Acoustics, Speech and Signal Processing*, 2: 711–714, Glasgow, UK.

Seneff, S. (1992a) A relaxation method for understanding spontaneous speech utterances. In *Proceedings of the DARPA Speech and Natural Language Workshop*, Morgan Kaufmann Publishers. Los Altos, California, USA.

Seneff, S. (1992b) Robust parsing for spoken language systems In *Proceedings of the IEEE International Conference on Acoustics, Speech and Signal Processing*, 189–192, San Francisco, California, USA.

Seneff, S. (1992c) TINA: a natural language system for spoken language applications. *Computational Linguistics*, 18(1): 61–86.

Seneff, S., McCandless, M. and Zue, V. (1995) Integrating natural language into the word graph search for simultaneous speech recognition and understanding. In *Proceedings of the European Conference on Speech Communication and Technology*, 1781–1784, Madrid, Spain.

Seneff, S., Meng, H. and Zue, V. (1994) Language modeling for recognition and understanding using layered bigrams. In *Proceedings of the International Conference on Spoken Language Processing*, 317–320, Banff, Canada.

Seo, J. and Simmons, R. (1989) Syntactic graphs: a representation for the union of all ambiguous parse trees. *Computational Linguistics*, 15(1): 19–32.

Sessler, G. M. (1996) Silicon microphones. *Journal of the Audio Engineering Society*, 44(1/2): 16–21.

Sessler, G. M., West, J. E. and Kuhl, R. A. (1989) Unidirectional, second order gradient microphone. *Journal of the Acoustical Society of America*, 86: 2063–2066.

Sessler, G. M., West, J. E. and Schroeder, M. R. (1969) Toroidal microphones. *Journal of the Acoustical Society of America*, 46: 28–36.

Seymore, K. and Rosenfeld, R. (1996) Scalable backoff language models. In *Proceedings of the International Conference on Spoken Language Processing*, 232–235, Philadelphia, Pennsylvania, USA.

Shabes, Y. and Joshi, A. (1990) Two recent developments in tree adjoining grammars: semantic and efficient processing. In *Proceedings of Speech and Natural Language Workshop*, 48–53, Morgan Kaufmann Publishers, Los Altos, California, USA.

Shank, R. (ed.) (1975) *Conceptual Information Processing*. North Holland, Amsterdam, The Netherlands.

Shank, R. and Colby, K. (1973) *Computer Models of Thought and Language*. Freeman, San Francisco, California, USA.

Shannon, C. E. (1951) Prediction and entropy of printed English. *Bell Systems Technical Journal*, 30: 50–62.

Shieber, S., van Noord, G., Pereira, F. and Moore, R. (1990) Semantic head-driven generation. *Computational Linguistics*, 16(1): 30–42.

Shieber, S. M. (1986) *An Introduction to Unification-Based Approaches to Grammars*. Center for the Study of Language and Information, Leland Stanford Junior University, Stanford, California, USA.

Shikano, K., Lee, K.-F. and Reddy, R. (1986) Speaker adaptation through vector quantization. In *Proceedings of the IEEE International Conference on Acoustics, Speech and Signal Processing*, 2643–2646, Tokyo, Japan.

Shoham, Y. (1993) Agent-oriented programming. *Artificial Intelligence*, 60(1): 51–92.

Shukat-Talamazzini, E. G., Niemann, H., Eckert, W., Kuhn, T. and Rieck, S. (1992) Acoustic modeling of subword units in the ISADORA speech recognizer. In *Proceedings of the IEEE International Conference on Acoustics, Speech and Signal Processing*, 577–580, San Francisco, California, USA.

Shynk, J. (1992) Frequency-domain and multirate adaptive filtering. *IEEE Signal Processing Magazine*, 9(1): 14–37.

Silverman, H. F. (1987) Some analysis of microphone arrays for speech data acquisition. *IEEE Transactions on Acoustics, Speech and Signal Processing*, 35(12): 1699–1712.

Silverman, H. F. and Kirtman, S. E. (1992) A two-stage algorithm for determining talker location from linear microphone array data. *Computer Speech and Language*, 6: 129–152.

Simard, P. Y., Victorri, B., LeCun, Y. and Denker, J. (1992) Tangent prop – a formalism for specifying selected invariances in an adaptive network. In *Neural Information Processing Systems*, 4: 895–903, Morgan Kaufmann Publishers, San Mateo, California, USA.

Simmer, K. U., Kuczynski, P. and Wasiljeff, A. (1992) Time delay compensation for adaptive multichannel speech enhancement systems. In *Proceedings of ISSSE*, 660–663.

Singer, H. and Sagayama, S. (1992) Pitch dependent phone modeling for HMM based speech recognition. In *Proceedings of the IEEE International Conference on Acoustics, Speech and Signal Processing*, 1: 273–276, San Francisco, California, USA.

Singer, H. and Sagayama, S. (1993) Matrix parser and its applications to IIMM-based speech recognition. In *Proceedings of the IEEE International Conference on Acoustics, Speech and Signal Processing*, II: 295–298, Minneapolis, Minnesota, USA.

Singer, H. and Takami, J. (1994) Speech recognition without grammar or vocabulary constraints. In *Proceedings of the International Conference on Spoken Language Processing*, 2207–2210, Yokohama, Japan.

Singer, Y. (1996) Adaptive mixtures of probabilistic transducers. In Mozer, M., Touretzky, D. and Perrone, M. (eds) *Advances in Neural Information Processing Systems 8*. MIT Press, Cambridge, Massachusetts, USA.

Siohan, O. (1995) On the robustness of linear discriminant analysis as a preprocessing step for noisy speech recognition. In *Proceedings of the IEEE International Conference on Acoustics, Speech and Signal Processing*, I: 125–128, Detroit, Michigan, USA.

Siroux, J., Gilloux, M., Guyomard, M. and Sorin, C. (1989) Le dialogue homme-machine en langue naturel: un Défi? *Annales des Telecommunications*, 44(1–2): 53–76.

Sleator, D. and Temperley, D. (1993) Parsing English with a link grammar. In *Proceedings of the Third International Workshop on Parsing Technologies*.

Sloboda, T. (1995) Dictionary learning: performance through consistency. In *Proceedings of the IEEE International Conference on Acoustics, Speech and Signal Processing*, 453–456, Detroit, Michigan, USA.

SLS95 (1995) *Proceedings of the ARPA Spoken Language Systems Technology Workshop*, Austin, Texas; Morgan Kaufmann Publishers, Los Altos, California, USA.

Slustker, G. (1968) Nelineini metod analisa recevik signalov. *Trudi Nauchno-Isledova-Teliskogo Instituta Radio (NIIR)*, M(2): 76–82.

Smith, J. O. and Abel, J. S. (1987) Closed-form least-squares source location estimation from range-difference measurements. *IEEE Transactions on Acoustics, Speech and Signal Processing*, 35(12): 1661–1669.

Smolders, J., Claes, T., Sablon, G. and Van Compernolle, D. (1994) On the importance of the microphone position for speech recognition in the car. In *Proceedings of the IEEE International Conference on Acoustics, Speech and Signal Processing*, I: 429–432, Adelaide, Australia.

SNL94 (1994) *Proceedings of the 1994 Speech and Natural Language Workshop*. Morgan Kaufmann Publishers, San Mateo, California, USA.

Sondik, E. (1978) The optimal control of partially observable Markov processes over the infinite horizon: discounted case. *Operations Research*, 26: 282–304.

Soo, J. and Pang, K. K. (1990) Multidelay block frequency domain adaptive filters. *IEEE Transactions on Acoustics, Speech and Signal Processing*, 38(2): 373–376.

Soong, F. and Sondhi, M. (1988) A frequency-weighted Itakura spectral distortion measure and its application to speech recognition in noise. *IEEE Transactions on Acoustics, Speech and Signal Processing*, 36(1): 41–48.

Soong, F. K. and Huang, E. F. (1991) A tree-trellis based fast search for finding the n-best sentence hypotheses in continuous speech recognition. In *Proceedings of the IEEE International Conference on Acoustics, Speech and Signal Processing*, 705–708, Toronto, Canada.

Soong, F. K. and Juang, B. (1993) Optimal quantization of LSP parameters. *IEEE Transactions on Speech and Audio Processing*, 1(1): 15–24.

Soong, F. K. and Juang, B. H. (1984) Line spectrum pair (LSP) and speech data compression. In *Proceedings of the IEEE International Conference on Acoustics, Speech and Signal Processing*, 1: 1.10.1–1.10.4, San Diego, California, USA.

Sorin, C. (1994) Towards high-quality multilingual text-to-speech. In Niemann, H. and De Mori, R. and Haqrieder, G. (eds) *Progress and Prospects of Speech Research and Technology*, Infix, Munchen, Germany.

Sorin, C. (1996) *Quel Futur pour les Technologies Vocales? Les Entretiens de la Technologie*. Lannion, France.

Sorin, C., Jouvet, D., Dubois, D., Sadek, D. and Toulharoat, M. (1995) Operational and experimental French telecommunication services using CNET speech recognition and text-to-speech synthesis. *Speech Communication*, **17**: 273–286.

Sowa, J. (1984) *Conceptual Graphs: Information Processing in Mind and Machine.* Addison-Wesley, Reading, Massachusetts, USA.

Spragins, J. (1965) A note on the iterative application of Bayes' rule. *IEEE Transactions on Information Theory*, **11**: 544–549.

Sreenivas, T., Sigh, K. and Niederjohn, R. (1990) Spectral resolution and noise robust ness in auditory modeling. In *Proceedings of the IEEE International Conference on Acoustics, Speech and Signal Processing*, 817–820.

Staab, S. (1995) GLR-parsing of word lattices using a beam search method. In *Proceedings of the European Conference on Speech Communication and Technology*, 1777–1780, Madrid, Spain.

Stallard, D. and Bobrow, R. (1993) The semantic linker – a new fragment combining method. In *Proceedings of the Human Technology Workshop*, 37–42, Plainsboro, New Jersey; Morgan Kaufmann Publishers, Palo Alto, California, USA.

Steede, M. (1993) Lexical choice criteria in language generation. In *Proceedings of the 6th European Chapter of the Association for Computational Linguistics*, 454–459.

Steedman, M. (1989) Parsing spoken language using combinatory grammars. In *Proceedings of the International Parsing Workshop*, Carnegie-Mellon University, Pittsburg, Pennsylvania, USA.

Steeneken, H. and Van Leeuwen, D. (1995) Multi-lingual assessment of speaker independent large vocabulary speech-recognition systems: the SQALE project. In *Proceedings of the European Conference on Speech Communication and Technology*, 1271–1275, Madrid, Spain.

Steeneken, H. J. M. and Houtgast, T. (1980) A physical method for measuring speech-transmission quality. *Journal of the Acoustical Society of America*, **67**(1): 318–326.

Steinbiss, V., Ney, H., Haeb-Umbach, R., Tran, B.-H., Essen, U., Kneser, R., Oerder, M., Meier, H.-G., Aubert, X., Dugast, C. and Geller, D. (1993) The Philips research system for large-vocabulary continuous-speech recognition. In *Proceedings of the European Conference on Speech Communication and Technology*, 2125–2128, Berlin, Germany.

Steinbiss, V., Noll, A., Paeseler, A., Ney, H. and Bergmann, H. (1990) A 10,000-word continuous speech recognition system. In *Proceedings of the IEEE International Conference on Acoustics, Speech and Signal Processing*, **1**: 57–60, Albuquerque, New Mexico, USA.

Steinbiss, V., Tran, B.-H. and Ney, H. (1994) Improvements in beam-search. In *Proceedings of the International Conference on Spoken Language Processing*, 2143–2146, Yokohama, Japan.

Stephenne, A. and Champagne, B. (1995) Cepstral prefiltering for time delay estimation in reverberant environments. In *Proceedings of the IEEE International Conference on Acoustics, Speech and Signal Processing*, 3055–3058, Tampa, Florida, USA.

Stern, R. M. (1988) An overview of models of binaural perception. In *Proceedings of the National Research Council CHABA Symposium*, Washington D.C., USA.

Stern, R. M. and Trahiotis, C. (1995) Model on binaural perception. In *Proceedings Conference on Binaural and Spatial Hearing*.

Stevens, K. (1992) Speech synthesis methods: hommage to Dennis Klatt. In Bailly, G. and Benoit, C. (eds) *Talking Machines: Theories, Models and Designs*, North-Holland, Amsterdam, The Netherlands.

Stock, O., Falcone, R. and Insinnamo, P. (1989) Bidirectional chart: a potential technique for parsing spoken natural language sentences. *Computer Speech and Language*, **3**(3): 219–223.

Stolcke, A. (1995) An efficient probabilistic context-free parsing algorithm that computes prefix probabilities. *Computational Linguistics*, **21**(2): 165–201.

Stolcke, A. and Segal, J. (1994) Precise n-gram probabilities from stochastic context-free grammars. In *Proceedings of the Annual Meeting of the Association of Computational Linguistics*, 74–79, Las Cruces, New Mexico, USA.

Stone, M. (1974) Cross-validatory choice and assessment of statistical predictions. *Journal of the Royal Statistical Society*, **36**(2): 111–147.

Strawson, P. (1971) *Logico-Linguistic Papers*. Methuen, London, UK.

Streit, R. L. and Barrett, R. F. (1990) Frequency line tracking using hidden Markov models. *IEEE Transactions on Acoustics, Speech and Signal Processing*, **38**(4): 586–598.

Sun, D. X. (1995) Robust estimation of spectral center of gravity trajectories using mixture spline models. In *Proceedings of the European Conference on Speech Communication and Technology*, **1**: 749–752, Madrid, Spain.

Svendsen, T. and Soong, F. K. (1987) On the automatic segmentation of speech signals. In *Proceedings of the IEEE International Conference on Acoustics, Speech and Signal Processing*, 77–80, Dallas, Texas, USA.

TAGs (1994) Special issue on tree adjoining grammars. *Computational Linguistics*, **10**(4).

Tait, J. (1983) Semantic parsing and syntactic constraints. In Jones, K. S. and Wilks, Y. A. (eds) *Automatic Natural Language Parsing*. Ellis Horwood/Wiley, Chichester, UK.

Takahashi, S., Aikawa, K. and Sagayama, S. (1997) Discrete mixture HMM. In *International Conference on Acoustics, Speech and Signal Processing*, 971–974, Munich, Germany.

Takahashi, J. and Sagayama, S. (1994) Telephone line characteristic adaptation using vector field smoothing technique. In *Proceedings of the International Conference on Spoken Language Processing*, 991–994, Yokohama, Japan.

Takahashi, J. and Sagayama, S. (1995a) Vector-field-smoothed bayesian learning for incremental speaker adaptation. In *Proceedings of the IEEE International Conference on Acoustics, Speech and Signal Processing*, **I**: 696–699, Detroit, Michigan, USA.

Takahashi, S. and Sagayama, S. (1995b) Four-level tied-structure for efficient representation of acoustic modeling. In *Proceedings of the IEEE International Conference on Acoustics, Speech and Signal Processing*, 520–523, Detroit, Michigan, USA.

Taylor, M., Niel, F. and Bouwhuis, D. G. (eds) (1989) *The Structure of Multimodal Dialogue*. North-Holland, Amsterdam, The Netherlands.

Tebelskis, J., Waibel, A., Petek, B. and Schmidbauer, O. (1991) Continuous speech recognition using linked predictive networks. In Lippmann, R. P., Moody, R. and Touretzky, D. S. (eds) *Advances in Neural Information Processing Systems* 3: 199–205, Denver, Colorado, USA; Morgan Kaufmann Publishers, San Mateo, California, USA.

Teich, E. and Bateman, J. (1994) Towards the application of text generation in an integrated publication system. In *Proceedings of the International Workshop on Natural Language Generation*, 153–162, Kennebunkport, Maine, USA.

Tibrewala, S. and Hermansky, H. (1997) Sub-band based recognition of noisy speech. In *International Conference on Acoustics, Speech and Signal Processing*, 1255–1258, Munich, Germany.

Tierney, J. (1980) A study of LPC analysis of speech in additive noise. In *IEEE Transactions on Acoustics, Speech and Signal Processing*, **28**: 389–397.

Tohkura, Y. (1986) A weighted cepstral distance measure for speech recognition. In *Proceedings of the IEEE International Conference on Acoustics, Speech and Signal Processing*, 761–764, Tokyo, Japan.

Tokuda, K., Kobayashi, T. and Shiomoto, S. (1990) Adaptive filtering based on cepstral representation – adaptive cepstral analysis of speech. In *Proceedings of the IEEE International Conference on Acoustics, Speech and Signal Processing*, 377–380, Albuquerque, New Mexico, USA.

Tomlinson, M. J., Russell, M. J., Moore, R. K., Buckland, A. P. and Fawley, M. A. (1997) Modeling asynchrony in speech using elementary single-signal decomposition. In *International Conference on Acoustics, Speech and Signal Processing*, 1247–1250, Munich, Germany.

Tonomura, M., Kosaka, T. and Matsunaga, S. (1995) Speaker adaptation based on transfer vector field smoothing using maximum a posteriori probability estimation. In *Proceedings of the IEEE International Conference on Acoustics, Speech and Signal Processing*, I: 688–691, Detroit, Michigan, USA.

Torkkola, K. (1993) An efficient way to learn English grapheme-to-phoneme rules automatically. In *Proceedings of the IEEE International Conference on Acoustics, Speech and Signal Processing*, II: 199–202, Minneapolis, Minnesota, USA.

Traber, C. (1992) Fo generation with a database of natural fo patterns and with a neural network. In Bailly, G. and Benoit, C. (eds) *Talking Machines: Theories, Models and Designs*, North-Holland, Amsterdam, The Netherlands.

Trancoso, I. M., Viana, M. C., Silva, F. M., Marques, G. C. and Oliveira, L. C. (1994) Rule-based vs neural network-based approaches to letter-to-phone conversion for Portuguese common and proper names. In *Proceedings of the International Conference on Spoken Language Processing*, 1767–1770, Yokohama, Japan.

Tribolet, J. (1977) A new phase unwrapping algorithm. *IEEE Transactions on Acoustics, Speech and Signal Processing*, **25**: 170–177.

Tribolet, J., Rabiner, L. and Sondhi, M. (1979) Statistical properties of an LPC distance measure. *IEEE Transactions on Acoustics, Speech and Signal Processing*, **27**(5): 550–558.

Tsuboi, H. and Takebayashi, Y. (1992) A real-time task-oriented speech understanding system using keyword-spotting. In *Proceedings of the IEEE International Conference on Acoustics, Speech and Signal Processing*, 197–200, San Francisco, California, USA.

Vaidyanathan, P. P. (1987) Quadrature mirror filter banks, *m*-band extensions and perfect-reconstruction techniques. *IEEE ASSP Magazine*, 4–20.

Van Coile, B. (1991) Inductive learning of pronunciation rules with the DEPES system. In *Proceedings of the IEEE International Conference on Acoustics, Speech and Signal Processing*, 745–748, Toronto, Canada.

Van Coile, B., Leys, S. and Mortier, L. (1992) On the development of a name pronunciation system. In *Proceedings of the International Conference on Spoken Language Processing*, 487–490, Banff, Canada.

Van Compernolle, D. (1990) Switching adaptive filters for enhancing noisy and reverberant speech from microphone array recordings. In *Proceedings of the IEEE International Conference on Acoustics, Speech and Signal Processing*, 833–836, Albuquerque, New Mexico, USA.

Van Compernolle, D., Ma, W., Xie, F. and Van Diest, M. (1990) Speech recognition in noisy environment with the aid of microphone arrays. *Speech Communication*, **9**(5–6): 433–442.

Van Santen, J., Olive, J., Hirschberg, J. and Sproat, R. (eds) (1996) *Speech Synthesis*. Springer-Verlag, Berlin and Heidelberg, Germany.

Van Summers, W., Pisoni, D., Bernacki, R., Pedlow, R. and Stokes, M. (1988) Effects of noise on speech production: acoustic and perceptual analyses. *Journal of the Acoustical Society of America*, **84**(3): 917–928.

Van Veen, B. D. and Buckley, K. M. (1988) Beamforming: a versatile approach to spatial filtering. *IEEE ASSP Magazine*, April, 4–24.

Vapnik, V. (1982) *Estimation of Dependences Based on Empirical Data*. Springer-Verlag, Berlin, Germany.

Vapnik, V. (1995) *The Nature of Statistical Learning Theory*. Springer-Verlag, Berlin, Germany.

Varga, A. and Moore, R. (1990) Hidden Markov model decomposition of speech and noise. In *Proceedings of the IEEE International Conference on Acoustics, Speech and Signal Processing*, 845–848, Albuquerque, New Mexico, USA.

Veilleux, N., Ostendorf, M. and Wightman, C. (1994) Parse scoring with prosodic information. In *Proceedings of the International Conference on Spoken Language Processing*, 1605–1608, Banff, Canada.

Velichico, V. M. and Zagoruiko, N. G. (1970) Automatic recognition of 200-words. *International Journal on Man-Machine Studies*, **2**: 223–232.

Vicens, P. (1969) Aspects of speech recognition by computers. Ph.D. thesis, Stanford University, Stanford, California, USA.

Vidal, E., Casacuberta, F. and Garcia, P. (1995) Syntactic learning techniques in language modeling and acoustic-phonetic decoding. In Ayuso, A. R. and Soler, J. L. (eds) *New Advances and Trends in Speech Recognition and Coding*, 157–173, NATO Meeting/ASI Series volume, Springer-Verlag, New York, USA.

Vidal, E., Pieraccini, R. and Levin, E. (1993) Learning associations between grammars: a new approach to natural language understanding. In *Proceedings of the European Conference on Speech Communication and Technology*, No. 3, 383–386, Berlin, Germany.

Vintsjuk, T. (1968) Speech discrimination by dynamic programming. *Kibernetika*, **4**: 81–88.

Viswanathan, V. and Henry, C. (1986) Evaluation of multisensor speech input for speech recognition in high ambient noise. In *Proceedings of the IEEE International Conference on Acoustics, Speech and Signal Processing*, 85–88, Tokyo, Japan.

Vitale, T. (1991) An algorithm for high accuracy name pronunciation by parametric speech synthesizer. *Computational Linguistics*, **17**(3): 257–276.

Viterbi, A. J. (1967) Error bounds for convolutional codes and an asymptotically optimum decoding algorithm. *IEEE Transactions on Information Theory*, **13**: 260–269.

Vogl, T., Mangis, J., Rigler, J., Zink, W. and Alkon, D. (1988) Accelerating convergence of the back-propagation method. *Biological Cybernetics*, **59**: 257–263.

von der Malsburg, C. (1973) Self-organization of orientation sensitive cells in the striate cortex. *Kybernetik*, **14**.

Vysotsky, G. (1994) Voicedialing SM – the first speech recognition based telephone service delivered to customer's home. In *Proceedings of IVTTA'94*, Tokyo, Japan.

Waast, C. and Bahl, L. R. (1995) Fast match based on decision tree. In *Proceedings of the European Conference on Speech Communication and Technology*, 909–912, Madrid Spain.

Waegner, N. and Young, S. (1994) A trellis-based language model for speech recognition. In *Proceedings of the International Conference on Spoken Language Processing* 245–248, Banff, Canada.

Waibel, A. (1989) Prosody and speech recognition. Morgan Kaufmann, San Mateo California, USA.

Waibel, A. (1989) Modular construction of time-delay neural networks for speech recognition. *Neural Computation*, **1**: 39–46.

Waibel, A., Hanazawa, T., Hinton, G., Shikano, K. and Lang, K. (1989a). Phoneme recognition using time-delay neural networks. *IEEE Transactions on Acoustics Speech and Signal Processing*, **37**: 328–339.

Waibel, A., Sawai, H. and Shikano, K. (1989b) Modularity and scaling in large phonemic neural networks. *IEEE Transactions on Acoustics, Speech and Signal Processing* **37**: 1888–1898.

Wakita, H. (1972) Estimation of the vocal tract shape by optimal inverse filtering and acoustic-articulatory conversion methods. Speech Communication Research Laboratory, Santa Barbara, California, USA.

Wallach, H. (1949) On sound localization. *Journal of the Acoustical Society of America* **10**: 270–274.

Wallerstein, F., Amano, A. and Hataoka, N. (1994) Implementation issues and parsing speed evaluation of HMM-LR parser. In *Proceedings of the International Conference on Spoken Language Processing*, 9–12, Yokohama, Japan.

Waltz, D. and Pollak, J. (1984) Phenomenologically plausible parsing. In *Proceedings National Conference on Artificial Intelligence*, 335–339, Austin, Texas, USA.

Wang, A. and Hirshberg, J. (1992) Automatic classification of intonational phrase boundaries. *Computer Speech and Language*, **6**(2): 175–196.

Wang, H. and Itakura, F. (1991) An approach of dereverberation using multi-microphone sub-band envelope estimation. In *Proceedings of the IEEE International Conference on Acoustics, Speech and Signal Processing*, 953–956, Toronto, Canada.

Wang, H. and Kaveh, M. (1985) Coherent signal-subspace processing for the detection and estimation of angles of arrival of multiple wide-band sources. *IEEE Transactions on Acoustics, Speech and Signal Processing*, **33**(4): 823–831.

Ward, W. (1990) The CMU air travel information service: understanding spontaneous speech. In *Proceedings of the DARPA Speech and Natural Language Workshop*, 127–129, Hidden Valley, Pennsylvania, USA.

Ward, W. (1991) Evaluation of the CMU ATIS system. In *Proceedings of the 1991 Speech and Natural Language Workshop*, 101–105. Morgan Kaufmann Publishers, San Mateo, California, USA.

Ward, W. and Issar, S. (1994a) Integrating semantic constraints into the sphinx-II recognition search. In *Proceedings of the IEEE International Conference on Acoustics, Speech and Signal Processing*, **II**: 17–19, Adelaide, Australia.

Ward, W. and Issar, S. (1994b) Recent improvements in the CMU spoken language understanding system. In *Proceedings of the ARPA Human Language Technology Workshop*, 208–211, Plainsboro, New Jersey, USA.

Ward, W. and Issar, S. (1995) The CMU ATIS system. In *Proceedings of the ARPA Spoken Language Systems Technology Workshop*, Austin, Texas; Morgan Kaufmann Publishers, San Mateo, California, USA.

Ward, W., Isaar, R., Huang, X., Hon, H., Hwang, M., Young, S., Matessa, M., Liu, F. and Stern, R. (1992) Speech understanding in open tasks. In *Proceedings of the 1992 Speech and Natural Language Workshop*, Morgan Kaufmann Publishers, San Mateo, California, USA.

Waterhouse, S., Kershaw, D. and Robinson, T. (1996) Smoothed local adaptation of connectionist systems. In *Proceedings of the International Conference on Spoken Language Processing*, 1309–1312, Philadelphia, Pennsylvania, USA.

Watrous, R. (1994) Speaker normalization and adaptation using second-order connectionist networks. *IEEE Transactions on Neural Networks*, **4**(1): 21–30.

Weintraub, M. (1993) Keyword-spotting using SRI's DECIPHER® large-vocabulary speech-recognition system. In *Proceedings of the IEEE International Conference on Acoustics, Speech and Signal Processing*, **II**: 463–466, Minneapolis, Minnesota, USA.

Weisberg, S. (1980) *Applied Linear Regression*. John Wiley & Sons, New York, USA.

Weizenbaum, J. (1966) Eliza – a computer program for the study of natural language communication between man and machine. *Communications of the Association for Computing Machinery*, **9**: 26–45.

Welch, J. (1977) Automated data entry analysis. Technical Report RADC TR-77-306, Rome Air Development Center Report, Griffis Air Force Base, New York, USA.

Werbos, P. (1974) Beyond regression: new tools for prediction and analysis in the behavioral sciences. Ph.D. thesis, Harvard University, Cambridge, Massachusetts, USA.

Werbos, P. (1988) Generalization of backpropagation with application to a recurrent gas market model. *Neural Networks*, **1**: 339–356.

Wetherell, C. S. (1980) Probabilistic languages: a review and some open questions. *Computing Surveys*, **12**(4): 361–379.

White, G. M. and Neely, R. B. (1976) Speech recognition experiments with linear prediction, bandpass filtering and dynamic programming. *IEEE Transactions on Acoustics, Speech and Signal Processing*, **24**(2).

White, H. (1989) Learning in artificial neural networks: A statistical perspective. *Neural Computation*, **1**(4): 425–464.

White, L. B. (1992) Cartesian hidden Markov models with applications. *IEEE Transactions on Signal Processing*, **40**(6): 1601–1604.

Widrow, B. and Stearns, S. D. (1985) *Adaptive Signal Processing*. Prentice Hall, Englewood Cliffs, New Jersey, USA.

Wiener, N. (1966) *Extrapolation Interpolation and Smoothing of Stationary Time Series*. MIT Press, Cambridge, Massachusetts, USA.

Wightman, C. and Ostendorf, M. (1991) Automatic recognition of prosodic phrases. In *Proceedings of the IEEE International Conference on Acoustics, Speech and Signal Processing*, 321–324, Toronto, Canada.

Wightman, C. and Ostendorf, M. (1994) Automatic labeling of prosodic patterns. *IEEE Transactions on Speech and Audio Processing*, **2**(4): 469–481.

Wildfire, H. (1994) Speech recognition update, No. 16.

Williams, R. and Zipser, D. (1989a) A learning algorithm for continually running fully recurrent neural networks. *Neural Computation*, **1**: 270–280.

Williams, R. and Zipser, D. (1989b) Experimental analysis of the real-time recurrent learning algorithm. *Connection Science*, **1**: 87–111.

Willshaw, D. J. and von der Malsburg, C. (1976) How patterned neural connections can be set up by self-organization. *Proceedings of the Royal Society of London B*, **194**: 431–445.

Wilpon, J. G., Lee, C. H. and Rabiner, L. R. (1991) Improvements in connected digit recognition using higher order spectral and energy features. In *Proceedings of the IEEE International Conference on Acoustics, Speech and Signal Processing*, **1**: 349–352, Toronto, Canada.

Wilpon, J. G., Lee, C. H. and Rabiner, L. R. (1993) Connected digit recognition based on improved acoustic resolution. *Computer Speech and Language*, **7**(1): 15–26.

Wilpon, J. G., Rabiner, L. R., Lee, C.-H. and Goldman, E. R. (1990) Automatic recognition of keywords in unconstrained speech using hidden Markov models. *IEEE Transactions on Acoustics, Speech and Signal Processing*, **38**(11): 1870–1878.

Winograd, T. (1983) *Language as a Cognitive Process*, volume 1 of *Syntax*. Addison-Wesley, Reading, Massachusetts, USA.

Winograd, T. and Flores, F. (1986) *Understanding Computers and Cognition: A New Foundation for Design*. Ablex Publishing, Northwood, New Jersey, USA.

Winston, P. (1992) *Artificial Intelligence*, 3rd edition. Addison-Wesley, Reading, Massachusetts, USA.

Winters, J. and Rose, C. (1989) Minimum distance automata in parallel networks for optimum classification. *Neural Networks*, **2**: 127–132.

Witten, I. H. and Bell, T. C. (1991) The zero-frequency problem: estimating the probabilities of novel events in adaptive text compression. *IEEE Transactions on Information Theory*, **37**(4): 1085–1094.

Wolferstetter, F. and Ruske, G. (1995) Structured Markov models for speech recognition. In *Proceedings of the IEEE International Conference on Acoustics, Speech and Signal Processing*, 544–547, Detroit, Michigan, USA.

Woodard, J. P. (1992) Modeling and classification of natural sounds by product code hidden Markov models. *IEEE Transactions on Signal Processing*, **40**(7): 1833–1835.

Woodland, P., Pye, D. and Gales, M. J. F. (1996) Iterative unsupervised adaptation using maximum likelihood linear regression. In *Proceedings of the International Conference on Spoken Language Processing*, 1129–1132, Philadelphia, Pennsylvania, USA.

Woodland, P. C., Leggetter, C. J., Odell, J. J., Valtchev, V. and Young, S. J. (1995) The 1994 HTK large vocabulary speech recognition system. In *Proceedings of the IEEE International Conference on Acoustics, Speech and Signal Processing*, 73–76, Detroit, Michigan, USA.

Woodland, P. C., Odell, J. J., Valtchev, V. and Young, S. J. (1994) Large vocabulary continuous speech recognition using HTK. In *Proceedings of the IEEE International Conference on Acoustics, Speech and Signal Processing*, II: 125–128, Adelaide, Australia.

Woods, W. (1968) Procedural semantics for question answering. In *Proceedings AFIPS Conference*, **33**: 457–471.

Woods, W. (1975) What's in a link? In Bobrow, D. G. and Collins, A. (eds) *Representation and Understanding*, Academic Press, London, UK.

Wooldrige, M. and Jennings, N. (1994) Towards a theory of cooperative problem solvings. In Demazeau, Y., Muller, J.-P. and Muller, P. J. (eds) *MAAMAW'94*, Odense, Denmark.

Wooters, C. and Stolcke, A. (1994) Multiple-pronunciation lexical modeling in a speaker independent speech understanding system. In *Proceedings of the International Conference on Spoken Language Processing*, 1363–1366, Yokohama, Japan.

Wright, J., Jones, G. and Lloyd-Thomas, H. (1994) A robust language model incorporating a substring parser and extended *n*-grams. In *Proceedings of the IEEE International Conference on Acoustics, Speech and Signal Processing*, I: 361–364, Minneapolis, Minnesota, USA.

Wylegala, W. (1989) A 20,000-word recognizer based on statistical evaluation methods. *Speech Technology*, April–May, 16–18.

Yamada, H., Wang, H. and Itakura, F. (1991) Recovering of broad band reverberant speech signal by sub-band MINT method. In *Proceedings of the IEEE International Conference on Acoustics, Speech and Signal Processing*, 969–972, Toronto, Canada.

Young, S., Hauptmann, A., Ward, W., Smith, E. and Werner, P. (1989) High level knowledge sources in usable speech recognition systems. *Communications of the Association for Computing Machinery*, **32**(2): 183–194.

Young, S. J., Odell, J. J. and Woodland, P. C. (1994) Tree-based state tying for high accuracy acoustic modeling. In *Proceedings of the Human Language Technology Workshop*, 307–312, Plainsboro, New Jersey, USA.

Young, S. J. and Woodland, P. C. (1994) State clustering in hidden Markov model-based continuous speech recognition. *Computer Speech and Language*, **8**(4): 369–384.

Younger, D. H. (1967) Recognition and parsing of context-free languages in time n^3. *Information and Control*, **10**: 189–208.

Yu, Y. and Simmons, R. (1990) Extra output biased learning. In *International Joint Conference on Neural Networks*, Lawrence Erlbaum, Hillsdale, Washington, D.C., USA.

Zavaliagkos, G. (1995) Maximum *a posteriori* adaptation techniques for speech recognitions. Ph.D. thesis, Northeastern University, Boston, USA.

Zavaliagkos, G., Austin, S., Makhoul, J. and Schwartz, R. (1993) A hybrid continuous speech recognition system using segmental neural nets with hidden Markov models. *International Journal of Pattern Recognition and Artificial Intelligence*, 305–319. (Special Issue on Applications of Neural Networks to Pattern Recognition, I. Guyon (ed.).)

Zavaliagkos, G., Schwartz, R. and Makhoul, J. (1995a) Batch, incremental and instantaneous adaptation techniques for speech recognition. In *Proceedings of the IEEE International Conference on Acoustics, Speech and Signal Processing*, I: 676–679, Detroit, Michigan, USA.

Zavaliagkos, G., Schwartz, R., McDonough, J. and Makhoul, J. (1995b) Adaptation algorithms for large scale HMM recognizer. In *Proceedings of the European Conference on Speech Communication and Technology*, 1131–1134, Madrid, Spain.

Zelinski, R. (1988) A microphone array with adaptive post-filtering for noise reduction in reverberant rooms. In *Proceedings of the IEEE International Conference on Acoustics, Speech and Signal Processing*, 2378–2581, New York, USA.

Zhan, P. and Westphal, M. (1997) Speaker normalization based on frequency warping. In *International Conference on Acoustics, Speech and Signal Processing*, 1039–1042, Munich, Germany.

Zhao, Y. (1994) An acoustic-phonetic based speaker adaptation technique for improving speaker independent continuous speech recognition. *IEEE Transactions on Speech and Audio Processing*, 2(3): 380–394.

Zhao, Y. (1996) Self-learning speaker and channel adaptation based on spectral variation source decomposition. *Speech Communication*, 18(1): 65–77.

Zhao, Y., Atlas, L. and Marks, R. (1990) The use of cone-shaped kernels for generalized time-frequency representations of nonstationary signals. *IEEE Transactions on Acoustics, Speech and Signal Processing*, 38(7): 1084–1091.

Zissman, M. A. (1995) Overview of current techniques for automatic language identification of speech. In *Proceedings of the Automatic Speech Recognition Workshop*, 60–62, Snowbird, Utah, USA.

Ziv, J. (1985) Universal decoding for finite-state channels. *IEEE Transactions on Information Theory*, IT-31(4), 453–460.

Ziv, J. (1988) On classification with empirically observed statistics and universal data compression. *IEEE Transactions on Information Theory*, 34(2): 278–286.

Zolfaghari, P. and Robinson, T. (1996) Formant analysis using mixtures of gaussians. In *Proceedings of the International Conference on Spoken Language Processing*, 2: 1229–1232, Philadelphia, Pennsylvania, USA.

Zoltowski, C. B., Harper, M. P., Jamieson, L. H. and Helzerman, R. A. (1992) PARSEC: a constraint-based framework for spoken language understanding. In *Proceedings of the International Conference on Spoken Language Processing*, 249–252, Banff, Canada.

Zue, V., Glass, J., Goodine, D., Phillips, M. and Seneff, S. (1990) The SUMMIT speech recognition system: phonological modeling and lexical access. In *Proceedings of the IEEE International Conference on Acoustics, Speech and Signal Processing*, 49–52, Albuquerque, New Mexico, USA.

Zue, V., Glass, J., Goddeau, D., Goodine, D., Hirschman, L., Philips, M., Polifroni, J. and Seneff, S. (1992) The MIT system ATIS system: February 1992 Progress Report. In *Proceedings of the DARPA Speech and Natural Language Workshop*, Morgan Kaufmann Publishers, Palo Alto, California, USA.

Zue, V. and Laferriere, M. (1979) Acoustic study of medial /t,d/ in American English. *Journal of the Acoustical Society of America*, 66: 1039–1050.

Zue, V., Seneff, S. *et al.* (1993) The MIT ATIS system: December 1993 Progress Report. In *Proceedings of the DARPA Speech and Natural Language Workshop*, 66–71, Plainsboro, New Jersey; Morgan Kaufmann Publishers, Palo Alto, California, USA.

Index

Printed and bound by CPI Group (UK) Ltd, Croydon, CR0 4YY

03/10/2024

01040313-0013